Further Praise for The Hidden Words...

"Very impressive biography . . . great daring, always with good sense . . . a less patient and capacious book would not have done [Wordsworth] justice. Johnston has cleared away the accretions of nearly 200 years and given us the Wordsworth who in that painful dawn felt it was bliss to be alive." —Andrew Motion, *The Guardian*

"This magisterial biography recreates an entire literary era even as it accomplishes the almost awesome feat of transforming William Wordsworth into a human being." —*Parade Magazine*

"A rich study. . . . Unlike too many of his academic peers, Johnston has a real sense of humor." —*Wall Street Journal*

"Although Mr. Johnston paints Wordsworth as a flawed character, he also reclaims him as a swashbuckling young Romantic in the Byronic mode." —*The Economist*

"Extraordinary. . . . [Johnston] succeeds astonishingly well. . . . *The Hidden Wordsworth* is a great read. It makes itself accessible to general readers without condescending to them and without sacrificing any of the critical sophistication that specialists will be looking for. . . . Johnston's account of Wordsworth's youth must at this point be considered the one scholars need to reckon with. What most distinguishes *The Hidden Wordsworth*, however, is Johnston's success at merging biography and literary criticism." —*European Romantic Review*

"Johnston's stunning book enables the reader to explore a much more fascinating, complex and believable William Wordsworth than previously suspected, who was truly representative of a tumultuous era of transition not unlike our own day." —*The New Leader*

"A terrific new biography . . . recaptures the light in Wordsworth's eyes and puts the spring back in his stride." —Blake Morrison, *Independent on Sunday*

"Another book about the great man? Close to 1,000 pages and covering only the first 37 years of his life? By an American professor of English? It had better be good. It is, in fact, outstanding." —Ian McIntyre, *The Times* (London)

"The highest praise I can think of—it justifies its length. . . . I was quickly won over again by the sheer fascination of the detail and by the feeling that I was being brought remarkably close to the grain of Wordsworth's life." —John Gross, *Los Angeles Times*

"Johnston is a good writer and a passionate researcher, and he conveys that passion on every page." —Frank Wilson, *Kansas City Star*

THE HIDDEN WORDSWORTH

KENNETH R. JOHNSTON

W. W. Norton & Company
New York • London

First published as a Norton paperback 2001
Copyright © 2000, 1998 by Kenneth R. Johnston
All rights reserved
Printed in the United States of America

Excerpts from *An Evening Walk* (James Averill, editor), *Descriptive Sketches* (Eric Birdsall, editor), *'The Ruined Cottage' and 'The Pedlar'* (James Butler, editor), *Lyrical Ballads* (James Butler and Karen Green, editors), *Early Poems and Fragments* (Jared Curtis and Carol Landon, editors), *Home at Grasmere* (Beth Darlington, editor), *The Borderers* (Robert Osborn, editor), and *The Thirteen-Book 'Prelude'* (Mark Reed, editor) are used by permission of the publisher, Cornell University Press. Excerpts from 'The Prelude' by William Wordsworth are from *The Prelude 1799, 1805, 1850: A Norton Critical Edition*, edited by Jonathan Wordsworth, M. H. Abrams, and Stephen Gill. Copyright © 1979 by W. W. Norton & Company, Inc. Reprinted with the permission of the publisher. Some of the material in this book has been previously published in substantially different form in *Studies in Romanticism*, *The Age of William Wordsworth: Critical Essays on the Romantic Tradition* (Rutgers, 1987), and *Beyond Representation: Philosophy and Poetic Imagination* (Cambridge, 1996).

For information about permission to reproduce selections from this book, write to
Permissions, W. W. Norton & Company, Inc., 500 Fifth Avenue, New York, NY 10110

The text of this book is composed in Bembo with the display set in Weiss Titling.
Composition and manufacturing by Haddon Craftsmen Inc.
Book design by Charlotte Staub
Maps prepared by Suzanne Hull, Indiana University, Bloomington, Indiana.
Inset illustration on pg. 197 by Jim Hull, Indiana University.

Library of Congress Cataloging-in-Publication Data

Johnson, Kenneth R.
The hidden Wordsworth : poet, lover, rebel, spy / Kenneth R. Johnston.
p. cm.
Includes bibliographical references (p.   ) and index.
ISBN 0-393-04623-0
1. Wordsworth, William, 1770–1850—Childhood and youth. 2. Wordsworth, William, 1770–1850—Relations with women. 3. Poets. English—19th century—Biography. 4. Revolutionaries—Great Britain—Biography. 5. Spies—Great Britain—Biography. I. Title.

PR5882.J65 1998
821'.7—dc21
[B]   97-40317
                                                                         CIP

ISBN 0-393-32159-2 (pbk.)

W. W. Norton & Company, Inc., 500 Fifth Avenue, New York, N.Y. 10110
www.wwnorton.com

W. W. Norton & Company Ltd., Castle House, 75/76 Wells Street, London W1T 3QT

1 2 3 4 5 6 7 8 9 0

for
ILINCA

Contents

PART THREE

WHAT IS A POET? 1799–1807

A Tale of Two Titles

Preface to the Norton Paperback Edition

> To have an inquiry, whether into the construction of a legend, or the execution of a crime, is surely to require the telling of stories. And so the asking of questions and the relating of narratives need not, I think, be mutually exclusive forms of historical representation. And if in the end we must be satisfied with nothing more than broken lines of communication to the past . . . and our flickering glimpses of dead worlds fall far short of ghostly immersion, that perhaps is still enough to be going on with.
>
> Simon Schama, *Dead Certainties (Unwarranted Speculations)*

When *The Hidden Wordsworth* first appeared in 1998 it provoked, besides a heartening amount of praise and a few cries of dismay, several lively issues of emphasis and interpretation that I am happy to have the opportunity to address in its first paperback publication.[1]

In the book's Prologue, I make note of the fact that its working title, until just a few months before it went into production, was *Young Wordsworth: Creation of the Poet*. I have occasionally regretted that milder-sounding title, and considered reverting to it for the paperback edition. But 'name recognition' factors won out in favour of keeping the first printed title. And there are other reasons as well for sticking to it, in light of some of the controversies generated by the book's first appearance.

First, however, I should note the *text* of the book was always the same: the entire final draft had been written by the time its title was changed to *The Hidden Wordsworth: Poet, Lover, Rebel, Spy*. It was never a case of my deciding to write one of two very different kinds of books, one wildly sensational ('Hidden'), the other normal and common ('Young').

One good practical reason for changing from 'Young' to 'Hidden' seemed to be the argument of my original editors that the former might lead readers to expect a sequel: 'Old Wordsworth,' or 'Late Wordsworth.' I am far from discounting the interest of Wordsworth's life and works after his thirty-sixth year, but the focus of my interest in 'Young Wordsworth' was not so much chronological as developmental. That is, rather than considering his early years arbitrarily, according to the conventions of 'straight' biography (whatever that might be), as simply the first half of a long life, I was interested in his closely intertwined processes of self-discovery and self-creation. And for a very good reason, in Wordsworth's case, since this process is very much the matter of his posthumous masterpiece, *The Prelude*, which he – himself telling tales of two titles – called either 'The Poem on the Growth of My Own Mind,' or, when referring to its initial and long-preferred audience, 'The Poem to Coleridge.' Hence, my interest was – and is – in the things that Wordsworth did or didn't do, to create and simultaneously recognize himself as the 'Wordsworth' we think we know from literary history.

Even so, the originally preferred title in its brief virtual life – like the long-intended name of a baby that is suddenly changed at birth – never failed to provoke a similar response among readers: 'Young Wordsworth? Was Wordsworth ever young?' Of course, we all know he was born, had been a child, a teenager, and so on, but somehow he never seems to have been *young*. And this is very odd, because his masterpiece is all about being young (*The Prelude* ends with him at age *c.* 25–27), many of his best known poems are about children, and he wrote some of the most famous lines in English about being young: 'Bliss was it in that dawn to be alive, / But to be young was very heaven!' (We usually say these lines are 'about' the French Revolution, but I would submit that for Wordsworth the more important subject was that *he* was young in that dawn.)

But, faced with good practical reasons for changing my title, what should I change it to? 'The Hidden Wordsworth' emerged from a long list of possible alternatives, some fanciful, some – like this one – merely generic: the unknown Wordsworth, the invisible Wordsworth, Words-worth incognito, the undiscovered Wordsworth, the hidden Wordsworth, the radical Wordsworth, the Wordsworth we never knew, and so on. My choice of 'hidden' seemed to be mysteriously confirmed when I ran across an already-written sentence in my Epilogue: 'the young Wordsworth is the hidden Wordsworth.' At that point in my own self-discovery, it seemed providential: it was just a matter of switching subject and predicate, and young Wordsworth became the hidden Wordsworth. Each adjective is clearly and crucially an aspect of the other – of, roughly, form (hidden) and content (young), or of topic (youth) and method (hiding).

But this new title struck a few reviewers, especially in England, as 'sensational', an impression further heightened in some instances by the fact that its author was an American, as if the two qualities, sensational and American, went together. I could see what they meant, so far as national stereotypes went – as if I were to assume that the words 'conventional' and

'English' went together. Sometimes they do, but I hope we all know enough concrete cases to the contrary to be able to resist national stereotyping as a valid critical perspective.

More important is the fact that none of the words in the title, including the sub-title, were sensational so far as they concerned Wordsworth's youth and young manhood. All of them – and more – are documented and reasoned out in the book. Many aspects of his youth *were* hidden, the affair with Annette Vallon and their illegitimate child being only the most famous case in point. But calling them 'hidden' does not necessarily imply that they were 'undiscovered', nor did I claim they were. I believe I have uncovered my fair share of facts (and interpretations thereof), both hidden and undiscovered, but I readily acknowledge that many of these hidden features have been discovered by others, the incest theory of William's relation to Dorothy being one of the most controversial cases in point. In this case, I could hardly claim to be discovering a possibility that I acknowledge to be more than forty years old. But some readers, wound up to take umbrage from preconceived positions at the mere thought, seemed to have skipped right over my plain statement that I, too, find it 'hard to conceive of a physically incestuous relation' between this brother and sister. To make myself still plainer, I have here revised that statement: 'I do not believe there was a physically incestuous relation' between them. But the rest of the sentence, which is the real point and heart of the matter in a story of poetic self-creation, remains the same: 'it is equally hard to believe that the possibility did not cross their minds, whether as a temptation or a threat.'

As with 'hidden' in the main title, so too with 'Poet, Lover, Rebel, Spy' in the original sub-title: all documented, and, where interpreted or speculated on, the grounds for interpretation and the presence of speculation are all clearly set forth, for readers to agree or disagree. For as Francis Parkman, nephew of that 'dead certainty' who is the subject of Simon Schama's 'unwarranted speculations,' said, 'faithfulness to the truth of history involves far more than research, however patient and scrupulous, into special facts. [The narrator] must himself be, as it were, a sharer or spectator of the action he describes.'[2] It follows that readers must be prepared to share those roles.

Of Wordsworth's four title roles, 'spy' got more than its fair share of most readers' attention, for reasons that I – speaking of national stereo-types – have come to feel are more British than American. The United States is a much younger country than the United Kingdom and, perhaps for that reason, has had much less experience with espionage, certainly among major cultural figures. British newspapers, confronted with 'Spy Wordsworth,' could immediately trot out Christopher Marlowe, Daniel Defoe, Graham Greene, and others for (depending on the newspaper) sensational titillation or moralistic reproof. But the American popular imagination seems to be more stimulated by criminals than by traitors, and many Americans, pressed to name a 'famous' spy, can come up only with Benedict Arnold at one end of our history (more traitor than spy) and Julius and Ethel Rosenberg at the other (more famous as victims than as traitors). The name of Arnold is forever marked with shame in American annals, whereas his British opposite number, Major John André, was apotheosized with a tomb in Westminster Abbey after his execution in New York. So too with spy novels: the English literary landscape is littered with them, but they are very thin on the ground in the States. James Fenimore Cooper's *The Spy* (inspired in part by Arnold's treason) fits the bill generically but certainly not in terms of literary value, although, again instructively, the title character is justified for spying against – who else? – 'perfidious Albion.'

Nonetheless, it is true that 'spy' involved the greatest amount of poetic licence in my subtitle, since what I opined to be Wordsworth's possible sub-contracted messenger service for the Home Office while in Germany in 1798–99 hardly amounts to cloak-and-dagger spying. Still, my jingling adaptation of that one term from John le Carré's *Tinker, Tailor, Soldier, Spy* seemed harmless enough, given my large task of trying to shift the ponderous weight of Wordsworth's entrenched reputation for stodginess. And, of all the claims implied by my sub-title, it also seemed that this one was perhaps – other than 'Poet' – the most clearly documented, by item No. 1994.125 in the Wordsworth Trust Library, the entry in the Duke of Portland's paybook allotting nearly £100 to 'Mr Wordsworth.' Now, however, that document has been further examined, both by me and by Professor Michael Durey of Murdoch University in Australia.[3] Professor Durey shows, thanks to his knowledge of a Home Office voucher system of which I was unaware, that it refers to Robinson Wordsworth, the poet's cousin.[4] This discovery thus fulfills the 'disconfirming possibility' that I myself provided – but does not, I think, affect my stated opinion that if the entry referred to 'a Richard, a John, a Christopher, or a Robinson [it] would be almost as interesting' (Chapter 25).

(Nor was the initial discovery one I can claim for myself, or, when all is said and done, one I was very happy to have to account for, in the biographical framework I had been constructing until that day in 1993 when Robert Woof and Jeff Cowton of the Wordsworth Library drew Portland's paybook and its intriguing entry to my attention. The real scandal, though, would have been if, confronted with this information, I neglected to mention it, or to give the fullest account of it that I could.)

There are still plenty of intriguing connections between young Wordsworth and the Home Office's secret service of the 1790s, but with 'spy' under suspicion, it has seemed prudent to remove the rest of the 'swashbuckling' sub-title. This is not because the other items in it are likely to be disconfirmed, but because they have had, all along, the side effect of limiting the full scope of the book's claims. Too many reviewers used them as handy pegs on which to hang their response, as if my discussion of the hidden, young Wordsworth were limited to just those four roles. In fact, there were many more, some hidden, some under-recognized, a few undiscovered, and several as important as any of the sub-titled four (always excepting 'Poet'). These include: (1) Wordsworth's and his father's unwavering allegiance to the dominant conservative Whig interest in the north, represented first by Sir James Lowther and later by his cousin William; (2) Wordsworth's quite academically successful and very sociable years at Cambridge University, a far cry from the pose of being 'not for that hour, nor for that place' he created for his developing, lonely, 'romantic' self in *The Prelude*; (3) his clandestine trip back to France in the dangerous autumn of 1793, just when the Reign of Terror was starting in earnest; (4) his legacy-hunting manoeuvres between the two Calvert brothers, William and Raisley, in 1794; (5) his participation in plans to publish a radical anti-war journal, *The Philanthropist*, in 1795; (6) his strong efforts to control – not indulge – the currents of the passion he and his beloved sister felt passing between them; (7) his initially halting but eventually quite confident attempts to manipulate the literary market-place's reception of his works; and, of course, his poetic development through all of this.

Of these, my personal favourite has always been the difference between Wordsworth's actual experience at Cambridge and his poetic account of it in Book III of *The Prelude*. Not because the former is fact and the latter fiction, but because the difference between the two is, as I hope it is in all these cases, *instructive*. Paradoxically, readers and reviewers have commented more favourably on my reconstruction of his 1793 trip back to France (Chapters 15 and 16), even though this is based on much slimmer evidence than any of the things I have to say about Wordsworth's relations with his lover, his sister, or the Home Office – the topics which have exercised my critics most. Most gratifying, however, has been the virtually unanimous critical agreement that my biography has fulfilled the promise of its working sub-title: 'Creation of the *Poet*.'

But after introducing Wordsworth in each of these roles, I have come to wish I could quietly murmur, 'nothing necessarily wrong with that.' Perhaps the very mention of the words 'hidden,' 'lover,' and 'spy,' in company with the name 'Wordsworth,' breathes scandal into some readers' minds, but I do not in Wordsworth's case see anything particularly scandalous about them. Like all the roles I find him trying out, they seem to me items in the list of charges he was prepared – reluctantly or not – to pay as part of the cost of the 'Creation of the Poet.' In short, the purpose of the book, then and now, is not to expose Wordsworth to the muck-raking zeal of a sensationalistic American biographer, but rather to appreciate the extraordinary difficulties and risks he took to 'come through' when and as he did. None of these roles are cause for alarm or scandal – except insofar as they jar with the image of prudential morality Wordsworth constructed for himself in the latter half of his life. He had good reasons for adopting that protective covering too. But he paid a cost for it as well: compared with the young roles he subsequently hid away, the image of the grand old man of the Lakes has been a hard one for many readers of poetry to warm to.

And so I am finally content to stick with my apparently sensational title, since it is topically just as accurate as *Young Wordsworth: Creation of the Poet*, and probably more revealing as to his *acts* of self-creation. It may indeed be preferable, despite its ruffling of some sensibilities, precisely because of the challenge it gives to presuppositions about 'stuffy old Wordsworth,' which are as limiting in their way as excessive reverence toward our sacrosanct nature poet. What Conor Cruise O'Brien has said about Thomas Jefferson can be applied verbatim to Wordsworth: '[He] is much more interesting, if less holy and more fallible, than his biographers would allow him to appear.'[5] Nor is this simply a matter of biographical accuracy. Instead, the challenge should lead readers, both pro- and contra-Wordsworth, to recognize the many ways in which the drama of his younger years inflects and charges his poetic development with far more 'emotion' than our own self-induced 'tranquillity' about him has allowed us to realize.

It may seem odd for an author to reassure his readers that they are not missing much in a substantially shorter (by about a third) version of his original work, but that is essentially true for this paperback edition. Most of the cuts have been of footnotes and endnotes, which are now trimmed to a referential minimum. Appendices and explanatory background notes and tables have also gone, along with some asides and digressions which, while helpful in sketching the context of certain interpretations and speculations, tended to interrupt the main lines of reportage, which here stand out more clearly for not having to carry this protective baggage. No claims have been withdrawn, though the Wordsworth family's connections to the Home Office's secret service have been adjusted in light of Professor Durey's new evidence. Nor have I tried to extend any lines of interpretation beyond what I say here in the preface. I have kept most of the jokes as well, feeling that Wordsworthian interpretation can always use some lightening up, despite those few reviewers who were not amused. As warrant for my good humour, I take the fact that two of the most hysterically (I use the word advisedly) funny writers in English, Samuel Coleridge and Charles Lamb, were Wordsworth's lifelong friends, and among his most profoundly insightful admirers, but they frequently (though rarely to his face) punctured his airs when his severe impassiveness slid over into pomposity. Though reviewers have for the most part treated *The Hidden Wordsworth* nearly as well as an author could wish, some occasionally took on the high-toned moralistic airs of his other friend, Robert Southey, in defending him. I am happy to remain in the snug, smoking and drinking and laughing with Lamb and Coleridge.

I'm also glad of the opportunity to correct a number of typographical and editorial slips, as well as some plain errors of my own. Some of these are just minor lapses in names, though occasionally there were major lapses in dates, such as my one mistaken reference to Wordsworth's birthday (7 April) being the same as Shakespeare's (23 April) – a confusion I feel sure Wordsworth would forgive me. Probably the most egregious mistake was my own commission of an 'error' I attributed to thousands of readers – that the little girl in 'Surprised by Joy' was Wordsworth's legitimate daughter, Catherine. In fact, she is. The sonnet I had in mind was 'It was a beauteous evening, calm and free,' where the little girl is indeed his illegitimate daughter, Caroline Vallon Wordsworth. I am grateful to many kind readers for pointing out these lapses to me, especially to colleagues who sent me detailed lists of chapter and verse in the interests of more accurate scholarship: Ernest Bernhardt-Kabisch (Indiana University), James Butler (LaSalle University), Geoffrey Carnall (University of Edinburgh), Bruce Graver (Providence College), Everard King (University of Newfoundland), and Leon Waldoff (University of Illinois). Donald Lamm has stuck with me through thick and thin, even as the book has migrated from one publisher to another, and Will Sulkin and Jörg Hensgen have made it feel welcome in a new house.

Still, in the end I am ruefully forced to agree with those reviewers who said that Wordsworth remains hidden even after *The Hidden Wordsworth*. It is hard to see or to present Wordsworth in anything like the unbuttoned deshabille of a Lamb or a Coleridge. My in-a-word description for him is 'impressive'. I might now go further, and say 'severe,' or downright 'scarey,' or, in the language of a man speaking to man, just plain 'tough.' A man who struggled with his emotions so much that his lifetime goal was to recollect them in tranquillity was not a man given to emotional display, doubtless because he knew its destructive force, for himself and very likely for others.

To see Wordsworth plain is to feel the full *personal* force of mountaintop passages like the Climbing of Snowdon or the Crossing of the Simplon, as critics like A.C. Bradley, Geoffrey Hartman, Harold Bloom, Thomas Weiskel, and Jonathan Wordsworth have done. For all their individual differences, these critics all agree that what we are reading in those and other passages of the Sublime Wordsworth are not landscape descriptions, nor finally anything very much at all about the world of nature, but rather entering into 'the haunt and main region of [his] song . . . the Mind of Man.' This Wordsworth is not hidden either, but, like others I have pointed out, stands directly in front of us, could we but recognize him. Recognizing that, however, entails acknowledging that there are aspects of our life – especially when we place ourselves in the presence of minds mightier than our own – that are not biographically representable, but will always leave us with 'blank misgivings . . . moving about in worlds unrealized,' 'forever voyaging through strange seas of thought, alone.'[6]

Illustrations

18 Dorothy Wordsworth, pencil drawing. *The Wordsworth Trust, Dove Cottage.*

19 Helen Maria Williams, by John Singleton. *Copyright © The British Museum.*

20 Presumed miniature portrait of Annette Vallon. *The Wordsworth Trust, Dove Cottage.*

21 Jean-Louis Carra (1742–1793). *de Lamartine, Alphonse Marie Louis, Histoire des Girondins.*

22 Antoine Joseph Gorsas (1751–1793). *de Lamartine, Alphonse Marie Louis, Histoire des Girondins.*

23 Henri Grégoire (1750–1831), in detail from Jacques-Louis David's *Oath of the Tennis Court, June 20, 1789. Réunion des musées nationaux, © photo RMN.*

24 Michel Beaupuy (1755–1796). *Permission granted by M. Henri de Beaupuy, photo courtesy of The Wordsworth Trust, Dove Cottage.*

25 Thomas Holcroft and William Godwin at the 1794 Treason Trials, by Sir Thomas Lawrence. *Private collection.*

26 John Thelwall addressing crowds behind Copenhagen House, Islington (detail from James Gillray, *Copenhagen House*, 16 November 1795). *The Lilly Library, Indiana University.*

27 Daniel Isaac Eaton, by W. Sharpe. *By courtesy of the National Portrait Gallery, London.*

28 Joseph Johnson, by W. Sharpe. *By courtesy of the National Portrait Gallery, London.*

29 Francis Wrangham. *By courtesy of the National Portrait Gallery, London.*

30 Samuel Taylor Coleridge (1798). *By courtesy of the National Portrait Gallery, London.*

31 Robert Southey, by James Sharples. *City of Bristol Museum & Art Gallery.*

32 Charles Lamb, by Robert Hancock. *By courtesy of The Wordsworth Trust, Dove Cottage.*

33 William Henry Cavendish Bentinck, 3rd Duke of Portland, by J. Murphy. *By courtesy of the National Portrait Gallery, London.*

34 Richard Ford. *By permission of Sir Brinsley Ford, C.B.E. Photo: Eileen Tweedie.*

35 George Canning, by John Hoppner (1800). *Provost and Fellows of Eton College. Photograph Courtauld Institute of Art, London.*

36 *The New Morality*, by James Gillray (7 August 1798). *The Newberry Library, Chicago.*

37 'Coleridge & Co', detail from *The New Morality. The Newberry Library, Chicago.*

38 Town End, by T. M. Richardson. *The Wordsworth Trust, Dove Cottage.*

39 Walter Scott, from portrait by Henry Raeburn. *Courtauld Institute of Art, London.*

Maps

Acknowledgments

This book was begun with the support of a fellowship from the National Endowment for the Humanities, and ended with similar support from the John Simon Guggenheim Memoral Foundation, for both of which I am deeply grateful.

Throughout the time of its research and composition, I have received unflagging co-operation from Indiana University, especially successive chairs of its Department of English, the dean of its College of Art & Sciences, and Kenneth R.R. Gros Louis, the chancellor of its main, Bloomington, campus. My research was facilitated by the splendid resources and personnel of the Indiana University libraries, particularly the English collections under the supervision of Anthony Shipps and Perry Willett, as well as those in the Lilly Rare Book Library, directed by William Cagle when I started and by Lisa Browar when I finished.

No serious biographical study of Wordsworth can be attempted without the unique collections of the Wordsworth Library in Grasmere, to which I am also indebted personally for friendships with Robert and Pamela Woof, Jeff and Gill Cowton, Sally Woodhead, and others among the modern 'Grasmere Volunteers.' These debts have at times been inseparable from those I owe to the Wordsworth Summer Conference for invitations to lecture and their kindnesses, from Jonathan Wordsworth (critical inheritor), from Sylvia and the late Richard Wordsworth, and from its American representative, Marilyn Gaull.

Thanks as well to all those in other libraries and archives who made my work easier simply by doing theirs so well: the Public Records Office at Kew, as well as PROs at Carlisle (for Cumberland), Kendal (for Westmorland), Winchester (for Hampshire and the Wickham Papers), Halifax, and Norfolk (for Cookson records at Forncett); and to the Manuscripts and Prints collections of the British Museum, the Bristol University Rare Book Library (for the Pinney Papers), the Guildhall Libraries (Jeremy Smith), the Hawkshead School (John West), the Kendal Public Library, the Bibliothèque National, the Royal Post Office archives (for the Freeling Papers), and the Scottish PRO in Edinburgh.

Many friends and colleagues have helped make this book a reality. First mention must go to four who read and commented on the entire manuscript at various stages: Mark Reed, intrepid chronologist of Wordsworth's life from 1770 to 1815, Stephen Parrish, the Grasmere gourmet, Donald Lamm of W.W. Norton, who gave it the editorial attention it needed and (I hope) deserved, and Otto Sonntag, who caught, queried, and corrected more copy mistakes than I care to remember, knowing that those remaining are entirely my own. Others have read parts of the manuscript with insight and generous criticism: Linda Charnes, Jared Curtis, Morris Dickstein, Mary Favret, Marilyn Gaull (editor of *The Wordsworth Circle*), Bill Hamilton, Hilary Hinzmann, John Kerrigan, Christoph Lohmann, Richard Matlak, Jerry McGann, Stuart Proffitt, Nick Roe, Michael Rosenblum, Stuart Sperry, David Wagenknecht (editor of *Studies in Romanticism*), John Wright, Dean Young, and, last but always first, Ilinca Zarifopol-Johnston.

For other help and advice I am grateful to M. H. Abrams, J. V. Beckett, Ernest Bernhardt-Kabisch, Harold Bloom, Jim Chandler, Linda David, Richard Eldridge, Paul Elledge, Stephen Gill, Don Gray, Susan Gubar, Geoffrey Hartman, Suzie Hull (inventive cartographer), Michael Jaye, Herb Kaplan, Susan Nelson, James Riley, Gene Ruoff, Sharon Setzer, Michael and Mona Shea, Michael Shelden, David Simpson, Elizabeth Sparrow, Murray and Aneta Sperber, Orrin Wang, and Carl Woodring.

Special thanks to Mr and Mrs Russell Gore-Andrews for a tour and an excellent lunch at their home, Racedown Lodge, and to the present owners of Robert Jones's house at Plas-yn-Llan near Ruthin, in Wales, for letting a by-passing stranger have a look around.

My labours have been lightened by two tireless research assistants, Michele Thomas and Heather E. Frey.

A Note on Money

Wordsworth was a man getting and spending like other men, though he deplored the process more memorably than the rest of us. As a member of the new professional class slowly rising out of the old country aristocracy, he was keenly aware from childhood of the value of a pound. In the biography of his young manhood, three sums have special importance: the approximately £8000 Sir James Lowther owed John Wordsworth Sr. at the time of his death, but refused to pay to his heirs; the £900 Raisley Calvert bequeathed to Wordsworth at the time of his death in 1795; and the £100 per year Wordsworth blithely said was all he would need to live an independent life.

Comparative historical economics is not an exact science, and there is no simple way to multiply the value of a late eighteenth-century pound to arrive at today's values. But the following comparisons give an idea of what these sums would have meant to young Wordsworth in terms of the kind of life they could buy.

A church 'living' producing about £300 per year was considered sufficient for a young university graduate to get married and set up housekeeping. Oliver Goldsmith's country parson in *The Deserted Village* (1770), 'passing rich at forty pounds a year,' provides a comparison from a generation earlier. Wordsworth's uncle William Cookson was engaged for almost ten years, waiting for such a post, before he gave up his university fellowship and finally married the Penrith vicar's daughter. A parson getting £400 a year could afford to keep five or six servants. A two-room country cottage in the north of England could be rented for £2 a year, and a whole house for £6; Sir Robert Walpole's London town house rented for £300 annually. In 1792 a man in Kendal could support a wife and three children on £30 a year, £20 of which went for food, and still live comfortably. But this was near the bottom of decent levels of existence.

Wordsworth lived within these ranges. His father started out with almost nothing, as a member of the 'decayed' lesser gentry, worth £200–1000 a year. But at his death his personal estate, independent of the

Lowther debt, brought in more than £10,000 at forced-sale prices.

These comparisons are accurate until the mid-1790s, when the cost of living approximately doubled as a result of economic dislocations caused by the war with France – a special hardship for people trying to live on a fixed income. At the upper end of the scale, members of the English landowning aristocracy were better off than many European princes, with average annual *incomes* of £10,000.

A Note on Texts

Editions of *The Prelude* pose a special problem for a biography concentrating on Wordsworth's development, since different versions of this poem developed alongside his life. The Cornell University Press edition is definitive for the three major stages of the poem's growth: *The Prelude, 1798–1799*, ed. Stephen Parrish (1977); *The Thirteen-Book Prelude*, 2 vols., ed. Mark L. Reed (1991); *The Fourteen-Book Prelude*, ed. W.J.B. Owen (1985). I follow convention in referring to these versions by their dates of completion or (in the case of the fourteen-book version) publication: as *1799, 1805*, and *1850*. (*1805* signifies the AB-Stage MSS in Reed's edition: that is, MSS A and B of the poem, or Dove Cottage MSS 52 and 53.) However, when referring to editorial matter, I use a short form of the Cornell title (for example, *Thirteen*, for Reed's edition).

The 1805, thirteen-book version of *The Prelude* is the one closest to the time frame of this biography, and hence the one I cite most frequently; all otherwise unattributed citations to books and line numbers throughout (for instance, X.348–49) are to this version. For readers' ease of reference, I have used the Norton paperback edition combining all three versions, *The Prelude: 1799, 1805, 1850*, ed. Jonathan Wordsworth, M.H. Abrams, and Stephen Gill (New York: W.W. Norton, 1979). Variations between the Norton version of *1805* and Reed's scholarly edition are for most readers' purposes not important.

For Wordsworth's other poems, I have used the Cornell University Press editions as my basic reference text, occasionally referring to and quoting from the older edition of Ernest de Selincourt for additional information: *The Poetical Works of William Wordsworth*, 5 vols. (Oxford, 1940–49). I have also made use of John O. Hayden's two-volume edition, *William Wordsworth: The Poems* (New Haven: Yale University Press, 1981; first published 1977 in England by Penguin Books).

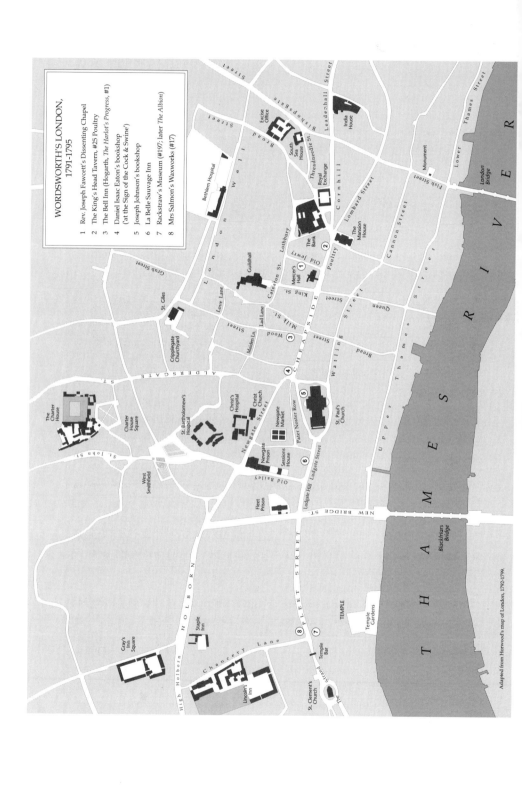

WORDSWORTH'S LONDON,
1791–1795

1   Rev. Joseph Fawcett's Dissenting Chapel
2   The King's Head Tavern, #25 Poultry
3   The Bell Inn (Hogarth, *The Harlot's Progress*, #1)
4   Daniel Isaac Eaton's bookshop
    (at the Sign of the Cock & Swine')
5   Joseph Johnson's bookshop
6   La Belle Sauvage Inn
7   Rackstraw's Museum (#197; later *The Albion*)
8   Mrs Salmon's Waxworks (#17)

Adapted from Horwood's map of London, 1792-1799.

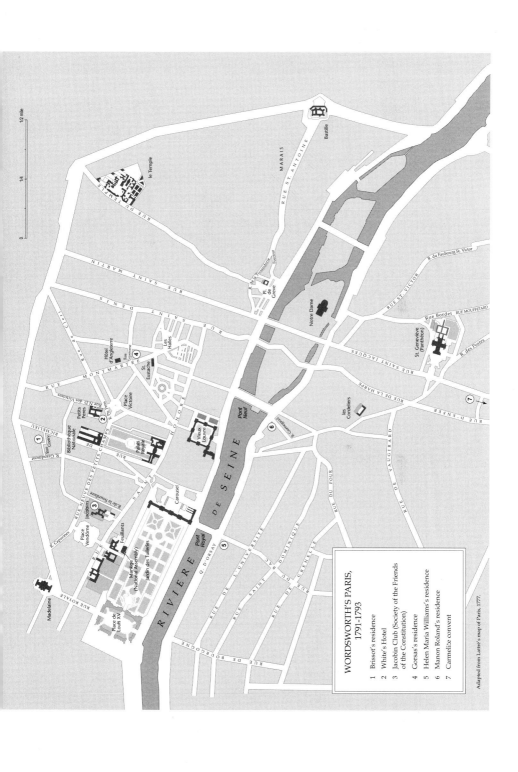

WORDSWORTH'S PARIS,
1791-1793

1 Brissot's residence
2 White's Hotel
3 Jacobin Club (Society of the Friends
   of the Constitution)
4 Gorsas's residence
5 Helen Maria Williams's residence
6 Manon Roland's residence
7 Carmelite convent

Adapted from Lattré's map of Paris, 1777.

Bliss was it in that dawn to be alive,
But to be young was very heaven!
(*The Prelude* [1805], X.692–93)

*****

I ask what is meant by the word Poet? What is a Poet? To whom does he
address himself? And what language is to be expected of him? He is a man
speaking to men . . .

 The obstacles which stand in the way of the fidelity of the Biographer
and Historian . . . are incalculably greater than those which are to be
encountered by the Poet who has an adequate notion of the dignity of his
art . . . there is no object standing between the Poet and the image of
things; between this, and the Biographer and Historian there are a
thousand.

 Emphatically may it be said of the Poet, as Shakespeare hath said of
man, 'that he looks before and after.' He is the rock and defence of human
nature; an upholder and preserver, carrying everywhere with him
relationship and love.

(Preface to *Lyrical Ballads*, 1802)

*****

. . . I could no more
Trust the elevation which had made me one
With the great family that here and there
Is scattered through the abyss of ages past,
Sage, patriot, lover, hero . . .
(*The Prelude* [1805], XI.60–64)

PROLOGUE

Images of Wordsworth

Difference is especially desirable in the field of Wordsworth studies, which has tended to be extremely familiar with its object of study.[1]

Looking at Wordsworth's earliest portraits, one is forcibly reminded that he was not an immediately attractive man, especially compared to his great literary contemporaries, almost all of whom *look* Romantic. But Wordsworth, from first portrait to last, looks calm and resigned at best, sleepy or weary at worst. He often looks better with his eyes closed, and his life-mask, though it looks like a death-mask, is an improvement over some of his pictures. William Shuter's portrait, taken when Wordsworth was twenty-eight, has the liveliest expression of the more than eighty portraits, sketches, and busts produced during the poet's lifetime. The earliest portrait (1798), it was also the last to catch Wordsworth smiling, capturing that incongruous 'convulsive inclination to laughter about the mouth' which William Hazlitt, then a young portrait painter himself, noted, adding that it was 'a good deal at variance with the solemn, stately expression of the rest of his face.'

Hazlitt, as it happens, is the only artist to have been suggested as the painter of the odd man out among the four portraits I have reproduced. It presents a very different image of Wordsworth from those we are used to. Weird, disturbing, 'like a spy in a thriller' (my friends say), both its subject and its author are unknown. Yet its mysterious, unsettling quality tempts me to make it a pictorial emblem for *The Hidden Wordsworth*.

It is plausibly Wordsworth. That at least was 'the consensus of opinion of those who visited the poet's birthplace during the centenary celebration' of his death, the year (1950) in which it was discovered – perhaps too coincidentally – in a garage in the Lake District.[2] It has been claimed to be one of the two portraits, both now lost, that Hazlitt painted of Words-worth and Coleridge in 1803.[3] According to other accounts, however, Hazlitt's 'evidently lugubrious portrait appears to have been destroyed,' and the most recent evidence indicates it was probably burned. But its destruction is not certain, and no other identification has been proposed for the picture we have, other than that it probably dates from *c.* 1800–1820, and that it seems to be a North of England subject, perhaps (if not

Wordsworth) an itinerant preacher.[4]

The chance that the picture *is* Hazlitt's portrait of Wordsworth, and that it thus pictures him just as he began to expand 'the poem on the growth of my own mind' (*The Prelude*) into a time-frame coterminous with this biography, makes it an appropriate symbol for a young man who in many ways hid himself from the gaze of posterity, covering over or destroying aspects of his life he did not want us to see.

How to describe the expression on that face? The rest of Hazlitt's first impression of Wordsworth fits it nicely: 'There was a severe, worn pressure of thought about his temples, a fire in his eye (as if he saw something in objects more than the outward appearance), an intense high narrow forehead, a Roman nose, cheeks furrowed by strong purpose and feeling.'[5] This in fact sounds more like the disputed portrait than it does any of the others of young Wordsworth. The fire is gone from the eyes of all other Wordsworth portraits after Shuter's.

Robert Southey supplied a sub-title for the portrait Hazlitt painted of Wordsworth that also fits the disputed portrait well: 'At the gallows – deeply affected by his deserved fate – yet determined to die like a man.' Wordsworth himself studied Hazlitt's image carefully, and his description of it to Charles Lamb in 1816 fits the disputed picture better than it does any of his known portraits. He reported that his brother Richard 'was literally *struck* with the strength of the signboard likeness; but never, till that moment, had he conceived that so much of the diabolical lurked under the innocent features of his quondam playmate, and respected Friend and dear Brother.'

The Hidden Wordsworth is a portrait in words that attempts to restore the fire to Wordsworth's eyes, to overcome his own strenuous efforts to damp his youthful passions down. With its urban revolutions and Alpine scenery, French mistresses and passionate sisters, secret agents and furious guardian uncles, Wordsworth's young life was a most exciting one: Byron might have envied it. I see Wordsworth's youthful face like the eyes in the unknown portrait: not calm but alert, the expression not pleasant but questioning, calculating, perhaps a bit startled – or a bit frightening.

By contrast, Wordsworth's uniformly calm gaze in all his other portraits matches the remarkable consistency with which he and his works have been perceived by the public. The young, unsettling Wordsworth has been replaced by the sedate and boring older poet. From twenty years before his death until a hundred years after it he was, above all, *revered*. His youthful self has become to a large degree a prisoner of the later image that he himself created.

Wordsworth's name always provokes one immediate association: Nature. He is Our Nature Poet. But from the beginning, many people's reverence for him has stimulated others' irreverence; not infrequently, both attitudes are expressed by the same person. Robert Browning celebrated Wordsworth's 'mild and magnificent eye' even as he lamented his 'Lost Leader.' From Byron and Shelley through Browning and Swinburne to Eliot and Pound, there have always been significant demurrals to Wordsworth's greatness. For some readers, he is the poet they love to hate. Others try to divide him into two distinct poets, as Matthew Arnold did: the (bad) philosophical poet and the (good) lyrical one, or the reactionary and the radical, or the silly and the profound, or simply the Good and the Bad Wordsworth. Often these disparate Wordsworthian identities speak in very different voices, as a nineteenth-century parodist ventriloquized them: 'one is of the mountain steep,' the other 'of an old, half-witted sheep.'[6]

But there is one image, or story, that we have not seen fully – *young* Wordsworth. Was Wordsworth ever young? On the evidence of his portraits, he seems to have looked old from a very early age, and his thoughts about death can almost be called precocious. But he was young once too, and this book is an effort to show him as he was then, even to suggest that his young life was his most important life.

But there is more to that young life than we have yet seen, certainly more than I expected to find when I set out writing this book: my research has outstripped my hypotheses. Almost more interesting than the new facts about his political life and his sex life – and his poetical life – is the Wordsworthian cover-up: the systematic and very successful efforts he made to bury his 'juvenile errors' from the sight of his contemporaries and from posterity. But though he covered them up, they did not disappear: many of them stare us in the face from the pages of his greatest poetry, like purloined letters we have not seen because they're so obvious – and because they were written by Wordsworth, that irreproachable name.

Repeatedly, when we can establish corroborated facts for an event in Wordsworth's life, his verse tends to confirm it, only silently or meta-phorically, drawing our attention away from the facts, not toward them. What seem to be metaphors often turn out to be literalisms. A small example: in Book X of *The Prelude*, speaking about his disaffection from England in her war against revolutionary France, Wordsworth says he sat 'like an uninvited guest' in a village church when 'prayers were offered up . . . for our country's victories.' The simile is a good one for expressing feelings of alienation, but its literal force is even stronger, for at that moment – when news of the Allied victory at Valenciennes on 28 July 1793 reached England – Wordsworth (not normally a church-goer in his young manhood) was precisely an *in*vited guest, at the home of his college friend Robert Jones, at Plas-yn-Llan in Wales, where Jones's father was the local vicar. So young Wordsworth felt estranged not only from his country and its national religion, but even from the affections and hospitality of his closest friend.

A larger example of our sanitized reading of Wordsworth is the way in which we tend to interpret his statement about his involvement in the French Revolution: 'Bliss was it in that dawn to be alive, / But to be young was very heaven!' These words, the second most famous in English about the Revolution (after Dickens's 'It was the best of times, it was the worst of times . . .'), are quite regularly treated as a *generalization* about the attitudes of Wordsworth's generation, rather than his very particular expression of his own experience. Blissful youth has been a hard concept to attach to the Wordsworth of posterity, let alone his full hyperbole: *heavenly* bliss. That this kind of language matches up exactly with his expressions of sexual joy over his love affair with Annette Vallon ('pathways, walks, / Swarmed with enchantment, till his spirits sunk / Beneath the burden, overblessed for life' [IX.593–95]) should not surprise us; rather, it confirms the intensity of his early adult experiences. And that these emotions should be attributed in *The Prelude* to two characters named Vaudracour and Julia, rather than William and Annette, is only another species of metaphor.

These kinds of literal metaphors, or particular generalizations, have special importance for Wordsworth's biography. They imply that much of his poetry is even more autobiographical than we realize. Not that Wordsworth's poetry is literally 'true.' Great care must be exercised in interpreting the facts of his metaphors. But it is not surprising that the poet who often wrote as if 'there were nothing else but him and the universe' (Hazlitt) should frequently take his metaphors from himself, from his own experience. As Shelley said, 'He had as much imagination as a pint-pot,' and 'never could / Fancy another situation . . . than that wherein he stood' (*Peter Bell the Third*, IV.viii). Shelley, however, went on to say, 'Yet his was individual mind, / And new created all he saw . . . and refined / Those new creations . . . by a master-spirit's law.'

The Hidden Wordsworth is an account of how Wordsworth transmuted the facts of his life into poetry – and into an image of himself as 'The Poet.' He was a poet with remarkably low powers of invention and remarkably high powers of imagination. He almost could not make up a story on his own: he used literary sources, or he asked people (especially poor ones) about the facts of their experience. Nor are his facts always facts: for example, when late in life he told his neighbour, Isabella Fenwick, about the circumstances of many of his poems' composition, he frequently neglected to mention clear literary sources, and even clearer facts about his own personal involvement with the persons or actions described. Nothing wrong here: it was all part of his continuing creation of 'The Poet'; he was no more obligated than any writer to anatomize himself for posterity. Indeed, given his extreme literalism, he was more obligated than many to *cover* that anatomy. And he did.

Wordsworthian biography does not need more facts, though these are always welcome, so much as its needs more interpretation of the facts we have, and speculation about those we don't – and about why we don't. If I had an axe to grind when I started, it was from feeling that there's more here than meets the eye, or more than has yet met our eyes, like that shifty portrait (whether lost or found) by Hazlitt. Anyone who studies Wordsworth's young life for long comes to agree with the feeling of the distinguished historian E. P. Thompson that there is something secretive about it. For a long time Wordsworth's supposed youthful 'crisis' was thought to be a kind of nervous breakdown, but lately the finger of suspicion has turned back to his politics, as it did for his contemporaries.

Suspicion is a methodological necessity for writing about England in the 1790s, especially about someone who claimed that 'to be young [then] was very heaven.' The practice of sweeping youthful enthusiasms under the carpet reaches epidemic – and epic – proportions for these years. Much of England's domestic policy in the nineteenth century was predicated on a deep need to bury the spectre of revolution which began stalking Europe in 1789 and continued to do so, with only brief interruptions, until 1917. The biographical correlative to this is that most people who wrote autobiographies drastically played down any involvement they might have had in the Jacobinism of the 1790s. The suppression, elision, or revisionary doctoring of one's radical republicanism in the 1790s was carried out as ruthlessly and with as utter seriousness of purpose in nineteenth-century biography as the suppression of youthful fascism or communism in the 1930s has been in twentieth-century. And for much the same reason: equally ruthless and serious enemies were watching with eagle eyes, ready to pounce on and exploit 'juvenile errors,' to the ruination of lives and, especially, of *careers*. Tom Paine, William Godwin, and Mary Wollstonecraft were the most famous victims of this long cultural witch-hunt, as were Shelley and Byron in different ways. But Wordsworth is no exception; indeed, he helped establish the rule. He seems forthcoming about his years in France, but by admitting that 'juvenile errors are my theme,' he seems to excuse himself in the act of confession without confessing all. He suppressed even more completely his dangerous involvement in *English* radical reform politics. And of course posthumous publication of *The Prelude* guaranteed his immunity.

My 'method' often consists of no more than raising questions. My rule of thumb has been: when there's a choice of possibilities, always respect and investigate the riskier one. I have tried to approach his life both as a lover of his poetry and as a modern investigative reporter. Since these two positions might define for many the apex and the nadir, respectively, of contemporary morality, I hope the result achieves something of a balance. It attempts to treat Wordsworth according to the standards – and with the same respect and gravity – he accorded his poetical subjects: (1) 'I have at all times endeavoured to look steadily at my subject,' (2) 'I have wished to keep my Reader in the company of flesh and blood,' and (3) 'in a selection of language really used by men.' Even without the new evidence I have found, there were many remarkable things about young Wordsworth's life that no one seems to have remarked, ordinary questions about everyday life that seem off-limits for him, as though he had been granted a diplomatic poetical immunity. Case in point: can it really be true, as the extant biographical record suggests, that he engaged in no sexual inter-course between leaving Annette Vallon pregnant in October 1792, and marrying Mary Hutchinson in October 1802? That is, between his ages twenty-two and thirty-two, a young man's sexually most active time of life? The fact would be extraordinary if true, and would certainly go far to explain a pervasive sexlessness in much of his work. While I can't exactly disprove it, his writings of this period upon closer scrutiny evince a remarkable, if subterranean, sexuality that suggests his facts of life were different – and in this case, more normal – than we think.

When something seems to be going on, but there's no hard evidence for an answer, I will at least hazard an educated guess. For example, I take seriously the possibility that Wordsworth did return to France secretly in the autumn of 1793. Repeatedly, I found myself chewing over facts that other biographers have recorded, or on the conclusions they have drawn – or refused to draw – and coming up with markedly different results. On such topics as: Wordsworth's father's business arrangements with Sir James Lowther; or Wordsworth's connections with William Wilberforce, the rich Yorkshire playboy turned anti-slavery hero; or his familiarity with the prostitutes in Cambridge; or his participation in political journalism in London in 1795; or his role in the 'Spy Nozy' incident in Somerset in 1797. My conclusions on these topics made it less surprising when I came across evidence pointing to knowledge of Wordsworth and his family on the part of persons in charge of England's newly reorganized Secret Service.

With a succession of portraits like this, why attempt another? Because, except for the great French scholar, Emile Legouis, a hundred years ago (1896), no one has attempted to draw the youthful poet's portrait since.[7] Legouis succumbed in homage almost immediately. His book, *The Early Life of William Wordsworth, 1770–1798*, ground-breaking as it was and important as it still is, is plainly sub-titled, 'A Study of *The Prelude*,' and what appears as biography is actually textual commentary. It instituted for nearly a century the common practice of interpreting Wordsworth by his own words, in which the biographer's work became essentially a matter of retroactive confirmation, reporting back on the gross details out of which Wordsworth revised and refined himself. For the biographer of Wordsworth's early years must confront his subject's own account of himself at every turn; and one's excitement at many an apparent discovery is immediately qualified by the realization that the biographical subject has been there before you, taking notes and writing poems on himself.

Every portrait is an interpretation. Mine stresses Wordsworth's self-creation, or what is now sometimes called 'self-fashioning.'[8] This is not the 'natural,' or inevitable, growth to greatness which Wordsworth laid down in *The Prelude*, where everything appears 'all gratulant, if rightly understood.' It is rather the sequence of actions and decisions, many far from 'gratulant,' that includes accidents, false starts, mistakes, and bad faith – and the adjustments, compromises, and changes of mind and life-plan that they entailed. *The Prelude* includes a fair share of these, but by no means all of them. *The Hidden Wordsworth* shows that his young life was not so fortunate, but that it is the immediately recognizable story of a young man becoming an adult, with the usual measures of bad luck and bad decisions: an ordinary life, with ordinary decisions, temptations and failures, out of which came extraordinary achievements.

When it comes to self-creation, Wordsworth wrote the book on it. The biggest obstacle to an account of Wordsworth's self-creation is his own self-portrait in *The Prelude*, which hangs like a golden curtain in front of all other portraits of him. Over eight thousand lines long, it is one of the greatest long poems in modern English, and one of the great English originals in the literature of self-portraiture. It is not Wordsworth's biography, but neither is it his autobiography: his early life was both the same as, yet very different from, *The Prelude*'s account of it. It is a full-length portrait of the artist as a perennially young man, meticulously worked over for forty-five years by the ageing master. Exactly the reverse of Dorian Grey's picture in his attic, which absorbs the horrid scars of his life of sin, the *Prelude*-picture kept Wordsworth forever young while the man aged. It was endlessly retouched and revised, and published and reproduced for posterity in several different versions. By not publishing *The Prelude* when he first completed it in 1805, Wordsworth's subsequent life and writings themselves became in a way posthumous, like *The Prelude* itself.

But though we have *The Prelude*, we don't have all of the years it covers, either in detail or interpretation. For example, among *The Prelude*'s many omissions, there is no mention of Wordsworth's privileged social position, of his many friends at Cambridge, of his mistress Annette Vallon and their daughter Caroline, nor of his clandestine political writings. Apparently a less biographical omission, but in its way even more striking, are the nearly 8000 lines of poetry he wrote between 1784 and 1800 – as many as in *The Prelude* itself – of which *The Prelude* mentions or alludes to barely a quarter. We must try to see what Wordsworth left *out* of his self-portrait, before we accept that it all turned out for the best.

Wordsworth was one of the first poets, as Werner Heisenberg was one of the first physicists, to discover life's great Uncertainty Principle: that observation, no matter how scientific, subtly changes the nature of the object under observation. Mass cannot be held constant relative to velocity, any more than identity can be held constant to life. In this respect, science has at last caught up with poetry, as Wordsworth predicted: 'the Poet will . . . be at the side [of the man of Science], carrying sensation into the midst of the objects of Science itself. The remotest discoveries of the Chemist, the Botanist, or Mineralogist, will be as proper objects of the Poet's art as any upon which it can be employed . . . *and the relations under which they are contemplated* by the followers of these respective Sciences shall be manifestly and palpably material to us as enjoying and suffering beings.' There *is* an object standing even between the Poet and Things, and it is precisely his 'image' of them. Ditto the biographer; ditto-ditto, a thousand times over, the Wordsworthian biographer.

One can still go to most of the places Wordsworth went, as I have. Some of them have not changed much – the older buildings of Cambridge University, for example, may have changed less than the hills of Cumberland, where thousands – nay, millions – of hikers' footsteps, many of them trying to follow Wordsworth's, have created real erosion problems and altered the landscape. Wordsworth's Cambridge, London, and Paris are still monuments of culture, but so is Wordsworth, now. Not only is he a monument, as Coleridge predicted he would be – 'the Giant Wordsworth, God love him' – but so is the *idea* of the Poet which he did so much, with Coleridge's great help (God love him for it), to erect. 'Thy monument of glory will be raised,' he said to Coleridge, and the monument is called 'Wordsworth.' Hence a biography of Wordsworth, charting the creation of the Poet, must acknowledge from time to time that such self-creating is something we all do, and feel free to comment or intrude upon the distance between him and us, which is yet another cause of the distorting discrepancies and weird looks we get when we try to look that subject in the face.

PART ONE

THE CHILD IS FATHER

1770–1790

CHAPTER I

The Ministries of Fear and Beauty

Cockermouth and Penrith, 1770–1779

> Fair seed-time had my soul, and I grew up
> Fostered alike by beauty and by fear . . .
> (I.305–06)

The earliest picture we have of young Wordsworth is his snapshot of himself as a little noble savage, jumping into the River Derwent behind his home at Cockermouth, in the northwest corner of the English Lake District. He is naked, tan, and alone: the wild child of Cumberland. His only playmates are flowers, and they are violently beaten down. No parents are in sight.

> I, a four year's child,
> A naked boy, among the silent pools
> Made one long bathing of a summer's day,
> Basked in the sun, or plunged into thy streams,
> Alternate, all a summer's day, or coursed
> Over the sandy fields, and dashed the flowers
> Of yellow grunsel; or, when the crag and hill,
> The woods, and distant Skiddaw's lofty height,
> Were bronzed with a deep radiance, stood alone
> A naked savage in the thunder-shower . . .
> (*1799* I.17–26)

The river Derwent was a companion who 'loved / To blend his murmurs with my nurse's song,' and Mount Skiddaw was a distant father-figure, against whose 'lofty height' this rambunctious boy dared to measure himself: at that time, Skiddaw was thought to be the highest mountain in England.

With this kind of writing, begun in 1798–99 and unmatched since, Wordsworth introduces himself as Nature's child in the poem 'on the

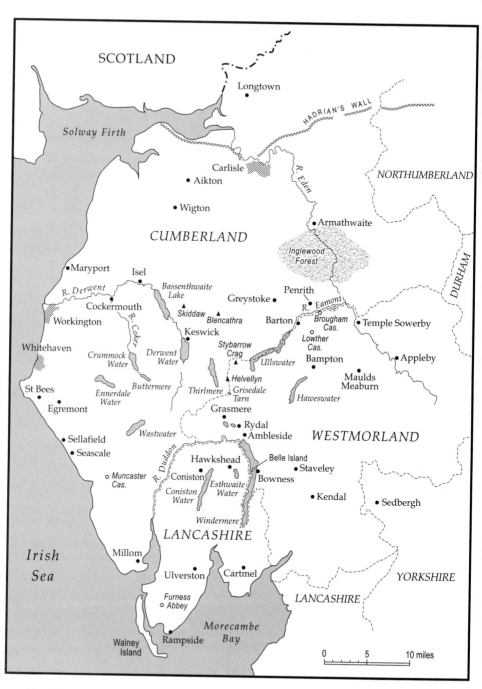

Cumberland, Westmorland, and Lancashire, with the English Lake District

growth of my own mind.' Another picture represents his childhood as a 'fair seed-time,' 'fostered alike by beauty and by fear,' making his growth seem more vegetable than human. In this view, he was fostered not by John and Ann Wordsworth but by Fear and Beauty, the main categories of aesthetic fashion in eighteenth-century Europe. The child Wordsworth seems not only at home in nature, but at one with it. The dominant impression, as *The Prelude*'s narrative begins, is of a child beyond the pale of civilization – those 'fretful dwellings of mankind' whose troubles, he suggests, the Derwent soothed him *not* to hear. He heard nature, not other people, not society.

But if we widen our camera's focus on that naked four-year-old in the river to include what stands behind him, what comes gradually into view is the largest, newest (built 1745), and most splendid house in Cockermouth in 1774, so large and splendid that it remains unmatched in the town to this day: this was his 'father's house.' Wordsworth's birthplace was a spacious town mansion, with impressive drawing rooms on the first floor and a subterranean ground floor that opened out at the rear to an exquisite long garden running down to the river Derwent.

But it was not truly his 'father's house.' It was the designated residence for the Cockermouth agent of Sir James, the fifth Baronet Lowther (1736–1802), the most powerful, feared, and hated aristocrat in all of Cumberland and Westmorland. Later known as the 'bad' or 'gloomy' Earl of Lonsdale, James Lowther was a man so irascible in all his personal dealings, political and domestic, that Thomas Carlyle's brother believed only his wealth kept him from being committed to a madhouse: 'more Detested than any man alive, a Shameless Political Sharper, a Domestick Bashaw, and an Intolerable Tyrant over his Tenants and Dependents.'[1]

John Wordsworth, the poet's father, was one such tenant and dependent of Lord Lowther, and one of the key agents in a ministry of fear by which Lowther sought to achieve his life's ambition: political control of Cumberland and Westmorland. It is ironic that the man whose name above all is associated with the English Lake District, William Wordsworth, should have been, as a child and young man, one of the many victims of the man above all in the eighteenth century who sought to stamp his name on Cumberland and Westmorland. But James Lowther's career is much more than mere background to Wordsworth's poetical life. The facts of his father's – and later his own – connections to the house of Lowther are often glossed over, as if the Wordsworths were innocent victims of Lowther's villainy. But their relations were much more complicated, so much so that we can leave the 'infant babe' Wordsworth to 'sleep upon his mother's breast' for a few years after his birth in 1770, to devote some attention to his father's career.

The Lowthers have been called the region's one indigenous aristocratic family. They were grander than the Le Flemings, Wordsworth's eventual landlords at Rydal Mount, and were not absentee landlords like their main opponents, the powerful young Duke of Portland, or the notoriously debauched Charles Howard, Earl of Surrey and future Duke of Norfolk, who owned Greystoke Castle near Penrith. Lowthers had been leaders in the Border Wars against Scotland, and today almost every town in Cumberland and Westmorland (modern Cumbria) has its Lowther Street or Lonsdale Square, or both. There are very few named after Wordsworth.

James Lowther inherited his uncles' and grandfather's political acumen, commercial orientation, and puritanical thriftiness. He had 'no opinion of anyone that is not punctual in business, a head not turned to it and that do not look strictly and principally into their own affairs.'[2] He had no patience for the feelings of other people, especially underlings, and little enough for those of his peers or superiors, including his wife, Lady Mary Stuart, though he took care not to offend her father, Lord Bute, Prime Minister from 1762 to 1763, and for fifteen years at mid-century the most powerful man in England.

He had hoped for a trade ministry in Lord Bute's government, to aid his shipping interests in Whitehaven, but he was too unpredictable to be trusted; the King thought his support 'scarce worth gaining.'[3] Disappointed in this ambition, he set about establishing personal control over Cumberland and Westmorland, with occasional thrusts into Lancashire and Yorkshire.[4] In Westmorland, the Lowther interest was returned to Parliament uncontested for over a hundred years, from 1775 to 1880, except for one year of disputed occupancy.[5]

The story of electoral politics in mid-eighteenth-century England is more diverting than much of its poetry; even the rambunctious novels of Fielding and Smollett are hard pressed to match it. A hundred years after the Glorious Revolution of 1688, representative democracy (so called) had settled down to a continuation of baronial warfare by other means, principally the buying and selling of votes, a process lubricated with vast amounts of free drinks. This was not quite as corrupt as it sounds, for freeholders who owned the requisite income-producing acreage for enfranchisement could drive hard bargains with large landowners to deliver their votes. Life depended on the pursuit of one's *interests* through one's *influence*. The pursuit of 'interests' in politics may sound corrupt to naive modern ears, but in those franker times that was all there was. 'All classes, even the lowest, asked or intrigued for places and promotions, for themselves, their relations, their protégés; and the most highly placed were the most ruthlessly insistent.'[6]

The main reason to seek control of a large number of parliamentary seats in eighteenth-century England was not party loyalty, still less national policy. The real reason was simply to get enough local power to 'make a great deal of [one's] affairs go on with great ease and quietness.' So said another of Lowther's agents, when urging him to extend his influence by taking over the Cockermouth seat.[7] Lowther took over Cockermouth in 1756 by his characteristically direct method of buying up almost all the burgage rents in town – narrow strips of property whose title deeds carried ancient voting rights – at the astronomical cost of £58,000 (over half a million, in modern terms), including Wordsworth's future birthplace.[8] He very probably owned the Derwent's 'sandy fields' with their 'yellow grunsel' that Wordsworth played in, and many a neighbouring 'crag,' 'hill', and 'wood' as well, if not Skiddaw's 'lofty height' itself.

John Wordsworth's life was devoted to Lowther, and Lowther was the domineering presence on the Wordsworth family, filtered through their father. Lowther consumed people who could not stand up to him, and so he did John Wordsworth. John Wordsworth, Sr. was Lowther's law or land agent. In the late twentieth century, this sounds like the overseer of an estate. But in the mid-eighteenth century it signified mainly a political agent, comprising the tasks of borough-monger, ward heeler, vote canvasser, election rigger, briber, and payer-off of innkeepers – none of which were regarded as reprehensible or, within reason, illegal activities. Such agents were not popular, since they tended to treat people as their master treated them. With an employer like this, and with enormous responsibilities in record-keeping, rent-collecting and vote-delivering, all involving large sums of money, Wordsworth's father's house was frequently one of the most 'fretful dwellings of mankind.' In this service, John Wordsworth was expected to keep scrupulous accounts and give accurate intelligence. In addition to dealing with innkeepers, he might also be expected to spread rumours, forge documents, manipulate opinion, and abuse the trust of his public offices to further the interests of his employer. All this would be considered 'honest' behaviour, where the standard of honesty was loyalty to one's employer, not necessarily public morality. One of John Wordsworth's letters gives the gist of this field lieutenant's reports to his general:

> At Grey southern [an election district] Lord Egremont's people have not been able to stir a Jot. They could not even get a hand to the Petition for Leave to carry in the Bill; so that this matter is over for the present session. I have not yet received the article for the purchase of Mrs Tiffin's Royalties in Grey southern but shall have it in a day or two and will then send the copy.[9]

The freeholders of Westmorland and Cumberland fiercely resisted Lowther's efforts to acquire total command of the two counties,[10] especially during the three decades of William Wordsworth's birth, growth, estrangement from, and return to his native country. Lowther's political ambitions were not an abstract historical process for him, but one in which his father was a principal actor who paid a high price for his actions in local unpopularity. By simultaneously associating young Wordsworth with the dominant social power in his home region, while alienating him from its popular base, James Lowther determined much of the poet's wandering life during the formative years of his manhood. But young Wordsworth was not a natural rebel: both prior to and immediately following this twenty-year period, he and his family unhesitatingly allied themselves with the Lowther interest and worked actively for it. Thus Dorothy Wordsworth, who at nineteen called Lord Lonsdale 'the greatest of tyrants,' would before she was fifty stoutly maintain that 'for my Part I wish not success to any opposers of the House of Lonsdale; for the side that house takes is the good side.'[11]

John Wordsworth held forth at Cockermouth, one of the three 'urban' boroughs in the two counties, along with Carlisle and Appleby. Each had two seats in parliament which, along with the two county boroughs themselves, made a regional total of ten. Cockermouth and Appleby were both 'pocket' and thoroughly 'rotten' boroughs, much less populous than unrepresented urban centres like Kendal and Whitehaven.[12] Whitehaven's population was over 12,000, while Cockermouth consisted of one road enclosed between the Derwent and a wall, with access to the countryside through gates at either end of the street.[13] For the twenty years of his tenure at Cockermouth (1764–1783), John Wordsworth was active in Lowther's successful campaign to extend his parliamentary interest to all ten seats. This was the period from Lowther's greatest debacle, the infamous election of 1768, to the time of his greatest triumph, the election of 1784, when his interest helped the younger Pitt to an ascendancy that lasted nearly twenty years. When Lowther first took up the seat for Cumberland in 1757, following the deaths of his father and two uncles in rapid succession, the family held only one seat in parliament.[14] But during the next twenty-odd years, thanks to the hard work of agents like John Wordsworth, he came to control as many as nine of the region's seats. In one combination or another, these nine seats were known as 'Sir James's Ninepins.'

John Wordsworth had difficulty in bending himself to Lowther's rod, and he was not nearly strong enough to stand up against it.* He worried that his terms of office – defined as agent and bailiff – had not been spelled out clearly enough regarding salary and expenses. He pleaded with his cousin, Captain Hugh Robinson, to intervene for him, because nothing had been settled though he had been in Cockermouth nine months. 'I

---

* James Boswell was more suited to dealing with Lowther than John Wordsworth. He was closely associated with him for four years, 1786–1790, the last two as his recorder for Carlisle. Their tempers clashed constantly, but when Boswell tried to resign his post – in order to finish his biography of Samuel Johnson – he was refused and 'dragged away, wretched as a convict,' to canvass for his master. On the trip north they quarrelled so furiously there would have been a duel, except for the fact that they had but one pistol between them. (Owen, 299–302.)

really hope Sir James will have no such thoughts as those of deferring the main business any longer.'[15] His fears were well founded, but he did not have – being only nineteen at the time – the foresight or courage to make his prospective employer sign a contract of obligations.

But John Wordsworth was not simply a naive victim of these hardball politics; he was a willing and expert player in the game. As a practising attorney keen to acquire a fortune, he 'took into his keeping most of the estates Sir James Lowther purchased for his election purposes,' and his own account book charts the steady growth of what would have been the young Wordsworth's inheritance. It shows that John Wordsworth owned nearly twenty parcels of property throughout the district, from a seventy-acre farm at Sockbridge to individual crofts and barns dotted across the countryside, which produced more than £100 a year in rents. In addition, he had smaller investments like cattlegates, which controlled livestock's access to pasturage; these might only return a pound a year, or less, but they added up: on the High Moor, he and Lowther were the two biggest owners, holding more than a third of fifty-six such gates between them, and thus effectively controlling the market there.[16]

Agents like John Wordsworth were less salaried employees than junior partners in an entrepreneurial business in which elections were only one of the variables to be monitored and controlled as best one could, like the price of labour. It was expected that agents would often lay out their own money for bribes, retainers, and other kinds of payments, in expectation of remuneration by their lord, but also in anticipation of other kinds of returns: offices, favours, rents, and other *quid pro quo* that they could hold as their own, with or without their employer's knowledge. The great lords' power was both dispersed and disguised by investing it in the hands of their underlings through the distribution of 'loaves and fishes,' as the spoils of office were genially known: a whole host of minor offices of little power or remuneration but of great usefulness whenever land or water rights were to be exercised for mining, fishing, and timbering ventures. There were sheriffs, coroners, distributorships, seigneuries, customs and port officers, and so on. Sometimes the fees charged by these offices were paltry sums, but they could be administered on an *ad hoc* basis according to what the official thought he could get away with. In the same year of 1774 when Wordsworth remembered himself as Nature's savage child, his father was made Coroner of the Seigniory of Millom, a little office for a large stretch of seacoast running from the mouth of the Duddon almost to the mouth of the Derwent,[17] and he also held the semi-official title of 'Steward of Ennerdale.'[18]

Active landlords like the Lowthers aided the independent business interests of trusted stewards by way of loans, partnerships and political influence. John Spedding, whose son was one of William Wordsworth's best friends, rose from an impoverished orphan serving-boy to the lesser ranks of the Cumberland gentry.[19] John Wordsworth, starting out from a social position close to where Spedding ended, and with professional education and a small estate to boot, certainly expected to rise to a proportionately higher rank.

Such professional inheritances had ample precedent: Wordsworths had long worked in the Lowther interest.[20] Wordsworth's paternal grandfather, Richard, had first come to Westmorland from South Yorkshire in 1700, to recoup his fortunes with the then-baron Lonsdale.[21] He was agent for James Lowther's father's Westmorland estates from 1728 until his death, during which time he was Clerk of the Peace and Receiver General of Westmorland.[22] He left the position of estate steward in 1738, but this was a mere technicality,[23] for loyal service to one's patron carried over into the government posts. This Richard Wordsworth particularly distinguished himself for loyalty in 1745, when he spirited away the county monies to Patterdale to protect them from the invading Jacobite armies of Bonnie Prince Charlie, while his wife, Wordsworth's grandmother, coolly entertained the rebel officers at their home in Penrith.[24] John Wordsworth took over some of his father's responsibilities immediately upon his death in 1760, when he was only nineteen years old. This is four years earlier than has usually been thought, and four years before his removal to Cockermouth.

The poet's uncle Richard (1733–1794), who was disinherited from the family's small estate at Sockbridge in favour of John Wordsworth, Sr. for marrying against his father's wishes,[25] was named Collector of Customs at Whitehaven, Cumberland's major seaport. Whitehaven was at the time second only to London in tonnage of materials that passed in and out of its harbour,[26] thanks largely to vast increases in profitable trade from North America, especially in Virginia tobacco. If James Lowther bought Cockermouth, it is not too much to say that he and his brothers and their agent Richard Wordsworth *made* Whitehaven, since they laid out its streets on a plan (apparently never paid for) prepared by the great architect and planner Robert Adam, and improved its harbour by way of improving their trading business, in one of the earliest examples of centralized town planning in England.[27]

But the most successful of all the Wordsworth clan was John ('Jack') Robinson, John Wordsworth's first cousin, who also started out as a Lowther agent, and was 'qualified' for Parliament in 1764 by Lowther's vesting in him the minimum financial requirement of £2000 a year.[28] Robinson held the ultra-safe Appleby seat until 1774, when he broke with his patron on the issue of the rights of the American colonists. Robinson then joined Lord North's administration, moved to the seat for Harwich, and soon became treasury secretary and the government's leading polltaker, political strategist and paymaster.[29] Lowther never forgave him.

Many elements of Lowther's policy and personality, and John

Wordsworth's role in furthering the one and suffering the other, came out illuminatingly in the election of 1768, a Pyrrhic victory that made the names of Lowther and Wordsworth hated for years to come. Wordsworth's father was very active in the Cumberland contest, and what Lowther's uncle said of his agent John Spedding could as well have been said of John Wordsworth: 'it is notorious in the country that you are my agent in everything.'[30]

Lowther had decided to run candidates for both of the Cumberland county seats, thereby upsetting the agreed-upon balance of power between his family and the Howards, that each should have one of the two seats.[31] Usually seats were disposed of by aristocrats casting lots, so as to avoid the tremendous cost in bribes and 'entertainments' of a contested election.[32] Contests were the exception rather than the rule, on a principle enunciated by James Lowther's great-grandfather: 'The first thing that contributes to a national settlement must be unanimity in elections.'[33] One item in John Wordsworth's hand from this election reads, 'Lent freemen in notes £680 which after they were polled were ordered to be cancelled.'[34] Did Wordsworth's father double-cross the freemen, or did the freemen vote differently than they were supposed to? And in 1772, four years after the election and two after Wordsworth's birth, some friends of Mrs Perle, an innkeeper at Cockermouth, applied to Lowther for payment of 'her Election Bills,' the hefty sum of £500, of which only £181 had been paid since the election. Mrs Perle had 'applied to Mr Wordsworth about two years ago for more money, and that she found from his answer that she had no expectation of any payment from him, and as he then told her that all the Cockermouth bills were then before [Lowther], she has waited since that time without giving any further trouble, in hopes of hearing from some of your agents.' Her friends said they wouldn't have bothered Lowther about the matter if they hadn't been solicited by people from Lorton who frequented her house, and who 'served you at the Election, notwithstanding they are Tenants to Lord Egremont.' Lowther would get the point of this thinly veiled threat of political defection.[35]

Not everything was so venal in this operation, however. Sometimes votes were bought outright, but this was frowned on if the sums were too high: not because it was illegal and immoral, but because it inflated prices on the election markets. In addition to the deals made before elections for favours in exchange for votes, there was the much livelier business of the 'canvass' of votes, a euphemism for the punch, pies, and tobacco provided free throughout the polling period, which could run as long as two weeks.[36] By far the largest item in all the money handled by John Wordsworth and other election agents was for paying publicans who kept their inns open for drinks on the house. Jack Robinson's account to Lowther for his first election in 1757 gives the flavour – or flavours – of these festivities:

'There are 7 houses fixed for the entertainment of your friends . . . Ordinarys 130 – Wine 10 Dozen. Punch and ale proportionable – . . . It is proposed also to have 13 other houses, for taking off the lower class as much as may be from the better houses . . . besides likewise some ale from the other houses for the mob . . .[37]

'Punch and ale proportionable' was the working slogan in these elections that would make a Chicago alderman blush. The election of 1768 has been reckoned to have cost nearly £100,000 pounds, mainly in this kind of expenditures. More cautious estimates put the figure at 'only' £30,000,[38] but since John Wordsworth's records alone show £24,000 paid out between January 1767 and April 1769, mainly for innkeepers' bills, they suggest that the higher estimates may not be excessive. All in all, approximately 10,000 votes were cast in the five boroughs, an exceptionally high number due to the artificial inflation of the voter rolls, that proved the proverbial wisdom of avoiding election contests to avoid costs.

But Lowther's victory was challenged by Portland in parliament, who was able to prove that the Cockermouth sheriff, Giles Lawson, had improperly cancelled votes for his opponent, Portland's man, Henry Curwen, one of Lowther's competitors in the coal-mining business. Lowther's defence was prepared by John Wordsworth, who set about a counter-attack, claiming that Portland's other candidate, Henry Fletcher, had 'paid the Bills of the Innkeepers after the Election' and bought votes in exchange for reduced tythes for some of his tenants – who readily acknowledged they would not have voted for him otherwise.[39] Many MPs had a hard time keeping a straight face when such normal practices were proffered as 'charges,' but they did not affect the verdict, which turned solely on Sheriff Lawson's inconsistently allowing some voters to participate in the poll while forbidding others.[40] Sometime during the proceedings, the Wordsworth house in Cockermouth was searched by officers, but they found nothing incriminating.[41] Nonetheless, Lowther lost his Cumberland seat, with no kind thoughts for the agent who had prepared his unsuccessful defence. Lowther himself was not greatly incommoded by losing his Cumberland seat, for he served out the rest of the term simply by switching over to his safe Cockermouth seat. But this setback may have cost John Wordsworth his own parliamentary career, since in the election of 1780 Lowther put another of his agents, John Garforth, into the Cockermouth seat.[42]

There may have been costs – and benefits – for the Wordsworth family from the other direction as well, as we shall see in 1799, when the Duke of Portland's secret accounts book – then Home Secretary, in charge of domestic security and espionage – records a payment of nearly £100 pounds to 'Mr Wordsworth,' either the son or the nephew of his old antagonist's chief agent in this *cause célèbre*.

A typical compromise was eventually worked out whereby the Lowther and Portland interests agreed again to divide the two Cumberland seats between them, so there would be no more contested elections. But for the population at large feelings were let loose that did not disappear for many years. A pamphlet war of squibs and cartoons ran for years, portraying Lowther as 'Satan in All His Glory' (see cartoon) and his minions as fools and traitors.*

We can only guess at the effect all this power-brokering and borough-mongering had on Wordsworth as a small child, but he would have been conscious of it by the time he was four or five, given his preternatural ability to recall sensations from early childhood. The effects of a direct, personal, familial involvement in the Lowther 'interest' did not simply stop with his father's death, but continued for nearly twenty years afterwards, while the Wordsworth childrens' guardian uncles were suing Lowther to recover John Wordsworth's money.

Dorothy Wordsworth's recollections illustrate the psychological cost to the children of their father's exploitation by his employer. She reflected that 'it is indeed mortifying to my Brothers and me to find that amongst all those who visited at my father's house he had not one real friend.'[43] By age fifteen, when she wrote this letter, she had come to the disillusioned realization that 'all those who visited . . . my father's house' had done so only because of their father's identification with Lowther. On another occasion, she speculated that 'my uncle Kit [Christopher Cookson Crackanthorpe] . . . having always espoused the cause of the Duke of Norfolk, has incensed him [Lowther] so much that I fear we shall feel through life the effects of his imprudence.'[44] This, plus the defection of Wordsworth's cousin Jack Robinson to the opposition, did indeed work against the Wordsworth childrens' interest. The Crackanthorpes of Newbiggin Hall near Penrith were another old gentry family on the way up, but their wagon was hitched to a different lord. They were not proud

---

* The 1768 election was but a skirmish in a longer war between Lowther and Portland, from 1765 to 1787, over rights to Inglewood Forest north of Penrith. Charges, judgements, and appeals went back and forth for years until the Court of Exchequer decided that Lowther's claims, though legally valid, were invalidated by the Dukes of Portland having been in 'undisturbed possession' of the forest for over sixty years. Like the 1768 election, this was no mere local dispute, but one with national political implications. The new Duke of Portland was a prime recruit of the Rockingham Whigs in 1765, which put him in opposition to Lord Bute, James Lowther's father-in-law. Legal activities were especially intense in 1767–1771, throwing 'the whole county of Cumberland . . . into a state of the greatest terror and confusion'; 400 ejectments against Portland's small landholders were served in one day, after Lowther's initial victory (*Annual Register*, 1771, p. 56). John Wordsworth would have served some of these writs of ejectment.

of their daughter's (Wordsworth's grandmother) marriage alliance with the Cookson family, who were 'in trade,' and they ignored the Wordsworth connection completely when they compiled their family tree.[45]

These family connections lead us back to Wordsworth's mother and her ministry of beauty, and require a change of scene. Wordsworth spent nearly half of his first eight years in his maternal grandparents' rooms above their linen shop in Penrith, not in his father's grace-and-favour mansion at Cockermouth.[46] He was at Penrith mainly in the winter, when he attended Dame Birkett's school, along with his sister Dorothy and Mary Hutchinson, his future wife, the daughter of a local tobacco merchant and granddaughter of the postmaster, to whom he was already related by marriage.[47]

It is not difficult to understand why the children spent so much time in Penrith. Ann Wordsworth had three younger children after Richard and William (Dorothy, born 1771; John, 1772; Christopher, 1774), and could certainly use the help of her parents' more established household. Her husband was not at home regularly, travelling the length and breadth of Cumberland for Lowther. The Cockermouth house, though large and well-staffed, was an important political headquarters, not the most peaceful place to raise children, especially after the crisis of 1768. And this was exactly when the children began to arrive: Richard was born that year. So frequent shifts to Penrith were desirable for family reasons, but politics couldn't be escaped so easily. In spending so much time with the Howard-supporting Cooksons in Penrith, Ann Wordsworth and her children were, in effect, consorting with the enemy.

These tensions were palpable in the rooms above their grandfather's neat white-and-red house on Cornmarket square, off Castlegate.[48] (Though the street has been sentimentally re-christened Poet's Walk, the house was occupied in 1992 by Jackie's Unisex haircutters, an illustration of the Lake District's insouciance toward its native poet.) As adults, the Wordsworth children registered regretful feelings toward Cockermouth, a birthplace they rarely visited in later years. But their feelings toward their grandparents and their uncles in Penrith were actively negative. Their father was not there, and his job was a source of irritation to the Cooksons.

The Cooksons were small town tradespeople, linen drapers and church wardens. Their lives, like their house, were altogether more pinched and conventional than the reflected glories of the Cockermouth manse. Every indication that has come down to us about them is of disapproval and nagging correction of the Wordsworth childrens' behaviour. It may seem hard, in terms of conventional cliches, that grandparents should be so cold. But there were good reasons of class and politics to motivate the Cooksons' disapproval of the Wordsworth children.

The Cooksons were upwardly mobile too, but on a different line. William Cookson, the poet's maternal grandfather, had made a highly advantageous match in marrying Dorothy Crackanthorpe, heiress of Newbiggin Hall. When Uncle Kit (born 1745) inherited Newbiggin Hall on his mother's death in 1792, he quickly dropped his father's name and took his more prestigious middle name as his family name, becoming Christopher Crackanthorpe. This Uncle Kit, who was twenty-five when Wordsworth was born, kept up the line of complaint against the children as his parents aged.

Wordsworth's memories of his mother are few and dim, as he regretfully admitted: 'O lost too early for the frequent tear.'[49] But they are more definite than his recollections of his father. He was seven when he last saw her, just before she died in March 1778, resting in a chair in her bedroom at Penrith. The main image that emerges from his memories of her is one of unselfconscious good sense. She was the 'parent hen' around whom the children trooped. But she was so much the 'centre,' so much 'the heart / And hinge of all our learning and our loves,' that when she died the centre did not hold: 'she left us destitute, and as we might / Trooping together' (V.246–60). Their father was unable to hold the troop together.

When Wordsworth began to describe his mother's influence, he stopped himself, saying he did not wish to disturb her memory 'with any thought that looks at others' blame.' This probably refers to the harsh parenting of the Penrith Cooksons, but it also applies to John Wordsworth. It is a criticism of adults with too-strong plans for the children in their care, either constantly 'shaping novelties' and 'false unnatural hopes' for their future success, or else being full of 'feverish dread of error and mishap' (V.260–80), very unlike Ann Wordsworth's easygoing ways. John Wordsworth had very definite plans for his sons' careers, for what they *should* be, while the Cooksons had very definite feelings of what they should *not* be – i.e., dependent on them.

In the absence of clear physical images of Wordsworth's mother, we find numerous psychological ones, suggesting that his maternal experience was as strong in the inner realm of feelings as his paternal experience was in the external world of power politics. His image of himself as a 'naked savage' is one of the few images he retained from his childhood's male-dominated ministry of fear. He recollected many more images of his mother's ministry of beauty, even though she died five years before his father. All these memories concern women, but most of them concentrate on women in jeopardy, in pain, or dead.

One day he came home from school and proudly told his mother he had witnessed 'a woman doing penance in the church in a white sheet,' but complained that he had not been given a penny for his observance.[50] His mother commended him for having been present, and hoped 'that I should remember the circumstance for the rest of my life,' wisely adding that he was 'very properly disappointed' of his venal penny.

Was this only a lesson against base motives for virtuous behaviour? The circumstance was in fact a rather unusual one: a woman doing public penance, in a white sheet, in the Church of England, *c.* 1775. Such public penances had all but disappeared from the watered-down liturgical practices of late eighteenth-century Anglicanism, except in remote provincial places. The woman was doing penance for sexual sin: incontinence, incest, adultery, or, most probably, for having borne a child out of wedlock. Her penance was part of the 'Cleansing of Women' rite, one of the five stated orders in the *Book of Common Prayer* of 1741. After safely giving birth, a woman came to church to give thanks to God, and was readmitted to the congregation, in what amounted to a sort of Christianized purification rite for her 'uncleanness.' But if she were unmarried, the ceremony had to be preceded by the public penance which Wordsworth saw, and which his mother hoped he would always remember.

And he did. For though it is impossible to sort out the psychosexual reactions contained in such a memory, its recollection was not accidental. He composed a sonnet on this 'Thanksgiving After Childbirth' rite, and his 'imagined view' of the safely-delivered young mother kneeling penitently is presented as a refuge of 'safety' to her 'Heir,' who walks in 'courses fit to make a mother rue / That he was ever born.'[51] This is a very strange idea with which to end a poem about thanksgiving. Ann Wordsworth probably only wished her son to remember the shameful wages of sin, not those of fallen women particularly. Yet she did fear for, even if she did not live to 'rue' (as her parents and brothers abundantly did), the future of her second child. William was the only one of her five children about whose future life she was anxious; she is reported to have said that he would be remarkable either for good or for evil.[52] This is how he fashioned himself in *The Prelude*, where Beauty is associated with goodness, and the Sublime with strong disobedience. The insistent peacefulness of Wordsworth's later poetry should always be measured against the extreme violence of his thoughts and actions as a child.

'I was of a stiff, moody, and violent temper,' Wordsworth told his nephew, and as an example of his character he brought up a memory of another threatened woman.

> Upon another occasion, while I was at my grandfather's house at Penrith, along with my brother Richard, we were whipping tops together in the large drawing-room, on which the carpet was only laid down upon particular occasions. The walls were hung round with family pictures, and I said to my brother, 'Dare you strike your whip through that old lady's petticoat?' He replied, 'No, I won't.' 'Then,' said I, 'here goes;' and I struck my lash through

her hooped petticoat, for which, no doubt, though I have forgotten it, I was properly punished.

As with his recollection of the woman in white, his punishment faded in comparison with his transgression. Was his violence cause or effect? He seems to be recalling perfectly the logic of children, who often perceive punishment as a wrong far greater than the act that provoked it. Yet the crime, not the punishment, fills his memory. Why should 'that old lady' be picked out from the family portrait gallery for punishment? One explanation is that her big skirts made her a better target, or at least a more inviting target than the severe faces of the male portraits hanging there.

The young Wordsworth liked to dare and disobey, even if he had to take his own dares. Throughout his early childhood, his violence toward nature contrasted to Dorothy's more tender feelings. His recollected images of violence or shame upon women are matched by images of his own violence exercised in the company of his sister's tenderness. His heart 'doubtless wanted not its tender moods,' but he could not remember them. He 'better recollect[s]' breathing

> Among wild appetites and blind desires,
> Motions of savage instinct my delight
> And exaltation. Nothing at that time
> So welcome, no temptation half so dear
> As that which urged me to a daring feat.
> Deep pools, tall trees, black chasms, and dizzy crags,
> And tottering towers; I loved to stand and read
> Their looks forbidding . . .

This sounds promisingly humble, but it ends up wholly in Wordsworth's willfulness: '. . . read *and disobey*, / Sometimes in act, and *evermore in thought*.'[53] He had his gentler side, but more often than not it was embodied in Dorothy *at* his side.

Dorothy Wordsworth's extreme susceptibility to emotion in scenes of natural beauty is as well-attested a fact as William's violent responses to such scenes. This difference is beautifully captured in his recollection of their first vision of the sea. They were on their way to visit their cousins in Whitehaven, and as they came up over the crest of the enormous hills that surround the town, they saw all at once the whitecaps that give the town its name, rushing into the crablike arms of the harbour breakwater on one of that coast's perpetually windy days. Dorothy, 'when she first *heard* the voice of the sea from this point, and beheld the scene spread before her, burst into tears.'[54] The family at Cockermouth often mentioned this incident, 'as indicating the sensibility for which she was so remarkable.'

Wordsworth, by contrast, remembered 'being *struck*' by the panorama of town and harbour, and identified himself emphatically with the waves' striking motion – 'the white waves breaking against its quays and piers.' This matches the 'mysterious awe with which I used to listen to anything said about storms or shipwrecks.'[55] This sounds appropriately adventuresome for a boy, but storms and shipwrecks were not romantic matters for a boy whose uncle was chief of customs at Whitehaven, and whose relations were heavily invested in a 'family bottom' of the East India Company, on a coast where storms and shipwrecks were very frequent disasters.

Poems like 'The Sparrow's Nest,' 'To a Butterfly,' and 'To a Daisy' have high standing in many peoples' admiration of Wordsworth, but it might truly be said that the Wordsworth they love is Dorothy, not William, since sparrow, butterfly, and daisy all stood in as much danger from him as that old lady in petticoats. Dorothy recalled that William wanted to kill all white butterflies 'because they were Frenchmen' (French soldiers wore white).[56] He chased after them ferociously:

> A very hunter did I rush
> Upon the prey; with leaps and springs
> I followed on from brake to bush;

Not so Dorothy: 'But she, God love her! feared to brush / The dust from off its wings.'[57]

He chased one butterfly through the 'green courts' of Cockermouth Castle, a few hundred yards east along the Derwent from his home. There, in a poem originally titled 'Castle to the Author,' his violent temperament got a lesson he never forgot. Entering by chance the 'soul-appalling darkness' of its dungeon, his 'young thoughts' were suddenly made 'acquainted with the grave.'[58] The scene, with him and Dorothy playing in it, is in effect a miniature of the twin ministries of Beauty and Fear, for the castle was not then a picturesque medieval ruin, still less the renovated family home it is today. It was the seat of the old Earls of Egremont and later of the Howard family, both traditional Lowther enemies, and the precise location of the polling place where Wordsworth's father helped fight latter-day versions of the old barons' wars.

His last clear recollection from his first eight years, before he, 'fair seed,' was transplanted to school at Hawkshead, brings this pattern of feminine Beauty and masculine Sublimity to a dramatic conclusion. He made it famous by identifying it as one of the two 'spots of time' which he said were central to the growth of his mind – the other being his imagined guilt for his father's death in 1783. Both, that is, are associated with his parents' deaths, and with their replacement by Nature's emotional foster-parents, beauty and fear.

One day when he was five or six he rode out from Penrith with his father's servant, James. He was just learning to ride, just being initiated into men's activities. Somehow they became separated. It seems very inattentive of James, but perhaps the disobedient boy separated himself from the servant and rode down off the road (the present A686) toward an abandoned quarry. He, with an ear attentive to 'tragedies of former times,' well knew the superstition of the place. Here, 'in former times / A man, the murderer of his wife, was hung / In irons.' His memory conflated two local stories,[59] adding to a recent (1767) Penrith homicide a much older (1672) Hawkshead superstition of matricide, or wife-murder. All was gone, of gallows, chains, and bones associated with those public executions, except that 'a long green ridge of turf remained / Whose shape was like a grave,' in which 'the murderer's name' in

> . . . monumental writing was engraven
> In times long past, and still from year to year
> By superstition of the neighbourhood
> The grass was cleared away; and to this hour
> The letters are all fresh and visible.
> (XI.293-98)[60]

Like the spirit of Cockermouth Castle, this scares even the little boy who liked nothing better than destruction and disobedience. It still scared the man in his early thirties who wrote about it.

Certainly there are enough reasons of the usual sort to explain everything away, if we want to: he was lost, he was scared, and he may have been disobedient. But he remembered, or added, much more about the scene, elements having to do with a violated woman. Thoroughly frightened, he dismounted and struggled back up the slope to the road, where he found not James but another woman whose image never left him.

> . . . reascending the bare slope I saw
> A naked pool that lay beneath the hills,
> The beacon on the summit, and more near
> A girl who bore a pitcher on her head
> And seemed with difficult steps to force her way
> Against the blowing wind.
> (*1799*, I.313–19)

That's all. By way of further explanation, he only offers a repetition of the same three elements: beacon, pool, and woman:

> It was in truth
> An ordinary sight, but I should need
> Colours and words that are unknown to man
> To paint the visionary dreariness
> Which, while I looked all round for my lost guide,
> Did at that time invest the naked pool,
> The beacon on the lonely eminence,

> The woman and her garments vexed and tossed
> By the strong wind.

> > (*1799*, I.319–27)

An ordinary sight, but extraordinary poetry, much odder than it appears at first glance. The girl, who firmly pursued an ordinary purpose in his first perception of her, has become a woman whose clothes are being violently disturbed in the second. Is the wind masculine like the murderer?

Penrith Beacon, 'the beacon on the summit,' was a relatively new piece of military hardware, dating from 1719, when it was erected as part of an early warning system for national rebellions like those of 1715.[61] It had most recently been activated in the Jacobite uprising of 1745, when the Scotch rebels marched down that same road. This was in fact the last time the beacon was ever used for its intended purpose, and the Wordsworths' role in 'The '45' was proudly recounted at family gatherings.[62] But such gatherings almost always contain hidden contests, and dead grandfather Wordsworth's loyalty to Lowther and the king was complicated by live grandfather Cookson's sympathy for the rebel cause. At every level, from violence in the family to violence in the state, and ambivalence about which grandfather was right, the Penrith Beacon focused the historical and personal forces brought to bear on the young Wordsworth.

The child Wordsworth was violent, moody, and melancholy. He was a paragon only of extremes – whether for good or evil, even his mother was in doubt. He loved nature mainly to destroy it, or to feel the thrill of his destructive impulses in contrast to his sister's tender sympathies. When his mother was near death, his busy and efficient father was too busy and efficient for his children's good. Dorothy was packed off to relatives in anticipation of the coming sad event, right after Christmas 1777.[63] After Ann Wordsworth's death in March 1778, John Wordsworth kept his four boys, aged ten, eight, six, and four, with him at Cockermouth for a while. But he never recovered his former cheerfulness, and was kept as busy as ever by his harsh taskmaster, who faced another important election in 1780. Deprived of what little maternal presence seven-year-old Dorothy might have provided, they trooped around awkwardly, a reproach to their father.

Toward the end of 1778 it was clear they could not make a home at Cockermouth, and they were sent back to Penrith, where they were not welcome. So, at the awkward school-beginning time of Whitsuntide (May) 1779, William, just turned nine, and his older brother Richard were packed off to Hawkshead school by their grandfather, who shortly thereafter presented their father with 'a very big bill.'[64] They returned home to Cockermouth rarely, and after Christmas 1783 not at all. Even before John Wordsworth's death, these were melancholy vacations;

Wordsworth more poignantly recalled throwing himself onto his father's library rather than into his arms on these vacations. But perhaps I judge John Wordsworth too harshly. Perhaps he sought rather to remove the boys from the unpleasantness surrounding his own unpopular reputation, in the house fearsomely regarded as a field headquarters for the ministry of fear emanating from Lowther Castle.

CHAPTER 2

The Vale of Esthwaite

Hawkshead and Colthouse, 1779–1787

> Beloved Hawkshead . . . thy paths, thy shores
> And brooks, were like a dream of novelty
> To my half-infant mind . . .
>
> *(1799*, i.261–63)

The village of Hawkshead, in the little Lancashire valley of Esthwaite, can well claim to be the heart of that imaginary country called 'Wordsworthshire.'[1] By far the largest number of famous passages describing Wordsworth's sublime experiences in nature derive from his years spent at the grammar school there, from May 1779, until October 1787, when he departed for Cambridge. But before admiring Hawkshead's imaginative reconstruction by the twenty-eight-year-old poet who wrote those passages, we should try to enter into the frame of mind of the nine-year-old who arrived there at Whitsuntide 1779.[2]

The dominant impression of Wordsworth's Hawkshead memories is one of boisterous release: the explosion into a new psychic space of an emptied-out sensibility. Motherless, practically fatherless, separated from all his siblings except the sombre Richard, Wordsworth burst into the region, desperately attaching himself to its places and persons. His sense of himself at Hawkshead was so keen because, with his emotional and intellectual precociousness, he was entering a second childhood with the awareness that this would be all the childhood he was likely to have. But this sudden and by no means entirely happy consciousness of himself *as a* child bulked large in the emotional baggage Wordsworth brought with him. There is plenty of evidence that other boys also had a wonderful time at Hawkshead school, but coming when and as he did, Wordsworth exploded into the Vale of Esthwaite as if shot from an emotional cannon. And he was, we have seen, already a highly volatile projectile.

His special consciousness of himself as a child was closely connected to an awareness of himself in that place, markedly different from his later feeling at Cambridge, 'that I was not for that hour / Nor for that place.' Here, he definitely *was* for that hour and that place, and for all the neighbouring places which soon entered into his consciousness: Colthouse, Coniston, Windermere, Furness, Grasmere, and many points in between. Wordsworth's Hawkshead years appear in retrospect as one long, non-stop career of boyish jaunts, climbs, rides and races. To judge from *The Prelude*'s account, 'one would say that because they were boys and happy they were all more or less poets.'[3] Round the clock, day and night, summer and winter, 'from week to week, from month to month . . . the year span round / With giddy motion' (*1799*, ii.46–7). The active focus of Wordsworth's life during these years was less the school than the vale of Esthwaite itself, and the valleys, hills and lakes around it, as far off the coast of the Irish Sea, twenty-five miles away. These passages in *The Prelude* are everybody's favourites, and Wordsworth knew how good they were, for he scattered them judiciously throughout the poem as thematic flashbacks. If they were excerpted and arranged sequentially they would read like a dream-childhood in The Valley of Happy Boys. They are a fast-paced, non-stop narration of boyish larks and sports, up hill and down dale, pell-mell in every direction, on foot, horseback or in boats, full speed ahead, and the devil take the hindmost. They may be too good to be literally true, but their truth is in their imaginative power, and his releasing his imagination into these recollections of boyhood is a very large part of what made Wordsworth the poet he is – a large part, that is, of his self-creation.

For the next eight and a half years, the boys' lives were effectively divided into spring and winter half-years. John joined them in 1782 and Christopher in 1785, just before Richard left.[4] School took up 'three divisions of the quartered year,' and they went home only twice a year, for a month at Christmas and for six to eight weeks in the summer, from late June to late August. 'Home,' moreover, varied both geographically and emotionally. At Christmas, it was Cockermouth until 1783, when John Wordsworth died. After that, they went to Whitehaven with their paternal uncle Richard and his large happy family of nine children. Summers were divided between Cockermouth and Penrith, but again only through 1783, and sometimes they stayed longer and returned earlier to Hawkshead.[5]

For more than three-quarters of every year they lived with old Ann Tyson and her husband Hugh, a carpenter. Until late 1783 – a decisive year in many ways – they lived in a house at the end of Vicarage Lane in the centre of Hawkshead. After that they moved out to Green End Cottage in the tiny hamlet of Colthouse, a small collection of houses about a half-mile east of Hawkshead. In these residences, and in Ann Tyson, they were extremely fortunate. About sixty of the school boys stayed in the headmaster's large house in town, near the school, but the rest stayed with individual families like the Tysons.[6] Married in 1749, the Tysons had no children of their own. Ann had sold groceries and dry goods in a small way since 1759, but by 1779 she and Hugh were old folks (sixty-six and sixty-five, respectively), ready to take up the more domestic work of boarding schoolboys.[7] Starting with Richard and William, the Wordsworth boys were her main source of income for the better part of thirteen years, until Christopher departed for Cambridge in 1792.[8] John Wordsworth may have erred in separating Dorothy from her brothers for so long, but by luck or design he did well to keep his boys together as a group during all their school years, and in a family setting. In Ann Tyson they got a surrogate mother for Ann Wordsworth, and simultaneously a loving stand-in grandmother for the censorious Dorothy Crackanthorpe Cookson. Although a simple, uneducated woman, there is no mistaking this Ann's importance to the boys in Wordsworth's tribute to his 'grey-haired dame':

> With thoughts unfelt till now I saw her read
> Her bible on the Sunday afternoons,
> And loved the book when she had dropped asleep
> And made of it a pillow for her head.
>
> (IV.218–21)

For the better part of these eight years, Wordsworth's life was one great round of seasonal activities. In good weather, he fished, flew kites, and set traplines to snare woodcocks; both fish and birds brought a good price at market, augmenting their 'little weekly stipend.' (In fact, Ann Tyson's accounts show a healthy outlay for large cuts of meat.[9])There was an enormous amount of what would now be called hiking or fell-walking, but then it was only basic transportation. Rock and cliff-climbing were not undertaken just for the fun of it, but to find and destroy ravens' nest and eggs, since these large birds often attacked young lambs. During one of these excursions, in 1783, one of the local boys, John Benson, lost his nerve and became 'crag-fast': frozen with terror and unable to move in any direction.[10] The older boys hurried down to find some adult workmen to rescue him, but one, the youngest of the group, stayed behind to imagine the sublime possibilities of the situation:

> Oh, when I have hung
> Above the raven's nest, by knots of grass
> And half-inch fissures in the slippery rock
> But ill-sustained, and almost, as it seemed,
> Suspended by the blast . . .
>
> . . . oh, at that time
> While on the perilous ridge I hung alone,
> With what strange utterance did the loud dry wind

Blow through my ears; the sky seemed not a sky
Of earth, and with what motion moved the clouds!
(I.341–50)

The excitement of these exploits was heightened both by competition and, not infrequently, by disobedience: stealing woodcocks from someone else's traps, or 'borrowing' a boat for a night-time joy ride. In great contrast to Penrith, no one seems to have disciplined Wordsworth very much at all in Hawkshead, but at these special moments he himself supplied the missing authority, larger and more grave than any father or schoolmaster. After snatching 'the bird / Which was the captive of another's toils,' he felt 'Low breathings coming after me . . . steps almost as silent as the turf they trod' (I.326–27, 330–32). Over on more distant Ullswater, hidden cliffs rose above the shore's horizon as he stroked a stolen boat further out into the lake, and 'the huge cliff . . . with measured motion, like a living thing / Strode after me' (I.409–12).

As they got older, the boys branched further afield, packing picnics and renting boats or horses for the day. They raced boats from the ferry-landing narrows at the middle of Windermere out to the little islands scattered there like so many inviting targets for boyish daring: Lady Holme, Hen Holme, Crow Holme, Longholme and Ramp Holme. Or, over to the west on quieter Coniston Water, they trolled the shore, confidently stopping to borrow butter and a chafing dish from the caretakers of the Le Flemings' dilapidated Coniston Hall, so after they caught their trout they could eat it too. Still older, when they could command attention as sons of worthy gentlemen of the region, they would saunter into the old White Horse Inn at Windermere and spend the afternoon bowling on the back lawn, ordering up strawberries and cream for refreshment.

These activities, mainly from Book II of *The Prelude* and after 1783, are more adult, less crossed by the excitement of danger or disobedience. But in the best of them, the rides down to Furness Abbey on the coast and back along Morecambe Bay, Wordsworth admits their 'sly subterfuge' upon 'the good old innkeeper,' 'for the intended bound / Of the day's journey was too distant far / For any cautious man' (II.106–08). The reckless boys did not tell the innkeeper how hard they would have to push their rented steeds to get them back within the appointed time: 'With whip and spur we . . . flew / In uncouth race . . . / In wantonness of heart . . . / We scampered homeward . . . / Lighted by gleams of moonlight from the sea, / We beat with thundering hoofs the level sand' (II.122–44, *passim*.).

But all this activity was frequently cut short or crossed for him by moments of silence, solitude, and fear. He often emphasizes the speed of his exploits by a sudden sharp contrast, as when ice-skating he 'glanced sideway' into one of Esthwaite's small bays, and 'stopped short . . .

reclining back upon my heels,' as only an expert skater can. His visual illusion – 'yet still the solitary cliffs / Wheeled by me' – is entirely accurate, for the upper body, head, and eyes are still experiencing a movement of perhaps twenty miles an hour, while the feet stand still. On this perceptual basis he builds a huge metaphorical leap: 'as if the earth had rolled / With visible motion her diurnal round' (*1799*, i.179–82). On the wild horseback rides to Furness Abbey, the sound of their 'thundering hoofs' was cut so sweetly by the song of a 'single wren' when they lay resting, 'that there *I could have made / My dwelling-place, and lived forever there, / To hear such music.*' Here, as at other moments on Coniston and above Grasmere, Wordsworth's perception of a peaceful moment seems to have sunk down unimpeded onto his naked psyche, imprinting for later decipherment the idea that these places might supply what he most desperately lacked, a home.

At other moments, the silences deepened further, to death. His first picture of himself at Hawkshead, 'in the very week / When I was first transplanted to thy vale' (actually it was the first month), catches him in perfect psychological focus,

> when thy paths, thy shores
> And brooks, were like a dream of novelty
> To my half-infant mind . . .
> (*1799*, i.259–63)

But as he crossed one of the two or three 'ear-shaped' peninsulas that bulge out from Esthwaite Water's smooth shores, a nightmare gradually unfolded before his mind, dreaming on the scene. With dusk coming on, he saw 'distinctly on the opposite shore . . . a heap of garments.'

> Long I watched,
> But no one owned them; meanwhile the calm lake
> Grew dark, with all the shadows on its breast,
> And now and then a fish up-leaping snapped
> The breathless stillness . . .
> (V.462–66)

Here the contrast came in reverse, shock *after* calm, as death rose up next day when men went out in boats to investigate the 'plain tale' of those 'unclaimed garments.'

> At length, the dead man, 'mid that beauteous scene
> Of trees and hills and water, bolt upright
> Rose with his ghastly face, a spectre shape –
> Of terror even.
> (V.470–73)

Revising these lines in 1805, Wordsworth credited his reading of the

Arabian Nights and other fairy tales for not being too terrified by this scene in 1779. But the fact that the drowned man was a schoolmaster in the nearby hamlet of Sawrey seems a reason at least as significant for the incident's impressing itself on the motherless nine-year-old's memory.

Death's strongest impress on him in Hawkshead came with his father's death in 1783. But it came also in imaginations of his own death. His description of the deceased 'Boy of Winander' is, as its manuscripts make clear, a description of himself. He and his friend William Raincock loved to blow 'mimic hootings to the silent owls' roosting in the woods across the lake, 'And they would shout / Across the watery vale, and shout again, / Responsive to his call.'

But sometimes the boy was frustrated by the owls' refusal to take the bait.

> Then, sometimes, in that silence, while he hung
> Listening, a gentle shock of mild surprise
> Has carried far into his heart the voice
> Of mountain-torrents; or the visible scene
> Would enter unawares into his mind
> With all its solemn imagery, its rocks,
> Its woods, and that uncertain heaven received
> Into the bosom of the steady lake.
>
> (18–25)

Nature entered into him, not vice versa. The smooth, calm 'bosom' or 'breast' of the lake in both episodes is pierced by, or calmly rebukes, violent human actions. That Wordsworth should present this boy as one of two twelve-year-olds at the school who actually did die of disease in 1782 – when he himself was twelve – is his way of underwriting the significance of the experience with a kind of metaphysical shorthand.[11]

For biographical purposes, we can add back the names of the boys who were with Wordsworth when he experienced these things, and subtract the names of the metaphysical abstractions with which he peopled these scenes when he wrote about them (e.g., 'Wisdom and Spirit of the Universe'). Not because the former are truer than the latter, but because the latter did not have names for young Wordsworth, *c.* 1780, except as conventional religious pieties. We may also be curious to know why the names of the former dropped out of most of his accounts of his formative boyhood experiences.

Who were these wild boys of Esthwaite? Wordsworth's friendships pose an interesting question. There is no indication in the poetry or in his prose recollections that he was particularly the leader in these exploits, but every indication that he was very much one of the group,[12] as he very rarely is elsewhere in his poetry. Neither his appearance nor his manners were conventionally attractive, yet he always had good, supportive, though often long-suffering friends. He was a serious-looking boy (some said 'horse-faced'), who developed rapidly into a large-boned, strongly-built young man, with a heavy mouth and a prominent nose.[13] His face in repose could appear tough and forbidding; when he laughed he looked even worse. But he was strong and healthy; in all his eight years at Hawkshead there is no record in the accounts of his ever requiring a doctor or medicine. He later compared himself to a craggy mountain eminence; this was not merely poetic license or regional propaganda, but the closest resemblance to himself he could find in his chosen landscape.

But unlike the mountain, he was restless. We see this in his outdoor activities, we see it in his conversation, and we see it affecting his friends. He was even restless in his sleep. Thomas Maude, one of a set of brothers who roomed with him at Colthouse recalled 'he was the uneasiest bedfellow I've ever had.' If he couldn't sleep he thought nothing of going out for a walk at one in the morning or even later.[14]

Wordsworth's friends were often very different from him, and this preference for difference began to emerge at Hawkshead. It suggests that Wordsworth's youthful personality was neither as comforting nor as pompous as it later became. He was, in a word, impressive. People were drawn to him, rarely he to them. He does not seem to have gone out of his way to appeal to anyone, unless he thought they might do him some good. This is not to say that he did not care for other people's opinions, nor was he unfriendly. Indeed, he seems to have had a special genius, and need, for friendships, especially of men somewhat older than himself – understandable in a boy whose father died at the beginning of his crucial teenage years. But Wordsworth was a high-risk friend. During his young manhood, he had three close male friends, all of whom came to rue their association with him: John Raincock Fleming at Hawkshead, William Mathews at Cambridge, and Coleridge in Somerset. They all attached themselves to his imaginative development, and they all fell foul of it for one reason or another. There is no need to apportion blame: if Wordsworth disappointed them, perhaps they disappointed him too.

Our earliest glimpse of the boy Wordsworth, while he was still living in the village of Hawkshead, comes down to us with the veracity of eye-witness report. Philip Braithwaite (1764–1849) was a poor crippled boy who was thrown on to parish relief by the death of his father, a local hatter. A great-uncle took him into his blacksmithy, but soon cast him off again, and he was apprenticed to a farmer, where an accident made his deformed leg worse. In 1781, to help make him employable, he was allowed into the reading, writing and arithmetic classes at the grammar school, even though they were for much younger boys, and he was boarded with Ann Tyson. He and Wordsworth shared a room and carved their names on the window seat:

PHIL^P BRAITHWAITE
1781
WM WORDSWORTH

Philip lived to eighty-five, and old people at the beginning of the twentieth century remembered talking to him when they were young. He said that while at the Tysons he never had much conversation with Richard Wordsworth, 'but that William talked to him quite a lot, and was always asking him questions about one thing or another, anything in fact that he, Philip, happened to know something about because of his greater age and wider experience.'[15]

This picture of Wordsworth as a pesky questioner is preserved in a passage from *The Prelude* where Wordsworth recalls pumping Philip for particulars of his trip to London. Their exchange is typical of many other important instances of flawed communication in Wordsworth's poetry, where what is *not* said is more important than what is.

> I well
> Remember that among our flock of boys
> Was one, a cripple from the birth, whom chance
> Summoned from school to London – fortunate
> And envied traveller – and when he returned,
> After short absence, and I first set eyes
> Upon his person, verily, though strange
> The thing may seem, I was not wholly free
> From disappointment to behold the same
> Appearance, the same body, not to find
> Some change, some beams of glory brought away
> From that new region. Much I questioned him,
> And every word he uttered, on my ears
> Fell flatter than a cagèd parrot's note,
> That answers unexpectedly awry,
> And mocks the prompter's listening.
>   (VII.93–108)

So marvellous was Wordsworth's imaginative conception of London that he imagined a cripple might be cured just by going there. Philip Braithwaite was notably 'queer' or touchy all his life about both his disability and his poverty, and his irascibility fits the type and matches the edginess of some of Wordsworth's other boy friends.

This sense of an edge is notably missing in Wordsworth's best friend at school, John Fleming. Born John Raincock, his parents changed his name in 1779 to honour his inheriting Rayrigg, a large estate on Windermere, from his mother's uncle. Two years older than Wordsworth, born and raised in Penrith, he left Hawkshead in 1785, proceeding duly to St

John's, Cambridge, where he graduated in 1789. He is memorialized in Wordsworth's first published volume, *An Evening Walk* (1793): 'Friendship and Fleming at the same.' He and William used to walk the five miles around the lake in the early morning, talking and memorizing school verses, especially from Thomson's *The Seasons* (1726), the most popular poem of the eighteenth century, whose subject was more or less the very action they were performing at such moments: enjoying the natural world as landscape scenery. Sometimes they worked up verse compositions of their own, quietly murmuring and musing together as they strolled along, a very intimate kind of communication. No one other than Coleridge or Dorothy – and Fleming – ever accompanied him in these exercises.

Fleming is remembered, but not named, in *The Prelude*'s account of these walks:

> five miles
> Of pleasant wandering – happy time, more dear
> For this, that one was by my side, a friend
> Then passionately loved. With heart how full
> Will he peruse these lines, this page – perhaps
> A blank to other men – for many years
> Have since flowed in between us, and, our minds
> Both silent to each other, at this time
> We live as if those hours had never been.
>
> (*1799*, ii.380–88)

This is an odd message to send to an old, or former, friend. We can always wave off Wordsworth's oddities, in this case calling it merely a conventional detail of stylized regret for the lost joys of youth. We all have such long-lost friends. But how many do we remember for so long, *as* forgotten? Is Fleming only supposed to regret his own boyhood, or is he also to be reminded how long their minds have been 'silent' to each other – i.e., out of mental sympathy with each other? 'We live as if those hours had never been' is a powerful line. Set against 'passionately loved,' it suggests that something else is going on here, recrimination perhaps as much as regret. Mary Moorman rarely criticizes Wordsworth, but she does not disguise anomalies: Wordsworth and Fleming 'formed a passionate friendship of which a mutual love of poetry was the basis, but, though in later life they were neighbours, Fleming living at Rayrigg and Wordsworth at Grasmere, intimacy did not continue.'[16] Though late in life Wordsworth recalled Fleming in a list of his former '*intimate* acquaintances' at college – all then dead[17] – Fleming probably became too conventional for Wordsworth's taste, stuck in the conventions of their youth (Thomson's landscape poetry), and was left behind.

This view of the risks of a Wordsworth friendship is strengthened when we contrast Wordsworth's relations with John Fleming's brother, Fletcher

Raincock (1769–1840), the 'Fleck' of many a Hawkshead escapade, including the rescue of John Benson from the ravens' crags. Fletcher was the ring-leader of Wordsworth's Hawkshead gang. He chatted up the Castlehow boys, the local bandits, and delighted in school tricks against the masters, not being particularly afraid of punishments. He also went to Cambridge, distinguishing himself as second Wrangler and fellow of Pembroke, and lived out an active legal and political career in the north, serving as the last Recorder of Kendal (1818–1840). He also acted as agent for the Lowther family at their Appleby elections.[18] He was remembered in Liverpool as 'one of the most remarkable characters of his day' for his legal powers, his 'gluttonous' reading, his habit of producing odd bits of information, his agreeably eccentric conversation, and his originality.[19] In short, he sounds about as different from his brother as can be – and very much the kind of person Wordsworth liked, though Wordsworth himself is never recalled in such affectionate detail. Fletcher Raincock even looked like Wordsworth, or worse: 'He was a man with a very plain face and ungainly gait. On one occasion, in cross-examining a female witness who had used once or twice the then newly-coined word "humbugging", Mr Raincock inquired what she meant by "humbugging"? "Whoi if oi war to ca' yer a handsome mon, that ud be humbugging." '[20]

Another such eccentric high in Wordsworth's esteem was Robert Hodgson Greenwood (1768–1839), 'the minstrel of our troop,' in Wordsworth's phrase, or 't' lad wi' t' flute,' in Ann Tyson's.[21] After an afternoon of bowling or boating, the boys sometimes put Greenwood on one of the small rocky islands near the Windermere ferry, 'and left him there, / And rowed off gently, while he blew his flute / Alone upon the rock' (II.174–76). This is another of those moments of precocious aestheticizing, like the walks with Fleming, which Charles Farish and his brother William, the school's star poets before Wordsworth, memorialized in *The Minstrels of Winandermere* (published 1811). Greenwood lived with Wordsworth at Ann Tyson's during his last year and a half there, and they both left for Cambridge from Hawkshead in October of 1787. Like Fletcher Raincock, Greenwood as a man was known for his dry, eccentric humour. Wordsworth, writing to his new friend William Mathews in 1791, gives a picture of Greenwood's personality: 'He is in Yorkshire with his Father, and writes in high spirits, his letter altogether irregular and fanciful. He seems to me to have much of Yorick in his disposition [i.e., the 'Yorick' of Laurence Sterne, author of *Tristram Shandy*]; at least Yorick, if I am not mistaken, had a deal of the male mad-cap in him, but Greenwood out-mad-caps him quite.'[22] One would like to know what distinction Wordsworth was trying to make in calling him a '*male* mad-cap': it may be a collegiate code for homosexuality. The implications of such a suggestion are neither irresponsible nor implausible. Several young men attached themselves passionately to Wordsworth between 1787 and

1798, as did several young women, and some of both sexes had occasion to be disappointed by him.

Wordsworth first appeared in print in company with Greenwood. Both sent poems to the *European Magazine* which appeared in March 1787. Wordsworth's was a throbbing tribute to Helen Maria Williams, one of the most successful members of the popular school of Sensibility. It was signed 'Axiologus', a Latin pun on his name (*axiom*, value or worth + *logos*, word).

More than a dozen other names can be associated with Wordsworth's years in Hawkshead and Colthouse, but these are the most significant ones. There was something a bit eccentric about his best friends, and we can infer that he had, or enjoyed, similar qualities himself. Wordsworth also knew and played with town boys in the neighbourhood, like John Benson and 'Tailor' Tyson. By way of contrast with William's rough and ready bunch, Thomas Gawthorp, a fellow boarder at the Tysons', was notably spoiled with large expenditures for coal, wine and velvet. He dutifully followed the typical Hawkshead-Cambridge career of successive university fellowships and church rectorships which Wordsworth was supposed to follow but didn't.[23]

'Thee and thy grey huts, my darling vale'

The Vale of Esthwaite was not as attractive in Wordsworth's time as it is today. People were then just beginning to look at nature like a picture, as 'picturesque,' and beginning to regard the Lakes as a place to enjoy their hard-earned leisure. Windermere, the region's largest and most accessible lake, had begun to develop a tourist and resort business, as had Grasmere, following Thomas Gray's discovery of 'this little unsuspected Paradise' in 1770.[24] But they were both on the main north–south road, while Esthwaite was literally a backwater. We have learned to look at it with eyes made quiet by two centuries of applied Wordsworthianism, but the idyllic vista of the vale today was not the image it presented in 1780. This is especially true of the village, which today looks like a movie set for *Brigadoon*, with its well-preserved nooks and crannies, trim tea rooms and souvenir shops. One half expects the residents to prance out singing and dancing in regional costumes. In fact, 'a smart assembly room' was built for dances and other public assemblies in 1790 at the height of Hawkshead's prosperity, partly at the instigation of the 'new people.' Few realized that these signs of prosperity were among the last vestiges of its old resource market economy, and the first signs of a new economy based on touristic services and organized leisure.

But in 1779 life was different there, and much different than it appears in *The Prelude*. 'Nature' in Wordsworth's Hawkshead was mainly a resource for industry, especially the coal and armaments industries, not for tourism. Landowners around Hawkshead were felling and burning their trees on Furness Fells and in Grizedale Forest as fast as they could to make charcoal, for the huge Blackbarrow Foundry Company, established in 1711, or for its main competitor, the Newlands Mills Company in Ulverston.[25] The main products of these companies were cannon and shot for the British navy, increasingly lucrative contracts as the eighteenth century wore on.

Besides timbering, there was also slate quarrying, Coniston slate being one of the prime grades for this expanding construction market.[26] Wordsworth and some other Colthouse boarders once inflicted a strange revenge upon 'Old Slaty,' a Quaker slate merchant who lived nearby and frequently complained about the boys' noisy antics. They would stand in a row and stare at him in total silence as he rode by, until one day they quite unnerved the old man. He stopped to talk, but they suddenly sprang to attention and saluted like soldiers, a clever if mean insult to the peaceable Quaker. He wheeled about and made as if to whip them, but then apologized for losing his friendly temper, and tried to recoup his shame by pointing out the moral differences in their situation, much to Wordsworth's disgust.[27]

Lumber, slate and coal were relatively speaking new industries in the region, which had subsisted for centuries on wool. With the invention of the spinning jenny and other industrial improvements, the large wool factories in Kendal expanded rapidly, though a generation-long war with France and the simultaneous boom in American cotton soon brought it all to an end. The war against the American colonists was very unpopular in Kendal because it interrupted the profitable trade in its specialty, the light woollen cloths, known as Kendal Cottons, which were much in demand in Virginia and Maryland.[28] Hawkshead was the main wool market in the southern part of the region, because the vale of Esthwaite, with easy access at its southern end to the ferry across Windermere, was the shortest and quickest route by which these raw materials could be extracted from the north, since there were no good ports on the coast nearby. The ferry itself was no small rural curiosity, but a link as important to the region as any Suez or Panama Canal, and a profitable franchise worth a tidy thirty guineas a year.[29]

With all these labour-intensive industries and their many subsidiaries (cartage and hostelry, for example) came workers of all types and their families: miners, loggers, charcoal burners, saddlers, joiners, pedlars, etc., in addition to the local sheepherders and stone and slate 'wallers.' Another kind of labour force was represented by the steady traffic of mostly sickly discharged veterans straggling down from Whitehaven and Workington, the walking wounded from the American war, and those ravaged by malaria and other tropical diseases in police actions against slave rebellions on British sugar plantations in the Caribbean.

Wordsworth and his friends talked to all these people working in or travelling through the valley. Wordsworth in particular entered into conversation with them, asking questions about where they were from, what they did, and what had happened to them along the way. He is said to have made friends with all ages; he was a boy who 'listened'.[30] These experiences were the personal source of the most common situation or 'plot' in Wordsworth's early poetry: a wayfaring observer, the poet-figure, meets a travelling man or woman, usually poor, and asks him or her how they came to be so. The Hawkshead boys were well placed for these kinds of encounters. They were boarders, away from home, and almost all sons of gentlemen or well-to-do tradesmen, who would feel no reserve, past a certain age, about accosting passing labourers and engaging them in conversation. To use an American analogy, Wordsworth and his friends were Tom Sawyers playing at being Huck Finn, privileged even if – like Tom and William – orphaned.

He was in daily contact with old Hugh Tyson, who was a man of all work around the village. He went fishing at an early age with John Martin, a weaver, who took him on a five-mile jaunt over two ranges of fells to the River Duddon, and then carried him home piggyback much of the way, when a luckless day ended in a driving downpour.[31] He had a particularly wide acquaintance among the pedlars or packmen in the neighbourhood. Most of them were Scots, and lived in Outgate, a collection of poor hovels a mile north of Hawkshead. In various composites, they helped to model the character of 'the venerable Armytage,' the philosophical pedlar in Wordsworth's first major narrative poem, 'The Ruined Cottage' of 1797–98. The degree to which he was capable of identifying himself with such characters should not be underestimated. 'Had I been born in a class which would have deprived me of what is called a liberal education, it is not unlikely that, being strong in body, I should have taken to a way of life such as that in which my Pedlar passed the greater part of his days . . . I . . . freely acknowledge that the character I have represented in his person is chiefly an idea of what I fancied my own character might have become in his circumstances.'[32] This may be wishful thinking, but it was a fantasy that gave strong motivation to his imagination. What he seems to have wanted most from the pedlars was stories of their travels, Armytage's main stock in trade.

There is no record of Wordsworth's associating with the loggers and charcoal burners further back in the hills. But among the 'wallers' were two of the valley's day-labourers, Frank and Jonathan Castlehow, 'the Castlehow robbers,' as they were melodramatized later in the nineteenth century.[33] These tough men were from a still-lower rung on the social ladder than pedlars. They did not plead for poor relief, but worked when they could and stole or otherwise helped themselves when they couldn't. They had hideouts scattered about the vale, and hovels on Hawkshead Moor and Hawkshead High Cross where they lived with their extended families.[34] It was to one of the latter that a party of local authorities, including Mr Varty, the grammar school writing master, came in August or September of 1784 to arrest Frank's son Jonathan – the very boy, though he was as big as a man, who had rescued 'crag-fast' Johnny Benson. But as they approached he burst from the back door and took off toward the west, leading his pursuers on a magnificent chase for several miles. They finally caught up with him in Little Langdale, only to discover that 'he' was his sister Ruth, 'a strapping young woman two or three years younger than he, and nearly as tall.'[35] Jonathan had made good his escape while she decoyed his captors.

The school boys enjoyed the escapade out of loyalty to their one-time saviour, and because it embarrassed their master. When the fall term began, they started an oral ballad-composing marathon on the incident, raising and lowering their voices with clever calculation so Mr Varty would hear just the parts least complimentary to him. Bill Wordsworth started the verses out well, for he was just at that time beginning to show signs of becoming another one of the school's excellent verse writers. But Fletcher Raincock and Ted Birkett outstripped him – to their grief, for they were the ones Reverend Taylor caught and punished. Something of William Taylor's wisdom as a teacher is indicated by the fact that part of his punishment was to make the boys write out their own verses in full.

Other out-of-the-way character types in Esthwaite still more important to Wordsworth than outlaws were the men who had missed out on the eighteenth century's great leap on to the bandwagon of the rising middle class. These were men who had had good prospects but failed to realize them and retired to remote spots like Esthwaite to eke out the rest of their existence and rue their great expectations. They seem to have appealed to Wordsworth a good deal anyway, but after his father's death and his own subsequently disappointed expectations, they flowed back into his imagination with added force. Men like this usually have time on their hands and bitterness to spare. They are happy to find audiences of eager youngsters who are just rising on to the crest of their opportunities, the better to caution or cynically puncture their optimism. The most well-known of these Esthwaite prototypes to survive in Wordsworth's poetry are the composite characters of 'Matthew' in 'The Two April Mornings' and 'The Fountain' and several other poems and fragments, and the disappointed builder of the yew-tree seat in one of the earliest-composed of the 1798 *Lyrical Ballads*. But there are others as well.

Three men melded into one for Wordsworth's Matthew poems: John Harrison (1709–1789?), a failed businessman turned local schoolmaster and tutor, Thomas Cowperthwaite (d. 1782), ironmonger, and John Gibson (1728–1800), a tipsy attorney. They each shared elements of Matthew's disappointed life-story: rural retreat, an ironical, facetious temperament, expressed in song, doggerel verse and exaggerated literary allusions – aided, in Gibson's case, by liquid spirits.

Harrison, having 'failed more than once in business,' went off to Liverpool but came back to Hawkshead with three young children after his wife died, and 'set up as a wool merchant, but the Kendal buyers were too smart for him, and soon had him out of business' again.[36] He then set up a school and tutoring service, which specialized in women's education. He took over the remnants of a school for village children and kept it up, as 'Mr John,' for the next thirty-four years, though he rarely made enough to keep both himself and his pony comfortably.[37] The pony was important, not only for the fishing expeditions which were his chief recreation, and on which Wordsworth and other boys loved to accompany him (he let them ride the pony while he fished), but also for his tutoring. He held evening classes in different parts of the parish at different times of the year, from poor Outgate in the north to Far Sawrey in the south. His speciality was teaching young women and girls how to write, and 'from about 1750 there was a notable increase in the proportion of Hawkshead brides who could sign their names.'[38] Wordsworth wrote more poems (especially epitaphs) on his Matthew figure than he published, and one of these unpublished poems records this special aspect of 'Mr John's' tutelage:

> Ye little girls, ye loved his name,
> Come here and knit your gloves of yarn,
> Ye loved him better than your dame
> – The schoolmaster of Glencarn.*
>
> For though to many a wanton boy
> Did Matthew act a father's part,
> Ye tiny maids, *ye* were his joy,
> Ye were the favourites of his heart.
>
> Ye ruddy damsels past sixteen
> Weep now that Matthew's race is run
> He wrote your love-letters, I ween
> Ye kiss'd him when the work was done.
>
> Ye Brothers gone to towns remote,
> And ye upon the ocean tost,
> Ye many a good and pious thought
> And many a [*word lacking in MS*] have lost.
>
> (*PW*, IV.454)

The interweaving of details from John Harrison's life with those of the sons of John Wordsworth could hardly be tighter than in the last stanza:

---

* The Scotch place-name is one of Wordsworth's typical distancing devices; it associates the story with a location more renowned for legend and folklore, and also serves to deflect its autobiographical reference.

Richard was sent away to law-clerking, first in Whitehaven and soon to London, and John apprenticed to the sea in his mid-teens. These biographical correspondences make me suspect that the 'wanton boy' of line 5, who seems jealous of the schoolmaster's attention to girls, is young Wordsworth, in search as always of a father. If this is the case, we can hardly dismiss those 'ruddy damsels past sixteen' as stock figures, for they are surely the same as the 'frank-hearted maids of rocky Cumberland' (VI.13) with whom Wordsworth began dancing and flirting at about age sixteen, and among whom he cut a particular figure when he returned from Cambridge for his first summer vacation.

Thomas Cowperthwaite, the ironmonger, was one of the old men who on pleasant evenings sat on the benches in the Hawkshead churchyard, behind the grammar school, looking out across the valley. His gravestone, set against the same church wall, notes his 'facetious' disposition. During his early years living in town, the boy Wordsworth often sat and talked with these men. Having fewer expectations for a career than Harrison or Gibson, Cowperthwaite had less obvious disappointments in life. But he was the actual rhyme-maker of the three, and one quatrain attributed to him is about his failure to make his mark on life in that place.

> The last of my Name in this Conny Spot,
> That's what I'm destined to be;
> My Course it's near run, decided my Lot,
> And there's no one to rue it but me.[39]

This was a life lesson that Wordsworth took much to heart.

The third major Hawkshead ingredient in Wordsworth's Matthew character was 'Little John' Gibson, an attorney well known to John Wordsworth from consultations about his customary rights and rents in the seigniory of Millom, fifteen miles down the road in Broughton-in-Furness. 'Little John' had more 'quips and pranks' than either Harrison or Cowperthwaite, and shared with them the sense of regret for the course of his life, expressed in the ambivalent terms of love and sorrow that catalyse these men together in Wordsworth's imagination.

Gibson was an avid practical joker whose antics delighted generations of Hawkshead schoolboys. One of his best tricks was to prop a scarecrow up at a roadside gate on cloudy nights and then, being an excellent mimic, to greet passers-by and hold them in conversation as long as he could, until they lost patience with what they took to be, variously, an old soldier, a wandering beggar, a drunk or a village idiot. Thus Gibson's antics are comic anticipations of such well-known Wordsworth poems as the lines on the Discharged Veteran, 'The Old Cumberland Beggar', 'The Waggoner', and 'The Idiot Boy.'

The most important to Wordsworth personally of the disappointed-gentleman types in his Esthwaite experience was William Braithwaite of

Satterhow (no relation to Philip), one of many Hawkshead graduates who followed the preferred route to St John's, Cambridge (BA 1776, MA 1780). He took orders, but was not offered a living until he received two pluralities in the south in 1787, just as Wordsworth was preparing to leave for Cambridge. Braithwaite's frustrations can hardly *not* have been in Wordsworth's mind in the early 1790s when his uncles were urging him to take orders and promising to arrange church livings for him. Wordsworth considered him 'a man of talent and learning.' He is the original of the disaffected misanthrope of the 'Lines, Left upon a Seat in a Yew-tree, which stands near the lake of Esthwaite, on a desolate part of the shore, commanding a beautiful prospect.' Wordsworth probably met him around 1785, when he was thirty-two, in the deepest trough of his disappointments, and a well-known neighbourhood melancholic. His yew-tree seat looked out over the lake at Waterside, less than a mile south of Ann Tyson's cottage, close to the local poorhouse, along a bleak stretch of road supposed to be haunted by the 'Waterside Boggle,' an old woman with glaring red lantern eyes. Braithwaite found this charming spot appropriate for brooding on the world's neglect of his talents, finding in its desolation 'an emblem of his own unfruitful life.' The spot was directly in the route of Wordsworth's and Fleming's favourite morning walk around the lake. Braithwaite was a man of the place, yet he was out of 'place' due to expectations raised by his education, which had been disappointed: 'descendant of a long line of local Statesmen who was so untypical of his class, *at any rate at that time in his life.*'[40]

William Braithwaite brings us near to the upper reaches of Esthwaite society, the local gentry who were Wordsworth's own social peers. He may have met Braithwaite at Belmount, the splendid new four-storey country house resembling Wordsworth's Cockermouth townhouse, built in 1774 by the Reverend Reginald Brathwaite [*sic*], the vicar or stipendiary minister of Hawkshead from 1769 to 1809. This kind and jovial man, also of St John's, Cambridge, exerted much good effort in the parish, 'at a time when the ministration of the clergy was at its lowest ebb.'[41] All over England, younger sons of gentry families were ordained simply so they could collect church-livings, as profitably as aristocrats pocketed boroughs. Reginald Brathwaite also held other livings, but unlike William Braithwaite he made his home and did his work in his principal one. One of his plurality livings was the post of Prebendary of St Cross in Llandaff Cathedral in Cardiff, which he had from his neighbour, Bishop Richard Watson of Calgarth Hall, about two miles due east of Belmount across Windermere lake. This is one of several close associations between Watson, the leading Whig bishop in the House of Lords, and people Wordsworth knew well – John Fleming was another – that may have affected Wordsworth's decision to write his violently republican 'Letter to the Bishop of Llandaff' in 1793.

Young William spent a good deal of time at Belmount, which he recalled fondly in later years.[42] Mrs Brathwaite's daughter recalled the young Wordsworth as an 'eager young boy,' full of questions, just the impression we have of him in almost all his associations in the valley.[43]

At Belmount he often met and talked to Gilbert Crackenthorp [*sic*], not quite a relation but a member of the junior line of grandmother Crackanthorpe's Newbiggin Hall family. This Crackenthorp was another, milder version of the disappointed-talent that appealed to William. He had been headmaster of the Kendal grammar school until 1774, but retired early because his frank admiration of the Hawkshead school daunted his own prospects. Gilbert Crackenthorp lacked ambition, but was a source of much conversation, and sometimes of small loans, to the Wordsworth boys, for he was well-off, being the owner (through his wife) of the White Hart Inn and Coffee House in Kendal, the regional centre for newspapers and lending libraries. The high point of his life had come at age thirty, when he dared to preach before the assembled officers of the Young Pretender who attended his church during the invasion of 1745, when other Wordsworth kin were reacting in different ways.

In Gilbert Crackenthorp's leisured style of existence we enter into the class of 'new' gentry who were beginning to populate the Lake District. To them, the trees of the region were more a source of picturesque enjoyment than of profits from charcoal, though the two uses were by no means mutually incompatible. Sometimes called 'strangers' or 'moderns,' these folk were either local gentry or, increasingly from about 1780, summer people who found in the Lakes a more cultured form of leisure than the hunting, gaming and drinking amusements of the average Squire Booby. Wordsworth by his age and class, and by the accident of his time and place of birth, was right on the edge of this social change. His father was the agent of one of the most ruthless of the land-exploiting aristocracy; had he lived, John Wordsworth might have become a commercial success like Michael Knott, or a political one like John Garforth. In the event, his son the poet became a kind of ideological apologist for the newer, leisure sense of landscape, but in ways that associated it with the older socio-economic organization of the region – i.e., the communities of free-holding 'statesmen,' or 'estatesmen.' Wordsworth's treatment of them wavers unsteadily between penetrating insights into the human costs of economic displacement, and complacent commodification of the locals for middle-class tourist consumption.

Often the visually most attractive land was the least economically useful. For example, the islands of Windermere were virtually useless for farming, grazing, or timbering, but made excellent locations for splendid vacation homes. The high points of the new life style were its 'summer gaieties': regattas, hunts, plays, elections of queens, and dances and balls. One summer renter active in them was William Wilberforce (b. 1759), MP from Hull and future opponent of slavery, who spent several summers from 1780 at Rayrigg.[44] He wrote to his mother, 'Boating, riding and continual parties at my own house and Sir Michael le Fleming's, fully occupied my time until I returned to London in the autumn.'[45] It is likely that Wordsworth met Wilberforce at many similar gatherings, for Wilberforce was the best friend of his kindlier Penrith uncle, William Cookson, and had helped Cookson to the living at Forncett in Norfolk that finally allowed him to marry.[46] Wordsworth later expected to get exactly this kind of help from Jack Robinson, and possibly from Wilberforce himself. Shared experiences of this sort helped form an immediate bond when they met again later as adults.

Wordsworth and the other Hawkshead boys, active in their own boat races, eagerly joined in these more organized regattas as keen competitors. But they were especially in demand for the dances. This resource of socially accomplished boys accounted for Hawkshead's 'superiority' in young Maria Spedding's eyes, writing to Reverend Brathwaite's step-daughter Martha Irton at Belmount, because 'so great a majority of Beaux can seldom be boasted of in this part of the world.'[47] The Wordsworth account books show sums being laid out from 1784 for dancing instruction for the boys from Mr Mingay, who taught 'the most fashionable Dances, now in Use at Court and the first Assemblies in Great Britain.'[48]

Mingay was so much in demand that he opened a 'Military Academy,' a kind of finishing school for extracurricular accomplishments (dancing, music and fencing, as well as French, accounting and navigation) adjacent to the grammar school. He taught the boys to dance well, and Wordsworth was as skilled a dancer as he was a skater until late in life, thanks to his Hawkshead tuition. 'Wordsworth dancing' sounds like an oxymoron, given his conventional image. But like skating it is a rhythmic activity well suited to a poet who developed a unique method of composing outdoors out loud, striding back and forth to the five-beat cadences of his own chanting.

The ferry landing on Windermere was much frequented on dance nights, either to cross the lake to estates like Rayrigg or to get out to estates like the newly redone mansion of John Christian Curwen on Belle Isle, as Longholme had been renamed in the fashionable refurbishing of the region. Curwen was one of the area's leaders in timbering, charcoaling, and quarrying, and the moving force behind the enclosure of Claife Heights, the ridge above the ferry crossing, planting 30,000 larches there 'by the desire of my respected friend Dr Watson, Bishop of Llandaff.'[49]

This Christian-Curwen connection can serve as an emblem to conclude our tour through Wordsworth's Hawkshead, for it connects back to his own family in ways that illuminate the complex texture of Lake District society out of which Wordsworth emerged. John Christian's father had been one of the most active political agents of the old Duke of Somerset's struggles at Cockermouth against the encroachments of the Lowther interest.[50] The Curwen family was one of the new sources of opposition to Lowther's encroachments – which is to say they were competitors in business. Henry Curwen was the man who replaced Lowther as MP for Cumberland in the disputed election of 1768. John Christian (born 1756), following his father's footsteps, was the Curwens' agent and joined the family as an in-law when he married the heiress Isabella Curwen, taking her name as well as all her property, as his second wife in 1790. Curwen was a staunch 'Old' or 'Country' Whig reformer, as Lowther had been originally, but he stayed with his party and principles after Lowther switched to Pitt and the proto-Tories in 1784.

John Christian's uncle was a Cockermouth attorney, and his two sons (i.e., John Christian's cousins) played important roles in two late eighteenth-century legal actions, one small and petty, the other forever famous, against the injustices of entrenched established privilege. Edward Christian was the Wordsworth family's lawyer in their unsuccessful action against Lord Lowther. But his brother, Fletcher, Wordsworth's slightly older Cockermouth neighbour and Hawkshead schoolmate, became first mate of a ship called *Bounty*, under the infamous Captain Bligh.[51]

CHAPTER 3

'While we were schoolboys'

Hawkshead Education and Reading

> a scanty record is deduced
> Of what I owed to books in early life;
> *Their later influence yet remains untold.*
> (V.630–32; italics added)

In Wordsworth's Hawkshead, the boys always seem to be running, never reading; it's hard to find the school in the midst of all this activity. The first two books of *The Prelude* both have 'School-Time' in their titles, but there is not a line in them describing school activity: no masters, no subjects, no punishments, no tedium, nothing. As far as they tell it, Wordsworth's Hawkshead curriculum was entirely extra-curricular. He was at an excellent school at the top of its form, but in *The Prelude* he had an interest in minimizing his debt to culture and society, relative to nature. But *The Prelude* is not his biography, and we have to hold ourselves at a distance from his romantic nature myth to recognize that most of his time in Hawkshead was in fact spent in school, and that he was an excellent, very bookish student.

Scholars charmed by the energy of Books I and II of *The Prelude* have speculated that Hawkshead grammar school's educational philosophy was influenced by the theories of Rousseau, stressing children's natural innocence.[1] This we may very much doubt. Wordsworth's *description* of it was indeed influenced by his admiration for the more optimistic, less manipulative parts of Rousseau's pedagogical theory. But the academic discipline at Hawkshead grammar school was hard old-fashioned classicism, combined with hard new-fashioned mathematics, and the value of the boys' freedom out of class was more accidental than philosophically inspired.

Founded in 1585 by Edwin Sandys, Archbishop of York, who was born at Esthwaite Hall, the school was one of about four hundred grammar schools in Great Britain to which the gentry and well-to-do merchants could send their sons; sons of the very rich were still tutored at home.[2] It was also one of the best, both in its traditional classical curriculum and in its modern scientific one. The school's proximity to Scotland helped it participate in the 'Northern Enlightenment,' evident in its strong emphasis on mathematics. Then as now, schools that specialized in preparing students for admission to the most prestigious universities often provided a more rigorous education than the universities themselves. Hawkshead was prodigiously successful in placing students at Cambridge and helping them to succeed there. Sandys had gone to St John's College, Cambridge, and so did many of the Hawkshead schoolboys, where they did very well indeed: four of the six senior wranglers at Cambridge between 1788 and 1793 came from Sandys's school.

There were great expectations behind John Wordsworth's expedient decision to send the Wordsworth boys to Hawkshead. Although founded as a charity school for local boys, it had by Wordsworth's time become a thriving establishment for the preparation of sons of the rising middle class. Only about ten percent of its hundred students were still charity boys, and they were usually on one- or two-year rotating scholarships. The school's endowment kept tuition down to a 'cockpenny' per year, about a guinea and a half, derived from an ancient custom of awarding prize money to the student with the best fighting cock. Room and board cost thirty to forty pounds per year on a national average, but charges for each of the Wordsworth boys' 'Sabine fare' ran less, in the twenty-pound range.[3] Lawyers and estate agents like John Wordsworth, local squires, wool merchants from Kendal and slate traders from Coniston, and other gentry from as far away as Carlisle and even Edinburgh were happy to pay these charges for a school that could virtually assure their sons a place at Cambridge.[4]

This was the route Wordsworth was supposed to follow, and he had every intention of doing so. By all accounts he did very well, in both the classical and modern parts of the curriculum. He was so well prepared in languages and mathematics that some of his dilatoriness at Cambridge can be explained as the result of boredom. One of his masters once left him alone in his office for a moment, looking at Newton's *Opticks*; he found him still poring over it an hour later, when he returned after a delay, and was astonished to hear the boy ask if he could take the book with him to read more.[5]

The literary curriculum was of course in Greek and Latin, included the standard authors (Anacreon, Homer, Ovid, Virgil), and moved smartly along from linguistic to literary training, as translating led to 'imitating' the classics in both English and the original language, a popular genre throughout the eighteenth century. Wordsworth was quickly awakened from his dame-school slumbers by Mr Shaw, one of the ushers, 'who taught me more of Latin in a fortnight than I had learnt during two preceding years at the school of Cockermouth.'[6] Translation was still a dominant literary genre; the mighty achievements of Dryden's Virgil (1697) and Pope's Homer (1715–25) remained unsurpassed for at least another century. The curriculum was arranged to take the boys up the ladder of genres from epigrams to lyrics to epistles and narratives, and finally to epics. Wordsworth expressed an early independence by preferring Ovid over Virgil. 'Before I read Virgil I was so strongly attached to Ovid, whose Metamorphoses I read at school, that I was quite in a passion whenever I found him, in books of criticism, placed below Virgil [i.e., almost always].'[7] This was a mildly naughty predeliction, for Ovid is the classical 'nature poet' whose Just-So stories reveal natural forms as the result of men or women's attempt to escape from – or the consequences of their not escaping from – the lascivious embraces of the gods.

Thanks largely to his Hawkshead training, Wordsworth was a lifelong student and master of languages, in fact a formidable linguist. His knowledge of – and debts to – a variety of literary traditions are usually not appreciated, because it often suited his purposes to minimize such debts in the interest of promoting his views about 'natural' imaginative creativity.

Wordsworth was not simply the beneficiary of large socio-cultural educational trends, however. They had a human face in Hawkshead, and its name was William Taylor (1754–1786), schoolmaster from 1782 till his death, during Wordsworth's critically important twelfth through sixteenth years. There were three other masters during Wordsworth's years at the school, but none of the others had anything like Taylor's impact on him.

Taylor's influence on the young Wordsworth was underscored with the psychological authority of a deathbed commission. Before he died, in June 1786, Taylor called in some of the older boys to say a last goodbye: 'He . . . said to me, "My head will soon lie low".' Wordsworth never forgot the encouragement Taylor gave him: '[he] Would have loved me, as one not destitute / Of promise, nor belying the kind hope / Which he had formed when I at his command / Began to spin, at first, my toilsome songs' (X.510–14).

William Taylor was a Cambridge graduate, and like many eighteenth-century schoolmaster-vicars combined his duties with a cultured love of literature, though he was also well trained in mathematics. He had excellent ideas about literary instruction. He set his young charges to imitate not only the best classical models but also a wide range of contemporary literary ones: not just Homer, Ovid, and Virgil, but also Gray, Collins, Goldsmith, and other mid-century poets of 'Sensibility,' who reacted sentimentally against the urbane, satiric verse of Dryden, Pope, and Swift. These poets, many of whom lived unhappy, reclusive lives and wrote poems to match, raised a self-consciously minor poetry to the status of a major genre, or at least a very popular one, in the half-century between the deaths of Pope and Swift in 1744 and 1745 and the publication of *Lyrical Ballads* by Wordsworth and Coleridge in 1800. They were the poets of an Age of Prose. To be sure, the Hawkshead boys read Shakespeare, Spenser, Milton, Dryden and Pope as well. But Taylor and his ushers lent the boys their own books, and encouraged them to join book clubs and lending libraries in Kendal and Penrith, where the boys read Gray, Goldsmith, Thomson, Collins, Cowper, Burns, Akenside, Williams, Shenstone, the Warton brothers (Joseph and Thomas), Percy, Smith, Beattie, Chatterton, Crabbe, Langhorne, Carter, and Aikin. Few twentieth-century readers who are not literary specialists will get very far in that list before starting to inquire, '*Who?*' It was as if students born in 1970 were, as they finished high school in the late 1980s, reading not only Eliot, Yeats, Pound, Stevens, and Frost, but also Larkin, MacNeice, Hughes, Harrison, Muldoon, and Heaney – or, in the United States, Lowell, Sexton, Wright, Rich, Nemerov, and Levine.

These long roll calls give the lie to Wordsworth's disingenuous claim in 1791 to William Mathews, one of his best college friends, who had asked him for some contemporary reading suggestions: 'God knows my incursions into the fields of modern literature, excepting in our own language three volumes of *Tristram Shandy*, and two or three papers of the *Spectator*, half subdued – are absolutely nothing.'[8] The facts are far different.[9]

Wordsworth's future course of development is best charted through his Hawkshead reading in contemporary poetry. Even if he did not read the complete works of all the poets listed above, it is still a remarkable range, and anticipates much of his later achievement. Hour for hour, book-reading took up as much of his time as ice-skating, bird-nesting, horseback-riding, and boat-racing. Just as he knew Philip Brathwaite, John Gibson, and the Castlehow boys, so too he knew and 'conversed' with Helen Maria Williams, Joseph Warton, James Thomson, and many others, and the traces of *these* boyish acquaintances can be followed in the textures of his work with as great – if not greater – confidence as his references to boyhood games and sports in Hawkshead. Even when Wordsworth wandered at night, or when he and his friends played at minstrelsy, they were not 'just being boys,' they were trying on ready-to-wear cultural fashions.

A common understanding of the influence of contemporary eighteenth-century poets on Wordsworth's youthful development simply takes him at his word in the preface to *Lyrical Ballads* and grants him high cultural status as a wholly original Romantic poet. A somewhat more sophisticated approach allows that he was indeed influenced in his youth by the 'poetic diction' of his Sensibility predecessors, but asserts that he recognized the error of his ways and created the new poetry of ordinary language for which he is deservedly famous, 'a man speaking to men.' A still more comprehensive view recognizes that these poets influenced not only his immature juvenile verse but that their signatures can be traced even in the revolutionary work of Wordsworth's first maturity, *whose novelty is presented by him as if it* rejected *the habits of thought, diction, and imagery characteristic of the poetry of Sensibility*. This 'later influence' has indeed, for the most part, 'yet remain[ed] untold,' as Wordsworth plainly admitted in his discussion of his early reading. In his notes to his poems he was not forthcoming about these influences, usually associating the poems with their time and place of composition but saying little or nothing about their literary debts. There is nothing unusual or reprehensible about this: Wordsworth is not required to be the scholar of his own work. But when time and place and local inspiration are wholly substituted for other influences we have not learned all we should about the process of Wordsworth's self-creation.

The poetry of Sensibility permeates the great work of Wordsworth's first maturity: that of the Poet of *Lyrical Ballads*. Just a few salient examples will show its strong influence in the themes and subjects of his poetry, as well as in other aspects of his style. Equally noteworthy in the Poet's self-creation are the ways in which the careers and 'life styles' of these men and women provided models for Wordsworth to follow – and ultimately to reject. Not only what they wrote and how they wrote it, but also the career-conditions these poets established to give themselves time to write, were matters of keen estimation for the young Wordsworth, especially the degrees to which these writers depended on the old system of patronage or on the emerging new one of marketplace capitalism.

In varying degrees, the two dozen or so poets that Wordsworth read and imitated at Hawkshead all wrote elaborate descriptions of rural scenes of natural beauty, with intermittent scenes of Sublime terror and apostrophes to mytho–religious 'Powers!' that were vaguely orthodox or Deistic. Their descriptions were marked by a new realism, or attention to detail, and an interest in describing common rural sights and objects (such as sunsets and peasants' cottages) that had not appeared much in English poetry before. They often expressed a desire for simplicity in life and expression, in language that was anything but simple. These elements were frequently cast into the theme of returning, sadder but wiser, to one's 'native vales', sometimes motivated by loss of youth, love, and success in the larger world, and sometimes in revolted reaction against the high degree of corruption in urban centres, particularly London. In this outline of elements, we can already see the vague outlines of Wordsworth's poetical career image.

The desire to go back to simple places with simple manners and sincere language was often extended historically into a broad programme for recovering older, more genuine ways of living and speaking. Sometimes this focused on the era just before the national trauma of the Civil War, the reign of Elizabeth I, but more often it tried to go 'all the way' back, not only to the antique Greek and Roman patterns of England's Neo-Classical myth, but to ancient or fictitious traditions of Welsh, Scottish, and generally Celtic bards and minstrels, as in Percy's *Reliques of Ancient English Poetry* (1765) and Beattie's *The Minstrel* (1770). The semi-fictions of James Macpherson's *Fragments of Ancient Poetry Collected in the Highlands of Scotland* (1760), 'translated' from fragments of oral tradition about third-century Gaelic warrior-bards named Fingal and Ossian, and the brilliant if fraudulent imitations of Thomas Chatterton's 'Rowley Poems' (1770), which he claimed to have recovered from fifteenth-century manuscripts in Bristol, were another part of this enthusiasm for native origins. It is not hard to associate much of Wordsworth's oeuvre with this broad programme.

Sophisticated theorists of the simple life diffused it into fashionable intellectual life. Hugh Blair's *Critical Dissertation on the Poems of Ossian* (1763) is one source for the literary impact of these ideas on Wordsworth, as were the various literary essays and dissertations of Blair's fellow Scot, James Beattie.[10] Thomas Warton's history of English literature (1774–1781) is generally acknowledged to be the first systematic attempt to establish a *history* of English poems that had heretofore been taken for granted. By the time Wordsworth arrived at Hawkshead, such views were nearly official culture: Thomas Warton was named poet laureate in 1775.

The philosophical basis for the liberating value of emotion, against the rigid claims of reason, had long been reasserted, most notably by Anthony Ashley Cooper, the third Earl of Shaftesbury (1671–1713). But a poet was wanting to make them good. Calls for original new bards went out regularly, but in poems whose melancholy tone undercut their effectiveness. They simply re-expressed the problem. Manifestoes of imaginative freedom were written in the most regretful ways imaginable, enlivened with merely histrionic exclamation marks. Joseph Warton – for the movement was most often called 'the school of Warton' – said forthrightly in the 'Advertisement' to his *Odes on Various Subjects* (1746) that 'the fashion of moralizing in verse has been carried too far,' and that his poems were 'an attempt to bring Poetry back into its right channel': more imaginative and descriptive, and less didactic. His first ode, 'To Fancy,' calls for 'some chosen swain' who sounds very like Wordsworth's later estimation of himself as 'a chosen Son': 'Like light'ning, let his mighty verse / The bosom's inmost foldings pierce; / With native beauties win applause, / Beyond cold critic's studied laws.' But Warton could not do it himself: he kept up his spirits with some odes on Liberty, Health, and against Superstition, but gradually he turned away from his intellectual message toward his melancholy medium, with odes on Evening, Solitude, and Despair. Similarly, William Collins's 'Ode on the Poetical Character'

(1746) starts strong but ends weak: England's poets were once inspired by godlike power, but 'Heav'n, and *Fancy*, kindred Pow'rs, / Have now o'erturned th'inspiring Bow'rs.'

'The first poem from which he [Wordsworth] remembered to have received great pleasure,' an 'Ode to Spring' attributed to Elizabeth Carter, is not by her but by Anna Aikin, later best known as Anna Barbauld (1743–1825), a consistently successful author of poems for both children and adults.[11] Both Carter and Aikin were typical of many writers in the late eighteenth century who were trying to write new poetry in old ways. Elizabeth Carter (1717–1806), in her *Poems on Several Occasions* (4th ed., 1789), composed many elegies and odes in the new Sentimental style, including several that anticipate its Romantic revival, such as her 'Ode to Melancholy.' But Carter and Barbauld were not typical of the poets that influenced Wordsworth at Hawkshead. Their combination of emotion with natural metaphors was still strongly framed by didactic abstractions, just the sort of thing Joseph Warton wanted to get away from. They were entirely appropriate for William Taylor to introduce into the Hawkshead schoolroom, but different from what he offered his older, more intelligent boys.

Yet Carter and Barbauld were typical of Wordsworth's earliest influences in another way: they were women, who continued Ann Wordsworth's 'Ministry of Beauty' to her son in literary terms. Wordsworth's share in the sector of the literary market sometimes called 'women's writing' is notable, because his first productions were so conversant in this mode, and because his poetic revolution depended in part on distinguishing what he was doing from its characteristic and highly successful productions: novels and poems of sentiment and romance. Though Wordsworth is, as Coleridge said, one of the most 'masculine' of poets (referring to his ability to distance himself emotionally from his subjects), he like the other major Romantic writers sought to retain a 'feminine' valuation of emotion that was supposed to be part of women writers' natural stock in trade.[12]

Much stronger feminine influences on the young Wordsworth's reading and writing were Charlotte Smith and Helen Maria Williams. Wordsworth's first published poem was addressed to Williams, and he went to France in 1791 with a letter of introduction to her from Smith, to whom he was distantly related by marriage: she was John Robinson's sister-in-law. From Helen Williams, Wordsworth got emotion and lots of it. 'She wept' is the opening phrase of his 'Sonnet on Seeing Miss Helen Maria Williams Weep at a Tale of Distress.' Tears are shed on virtually every page of her *Poems* of 1786; one of her special effects was to represent tears as falling on the very page we are reading. Williams's locales and situations were also familiar to Wordsworth. Her 'Edwin and Eltruda: A Legendary Tale' opens 'where the pure Derwent's waters glide . . . [and]

A castle rear'd its head' – that is, Cockermouth Castle, a neighbourly setting for a fantastic love story of immediate adolescent interest to Wordsworth.

Extensive borrowings from Helen Williams's friend Charlotte Smith (1749–1806) have been found in many of Wordsworth's poems, particularly *An Evening Walk*, 'Tintern Abbey,' and 'Elegiac Stanzas,' especially from her *Elegiac Sonnets*, first published in 1784.[13] Wordsworth's own copy is inscribed, 'St John's Cambridge '89.'[14] In 1833 he backhandedly acknowledged his debt to her in a note to his 'Stanzas Suggested in a Steamboat off St Bees' Head': 'The form of the stanza in this poem, and something in the style of versification, are adopted from the 'St Monica,' a poem of much beauty upon a monastic subject, by Charlotte Smith: a lady to whom English verse is under greater obligations than are likely to be either acknowledged or remembered. She wrote little, and that little unambitiously, but with true feeling for rural nature, at a time when nature was not much regarded by English poets; for in point of time her earlier writings preceded, I believe, those of Cowper and Burns.'[15] This is really quite disingenuous, especially the vague 'I believe,' from the poet who had, by 1833, established in perpetuity the priority of *his* claims on true feelings for rural nature.

The dominant theme of her poems is the loss of youth and happiness, in contrast to the constant beauty of her beloved home district. She celebrates her beloved River Arun in much the same way that Wordsworth does the River Derwent, and the difference in quality between her expressions of this theme and his is moot. Smith: 'Ah! hills beloved! – where once, a happy child, / Your beechen shades, "your turf, your flowers among." / I wove your blue-bells into garlands wild, / And woke your echoes with my artless song' ('To the South Downs,' ll. 1–4). Wordsworth: 'Fair scenes! with other eyes, than once, I gaze, / The ever-varying charm your round displays, / Than when, erewhile, I taught, "a happy child," / The echoes of your rocks my carols wild' (*An Evening Walk*, ll. 17–20). Smith identifies her internal quotation (from Gray) in a note; but Wordsworth's quotation – of Smith (he removed the quotation marks in his final 1849 edition) – was not attributed until 1982, with the deadpan scholarly comment, 'It seems clear that the . . . passage contains Wordsworth's first acknowledgment of his obligations to Charlotte Smith's poetry.'[16] If this be acknowledgment, what constitutes neglect?

However, the male poets of Sensibility were stronger influences on Wordsworth, not because they were better poets, but because they enjoyed by right of cultural tradition precisely what the women poets lacked: careers whose patterns could be studied and imitated by young admirers.

James Thomson's 'Winter' (1726) and *The Seasons* (1730) anticipated Joseph Warton's call to return poetry 'into its right [descriptive] channel' by nearly a generation, and became one of the most popular poems in

Europe. Thomson described the appearances of the seasons elaborately but not naturally. Or rather – since what constitutes a 'natural' description of natural phenomena is impossible to say – he used very ornate diction to describe many ordinary natural occurrences. Wordsworth's debt to *The Seasons* was first incurred by adapting Thomson's descriptions directly to his Hawkshead activities.[17] For example, nutting, where Wordsworth picked up Thomson's idyllic swains and virgins –

> Ye swains, now hasten to the hazel bank . . .
>> In close array
> Fit for the thickets and the tangling shrub,
> Ye virgins, come . . .
>> . . . the clustering nuts for you
> The lover finds amid the secret shade;
> And, where they burnish on the topmost bough,
> With active vigour crashes down the tree . . .
>> ('Autumn,' ll. 611 ff.)

– and transferred their emotions to his own sexual intercourse with the natural scene:

> . . . the hazels rose
> Tall and erect, with tempting clusters hung,
> A virgin scene! – A little while I stood,
> Breathing with such suppression of the heart
> As joy delights in; and, with wise restraint
> Voluptuous, fearless of a rival, eyed
> The banquet . . .
>> Then up I rose,
> And dragged to earth both branch and bough, with crash
> And merciless ravage
>> ('Nutting,' 19–25, 43–45)

Similarly, where Thomson's 'shepherd stalks gigantic' through the fog ('Autumn,' 727), Wordsworth's follows him, 'In size a giant, stalking through the fog' (VIII.401).[18] When Thomson's 'western sun withdraws the darkened day' ('Autumn,' 1082), Wordsworth's 'western clouds a deepening gloom display.'[19]

At this point, we may simply feel we have reached the limits of what sixty years of stylized descriptive language can do with sunsets. But Thomson's introduction to 'Autumn' is so like Wordsworth's in 'The Ruined Cottage' that it's clear his early reading of Thomson went far beyond sharing common literary conventions. ''Tis raging noon; and, vertical, the Sun / Darts on the head direct his forceful rays. / O'er heaven and earth, far as the ranging eye / Can sweep, a dazzling deluge reigns; and all / From pole to pole is undistinguished blaze' ('Autumn,' 432–36). Here is Wordsworth's similar scene: '''Twas Summer, and the sun was mounted high, / Along the south the uplands feebly glared / Through a pale steam, and all the northern downs / In clearer air ascending shewed far off / Their surfaces on which the shadows lay / Of many clouds far as the sight could reach' ('The Ruined Cottage,' 1–6). These close verbal parallels continue for nearly fifty lines, encompassing the figure of the wanderer whom Thomson uses as a foil to his narrator, exactly as Wordsworth does with his Pedlar: 'Thrice happy he, who on the sunless side / Of a romantic mountain, forest-crowned, / Beneath the whole collected shade reclines' ('Autumn,' 458–60). Wordsworth: 'Pleasant to him who on the soft cool grass / Extends his careless limbs beside the root / Of some huge oak whose aged branches make / A twilight of their own' (10–13). The story that Wordsworth proceeds to tell in this setting shows great advances upon Thomson, but the close similarity of the two passages indicates that Wordsworth's advance depends upon Thomson's text as much as – if not more than – the personal observations of landscapes and poverty in Dorset to which Wordsworth attributed his descriptions.

Thomson was a precursor of the new school, and, as a Scotsman who succeeded in London, he also anticipated the frequency with which practitioners of the new descriptive poetry hailed from the north. Thomas Percy, James Beattie and Robert Burns were other authors in this northern constellation that Wordsworth read toward the end of his Hawkshead years. Each in his own way called for a national cultural revival to rise from approximately the region where Wordsworth lived, and each located the source of a new imaginative power in a romantically historicised 'north countrie' setting, peopled by simple folk following rural pursuits far from urban corruption, and speaking native dialects.

Thomas Percy (1729–1811) changed his name from Piercy when he took up his first parish, in Northampton, after his MA from Oxford. Although a grocer's son in Shropshire, he associated himself with the Percys of the north for both cultural and practical reasons; he eventually became chaplain and secretary to the Duke of Northumberland.[20] He dedicated his famous *Reliques of Ancient English Poetry* (1765) to the Countess of Northumberland, a well-known 'romantic' diarist. His career as a literary priest, like many of these authors' lives, was another influence on Wordsworth, who was intended for the same profession, and who knew these writers' lives well from the biographical notices and memoirs which prefaced their works.

Percy's essay on 'The Ancient English Minstrels' stimulated young Wordsworth's developing sense of himself as a poet. It stresses the northern associations of minstrelsy – signifying Scotland and England north of the Humber. 'There is hardly an ancient Ballad or Romance, wherein a Minstrel or Harper appears, but he is characterized by way of eminence to have been "of the North Countrie": and indeed the prevalence of the Northern dialect in such kind of poems, shews that this representation is real.'[21] Such nearby geographic identifications enthused the self-conscious 'Minstrels of Winandermere,' Charles and William Farish, Robert Greenwood, and William Wordsworth. Many of the ballads have Lake District settings, like 'The Nut-Brown Maid,' a popular favourite, who is sorely tested by her lover, 'a squyer of low degre,' but finally taken home in triumph 'to Westmarlande, / Which is myne herytage.'

Within five years Percy's call for a modern revival of old minstrelsy was taken up by James Beattie. The first version of *The Minstrel* (1770) was so successful that a second installment was called for; Books I and II were published together in 1774. Like Percy, Langhorne, Crabbe, and others in this group – including Wordsworth – Beattie came of poor but respectable professional gentry background. But he achieved his independence by stitching together schoolmastering jobs and low-level church appointments. He had made a stout defence of Scotland's honour against Charles Churchill's hilarious attack, *The Progress of Famine* (1763), which put its finger exactly on the way these 'rude' bards were condescendingly adopted by London:

> *Thence* simple bards, by simple prudence taught,
> To this *wise* town by simple patrons brought,
> In simple manner utter simple lays,
> And take, with simple pension, simple praise.

Beattie's *Minstrel* was well received by the conservative old literary lions in London, as well as by the young literary cubs in Hawkshead. Wordsworth and his friends adopted the style and manners of this ersatz chivalric minstrelsy, in Charles Farish's *The Minstrels of Winandermere* and in the boys' picturesque placing of Greenwood, 'the minstrel of our group,' on the Windermere 'holmes' for relaxing, pseudo-sophisticated sunset concerts. The Hawkshead boys aped the mannerisms of Beattie's poem with a devotion akin to late twentieth-century teenagers' adopting the dress, style, speech and mannerisms of contemporary rock music stars, and their youthful minstrelsy on the lakes echoes in the sound of amateur rock-and-roll groups practising in garages and basements around the world.

The earliest commentator to recognize Beattie's influence on Wordsworth was his sister Dorothy. In her charming letters of 1787 to her friend Jane Pollard, recording her rediscovery and exploration of her long-lost brothers, she presents 'my dear William' as a version of Beattie's model: ' "In truth he was a strange and wayward wight fond of each gentle &c. &c." That verse of Beattie's Minstrel always reminds me of him, and indeed the whole character of Edwin resembles much what William was when I first knew him after my leaving Halifax – "and oft he traced the uplands &c, &c, &c." [22] Doubtless she was prompted in this identification by the favourite parts of Beattie that William read or recited to her, which are reflected in various ways throughout his works. When he represented himself as 'singled out . . . from a swarm of rosy boys . . . For my grave looks, too thoughtful for my years' (*The Excursion*, I.56–59), he was adapting Beattie's words for Edwin: 'no vulgar boy, / Deep thought oft seem'd to fix his infant eye' (I.16).

Robert Burns (1759–1796) took the innovations of his fellow Scots Thomson and Beattie a big step further by writing many of his poems in the language of southern Scotland, and on contemporary topics. Wordsworth purchased Burns's most important volume, *Poems, Chiefly in the Scottish Dialect* (1786), from the Penrith book club as a present for Dorothy before he went to Cambridge in 1787, having read it enthusiastically during his last year at Hawkshead. [23] Burns's use of Scottish (though a third of the poems are in standard English) marks a shift in theme and focus not present in the tamer innovations of Beattie and Thomson. Like all the writers of Sensibility, they were mild rebels, proffering their works from the margins of contemporary literature as self-consciously minor productions hopeful of acceptance by mainline culture, symbolized by the 'Great Cham,' Samuel Johnson.

But Robert Burns was not such a co-optable rebel. He interwove poems about the proper language and subjects for poetry with poems about country manners and problems. On the first manuscript page of 'The Ruined Cottage,' Wordsworth penned an epigraph from Burns, the first two and last two lines of this stanza from 'Epistle to J. L. L*****k [John Lapraik], an Old Scots Bard. April 1st, 1785':

> Gie me ae spark o' Nature's fire,
> That's a' the learning I desire;
> Then tho' I drudge thro' dub an' mire
>> At pleugh or cart,
> My Muse, tho' hamely in attire,
>> May touch the heart.

These are the same sentiments that Burns had prefixed to his own volume, in English:

> The Simple Bard, unbroke by rules of Art,
> He pours the wild effusions of the heart:
> And if inspir'd, 'tis Nature's pow'rs inspire;
> Her's all the melting thrill, and her's the kindling fire.

Burns's volume ends with 'A Bard's Epitaph' that uses the same sequence of challenges delivered to other, supposedly more useful vocations (soldier, priest, merchant, etc.) that Wordsworth later adopted in 'A Poet's

Epitaph' to arrive at a remarkably similar conclusion: 'Is there a Bard of rustic song / Who, noteless, steals the crouds among . . . / . . . Here pause – and thro' the starting tear, / Survey this grave' (7–8, 17–18). Wordsworth: 'But who is He, with modest looks, / And clad in homely russet brown? . . . / . . . Here stretch thy body at full length; / Or build thy house upon his grave' (37–38, 59–60). Both poems are indebted to the pastoral tradition of one shepherd piping a lament at the grave of another. But Burns invoked this tradition mainly to distinguish his poems from it: 'The following trifles are not the production of the Poet, who, with all the advantages of learned art, and perhaps amid the elegancies and idlenesses of upper life, looks down for a rural theme, with an eye to Theocritus or Virgil.' This, the lead-sentence of Burns's preface, helped prepare the way for Wordsworth's great preface of 1800.

The Scottish or Northern Revival was not the only kind of poetry that interested William Taylor and his best students. The contemporary English poets, George Crabbe, John Langhorne, and William Shenstone were also high on their lists of extracurricular reading. These were some of the first poets who took it upon themselves to describe the plight of the poor as a fit subject for serious poetry. The literature of Sensibility, with its large funds of pathos, expended much emotion on the poor, but predominantly in sentimental pastoral rhetoric like Thomson's and Beattie's. The one great poem that transcends this level before the 1780s is Gray's 'Elegy Written in a Country Church Yard' (1751), which purports to read 'the short and simple annals of the poor.' But we do not look to Gray to learn what poverty is like, still less what to do about it, unless we are disposed to accept his view that its greatest claim on our attention is to 'implore the passing tribute of a sigh.'

Crabbe's *The Village* (1783) was written against these fashions of affected pastoral representations of poverty, but it was not a protest poem in the modern radical sense. Crabbe, another of the many literary divines on Wordsworth's extra-curricular reading list, was surely 'against' poverty, but his best hope was for an enlightened aristocracy to take better paternal care of the peasants in their parishes, following the example of his patron the Duke of Rutland. Wordsworth read Crabbe as early as 1783, when the best parts of *The Village* were excerpted in the *Annual Register*, available at Hawkshead.[24] These were Crabbe's set-pieces of naturalistic description, the worn-out labourer, the parish poorhouse, the cheating apothecary, the jovial hunting parson, and the pauper's funeral.

Crabbe knew the world of parish politics that Wordsworth also knew from Cockermouth, where many social issues were resolved by 'the yearly dinner, the septennial bribe' (I.114). His exhausted old labourer anticipates Wordsworth's Simon Lee, the Old Huntsman: 'He once was chief in all the rustic trade; / His steady hand the straitest furrow made; / Full many a prize he won, and still is proud / To find the triumphs of his youth allow'd; / A transient pleasure sparkles in his eyes, / He hears and smiles, then thinks again and sighs' ('The Village,' 188–93).

The situation of Crabbe's labourer is the same as that of Wordsworth's 'Old Cumberland Beggar.' Both authors describe the same social phenomena: 'roundsmen,' paupers sent 'round the parish from house to house by the Overseer of the Poor to get work (for about sixpence a day) and food.'[25] But what Crabbe simply reports with pity, Wordsworth finds a way to celebrate as the occasion for virtuous philanthropy: 'the villagers in him / Behold a record which together binds / Past deeds and offices of charity.' Whether his view or Crabbe's description of villagers' 'ruthless taunts of lazy poor' is more accurate would depend a lot on the parish in question. Realism sides with Crabbe; Wordsworth's hopeful vision of moral good arising from existing social services is a desperate effort to fight shy of despair. Both men deplored the alternative, the poor house, which was in many parishes purposely left in a terrible state to discourage applicants. But though Crabbe represented the condition of the poor more realistically than the fashionable conventions of Picturesque description, he did not have a theory of language and its relations to culture and politics such as Wordsworth proposed in 1800.

In 1837, when he was nearly seventy, Wordsworth compared Crabbe to John Langhorne (1735–1779), 'our Westmorland Poet,' on the question of poverty as a subject for poetry, with a side glance at Shenstone:

['The Country Justice'] is the first Poem, unless perhaps Shenstone's Schoolmistress be excepted, that fairly brought the Muse into the Company of common life, to which it comes nearer than Goldsmith, and upon which it looks with a tender and enlightened humanity – and with a charitable, (and being so) philosophical and poetical construction that is too rarely found in the works of Crabbe. It is not without many faults in style from which Crabbe's more austere judgment preserved him – but these to me are trifles in a work so original and touching.[26]

Wordsworth made this subtle discrimination for an admirer who accepted the then new opinion that the great poet of the poor was now Wordsworth. He apportions value to Langhorne for content and to Crabbe for style, and modestly leaves unspoken the name of the poet who might be said to have united the two. He unfairly links Crabbe's 'austere' style to his ostensibly less charitable views of common life, for Crabbe was nothing if not a social critic. But this was probably only done to flatter Wordsworth's correspondent, who had sent him a critical notice on Langhorne. Today, Crabbe remains an important minor poet, but Langhorne is almost completely forgotten, except for his associations with Wordsworth, which are worth remembering because Langhorne also combined Lake District origins with poetical attentions to social suffering.

Possibly Wordsworth did not actually read Langhorne until he was at Cambridge,[27] but Langhorne's influence on him is close to Crabbe's, as his proprietary phrase, 'our Westmorland poet,' indicates. For their differences, we have only to imagine Wordsworth's reaction if he were called 'our Cumberland poet'! Langhorne, born in Kirkby Stephen and schooled in Appleby, was another instance of a local boy struggling through difficulties to make good. He did not have Wordsworth's social advantages, for his formal education ended with grammar school. But by dint of tutoring and schoolmastering he was able at age twenty-five to register for an extramural BD degree from Cambridge, the same age at which Beattie achieved the same shaky start, and the age at which Wordsworth would depart for London to throw himself into political journalism. Langhorne's path also led him toward London, 'the metropolis, that mart for genius and learning'[28] (Wordsworth would call it 'that mighty gulph . . . of talents' when he made the same move[29]), where he became a reviewer and writer for the *Monthly Review* from 1764 until his death in 1779.

His 'Ode to the Genius of Westmorland' was one of many contemporary stimuli to Wordsworth to praise the Muse in the Lakes. It runs over all the usual picturesque keys – 'wild groves,' 'mountains grey.' 'dark woods,' the poet claiming that he has caught from them 'the sacred fire, / That glow'd within my youthful breast,' and that he will eventually return to repay his debt to them. But Langhorne's 'Ode to the River Eden' (1759), the Lake District river that flows just east of Penrith into Solway Firth, points to even more specific similarities between these two poets' recognition of their muse in the features of their childhood landscape.

> Delightful Eden! parent stream,
>   Yet shall the maids of Memory say,
> (When, led by Fancy's fairy dream,
>   My young steps trac'd thy winding way)
> How oft along thy mazy shore,
> That many a gloomy alder bore,
>   In pensive thought their Poet stray'd;
> Or, careless thrown thy banks beside,
> Beheld thy dimply waters glide,
>   Bright thro' the trembling shade.

This beginning and all that follows it prepares the way for perhaps the most famous of all Wordsworth's beginnings:

> Was it for this
> That one, the fairest of all rivers, loved
> To blend his murmurs with my nurse's song,
> And from his alder shades and rocky falls,
> And from his fords and shallows, sent a voice

That flowed along my dreams? For this didst thou,
O Derwent, travelling over the green plains
Near my 'sweet birthplace,' didst thou, beauteous stream,
Make ceaseless music through the night and day . . .

(*1799*, i.1–9)

Wordsworth's lines read almost like a translation of Langhorne into another language. But Wordsworth's memory – which must include his memory of Langhorne – shares many common elements of setting and attitude with Langhorne: the river as parent/nurse, the shady or "gloomy" alders, the flowers, the boyish play, the passage's movement toward sunset, and the question if imagination can respond adequately to childhood memories. Wordsworth's lines are of course remarkable for their clear, modern simplicity, though written only forty years later. But perhaps most telling, as his response to a remembered text, is the subtle symbolism by which (as with Crabbe) he transmutes Langhorne's allegorical and abstract personifications into organic metaphors. Langhorne pleasantly imagines old Father Time skipping like a boy, but Wordsworth much more impressively, yet without sacrificing the charm of the situation, manages to suggest that Skiddaw is something like a 'bronzed' primitive deity and he a little 'naked savage' worshipping before it.

Langhorne's 'Fables of Flora,' dialogues between flowers ('The Wilding and the Broom,' 'The Garden Rose and the Wild Rose') are a recognized influence upon Wordsworth's similar poems in the 1800 edition of *Lyrical Ballads* ('The Oak and the Broom' and 'The Waterfall and the Eglantine').[30] But Langhorne's defence of his allegories also anticipates Wordsworth's defence of rural and natural subjects. 'The scenery is formed in a department of nature, adapted to the genius and disposition of poetry; where she finds new objects, interests, and connections, to exercise her fancy and her powers.' 'The rural imagery, on which the fables are grounded, had not been before adapted to that species of poetry; and the moral is so naturally interwoven with the narrative, that its effect is more forcible and more pleasing, than when unconnected with the relation. . . . the mode of conveying instruction, by allegorizing the scenery of nature, must be considered as an acquisition to literature . . .'[31]

The stylized, artificial quality of nature in these and other contemporary poems owes more to William Shenstone (1714–1763), who was criticized during his lifetime for the excessive prettiness both of his poetry and of his carefully tended estate, Leasowes, near Halesowen. Shenstone's favourite topics are a veritable roll-call of Sensibility, featuring elegies on retirement, simplicity, death, friendship, domesticity, disinterestedness, humility, solitude and benevolence. Shenstone's 'Schoolmistress' is another prototype for Wordsworth's idyllic portrait of Ann Tyson, in parallels of feeling and tone rather than diction.

> Here oft the dame, on Sabbath's decent eve,
> Hymned such psalms as Sternhold forth did mete;
> If winter 'twere, she to her hearth did cleave,
> But in her garden found a summer-seat:
> Sweet melody!
>
> (118–22)

Wordsworth's idyllic descriptions of his Hawkshead 'School-Time' owe a debt to the idealized school in Shenstone's popular poem: 'In ev'ry village mark'd with little spire, / Embower'd in trees, and hardly known to fame, / There dwells, in lowly shades and mean attire, / A matron old, whom we Schoolmistress name.' The single longest section of Shenstone's poem describes the punishment of a wild, wayward boy, but ends with a caution against too severe punishments that might cramp future great spirits:

> E'en now sagacious foresight points to show
> A little bench of heedless bishops here,
> And here a chancellor in embryo,
> Or bard sublime, if bard may e'er be so,
> As Milton, Shakespeare, names that ne'er shall die!
>
> (245–49)

The immediate source of such sentiments is Gray's 'mute inglorious Miltons,' but the theme of a hoped-for new poetic saviour echoed through the works of almost all these poets, and it resonated loudly with Wordsworth at Hawkshead, stimulating thoughts about the creation of the Poet that became his master theme.

Wordsworth's sense of the power of his imagination is often expressed in the contrary terms of how great his loss would be if imagination should fail him. Hence it is not surprising that one of Shenstone's clearest influences on him should be in the Lucy poems, those privately coded meditations on the imagined death of his sister Dorothy, or, what amounted to the nearly same thing, a loss of his confidence in his developing genius. Many of Lucy's characteristics are borrowed from Shenstone's 'Nancy of the Vale.' The rivers Dove and Avona are far apart, but the maids the poets place on their banks are virtually twin sisters – one generation removed: ''Twas from Avona's banks the maid / Diffus'd her lovely beams, / And ev'ry shining glance display'd / The Naiad of the streams.' (Shenstone, 18–21) 'She dwelt among the untrodden ways / Besides the banks of Dove . . . Fair as a star, when only one / Is shining in the sky' ('She dwelt among the untrodden ways,' 1–2). And both poets work in very close concert with a personified Nature to try to possess the fair one: 'That Nature in so lone a dell / Should form a nymph so sweet!' (Shenstone, 37–38). 'Then Nature said, "A lovelier flower / On earth was never sown"' ('Three years she grew,' 2–3). Wordsworth's terse late note,

'1799. Composed in the Hartz Forest,' again identifies only the physical time and space of his poems' composition: their roots in creative memory very evidently go to 'hiding places' at least ten years further back, in Hawkshead. Shenstone's pastoral was not Wordsworth's only model; they both go back to Theocritus, but Wordsworth's poems are much more striking advances upon the possibilities of such models, and do not suffer by being set against their likely text-of-origin. Yet much of the polemical energy swirling around Wordsworth for most of his career was stirred up by readers of his own generation who had also grown up on poets like Shenstone, and who were profoundly unsettled to see how like yet how different he was from them, but were unable to put their finger on exactly what the difference was.

William Cowper's *Poems* (1782) and *The Task* (1785) were both critical and popular successes when they appeared in the middle of Wordsworth's Hawkshead years, but Cowper's influence on Wordsworth, though long felt, has only recently begun to get its due.[32] Lines like, 'I gaz'd, myself creating what I saw' (*Task*, IV.290), touch very closely on 'Tintern Abbey's' 'mighty world / Of eye and ear, both what they half create, / And what perceive.' This influence was first set in motion when Wordsworth, like all the other Hawkshead schoolboys, was set to write celebratory verses on the Bishop Sandys's school's bicentenary in 1785. They had immediately before them Cowper's new poem, 'Tirocinium: or, A Review of the Schools' (1785), which they were expected to refute, since it argued against public school education like theirs in favour of the older aristocratic idea of private education at home by tutors.

But Cowper's influence on Wordsworth is as broadly cultural as it is specifically literary. The cool, sensible blank verse of *The Task* is only a step or two from the limpid clarity of *The Prelude* at its best, but those two steps are the stride from talent to genius. Cowper's unassuming voice of personal meditation encouraged Wordsworth's self-examination, though Cowper stopped far short of Wordsworth's claims for his imagination: 'no prophetic fires to me belong; / I play with syllables, and sport in song' ('Table Talk,' 504–05). The similar motives but different outcomes of these two long poems make all the difference between a major Romantic poem and an amusing, intelligent, but finally unchallenging poem like *The Task*. Many of its episodes start out like those in *The Prelude*, but they never develop into visionary 'spots of time.' Cowper presciently imagined the fall of the Bastille: 'There's not an English heart that would not leap / To hear that ye were fall'n at last' (V.389–90). But his lines 'leap' nowhere near the height Wordsworth's heart leapt when the event actually occurred: 'Bliss was it in that dawn to be alive, / But to be young was very heaven!'

These moments of poetic influence are very close, but worlds apart.

Both *The Task* and *The Prelude* are preparatory, therapeutic poems. But one was written from the last stages of mental debility, while the other took its first steps toward recovery by imagining the creation of a new kind of mind. Cowper's 'warfare [was] within' (VI.935), as was Wordsworth's, but he raised the stakes of mental struggle much higher. There is no point using Wordsworth as a stick to beat Cowper. The point, rather, is to see how close Cowper, like all these poets of Sensibility, came to Wordsworth, and how far Wordsworth went beyond them.

The time, the place, the occasion, and the mastership of William Taylor combined to make Wordsworth's response to Cowper, his first extended verse production, an unexceptionally positive celebration of his school. What might not have been expected was that the assignment led Wordsworth into a course from which he never thereafter was fundamentally diverted: 'This exercise . . . put it into my head to compose verses from the impulse of my own mind.'[33]

CHAPTER 4

'Verses from the impulse of my own mind'

Wordsworth's Earliest Poetry

> Thirteen years,
> Or haply less, I might have seen when first
> My ears began to open to the charm
> Of words in tuneful order, found them sweet
> For *their own sakes* – a passion and a power –
> And phrases pleased me, chosen for delight,
> For pomp, or love.
>
> (V.575–81)

On 13 December 1783, William walked out, 'feverish, and tired, and restless,' to the road junction at Borwick Lodge, a mile and a half north of Hawkshead, to wait for the horses coming to take him and Richard and John home for Christmas. It was cold and misty, not a good day for mounting a lookout. But he was impatient, and so he went, alone. The horses finally came, but the boys were home barely ten days before their father died. John Wordsworth, like his wife, died of a cold, or from a 'dropsy' which aggravated it – the same immediate cause as Wordsworth's death sixty-seven years later. He had spent a night without shelter on ill-omened Cold Fell, after losing his way back to Cockermouth en route from finishing up some coroner's duties at Millom.[1] Millom is even further from Cockermouth than Hawkshead, so he must have been as eager as his sons to return home, if he was willing to travel by night.

The occasion of his father's death lodged deeply in Wordsworth's mind at – or *as* – the beginning of his writing career. His recollection of waiting for the horses stuck in his imagination a long time – at least twenty years, when it joined his other childhood 'spot of time' at Penrith Beacon to form the visionary diptych by which he symbolized the final resolution of *The Prelude*'s crisis: 'Imagination, How Impaired and Restored.' Both 'spots of time' are thus powerfully about the death of parents: his father in one, and a murdered wife in the other. He wrote his first version of this episode in 1787, four years after the event. He tries to intensify the feeling of loss by imagining his own death as well, and the cultural signature he put on it underscores its deep significance for him: 'In church-yard such at death of day / As heard the pensive sighs of Gray.'[2] Thus his 1787 fantasy about the loss he suffered in 1783 is framed in terms from William Taylor's death in June 1786, and his tombstone's epitaph from Gray's 'Elegy.' Such palimpsests of memory, composition, and revision are fundamental to the operation of Wordsworth's self-creating imagination.

His life changed dramatically with his father's death. In that same autumn of 1783 the Wordsworth boys had moved with the Tysons out of Hawkshead village into the little enclave of Colthouse, leaving the school-home they had enjoyed since 1779. Shortly after they returned from that sad Christmas, Hugh Tyson made another sad parallel in Wordsworth's life: he died, aged seventy, on 28 February 1784, and the boys had to attend another fatherly funeral.[3]

John Wordsworth's estate was sold off quickly in two spring sales. The first disposed of personal items like his watch and rings that would normally have been reserved for his sons, had the executor been more generous than Christopher Crackanthorpe. A second sale in May disposed of the rest of the household goods, netting £260.[4] The two uncles (Richard Wordsworth of Whitehaven was the other executor) were determined to raise as much cash as they could for the five children who now fell on to their care. They did quite well, even before confronting the question of James Lowther's debt to his deceased agent: by the time John Wordsworth's land holdings were liquidated, they had raised a total of about £10,500, or more than £2000 per child. Dorothy over-optimistically estimated that this would give them each £200 per year at interest: a modest lower-middle class income, but not enough to provide the cost of a university education. For that – and for William and Christopher only – the uncles would have to advance money in anticipation of Lowther's eventual payment of the expenses he owed his late steward.

Other painful events of the sort that local gossip delights in soon reached the boys' ears. On 24 May 1784, the new Lowther agent, Michael Satterthwaite, arrived to demand the keys to the Cockermouth house. By cruel coincidence, this was the very date on which James Lowther came into his full harvest of honours for the success of his protégé, William Pitt, in the parliamentary elections of 1783. Pitt, defeated in 1780 in his first run for parliament, had held Lowther's Appleby seat (formerly Jack Robinson's) as a courtesy in 1781–83, while he positioned himself for the next election, which came very soon, given the unpopularity of the government's unholy alliance between the liberal Fox and his conservative former opponent, Lord North. Lowther now officially abandoned the Country Whigs to join a new version of the Court Whigs (Pitt's followers were not yet called 'Tories'), and was rewarded for his help by being created Viscount Lonsdale, Viscount Lowther, and Earl of Lonsdale, on top of his former ranks, Baron Lowther of Lowther, Baron of Kendal, Baron of Burgh.[5]

Another cruel coincidence of the election that brought Pitt and Lowther into power was that the Wordsworths' other political refuge, Jack Robinson, was thrown out of it. He retained his seat at Harwich, but was no longer in the government, where his influence as secretary of the treasury and his established position as Lowther's enemy could have done the Wordsworth children untold good.

The balance of life was tipping against the Wordsworths, though the full force of the change didn't appear immediately. Wordsworth's verses on his father's death show that he only gradually came to realize how much he had lost:

> I mourn [now] because I mourn'd no more [then].
> For ah! the storm was soon at rest,
>
> . . . .
>
> Nor did my little heart foresee
> —She lost a home in losing thee . . .
>
> (441–42, 445–46)

When he returned to school in the autumn of 1784, the boys were assigned verses on a topic as old as school itself: the summer vacation. After all that had happened during the year, the assignment must have seemed a cruel joke to Wordsworth. It had been, after his mother's death 1778, the worst summer of his young life.

During the following Christmas vacation, December–January 1784–85, Wordsworth wrote what he called his 'first *voluntary* verses . . . after walking six miles to attend a dance at Egremont' (from Whitehaven, where he was staying with his cousins).[6] These verses also have not survived, but they were written during the first anniversary of his father's death. They were about returning to school after the winter holidays, and Wordsworth implies that he added them on to to his earlier verses on the summer vacation. To these compositions he gave the title 'The Pleasures of Change,' which fits all the topical possibilities, and was very much in the contemporary style: 'Pleasures of Imagination' (Akenside), 'Pleasures of Memory' (Samuel Rogers), and 'Pleasures of Hope' (Thomas Campbell). A slight oddity of Wordsworth's title is that *change* did not usually give much pleasure to the poets of Sensibility. But then, neither did it to Wordsworth, in the majority of his verses surviving from this period, which turn compulsively on changes in his life occasioned by John Wordsworth's death. If, in the over-simplifications of psychobiography, his mother's death made him turn to Mother Nature for a substitute, the loss of his father, the family provider, turned him toward poetry for restoration, but with a host of attendant guilt feelings. His earlier versions of the Waiting for the Horses seem in a way the most mature: they reveal his guilt for enjoying so much the poetry that his father's death had now rendered a suspect, unprofitable pastime, and nothing like a career.

When he returned to school for the spring term, the boys were assigned to write verses for the school's bicentenary, with Cowper's 'Tirocinium: or, A Review of the Schools' (1785) as their polemical foil. Praise of public education was the theme, against Cowper's strictures, but Wordsworth managed to work in fathers and their hopes for their sons in his contribution. These 'Lines Written as a School Exercise' are the earliest surviving lines of his poetry. Most of the poem is, as he said, 'but a tame imitation of Pope's versification, and a little in his style,' although at 112 lines it is a considerable teenage production in any style.[7] It gives an unexceptionably Anglican vision of Britain's progress since the Reformation: Religion and Science join together to drive out Superstition and advance the arts of this 'cheerful isle,' which heretofore had 'deemed all merit centred in the sword.' After paying his respects to religion and science, Wordsworth turns to the moral dimension of the school's curriculum: it quenches 'the passions kindling into flame,' shames Pleasure's 'blushing beauties,' and teaches 'the tender tear to flow.' Among Pleasure's 'blushing beauties' at Hawkshead are those 'ruddy damsels past sixteen' who commissioned John Harrison to write their love letters to the grammar school boys.

The reason why this moralistic section of the goddess of Education's speech comes as the conclusion of the poem is revealed by its next-to-last words:

> "*So* shall thy sire, whilst Hope his Breast inspires,
> And wakes anew life's glimmering, trembling fires,
> Hear Britain's Sons rehearse thy praise with joy,
> Look up to Heav'n, and bless his darling Boy."
>
> (99–102; italics added)

This sounds as bland as the rest of the poem: work hard, avoid temptation, and you'll be successful and your father will be proud of you. But it was a brave quatrain for a boy whose father had just died to recite publicly in front of all the other boys and their parents at the ceremony. As far as Wordsworth personally was concerned, the proper locution for the last line would be, 'Look *down* from Heaven, and bless his darling Boy.'

On the basis of his summer vacation and School Exercise lines, Taylor encouraged him to write more. This was more than a recognition of talent; it was a wise teacher's way of helping a favourite pupil deal with his grief. Taylor's personal literary tastes ran to the melancholy-sentimental, and his pedagogical methods were flexible enough to use verse-writing as a reward, punishment or encouragement.

*

A considerable amount of other poetry survives from Wordsworth's Hawkshead days, most of it written between 1785 and 1787. It would of course be possible to dismiss all of it as derivative, and no more interesting than what we would expect from a boy of his class and training at that time and in that place.[8] But they cannot be wholly dismissed as generic late eighteenth-century verse. He was somewhat exceptional in being considered 'rather the poet of the school,' though not more so than Robert Greenwood or the Farrish brothers, the Windermere minstrels.[9] We can hear the actual voice of his schoolmates' admiration in a marginal comment recorded over a hundred years ago: 'One day after he had gained some credit from his Master for some English Verses – a bigger boy took him by the arm and led him off into the fields, & when he had got him quite apart, gravely said to him, "I say, Bill, when thoo writes verse dost thoo invoke t'Muse?"'[10] It's like a moment from Joyce's *Portrait of the Artist as a Young Man*. It recaptures our school memories of awe at peers who do easily what we can't do at all, whether it be maths, drawing, sports or singing. One wonders why the bigger boy took him so far off. Was he embarrassed? Threatening? Probably the reason for distance, and confidentiality, was pragmatic: if poetry required invoking the Muse, could Bill show him how, so he could gain some much-needed credit with the master?

But the strongest reason for not passing over Wordsworth's earliest verses is that they have been preserved by a very reputable authority – Wordsworth himself. In several notebooks never thrown away during many shifts of residence and travels between 1787 and 1799 – not to neglect the ensuing fifty-one years at Grasmere and Rydal Mount – he kept by him many juvenile poems and fragments, amounting to well over a thousand lines of verse. This is exceptional: no comparable body of juvenile poetry in English exists for any major poet before him. These notebooks helped develop his lifelong habit of reading himself when no other books were available – or even if they were. It seems perfectly natural in retrospect that Wordsworth, the poet of childhood, should save them, but his doing so was by no means automatic. Facetiously, he said that he kept on composing after his 'School Exercise' because he'd been given a new notebook for it and it seemed a shame not to make use of the remaining pages.

He continued to write Greek, Latin and English verses in school, but the poems in the Hawkshead notebook were his own. They reflected the kind of verse he was writing in school, but they are markedly different from the style of the 'School Exercise' lines, clearly representing his *voluntary* selection of models among the many that William Taylor exposed him to. As such, they have a remarkable consistency: with very few exceptions they are all about love and death. Most often, his themes of love and death appear in conventional contexts – e.g., the aftermath of disappointed love affairs – and do not support very much psychological interpretation. Less often, Wordsworth presents love more broadly, as toward a parent or a place. Death is likewise generalized broadly to include the loss of a friend, an impending departure, or a generalized mood of melancholy. There are no satires or topical, occasional poems, and few narratives involving characters other than himself.

His translations of Anacreon and Catullus are suitably frank and sexy like their originals, and not the kind of poems he was assigned in school, if the 'School Exercise' is any indication. His imitation of Anacreon updates the Greek poet's instructions to a painter of ancient Rhodes by addressing instructions for a portrait of his lover to Sir Joshua Reynolds. Wordsworth cleverly substitutes local nature metaphors to describe the mistress's arching eyebrows (the moon's 'silver crescent') and her eye's 'lunar beams.' But when his description drops below her neck – everything that Anacreon dismisses with a sly glance – Wordsworth extends the original by several lines, to produce one of the sexiest – if most awkward – descriptions of Grasmere on record. Anacreon simply says, 'the rest / Be in a chastened purple drest, / But let her flesh peep here and there / The lines of beauty to declare.'[11] But Wordsworth pursues his innovative nature imagery to describe how the robe draped over the beloved's body is like a mist on Grasmere lake, which 'Hides half the landskip from the sight.' So far, so good. But then the metaphor takes over from the message, and he begins wandering through a thoroughly anthropomorphized landscape to some spots revealed with considerably more frankness than the peeping flesh Anacreon alluded to.

> While Fancy paints beneath the Veil
> The pathway winding through the dale,
> The cot, the seat of Peace and Love,
> Peeping through the tufted grove.
>
> (43–46)

If the landscape is the beloved's body and the mist is her robe, the explication of that 'seat' of Love behind the 'tufted' metaphor that Fancy imagines beneath the robe can go in only one direction. Wordsworth here achieves a transformation of landscape into sensual terms that parallels the more 'spiritual' transformations of his greatest poetry. In choice and execution, the translation reflects the preoccupations of any healthy sixteen-year-old, and participates in a centuries-old schoolboy tradition of finding a stimulus to classical translation in the promise of illicit erotic rewards.

Wordsworth's translations and imitations of Catullus are closer to the original than his Anacreontics, but equally erotic.[12] His Septimius and Acme (Catullus XLV) are more passionate than the standard English version, which reads: 'Then Acme, slightly bending back her head, kissed with that rosy mouth her sweet love's swimming eyes, and said, 'So, my life, my darling Septimius, so may we ever serve this one master as (I swear) more strongly and fiercely burns in me the flame deep in my melting marrow.'[13] Here is Wordsworth's version:

> But Acme lightly turning back her head
> Kissed with that rosy mouth th'inebriate eyes
> Of the sweet youth, and kissed again and said:
> 'My life, and what far more than life I prize,
> So may we to the end of time obey
> Love our sole master, as my bosom owns
> A flame that with far more resistless sway
> Thrills through the very marrow of my bones.'
> (13–20)

So too his Lesbia (Catullus V), where he adds contemporary details of lovelorn melancholy that are no part of his original. Catullus' poem is a hyperbole of kisses, mounting up to 'many thousands,' the better to befuddle any 'malicious person' who might give him and his lover the evil eye, 'when he knows that our kisses are so many.' For this aggressive policy of erotic economy, the teenage Wordsworth substituted intimations of loss. He raises the stakes to 'a million' kisses, but his conclusion is abrupt, original with him, and adolescently apocalyptic: 'That I for joys may never pine / That never can again be mine.' Why so pale and wan, young lover?

The title of 'Beauty and Moonlight' promises more of the same love-and-death motifs, but it was good enough for Coleridge to pick up years later and revise, as 'Lewti', for the *Morning Post*, and it almost got into *Lyrical Ballads*.[14] It is a cinematic version of Wordsworth's Anacreon translation, with a Hawkshead lover wandering 'high o'er the silver rocks' trying to forget his Mary. But he keeps seeing her in anthropomorphic imagery of land, sky, and sea. A waterfall seen through the trees reminds him, 'So shines her forehead smooth and fair / Gleaming through her sable hair.' But if the God of Love would let him really see her, then the metaphors of the poem might be returned to their right relation to human life, which is the main technical problem in all these poems.

> *Then* might her bosom soft and white
> Heave upon my swimming sight
> *As* these two Swans together ride [MS: heave]
> Upon the gently swelling tide. [MS: soft heaving wave]
> (31–34; italics added)

That is, better to see her breasts as swans than swans as her breasts: the former is ecstasy, the latter fantasy. The imagery of swans for breasts is a Renaissance figure, or *blason*, that Wordsworth took from Spenser and

Milton, but it curiously always caused him trouble whenever he tried to use it, as he frequently did throughout the 1790s.

The speaker of this poem could be the hero, who is also the villain, of the only ballad Wordsworth composed at Hawkshead, since the girl in both poems is named Mary. The date of this poem ('And will you leave me thus alone?') can be fixed with extraordinary accuracy at 23–24 March 1787, by Wordsworth's date on the manuscript.[15] The real-life biographies of its characters are well established in Hawkshead records, but his treatment of them is a surprising variation on the theme of love and death which dominates his juvenilia. It looks like a curse-poem to start with, as Mary tells William, who has jilted her, 'Be sure her Ghost will haunt thy bed / When Mary shall lie low.' The revenge of wronged lovers is a dominant feature of folk ballads, but Wordsworth's poem reverses this tried-and-true formula. Instead of seeing William haunted by Mary's curse, we observe her dawning realization that she has been abandoned, in a series of natural signs which the narrator interprets in lugubrious detail. Instead of haunting William, her ghost haunts *her*: 'oft her waft [ghost] was seen / With wan light standing at the door' – a sure folk-sign of imminent death.

It is tempting to imagine that this William and Mary are teenage fantasy prototypes of William Wordsworth and Mary Hutchinson, the Penrith playmate who would become his wife. But whatever the state of his feelings for her at age sixteen, the identities of the lovers in this ballad are too well known to allow such an easy identification. However, the poem's empathy for the young woman instead of the young man is not in doubt. Mary follows a round of activity in the vale of Esthwaite that is very similar to Wordsworth's. And when he gave her the words, 'My head would soon lie low,' we can be sure his identification with the poem's emotions is very deep, since these are, once again, his oft-repeated words from William Taylor's deathbed less than a year earlier.

The Mary of the poem is actually Mary Rigge (d. 1760), who had been a friend and confidante of Ann Tyson's, and whose parents still lived in the Green End house next to hers.[16] The Wordsworth boys stayed with the Rigges for two or three weeks in early 1784, during Hugh Tyson's final illness, when Ann was too busy to care for them. Mary's mother took such good care of them, and they were so quiet and well behaved that her husband – the stern father of the ballad – relented his initial opposition to having noisy boys in the house. From Mrs Rigge and Ann Tyson, the boys heard a lot about Mary Rigge's sad story, for it was one of the neighbourhood's scandals, and its actors were, with one exception, still very much alive. Mary had been seduced by David Kirkby, of Kirkby Quay on Coniston Water. She bore his child, baptized David Benoni on 17 June 1759, a year before her own death. Kirkby did not marry her, reserving his choice for one Agatha Sawrey, whom he married in 1762. Wordsworth made a note of the affair in a comment on *Peter Bell* (where he used the Biblical name Benoni) that conceals as much as it reveals: 'Benoni, or the child of sorrow, I knew when I was a school-boy. His mother had been deserted by a gentleman in the neighbourhood, she herself being a gentlewoman by birth. The circumstances of her story were told me by my dear old dame, Ann Tyson, who was her confidante. The lady died broken-hearted.' David Benoni was not a Sandys school-boy, but he was very much alive when the Wordsworth boys lived with his grandparents, and had received the hefty sum of £700 in June, 1786, when his grand-father died – two weeks after William Taylor.[17] Without drawing causal connections, it is not surprising, given this tissue of associations, that the Mary in the ballad should utter William Taylor's dying words.

The poem's reversal of the usual terms of the curse-ballad and Wordsworth's sophisticated manipulation of its natural symbols make it more than a 'feeble' imitation of a standard model.[18] He was able to accomplish so much with it because of the proximity of the persons involved to his residence – and to the facts of his own life. David Benoni, unrecognized by the natural father whose surname he bore, lost the grandfather who had raised him in June of 1786, the same month in which the recently orphaned William Wordsworth, now also a 'child of sorrow', lost the schoolmaster who was his most important father-substitute. David's inheritance was not as large as William's, but at least it was uncontested and paid immediately.

William in the ballad is something of a sadist. His emotional insen-sitivity makes him the anti-type of another poetical character Wordsworth adopted in this same period, February–March 1787, for his sonnet 'On Seeing Miss Helen Maria Williams Weep at a Tale of Distress,' which was good enough for the *European Magazine*, a leading London journal which favoured her verse to publish.[19] Thus by 1787 Wordsworth was a writer fully capable of imagining himself persuasively into states of mind diametrically different from his own. The well-known tears of Helen Williams, sprinkled liberally throughout her poetry, are the catalyst to the speaker's own: 'She wept. – Life's purple tide began to flow / In languid streams through every thrilling vein.' The sonnet swoops near to death-by-poetry, until 'a sigh recall'd the wanderer [Life] to my breast.' Yet the speaker is in doubt which was most valuable in his experience, the dying tear or the saving sigh. His tears, like Williams's, are a sign of virtue: the strongest moral guarantee in the world of Sensibility.

He wrote two other sonnets in the same mood, upon losses closer to his own experience: the coming departure from Hawkshead for Cambridge. These two sonnets also indicate some of the difference between what Wordsworth felt or wrote in 1787, and what he later *represented* himself as feeling then. 'Extract from the Conclusion of a Poem, Composed in Anticipation of Leaving School,' dated from 1786 by Wordsworth in 1843, is a published poem, included in his first collected works (1815), the earliest of his poems to be so retained. Because of later reworking, its polish sets it apart from the rest of the juvenilia, especially 'The Vale of Esthwaite', which it was supposed to conclude.[20]

> *1787:*
>
> As Phoebus, when he sinks to rest
> Far on the mountains in the west,
> While all the vale is dark between
> Ungilded by his golden sheen,
> A lingering lustre softly throws
> On the dear hills where first he rose.
>
> *1815:*
>
> Thus, while the Sun sinks down to rest
> Far in the regions of the west,
> Though to the vale no parting gleam
> Be given, not one memorial gleam,
> A lingering light he softly throws
> On the dear hills where first he rose.

The latter version's subtle connection between the speaker's memory and the setting sun is exactly the kind of relation the young Wordsworth failed to establish successfully in most of his other early poems, where his metaphors become so intricate we lose their point. The earlier version expresses a teenager's fear of dying, not the reflective views of a forty-five-year-old man. The published version doesn't look like a sonnet, but it is; its simple four-beat lines are an example of primitive *style* rather than of juvenile poetry strictly speaking.

Quite different is the other 'farewell' sonnet, dated *c.* 23 October 1787, perhaps the very day he departed Hawkshead for Cambridge.[21] Not revised for later publication, it is a poem much more like his other early creations.

> What is it that tells my soul the Sun is setting?
> For not a straggling ray tell[s] her he is in the
> Eas[t] or west[;] 'tis the brown mist which
> descends slowly into the valley to [shed?] [?]
> that burden of [ghosts?]. See where a
> son of other worlds is sailing [s]lowly or the
> lake – no! 'tis the taper that twinkling in the
> cottage casts a long wan shadow over the [lake?].
> Lo[ud] howls the village dog. Spirit of these
> Mountains I see thee throned on Helvellyn, but
> thy feet and head are wrapped in mist.
> Spirit of these mountains if thou can [?Speak]

bid the mist break from thy forehead, and nod
me thrice farewell. farewell [,] farewell.—
For [no?] more shall the ghosts leaning from
The rocks or look[ing] from the parting of the cloud
listen while thou instructed me in the lore
of Nature. Bid the mist break from thy brow
an[d] thrice nod me a Farewell.

Though an incomplete fragment, it needs only a little technical help to become a perfectly adequate sonnet. As a farewell poem, it is not saying goodbye to the region, but rather to the Gothic modes which the poet has used to represent it. Its message is, 'No more ghosts.' Its plea is simply for a more naturalistic way of interpreting meaning in landscape – the same issue, though with different content, that Wordsworth explored in the Mary Rigge ballad and 'Beauty and Moonlight.'

If this sonnet, like most of Wordsworth's earliest poems, claims that Nature chastened his overheated imagination, then 'The Vale of Esthwaite' is the text that the sonnet was written *against*. Very little of what we have seen of Wordsworth's life, reading and writing at Hawkshead prepares us for the unrestrained Gothicism of this extraordinary poem. Its innocuous title is the first of many surprises; it might better have been called 'Revenge of the Phantom Minstrel'. As a personal narrative poem summing up his eight years at Hawkshead, 'The Vale of Esthwaite' sounds a cautionary note for any estimate of the range of Wordsworth's youthful imagination: not because it is so bad, but because it is at once so powerful and so powerfully out of control. His later characterization of it as 'a long poem running upon my own adventures, and the scenery of the country in which I was brought up' is laughably inaccurate, unless we reflect that his sense of 'adventure' (and equally of 'scenery') could be as strongly mental as it was physical. It reads like the nightmare underside of the splendid boyhood adventures recounted in *Prelude* I & II. It is Hawkshead-by-Night, or what ran through Wordsworth's mind on those night-time rambles he loved. Of course, it can be pigeon-holed as 'conventional' Gothicism, but that only explains away what surely wants explaining, when a convention is allowed to run loose at such length. Published texts of its fragmentary manuscripts run to nearly 600 lines, by far the longest of Wordsworth's juvenilia, but the condition of the manuscripts suggest that almost twice that number of lines have been torn out at various points in the notebooks to supply the 'thoughts and images . . . which have been dispersed through my other writings.'[22]

The uncertain and probably unhappy future of his life was becoming pretty apparent by 1787 when Wordsworth came to write it. In May of that year Richard Wordsworth and Christopher Crackanthorpe finally faced up to the fact that they would have to bring suit against Lowther to get the more than £4600 still outstanding in his accounts with John Wordsworth.[23] No one knew, though some perhaps dreaded, how long Lowther would hold out: he stalled for five more years before they got him into court, and even when the judgment came in their favour it produced no action. Suing James Lowther was not simply a personal lawsuit; it was an action against a vast, powerful sociopolitical institution, a kind of international corporation.

'The Vale of Esthwaite', though still in Wordsworth's earliest stages of self-mining, is much more concerned with what the mind imagines than with what the eye sees. Its sprawling shapelessness suggest 'automatic' writing of the most therapeutic kind. He used the materials of landscape description, the machinery of Gothic horror, and the motives of his own mind – especially his impending vocational choices – to produce a psycho-sexual monodrama of a Lake District minstrel's quest for meaning in life.

There can be no complete or unified version of such a fragmentary poem, but this does not make much difference, since for all its weird grotesquerie 'The Vale of Esthwaite' is very much of a piece, holographically. No matter where you slice into it, you find yourself reading the same poem. This is exactly what we should expect of such a compulsive text: reading it is like hearing someone recount a dream or a nightmare, and interpreting it requires some minimal skill in the interpretation of dreams. Like a dream, it is highly repetitive. What it mainly repeats is, as in many anxiety dreams, the speaker's fear of being destroyed: in this case, by a malevolent agent represented as a harp, a lyre, a bard, or a minstrel – the nightmare agents or secret police of poetry. But since it is not a dream but a consciously-produced poem, its forward movement is marked by its speaker's determined effort to stay *on* his subject, which is basically poetical landscape description. What could be more 'Wordsworthian'? But on the evidence of 'The Vale of Esthwaite,' we would have to say that for Wordsworth at age seventeen there was no more life-threatening, scarifying topic than that one. It is impossible for modern readers not to smile at its Gothic excesses, but we should not ignore the pathos of its situation, which is something like a young boy's exploring the very real sadness of his life in – for a modern equivalent – the plot, imagery and language of a comic book. No fancy critical skill is needed to reach this conclusion; the poem deconstructs itself over and over again before our very eyes. By its end – wherever we locate it – the poet seems to have lost the battle.

Generically, 'The Vale of Esthwaite' is yet another eighteenth-century imitation of Milton along lines first laid down by James Thomson: a walk through the landscape and the seasons, alternating between moods of L'Allegro and Il Penseroso. But this convenient arrangement is continually knocked askew by the interruption of a third term, the Gothic–Sublime, with life-threatening thrills of horror that make it impossible to maintain the usual balance between charming beauty and pleasant melancholy. The demonic bard-figures are always associated with these Gothic interruptions. Statistically, less than ten per cent of the extant text is in the L'Allegro mood, and while Il Penseroso gets almost thirty per cent of the total, the Gothic passages take up fully forty per cent of the whole. In his melancholy passages, Wordsworth tried to be serious and mature; these are the parts of the poem containing benevolent 'social' references to village poverty. The Gothic parts are intensely personal, and, not surprisingly, are the best parts of the whole, if you like that sort of thing, which Wordsworth clearly did. Yet they also repulsed him; such was his double bind. The remaining twenty per cent of the lines are autobiographical: self-pitying thoughts about his coming change of scene, and the hard life awaiting him: 'full soon must I resign [the cheering joys of Fancy] / To delve in Mammon's joyless mine' (Text 1.V.13–14). The only human agents able to offer him any support are John Fleming's friendship and Dorothy's confidence.

Wordsworth was saying farewell to the dearest spot he knew on earth, and he dreads the thought so much that it returns *as* dread to haunt the beloved landscape: the return of the repressed. He goes to face 'the real world', but his vision is complicated not only by 'Mammon,' but by his realization that his growing attachment to poetical Fancy is going to complicate his work in Mammon's 'joyless mine.' No minstrels need apply. In light of the family plan that he should achieve honours at Cambridge, proceed thence to a fellowship, possibly a professorship, or at least ordination, the attractions of a life of poetry appeared to this serious teenager like nightmarish delusions of his own badly conflicted motives.

What happens at the beginning of the poem happens repeatedly throughout it. It starts with a command, 'avaunt!,' and that is its password throughout, as the speaker tries to ward off the various spectres that try to kill him. He starts out with the morning lark for his usual walk around the beautiful 'lake's lovely bosom.' Ann Tyson's terrier was with him, recast for poetic purposes as 'the shepherd's restless dog.' Then, 'at noon I hied to gloomy glades.' This is the standard next move for L'Allegro to become a bit more *penseroso*, but things quickly get out of hand. In three lines Wordsworth accelerates himself from 'gloom' to religion to superstition to horror, a woman in a black dress ('She wove a stole of sable thread'), and then all hell breaks loose, or rather the precisely articulated hell of this poem:

> And hark[!] the ringing harp I hear
> And [lo!] her druid sons appear.
> Why roll on me your glaring eyes[?]
> Why fix on me for sacrifice[?]

That these lines are imitated directly from Helen Maria Williams is less important than the special use Wordsworth puts them to.[24] There are many demons in eighteenth-century Gothic poems and novels, and plenty of ancient bards, druids, and harps, but few in which the harps are identical to demonic instruments of destruction. The trademark – or psychic scar – of 'The Vale of Esthwaite' is that the demons represented *in* the text have taken over control *of* the text.

All this is made more poignant and realistic in the latter portions of the text, where he refers to his father's death and to Dorothy and John Fleming. But the poem can only be 'the shipwreck of the thought' it means to be conveying, so long as 'fancy in a daemon's form / Rides through the clouds and swells the storm, / To . . . sweet Melancholy blind, / The moonlight of the Poet's mind' (Text 1.V.2–6). At the very end of the poem he asserts bravely that he'll still be able to think of the beauties of Nature and Art even while toiling in Mammon's mine. This is not the main problem of 'The Vale of Esthwaite', which has been, rather, that Fancy all too regularly takes on a demonic form that throws him into a terror and a darkness far worse than Mammon's gloom. Poetry, his own career dream, not Mammon, his uncles' plan, is the enemy, and this is the source of the contradictions between his projected life plan and his personal desires that 'The Vale of Esthwaite' tries but fails to overcome.

Wordsworth returned to Penrith after graduating in June 1787. Christopher Crackanthorpe knew that school was out and the boys ready to come home, but did not send horses for the boys because they had not specifically requested them – nor had any family member attended the closing ceremonies. The homecoming tragedy of 1783 was being replayed as farce. William finally hired a horse himself to ride to Penrith to see what was the matter. Dorothy related the incident to her friend Jane Pollard in Halifax with shrewd insight into Crackanthorpe's mean punctilio. Their guardian's treatment of them affected the servants, who did not miss an opportunity to make snide comments about the children's lowered expectations. Because of William's strongly independent bearing they particularly delighted in thwarting his requests with variations on the theme of 'Who does he think he is, a gentleman?'

The situation that summer was all the more painful because it was the boys' first reunion with Dorothy since their mother's death nine years earlier. The happiness of the occasion was deeply scarred by their sense of what they had lost: parents, prospects, a whole world of possibilities. They frequently wept together. Yet they were also happy together: William and Dorothy and Mary Hutchinson had some fine rambles about the country-side, including a return visit to Penrith Beacon, reinforcing its earlier emotional associations with new intensities from this time of school ending and family reunion, and laying powerful depth charges in Wordsworth's young imagination.

William returned to Hawkshead and Ann Tyson many weeks before he departed for Cambridge: further evidence of the mutual distaste with which he and Crackanthorpe now regarded each other. Dorothy returned not to Halifax and her Aunt Threlkeld but to Forncett (near Norwich), to live with her kindlier uncle, the Reverend William Cookson, whose personality was not so distorted as his brother's by a fixation on social advancement. As a younger son, Cookson had lesser expectations in this direction anyway. But he was working his mild, stolid, yet expertly calculating way up the social ladder via influential friends like William Wilberforce, MP for York and one of Pitt's closest friends. The Forncett vicarage was the prime stock in Cookson's portfolio of non-resident 'livings' and preferred ecclesiastical appointments, that had allowed him at last to marry the daughter of the Penrith vicar after a courtship of seven passion-deadening years. Such arrangments, which were also characteristic of several of the poets of Sensibility who influenced young Wordsworth, marked out the late eighteenth-century path of advancement that he expected to follow, and Cookson's hard experience in this road eventually made him a severer, more knowledgeable critic of his young nephew than Christopher Crackanthorpe, who mainly resented the money.

CHAPTER 5

Stranger, Lounger, Lover

Residence at Cambridge

> . . . I had . . . a strangeness in my mind,
> A feeling that I was not for that hour
> Nor for that place. But . . .
>
> We sauntered, played, we rioted, we talked
> Unprofitable talk at morning hours,
> Drifted about along the streets and walks,
> Read lazily in lazy books . . .
>
> (III.80–82, 251–54)

Wordsworth set out for Cambridge with his maternal uncle William Cookson and paternal cousin John Myers in late October of 1787. The boys were full of enthusiasm; William in particular 'had raised a pile upon the basis of the coming time' of fantastical proportions. But they would need help making their way in the world: Wordsworth was an orphan, and Myers's mother had died earlier that year. William Cookson was just the man to help them.

Cookson was much more than an uncle at this moment: he was a fellow of St John's College, one of two fellowships the college reserved for men from Cumberland, at least one of which was usually held by a Hawkshead graduate.[1] This meant he was one of fifty-five fellows of the autonomous corporate body which legally owned and administered the college and the forty-six church livings in its gift, each paying about £300 per year. Neither Cambridge nor Oxford was truly a national university.[2] They were still Anglican foundations whose primary social function was to supply parishes with priests. By the late eighteenth century the priests-to-be were much more interested in the process than most parishes, and it was said that 'the emoluments of Cambridge have been its ruin, as a place of genuine education.'[3] In the normal course of events, students elected to fellowships stayed on at college after their BA, advanced to their MA by payment of a fee, and then drew an annual stipend of about £200 until a living became vacant. About two per year opened up, on average, in the larger colleges.[4] Upon being awarded a living, a fellow was released from his vows of celibacy, and, if he had cultivated his marriage prospects well – as Cookson had – retired to a country parish to begin his adult life of religious leisure and good works.[5] Cookson knew a fellowship would be waiting for William on graduation because he would soon vacate his own fellowship to get married: both King George and Pitt had assured Wilberforce that his 'fat little Canon's' long wait for a living was almost over.[6]

Besides his fellowship, William Cookson had other important connections with which to ease his nephews' transition into adult life via the university. Now thirty-three, he had spent nearly five years (1781–86) as preceptor to George III's sons, particularly the fifth, Ernest Augustus, Duke of Cumberland (1771–1851), in the palace at Kew.[7] He regularly held long conversations with the concerned monarch about all his sons' progress – those unimpressive, when not actively infamous, boys who grew up causing great concern for the crown's succession during the Regency period. George, the Prince of Wales (b. 1762), was already beyond parental control, as the first 'Regency Crisis' (1788–89) made abundantly clear, when King George suffered the first of his fits of 'madness.' Tutors of royalty and nobility often became figures of considerable social importance in their own right. George III was 'completely devoted' to his tutor, John Stuart, eventually making him first lord of the treasury (i.e., prime minister) in 1762, as Lord Bute: Sir James Lowther's father-in-law.[8] Cookson was on familiar enough terms with the King to be teased by him about his weight, and this intimacy, plus George's entire satisfaction with Cookson's tutoring, made his appointment as one of the canons of the chapel royal at Windsor an easy matter.[9] William Cookson was one of 'the round pegs for whom the round holes of preferment are intended,'[10] and there was no reason at this time to suppose that his nephew William was not equally malleable.

Still more important for his young charges was Cookson's intimate friendship with Wilberforce, who was just emerging as the parliamentary champion of the fight against slavery. Their friendship dated from their college days at St John's ten years earlier. Wilberforce was one of Pitt's closest friends. For several years begining in 1788, he spent weeks or months at a time at Cookson's house in Forncett, reading up to nine hours a day and using Cookson as a tutor to make up for his wasted time at Cambridge.[11] Cookson had recently helped Wilberforce (who was very rich) obtain a holiday property in the Lake District: he leased Rayrigg, the Windermere estate of Wordsworth's friend John Fleming, from as early as 1782.[12]

Wordsworth was very fortunate to have an uncle with William Cookson's connections, which were sure routes to preferment if his university career ended with even a modicum of success. In this respect, Cookson was a younger complement to John Robinson, who, though now sixty, was still active in court and government politics. He had by this time moved from his service in Lord North's prime ministership to being the trusted political agent for no less a client than George III himself. Using the electioneering skills he had learned in Cumberland, he was now the king's chief go-between in his relations with parliament, and had already demonstrated his usefulness to Pitt.[13] For young Wordsworth's prospects, Robinson's shrewd dealings were all to the good; it would be hard to name a man in England at the time more experienced in securing and dispensing places, especially the comparatively trifling matter of finding a place for a needy nephew after graduation. Robinson was alert to all these possibilities. He kept a keen eye on his nephew during this first year at college: 'my earnest recommendation to you is to stick close to the College for the first two or three years . . . . It will give me great pleasure to hear you go out high in your year, and I cannot by words alone express to you the satisfaction I shall feel in hearing you go out senior wrangler, strive for that, and establish a reputation at College which will go with you, and serve you thro' Life.'[14]

With two such uncles, young Wordsworth was, speaking in modern terms, never more than two phone calls away from the king or the prime minister of England throughout his years at Cambridge. One of the best measures of his independence is that he never placed those calls, or let others make them for him; and when he finally did make them, out of personal desperation, it was much too late, and his credit along those lines long since expended.

En route to Cambridge, the three Cumberland travellers spent their first night at the home of John Robinson's brother, Captain (later Admiral) Hugh Robinson, in York. The fifty-two-year-old captain had just married John Myers's sister Mary, aged twenty-two; she would bear him thirteen children in the remaining fifteen years of his life.[15] At dinner that night the family's expectations and interests were on everyone's mind when the captain pointedly commented, 'I hope, William, you mean to take a good degree.' William answered with a sweeping challenge to himself: 'I will be either senior wrangler or nothing!'[16] The boast was not idle. He was the most favoured student in his year at Hawkshead, and one of the best in the past several years. The school had a steady record of high-ranking wranglers for many years, most of them at St John's, where several of the fellows were always sure to be Hawkshead alumni: Cookson's friend Edward Christian, Hawkshead master in 1781, was now a Johnian fellow and professor of law.[17]

That Wordsworth more nearly achieved the other alternative in his ultimatum – 'nothing!' – is the real story of his Cambridge years. But, backed by family support and buoyed by his own confidence, he rolled into Cambridge three or four days later, along the northwest road from Huntingdon, over the Cam at Magdalene Bridge, into Bridge Street, 'and at the Hoop we landed, famous inn.' The Hoop Inn, or Hotel, was indeed very much at the centre of Cambridge life, being the unofficial head-quarters of the Whig party until well past the middle of the nineteenth century.[18] Located near the three-way intersection of the main northwest-southeast road (Bridge Street and Sidney Street), the east-west road to Newmarket (Jesus Lane), and High Street (now St John's Street), the north-south road to Trumpington, it was physically at the centre of Cambridge as well. It was the main hotel for families of students at St John's College, which stood just across the street.

Just as the world of personal social connections that Wordsworth now entered was by modern standards extremely small, so too was its university outpost. From St John's College at the top of the High Street to Peterhouse at the bottom was less than a thousand yards, and all but five of the colleges were strung along that axis. The town centre was not much different in its physical layout than it is today.

But in other respects it differed greatly. The sixteen oldest colleges were there in all their Gothic splendour, one of the largest and most coherent groupings of well-preserved Gothic-Renaissance buildings in Europe. But the town, with less than 10,000 inhabitants living in fourteen different parishes, was small and miserable, a far cry from today's upscale urban milieu. On fine days, it presented a vision of rural simplicity surrounding Gothic magnificence. But on bad days it was all mud and flowing gutters, and every night the streets nearest the university were filled with drunken roistering students, making passage dangerous.[19] Town-and-gown fights or riots went on constantly, for despite the town's dependence on the university, relations between the two were extremely hostile, producing 'a state at times comparable to petty warfare.'[20] The streets were unpaved and completely dark at night; the first citywide illuminations were not installed until 1796. One of the arguments against streetlighting was that the students and the 'snobs' (as students called all townspeople) would recognize each other more easily and fight even more. But at least the traffic was not bad; only three people in town kept carriages, one of them Richard Watson, professor of chemistry and bishop of Llandaff, the Lake District boy whose successful ascent up the ladder of place and preferment was legendary, and often held up to young Wordsworth as a model – or a reproach.

'The Evangelist St John my patron was'

The massive entrance to St John's three 'gloomy courts' was on High Street, just off the main Cambridge intersection. Wordsworth's 'nook obscure' was Room 23 in the southwest corner of First Court, up Pump staircase, above the busy kitchens with their 'shrill notes of sharp command and scolding intermixed.'[21] Its courts are not 'gloomy' today (East Anglian weather permitting), in their manicured beauty, but in Wordsworth's time the courts and cellars were all work areas, piled up with coal and wood, and bustling with porters and shoeblacks, laundresses and cooks, 'gyps' (menservants assigned to each entryway) and bed makers. The kitchens were huge subterranean places, with fireplaces as big as rooms, and 'cooks, sub-cooks, and scullions in abundance, as black and greasy as so many devils.'[22] Wordsworth's small, cheap room looked out on the dark squalor of Back Lane toward the splendid chapel of Trinity College, designed by Christopher Wren. His bedroom was but a closet, and he used to pull the bed out into his 'keeping room' at night to have a view of the chapel spires through his little window.[23]

St John's was one of the two largest Cambridge colleges, along with Trinity, its next-door neighbour and constant rival. In various college publications one detects a slight note of restive inferiority with regard to Trinity, which has more often attained a reputation for academic excellence, as measured in famous names, like Newton. A similar paradox afflicts the relationship between St John's and Wordsworth, in that the man 'almost universally regarded as the greatest of the Johnians'[24] was one of its least distinguished students. Yet university records and chronologies must frequently use him as a reference point ('Wordsworth's year,' 'friend of Wordsworth,' etc.). Some of St John's lagging reputation came from its long association with conservative positions and professors, especially in religious matters; it is directly across the street from the university divinity school.[25]

In the Civil War, St John's was a Royalist college in a parliamentary town, used as a prison by Cromwell's troops. High Church orthodoxy returned in 1661, but for the next hundred years St John's went into a steady decline that leaves its own historians puzzled.[26] At the time Wordsworth arrived, its reputation was reviving, thanks to the energetic reforms of Samuel Powell, master from 1765 to 1775, mostly involving more rigorous examinations – which had a direct effect on Wordsworth. But with about 200 students and fifty fellows, and generally low enrollments throughout the eighteenth century, living conditions were fairly spacious through its three courtyards.

Wordsworth was one of the forty-four students who entered St John's as freshmen that year. The number was low, but up significantly from the doldrums of the 1760s and 1770s. Among the students who started with him, or already there, were many known to him from Hawkshead. Far different than the solitary existence portrayed in *The Prelude* and rehearsed in his standard biographies, the full range of Wordsworth's friendships and acquaintances included more than two dozen names.[27]

Also entering with Wordsworth and Myers were Thomas Gawthorp, who had roomed with Wordsworth at Ann Tyson's the previous year.[28] Other Hawkshead boys entering other colleges in 1787 included Robert Greenwood, the minstrel of Windermere, next door at Trinity, and John Millar at Jesus. Many of William's best friends were already at nearby colleges: John Fleming and William Penny at Christ's; Fleming's brother Fletcher Raincock at Pembroke; Charles Farish, another of the 'minstrels,' at Queen's (Farish's brother John was a tutor at Magdalen), as was James Losh from Carlisle, whose younger brother William had been with Wordsworth at Hawkshead.[29] This gallery of familiar faces lengthened in subsequent years: Thomas Maude, also a boarder at Ann Tyson's with the Wordsworths, came up to St John's the next year (he, not Wordsworth, would succeed William Cookson as rector at Forncett), and Reginald Brathwaite, son of the Hawkshead vicar at whose Belmount country house Wordsworth had been so well received, came in 1790.[30] At least thirteen other Hawkshead boys arrived at other colleges between 1787 and 1790. When Wordsworth says he felt 'a strangeness in his mind,' that he was 'not for that place,' the reference must be understood as strictly subjective, for there was no place in England that could have been less strange and more familiar to him in personal terms than St John's College. In fact, there was no place on earth, in default of a family home, that stood more ready to give the young Wordsworth a warm, comfortable reception than Cambridge University.

College friendships are always important, but in eighteenth-century England, with a much smaller population and far fewer participants in public life, college associates were central to one's mature life. The inner circle of Pitt's government – and of his Foxite opponents – was peopled to an extraordinary degree by Cambridge men (such as Wilberforce). Not only Wordsworth's friends but also the people he knew *of* (and vice versa) at college are significant data for charting his development, as persons who might be expected to remain more or less aware of him as 'someone-I-knew-at-university.' For example, among students already at St John's in 1787 was a young man named Robert Stewart, later Viscount Castlereagh, the Pitt protégé who helped put down the Irish rebellion of 1798 and who as foreign minister would put together the coalition which finally brought Napoleon down.

At other colleges, Wordsworth also knew Francis Wrangham and John Tweddell of Trinity, members of the brilliant class of 1790. Two friends from Pembroke were Thomas Middleton, Coleridge's school friend and future liberal bishop of Calcutta, and William Mathews, the unhappy son of a Methodist bookseller, Wordsworth's 'most intimate friend.'[31] Other noteworthy names that come close to Wordsworth's orbit are Thomas Malthus of Jesus, ninth wrangler in 1788, author of the famous *Essay on Population* (1798). (His father had been one of Rousseau's executors and his tutors were Gilbert Wakefield [at Warrington Academy] and William Frend, important Cambridge radicals known to Wordsworth in London in the early 1790s.[32]) On the other side of the political coin were future enemies: John Hookham Frere, another Cambridge contemporary (Caius, 1792), became, like Castlereagh, a member of Pitt's coterie: he was one of the main contributors, along with George Canning, future prime minister, to *The Anti-Jacobin* of 1797–98, which savagely attacked Coleridge, Southey and Lamb by name, and alluded knowingly to Wordsworth. Frere was one of several men who could have made Wordsworth's name well known to secret service agents in the Home Office in 1798 (Chapter 24).

Freshmen entering St John's were assigned randomly either to Edward Frewen or William Pearce as tutors. William Cookson saw to it that Wordsworth was assigned to his friend Frewen, and the chain of influence began to work immediately. There were over a hundred scholarships and 'exhibitions' available at St John's for financial aid, and Frewen secured Wordsworth a Foundress's scholarship and two small exhibitions worth about £10 each annually, from those designated specifically for students from Hawkshead or Cumberland.[33] Wordsworth's excellent preparatory school record entitled him to some of these, but his connections helped, for Cambridge was far from a pure meritocracy. These awards, and the cheap room he was assigned (£7 pounds a year[34]), should have covered his university expenses nicely, which were officially estimated at about £15 per year, not including tuition.[35] But Wordsworth's actual expenses for his first two years ran over £100 per year, and, in 1794, Mrs Richard Wordsworth, his guardian's widow, claimed £400 of Christopher Crackanthorpe, almost all of it laid out in payment for William's education.[36] Considering his scholarship, cheap room, and 'exhibition' awards, such a high rate of expense shows that he had not yet adopted his regimen of 'plain living and high thinking,' and his college life style shows where the money went.

As a gentleman's orphan, dependent on loans from his guardians which he was expected to pay back, he was entered at St John's as a sizar, the lowest category, one of seven in his year. The other ranks were nobleman (one in his year), fellow-commoners (four), and pensioners, the largest category (thirty-two). Sizar was a reduced-fee status, traditionally requiring such duties as waiting on tables, but luckily for Wordsworth's pride this had been discontinued in 1786. Sizars could be looked down on as irretrievably 'low' persons by fellow commoners or noblemen, but they were also elected to fellowships proportionally more than any other class of students.[37] They were expected to distinguish themselves by hard work: Newton had been a sizar, as had Paley, and that indefatigable Lakeland success story, Richard Watson. So had William Cookson. If the designation of sizar caused Wordsworth any pain, he had plenty of friendly company in which to assuage it, for Myers, Gawthorp, Greenwood, Farish and John Millar were all sizars. The *Gradus ad Cantabrigiam*, a contemporary handbook of student advice and slang, claims that the gap between sizars and pensioners at Cambridge was much smaller than that between Oxford's servitors and its pensioners, noting that their gowns were identical at St John's and that some sizars 'endeavour to vie [with pensioners] in fashionable frivolity.'* Wordsworth's self-descriptions and the family accounts show that he was one of these. He neither lived nor looked like a sizar: neither he nor his family were going to let his lower status show. He went 'to tutor or to tailors' with equal frequency, got himself 'attired in splendid clothes,' and purchased a 'lordly dressing gown' – i.e., as good as any of the young lords' who were his classmates, who included Lord Bute's grandson, James Lowther's nephew.[38]

Dress was very important at Cambridge, because it immediately distinguished members of the university from all other members of the surrounding community. Rowlandson's picture, *Bucks of the First Head* (see illustration), gives a good idea of what Cambridge students looked like. The two 'bucks' are probably fellow-commoners, their elaborately dishevelled costumes, long curly hair, and girlish good looks very much part of the 'effeminate' manners and appearance which writers of the time criticized, along with the violence and rampant sexual license which went arm in arm with it, as they are with the market girl. She would be one of the 'lady snobbesses' of the town who were a focus of constant interest, harrassment and satisfaction to those non-reading men whose sub-specialty was to be 'gay-men' or 'varmint-men.'

Cambridge students wore a sleeveless gown or 'curtain' at all times, fellows wore cocked hats, and the students, as Dorothy noted on her visit during Wordsworth's second year, had 'smart powdered heads with black caps like helmets,' which they were expected to touch in deference to senior college and university officials.[39] Hair could be curled in the 'Apollo' style, as well as powdered; the republican 'crop' did not come into fashion until a couple of years later. 'Gay silks, ruffles, and embroidery' were additional fashion accents,[40] which Wordsworth's account gives us to understand he did not stint. He later spoke of himself as 'a simple rustic,' but this was editing himself for poetical effect: his family had laid out 11s. 5d. for silk hose and velvet coats before he left Hawkshead,[41] and he powdered his hair till it 'glitter[ed] like rimy tree when frost is keen' – a description that strains to give a naturalistic twist to his wholly fashionable appearance. When he speaks of 'the surfaces of artificial life, / And manners finely spun, the delicate race / Of colours, lurking, gleaming up and down . . . woven with silk and gold . . . wily interchange of snaky hues'

---

* *Gradus ad Cantabrigiam* (London: 1824), 122–23. I will cite the *Gradus* throughout this chapter for specialized Cambridge terms.

(III.590–94), the very intricacy of his description (which owes something to Milton's Satan), plus his family's accounts, belie his claims that he was 'content with the more homely produce rudely piled / In this our coarser warehouse.' He had his own silks and satins and velvets, and his description matches very well the *Gradus*' definition of fellow-commoners: 'their gowns are richly trimmed with gold, or silver, lace – their caps are crowned with velvet, the tassels to which are of gold, or silver.'

He had 'smooth housekeeping within, and all without / Liberal and suiting a gentleman's array,' just like any other young gentleman. His housekeeping was 'smooth' because, although he had a small room, he had the services, along with the other students in his stairwell, of a 'gyp', who brought coal and meals and fended off tradesmen bearing bills, and a female bed maker who made up the boys' beds in the morning and turned them down at night. Gyps and bed makers were also available for services and favours beyond their normal duties.

Academic work was plainly not the highest priority for most men at Cambridge. In Wordsworth's descriptions, non-academic pursuits out-number academic ones by three to one. On the one hand, he shopped, went to parties, sauntered, played, 'rioted', rode horseback, sailed on the Cam, drank, laughed at the college fellows, walked out in the countryside, and dreamed of becoming a writer; on the other, he attended lectures and compulsory chapel, read both required and non-required books, dabbled in geometry, dealt in 'classic niceties' on themes and declamations, and worried about his future maintenance. This was the normal ratio for most students, and Wordsworth's account of it in *Prelude* III, one of the few extended descriptions of eighteenth-century university life in a major work of serious literature, is in fact quite unremarkable as to content. Almost everyone reminiscing about Cambridge in the eighteenth century mentions what Wordsworth does, and with roughly the same attitudes. Book III opens with Wordsworth's first sight of 'the long-backed chapel of King's College,' a focus so common that the *Gradus* defines it simply as 'Freshman Landmark.'

Students were considered to be adults. Masters and tutors rarely inquired into their domestic arrangements as long as they showed up often enough at chapel. Attendance at lectures and tutorials, while not tech-nically optional, quickly dwindled down to the 'reading men.' The proportions in Wordsworth's description of 'the lecturer's room' are just about right:

> All studded round, as thick as chairs could stand,
> With loyal students faithful to their books,
> Half-and-half idlers, hardy recusants,
> And honest dunces . . .

(III.65–68)

Here again, the ratio is three to one between frivolous and serious students. His own progress went steadily downward through the first three types he mentions, from faithful study, to increasing idleness, ending in hardy 'recusancy' – refusal to do the required work on the basis of principle. What that principle could have been for him at the time requires some speculation. In *The Prelude*, he says it was to preserve himself as a poet, but it can hardly have appeared so then.

The morning's lead-up to dinner at one, the most important official event of each day, was leisurely. Chapel was at seven, and attendance was required. There was a lively trade in bribes, conveyed via gyps, to the 'marker' who pricked pin holes after the names of absentees in the college lists. Breakfast was at eight, served in one's room, and then came the two classes in Classics and Maths, between nine and noon. A good hour was allowed for dressing for dinner, donning white waistcoats and white silk stockings, visiting the hairdresser, and so on.

At dinner, the fellows sat at the high table across one end of the hall, where they were joined by their noble students and fellow commoners. Pensioners and sizars crowded together at the tables running perpendicularly down the length of the hall. Sizars' meals were still sometimes made up from the leftovers of the high table, but so full, rich, and varied was the menu of these well-endowed establishments that one hardly ever hears, in all the university histories and reminiscences, a single complaint about the food, that staple gripe of modern-day college life. Descriptions of college meals fairly burst with calories and cholesterol: meat pies, pigeon pies, sirloins of beef, hams, tarts and plum puddings. One of the perquisites which the celibate fellows could enjoy, legitimately, as they waited for their benefices, was good food, and the amounts they were willing to spend on it spilled over to the benefit of their students.

After dinner, organized academic work was done for the day. Afternoons could be spent riding in the fields or rowing on the Cam in good weather, both of which Wordsworth did enthusiastically, going forth 'to gallop through the country in blind zeal / Of senseless horsemanship, or on the breast / Of Cam sail . . . boisterously.' This was exactly what he had done regularly at Hawkshead, and many of his fellow horsemen and boatsmen there were with him here. In *The Prelude*'s image of a better, simpler university where he might have done better, Wordsworth seems to be describing an imaginary 'Hawkshead University,' for the majority of student activities he includes were but a continuation of his grammar school pursuits, with a few 'mature' additions.

In cold and inclement weather, there was much 'good-natured lounging' in friends' rooms,[42] or 'reading lazily in lazy books.' 'Lazy' and 'lounging' are not vague general words here; these books designated a specific class of collegiate leisure reading. The *Gradus* glosses as, 'to lounge,' all the verbs from an epigram of Martial's – 'Prandeo, poto, cano, endo, lego, caeno' –

which Wordsworth adapted to describe his activities ('sauntered, played [i.e., gambled] . . . rioted . . . talked . . . Read lazily'). The 'most choice collection that the genius of Indolence could desire' was that of John 'Maps' Nicholson, who in addition to his bookshop hawked his wares aloud through all the college courts. His most popular authors and titles were 'Rabelais in English; several copies of the Reverend Mr Sterne's *Tristram Shandy*; Wycherley and Congreve's plays; *Joe Miller's Jest Book* [a.k.a. *The Wit's Vade-Mecum*], Mrs Behn's novels ['the English Sappho'], and Lord Rochester's Poems, which are very *moving!*'[43] Wordsworth ruefully admits his attraction to this kind of reading: he 'turned with sickly appetite' to the 'daily fare [of books] prescribed,' but

> I chaced not steadily the manly deer,
> But laid me down to any casual feast
> Of wild wood-honey; or, with truant eyes
> Unruly, peeped about for vagrant fruit.
>
> (III.524–30)

This is one of many naturalized allusions to *Paradise Lost* by which he tried to dignify his report of his Cambridge experiences. Eve ate the 'vagrant fruit' when she was tempted with godlike knowledge, but the 'truant' or 'vagrant' element in Nicholson's Lounging Library was obviously sophisticated erotic stimulation at best, dirty books at worst, exactly of the sort we could expect to appeal to young men on their own as adults for the first time in their lives.

At the end of the afternoon, one took tea or went out to coffee houses to read the newspapers. Evening chapel followed, and then the bed maker made her appearance and the gyp came in with the 'sizing' bill of fare, for ordering hot food from the college kitchens: part of a fowl or duck, a piece of apple pie or cake, or 'any little luxury that might tempt you, in addition to commons fare.' Most often these 'suppers, invitations, wine, and fruit' (III.41) were clubbed together in the rooms of a member of a group of friends; Wordsworth, Myers, Jones, Terrot, and Gawthorp formed one at St John's. The host would furnish bread, butter, cheese, and beer, and all would share the snacks they had ordered, sometimes roasting meat and sausages in the fireplace. These 'sizing parties' were the most enjoyable event of the day and the focus of students' social life. Wordsworth indulged in them at least as regularly as his more proper brother Christopher a few years later, and Christopher's diary shows they were very regular indeed.

'Buzzing' was a favourite strategy in these college parlour games. The decanter of wine was passed round, and a man receiving a nearly empty flagon could demand that the person passing it drink off the dregs in a single glass. But if the amount left exceeded the glass, the challenger had to finish what remained, and toss off a bumper of the newly filled decanter as well. Naturally, inexperienced boys got drunk fast. Toasts were proposed, first to a lady, then to a gentleman, and then to a friend. In these toasts, puns were very much in order, especially at St John's. Johnians were called Hogs or Pigs, and had presumptive rights to wretched punning, in a community where Latin and English word-play was a favourite mode of enlivening conversation.

The longest single episode Wordsworth recalls from his account of his Cambridge life occurred at just such a party. It was in the rooms of his friend, Edward Birkett, who had the honour of living in the rooms in Christ's College reputed to have been Milton's. Heavily invoking the great man ('O temperate bard!'), Wordsworth sat down with the 'others in a festive ring of commonplace convention' – that is to say, it was the usual routine. Wordsworth proposed the toast to Milton, 'I to thee poured out libations,' but he kept a mental reserve: 'to thy memory drank / Within my private thoughts.' They weren't drinking to Milton all the time, and soon his brain 'reeled,' 'Never so clouded by the fumes of wine / Before that hour, or since'. Wordsworth became a connoisseur of fine wines, and left a valuable cellar at his death, but we can take his claim straight-forwardly, since no one ever records him as drinking too much. Yet when he ends the episode by asking Milton's forgiveness for his 'empty thoughts' in 'the weakness of that hour,' he also clearly indicates that he continued to join regularly in such practices: 'In some of its unworthy vanities / Brother of many more' (III.326–27).

Suddenly hearing the chapel bell, he ran desperately to put in his appearance. He humourously sketches his 'ostrich-like' appearance, with white surplice thrown up over his shoulder for greater speed: easy to do, for the sleeveless gowns were short, being also known as 'cover-arse-gowns.' But this surplice, 'gloried in and yet despised,' gave him the right to cleave 'in pride through the inferior throng / Of the plain burghers,' standing at the back of the church. Curiously, this moment of shame combined with privilege also contains a slight Miltonic echo, of Satan's entrance into Pandemonium through the crowds of expectant demons after his successful mission to seduce Adam and Eve in Paradise:

> . . . he through the midst unmarked,
> In show plebian angel militant
> Of lowest order, passed; and from the door
> Of that Plutonian hall, invisible
> Ascended his high throne . . .
>
> (*PL*, X.441–45)

The sense of special status, as distinct from an 'inferior' or 'plebian' one, shows Wordsworth in the compositional moment still recalling his 'reeling' sense of identification with the great Cambridge rebel – or with his great villain – at college, when he bought his first personal copy of *Paradise Lost* and began to annotate it heavily.[44]

Very commonly these supper parties spilled out into the streets, where, as Wordsworth says, 'we rioted.' These fights occurred virtually every night during term time. Students met, boasted, argued and quarrelled in the taverns with each other or with the town 'snobs.' Between students, these fights sometimes led to sword duels. But between the students and the town boys, the fights were very frequent and very violent. In March of Wordsworth's first year, a drayman was killed in a fight with two students, who were let off on grounds of insufficient evidence.[45] One of the two, the notorious 'Turk' Taylor of Trinity, also assaulted Wordsworth's tutor outside the Union Coffee-House.[46]

These 'disgraceful tumults' broke out everywhere,[47] but especially outside Trinity Church in Sidney Street, exactly where Wordsworth passed on his run back to St John's from Birkett's room at Christ's. Townspeople could also attend college chapel services, and did so especially on Sundays, when the favoured place was 'The long-backed chapel of King's College.' Here the 'Cambridge Beauties' or lady-snobbesses flocked, 'emphatically be it understood, to see and be seen,' for 'King's cool shades' along the college Backs were a notorious trysting place: 'But ah how fatal oft these Walks do prove / To injur'd Innocence, and constant Love.'[48]

The most frequent cause of the street fights was women, not surprising in such an all-male environment, especially given their scarcity in a technically celibate society. Toasts were drunk much more frequently to 'virgin snobbesses' than to Milton: to the three 'Miss Go-to-beds,' friendly daughters of the master of the *Bull*, the 'Brown St Venus,' daughter of a cigar vendor, or to 'the Trinity Venus, one of the few . . . pretty virtuous bed makers of the time.'[49] The writer means pretty *and* virtuous, not *relatively* virtuous, but on the subject of bed makers the ambiguity is appropriate. The bed makers and other female servants employed by the colleges were the members of the opposite sex nearest the students, and thus the immediate focus of attention in a situation which was 'the greatest drawback of college-life . . . this lack of the society of virtuous females.'[50] Sometimes virtue preserved the women servants from affront, or their looks, as in the case of the 'wry-nosed beauty' and 'noseless Jenny,' or their age, for some were elderly, and more given to getting tipsy on students' wine than to seducing them. But often they were less interested in preserving their virtue than in catching one of these highly eligible young men, either in matrimony or in some other profitably compromising situation. Some 'matriculated tradesmen' (butlers, barbers, cooks and others permanently attached to a college) were called 'petticoat-professors' because they trained up their daughters almost from infancy to be 'ladies' in this trade.[51] Gyps' daughters were also very useful in such entrapments, especially with freshmen whose experiences with wine, women and mathematics were all about equally new.

Of course, many of the boys were willing victims and equally unscrupulous players in the game. When a Caius varmint-man proposed a toast to the 'virgin snobbesses,' he was met with the derisive cry, 'Aye, where are these maidens?'[52] J. M. Wright, our Trinity correspondent, tells how he came to 'understand' his bed maker while studying Greek tragedy at three in morning:

> Whilst musing over the choruses, the strophes and the anti-strophes, analysing caesuras and quasi-caesuras, I myself was being scanned by a fair household goddess, who tripping into my presence, in the most celestial accents, breathed apprehension lest I should ruin my health by such midnight meditations, and *looking* unutterable things, a language I then understood less than Greek (and of this I was ignorant enough), hastily withdrew, covered with confusion. Joseph-like, I retired to my solitary pillow, dozing away the few hours that intervened before the hour of chapel.[53]

With typical student archness, he casts himself as virtuous Joseph to the bed maker as Potiphar's wife. Wright, like Wordsworth, was a northern sizar, from Kendal, and also began his college days holed up in a high little room. But everyone was entitled to a bed maker's services. The *Gradus* took a longer, more sophisticated view of what these might be:

> They are not only adept at making beds (*secundum Artem*), but when they have had a mind to it, have shewn themselves very alert in helping to *UN*-make the bed they have made, *secundum Naturam*! Indeed, these their *natural* parts and endowments were at one time so notorious . . . that, by a most merciless and *unmanly* decree of the Senate, the whole sex was rusticated! . . . [But] O tempora! O Mulieres! there is no *scruple* in the present *Saturnian* age, respecting the admission of '*young maids*' into 'the students' chambers.'
>
> (*Gradus*, 7, 18)

Most fellows were considered 'men of gallantry'. The longer they stayed waiting for a living, the more restive they became under their celibate status. Getting married was the Catch-22 of fellowship life, for it solved one problem at the cost of another. 'The scheme therefore is – a wife and fellowship.'[54] 'Graces' or petitions were offered in the University Senate in the 1760s and 1770s for abolition of the celibacy requirement almost as frequently as petitions against the Test Acts in the 1770s and 1780s. Some fellows lived with their housekeepers – and their housekeeper's daughters – 'in a very equivocal capacity.'[55] It was said of William Chevallier, the master of St John's when Wordsworth arrived, who was nearly blind, that his 'dark hours' were 'cheered by Day' – i.e., Mrs Day, the wife of the town clerk, who lived more in the Master's Lodge at St John's than she did at home.[56]

Some women of the town did as well by their charms as college fellows did by their gallantry. Jemima Watson (no relation to Bishop Watson) 'lived in expensive lodgings, where she was in the habit of receiving some of the most fashionable men of the University.'[57] These might be fellows or wealthy noblemen, but most pensioners and sizars could not, by age and by pocket, keep company with such courtesans. For them, if they were not lucky with their bed maker or local girls, there was the 'rookery' at Barnwell, the theatre and brothel district out past Jesus College along the Newmarket Road. Plays were put on at Barnwell, the ancient site of an Augustinian nunnery, at the beginning of each academic year, and regularly featured 'rows between Cyprians and Gownsmen.' 'Cyprians' was the universal code word among educated eighteenth-century males for prostitutes (from Cyprus, birthplace of Venus), and the 'Barnwell Ague' is defined by the *Gradus*, in a rare moment of restraint, as 'French ***.'

Prostitutes were as common in Cambridge as nightly drinking, and presented an attractive threat to the college boys. Playhouses and taverns were subject to regulations against keeping any 'daughter or other women in [houses to which] there shall resort any scholars of the University of what condition soever.'[58] Such establishments were subject to arbitrary search and arrest by the proctors and sub-proctors who patrolled the streets every night

> 'to prevent rioting in the streets, knocking down snobs, too great a familiarity with a certain class of the fair sex. . . . Their powers are more particularly directed against the Cyprians, over whom they have unlimited control; being permitted by the statutes to enter by force *any house in the town*, suspected of concealing them, and afterwards to lodge them in the Spinning-House. . . . It would be easy enough for the University by means of the Spinning-House, to exterminate the whole race of these unfortunates, but they know human nature too well to act so madly. Whatever the saints may say to it, the Philosophers of Mathematical Cambridge know and feel them to be necessary evils . . .'[59]

Neither the collegians nor the fellows regarded the Cyprians in such an unfavourable light. They used them in a variety of ways, such as dressing them up in academic gowns and bringing them to church – a great inside joke among some Emmanuel students until an accident discovered the identity of one of these fair 'boys.'

Not all boys were licentious or promiscuous, of course. Many recoiled from such widespread public vice to become 'Simeonites,' followers of the evangelical preacher Charles Simeon at Holy Trinity Church.[60] Wilberforce is said to have held himself off from sexual adventures in his otherwise typical 'gay-man's' career, though he took tea in a well-known London brothel.[61] But every boy's experience was coloured in some way by this onslaught of sexuality, especially to the degree that he had not been exposed to anything like it before. It was in no way dissimilar from anything else we know about the sexual aspect of class relations in the eighteenth century, as a glance at Boswell's journals will confirm.

*

Where is Wordsworth in all this? We have seen a few tantalizing glimpses or possible identifications of him, but he deliberately cancelled these out in the final item of a list of 'deeper passions' from which, he says, he held himself off:

> . . . envy, jealousy, pride, shame,
> Ambition, emulation, fear, or hope,
> Or those of dissolute pleasure – were by me
> Unshared, and only now and then observed
>
> (III.532–35)

All of these could be called academic vices except the last, which was more likely to be extra-curricular than intramural. 'Dissolute pleasure' is certainly not reflected in Wordsworth's later life and reputation, yet the question is not impertinent. Sex is biologically relevant to his biography not only in normative terms, but also in relation to its more unusual features, such as his fathering a daughter at age twenty-one with a French woman four years his senior, his strangely passionate relations with his sister Dorothy, and his marriage to his childhood playmate at age thirty-two. It may be that Wordsworth's first sexual experience occurred in March of 1792, when he was twenty-one and living in a foreign country. But we want to know how he came to that moment prepared or unprepared for it. The facts of his life show him to have been a sexually attractive and active man, and his love letters to his wife are written in moving, passionate language.[62] His poetry makes this abundantly clear too, though its sexual element is frequently displaced on to a strongly feminized Nature, making it easy to ignore any overtones of actual human sexuality. But his best contemporary readers, like Shelley and James Hogg, did not miss it.* Given the facts of life between ages seventeen and twenty-one, and the facts of Cambridge between 1787 and 1791, the reputedly asexual quality of Wordsworth's poetry becomes an issue that asks for interrogation.

Given the extensive evidence of an atmosphere of sex and violence in Cambridge while Wordsworth was there, he could not have avoided its

---

* 'But from the first 'twas Peter's drift / To be a kind of moral eunuch, / He touched the hem of Nature's shift, / Felt faint – and never dared uplift / The closest, all-concealing tunic. / She laughed the while, with an arch smile, / And kissed him with a sister's kiss, / And said— "My best Diogenes, / I love you well – but, if you please, / Tempt not again my deepest bliss"' (Shelley, *Peter Bell the Third*, 313–22). Hogg's parodies are less serious, but equally insightful: Nature is the 'great wet-nurse of the human race,' and on her 'similitude / In dissimilitude, man's sole delight, / And all the sexual intercourse of things, / Do most supremely hang' ('James Rigg' and 'The Stranger,' in *The Poetic Mirror; or, The Living Bards of Britain*, 1816).

prostitutes and provocative 'snobbesses'. But how the sexuality they boldly offered filtered into his work requires careful reading of scattered evidence in *The Prelude*. The overall impression he gives of his Cambridge life is of hearty engagement in extracurricular social pursuits. True, there were solitary midnight walks, as at Hawkshead. But 'if a throng was near / That way I leaned by nature, for my heart / Was social and loved idleness and joy' (III.234–36). The words bear repeating, in light of Wordsworth's later image, because they are his own youthful self-description: *'My heart was social and loved idleness and joy.'* And a 'throng' was nearly always 'near.' Speaking in merely statistical terms of the facts of Cambridge life and the burden of his own commentary, it would be more likely than not that he had some experience with these women. But the issue, complicated for any teenager, was especially so for Wordsworth. There are many references to sexuality in *The Prelude* referring to the period between his seventeenth and twenty-first years, but they are not found in the Cambridge books. Instead, they are dispersed to other parts of the poem and must be transposed in order to be brought to bear on the subject.

When he says he 'laughed with Chaucer . . . beside the pleasant mills of Trompington' [sic], the next town down the river from Cambridge, he is directing us to more of his 'lazy,' 'lounging' reading. But to characterize Chaucer's gritty 'Reeve's Tale,' set in Trumpington, as a tale of 'amorous passion' is to sanitize it ridiculously. This Cantabrigian riposte to the Oxford-based bawdy of the 'Miller's Tale' was loyally included in every collection of Cambridge 'facetiae' (bawdy, satirical collegiate writings). It is a seamy tale of sexual revenge, wholly consonant with everything we can learn about daily town-gown relations in Cambridge, and since it was written four hundred years earlier, an indication of the marked consistency of university life in this respect. Wordsworth's enjoyment of the story was heightened by the fact that Allen and John, the two students who cuckold the thieving miller, are 'both northern men, both in one town were born,' like Wordsworth and his Hawkshead mates.

Wordsworth recalled that it was on his trip down to Cambridge with John Myers and William Cookson that he 'for the first time in my life did hear'

> The voice of woman utter blasphemy,
> Saw woman as she is to open shame
> Abandoned, and the pride of public vice.
> (VII.417–20)

He locates the spot with some care, 'southward two hundred miles . . . from our pastoral hills,' as if to establish a moral quarantine in the distance. The scene has been located in Stamford or Grantham on the Great North Road, with the explanation that the shock was all the greater because 'love children' who appeared in Lakeland were not banished or degraded into lives of raucous ugliness.[63] One hopes not, though the incident of the woman in white at Cockermouth and the tale of Mary Rigge at Colthouse, suggest that all was not quite so idyllic in those pastoral hills. But in any case, such 'blasphemy' would have been repeated many times in Wordsworth's hearing when he got to Cambridge – which may be why he does not mention it there, but instead associates it with his later experiences in London. Several of his recollections of seeing dissolute women in public are from London, but their placement in Book VII ('Residence in London') makes them appear chronologically later, whereas the specific details are from his Cambridge years when, as early as 1788, he first visited the city.

Student trips to London, it is not surprising to learn, were often undertaken for more refined or extreme versions of the fleshly pleasures of Cambridge. Coleridge knew the Cambridge-London circuit well: 'I formed a Party, dashed to London at eleven o'clock at night, & for three days lived in all the tempest of Pleasure . . . I again returned to Cambridge – staid a week – such a week! Where Vice has not annihilated Sensibility, there is little need of Hell!'[64]

Wordsworth loved London, but he also feared its temptations, and many of these temptations are cast in feminine roles. The whole of Book VII in *The Prelude* turns upon the story of Mary Robinson, the Maid of Buttermere, 'the artless daughter of the hills,' whose story of seduction and abandonment was a hit play in 1803. But he says it was 'at least two years before' Book VII's account of his first (1791) residence in London that he first began to visit there – that is, in December 1788 or January 1789, while he was still at Cambridge. Many of the images he recalls are feminine: the 'gorgeous ladies' of Vauxhall and Ranelagh gardens, or 'some female vendor's scream – belike / The very shrillest of all London cries.' He especially loved playhouses, 'whether some beauteous dame' appeared, 'or *romping girl* / Bounced, leapt, and pawed the air' (446, 454-55). These two ostensibly generic descriptions probably attach specifically to Sarah Siddons and Dora Jordan, the reigning Muses of Tragedy and Comedy, respectively, on the London stage throughout Wordsworth's young manhood.* The playhouse managers in London, as at Barnwell, 'were but a higher sort of brothel-keepers; pimps to the public,' and their establishments so indecent that one could not take a woman there, for 'sights scarcely to be imagined, much less described.'[65] Wordsworth's story of

---

* The identification of Dora Jordan as the 'romping girl' is virtually certain, since one of her most famous roles was that of Priscilla Tomboy in the operatic farce, *The Romp*. Her beautiful legs and sensual athleticism featured prominently in both her stage reputation and in the gross caricatures which greeted her liaison with William, Duke of Clarence, the future William IV. (Tomalin, 70–71, 121–23.)

Mary of Buttermere is crossed by a recollection very much of this kind: his sight of a prostitute's child amid 'chance spectators, chiefly dissolute men / And shameless women' – and including Wordsworth too, of course. He wonders with amazement how such innocence can appear there, 'A sort of alien scattered from the clouds,' when 'on the mother's cheeks the tints were false, / A painted bloom.' The whole episode is full of over-determined language, making us feel that Wordsworth's early experiences with sexuality provoked an almost destructive sense of contrast: whatever was not pure must be terribly contaminated.

But we see most of the fallout from his Cambridge experiences not in London but in the Lake District, during his first summer vacation. As with his poetic energies and his reputation, he displaced his sexual energies back into Cumberland and released them there.

CHAPTER SIX

Young Love-Liking

Summer Vacation, 1788

> Spirits upon the stretch, and here and there
> Slight shocks of young love-liking interspersed
> That mounted up like joy into the head,
> And tingled through the veins.
>
> (IV.324–27)

He set out alone from Cambridge in early June, heading back to Hawkshead and Ann Tyson, not to Penrith and Dorothy. Eager as he was to see her, he was even more eager not to see his uncle Crackanthorpe, and the feeling was mutual. The coach stopped at Ashbourne (beyond Derby) on a Sunday evening, and he took advantage of the break to rent a horse and ride over to Dovedale, which already had a reputation as one of England's prime picturesque locations. He described it in a unique notebook entry, worth listening to as the earliest non-poetic words we have from Wordsworth.

Cambridge to Hawkshead. June 8th. Saw nothing particularly striking till I came to Ashburn. Arrived there on Sunday evening and rode over to Dovedale. Dovedale is a very narrow valley, somewhat better than a mile in length, broken into five or six distinct parts, so that the views it affords are necessarily upon a small scale. The first thing that strikes you on descending into the valley is the River Dove fringed with sedge and spotted with a variety of small tufts of grass hurrying between two hills, one of which about six years ago was clothed with wood; the wood is again getting forward; the other had a number of cattle grazing upon it – the scene was pleasing – the sun was just sinking behind the hill on the left – which was dark – while his beams cast a faint golden haze upon the side of the other. The River in that part which was streamy had a glittering splendour which was pleasingly chastized by the blue tint of intervening pieces of calm water; the fringe of the sedge and the number of small islands, with which it is variegated. The view is terminated by a number of rocks scattered upon the side of one of the hills of a form perfectly spiral.[1]

What is potentially 'Wordsworthian' about the passage is its fixation on the contrasts in the scene. The phenomenon of hills in the east being brighter than those in the west due to the angle of the setting sun strikes anyone walking in mountainous country, but Wordsworth never tired of recording it, nor of its varied thematic possibilities (life-in-death, promise-in-despair, and the like). But the sentence about the 'streamy' river being 'chastized' by its own intervening sections of calm is pure proto-Wordsworth, anticipating such important later formulations as 'emotion recollected in tranquillity.' The moment had more than a passing interest for him. The Dove would return to his mind ten years later in the Lucy poem about a mysterious maiden he loved, where he drew out the contrasts between love and beauty, and loss and death, with maximum force and mystery: 'She dwelt . . . beside the streams of Dove, / A Maid whom there were none to praise / And very few to love . . . But she is in her grave, and, oh, / The difference to me!'

There is similar sense of *difference* between himself as a 'glittering' Cambridge personage and the calming, chastising effect on him of persons and places around Hawkshead in Book IV of *The Prelude*, 'Summer Vacation.' He returned to a community of 'frank-hearted' country girls who behaved according to rural standards of morality that, though far from unsexual, were worlds apart from the extraordinarily immoral sexual milieu of Cambridge. In *The Prelude*'s account of his summer of 1788, Wordsworth highlights his experiences with women, in strong contrast to the relative absence of such descriptions from his Cambridge years. The commonsense explanation, that things naturally look different after a year away at college, was intensified for him by a more important contrast, between the erotic energy of sex and that of art. His very first statement about the changes that had occurred at home concludes in terms of feminine beauty, very oddly expressed:

> 'Twas not indifferent to a youthful mind
> To note . . .
> . . . growing girls, whose beauty, filched away
> With all its pleasant promises, was gone
> To deck some slighted playmate's homely cheek.
> (IV.191–92, 197–99)

Promised to whom, and slighted by whom, one might wonder? At the end of this summer, he bade farewell not only to Cumberland's mountains, as we expect, but also to its girls, as we tend to forget:

> . . . and you,
> Frank-hearted maids of rocky Cumberland,

> You and your not unwelcome days of mirth
> I quitted, and your nights of revelry
>
> (VI.12–15)

These 'nights of revelry' are the focus of the two main incidents Wordsworth remembered from his vacation: his self-dedication to poetry at dawn after one dancing party, and his encounter with a discharged army veteran after another.

For nine weeks, Wordsworth stayed with Ann Tyson, the only mother he knew, at Colthouse, the only home he had. His sense of difference was heightened by his new status as a young gentleman, much in demand at both local parties and in high society resorts like John Fleming's Rayrigg estate, in the last summer it was leased by Wilberforce. Wilberforce had spent the month of May in residence at St John's, recuperating from the 'corrupt imaginations' and other side effects of his opium medication. It would have very been odd if he had not spoken to Wordsworth in college, the favoured ward of his best friend. The quiet of Windermere, along with prayer and Bible-reading, were his cure that summer, though the 'dissipation' of the parties continued.[2] Wordsworth was undergoing a similar regimen, but in different directions and with different results.

Ann was very proud of her charge, trotting him round to show off his 'fancy habilments.' But Wordsworth also felt a sense of inner change, which he associated with his increasing desire to write poetry, which he frequently experienced as an erotic sensation, a common writerly emotion, not limited to Romantic poets. Taking Ann's old 'rough terrier of the hills' as his companion, he resumed his poetry-composing walks around Esthwaite. He 'affect[ed] private shades like a sick lover,' and 'some fair enchanting image' would rise up in his mind, 'full-formed like Venus from the sea.' He discharged the erotic emotions raised by these full-bodied feminine images on to the dog: 'let loose / My hand upon his back with stormy joy, / Caressing him again and yet again.' The dog, though pleased, must have wondered what the reason was, and so can we. Wordsworth's summary of these poetry-composing walks continues the same strong language of physical exposure and sexual vulnerability:

> Gently did my soul
> Put off her veil, and, self-transmuted, stood
> Naked as in the presence of her God.
>
> (IV.140–42)

Poetry, and especially his feelings about it, took on an erotic charge. The image can be explained as a reference to Moses's interviews with God,[3] but Wordsworth has made a striking change in gender. The relationship between his soul and its 'God' (which is nothing less than his conception of his own identity) is that of a willingly submissive woman, perhaps a slave girl, giving herself up to her master's pleasure.

As he contrasted his new splendour with his homely old neighbours, he began to feel a new 'human-heartedness' about his love for them, which previously he had felt only 'as a blessed spirit / Or angel, if he were to dwell on earth, / Might love in individual [i.e., private] happiness' (IV.228-30). That is, he had felt, before this, like Raphael or Michael in *Paradise Lost*, observing the human life of Adam and Eve without revealing themselves as God's messenger – or like Satan, who looks long and lasciviously on Eve in just this way. But now Wordsworth actually began to feel like a human being himself, and sexual awakening contributed mightily – as it does for all of us – to de-etherealizing his sense of what love meant.

His new sense of contrasts and connections between himself and other human beings came to him most strikingly as he returned to Colthouse after two dances in that busy social summer. These dances were as glittering as the 'streamy' River Dove:

> . . . a swarm
> Of heady thoughts jostling each other, gawds
> And feast and dance and public revelry
> And sports and games – less pleasing in themselves
> Than as they were a badge, glossy and fresh,
> Of manliness and freedom
>
> (IV.272–77)

Like the 'vagrant fruit' of his collegiate 'lounge' reading, all these activities 'seduce[d] [him] from the firm habitual quest of feeding [i.e., nutritious] pleasures,' yet there is a relish in his description of them that suggests either the thrill of seduction or the agonies of puberty. The language could certainly suggest sexual initiation, though what a 'glossy and fresh' badge of manhood might be is hard to say. The clear sense of the lines is that he didn't actually like the parties and the thoughts they stimulated, but he felt at least that he had 'earned his badge' of manhood there: he was a man. The only other time Wordsworth used such language was to describe his pleasure at seeing actresses in London playhouses during visits from Cambridge: 'something of a girlish childlike gloss / Of novelty survived for scenes like these' (VII.479–80). Here the 'gloss' is 'girlish', not manly, but in both cases his sense of pleasure is strongly gendered. Probably one should not push the sense further than to imagine a *new* badge, and yet the two contexts, put together, are sensually suggestive.

A very important aspect of Wordsworth's greatness is the way he lets his poetry reveal conflicts that he cannot wholly resolve. Rather than admit that this new 'human-heartedness' involved – not unusually – sexual awakening, he instead goes on for over a hundred lines, worrying the idea this way and that. In weary '*chastisement* of these regrets,' he recalls a moment of dedication at dawn he experienced after one of these dances. So pious has Wordsworth's after-image become that most readers ignore the fact that his Dawn Dedication did not come in chastisement of his 'heartless chace of trivial pleasures,' but of his *regretting* them. The dance had been a 'promiscuous rout', and there is no doubt about the nature of Wordsworth's behaviour there:

> I had passed
> The night in dancing, gaiety and mirth –
> With a din of instruments, and shuffling feet,
> And glancing forms, and tapers glittering,
> And unaimed prattle flying up and down,
> Spirits upon the stretch, and here and there
> Slight shocks of young love-liking interspersed
> That mounted up like joy into the head,
> And tingled through the veins.
>
> (IV.319–27)

This is a convincing physiological description of sexual stimulation. But he goes no further here: the lines continue, 'Ere we retired . . . the sky was bright with day.' It is clear he mildly disapproves of the dance, but we can also see that he knows what he's talking about, despite his Miltonic diction. The metaphors push the passage beyond its evident intention, in a clear example of the 'deconstructive' force of figurative language. Wordsworth doth protest too much his dancing feet and glancing eyes, but his language of sensual indulgence also exposes what he seeks to disapprove in his youthful character. The girls' forms are not only 'glancing' in the light, but glancing *at him*, causing those 'slight shocks' of glandular reaction, from head to veins.

Leaving the party, he walked the two or three miles home over Claife Heights and beheld a sunrise of 'memorable pomp . . . more glorious than I ever had beheld.' Compared with the sharp contrasts of his provocative 'glittering/glancing' dance flirtations, this is a comprehensively unified landscape, where the maximum number of contrasts are allowed in, the better to be hierarchically ordered:

> The sea was laughing at a distance; all
> The solid mountains were as bright as clouds,
> Grain-tinctured, drenched in empyrean light;
> And in the meadows and the lower grounds
> Was all the sweetness of a common dawn –
> Dews, vapours, and the melody of birds,
> And labourers going forth into the fields.
>
> (IV.333–39)

The easy modulation from heavenly brightness to earthly calm shows how much Wordsworth became master of the landscape idiom he first essayed at Dovedale. But the dawn's direct *connection* with the dance's 'promiscuous rout', not merely its chastising contrast, is pointedly enforced. The laughing sea echoes the girls' 'gaiety and mirth' at a more comfortable distance, and 'empyrean light' heightens, not darkens, the ballroom's glittering tapers. The relation between the two scenes is cumulative, not contrastive. The moment of dedication came to him because he was in a very stimulated and alert state of mind, fulfilling, not frustrating him. Certainly sin is on his mind when he says that 'vows were then made for me . . . that I should be – else sinning greatly – / A dedicated spirit' (IV.341–44). He was beginning to imagine that he too might go forth to labour in a field, of poetry. But that labour is stimulated by those 'shocks of young love-liking . . . that mounted up like joy into the head,' which are in turn akin to the 'stormy joy' with which he caressed his terrier, 'again and yet again,' when 'Some fair enchanting image . . . rose up, full-formed like Venus from the sea.'

The sexual 'feel' of these dance descriptions in *Prelude* IV is strongly confirmed when we read back to the passages from *Paradise Lost* to which they allude. They were not composed until about 1804, but they are written *about* a time when he was thoroughly and self-consciously steeped in Milton, and much given to refracting his own experience through Milton's poetry, as we saw at his Cambridge 'sizing' parties. Some key terms in Wordsworth's vocabulary do not achieve their full force and meaning until *Paradise Lost* is brought to bear on them as a defining context.[4] In the Dawn Dedication, 'grain-tinctured' (i.e., red) comes from 'sky-tinctured grain' in Milton's description of Raphael descending to Paradise to warn Adam and Eve that their enemy is in the garden (*PL*, V.285). The little phrase, 'and the melody of birds,' comes from Book VIII, when Adam describes to Raphael 'the sum of earthly bliss' he felt in Nature – 'I mean of taste, sight, smell, herbs, fruits, and flow'rs, / Walks, *and the melody of birds.*' But all of this bliss was surpassed when Adam discovered Eve:

> . . . here
> Far otherwise, transported I behold,
> Transported touch; here passion first I felt,
> Commotion strange, in all enjoyments else
> Superior and unmoved, here only weak
> Against the charm of beauty's powerful glance.
> (*PL*, 528–33)[5]

It is impossible to dismiss these echoes as adventitious, given the similarity in subject matter. Wordsworth's 'slight shocks' parallel Milton's 'commotion strange,' and 'glancing forms' is close to 'beauty's powerful glance.' But no echo of Milton by Wordsworth is ever innocent, even if unconscious – and probably even less innocent then.

These links between sex and art were confirmed at a second dance that summer, which ended in a much sterner confrontation, between young Wordsworth and a sickly veteran recently discharged from terrible service in the Caribbean. Wordsworth now imagined his whole mind as a dance party:

> Strange rendezvous my mind was at that time,
> A party-coloured shew of grave and gay,
> Solid and light, short-sighted and profound,
> Of inconsiderate habits and sedate,
> Consorting in one mansion unreproved.
>
> (IV.346–50)

This mixture of grave and gay, short-sighted and profound, is a like a vacation version of Cambridge's 'hard reading' and 'gay men.' And when are 'consortings' in 'mansions' subject to 'reproof'? One can almost hear the Cambridge proctors' reproofs for the illicit behaviour in the Barnwell 'mansions,' and when Wordsworth goes on to characterize his thoughts that summer as 'transient and loose' (IV.354), we can hear, further, the proctors' formal language of complaint against those 'lewd women,' the Cambridge Cyprians.

Wordsworth said his encounter with the veteran proved that,

> ... when – by these hindrances
> Unthwarted – I experienced in myself
> *Conformity as just as that of old*
> *To the end and written spirit of God's works,*
> Whether held forth in Nature or in man ...
>
> (IV.355–59; italics added)

This is because he is directly following Michael's warning to Adam about the danger of chasing after loose dancing women:

> Judge not what is best
> By pleasure, though to nature seeming meet,
> *Created, as thou art, to nobler end*
> *Holy and pure, conformity divine.*
>
> (*PL*, XI.603–06; italics added)

Wordsworth's lead-up to his encounter with the discharged veteran, like the dance before the Dawn Dedication, is highly sensual. It was another one of that summer's 'primitive hours' that was not cancelled by, but somehow confirmed by what followed. Again, he establishes a sense of vocation via sexually charged language, mediated through Milton.

He was walking along the familiar road up from the Windermere Ferry toward Colthouse, in a dreamy mood of physical well-being and adolescent fantasizing:

> the listless sense
> Quiescent and disposed to sympathy,
> With an exhausted mind worn out by toil
> And all unworthy of the deeper joy
> Which waits on distant prospect – cliff or sea,
> The dark blue vault and universe of stars.
>
> (IV.379–84)

No dawn dedication is forthcoming here: he was 'unworthy' of it. Given his age, situation, and the whole context of sexual alertness he sketches, it does not seem too much to say that more than a few of the pictures running through his mind on this night must have been sexual ones:

> O happy state! what beauteous pictures now
> Rose in harmonious imagery; they rose
> As from some distant region of my soul
> And came along like dreams – yet such as left
> Obscurely mingled with their passing forms
> A consciousness of *animal delight*,
> A self-possession felt in every pause
> And every gentle movement of my frame.
>
> (IV.392–99; italics added)

It could sound like a young man reflecting on recent sexual fulfillment, or anticipating it, or simply musing enjoyably upon it, if the man were not the 'Wordsworth' we have come to presume we know in advance from the cultural history he constructed for himself.

Suddenly he saw the gaunt man leaning on a mile-stone, quietly groaning. Alarmed, he slipped 'back into the shade of a thick hawthorn' where he could observe him. The man looked like the Cockermouth beggars and Hawkshead pedlars Wordsworth had known all his life, but he was a veteran of dangerous military police work, protecting England's lucrative West Indian sugar plantations from slave uprisings. Overcoming his initial fear, Wordsworth stepped out and saluted the man. He learned the man had been discharged ten days before, probably at Whitehaven. Wordsworth could have taken him home to Ann Tyson's house, but instead he lodged him safely with a labourer in the woods, whom, he knew, 'will not murmur should we break his rest.'

Wordsworth does not say directly that his preceding 'consciousness of animal delight' was cancelled out by playing Good Samaritan to the veteran, but that is the general impression from the juxtaposition of these two passages. We go from 'a consciousness of animal delight . . . felt in . . .

every gentle movement of my frame' to an encounter with a man who, far from wearing any 'badge, glossy and fresh, of manliness and freedom,' seems to have been *un*manned, or wounded in and by his very manliness, especially in Wordsworth's first draft of the incident.

> He was in stature tall,
> A foot above man's common measure tall,
> And lank, and upright. There was in his form
> A meagre stiffness. You might almost think
> That his bones wounded him. His legs were long,
> So long and shapeless that I looked at them
> Forgetful of the body they sustained.
> His arms were long & lean; his hands were bare;
> His visage, wasted though it seem'd, was large
> In feature; his cheeks sunken; and his mouth
> Shew'd ghastly in the moonlight.[6]

Wordsworth does not explain the relevance of this encounter to his sensual feelings before it, still less to his other post-dance experience. Book IV ends abruptly at this point, in its first version, after Wordsworth has seen the veteran safely to rest, 'Then [I] sought with quiet heart my distant home.' (His home was not 'distant'; it was only a mile or so up the road.) But in his final manuscript of *The Prelude*, Wordsworth added three lines which challenge his readers to try to interpret these contrasts, these 'obscure minglings' of spiritual dedication and sexual awakening he felt that summer, though few editors have seen fit to include them in printed texts of the poem:

> This passed, and he who deigns to mark with care
> By what rules governed, with what end in view,
> This Work proceeds, *he* will not wish for more.
> (1850 IV.469–71; Wordsworth's italics)[7]

The date, place and persons of Wordsworth's first sexual experiences, if there were any before March 1792, remain matters of speculation and opinion. I am inclined to place them somewhere in Cambridge, London, or with the 'frank-hearted maids of rocky Cumberland' between 1787 and 1790. But the probability is almost equally strong that he held himself off from indulgence, if not from initiation, and displaced his erotic energies not into Methodism or Evangelism but into poetry. Some readers may insist that they are not clinical psychologists, and therefore not interested in Wordsworth's early sexual experiences. But since imaginative *development* is his master-topic, we cannot but be interested in suggestions that his imaginative awakening was tied to his sexual awakening. And, since nothing is more common in general human experience than this connection, we must be all the more interested because we find it apparently so markedly *absent* from Wordsworth's account of his imaginative growth, and from most critical intepretations of his account. There can be no doubt that sexual images, situations and feelings are present in his account of his first being alone with his sense of himself as a poet. An interpretation correlating exactly with biographical reality is impossible: the possibilities are polymorphous. The content of Wordsworth's poetry is rarely sexual, and no one will ever call him sexy. But in the larger sense of imbuing his readers' poetic pleasure with deeply erotic feeling, Wordsworth is one of the most sexual poets in the language.

After spending the first part of the summer at Hawkshead, he went to Whitehaven to visit Richard and his cousins, and then to Penrith to be with Dorothy and Mary Hutchinson. In August, he roamed again with Dorothy through their early childhood haunts around Penrith, renewing the delightful novelty of their first reacquaintance the previous summer. His descriptions of this time in *The Prelude* are suffused with a spirit combining first love and brotherly love that connect them to other parts of his account of this vacation. To Dorothy, he appeared doubly changed: the successful schoolboy she first saw in 1787 was now an impressive college gentleman. Dorothy appeared to him 'with a joy / Above all joys, that seemed another morn / Risen on mid-noon' (VI.211–13). The last phrase repeats Milton word for word, describing Adam's amazement at seeing Raphael's splendour in the Garden at noon.

At the ruins of Brougham Castle on the south edge of Penrith, William stressed his 'fraternal love' for Dorothy by linking the castle to poetical composition. He recalled the legend that Sir Philip Sidney had composed part of his *Arcadia* there for *his* sister, the Countess of Pembroke, 'in sight of our Helvellyn,' on the banks of the River Eamont, 'hitherto unnamed in song' – unnamed, that is, until this moment of its being named in *The Prelude*. That Sidney did not compose his poem there is not important; Wordsworth is linking the two because of his newly reawakened love for his sister.

He describes his and Dorothy's adventures with light suggestions of danger and eroticism. They climbed up 'in danger through some window's open space' to look abroad from the castle's walls. Or they would climb even higher, to 'the turret's head,' and 'lay listening to the wild-flowers and the grass / As they gave out their whispers to the wind.' His slight personification of the weeds gives a queer sense of overhearing something, as if the flowers and grass were whispering to each other, like the listening brother and sister. Lying down outdoors somewhere with Dorothy is something he seems to have done almost every time he visited her, weather permitting, a practice they continued once they started living together in 1795. More than just neutral relaxation and sensory enjoyment, the habit seems occasionally to have overtones of sexual sublimation or therapy, overtones that become stronger in the later 1790s, reaching their climax after William's engagement in spring of 1802.

Just at this intimate moment in Brougham Castle, comes the necessary, chastising addition: 'Another maid there was.' This was Mary Hutchinson, now 'first endeared' to him 'By her exulting outside look of youth / And placid under-countenance.' Both Mary and Annette Vallon, Wordsworth's only two known sexual loves, were mediated to him through Dorothy's presence. Just how Dorothy mediated these loves, or even what, precisely, she was mediating, is too complicated to say. But it is quite clear that she was the tutelary spirit at the crux in Wordsworth's creative psychology where sexual and poetic inspiration come close together.

With Mary and Dorothy, he visited another poetically charged childhood spot, Penrith Beacon, on the northeast edge of town, where he had had the terrifying experience of seeing the murderer's grave at age five or six. But his effort to link his feelings of awakening love with his earlier feeling of terror at the place results in a contrast so strong that the passage almost breaks in two, marked by a desperate dash:

> And o'er the Border Beacon and the waste
> Of naked pools and common crags that lay
> Exposed on the bare fell, was scattered love—
> A spirit of pleasure, and youth's golden gleam.
> (VI.242–45)

Mary's presence is not recorded in the *1799* version, which deals solely with his childhood. Given the terrible associations of the place for Wordsworth, his wish to revisit it as a grown-up and re-christen it with healthy romantic and fraternal emotions is understandable, though perhaps ill-advised. But the strain of the effort shows through.

On 27 August there was a wedding in the family. Uncle Christopher Crackanthorpe, aged forty-three, married Charlotte Cust of Penrith. Both Cookson uncles married in this year (William in October), having been freed to do so, financially, by the death of their father, Wordsworth's maternal grandfather, the previous December. William and Dorothy attended the Crackanthorpe-Cust nuptials, but they did not include the newlyweds in the 'golden gleams' of love they had been scattering over the countryside. Dorothy fairly spat out her contempt of Charlotte Cust and her sisters: 'a mixture of Ignorance, Pride, affectation, self-conceit, and affected notability . . . so ill-natured too.'[8] The Custs' affectation of nobility had a material effect on the Wordsworth children, no doubt influencing Dorothy's contempt, since the Custs, not content with marrying the heir to Newbiggin Hall, induced Crackanthorpe to extract an additional £500 from old Dorothy Cookson (d. 1792), an amount that William considered to belong by right to her grandchildren. He felt so strongly about it that when Uncle

Kit died eleven years later, he refused to attend the funeral or pay his respects to the family.[9]

Old William Cookson's death also stimulated a flurry of activity on the Lowther case. In January a bill and a summons were delivered to the Earl, but in the Easter court term he obtained an injunction against the Wordsworth executors, maintaining that John Wordsworth had agreed to do all his business for £100 a year. Recalling John's confused and uncertain letter in 1764 to Captain Robinson, we cannot say that Lowther was actually lying, though we can be sure he was always calculating. In May, Crackanthorpe and Richard Wordsworth obtained an order *nisi* dissolving this injunction, but Lowther then embarked on various delaying tactics which kept matters in limbo for three more years.[10]

With these unpleasant reminders of the obstructions that lay in the course of his young life, Wordsworth returned to Hawkshead to get himself ready to return to Cambridge. He may have returned briefly to Penrith for the happier occasion of William Cookson and Dorothy Cowper's wedding on 17 October, departing for Cambridge the next day, while Dorothy accompanied the newlyweds to their new home in Norfolk.[11]

William tried to capitalize on his recent associations of love and poetry by starting to compose *An Evening Walk*, addressed 'To a Young Lady from the Lakes of the North of England.' The poem is, in part, an aesthetic re-claiming of the Lake District in Dorothy's name, and its inspiration and subject matter place its genesis in the summer vacation of 1788.

Biographically *An Evening Walk* is another version of 'The Vale of Esthwaite' composed the previous summer, but with the Gothic ghosts removed in favour of Sentimental emotions, by virtue of Dorothy replacing Wordsworth's dead father as the family spirit in the poem. Where 'The Vale of Esthwaite' turned on Wordsworth's fear that his attraction to poetry would unsuit him for labour in 'Mammon's mine,' his 1788 reprise of the same material is based on an *assumption* of worldly failure, modified only by wishful thinking about spending his life together with Dorothy in these delightfully melancholy scenes. Otherwise, it is much the same poem, only in a different genre: loco-descriptive idyll rather than Gothic horror story. The former poem's nightmare walks around Esthwaite Water are expanded to a larger itinerary through the Lake District, though most of its scenes are still drawn from the Hawkshead neighbourhood.

An Evening Walk is nearly unreadable to twentieth-century tastes, especially in its first published version of 1793, which is full of horrendous examples of the 'poetic diction' Wordsworth made much of his reputation by attacking. But it is a creditable piece of description and meditation in the mode of Sensibility. Its aims at little more than a sequence of verbal picture postcards, though its participial cinema is closer to amateur video than anything as definite as a snapshot: gerunds predominate over verbs to keep the action moving, but they also render it inconclusive.

The speaker is a young man who was happy as a child, but now is older and sadder, if not wiser. He has wandered 'far from my dearest friend.' His itinerary is approximately that of Wordsworth's life, from Cockermouth to Hawkshead. Following the course of the river Derwent, out on to Derwentwater and past the falls of 'high Lodore' near its southern tip, the speaker climbs over the Borrowdale fells, down into Grasmere, past Rydal, to Winander and Esthwaite. Thus the poem, autobiographical like virtually everything the young Wordsworth wrote, is a stylized record of his freshman's despondency, stimulated not only by the recollections of his and Dorothy's happy childhood, but also by the recent joys of their few brief weeks together, and complicated by fresh reminders that they were not much loved by the adults who held their lives and futures in trust.

But all this is apparent only in the poem's framework. The bulk of it consists of more and less successful attempts to capture landscape in language, recapitulating his poetry-chanting walks with John Fleming three years earlier, and also 'those walks, well worthy to be prized and loved,' when his companion was Ann Tyson's terrier. Even at this early stage, the chronological layers one uncovers in the palimpsest of a Wordsworth poem are numerous: Dorothy in *An Evening Walk* substitutes for father, Fleming, and terrier all at once, and her role is adjusted to perform the diverse functions of each: family romance and tragedy, social friendship, and sexual surrogate.

Any psychological interpretation of the poem must be cautioned by the recognition that its personal elements are pressed into utterly conventional material that Wordsworth borrowed wholesale from other poets. The borrowings do not negate the personal elements, but they do illustrate clearly how young Wordsworth managed his emotional life in terms of poetic vocation. Wordsworth's notes to the 1793 edition acknowledge ten borrowings from other poets; the definitive scholarly edition (1984) adds twenty-three more, sometimes aided by Wordsworth's use of unattributed quotation marks (another convention), sometimes not. This rate of borrowing from one's predecessors is not unusual in eighteenth-century poetry, but Wordsworth strains credulity in his claim to Isabella Fenwick in 1843 that 'there is not an image in it which I have not observed; and now, even in my seventy third year, I recollect the time & place where most of them were noticed.' By 1843 he had himself fallen under the sway of the poetic myth of originality which in the summer of 1788 he had little thought of creating.

It is the *literariness* of *An Evening Walk*, not its naturalness, that is most relevant to Wordsworth's self-creation: namely, the increased extent to which he was beginning to consider becoming an author of some sort. 'The poet's soul was with me at that time . . . a thousand hopes were mine . . . a daring thought, that I might leave some monument behind me' (VI.55–68, *passim.*) The literary borrowings in the poem are themselves proof of a new kind of confidence, apparently modest, natural, and 'feminine,' but undergirded by an aggressiveness toward previous literary history unmatched by any English poet since Milton.

> The *instinctive humbleness,*
> Upheld even by the very name and thought
> Of printed books and authorship, began
> To *melt away*; and further, the dread awe
> Of mighty names was *softened down*, and seemed
> Approachable, admitting fellowship
> *Of modest sympathy.*
>
> (VI.69–76; italics added)

The first sign of this 'fellowship' of sympathy was *An Evening Walk* itself, into which he modestly admitted so many 'mighty names.'

It was in this frame of mind that he returned to Cambridge, and began unravelling his public, university career in earnest.

CHAPTER SEVEN

Weighing the Man in the Balance

> . . . of important days,
> Examinations, when the man was weighed
> As in the balance; of excessive hopes,
> Tremblings withal and commendable fears,
> Small jealousies and triumphs good or bad—
> I make short mention.
>
> (III.64-69)

When Wordsworth got back to college in October, he decided to turn over a new leaf, the excellent resolution of many a junior soph, as second-year men were known at Cambridge:

> the bonds
> Of indolent and vague society
> Relaxing in their hold, I lived henceforth
> More to myself, read more, reflected more,
> Felt more, and settled daily into habits
> More promising.
>
> (VI.20–25)

Yet in that 'indolent and vague society' he had placed in the first and second classes in his two 1787–88 exams. But now, reading, reflecting, and *feeling* more, he set off on an ambivalent course, taking only parts of his college exams during the next two years.

People think that Wordsworth spoiled his academic career and chances for future advancement by failing to take his exams. In fact, he took more exams than many other undergraduates, especially among the 'non-reading' category. He did not take the mathematical part of his 1788–89 and 1789–90 college exams, but not taking the whole exam did not, in and of itself, spoil his chances for the honours degree which would lead to a fellowship.

Honours degrees, signifying placement in one of the three classes in the

Tripos listing (wranglers, and senior and junior optimes), required some excellent performance in the university-wide examinations held in the Senate House in January of a student's final year. But the college exams – if one's college had any – were intended only to prepare students for the final exams, and to establish a preliminary estimate of the class in which they might be placed there. Students at St John's had to take more examinations than any other students at Cambridge: two a year. Trinity, the other large college, had one annual exam, but some of the smaller colleges had none. St John's twice-yearly examination system had only recently been instituted, to halt the college's alarming slide into mediocrity, and the reform had its intended effect. By the time Wordsworth arrived, St John's was again one of the 'preeminent' colleges.

Hence Wordsworth had to sit for six examinations before his final year. He had done very well in his first-year exams, when the classics subject was the last book of Xenophon's *Anabasis* (in Greek), and, in mathematics, basic algebra. Wordsworth, who had already read the first six books of Euclid's *Elements* (the second-year maths text) and knew both simple and quadratic equations, was so well prepared in mathematics that he did not need to attend many of his Maths classes. 'Accordingly,' he said, 'I got into a rather idle way, reading nothing but classic authors according to my fancy, and Italian poetry.'[1] Both Wordsworth and Myers had finished in the first class, as did nearly half of the other freshmen, including Robert Jones from Wales and William Terrot from Scotland, two of William's new friends. After the first Christmas break, the distinction between 'reading' and 'non-reading' men began to emerge. Most students were 'non-reading' men: they would not compete for honours degrees, but do only the minimum necessary to pass the university exams in January of their fourth year. In this respect, Wordsworth's university career is very typical; well over half of the students in his year did not compete for honours. But he actually read quite a lot, both in required and non-required texts: he could technically be classed as a 'reading non-reading' man. In the spring 1788 exam, Wordsworth slipped to second class, though Myers stayed in first. This was not very serious, as college exams had little bearing on the degree one would finally receive. They didn't count, except as predictors of the groupings in which boys would compete in the mathematical exams of their final year.

In the next two years William consistently distinguished himself in the classical literature and history sections. In December of 1788, he was listed first among those 'who did not go thro' the whole of the examination and yet had considerable merit.'[2] Every placement on any list at competitive Cambridge signified an important value judgment. He was 'in excellent spirits' when Dorothy saw him during a one-day visit with the Cooksons in November, and he felt even better after this exam.[3] The texts set for it were *Oedipus at Colonus*, the first six books of Euclid, and Thomas

Rutherford's *Institutes of Natural Law* (1756), which alternated with Paley's *Moral Philosophy* (1785) as the standard philosophy text. Since he had already read Euclid at Hawkshead, he could at least have taken a stab at the mathematical section of the exam: his cousin John Myers did, and achieved a first.

There is no evidence that Wordsworth, as a literary person, did not like mathematics. Quite the contrary. He goes out of his way in *The Prelude* to deliver a tribute to 'the pleasure gathered from the *elements* of geometric science': that is, Euclid's *Elements*, as the first six books were collectively known. In Book V, he pairs geometry with poetry as the two human creations most worth saving from an apocalyptic deluge. His praise of geometry used the same ecstatic rhetoric of 'Indian awe and wonder' which he reserved elsewhere in *The Prelude* for celebrating the powers of Imagination itself.

As for natural philosophy, he was as conversant in its contemporary styles of argument as any other intelligent young man, if not more so. In 1793–94 he would propose to William Mathews to start a journal by drafting a whole series of essays in this vein, and his fragmentary 'Essay on Morals' (1798) shows him finally turning away, in revulsion, from its mechanical modes of argument. Not only could he have, with no very large expenditure of effort, done better on his college examinations than he did, he could easily have placed himself along with most of his friends at the top of his class – as his family knew very well. No wonder he says, 'I make short mention,' of the Cambridge exams and his performance on them.

Even if a student didn't like maths, however, there were prestigious literary prizes to be won, which could be used as leverage to gain fellowships by other means: the Greek and Latin odes and epigrams, the two Chancellor's medals and the two Smith prizes. A brilliant freshman named Coleridge carried off the Greek prize in 1792. College officials coveted these awards nearly as much as wranglerships for their students. None were won by St John's in 1791 or 1790, though normally it got one or two, and with desire so keen, a strong candidate who refused to compete was *persona non grata*. St John's winning ways resumed in 1792, the year after Wordsworth graduated.[4]

Wordsworth gave early evidence that he would snub this route to preferment as well. In March of his second year William Chevallier, the Master of St John's, died. According to custom, undergraduates wrote elegies in Latin or English and pinned them to the coffin. Wordsworth did not contribute any verses, to the mortification of his Uncle Cookson – not because it showed insufficient grief, but ' "because," he said, "it would have been a fair opportunity for distinguishing yourself." '[5] This was true. Wordsworth was an excellent young poet, with a marked predelection for the elegiac mode, especially when it came to dead schoolmasters. But William Chevallier was a far cry from William Taylor, though

Wordsworth pled ignorance of the deceased rather than disapproval of his morals as his excuse. 'I did not regret, however, that I had been silent on this occasion, as I felt no interest in the deceased person, with whom I had had no intercourse, and whom I had never seen but during his walks in the college grounds.'[6]

The low quality of the poetry may also have influenced his decision. Tom Butler of Trinity, a friend of Francis Wrangham and Basil Montagu, regaled a supper party on the night after the funeral with some terrible verses he claimed to have snatched off the pall as it passed through the chapel doors. He was having fun at the Johnians' expense: he had composed them all himself. But, recalling Chevallier's reputation for 'gallantry,' Butler's jokes show that the occasion was not one of very deep grief for anyone, except perhaps Mrs Day, the master's mistress. 'No buck was he, no Don Diego queer, / No gallant youth, and yet a Chevallier!'[7] But Wordsworth stubbornly held himself off from the cynicism of both his adult mentors and his fellow students.

In the May exam two months later, Wordsworth and Jones 'distinguished themselves in the classic.' Myers and Terrot, still taking the whole exam, dropped into the third class. The set texts now were the final book of Livy's *History of Rome*, elementary mechanics, and selections from Locke's *Essay on Human Understanding*. Livy's account of Hannibal's march on Rome struck a deep chord in Wordsworth. Young Hannibal vows to avenge his father's defeat by the Romans, rises through difficulties to a position of leadership, where his own provocative policies make war inevitable. His amazing feats of crossing Spain and the Alps with his elephants and Numidian cavalry give the book a glorious feeling of high adventure, and the initial defeats Hannibal inflicts on the Romans in northern Italy add a satisfying sense of psychological justice.[8] These kinds of stories – avenging defeats wreaked upon worldly powers by an orphan or some other outcast – appealed terrifically to Wordsworth's imagination. At the beginning of *The Prelude* he gives a list of possible epic topics he might have written about if he weren't writing about himself; almost all of them correspond to this pattern.[9] His own Alp-crossing in *Prelude* VI is described with a military rhetoric reminiscent of Livy's descriptions of Hannibal – reinforced, by the time of its composition, with overtones from contemporary accounts of Napoleon's equally astounding feats of generalship.[10] He eventually cast his early life as a version of the same story: the orphan boy from a remote district single-mindedly overcoming the entrenched political and poetical powers of eighteenth-century Europe.

But this was not what St John's examiners were looking for, not at all. The questions on Livy, like virtually all classical texts set at Cambridge during the eighteenth century, reflected a curriculum whose ideological bias was thoroughly republican and anti-imperial. Whether from Xenophon, Thucydides, and Demosthenes in Greek, or from Livy,

Tacitus, and Juvenal in Latin, there was a consistent emphasis on texts and questions that stressed individual, republican virtues, as contrasted to accounts of foreign or domestic imperial corruption. Despite its Tory traditions, St John's did not differ from its Whiggish sisters in this respect.[11]

Though Wordsworth did not take the exam on Locke, he certainly read the *Essay on Human Understanding*, one of the great books of the age, and, along with Newton's *Principia*, one of the two foundational books of eighteenth-century Cambridge.[12] A contemporaneous question on Locke from Trinity College shows how his theory of association of ideas helped to frame Wordsworth's variations on the theme in 'Tintern Abbey' and *The Prelude*: 'The ideas as well as the children of our youth often die before us, and *our minds represent to us those tombs to which we are approaching*, where, though the brass and marble remain, yet *the inscriptions are effaced by time and the imagery moulders away*.' This powerful passage, from Book II of Locke's *Essay*, lies immediately behind Wordsworth's desperate realization of the need to record everything that he could about the foundations of his mental growth while he still recalled them:

> Oh mystery of man, from what a depth
> Proceed thy honours! I am lost, but see
> In simple childhood something of the base
> On which thy greatness stands . . .
>   The days gone by
> Come back upon me from the dawn almost
> Of life; the hiding-places of my power
> Seem open, I *approach*, and then they *close*;
> I see *by glimpses* now, when age comes on
> May *scarcely see at all* . . .
>   (XI.328–31, 333–38; italics added)

After his June 1789 exams, Wordsworth went north via Forncett to visit Dorothy. There, hidden away in the rolling flats of East Anglia, she was busy with a Sunday School she had started and other useful projects around the Cooksons' three parishes, exercising her nervous energy with a scope never before possible in her life. The yellow brick parsonage where she lived with her uncle and aunt still stands; it is pleasant to imagine the Church of England primary school beside it as a descendant of Dorothy's school. William accompanied her on her rounds through Cookson's parishes, and drafted a sonnet which began as an English idyll along these remote Norfolk country lanes:

> Sweet was the walk along the narrow lane
> At noon, the bank and Hedge-rows all the way
> Shagged with wild pale green Tufts of fragrant Hay,
> Caught by the Hawthorns from the loaded wain . . .[13]

But he ended it in the conventional manner of *An Evening Walk*, going from noon to night, happiness to sadness, ending in 'melancholy's idle dreams,' and straying 'through tall, green, silent woods and Ruins grey.'

But such conventional melancholy may also have been Wordsworth's actual emotions when he got back to Hawkshead, for 1789 was a much lonelier summer than the previous one. Ann Tyson was giving up her boarding establishment, Dorothy was gone, and Mary Hutchinson left early in the summer to live with her brother in Durham.[14] He wandered about alone, probing down into the Apennines between Lancashire and Yorkshire. He worked some more on *An Evening Walk*, and again paid family visits to Whitehaven and Penrith. He was becoming more and more of a family problem, and had to fend off increasingly pointed inquiries about what he was going to do. He was well received by his paternal cousin Mary Wordsworth Smith at Broughton-in-Furness, but his visit at Penrith was so short – a couple of hours – as to be rude.[15] Christopher Crackanthorpe and his unpleasant new wife were the only family members left there, besides old Mrs Cookson. Wordsworth was in an impossible dilemma with this uncle. On the one hand, Crackanthorpe complained that William did not spend enough time with them: 'I should have been happy if he had favoured me with more of his company, but I'm afraid I'm out of his good graces.' This was plain snideness, for the fact was that William was out of *his* good graces. But on the other hand, Crackanthorpe complained that William was shamefully extravagant at Cambridge, 'considering his expectations,'[16] and this charge was unanswerable. The unavoidable sticking point was that *any* expense provided grounds for chiding, given his apparent intention to flout family expectations by not taking his maths exams.

He was going nowhere fast in this summer of 1789, when the world suddenly began speeding up to modern velocity. One would like to know just where William Wordsworth was standing when he heard the news of the fall of the Bastille, because we have just such a detailed account of what he was doing when he heard the news of Robespierre's death five years later, in July 1794: the end of the Terror, and effectively the end of the Revolution. Probably his reaction to the news of the Bastille was much milder than his ecstatic response to the death of Robespierre; it was certainly favourable, as the news was widely received in England at the time. But for Wordsworth personally, the summer of 1789 was silent, solitary and sour: the kind of going-nowhere, doing-nothing period that sometimes provokes adolescents into exaggerated, compensatory overreactions.

He faced his last set of college exams in 1789–90. The December 1789 exam is the only one for which there is no record of Wordsworth's participation, although his two friends Jones and Myers continued to 'distinguish themselves in the classic.' The classical texts were Demosthenes' *Olynthiacs*, I–II, and his first *Philippic*, all urging Athens to take a stronger stand against of Philip of Macedon. The other two topics were optics and Bishop Butler's *Analogy of Religion, Natural and Revealed, to the Constitution and Course of Nature*. The latter was one of the century's standard rationalist defences of Christianity, and Wordsworth had to know it for his final exams a year later. Optics was one of the most popular scientific subjects of the eighteenth century; writers from Newton to Blake to Goethe were deeply engaged by it; Wordsworth had read Newton's *Opticks* with great interest on his own during his last year at Hawkshead. His interest in the anatomy of visual perception was stimulated by Edward Young's popularizations of Newton, as we recognize from 'Tintern Abbey's' line about 'the mighty world / Of eye, and ear, —both what they half create, / And what perceive,' adapted from Young. Again, the distance between what the exam required and what Wordsworth already knew about or was interested in is not very great, making the question of why he didn't take it all the more puzzling.

But almost half of Wordsworth's class failed to sit for this exam, so again his behaviour followed that of the majority.[17] One might guess that the news of revolution from France and its ripple effect in university life distracted Wordsworth and many others. But the examiners were quite ready to give their questions a contemporary application, for example by suggesting parallels between the Athenian context of Demosthenes' orations and a very widespread view of the condition of England at this time: 'its ancient liberties in a state of decay, with a government full of placemen and pensioners and a legislature that no longer represented the citizens,' all under the sway of an absolute monarch: Philip of Macedon, or Louis XVI (as he had been until just six months earlier), or George III as he seemed to want to become.[18]

The French Revolution immediately became a favourite illustration for freshening up the standard theme of Liberty in classical declamations. The brilliant John Tweddell's 'Address to Liberty' in the spring of 1790 set a new standard for outspokenness: '[he] took every opportunity of speaking his sentiments most freely, and, to those who watched the signs of the times, most indiscreetly.'[19] But within a few years this theme decayed into another hackneyed academic topic. By 1796, Charles Le Grice, a close friend of Coleridge and Lamb, was parodying the fervent declamations of the early 1790s in a 'General Theorem for a College Declamation':

> Three or four Sidneys, and Hampdens, and Lockes,
> And on the present times at least three or four knocks . . .
> Three or four tears with Sympathy's sigh,
> Three or four sweet things of I myself I,
> Three or four hurricanes, three or four ravages,

> Three or four Monarchs who are three or four savages . . .
> Three or four marks of interrogation,
> Three or four Os! of dire exclamation,
> With pause, start, and stare, and vociferation,
> Whatsoe'er be the theme, make a fair Declamation.[20]

Two of Wordsworth's longest poems of the 1790s, *Descriptive Sketches* and the Salisbury Plains poems of 1793–95, contain this same odd mix of introspective sentiment ('Sympathy's sigh', and 'I myself I') with vociferous political outbursts. The point is not that he was influenced by Le Grice, but his total familiarity with this rhetorical manner from college exercises.[21]

In his sixth and final college exam, in June 1790, Wordsworth's name appears, again coupled with Jones, Myers, and Thomas Gawthorp, his old Hawkshead housemate, as having 'considerable merit in the subjects which they undertook.'[22] By now barely a third of the class of '91 was taking the whole exam, and Wordsworth and his friends were part of a small group of eight students who did very well, but not enough. The subjects were plane and physical astronomy, the Gospel of Matthew, and three satires of Juvenal: Satire III, on country virtue versus city vice; X, on the heroism of the virtuous life, the basis for Johnson's 'Vanity of Human Wishes;' and XV, dedicated to the proposition that all men are capable of high moral feeling. Wordsworth again did the classical part, which inevitably heightened his awareness of social ills, of simple country life as one sort of answer to them, and of satire as a way of addressing them. His own Juvenal imitation, of Satire VIII, still five years off, would attack the nobility for failing to exercise the virtue incumbent upon their elevated status, citing as one particularly debased example the house of Lowther. Nor would the astronomy topic have been so terribly forbidding, for it is the spiritual heart of Newton's *Principia*, attempting to demonstrate God's power by quantifying the astronomical forces, as Wordsworth said: 'there . . . did I meditate / Upon the alliance of those simple, pure / Proportions and relations, with the frame / And laws of Nature' (VI.143–46). Wordsworth owned a copy of John Bonnycastle's *Introduction to Astronomy* (1786), which illustrated Newton with quotations from Milton, Thomson, and Young.[23] This is another instance among several where he had the required text, and read it well enough for certain parts to stick with him for years, but did not take the exam given on it at the time.

As a non-reading man, he participated but minimally in the oral Latin 'Acts & Opponencies' of the third and fourth years.[24] These oral disputations were usually excruciatingly boring, especially for students of Wordsworth's gifts, not to mention for the faculty who had to administer them. They allowed a very broad, not say laughable, range of achievement, and Wordsworth's strong command of Latin could have made him a formidable opponent. One was expected to defend a set (an 'Act') of three propositions, one moral and two mathematical, and each student also opposed someone else's 'Act.' One chose the propositions one wished to defend, usually lifted from a standard text like *Johnson's Questiones Philosophicae*. By custom, one invited one's opponent to tea before the disputation to talk over subjects and strategies. There was a good deal of self-interest on the part of everyone involved not to produce any untoward surprises, since every opposer knew he would have to be a proposer in his turn. On the other hand, there was also a great deal of self-interest in showing up brilliantly, if one aspired to a wranglership, so the ordeal placed students in a dilemma of mutual dependence and deceit.

These mock debates epitomized the pressures of the Cambridge exam system, with its emphasis on performance over substance. Left over from the age of religious disputation, they rewarded, in an age of supine religious energy, memorization and verbal facility over independent thinking. They were nightmares for dull students who were actually trying to get a good degree, and occasions of high drama for brilliant students who tried to succeed with displays of wit and erudition. For Wordsworth and his friends, smart enough to do well and intelligent enough to recognize the abuses of the university examination system, they were an artificial exercise that was not worth the effort if one 'set the pains against the prize' (III.632). Byron's conclusion would be surprisingly similar: 'The premium can't exceed the price they pay.'[25]

By not taking the maths sections of his college maths exams in 1788–89 and 1789–90, Wordsworth came to his Senate-House exams in January 1791 already in one of the two lowest categories, the seventh or eighth class: the *hoi polloi* who would be matched against each other only to determine their relative merit and to be sure they did not deserve 'plucking': given no degree at all. The minimal standard was so low that Wordsworth could have passed much of this exam in his freshman year. All that was required were some demonstrations from the first two books of Euclid's *Elements*, some ability to solve simple and quadratic equations, and familiarity with the arguments in the early parts of Paley's *Moral Philosophy* and Butler's *Analogy*.[26]

The experience of the university exams was, however, much more traumatic than college exams, or the Acts and Opponencies. They brought maths rather than moral philosophy to the fore. The morning of the first day of the week was the worst. Examiners read mathematical problems aloud, in Latin, and proceeded to the next problem as soon as the fastest student finished the first one, creating a nightmarish atmosphere of falling ever further behind. There was some temporary relief in the 'window problems,' where each student was given a sheet of problems to solve by himself, standing by the light of the windows, as examiners proceeded on to other classes. But following this, students were called upstairs in pairs and rigorously set against each other in head-to-head competitions aimed at discovering the smallest degrees of superiority or inferiority between them. It was not uncommon for students to faint or fall into fits before or during this ordeal, sometimes not recovering their mental composure or consciousness for hours or days afterwards. John Tweddell, 'the English Marcellus' and the star of 1790, almost lost his mind when he found he had placed only as a senior optime, not a wrangler.[27] One cheers for some students' acts of semi-rebellion, such as Blackburn of Trinity in 1790, who refused for two days to answer any question, but who, when threatened with 'plucking,' contemptuously rattled off answers to the hardest questions posed, and finished as fourteenth senior optime.[28]

Furthermore, the whole examination system was notoriously corrupt, and Wordsworth's not taking an honours degree also meant that he chose not to avail himself of a wide range of perfectly acceptable alternate routes to preferment. The least objectional of these was the *aegrotat* degree, awarded to students who claimed to be ill at examination times, 'though commonly the real complaint is much more serious; *viz. indisposition of the mind*' (*Gradus*). This kept one in the class to which one had been preliminarily assigned, albeit at the bottom of it. One or two of these were awarded every year, and three in 1791 – Wordsworth's year – one to a Johnian.[29] There were also four honorary senior optime degrees every year which moderators awarded at their discretion, often to deserving students who, like Wordsworth, didn't study mathematics.[30] Even fellowships could be awarded without taking the exams.[31] But such arrangements required a little negotiating, a little politic use of one's connections, and some seemly subservience, none of which Wordsworth would bend himself to.

Then there was outright jobbing or exam fixing: 'men of commanding talents and great acquirements scrupled not, as Examiners, for the sake of making money, to assign the highest honours in the power of the University to bestow, not on the most deserving, but upon those who had been fortunate enough to avail themselves of their instruction as Private Tutors!'[32] Sometimes this took the 'higher' form of deciding that a student's moral excellence outweighed his mathematical deficiencies, and promoting him over others who had better test results. A Clare Fellow claimed to owe his election to his 'never absenting himself from chapel, night or morning, during the whole period of his residence.'[33] Given some colleges' grim fixation on these observances, and some students' (like Wordsworth's) extreme detestation of them, the claim is not unlikely. Wordsworth's complaint against compulsory chapel attendance is the single longest item (III.407–59) in his extensive bill of complaint against Cambridge, and is all the more interesting because his brother Christopher was noted, as Master of Trinity, for rigorously enforcing this requirement.*

At the lowest level of test jobbing were 'pupil-mongering' fellows who simply gave precedence to students who had paid them well as private tutors, independent of their exam performance. If artificially competitive exams were the outward sign of Cambridge's intellectual debility, private tuition and its corruptions were the internal motors that kept the system going. Given the exams' emphasis on rapid recall, students were glad to pay for the services of fellows who had recently done well on the same exams; indeed, it was commonly assumed to be almost the only way to prepare successfully for the exams.[34] Some fellows supplemented their college incomes by more than a thousand pounds a year by such pupil-mongering.[35] Such a system of tuition, intended to overcome deficiencies in the regularly-assigned teachers, drastically undercut them instead, and created ever-higher levels of competition among the students who were determined to succeed. In 1833 Wordsworth warned a new Cambridge graduate against taking on pupils in this way, calling it 'an absolute blight' on 'the blossoms of the mind . . . setting to take fruit.' He meant the tutor's mind, not his students'.

On balance, Wordsworth's collegiate examination career was considerably better than most of his biographers have allowed, from their being too much under the sway of his dramatized self-presentation in *The Prelude*. In his college, he placed in the first class once, second once, received three honourable mentions, and failed to sit for only one exam. These supposed 'failures' are often extenuated on the basis of (1) his love of nature and poetry, (2) his lower social status, and (3) his provincial origins and northern accent or 'burr.' The second of these, as we saw in Chapter 5, was much less determining than modern assumptions suppose, while the first is based on a misunderstanding of Cambridge's intellectual context. As to northern accents, they were doubtless occasionally laughed at, but there were so many boys and faculty from the north that such condescension would have run its own risks.

Poetry and literature were oft-lamented casualties of the mathematical tripos system. The mathematical tripos had only been fully instituted in 1748, and a classical literary exam was reinstituted early in the nineteenth century. So Wordsworth was at Cambridge during the half-century it was

---

* Christopher Wordsworth earned a reputation as a strict, dour master at Trinity, strong on chapel and firmly against drinking, as a description of *c.* 1820 indicates: 'Apropos to masters, W——d begged pardon of the Trinitarians, but could not help d——g the whole race of "Milk & Waters." Hereupon, the Wordsworthians looked milk-and-watery' (*Facetiae*, 187). When he added a second compulsory chapel service on Sundays to the daily requirement, a Society for the Prevention of Cruelty to Undergraduates was formed (Benstead, 157)

most inimical to literature. Traditionally it had not been so; Cambridge's list of poetical lights is longer and brighter than Oxford's: Spenser, Marlowe, Jonson, Herbert, Crashaw, Marvell, Milton, Cowley, Dryden, Otway, Prior, Collins, Smart, and Gray, to mention only the standard anthology names; Chaucer, Butler, and Donne can be added by association; Coleridge and Byron and Tennyson of course came afterwards. (Tennyson's father was a Johnian of Wordsworth's year who also took a pass degree from dislike of mathematics.[36]) Such stifling of the literary was particularly associated with St John's because of its strong emphasis on mathematics, rigorously enforced by its twice-yearly exams.

Hence we come to the question that every student of Wordsworth has asked, just as every member of his family must have: Why, given his superior intellectual powers, his excellent family connections for future preferment, and the strong necessity of providing for himself and repaying the guardians who had invested their money in him, did he not do better? Far from being 'senior wrangler or nothing!' it took considerably more effort, though of a negative kind, for him to end up with 'nothing' on the honours list than it would have taken to place himself among the twenty-one wranglers of 1791 (the largest number in years).[37] As the master of his college said, with an extreme of donnish understatement, on the bicentenary of Wordsworth's birth, 'for a Hawkshead boy of his ability, Wordsworth's Cambridge career was an exceptional one.'[38] Given Wordsworth's college exam record, the questions that arose from family were not why he had done so poorly, but why, having done so well in what he did do, he could not have improved his prospects by doing a bit more?

The course he followed seems ridiculously, not sublimely, egotistical, and one explanation fits it very well: that he did not want to take examinations in which he would not show up well – that is, *best*. Merely by sitting the mathematical and moral/religious sections of the college exams, he would inevitably have landed in the second or third collegiate categories, since classifications were based on overall performance, and outstanding classics work pulled up mediocre mathematical work. Even the smallest calculation of his interests could have earned him a junior optime degree.

Wordsworth was in the most comfortable collegiate group: bright students who elected not to try for honours. Reading for honours was considered 'a slow sort of suicide,' but when Wordsworth parts himself from this company – 'Willingly did I part from these' – his explanation is dubious:

> I turn[ed]
> Out of their track to travel with the shoal
> Of more unthinking natures, easy minds
> And pillowy, and not wanting love that makes
> The day pass lightly on . . .
>
> (III.516–20)

But Wordsworth's friends were just as smart as he was, as we would expect them to have been, unless we imagine a wholly unknown group of 'easy' and 'pillowy' persons. No, as a later St John's master shrewdly noted, Wordsworth constantly saw his friends and acquaintances receiving honours of one sort or another, and he chose not to enter into competition with them, even though most of them were his intellectual inferiors.[39]

The Prelude would lead us to believe that his confidence in his future greatness made him reject Cambridge requirements, but this was not true when he wrote it (1803–04), and would have been a mere fantasy when he lived it. To have acted upon such a reason in 1790 would have been 'crazed' in mind indeed, however well it fits *ex post facto* with the later Romantic idealization of great writers' keeping faith with their art.

What he did have, that formed the basis of his foolhardy turn against Cambridge, was enormous, if almost desperate, pride and egotism, neither of which quite constitute self-confidence. Few things in the young Wordsworth's life are more 'romantic' in the colloquial sense than his rejection of Cambridge's opportunities. But we should be wary of *romanticizing* it: it cost him opportunities for church livings that were by no means incompatible with poetry, and it cost his family dearly. He could not know what the result would be, but eventually it was crucial to the creation of the Poet. He was a late bloomer whose psychological profile fits very closely the model for genius developed by Erik Erikson in *Young Man Luther*, particularly its elements of fatherlessness and a difficult, unforthcoming personality that nonetheless craved affection. It is clear from *The Prelude* that what he rejected was the Cambridge *system*: not the exams *per se*, but the personally humiliating subservience to a course of social advancement of which they were the prime instruments.

One of the best, least temporizing parts of Book III of *The Prelude*, 'Residence at Cambridge,' is also one of its least Romantic. Its concluding peroration shows his mastery of the tradition of allegorical satire of which he is supposed to be the enemy, but which writing about his Cambridge experiences brought forcefully into his mind. We can imagine the real names he saw behind each allegorical personification in this powerful passage, which harks back to bludgeoning denunciations of Bunyan's Puritan *Pilgrim's Progress* and Samuel Butler's Royalist *Hudibras*:

> And here was Labour, his own Bond-slave; Hope
> That never set the pains against the prize;
> Idleness, halting with his weary clog;
> And poor misguided Shame, and witless Fear,
> And simple Pleasure, foraging for Death;
> Honour misplaced, and Dignity astray;
> Feuds, factions, flatteries, Enmity and Guile,
> Murmuring Submission and bald Government

> (The idol weak as the idolator)
> And Decency and Custom starving Truth,
> And blind Authority beating with his staff
> The child that might have led him; Emptiness
> Followed as of good omen, and meek *Worth*
> Left to itself *unheard of and unknown*.
>   (III.630–43; italics added)

If we look for Words*worth* in this catalogue, rhetorical inevitability and his rights as a Johnian punster put him in the climactic position, which is verified by its echoing his self-presentation earlier in the book: 'So was it with me in my solitude . . . *Unknown, unthought of*' (139–41; italics added).

But his university failure was still worse than this, for he was not even true to himself. Book III of *The Prelude*, if recast as a letter home from college, would be enough to make any parent weep, with its tissue of weak excuses and temporizing admissions, self-blame and institutional critique, shoulder-shrugging insouciance and chin-out arrogance. In his later public life Wordsworth expressed conventional regrets for not having studied harder at Cambridge, but in the *Prelude* account he criticizes himself for having given in as much as he did to the exam-and-preferment system.[40] Some excellent students followed this independent course of action, and were often rewarded for their hardy perseverance. The young Pitt, for example, spent an extra two years reading history, politics and government with famous results, and Wilberforce put himself under the tutelage of William Cookson to recover his wasted time at college. To a considerable degree, Wordsworth also did this. He read classical literature, much more than was required, and also modern literature and modern European languages. He hired an Italian tutor, Augustino Isola, a friend of Gray's, who had tutored young Pitt. He also taught himself Spanish, and his French was already quite good, thanks to Mr Mingay at Hawkshead. It was almost unheard of for sizars to study modern languages, as this instruction was offered mainly for noblemen and fellow commoners in preparation for their grand tour of the Continent.[41] In a sense, this is what Wordsworth was doing too, only his grand tour would be made on foot. But members of his family were not slow to see a presumptive arrogance in his study of modern languages and his desire to go abroad.[42]

But he did not have the courage to break off college work and follow his own bent single-mindedly. He continued to post 'distinguished' exam performances on parts of the exam, results that inevitably drew attention to the parts that he was omitting. His failures toward himself were very much like his failures toward the system, exposing the neither-this-nor-that, 'amphibious,' 'spungy texture' of his mind, which he compared to a floating island of weeds and flowers that drifted about Derwentwater.[43] He sampled all the options of Cambridge: its 'deep quiet and majestic thoughts,' its 'empty noise and superficial pastimes,' its 'forced labour, and more frequently forced hopes.' But none of it added up. Instead, it produced only 'a treasonable growth of indecisive judgements that impaired / And shook the mind's simplicity' (III.210–16).

Wordsworth was still an adolescent, not a romantic epic hero, and hence fundamentally honest in his self-presentation in *The Prelude*. It is the most typical adolescent behaviour to rebel *partially* against authority, to refuse to do what is required of it, and yet not to do what the young person says he most desires to do, because he does not know himself. Like Stephen Dedalus, who also left for the Continent rather than take his university degree, Wordsworth's refusal to complete his university exams was a romantic 'Non serviam,' delivered with the same Miltonic overtones – and subject to the same critique of histrionic adolescent posturing – as Joyce's later portrait of the artist as a young man.

CHAPTER EIGHT

Something of a Republic

Politics at Cambridge

> Nor was it least
> Of many debts which afterwards I owed
> To Cambridge and the academic life,
> That something there was holden up to view
> Of a republic, where all stood thus far
> Upon equal ground, that they were brothers all . . .
>
> (IX.226–31)

William's return to Cambridge in the autumn of 1789 had dramatically raised his consciousness of events in France. The Revolution was being avidly discussed, especially by popular young fellows who not only favoured events in France but were also outspoken partisans of reform at home, and hoped to begin with the university itself. 'Long before 1789 the republican ideal had had extensive circulation at Cambridge; with the French Revolution to give it support, it must have been well-nigh irresistible.'[1]

Chief among the university's revolutionary enthusiasts was William Frend, brilliant fellow of Jesus College ('Frend of Jesus,' inevitably), who had been touring in Europe during the summer and felt the aftershocks radiating out from the epicentre at Paris. He narrowly missed the attack of the populace of Ghent on the imperial garrison there, heard rumours of other short-lived 'revolutions' breaking out in Germany, and got firsthand reports on events in France from William Priestley, son of the famous Unitarian scientist and reform politician Joseph Priestley.[2] Frend's tales of these events aroused wide interest among the students because he was a dedicated clergyman as well as a popular teacher. He had been publicly involved in university reform issues since October 1787, the very month that Wordsworth first arrived at Cambridge.

The political life of 'unreformed' Cambridge was far more active than in orthodox Oxford. Throughout the 1770s and 1780s it was a simmering cauldron of mixed issues that came to a boil in 1789–90, Wordsworth's third year at college. It was real politics now, going beyond the preferment politics which governed so much of student and faculty behaviour, though the two were intimately connected, as Frend's career shows.

He had renounced his Anglican faith in the spring of 1787, following a close study of the church's Thirty-Nine Articles; other fellows like John Jebb of Peterhouse had come to similar conclusions. There was a continuous line of such 'dissentience' in eighteenth-century Cambridge, going back to Edward Law of St John's and Francis Blackburne of St Catherine's, northern men (Blackburne attended Hawkshead) who both died in 1787.[3] All these men were theorists of perfectibility: committed Protestants who based their scriptural research on Newtonian logic and Lockean psychology, and followed wherever they led, in full confidence that reason and revelation could not be ultimately irreconcilable. (Jebb's brother, one of the King's physicians, told his master that his brother would be a reformer even in heaven.[4]) Their decisions were not taken lightly. They usually began with the Test Acts, the requirement that anybody wanting a university degree must subscribe to the thirty-nine articles of the Anglican creed, thus excluding Catholics and Dissenters. Nobody was much worried about the Catholics, still under the cloud of international conspiracy theories from the Jacobite risings forty years earlier. But many intelligent Dissenters were being denied their intellectual rights by the Test Acts, and rationalist research into the Articles often led to the conclusion that not only was the Test requirement unfair, but that the articles themselves were untenable, especially the doctrine of the Trinity, which not even differential calculus could prove. The great classicist Richard Porson was almost equal to the task, however. A friend once pointed out to him a buggy carrying three men, saying, 'There is an illustration of the Trinity.' 'No,' said Porson, 'you must show me one man in *three* buggies, if you can.'[5]

The intellectual route from opposition to the Test Acts, through doubts about the Trinity, to Unitarianism, and thence into republicanism, was the intellectual fast track of the era. Cambridge in the late 1780s was a hotbed of Unitarianism, which amounted to a sort of eighteenth-century 'green' radicalism. Its practitioners were more fervent in pursuit of good works, without faith in an afterlife, than most Anglicans, whose faith had settled down to mere conventions of theological good manners. Frend's mentor was Theophilus Lindsey (1723–1808), formerly a Fellow of St John's, one of the founders (along with Jebb) of the first Unitarian church in England, the Essex Street chapel in London, and a close associate of Priestley and Richard Price, the Dissenter whose 1789 sermon in praise of the Revolution provoked Burke's *Reflections*. Lindsey's letters to Frend about the rapid spread of Unitarianism in the north and west have all the urgency of a political campaign, and were of course regarded by the authorities in that light.[6] The university's charters were very strict against public expressions which tended to 'teach, or treat of, or defend any thing against the religion . . . received and established by public authority.'[7] Some fellows gave up Anglicanism but kept their opinions to themselves and were allowed to remain in college. Those who made their opinions public suffered the consequences, and William Frend was the most famous example.

Wordsworth's religious opinions at the time were so mild as to be nonexistent; he had no trouble subscribing to the Test Acts for his degree. But as he contemplated the life in orders he was supposed to follow, the successive acts of the drama of conscience that William Frend enacted during his college years made him feel keenly the exactions of the Cambridge system on the individual will.

Frend published his *Thoughts on Subscription* in the spring of 1788.[8] In the autumn of 1788, he widened both his audience and his target, publishing an *Address to the Inhabitants of Cambridge*, explicitly against Trinitarianism. This cost him his £150 tutorship, but he retained his fellowship. The dismissal threw him out of his university circle of 'dissentients' (oppositional thinking) into a larger group of political dissidents and Dissenters (oppositional actions) in both the university and the town. One of the respected leaders of the latter group was Robert Robinson, minister of a Baptist church (though he too slid into Unitarianism), and mentor of George Dyer, a close friend of Wordsworth's revered schoolteacher, William Taylor. In 1789, Dyer was living in Robinson's house when he published his own *Inquiry into the Nature of Subscription to the Thirty-Nine Articles*.[9] Given Wordsworth's deep feelings for Taylor, we can assume he had some contact with Dyer in Cambridge, as he did later in London. He would call Dyer's biography of Robinson 'the best in the language.'[10] Such hyperbolic praise for a merely workmanlike job signals feelings of solidarity for what these men represented, not impartial literary judgment.

Frend, buoyed by his new support, revised his Cambridge address in the autumn of 1789, publishing it as an *Address to the Members of the Church of England*. For this he was kicked out of the Society for the Promotion of Christian Knowledge, which Wilberforce had helped to found. Frend's writings over the next four years would be increasingly associated by his enemies with the rising spectre of Jacobinism, until he was finally dismissed from all university positions for the publication of his *Peace and Union recommended to the Associated bodies of Republicans and Anti-Republicans* (1793), a tract whose clear purpose was to *avoid* the increasingly intense polarization of opinions to which it fell victim. Many other writers urging academic or religious reform at this period suffered the same imputation of guilt by association from 'French principles.'

When Frend's university hearings finally came to an end, he had won all the moral and rhetorical points, to the great delight of crowds of student spectators (including Coleridge). But he lost all the technical and substantive ones. The vice-chancellor, Isaac Milner, assured Wilberforce that the trial was 'the end of the Jacobinical party as a *University* thing.' Milner wrote to Wilberforce as the surest way of reaching Pitt's ear, the better to increase Pitt's appreciation for Milner's role in putting down the threat.[11] This sequence describes perfectly the circles through which public politics were recycled as preferment politics, and reminds us that Wordsworth's connections along this circuit were of exactly the same order and magnitude as Frend's: Cookson to Wilberforce to Pitt.

Cambridge was very conservative or very radical, depending on which corners one looked into, but its atmosphere of political agitation was pervasive. There were university reformers and parliamentary reformers, but since the university itself was Pitt's rotten borough, the two were often indistinguishable. There was religious reform and political reform, from Dissenters through Unitarians to republicans. There were philosophical reformers who would find their great text in William Godwin's *Political Justice* (1793) and 'philanthropists' whose hero was Tom Paine.[12] There were practical politicians, Foxite Whigs, and other Whigs who increasingly supported Pitt, becoming the leading edge of the great wave of 'apostasy' which would roll back like a treacherous moral undertow through the 1790s, pulling under almost everyone of liberal persuasion with it. For the promise of liberal reform, it was the best of times; for liberalism's actual achievements, it was the worst of times. Oxford gained a reputation as 'the home of lost causes' in the nineteenth century, but in late eighteenth-century Cambridge, the cause of liberal reform was one long string of near-misses. The Test Act requirement was not abolished until 1870.

In all this, what tended to impress itself on undergraduates' minds was the sight of popular tutors and fellows, young, intelligent, and well-meaning, proposing changes in university regulations that affected the students themselves, and being punished, even deprived of their livelihood, for their actions. One 'grace' or petition after another was offered to the university senate, calling for greater or lesser reforms, and argued with scrupulous rationality, but almost all of them lost out. Some changes did get through, regarding the content of examinations, but on the big questions, of which the Test Acts were the cornerstone, there was no victory. Jebb and Robert Tyrwhitt had petitioned for their repeal in 1771, and Thomas Edwards, who helped Coleridge with the *Watchman* in 1796, offered another grace against them in December of 1787.[13] Charles James Fox offered his last bill against the Test Acts in parliament in March 1790, but it lost, 294 to 105, with Wilberforce active against it.[14] Had any of these academic initiatives won out, the political atmosphere in Cambridge would have been much less lively. But by constantly losing, the reformers effectively if unhappily kept politics in the forefront of everyone's mind.

Wordsworth's Christmas vacation in 1789 had its own political overtones. The three older brothers had a brief reunion in London. Richard was just finishing his first year with the firm of Parkin & Lambert, legal associates of Jack Robinson. He had been sent off to London by Christopher Crackanthorpe with very particular instructions, which repeated the advice given earlier to William: 'I would recommend it to you to pay attention to Mr Robinson as much as you conveniently can, as he has it much in his power to be of service to you in the future.'[15] John, for his part, had recently returned from the East Indies; he was to sail for India in January, aboard the *Earl of Abergavenny*, captained by his cousin John of Whitehaven, owned in part by Robinson, and named for Robinson's son-in-law, Henry Nevill, the second Earl of Abergavenny.[16] Wordsworth's cousin Thomas Myers married the earl's daughter; his sister was already married to Robinson's admiral brother. So young Wordsworth that Christmas was very much at the crossroads of several successful family ventures in law, trade and matrimony.

Dorothy's 1789 Christmas was equally eventful and well connected. Wilberforce spent the holidays with the Cooksons at Forncett, staying more than a month, and paid her much attention. He was much impressed with the school for parish children she had started, and gave her ten guineas to distribute to the poor 'in what manner I think best.'[17] He also gave her *A Practical Treatise on Regeneration* and the tireless Mrs Trimmer's *Economy of Charity*, a book about Sunday schools with 'some desultory hints towards improving the condition of the poor.' The Sunday school movement was just beginning in these years (William Frend had started one in his parish near Cambridge) and Dorothy's model and Wilberforce's advice show that it was as much a response to social crisis as of religious education. All in all, Dorothy found Wilberforce 'to be one of the best of men.' In fact, he had just been jilted, and might have been in a receptive mood at the time, though he soon made a resolve never to marry – which lasted for seven years. A marriage between Dorothy Wordsworth and William Wilberforce was not implausible, for he was rich enough for them both, and Dorothy, as the niece of his bosom-friend Cookson and an heir-dependent of Lord Lowther, a Wilberforce ally, needed no social apology. She had been introduced to the royal family at Windsor during one of Cookson's visits there as a canon of the Chapel Royal,[18] and the King was very pleased to meet a young cousin of his childrens' trusted tutor who was also the cousin of his chief political agent, Jack Robinson. Dorothy was even more ready than William to act in the family's political interest, urging her friend Jane Pollard to 'tell your Father I hope he will give

[Wilberforce] his vote at the next general election,' which was held in June.

As with the facts of prostitution in Cambridge and the rigors of the university exam system, the question regarding its political atmosphere must be, How far did all this agitation affect Wordsworth? He used the word 'republican' twice in talking about his university experience, and that word, eminently respectable today, was potentially treasonous in Wordsworth's Cambridge. Imagining a better university that 'should have bent me down to instantaneous service,' he describes a place whose 'majestic edifices' had a 'corresponding dignity within': 'a healthy sound simplicity, / A seemly plainness—name it as you will, / Republican or pious' (III.380–407). His offer of a 'pious' alternative – i.e., a simple religious community – shows how dangerous the 'republican' one – Roman, Swiss, or French – was construed to be.[19] Wordsworth also used his Cambridge experience to describe his receptiveness to the democratic impulses of the French Revolution:

> Nor was it least
> Of many debts which afterwards I owed
> To Cambridge and an academic life,
> That something there was holden up to view
> Of a republic, where all stood thus far
> Upon equal ground, that they were brothers all
> In honour, as of one community —
> Scholars and gentlemen—where, furthermore,
> Distinction lay open to all that came,
> And wealth and titles were in less esteem
> Than talents and successful industry.
> (IX.226–36)

This idealized view of Cambridge sits very ill with his account of it in Book III, and even less well with his actual performance there: who was he to invoke 'talents and successful industry'? But the more relevant point is that he recalled it as being 'something . . . of a republic' at a very pertinent point in time: the summer of 1792 when he was in France, and when, on 10 August, the National Assembly first declared France a republic.

These two sympathetic references do not make young Wordsworth a republican in 1787–91. Though he sympathized with the direction of liberal reform and republican sentiment, he also contained within himself background tendencies of a sharply opposite nature. His own personal, family politics, his *interests*, were Pittite all the way. Pitt was certainly not a republican, but then neither was any other politician of any standing at the time, including Fox, the florid, flawed leader of the Whigs during Wordsworth's young manhood.

This is much more than mere political background, for these same persons and issues held centre stage in British public life without significant interruption throughout Wordsworth's early development. The enormous change in the English political system in the half-century between 1783 and 1832 was very much centred on Pitt's career and his Cambridge power base. At the time of Wordsworth's arrival at college, Pitt owed his seat to 351 of the 554 university fellows who voted in the election of 1784, an actual victory margin of only 73.[20] In strictly numerical terms, Cambridge University was one of the rottenest boroughs. Wordsworth was personally familiar with these events – 'I had so often seen Mr Pitt *upon his own ground* at Cambridge.'[21] The arc of Pitt's career marked, though few people realized it at the time, nothing less than the creation of the modern Conservative party, to which the mighty events of the French Revolution were, for practical domestic purposes, frequently only a dramatic and sometimes useful propaganda backdrop. For not only was Pitt not a republican, it was an increasingly open question, by the time Wordsworth arrived in Cambridge in 1787, whether he was a Whig, or even a liberal. The actual political situation changed with lightning rapidity during the decade; its future outlines were revealed in their eventual form at the end of Wordsworth's third year at Cambridge, June 1790.

In 1780, Pitt, aged twenty-two, had finished last in a field of five in the university's parliamentary election, with 142 votes. In the election in 1784 Pitt stood again for Cambridge, having spent the intervening three years in James Lowther's seat for Appleby, and was elected, ratifying the King's controversial appointment of him as prime minister in 1783. Pitt and his friend George Henry Fitzroy (1760–1844), Earl of Euston and fourth Duke of Grafton, unseated the two 'old Whigs,' Pitt running first in the field. In 1785, Pitt, who along with Burke and Fox had been a supporter of the cause of the American colonists, and who was by definition a liberal reform politician, offered a mild bill for parliamentary reform. It lost, and he never offered another. In August of 1786, Fox and Sheridan and other Whig leaders were made 'freemen' of Cambridge. In the election of June 1790, at the beginning of Wordsworth's last Long Vacation – the same election for which Dorothy had been stumping for votes for Wilberforce – Pitt increased his university vote total to 510, fewer than 100 fellows failing to vote for him, and was elected high steward of the university.

In Wordsworth's Cambridge there was a constant political contention between the university Whigs who supported Pitt and those who felt betrayed by him. University fellows, like all political constituencies at the time, quickly switched their allegiances to match those of the person in power. Pitt was their source of preferment, master of the only market on which they could sell their vote. He came up to Cambridge about twice a year when the university was in session, 'usually with a Deanery or some preferment in his pocket.'[22] These were painful occasions, for Pitt was both arrogant and shy, the very antithesis of Fox personally, and most of the Fellows could not disguise their squirming lust for place, preferment, or a pension. Sometimes they would stupefy their benefactor with irrelevant displays of erudition, or alternatively confuse him with bizarre donnish humour. The system was certainly corrupt from a modern point of view, but it was normal and natural to those enmeshed in its contradictions, and within these limits it worked very well. One might hold almost any opinion, within reason, on such volatile issues as parliamentary reform, the slave trade, or the East India Company. Rather, the university connection to the political system was directly based on votes given to a candidate, from whom favours flowed down as a matter of course.

Though Wordsworth's failure to take an honours degree at Cambridge was a spectacular flouting of his family's expectations, his university career was never intended to be primarily an intellectual affair. Rather, he was supposed to become a fellow and join Pitt's majority, standing ready to deliver his vote whenever the next election was called, for his career interests lay, as we have seen, decidedly on the conservative, Pittite side. Hence his failure to prepare himself even minimally for the mathematical honours examinations was not only a personal failure, nor even simply a family matter; it had, in a manner of speaking, national ramifications. Lacking an inheritance, he did not have the land necessary to make him a 'freeman' or 'freeholder' eligible to vote in the Cumberland elections. But with an honours degree and a college fellowship he could have earned these same rights in Cambridge by his own intellectual exertions. He could have gone on reading and studying and writing whatever he liked, as Gray and Smart and many others before had done. With his connections, frayed though they were by two years of unfocused – but not undistinguished – study, a concerted effort from June 1790, to the following January could at least have landed him somewhere among the optimes.

To journey to Europe instead at this crucial time not only threw him out of the system of preferment politics for which he was well groomed by family and personal interests, it also drew him into systems of thought, and among people, opposed not only to that comfortable system of benefices and emoluments, but to the entire ideology of hierarchy on which it was based.

CHAPTER NINE

Golden Hours

The 1790 Walking Tour: France and Switzerland

> France standing on the top of golden hours,
> And human nature seeming born again.
> (VI.353–54)

In the summer of 1790, Wordsworth would have been well advised to join a Lakeland reading party to study for his university exams. But he decided to take a walking tour of Europe instead. With this act of disobedience, his career as a romantic poet may be said to have begun.

'William . . . lost the chance (indeed the certainty) of a fellowship, by not combating his inclinations,' Dorothy ruefully admitted.[1] It is almost impossible to overestimate the importance of this summer's tour in Wordsworth's development. In a life thus far marked by only small acts of disobedience, like slashing family portraits with a whip, this was a decisive act of rebellion, the culmination of his minor college lapses. But, like stealing the rowboat on Ullswater, which produced one of his visionary 'spots of time,' this initially clandestine tour became a three-month-long spot of time, opening an entire decade when Wordsworth's senses were always preternaturally heightened, because almost everything he did could be construed by his elders as a continuation of this one act of rebellion.

Seducing his good friend Robert Jones to his cause, he spent the month after his last college exams in June preparing for a tour of the Alps that all their friends agreed was 'mad and impracticable.' Drawing a draft of twenty pounds on his brother Richard – ostensibly for current college expenses – Wordsworth ordered special greatcoats for each of them, 'made light on purpose,' from a local tailor. Closeting themselves in the now deserted college, he and Jones sat down to plan a detailed itinerary.[2]

The idea was very much a Cambridge fashion. William Frend's 1789 tour had been all the rage in college talk, and though the French Revolution was still the main item of international news, beautiful landscapes were Wordsworth's primary motivation: 'Nature then was sovereign in my heart, / And mighty forms seizing a youthful fancy / Had given a charter to irregular hopes' (VI.346–48). But his political diction ('sovereign,' 'charter') suggests similarities between his own declaration of independence and the larger public sphere which encouraged it: "twas a time when Europe was rejoiced, / France standing on the top of golden hours, / And human nature seeming born again.' En route once more for the Picturesque Sublime, he was swept up in the world history of his times, and was himself 'born again' . . . as *Wordsworth*. His success at pulling off such a 'mad and impracticable' scheme, 'far beyond my most sanguine expectations,' gave an enormous boost to his confidence for pursuing other impracticalities, on almost a year-by-year basis, throughout the 1790s.

Wordsworth and Jones were making a new version of the grand tour. This had been a standard item in the education of wealthy young men for over a century. But they were going to Switzerland rather than Italy, and on foot for three months instead of in a carriage for two years, as Thomas Gray and Horace Walpole had done fifty years earlier (1739–41), when they too were Cambridge undergraduates. Gray's precedent was very much in Wordsworth's mind, since Gray's account of his tour was 'a favourite volume' with him.[3] In his poetical rendering of this tour, *Descriptive Sketches* (1793), Wordsworth remarked the 'great difference between two companions lolling in a post chaise, and two travellers plodding slowly along the road, side by side, each with his little knapsack of necessaries upon his shoulders.' Gray and Walpole did indeed 'loll' in their post chaise, but this was a model of tourism which Wordsworth tried at every turn to subvert. Gray had been called 'Miss Gray' at college: his contemporary Christopher Smart said his mincing walk made him look like a man who had just soiled his underclothes. Wordsworth was known to be both a poet and a walker, and he now brought these two talents together with an athletic energy that put Gray's delicate image of the poet to shame.

If his imaginative inspiration came from Gray, his practical information came from another Cambridge fellow, William Coxe of King's, whose *Sketches on the Natural, Civil, and Political State of Switzerland*, first published in 1776, had been republished with additions in 1779 and 1789 as *Travels in Switzerland*. Coxe emphasized economic and political matters more than landscape description, but he included enough of the latter, in the current idiom of the Sublime, for Wordsworth to respond to: 'What a chaos of mountains are here heaped upon one another! a dreary, desolate but sublime appearance: it looks like the ruins and wreck of a world.'[4] Wordsworth and Jones adapted their itinerary from Coxe, reducing it considerably, and for the most part running it in reverse, from southern to northern Switzerland.

The distance they covered and the pace they maintained could not have been accomplished without very detailed planning in advance, as a glance at any contemporary map of France and Switzerland makes clear. Europe was not signposted, paved and hostelled for pedestrian tourists. Well-off persons travelling by coach, between inns, could expect to advance reasonably well in settled regions, but not young men of uncertain class and dubious appearance, on foot in the mountains in unsettled times. Wordsworth noted this lightheartedly to Dorothy: 'Our appearance is singular, and we have often . . . excited a general smile . . . and our manner of bearing our bundles, which is upon our heads, with each an oak stick in our hands, contibutes not a little to that general curiosity which we seem to excite.'[5] But they knew exactly where they were going, almost every day of the way. This tour has become one of the archetypes of Romantic wandering, in cultural memory, but it was far from a lighthearted summer's *wanderjahr*, following wherever their fancy led. Rather, they were following Wordsworth's fancy, and the fact that they lost their way only two or three times during the whole summer indicates how well he supplied his fancy with facts. The huge impression made on Wordsworth by the few times they did get lost indicates, further, how much emotional energy he invested in his preparation for the trip.

On 10 July they set out, without Wordsworth telling any of his relatives he was leaving the country.[6] They went first to London, where William drew more money on his account, but did not contact Richard. In their haste to get out of reach they spent the first night barely beyond Greenwich, at Shooter's Hill. Proceeding through Canterbury to Dover, they crossed to Calais on 13 July and immediately fell into the first of many surprises that awaited them on this trip. Awaking on the morning of 14 July, they found themselves foreign observers of the world's first great celebration of modern state democracy. The Fête de la Fédération was of course scheduled to coincide with the first anniversary of the fall of the Bastille, but it was not a celebration of the Revolution as it is today. Rather, its main purpose was to dramatize Louis XVI's oath of loyalty to the new constitution, sworn like a marriage vow upon an 'altar of the country' in a huge amphitheatre in the Champs de Mars. Wordsworth and Jones could not have anticipated the effect it would have, by rapid degrees, on them.

All France was mad with joy at the prospect of freedom that lay before it, and liberal spirits everywhere were rushing to join its celebration. Helen Maria Williams, crossing the Channel from Brighton to Dieppe on the same day as Wordsworth, took a fast coach to get to Paris in time for the festivities, and the spectacle did not disappoint her: 'it required but the common feelings of humanity to become in that moment a citizen of the world.'[7] A year later Wordsworth would cross again, bearing a letter of introduction to Williams, but in 1790 her boundless political enthusiasm was not yet his. Still, he and Jones were enough struck by the joy they saw in Calais to spend the day there, observing the festivities. 'How bright a face is worn when joy of one / Is joy of tens of millions!' Gradually, their own faces came to wear a similar expression, for the first *quatorze juillet* was much more than a one-day affair. For the next two weeks, all through the French part of their trip, Wordsworth and Jones were in constant presence of this public ecstasy, passing by the 'gaudy reliques' of *la grande fête* in Paris.

But they were not distracted from their itinerary. They were heading for the Grand Chartreuse, and the deep cultural shift from Enlightenment to early Romantic Europe is clearly marked by the fact that this severe monastery, which had been for Gray and Walpole a fascinating distraction from their goal, Rome, was for Wordsworth and Jones the first object of interest on the way towards theirs, the Alps.

To get there as fast as possible, they enforced 'a march . . . of military speed.' Their pace was indeed extraordinary. Through the summer, covering 2000 miles on foot, they averaged nearly thirty miles a day, mostly on foot, including many days in difficult mountainous terrain. Figuring four miles per hour as a good pace, and even allowing full twelve-hour days in summer weather, they still must have been walking almost all of the time. They did not take much time to stop and look at the sights. In a tour of ninety days there were only four occasions when they spent two nights at the same place.

Neither old nor new cultural monuments distracted them. They ignored Amiens and Rheims and their famous cathedrals, and they were not tempted by revolutionary Paris, though it lay within fifty miles of their route. Instead, hurrying through the green fields of Picardy, they kept to the Calais–Paris public roads as far as Péronne. There, hewing to their southeasterly course, they branched off, and for 'three days successively [walked] through paths / By which our toilsome journey was abridged — / Among sequestered villages.' They came out at Château-Thierry, and a day and a half later, just a week after they set out from Calais, were walking alongside the Seine at Troyes.

They saw joy spread round them everywhere, but they were lonely and a bit homesick, making it easy to indulge in the fashionable melancholy which was considered the necessary emotional complement to Picturesque experiences. ''Twas sweet at such a time—with such delights / On every side, in prime of youthful strength — / To feed a poet's tender melancholy' (VI.375–77). Jones was too round and fat, and Wordsworth too tall and severe, to *look* very tender or melancholy, but they wore their mental fashion as best they could, even if it looked as awkward as their greatcoats bundled up on their heads.

Following the Seine through 'the vine-clad hills of Burgundy,' they came to Chalon-sur-Saône. There, both their mode and mood of conveyance

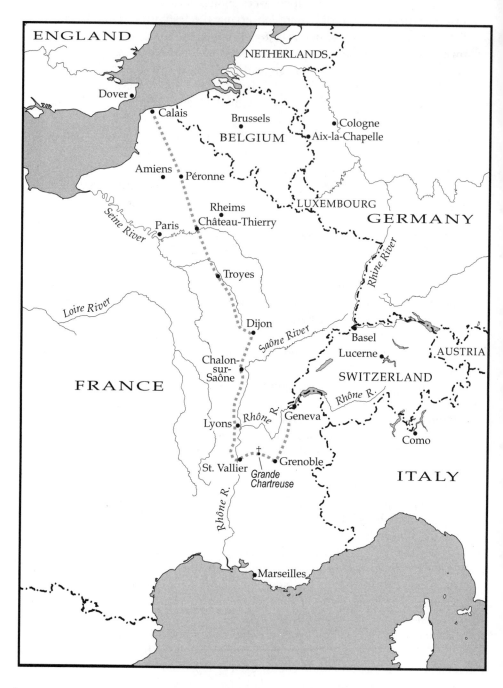

'A march it was of military speed': Wordsworth's and Jones's route across
France, July 1790

changed dramatically. They boarded a boat bound for Lyons, crowded with *fédérés* returning from the Fête de la Fédération. Over 100,000 provincial delegates, armed with symbolic swords, had attended the fête, and they were still streaming homeward two weeks later.[8] Confined with this 'merry crowd' in the narrow bounds of a river boat, Wordsworth and Jones soon found themselves in a new kind of community. Before this, they only '*saw* dances of liberty, and, in late hours / Of darkness, dances in the open air.' Now, although they were just 'a lonely pair of Englishmen' when they boarded the boat, by the end of the first day they found that they 'bore a name / Honoured in France, the name of Englishmen,' and were invited into the dance of freedom themselves. They chatted, they ate, they drank and, above all, they danced – Wordsworth's favourite physical activity after walking, and now once again crucial to his developing sense of himself, as it had been in the summer of 1788.

> In this blithe company
> We landed, took with them our evening meal . . .
>   . . . The supper done,
> With flowing cups elate and happy thoughts
> We rose at signal given, and formed a ring,
> And hand in hand danced round and round the board;
> All hearts were open, every tongue was loud
> With amity and glee . . .
> And hospitably did they give us hail
> As their forerunners in a glorious course . . .
>   (VI.401–12)

These were glorious moments for two very fortunate young men. They joined in 'dances of liberty' that were repetitions – overflowings – of those in Paris, caught up in the effervescence of a national political event that represented the hopes and dreams of the best spirits of the age. Their academic republicanism disposed them to endorse it, and their accidental tourism allowed them to enjoy it to the full.

Wordsworth sets out their welcome in no uncertain terms: they were 'Guests welcome almost as angels were / To Abraham of old' (VI.403–4). That is to say, in Wordsworth's retrospective editorializing, the Englishmen (*les anglais*) were received like the angels (*les anges*) who announced to Abraham the birth of a new nation. Never underestimate the power of a Wordsworthian figure of speech: he means to say that they, not the French delegates, carried the new annunciation. In the context of *The Prelude*, this was not a national miracle but a personal one, manifested in the growing self-consciousness of its young hero.

Wordsworth and Jones drifted downriver with the *fédérés* for three or four days to Lyons, where many disembarked. They continued on in a smaller boat on a swifter river, the Rhône.[9] Since the *fédérés* who contined south of Lyons were heading directly to the mouth of the Rhône, 'it is easy to recognize [among them] the delegates sent from Marseilles to the Federation.'[10] And, since Wordsworth finished his poem describing all this in 1792, when he was in Orléans and Blois, it is also easy to realize that some of the disgruntled *citoyens* who came back to Paris from Marseilles that summer, dragging their cannon, their grievances, and their radically new demands with them, would have included some of the very *fédérés* with whom he danced and drank in the happier days of 1790. The coincidence is worth emphasizing: young Wordsworth danced with the people who brought 'La Marseillaise' to Paris, and with it the Republic and the Terror.

More important for him and Jones at the time was the fact that they were no longer lonely. They were young, they were strong, they could speak the language well enough, and if they were not very handsome, they were something even more attractive at the moment: they were English. The sense of being recognized and welcomed as an interesting person outside of one's own country, simply by virtue of being *of* that country, is one of the delights of foreign travel for young people, and such recognition could hardly have come at a higher pitch than it did for Wordsworth on the Saône at the end of July 1790. It was on this boat trip, in this company, that Wordsworth's personal attachment to the ideals of the French Revolution began, and the attachment had as much to do with the lift it gave to his sense of himself as it did with those political ideals, abstractly considered. No longer by-passing observers of 'gaudy reliques,' he and Jones were now participants in a joyous community of fellow travellers.

They got off the boat at St-Vallier and started hiking across country. In two days, they reached the neighbourhood of the Chartreuse. On their third night (3 August) they stayed in a village near the monastery, and for the next two nights they were guests of the Carthusians themselves.

Thomas Gray's visit to the 'awful solitude' of the Chartreuse was Wordsworth's immediate motive for visiting it. Gray's response to it is still the most famous in English: 'In our little journey up to the Grande Chartreuse, I do not remember to have gone ten paces without an exclamation, that there was no restraining: Not a precipice, not a torrent, not a cliff, but is pregnant with religion and poetry. There are certain scenes that would awe an atheist into belief, without the help of other argument. One need not have a very fantastic imagination to see spirits there at noon-day.'[11]

Curiously, Gray's response was more 'romantic' than Wordsworth's. All these young Englishmen were predisposed to regard the monastery as a living relic of Catholic superstition. Gray emphasized the spirituality that seemed inherent in the monastery's natural surroundings, but Wordsworth gave as much attention to the religious institution itself. He did so partly because he was seeing a working monastery for the first time, reawakening his interest in England's ruined abbeys, such as Furness near Hawkshead.[12]

His sympathy was stimulated by the fact that he came to it at the very moment when it was about to pass out of existence, because of 'the gleam of arms' which now threatened it. The first goal of his tour was already under attack by new social order of revolution; the Grande Chartreuse thus became the first item in a growing catalogue of reversals that gradually became the basis for all Wordsworth's interpretations of the meaning of his tour.

The monastery was still in full operation in 1790, though monastic vows had been forbidden by the National Assembly in February. The final vote on the Civil Constitution of the Clergy had just been passed on 12 July, and the bad news must have reached the monastery just about the time Wordsworth arrived. Some of its treasures had already been appropriated, but it was not officially disestablished, and its inmates routed, until the summer of 1792, when for five months it was subjected to a 'dragonade' by troops.[13] (Around 1816–1819 he added a long passage on the Chartreuse to *The Prelude*, giving full vent to his now *post*-romantic feeling for the spiritual loss humanity incurred there, when 800 years of Christian observances were blasted away by the 'rage of one State-whirlwind' (*1850* VI.488).[14]

During the two days they spent there – their first rest after three weeks of haste – they walked through the St Bruno's woods, 'contemplating, with encreased pleasure its wonderful scenery,' and sampled the famous Chartreuse liqueurs.[15] In Vallombre, the Valley of the Shadow, they watched monks sworn to silence digging their own graves. For Wordsworth, the overwhelming impression was one of *solitude*, a special sense of place that eventually became his dominant frame of mind. His youthful reaction to it is caught in *Descriptive Sketches*' allusion to the 'parting Genius' of Milton's Nativity Ode, for this fits exactly with his earlier image of himself and Jones being welcomed by the *fédérés* as angels. For Milton, the 'parting Genius' was the mythological spirit of the classical world, sadly departing before the new spiritual reality of Jesus Christ. But for Wordsworth, who accurately guessed that they might well be 'the last, perchance the very last, of men / Who shall be welcom'd here,' the 'parting Genius' was now Christianity itself, and he the last among men who could appreciate its spiritual value even as its institutional forms disappeared. He imagined himself saving the spirit of religion as one might save an endangered species:

> who,
> If the ability were his, would dare
> To kill a species of insensate life,
> Or to the bird of meanest wing would say,
> Thou and thy kind must perish? Even so,
> So consecrated, almost, might he deem
> That power, that organ, that transcendent frame
> Of social being.[16]

This new Sublime is not religious, nor even in nature as it was for Gray, but in the mind of man – perhaps, as he entertained the thought, this one man alone.

Wordsworth and Jones left the Grand Chartreuse on 6 August, making for their next destination, Mont Blanc, the ultimate symbol of European sublimity. They went via Geneva because it was the easiest way to get there, but also because of its associations with that strangely enlightened mind whose ideas lay behind many of their beliefs about connections between nature and virtue: Jean-Jacques Rousseau, the 'Citizen of Geneva.' One of Wordsworth's primary wishes on the tour was to track the great philosopher of republican virtue and personal egoism. They visited Rousseau's lake district at the end of the tour, but from Geneva they passed into the provinces of Vaud and Vallais which he had glorified in *La Nouvelle Héloise* (1769), a book already regarded as one of the books responsible for seducing the European mind into revolution.[17]

At the 'higher part' of the lake, they passed through Montreux and by the Castle of Chillon that would captivate Byron a generation later. But Wordsworth made no mention of it; castles, like cities, were simply not on his mental map: he was already thinking himself into his role of 'mountain youth.'

The attention of the landscape-wandering public had been concentrated on Mont Blanc for over ten years, since the first modern attempts to scale it began in 1776. Its first ascent in 1786 by Michael Piccard was followed in 1787 by the more scientific Dr Horace Bénédict de Saussure, whose success in commercially marketing his achievement made it a popular item of touristic consumption.[18]

When Wordsworth and Jones reached Martigny, they checked their knapsacks and headed up the Col de Balme toward the great white mountain. They must have had Saussure's feat much in mind, for the days they spent there, 12–14 August, coincide almost exactly with the third anniversary of his renowned success (13–15 August 1787). Wordsworth and Jones did not expect to climb the mountain themselves: that remained a business for professionals. But getting to it involved them in their first mountain *crossing*, since the Col de Balme reaches 1526 metres above Martigny before descending down to the region of the Chamonix glacier (1037 metres). Coxe made high claims for it which raised Wordsworth's hopes: 'an extensive prospect, which many travellers consider as equal to the most sublime prospects in Switzerland.'[19] But again they encountered difference and disappointment.

> That day we first
> Beheld the summit of Mont Blanc, and grieved
> To have a soulless image on the eye

Which had usurped upon a living thought
That never more could be.
(VI.452–56)

This is a common experience. For though Mont Blanc is the highest point in Europe (4807 metres), and was still thought by many experts to be the highest point on earth,[20] it does not always look impressive. William Coxe, Wordsworth's tour authority, had a similar letdown. He and his companions had set off from the same place as Wordsworth and Jones, 'with the expectation of seeing the sun rise on the summit of Mont Blanc, but were disappointed . . . it did not impress me with that astonishment which might be expected.' It is too broad and round, and too often obscured by clouds and snowy mist to live up to its reputation, the very whiteness of its glare rendering it 'in many situations . . . less lofty in appearance than it is in reality.' Wordsworth's expectations of a 'sublime' experience were far beyond reality – how far beyond, he now began to suspect.

They needed a night's rest before they could take in the Vale of Chamonix, for they had been walking a very long time, over twenty-five miles by the time they reached the village on the night of 12 August. They had the recompense of seeing the mountain from one its most impressive perspectives, almost straight upwards from the little village lying nearly 4000 metres below it. All the next day, and part of the following day as well, they explored 'the wondrous Vale of Chamouny.' Wordsworth in *The Prelude* painted a set -piece of typical touristic amazement at the five brutal ice-rivers of the glacier cohabiting with the green fields and human activities between them.

There small birds warble from the leafy trees,
The eagle soareth in the element,
There doth the reaper bind the yellow sheaf,
The maiden spread the haycock in the sun,
While Winter like a tamed lion walks,
Descending from the mountain to make sport
Among the cottages by beds of flowers.
(VI.462–68)

This typological allegory follows Coxe closely: he also noted that the five glaciers are 'separated from each other by forests, corn-fields, and meadows': a sequence exactly repeated in Wordsworth's 'leafy trees . . . yellow sheaf . . . haycock in the sun.'[21] But this *Prelude* picture sits rather uneasily next to *Descriptive Sketches*' earlier version of what Wordsworth saw there:

At such an hour I heav'd the human sigh,
When roar'd the sullen Arve in anger by,
That not for thee, delicious vale! unfold

Thy reddening orchards, and thy fields of gold;
That thou, the slave of slaves, art doom'd to pine,
While no Italian arts their charms combine
To teach the skirt of thy dark cloud to shine;
For thy poor babes that, hurrying from the door,
With pale-blue hands, and eyes that fix'd implore
Dead muttering lips, and hair of hungry white,
Besiege the traveller whom they half affright.

(702–12)

This earlier version, though poetically awkward, is keenly observed human reality, its last four lines stunningly *sur*real, from an obviously frightened young poet. 'Dead muttering lips, and hair of hungry white' is a line to conjure with, not explain. The poetic diction of the loco-descriptive mode here profits by its artificiality, projecting landscape sights that the 'affrighted traveller' feels *should not be* in the landscape: this was not the kind of *blanc* he had come so far to see. No doubt the little girl is better off when transmuted into the maiden spreading her haycock in the sun. But the focus of Wordsworth's grief has shifted entirely in the interim, from 'a human sigh' for poverty to a disappointed expectation of sublime scenery.

CHAPTER TEN

Golden Days and Giddy Prospects

The 1790 Walking Tour: Switzerland and Italy

> . . . and such a summer night
> Did to that pair of golden days succeed,
> With now and then a doze and snatch of sleep
> (VI.654-56)

Lost in Sublimity

Their second touristic mission completed, Wordsworth and Jones returned to Martigny and reclaimed their knapsacks. Resuming their course up the Rhône next morning, they passed through Sion and came to Brig on 16 August. 'At Brig we quitted the Valais and passed the Alps at Semplon [sic] *in order to visit part of Italy*.'[1] Wordsworth's contemporary words are important, especially their matter-of-factness, because he subsequently built so much on – and beyond – the facts of what happened on 17 August 1790. *The Prelude* records a visionary experience of imaginative power, stimulated by Wordsworth's delayed realization 'that we had crossed the Alps' without realizing it. The highest point of their tour was missed by an act of consciousness which failed to register a fact of physical perception. His account of crossing the Simplon Pass has achieved a nearly iconic status, almost completely separated from its surrounding textual and historical environments. Wordsworth's crossing the Alps unawares is as important in the development of European Romantic culture as Goethe's trip to Italy in 1786, as Byron and the Shelleys' summer on Lake Geneva in 1816, or – since Wordsworth uses the same kind of rhetoric to describe it – as Paul's vision on the road to Damascus. But an account of the creation of the Poet requires that we restore as much as possible its enabling contexts.

Year by year, revision by revision, Wordsworth steadily raised the level of the tour's meaning for him, from his letter to Dorothy in 1790, through his 1792 composition of *Descriptive Sketches* (published 1793), through his

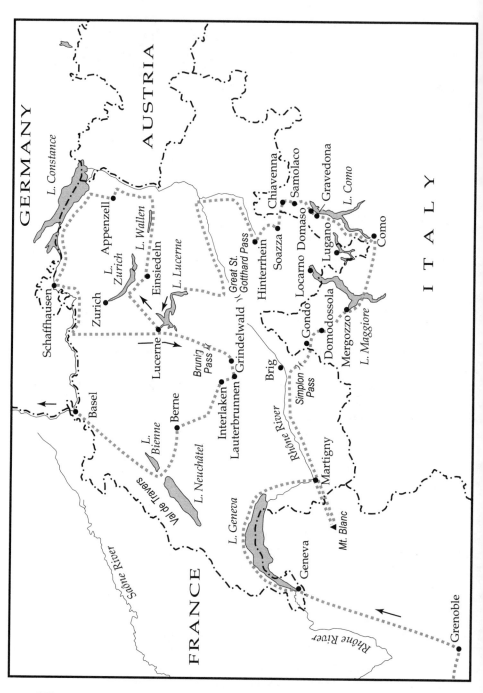

'Thence onward to the country of the Swiss': Wordsworth's and Jones's
route through Switzerland, July–August 1790

extensive (but unpublished) revisions of that poem in 1794, into his rewriting of the whole tour in 1804 for the 1805 *Prelude*, and beyond, to his 1808 drafting of the Grande Chartreuse passage and his 1816–1819 incorporation of it into *The Prelude*, to his preparations for a return pilgrimage with Dorothy and Mary in 1820, and finally into his composition of *Memorials of a Tour on the Continent, 1820*, published in 1822. These revisions are a paradigm of the way Wordsworth's imagination worked, and the 1790 tour is a paradigm for the kinds of experiences it worked upon.

But his contemporary letter to Dorothy makes clear that they were not crossing the Simplon primarily to have an Alpine experience; the thought foremost in his mind was simply to cross over into Italy. They were heading for their third main goal, the Italian Lake District. Their source-authority, Coxe, had added an extensive segment on the Italian lakes to his revised edition of his *Sketches,* and Wordsworth wanted to include it. As he and Jones toiled up the road from Brig, they were less concerned with an Alpine crossing than with whether they might get to Lake Maggiore by nightfall. This was one of their longest daily jaunts, a basis for Wordsworth's boast to Dorothy, that 'We have several times performed a journey of thirteen leagues [approximately thirty-nine miles] over the most mountainous parts of Swisserland, without any more weariness, than if we had been walking an hour in the groves of Cambridge.' But nearly a quarter of their time and distance on this day was taken up with wandering around, lost, near the top of the pass.

To climb from Brig to the top of the Simplon pass, a distance of sixteen linear miles (and 1300 vertical metres), is a matter of a long morning's walk. Baedeker recommends five hours for modern all-purpose hikers, but young men 'in prime of youthful strength' could do it faster, after a month of on-road conditioning. Wordsworth and Jones joined in with a troop of muleteers who were travelling 'along the road that leads to Italy,' as he says in 1805, revising it in 1850 to, 'the Simplon's steep and rugged road,' one of a number of revisions by which the 1805 text is altered to dramatize the experience, blurring the fact that in 1790 it was not conceived as such a *meta*physical crossing. They had little communication with the muleteers because the local dialects of French, German-Swiss, and Italian were terribly mixed up at such border-crossing junctions; Wordsworth's phrase, 'making of them our guide,' suggests the boys just tagged along behind.

After 'a length of hours,' sometime around noon, they stopped for lunch, 'having reached an inn among the mountains' (498–99). Just where Wordsworth had lunch on 17 August 1790, is a matter of some critical importance, for all the available evidence, as well as common sense and empirical observation, suggests that they were already at the top, or well past it – 'that [we] had crossed the Alps' – by the time they stopped for lunch. A small but significant difference would have been created in the history of European romanticism if one of the muleteers had happened to say, 'Okay, boys, we're just now coming to the top of the pass.' Again Wordsworth's revisions are revealing, for he does not mention the inn in 1850, saying only, 'We reached a halting place.'[2] Inns in mountain passes tend to be at the top, unless the way is very long – as it is not, here. There are two places where they might have stopped for lunch, either the spital erected by Kaspar Stockalper a hundred years earlier, or the inn in Simplon Village. But both of these places are well past the top of the pass: the spital two miles, the inn another four miles further on – and 500 metres lower down. Even if Wordsworth and Jones could not communicate with the churlish muleteers, they were both mountain boys and could hardly have misinterpreted the meaning of the relief they felt in their muscles as they eased their legs under 'the board' at noon. Their eagerness for sensation may have led them to doubt the evidence of their senses, for the Simplon, like the other great Alpine passes, does not look very dramatic at the top, being a 'wide, level glacial terrace.'[3] Wordsworth's language in both versions makes perfectly clear that they were already on the downhill slope. Taking their time over their leisurely lunch, they got up to pursue their erstwhile guides: 'we followed, / *Descending* by the beaten road' (1850: 'the beaten downward way').

Now their real mountaintop experience began, and it had to do not with *crossing* but with being lost. This loss quickly ramified in Wordsworth's mind into thoughts of losing one's way more generally, or even losing one's mind. The road, though 'beaten', was nothing like a highway.

> . . . the beaten road . . . led
> Right to a rivulet's edge, and there broke off;
> The only track now visible was one
> Upon the further side, right opposite
> And up a lofty mountain.
>
> (VI.502-06)[4]

The road *down* the mountain ran in the stream bed for a while, which in summer was useable as a road bed, particularly since its usual passengers were sure-footed mules and muleteers, not touring foreign gentlemen. The two Englishmen, not grasping this bit of local economy, crossed the stream and followed the upward path to a nearby mountain village.[5] Their misstep is easy to understand because the correct downward path swerves sharply left into the Gondo Gorge, while another path runs straight up a hill directly opposite the point at which the downward path entered the stream bed.

They crossed the stream and continued upward – or rather, since they had clearly already been 'descending . . . downward,' they changed course upwards. What they climbed was 'a lofty mountain' only by the courtesy that anything at this height might be called 'lofty'; it was steep, but it did not prevent them from 'climb[ing] with eagerness.' They continued on for three or four miles, the better part of an hour, and 'at length' their eagerness gave way to 'surprize and some anxiety / On finding that we did not overtake / Our comrades gone before.' The muleteers had not been very friendly before, but now, travelling without them, they suddenly seemed like lost 'comrades.'

Eventually, coming in sight of some huts they met a peasant, and after the double difficulty of discovering in a foreign language that they were lost in a foreign place, they figured out that the right road lay back down in the stream bed and, coincidentally, 'that we had crossed the Alps.' (524). Modern scholarship has made clear that the apostrophe to 'Imagination!' which interrupts *The Prelude*'s narrative at this point (VI.525–48) is the product of emotion recollected in the tranquillity of composition fourteen years later. The final version imagines all of human imaginative life as an endlessly rewarding mountain climb to infinity: 'our home is with infinitude – and only there.'

His confusion was real enough in 1790, though not yet formulated in such high language. To Dorothy, he said simply, 'The impressions *of three hours of* our walk among the Alps will never be effaced' (italics added). These three hours, so central to the definition of Romanticism as a faith in the transcendental powers of the human imagination, can be pinpointed as the three hours after lunch on 17 August 1790. If they walked four miles before meeting the peasant, one hour was lost in each direction, and the third hour in confusions before and after – or in the Gondo Gorge, for which Baedeker allows one and a quarter hours, though Wordsworth says it took them 'several hours at a slow step.' Thirty years later, the force of this intensely meaningful experience remained, when he found, again somewhat accidentally, the place where he had got lost thirty years before. Dorothy said it was 'impossible for me to say' how much seeing that little 'upright path . . . on the green precipice' moved her brother, 'when he discovered it was the very same which had tempted him in his youth . . . [disappointing] the ambition of youth.'[6]

Back on track, they now entered the Gondo Gorge, for which Wordsworth produced one of the best descriptions of Alpine landscape ever recorded, a description heightened line by line with metaphors in which the imagination finally outstrips altogether its mountain passage:

> The immeasurable height
> Of woods decaying, never to be decayed,
> The stationary blasts of waterfalls,
> And everywhere along the hollow rent
> Winds thwarting winds, bewildered and forlorn,
> The torrents shooting from the clear blue sky,
> The rocks that muttered close upon our ears —

> Black drizzling crags that spake by the wayside
> As if a voice were in them—the sick sight
> And giddy prospect of the raving stream,
> The unfettered clouds and region of the heavens,
> Tumult and peace, the darkness and the light,
> Were all like workings of one mind, the features
> Of the same face, blossoms upon one tree,
> Characters of the great apocalypse,
> The types and symbols of eternity,
> Of first, and last, and midst, and without end.
>
> (VI.556–72)

His comment to Dorothy about this time was more orthodox: 'Among the more awful scenes of the Alps, I had not a thought of man, or a single created being; my whole soul was turned to him who produced the terrible majesty before me.'[7] Yet his description is not merely referential. His allusion to Milton's description of God in the concluding lines means that he saw – or projected – the face of God on this trip. 'Him first, him last, him midst, and without end' (*PL*, V.165).[8]

Besides being sublime, the Gondo Gorge was also very dangerous. The path was barely wide enough to walk on, and was so close to the raging stream – really one long waterfall – that it was frequently rendered impassable, or, in the case of sudden thaws or rainstorms, instantly fatal. A friend of Gray's left this record from 1777: 'You go across pastures and over rocks, over unstable, swaying bridges, past the ruins of older and better bridges [unnerving observation!] . . . the rock face towers high above you and down below seems gnawed away by the pounding waves of the wild Toggia. The pass leads over colossal threatening ruins. The river beside us was sometimes almost hidden by mountains, and sometimes it tumbled like smoke into hideous depths below.'[9]

This was the sort of thing Wordsworth had come expecting to see; the Gondo Gorge is the only place in the Simplon Pass that merits a 'must-see' star in modern touring guides. But his imagination, already prepared for disappointment by his experiences at the Grande Chartreuse and Mont Blanc, was not satisfied enough by the Gondo Gorge. In the interim, only three hours by the clock but an instantaneous mental 'flash' that revealed 'the invisible world,' he found by personal experience that the Sublime was located exactly where Kant had already logically deduced that it must be, without ever leaving the University of Königsberg: in the mind of man.

Coming out of the dark gorge at last, they spent the night at another one of Stockalper's old spitals, in Gondo village. Here the trauma Wordsworth experienced began to sweep over him.

> That night our lodging was an alpine house,
> An inn, or hospital (as they are named),

> Standing in that same valley by itself,
> And close upon the confluence of two streams —
> A dreary mansion, large beyond all need,
> With high and spacious rooms, deafened and stunned
> By noise of waters, making innocent sleep
> Lie melancholy among weary bones.
>
> (VI.573–80)

Wordsworth's last two lines – 'making innocent sleep / Lie melancholy among weary bones' – are extraordinarily good, and biographically significant. The image is finally one of a charnel house. Sleep is disembodied from their 'weary bones': the cliché is recast with ghastly literalness, so that the two travellers are represented as lying down among the bones of their own bodies. Dorothy participated in her brother's horror of this experience with all the power of her vicarious imagination. Returning to the spot thirty years later, Wordsworth flatly refused to enter the spital, and even Dorothy could not persuade him to do so. 'I regret not having the courage to pass the threshold alone. I had a strong desire to see what was going on within doors for the sake of *tales of thirty years gone by*; but could not persuade William to accompany me.'[10] If he would not enter, neither would she. We are clearly in the presence of some kind of trauma when a fifty-year-old man in the broad light of day and in the company of his family and friends, amid all the luxuries of a more modern, well-heeled tourism, refuses even to enter a house where he had waking nightmares thirty years earlier, even though his dearly beloved sister pleads with him to do so.

'Making innocent sleep / Lie melancholy among weary bones.' Of what were they 'innocent,' and why? The lines contain an allusion from *Macbeth*, when Macbeth is trying to recoup his courage for the murder of Duncan, after funking his first attempt.

> Methought I head a voice cry 'Sleep no more,
> Macbeth doth murder sleep' — the innocent sleep,
> Sleep that knits up the ravelled sleeve of care,
> The death of each day's life, sore labour's bath,
> Balm of hurt minds, great nature's second course,
> Chief nourisher in life's feast —
>
> (II.ii.33–38)

Lady Macbeth brusquely interrupts him to ask, 'What do you mean?' No allusion is innocent in Wordsworth, and especially not this one, for more than 'innocent sleep' was murdered that night in Gondo village. Wordsworth's youthful innocence had been done in, by the disappointment of his own misplaced hopes. Everything that Macbeth laments he (Wordsworth) also needed: 'sore labour's bath,' 'balm of hurt minds,' 'great nature's second course.' His *mind* was hurt: what else is trauma? In ways as yet unclear to him, the whole motivation of Wordsworth's trip was being superseded, and he had invested – or squandered – a lot in following that motive. The tour was turning out to be disappointing, not in his uncles' terms, but in his own: not mountains, not 'mighty forms,' not the highest point in the natural world would give a 'charter' to his hopes. Somehow, his own mind would have to do so.

Yet if Wordsworth's consciousness could lose itself beyond recognition on the top of the Alps, then no *place* was safe for human consciousness, no place on earth: his mind was alienated from the earth on which it dwelt. Yet at this moment, his whole life was invested in the idea that Nature *could* underwrite his hopes, that 'great nature's second course' was always forthcoming, that there would always be a way or a path one could follow. If not, where will the mind go, or dwell, then? 'Apocalypse is not habitable,' Wordsworth would eventually see.[11] But his imagination could find no habitation in the Gondo spital, only a charnel house in which to rest his weary bones – the death of his 'innocent' youthful ambitions.

After Gondo Gorge, the Borromean islands are the next 'must see' sight for anyone following this route. They were highly artifical beauties, especially Isola Bella, which had been developed by Count Borromeo in the seventeenth century to approximate a Renaissance earthly paradise. A hundred years later, Wordsworth was seeing it at its natural best, for though the buildings were run down, the plantings had grown to magnificent effect, frequently compared to the Garden of Eden and the Hanging Gardens of Babylon.[12] Earthly paradises began to run much in Wordsworth's mind over the next two or three days. His descriptions of his entire tour, with their deep Miltonic substratum, veer back and forth between presenting it as a trip through Paradise, or one through Hell; soon this fundamental ambivalence began to show up in his actions, and rose to trouble the surface of his verse.

Rather than go north or south around Maggiore to get to Como, either route prodigiously long and circuitous, Wordsworth and Jones continued right across the lake to reach the other side on 19 August.[13] Years later he twitted some fatuous aristocrats in the Lake District for over-praising Windermere relative to Maggiore, Como, Geneva and Zurich – all points on his 1790 itinerary. He fired off some good comic rhymes based on his own experience: 'And [I've] seen the Simplon's forehead hoary / Reclined on the Lago Maggiore.'[14] It's always heartening to see Wordsworth able to laugh at himself, but the next two lines were not meant to be funny: 'At breathless eventide at rest / On the broad water's placid breast.' This position was perfectly appropriate both to his itinerary and his state of mind, drifting out across Maggiore on the 19th to look back up at Simplon's 'forehead hoary', another 'feature of the same face' that had scared him so badly two days earlier – all the more so as he was beginning to realize that the face he saw in the picture was not God's but his own.

Lost in Beauty

Coming to Lake Como the next day, Wordsworth and Jones had 'a pair of golden days' and two terrible nights. Or maybe not so terrible. Their visit to Como was intended to provide them with a real-life experience of ideal Beauty, to complement the Sublime of the Alps. About the latter Wordsworth could as yet say little, because he had not found it where he expected to. But he wrote at length to Dorothy about the beautiful effects of light and shade they saw on Como's shores as they passed along its 'pathways roofed with vines,' heading back up toward Switzerland. 'The lake is narrow and the shadows of the mountains were early thrown across it. It is beautiful to watch them travelling up the sides of the hill for several hours, to remark one half of a village covered with shade, and the other bright with the strongest sunshine.' Wordsworth's experiences seemed at last to match perfectly the expectations raised by Coxe. But where Coxe digressed into the region's military history, Wordsworth skirts close to his own sexual history.

The beauties he enjoyed at Como were not only those of the mountains and the lake, but also of the 'dark-ey'd maids' he saw there. That single phrase is all *The Prelude* says on the subject of women there, unless we press a bit on the Miltonic allusion in Wordsworth's metaphor for it: 'a darling bosomed up / In Abyssinian privacy' (591–92). Milton's line, 'where Abassin kings their issue guard' (*PL* IV.280), is about the Garden of Eden, which had come into Wordsworth's mind at Lake Maggiore, but any thoughts about bosoms and darlings were entirely his own. However, Milton is speaking of Satan's leering 'delight' at all he saw in Eden, especially the two creatures he spied on in their 'naked majesty' there, and Wordsworth's account of himself in *Descriptive Sketches* gives many indications that his experience at Lake Como had more to do with Satan's voyeurism in Eden than with the garden he presents in *The Prelude*. Like Satan, he was invisible – 'viewless' (*DS*, 92) – there, looking at the 'dark-ey'd maids' and questions of seduction, fall and ruin were very much on his mind as it ran through the various texts and subtexts which this adventure produced over the next thirty years.

Writing to Dorothy, he said nothing about dark-eyed maidens, but much about his mind's running 'thro a thousand dreams of happiness which might be enjoyed upon its banks, if heightened by conversation and the exercise of the social affections.'[15] This was yet another expression of their dream of living together some day on a lake somewhere, but it was not only that, nor did the thought arise merely from landscape. Passing along the lakeshore on 21 and 22 August, Wordsworth found himself increasingly attracted by the girls he saw, until, sometime between the mornings of the 22nd and 23rd, he parted company with Jones and went to seek one out. What happened then is a matter of conjecture, though Wordsworth seems to have been disappointed, or shamed, in his quest. But we can follow his long paper trail with some confidence to place him in such a spot at that time. The following account could be presented as a straightforward narrative ('he went there, he did this'), but to really appreciate the complex processes of Wordsworth's self-creation it is better to track his manuscript revisions and erasures, not just the paths he took alongside Lake Como.

In *Descriptive Sketches*, his account of the Como sequence of his tour (ll.80–175) swerves erratically between two topics, attractive landscapes and attractive dancing girls, with the landscapes repeatedly coming back into the narrative to correct the sensual lines of fantasy the girls stimulate in his mind. In fact, Wordsworth dropped nearly half of the lines from the 1793 version describing these girls, and drastically toned down those that remained when he first reprinted excerpts from the poem in his collected *Poems* of 1815. He further truncated these passages when he republished the entire poem in 1836 as a specimen of his juvenile work. And in *The Prelude*, as we have seen, they are reduced to a single phrase and a Miltonic allusion.

But it is not only the negative evidence of later revisions that suggests what is going on in these lines. We find it also in the proposed additions Wordsworth made in the margins and between the lines of his published poem in late 1793 and early 1794.[16] These revisions – never printed by him – give much more detailed physical descriptions of the girls, and of their effect on the willpower of the narrator who spies on them.

> The viewless lingerer hence, at evening, sees
> From rock-hewn steps the sail between the trees;
> Or marks, mid opening cliffs, fair dark-ey'd maids
> Tend the small harvest of their garden glades,
> Or, led by distant warbling notes, surveys,
> *With hollow ringing ears and darkening gaze,*
> *Binding the charmed soul in powerless trance,*
> Lip-dewing Song and ringlet-tossing Dance,
> Where sparkling eyes and breaking smiles illume
> The bosom'd cabin's lyre-enliven'd gloom.
>
> (92–101; italics added)

The last six lines, describing a glowering lust so strong that it hurts, disappear entirely in 1815. But in 1794, Wordsworth added to the passage at various points, 'the panting dance's neck revealing maze,' 'dewy lips prolong the magic strain / That locks in powerless trance the swimming brain,' concluding,

> Yes, sweet languor here the failing soul involves
> That from the best might steal their best resolves
> While breathe soft amorous wishes[17]

The next description is explicit enough as it stands:

> Soft bosoms breathe around contagious sighs,
> And amorous music on the water dies.
> Heedless how Pliny, musing here, survey'd
> Old Roman boats and figures thro' the shade,
> Pale Passion, overpower'd, retires and woos
> The thicket, where th'unlisten'd stock-dove coos.
>
> (114–19)

Wordsworth evidently thought this was too explicit, because he cut all but the first two lines in 1815 and 1836, since they retain the appropriately censorious notion of '*contagious* sighs.' Pliny the Younger appears here not simply because he was born on Como, but to represent a stern figure of Roman stoic virtue to shame, by contrast, 'Pale Passion, overpower'd.' And what *is* that personified figure of Passion retiring to do in that thicket, ostentatiously *not* listening to the stock-dove? Hard not to listen to a bird; harder still to 'woo' a thicket. The artificiality of the verse allows several interpretations, from pure lust or sheer fantasy, through flirtation or casual dancing, to masturbation or an actual sexual encounter, successful or otherwise.

Finally, we come to the climax:

> Farewell! those forms that, in thy noon-tide shade,
> Rest, near their little plots of wheaten glade;

[Clearly these are the same girls he saw earlier.]

> Those stedfast eyes, that beating breasts inspire
> To throw the 'sultry ray' of young Desire;
> Those lips, whose tides of fragrance come, and go,
> Accordant to the cheek's unquiet glow;
> Those shadowy breasts in love's soft light array'd,
> And rising, by the moon of passion sway'd.
> — Thy fragrant gales and lute-resounding streams,
> Breathe o'er the failing soul voluptuous dreams;
> While Slavery, forcing the sunk mind to dwell
> On joys that might disgrace the captive's cell,
> Her shameless timbrel shakes along thy marge,
> And winds between thine isles the vocal barge.
>
> (148–61)

Sultry rays, young desires, lips and breasts – all these are gone from this passage in 1815, but the last four lines remain because, like 'contagious sighs,' they contain their own moral censor, being a reference to the exploited social condition of the northern Italians under Austrian domination.

This 'sunk mind' is another attribute of the 'failing soul' musing on these girls. He feels tempted by their slavery, their easy availability, and is ashamed of himself as a result. The 1794 additions make the 1793 text's allusion to the casual prostitution of oppressed women more particular, and draw the 'sunk mind' much closer to its objects of desire: 'those eyes' become 'dark eyes,' and the lips' 'tides of fragrance' are, additionally, 'soft.' The 1794 additions also intensify the earlier statement about the threat of disaster for 'the best' that lurks in all this reckless beauty: 'Charms which in powerless trance the *wisest* view / Robb'd of their resolves all adieu.'[18] Farewell, that is, to all the high resolves I have begun to form for my life.

If we arrange all these alternating sequences of descriptions and reactions – from his contemporaneous letter to Dorothy and his later drafts and revisions of *Descriptive Sketches* and *The Prelude* – into a narrative sequence, we come close to what might have happened to Wordsworth on Lake Como between 20 and 23 August 1790.[19] On their second or third night along the lake Wordsworth and Jones were separated, by a thunderstorm (they said), and spent the night in two different towns, the only time they were apart during the entire tour. 'Interestingly enough, Wordsworth did not describe the mishap at the head of Lake Como in his letter to his sister Dorothy, just as he did not detail the mistaken path at the Simplon Pass.'[20] His omissions of these two incidents, one the apex of the frustrated Sublime, the other the nadir of frustrating Beauty, is indeed interesting.

The usual account is that on the night of 21 August, their second night along the lake, in the town of Gravedona, Wordsworth and Jones got up by mistake at 1:45 a.m. (i.e., early morning of the 22nd) and set off, aiming to 'behold the scene in its most deep repose' (VI.628–29). They wanted to see the sunrise on the lake. They heard four chimes and thought it was 4 a.m., not realizing that the local church bells rang once for the hour and once for each quarter. 'Coasting the water's edge as hitherto,' they 'soon were lost, bewildered among woods immense,' and had to sit on a rock overlooking the lake to wait for daybreak, a night whose terror Wordsworth described in Miltonic cadences and images that approach the power of his Gondo Gorge description:

> On the rock we lay
> And wished to sleep, but could not for the stings
> Of insects, which with noise like that of noon
> Filled all the woods. The cry of unknown birds,

The mountains—more by darkness visible
And by their own size, than any outward light —
The breathless wilderness of clouds, the clock
That told with unintelligible voice
The widely parted hours, the noise of streams,
And sometimes rustling motions nigh at hand
Which did not leave us free from personal fear,
And lastly, the withdrawing moon that set
Before us while she still was high in heaven —

(641–53)

These, he concludes, amazed at the contrast, 'were our food' that succeeded the 'pair of golden days' they had just had on that 'same delicious lake.' But was it only the clocks that confused them, or were they, as in the Gondo spital, 'unable to sleep from other causes'?

One notices immediately his convincing specificity, and his refusal to assign a pat meaning to this experience. Milton's seducing archangel was again on his mind when he composed these lines in 1804, not only in the well-known tag phrase, 'darkness visible,' but also in his archaic diction for their progress, 'coasting the water's edge,' which echoes Satan's nefarious approach to Paradise: 'Coasting the wall of heav'n on this side Night' (*PL* III.71). One thing seems clear: unpleasant as the experience was, it was not raining.[21] Therefore, if they were separated in a rainstorm, it must have been during the coming day or night, 22 August.

On the 22nd, Wordsworth stayed behind at Samolaco, the last town on the lake, while Jones went on ahead to Chiavenna, some ten miles further up. The explanation usually supplied is that they were separated by a thunderstorm and spent the night wandering in the woods between Gravedona and Chiavenna, a distance of more than twenty miles. But Dorothy's journal of 1820 gives three slightly different accounts of the misadventure, and it is not clear whether she refers to this incident outside Gravedona or to a subsequent one – or if they are both part of the same incident.

First she says she was interested in Gravedona 'for the sake of an adventure of our youthful Travellers recorded by my brother in the poem on his own life. They were parted in a thunder storm, and wandered all night in the forest between Gravedona and Chiavenna.'[22] The first sentence fits with the *Prelude* account, but the second doesn't: there, it is not raining, and they stay put. Dorothy's second account says that 'my Brother, when parted by mischance from his companion, had seen the moon hanging over the highest point of that same mountain [Colico], while bewildered in the forest on the opposite [i.e., west] side of the Lake.'[23] In this account they are separated and lost, and the appearance of the moon matches the *Prelude*'s account, but it does not seem to be raining. Finally, she speaks of a location closer to 'the upper small reach . . . called Chiavenna. The path my Brother had travelled, when bewildered in the night thirty years ago, was traceable through some parts of the forest on the opposite [west] side of the lake—then most dismal with thunder, lightning, and rain.'[24] Now it seems to have been raining very hard, and they are at a location near to, if not beyond, Samolaco, where Wordsworth is said to have spent the night.

Scholars have assumed that Dorothy made a mistake when she said that the incident of being separated in a thunderstorm appeared in 'the poem on his own life,' and it is easy to see how she might have conflated two incidents that may have occurred so close together. But barring the discovery of a manuscript which records such an incident, and given Dorothy's thrice-repeated emphasis on an event outside of Gravedona,[25] Wordsworth's account of their too-early rising and Dorothy's account of their being separated appear to refer to one and the same incident, or to two parts of an essentially single experience, running from 1:45 a.m. on 22 August to whatever time on the morning of the 23rd Wordsworth and Jones were reunited and continued on their way. If they stayed together till dawn, they were separated sometime before late afternoon, when they would have sought out lodgings. On the other hand, the only authority for its being a *rainstorm* that separated them is William's word to Dorothy.

What with one thing and another, these were two very disorienting days. If the storm started towards evening, they had plenty of time to reach Chiavenna before that.[26] Twenty miles in a day was nothing for these striders, and on this day of all days they had a *very* early start. It is possible that they lingered at the head of Lake Como before pushing on, but why should they linger there, and if the storm came on during the day, how could they get separated by it? Granted, it's possible. But it is nearly miraculous that they could have got lost, been reunited by word of mouth, and still left Chiavenna together in good time to cross back over the river and up the Forcola Pass to spend the next night (23 August) in the mountains at Soazza.

In *Descriptive Sketches*, these nights – if they *are* two nights – are in essence treated as one (201–42). But they are removed from their Como context, and attributed to the experience of the 'Grison gypsey' who appears next on their itinerary. The poem cannot be held to geographical accuracy or consistency, but the night outside Gravedona is unmistakeable in this passage: 'Heavy, and dull, and cloudy is the night . . . Glimmer the dim-lit Alps, dilated, round . . . insect buzz, that stuns the sultry woods . . . On viewless fingers counts the valley-clock,' and so on. Wordsworth introduces this passage with an equally unmistakeable thunderstorm, the details of which are taken from later parts of his tour. But their placement here tends to associate 'thunderstorm' with images that are clearly from the night, or nights, outside Gravedona, 21 or 22 August. He speaks of something disturbing the birds: 'and chattering breaks the night's respose' (230). (Compare 'the cry of unknown birds' from *The Prelude* [VI.644].) 'The bushes rustle near . . . with strange tinglings' (237–38), exactly as in *The Prelude*: 'sometimes rustling motions nigh at hand / Which did not leave us free from personal fear' (650–51). What are those 'strange tinglings'? Rhetorically, they are transferred epithets, describing a human reaction to a natural sound, like 'wooing' a thicket. This is one of only two occurences of the verb, to *tingle*, in Wordsworth's poetry, and the other comes in precisely the same kind of context: the 'slight shocks of young love-liking' he felt at the summer dances on Windermere, which 'mounted up like joy into the head / And tingled through the veins' (IV.325–27).[27] The wind is blowing – or somebody is walking – with sinister sound effects: 'the dry leaves stir as with the serpent's walk' (233).

Is Wordsworth again imagining the Garden of Eden, where one serpent actually could 'walk'? A quick check with Milton provides another uncanny confirmation that not only Milton, but also Milton's subject matter, is on Wordsworth's mind. For, turning to the place in *Paradise Lost* where Satan approaches Eve in serpent guise, we find: 'she busied heard the sound / Of rustling leaves but minded not' (*PL* IX.518–19). There too, a smooth-talking seducer in outlandish guise is approaching, and a woman is in danger. Wordsworth puts a sinister spin on his every perception; voices are heard, and attributed to 'Banditti.' His own fear, in *The Prelude*, is made the gypsy's fear, in *Descriptive Sketches*. But the gypsy is very likely a stand-in for another woman Wordsworth both lusted after and, as a result, feared or *feared for* at Lake Como, as he watched her 'with hollow ringing ears and darkening gaze,' and as he returned to approach her now. All this is lost in *The Prelude*, and displaced and disjointed in *Descriptive Sketches*, but it is recoverable. In *Descriptive Sketches*, he projects all these fears outward on to bears, bandits, and famished wolves coming to devour their prey. The complicated but intriguing textual evidence suggests that the spying, seducing Satanic figure is more in his mind than those poor dumb creatures of picturesque melodrama.

Hence it is worth considering, even if we cannot finally decide, in light of all Wordsworth's emotional and guilt-ridden language about Como's 'dark-ey'd maids,' that some kind of internal storm, corollary to – or substituting for – an external thunderstorm, led him to spend a night by himself and join up with Jones by appointment next day. The final passage in *Descriptive Sketches* does place him, alone, in the woods, visiting – or spying on – a 'far-off peasant's day-deserted home.' What he sees is a charming domestic scene that finally lays to rest all the preceding eroticism.

> Once did I pierce to where a cabin stood,
> The red-breast peace had bury'd it in wood,
> There, by the door a hoary-headed sire

> Touch'd with his wither'd hand an aged lyre;
> Beneath an old-grey oak as violets lie,
> Stretch'd at his feet with stedfast, upward eye,
> His children's children join'd the holy sound,
> A hermit—with his family all around.
>
> (168–75)

In these young faces we see again 'stedfast' eyes, but now they belong not to dark-eyed maids but to children listening to a 'holy sound.' A musical detail from the sexy dances – 'Where sparkling eyes and breaking smiles illume / *The bosom'd cabin's lyre-enliven'd gloom*' (100–01) – is repeated with a deadening difference: 'a hoary-headed sire / Touch'd with his wither'd hand an aged lyre.' The former cabin was 'bosom'd'; the latter, 'bury'd': two very different ways of being hidden.

Having come to the nadir of his sexual fantasies, where 'the sunk mind . . . dwell[s] on joys that might disgrace the captive's cell,' after hearing the 'shameless timbrel' of sexual slavery, he shakes these joys off for other images to restore his poem's moral equilibrium:

> I lov'd, mid thy most desert woods astray,
> With pensive steps to measure my slow way,[28]
> By lonely, silent cottage-doors to roam,
> The far-off peasant's day-deserted home;
> Once did I pierce to where a cabin stood . . .
>
> (164–68)

Taken literally, these lines indicate that he went to a peasant's cottage during the day, when he knew the man of the house would be away – and found a grandfather and his grandchildren instead. That this incident occurred on a Sunday – and the day he and Jones were parted was Sunday, 22 August – is suggested by lines preceding it, as well as by the 'holy sound' of the grandfather's lyre. The speaker is watching the lake very early in the morning, when it is 'still hid from morning's ray,' and hears 'the matin-bell / Calling the woodman from his desert-cell.' Wordsworth and Jones were certainly awake before dawn on that sleepless night. The woodman goes to church by boat, evidently passing near an observer who can hear him, but not see him, from the shore: 'the sound of oars, that pass, / Spotting the steaming deeps, to early mass.' The word 'desert-cell' links up with what seems like a repetitive tic in the following report, of 'The far-off peasant's day-*deserted* home.' That is to say, deserted *for the day*. Or, to put all bluntly, has Wordsworth watched his chance to go back to a cottage near a 'little plot of wheaten glade' where one particular girl caught his eye on the 21st?[29] And did he find instead, perhaps not without some relief, that she and the other adults were gone, leaving only the grandfather and grandchildren at home?

When he and his family returned to this neighbourhood in 1820, Wordsworth set off for a day's walk by himself. Or rather he set off with Henry Crabb Robinson but returned alone: 'and at 7 o'clock W. arrived enchanted with *his* rambles. He had found, high up on the hills, cottages within pastoral hollows, among groves of chestnut trees and olives – every cottage with its garden and vineyard. From those sequestered places he had descended by a direct road to the palace.'[30] This could be interpreted as the behaviour of a man well pleased with himself, who had 'lov'd,' thirty years before, 'mid thy most desert woods astray . . . by lonely, silent cottage-doors to roam,' and whose special enjoyment on his return tour was to search out places where he had got lost before. They certainly sound like the same kinds of places, and the way in which he found them, and returned from them ('descended . . . direct'), sounds as if he knew his way around the area. A return visit to a scene of sexual initiation would be hard to resist, given the time and opportunity, and especially given Wordsworth's fascination with his own development as the master-subject of his poetry.

In *The Prelude*, all this is generalized out on to the 'impassioned . . . beauty' of the landscape, in contrast to the specificity of *Descriptive Sketches* and the Gravedona passage. Fair enough: different poem, different time, different purposes. But to the extent that these biographical issues lie behind any account of his experiences on Lake Como, his apology in *The Prelude* for the 'undisciplined verse' he wrote about it in *Descriptive Sketches* sounds even more pompous than it already does, lacking any life context:

> . . . [Como:] ye have left
> Your beauty with me, an impassioned sight
> Of colours and of forms, whose power is sweet
> And gracious, almost, might I dare to say,
> As virtue is, or goodness—sweet as love,
> Or the remembrance of a noble deed,
> Or gentlest visitation of pure thought
> When God, the giver of all joy, is thanked
> Religiously in silent blessedness —
>
> (VI.607–15)

There's too much pious mumbling here, trying to link up beauty, passion and love with nobility, purity, and God. Not because the two groups of subjects are incompatible, but because the speaker seems to feel they are, with his awkward 'almost, might I dare to say.'

In *The Prelude* he simply stops here, but with language about where his poem is heading that we can now interpret as referring to the nature of the events he is recording as much as to the formal proportions of his poem:

> But here I must break off, and quit at once,
> Though loth, the record of these wanderings,
> A theme which may *seduce* me else beyond
> All reasonable bounds.
>
> (658–61; italics added)

In *The Prelude*, this statement refers to the proportions of his poem, the 'circuitous' path that led him to 'tender thoughts' about Lake Como. But in *Descriptive Sketches* and its various revisions and corollary texts, seduction is a temptation threatening the proper – 'reasonable' – course of his life.

Any real-life scenario constructed from these texts is of course subject to challenge as an overly ingenious reading of scenes and figures that are wholly conventional, especially in a poem as artificial as *Descriptive Sketches*. Yet Wordsworth is also the most literal and matter-of-fact of all major English poets. Like Gray, he wove the conventions of his genres into his own experience, but, being Wordsworth, and invention not his forte, the possibility that he is using literal representations of his own personal experiences is proportionately much higher. Given the various strands of evidence, the burden of disproving the scenario sketched here would seem to fall on those who want to maintain either the young Wordsworth's moral chastity, or his strict allegiance to the conventions of his genres.

A major shift occurs after Lake Como in both poems Wordsworth wrote about the 1790 tour, which further suggests that there was something critical about his experiences there. He and Jones were at this point precisely halfway through their itinerary: one month and eight days had passed, and one month and eight days remained, before their last recorded stopping-place, at Aix-la-Chapelle on the German-Belgian border. In *The Prelude*, the account of the tour finishes at this point, except for a brief reference to their final dash across Belgium, skipping all of Switzerland in between. In *Descriptive Sketches*, though only a quarter of the poem has passed, he shifts from the particularity of his first two sketches (Chartreuse and Como) to geographical and moral generalizations: from this point on, there are only a half dozen place-names, but much more moral allegory, drawn from the everyday lives of Swiss peasants, who are usually viewed from a considerable distance up on the mountains. Thus the two poems give different accounts of two separate parts of the tour. *The Prelude* concentrates almost entirely on the first, southern half of it, while *Descriptive Sketches*, after a detailed opening look at Chartreuse and Como, moves into Switzerland and spends most of its time on the second, northern half of the tour.

Going from Lake Como to Lake Lucerne, there was only one way to go, dictated by the rivers and passes through the mountains. They crossed over the Forcola Pass on 23 August. Crossing the San Bernardino Pass at 2805 metres, they came down into Hinterrhein, cradle of 'th'indignant waters of the infant Rhine.' For four days they followed first one, then the other of the Rhine's source-streams (Hinter and Vorder), up through the Via Mala, whose name stimulated Wordsworth to a heavy allegory about 'life's long deserts with its charge of woe,' in which their collegiate summer walking tour suddenly becomes part of 'a mighty caravan of pain,' representing all of human life.

Coming down along the Vorderrhein on 26 August, they crossed without comment the taxing Oberalp Pass, arriving at the base of the Great St Gotthard on 27 August. Alpine mountain crossings were becoming routine.

They reached Lake Lucerne the next day, a week after leaving Lake Como. Moving out into the 'open vale serene' of Urseren (a name combining the canton, Uri, with its habitual adjective), Wordsworth paints an Alpine scene of almost complete generality: 'On as we move, a softer prospect opes, / Calm huts, and lawns between, and sylvan slopes.' But it was on 'Uri's lake' (Lucerne) that Wordsworth painted the sunset that is the poem's best descriptive sketch, and that was immediately recognized as such when it was read by Samuel Coleridge three years later in an undergraduate discussion group at Cambridge that included the poet's brother.

> . . . the Sun walking on his western field
> Shakes from behind the clouds his flashing shield.
> Triumphant on the bosom of the storm,
> Glances the fire-clad eagle's wheeling form;
> Eastward, in long perspective glittering, shine
> The wood-crown'd cliffs that o'er the lake recline;
> Wide o'er the Alps a hundred streams unfold,
> At once to pillars turn'd that flame with gold;
> Behind his sail the peasant strives to shun
> The west that burns like one dilated sun,
> Where in a mighty crucible expire,
> The mountains, glowing hot, like coals of fire.
>
> (336–47)

Coleridge, writing years later with the undimmed enthusiasm of hindsight, declared that 'seldom, if ever, was the emergence of an original poetic genius above the literary horizon more evidently announced.'[31] But though this apocalyptic passage is indeed the best thing in the poem, Coleridge also noted that it 'demanded a greater closeness of attention, than poetry, (at all events, than descriptive poetry) has a right to claim.' Many admirers of Wordsworth's 'nature poetry' have consistently ignored this apt observation. Coleridge had recognized what Wordsworth was only beginning to sense in 1790, that his poetry did not describe landscapes, but the mind at work on them.

From Lake Lucerne they crossed over to Zurich to visit the convent of Einsiedeln. This was only the second cultural monument they sought out on the tour, and Wordsworth's empathy with the credulous pilgrims coming to the Black Madonna is similar to his plea that the Chartreuse might be spared from revolutionary violence: 'Oh give me not that eye of hard disdain / That views undimm'd Einsiedlen's [sic] wretched fane.' When he says that 'there are [those] who love to stray' out at evening to watch the pilgrims, he's referring to himself: 'I forlorn dejected weary slow / A pilgrim wandering round this world of woe.'[32] His note on the little outdoor sheds provided for the pilgrims combines, in effect, two versions of himself: 'Under these sheds the sentimental traveller and the philosopher may find interesting sources of meditation.' The pilgrims were neither sentimental nor philosophical, but he was both, and very much in transit from the first role to the second at precisely this moment.

Leaving Einsiedeln on 1 September, they spent a day and two nights 'visiting the romantic valley of Glarus,'[33] only their fourth two-night stay in fifty days. From Glarus they skirted Lake Wallen (Walensee) and turned north again along the Rhine to reach Lake Constance on 6 September. The sight to see at Lake Constance was the Rhinefall near Schaffhausen, west of Konstanz, to which they dutifully proceeded. In what had become by now a regular pattern, they were again disappointed. By now he could recognize what was happening: anything he hoped for (Mont Blanc, the Simplon Pass) would be less grand in reality than what it was in imagination. Conversely, those places where he had not expected much often surprised him, not because of the scenery but because of the *people* there – the French *fédérés*, the Como dancers.

They dropped back south into the heart of Switzerland, returning to Lucerne on 10 September. Then they undertook a westward circuit, past Interlaken's twin lakes to Neuchatel and Bienne, Rousseau country. They re-entered 'the very heart of the high Alps at Grindelwald and Lauterbrunnen.'[34] The next four days were the centre of their purest *Alpine* experience, as they passed in sight of the splendid mountains whose names Wordsworth explained by using Cumbrian equivalents: 'As Schreck-horn, the pike of terror. Wetter-horn the pike of storms, &c. &c.'[35] The smaller lakes they passed, Sarnen and Lugern, also put him in mind of home: 'Those two lakes have always interested me especially, from bearing in their size and other features, a resemblance to the North of England.'[36]

On 12 September they passed over the Brunig Pass into Unterwalden, a crossing 'well remembered by my brother; he and his companion, owing to the jealousies and disorders of the French Revolution [were] rudely treated by persons stationed there.'[37] As foreigners, and obviously not aristocrats, they were taken as fellow-travellers in the modern sense. Wordsworth drew an invidious contrast between the beauty of the country and its people, 'with regard to manners.' He had come to Switzerland nurturing a Rousseauistic fantasy about direct correlations between man and nature: 'my partiality to Swisserland excited by its natural charms induces me to hope that the manners of its inhabitants are amiable.' But now a different kind of correlation has been suggested to his mind: 'I cannot help frequently contrasting them to the French,' whose absence of class-feeling had so impressed him a month earlier: 'that politeness diffused thro the lower ranks had an air so engaging, that you could scarce attribute it to any other cause than real benevolence.' But he realized that this new class *un*consciousness came from a deeper cause than nationality: 'I must remind you that we crossed it at the time when the whole nation was mad with joy, in consequence of the revolution.'[38]

Posting his journal letter from Berne on the 16th, he and Jones headed for their final goal, the lakes of Neuchatel and Bienne, Rousseau's visionary haunts. They rowed out to the Isle of St Pierre in the lake of Bienne, where Rousseau sought refuge in 1763 from a mob, and which he lovingly memorialized both in his *Confessions* and *The Reveries of a Solitary Walker*.[39] The island becomes, in Rousseau's representation of it, the very symbol of his imaginative project – which is to say, of himself:

> . . . the ardent desire I had to end my days in that island, was inseparable from the apprehension of being obliged to leave it. I felt a singular pleasure in seeing the waves break at my feet. I formed of them in my imagination the image of the tumult of the world contrasted with the peace of my habitation, and this pleasing idea sometimes softened me even to tears. . . .[40]

Here at last – and perhaps saved for last – was a cultural monument that was simultaneously a natural beauty, and one that piqued a more than merely historical interest in Wordsworth's mind, thinking of all the islands in Windermere he had so often rowed out to with his 'minstrel' friends, and of the melancholy Reverend Braithwaite watching the little waves of Esthwaite break at the foot of his yew-tree seat.

Reaching Basel early on the morning of 21 September, they bought a boat and set out down the Rhine the next day. Their aim was to travel north until they were due east of the Channel ports and then strike out cross-country again. They spent a week on the river, selling their boat at Cologne and spending their last recorded itinerary night at Aix-la-Chapelle on 29 September.

More danger awaited them when they disembarked. As luck would have it, on this incredible trip for coincidences, they walked right through another country torn by revolution and counterrevolution. A Belgian revolution had risen up in imitation of the French, and the République des

Etats-Unis been declared in January of 1790, the first independent Belgian republic.

Wordsworth saw only the Belgian, optimistic half of this, and his account of it stresses that he knew little about the details of politics, which was true enough at the time:

> We crossed the Brabant armies on the fret
> For battle in the cause of Liberty.
> A stripling, scarcely of the household then
> Of social life, I looked upon these things
> As from a distance—heard, and saw, and felt,
> Was touched but with no intimate concern —
>
> (691–96)

Wordsworth exaggerated this enthusiasm in order to distance himself from it – 'I needed not that joy' – because by 1804 he was attuning himself to a deeper joy in nature. But vague references to 'the cause of Liberty' were his wisest course here, anyway, since the reasons for the Brabançonne (Brabant) Revolution of December 1789 were very murky, politically. It was in large part an aristocratic and clerical *conservative* reaction against the relatively enlightened religious policies of the Austrians, and the constitution adopted on 11 July included no declaration of the rights of man or provisions for religious freedom. The new Holy Roman emperor, Leopold II (1747–1792), soon decided to restore law and order. He retook some provinces in the summer, and early in October, just as Wordsworth and Jones were crossing the territory, he was marshalling his forces for a decisive assault on the capital. Leopold was 'perhaps the only Hapsburg ruler who was a genuine constitutionalist'.[41] On the other hand, he was the brother of Marie Antoinette and no republican, so Wordsworth's pose of distant naïveté was a shrewd one.

Having entered France on the very day of her feast of federation, Wordsworth left Belgium just in the days that its brief feast of *apparent* republican enthusiasm was about to be spoiled. Between July and October of 1790, the fortunes of republican revolutions began to shift in less optimistic directions, and William Wordsworth and Robert Jones walked through or around much of it. One thing above all the tour left in Wordsworth's heart: the desire to get back to France as soon as possible, though in the event it took a year's doing – and undoing – to bring it about.

PART II

OF THE MAN

1790–1799

CHAPTER ELEVEN

The Mighty City

London, 1791

> O, blank confusion, and a type not false
> Of what the mighty city is itself . . . !
>   (VII.696–97)

Disembarking at Dover, Wordsworth had planned to unwind for a few weeks with Dorothy at Forncett. In a letter from Basel about 21 September, he said he would be home in two or three weeks, with 'no necessity for me to be in Cambridge before the 10th of Novbr.' This was the last possible date at which he, as a thorough 'term trotter', could still meet the residency requirement. Disingenuously, he hoped that his uncle Cookson, knowing that he had 'given up all thoughts of a fellowship . . . may perhaps not be so much displeased at this journey.'[1]

Who was he kidding? Had he forgotten that he had left the country three months earlier without telling a soul, knowing how 'mad' his adventure seemed to anyone who cared for him? His optimistic self-presentation was diverging more and more from the perspective of his elders. If the Cooksons had welcomed him for a visit, they would have appeared to condone the madcap jaunt which had put the final tap to their ward's fellowship hopes, the very fellowship that Cookson had vacated – and connived to keep open for two years – so that his nephew could get it. There would be no friendly homecoming at Forncett.

So, after stopping briefly in London to present Richard with his next request for funds, he returned to Cambridge around 20 October.[2] As 'Questionists,' fourth-year men only had to be in residence for the term before their final exam in January. Instead of delicately conveying the raptures of his European experience to Dorothy, Wordsworth spent most of the next six weeks 'exulting' over his friends, triumphing in the success of the scheme which they had scoffed at. His bragging was not attractive, and he did not enjoy the popular success that William Frend had won the previous year for his 'revolution' tour. But Jones's good humour helped soften Wordsworth's hard edges, and the occasion was an excellent excuse for parties with their lively social group. At least he paid for many of the toasts, for he settled a wine bill of over five pounds with Messrs. Wilkinson & Crossthwaite on 6 November.[3]

After six weeks of non-stop celebrations, he travelled fifty miles north through Newmarket and Thetford to Forncett for the Christmas holidays. The Cooksons' displeasure had cooled enough to make the visit acceptable. It was after all vacation time, he had nowhere else to go, and Dorothy longed to see her favourite brother. He spent most of his time with her, and as little as possible in strained conversation with his uncle. Brother and sister had not seen each other for more than a year, and she was in an ecstasy to hear the details of his great tour. There was no question of 'relapsing into Egotism' now; it was all egotism: anything he said was interesting simply because he was saying it. They walked outside in the garden behind the parsonage for nearly four hours every day, two hours in the morning after breakfast and two in the afternoon after tea.[4] Years later, Dorothy recollected 'the tales brought to me the following Christmas holidays at Forncett; and often repeated while we paced together on the gravel walk in the parsonage garden, by moon or star light.'[5] These tales began to form 'the shapeless wishes of [her] youth' into the image of the brother of whom she was becoming 'particularly fond.'

In her letters to Jane Pollard, Dorothy transcribed *verbatim* not only her brother's descriptions of Switzerland but also his loving expressions of regard for her. The question of what William was going to do with his life was closely entwined with Dorothy's similar concerns for herself. She was preoccupied with questions of marriageability – natural in a young woman of nineteen. Her growing conviction that she would not marry, even if she received a proposal, was another version of the family problems being created by William's refusal to take up a paying profession. Her dependent financial position made her less eligible for marriage, but not marrying also meant that she would continue to be a drain on family finances. Unlike Richard, John, and Christopher, neither she nor William were producing income, or seemed likely to start doing so. They were entirely a liability in the family's scrupulous account books.

Dorothy both invites and rejects Jane's teasing about her prospects. She asked her not to mention the subject of Wilberforce again, giving Jane instead the measure of her brothers, confessing that 'you are right in supposing me partial to William,' although allowing that 'when I next see Kitt I shall love him as well . . . his disposition is of the same cast as William's, and his inclinations have taken the same turn, but he is much more likely to make his fortune; he is not so warm as William but has a most affectionate heart, his abilities though not so great perhaps as his brothers may be of more use to him as he has not fixed his mind upon any particular species of reading, or conceived an aversion to any.' Christopher's malleability was the making of his fortune, but William's 'warmth' won her affections, even more than his poetry, which she well knew was 'not the most likely thing to produce his advancement in the world.'[6] One way and another, Dorothy was casting William as her lifetime companion, the hope of her life.

He, amid all this speculation about future prospects, lounged about reading Richardson's *Clarissa Harlowe*, that eight-volume masterpiece of the epistolary novel. This especially annoyed the frowning Cooksons because it openly exhibited his disdain for the kind of serious reading that his brother Kit was bending himself down to. His choice of *Clarissa* is not entirely incidental to this milieu of marriages and prospects. Richardson's detailed exposure of the vices of seduction, prostitution and calculated rape in eighteenth-century England, though nearly half a century old, had not lost any of its currency. Thoughts of how young women could be given – or taken – away were not only a diversion but also cause for reflection in young Wordsworth, as he contemplated his own slim prospects, and saw how Dorothy projected hers upon him.

Taking this *Clarissa* with him, Wordsworth returned to Cambridge in mid-January to endure the rigors of the Senate House final university examinations, which commenced at eight o'clock on Monday morning, 17 January 1791, and lasted for three days. This combination oral and written exam was finely calculated to drive weaker natures to distraction, but for Wordsworth and his friends these terrors were remote, and hence all the more contemptible. They would not get honours, but they could hardly fail, and they didn't. He stayed calm by reading *Clarissa*, and participated in the spirit of the exams only to cheer on the members of his set who actually were seeking honours.

They were few enough. Only two of his close friends gained honours: Robert Greenwood was sixteenth wrangler, and William Terrot came eighth senior optime. But one statistic an insider like William Cookson might brood over was the fact that, although 25 per cent of the graduating Johnians accounted for approximately 25 per cent of the entire university's honours degrees in 1791, his brilliant nephew was not among them.[7] Given the high hopes and good connections with which Wordsworth had entered St John's in 1787, this was a bitter harvest indeed.

After being formally admitted to his BA degree on Friday, 21 January, William did not stay around long for celebration parties that, unlike his triumphal 'exulting' in October, held little praise for him. He went off at the earliest possible opportunity – that very weekend or the following Monday, 24 January – to bury himself, and the world's current valuation of him, in the 'blank confusion' of London.

He took a seat on the roof of the London coach to save money. He never forgot the end of the day's ride when, 'having thridded the labyrinth of suburban villages,' he passed over the 'threshold' into the city itself and was swept away: 'great God! / That ought *external* to the human mind / Should have such mighty sway, yet so it was' (VIII.700–02). The spot was most likely the turnpike gate where Mile End road becomes Whitechapel, near Bethnal Green. Cambridge coaches usually deposited their passengers on Ludgate Hill, in front of St Paul's at 'La Belle Sauvage' inn.

People rarely ask where Wordsworth lived in London. The question may seem irrelevant to our nature poet, but, not surprisingly, he stayed where almost everybody else stayed, in the old central hub of the City, where Cheapside splits into Threadneedle, Cornhill, and Lombard streets, and the Lord Mayor's Mansion House, the Royal Exchange, and the Bank of England face each other across the intersection (see map, p. xxvi). By far the greatest number of Wordsworth's urban references fall within the compass of less than a square mile around this central point: 'the renowned Lord Mayor,' 'the river proudly bridged' (Blackfriars), 'the giddy top and Whispering Gallery of St. Paul's,' 'the Giants of Guildhall' (Gog and Magog), and 'the Monument' (Wren's memorial of the Great Fire of 1666, at the top of Fish Street Hill). It was still very much the heart of everyday London, not the stark financial district of today, built on the ruins of the Battle of Britain. When he says, 'obscurely did I live, / Not courting the society of men / By literature, or elegance, or rank, / Distinguished' (IX.20–23), he means that he did not live in Westminster or in the fashionable new squares being constructed in the West End. It also meant he lived alone, not with his brother Richard, nor seeking out people of rank who might still – barely – have been disposed to help him, such as John Robinson or William Wilberforce.

His first contact in the city was Dorothy's adored 'Aunt' Elizabeth Threlkeld, an enterprising woman in the woollen trade, who frequently came to London on business.[8] She introduced William to Samuel Nicholson, a wholesale mercer who supplied her shop in Halifax as well as that of the Wordsworths' Newcastle cousins, the Griffiths. Nicholson lived in Cateaton Street (originally 'Cat Eaten,' now Gresham Street); Wordsworth often dined with him on Sunday evenings. After dinner, they would go round the corner to the Dissenting chapel in Old Jewry to hear the sermons of Joseph Fawcett, the future author of *The Art of War* (1795). Fawcett was at this time capitalizing on the spectacular revival of the old meeting house's reputation by the radical Dissenter Richard Price, especially his sermon of November 1789 in praise of the French Revolution. Price died in 1791, and Fawcett took his place, attracting 'the largest and most genteel London audience that ever assembled in a dissenting place of worship.'[9] He would later become Wordsworth's model for the disaffected Solitary in *The Excursion*: 'And there with popular talents [he] preach'd the cause / Of Christ and of the new-born Liberty.'[10]

Both Fawcett and Nicholson were members of the Society for Constitutional Information, and their religious faith in 1791 was inspired by the hope that the fires of France might be fanned into reform in England, to remove the political restrictions of the Test and Corporation Acts.

A likely address for Wordsworth would be Wood Street at its intersection with Maiden Lane and Lad Lane, just below Love Lane.[11] These punningly named streets were close to his reality, for Lad Lane connected Cateaton Street, where he met his Aunt Threlkeld and visited Samuel Nicholson, to Wood Street and Lothbury, two well-known urban reference points which establish the location, and the occupation, of his 'Poor Susan':

> At the corner of Wood Street, when daylight appears,
> Hangs a Thrush that sings loud, it has sung for three years:
> Poor Susan has passed by the spot, and has heard
> In the silence of morning the song of the Bird.
>
> 'Tis a note of enchantment; what ails her? She sees
> A mountain ascending, a vision of trees;
> Bright volumes of vapour through Lothbury glide,
> And a river flows on through the vale of Cheapside.
>
> (1–8)

There were rooks (not thrushes) at the corner of Wood Street and Cheapside in a large plane tree there, a natural landmark which still stands, though it is now a ten-storey-high sycamore tree visited only by starlings and pigeons. Wordsworth's Susan is ailing not simply because she misses her home in the country, but in all likelihood because she had been cast out from it by her father for sexual misbehaviour. This has led her where such transgression led most young girls in the late eighteenth century, into a life of prostitution in the streets. Love Lane was a euphemistically renamed version of the notorious Gropecunt Lane of Elizabethan times.

Wordsworth's original last stanza for the poem makes this connection:

> Poor Outcast! return—to receive thee once more
> The house of thy Father will open its door,
> And thou once again, in thy plain russet gown,
> May'st hear the thrush sing from a tree of its own.[12]

This was cut out in response to Lamb's objection, because it made too clear that Susan 'was no better than she should be': not a serving maid going to work but a prostitute returning *from* work, wearing a more provocative gown than her 'plain russet' homespun. Wordsworth's late note to the poem throws us even further off the scent of this working girl: 'This arose out of my observation of the affecting music of these birds hanging in this way in the London streets during the freshness and stillness of the Spring morning.' What it really arose out of, as much of his best poetry always did, was the contrast between a fresh spring morning when he set out lightheartedly for his day's walk, and a tired prostitute he met returning home: a country thrush turned city rook.[13]

Among the many ancient guilds thriving in the city, prostitution was one of the busiest. The 'chartered streets' of Blake's 'London' were right here, where commercial charters were drawn up, and where 'thro' midnight streets' he heard 'How the youthful Harlot's curse / Blasts the new-born Infant's tear / And blights with plagues the Marriage hearse.' By the estimate of police magistrate Patrick Colquhoun, nearly 5 per cent of the *total* population of the city at this time – about 50,000 women – was composed of prostitutes, in addition to another 5 per cent who made up the rest of the criminal classes.[14] This would mean (assuming that women constitute about half of any population) that every tenth woman Wordsworth saw was likely to be a prostitute. But their frequency was actually even greater, since many respectable women never ventured out into the public street for fear of insult or assault. The Wood Street and Poultry 'compters,' verminous little holding cells, were used particularly for prostitutes who tried to rob their patrons.[15] Wordsworth was familiar with the Poultry, the little street connecting Cheapside and the Mansion House; he mentions the famous turtles of its King's Head Tavern (no. 25, exactly at Mansion House corner) in his imitation of Juvenal.[16]

We can just make out one of these women, close to Wordsworth's residence, in a blurred snapshot from *The Prelude*:

> When the great tide of human life stands still,
> The business of the day to come unborn,
> Of that gone by locked up as in the grave;
> . . . empty streets, and sounds
> Unfrequent as in desarts; at late hours
> Of winter evenings when unwholesome rains
> Are falling hard, with people yet astir,
> The feeble salutation from the voice
> Of some unhappy woman now and then
> Heard as we pass, when no one looks about,
> Nothing is listened to.
>
> (VII.631–42)

This reads like a strong first impression. 'The business of the day' which has come to a standstill was at the Royal Exchange, where pimps and their prostitutes came out in the evening to traffic among the shops and stalls as the stock traders and commodity buyers left work. Wordsworth's 'winter evening' is some time in February 1791. The 'we' would be Wordsworth and Nicholson returning home, Wordsworth wondering about his pious companion – and himself – neither of whom looks at or says anything to the unhappy woman. She is standing in a doorway, as we learn from Wordsworth's wrestling with the lines in manuscript, which might read, 'From door or arch a word [?hesi] [?pollu] tant breathed.'[17] With this addition earlier words in the passage – 'human life,' 'unborn,' and 'the grave' – suddenly stand out not as metaphors, but as living responses to something actually seen in these mean streets.

Besides challenging his sense of what it meant to be a man in the city, Wordsworth's neighbourhood also contributed to his sense of what it meant to be a writer in this society. He was well aware that his hero Milton had been born in Bread Street, directly across Cheapside from Wood Street. A scandal had arisen around the disinterment of Milton's body in 1790, when St Giles was being repaired and a memorial to the poet proposed.[18] Some enterprising parish clerks with inside knowledge saw a chance for big profits and dug up the body the night before the official disinterment was scheduled. Before they were caught, they had sold off one rib, ten teeth and several handfuls of hair. The scandal enjoyed a lively public life until 1793, when Samuel Whitbread, the Whig brewer, placed a memorial to the poet inside the church. The ironies for poetic reputation in the incident were not lost on Wordsworth, nor the symbolism of Milton's residence's proximity to Grub Street, the degraded antipodes of literary sublimity.

His thoughts were further stimulated in this direction by the enormous publicity leading up to the publication of Boswell's *Life of Johnson* in early May, and the huge success it immediately enjoyed.[19] The competition to write the first, or best, biography of – as it then seemed – England's last great literary figure had been intense since Johnson's death in 1784, and Boswell was preceded by two successful competitors, John Hawkins and Hester Thrale Piozzi. The literary press had been whipping up the competition between the rival biographers ever since Hawkins's biography appeared in 1787. Although Boswell's brilliant work carried the field with posterity, one side effect it produced was a spate of gloomy reflections that there no longer seemed to be any writers of Johnson's stature, especially in poetry. Boswell's success drew more attention to the vacuum, and we can easily imagine young Wordsworth reflecting on it as he turned past Milton's old church on the corner of Wood Street on his way home.

What should he do in London? What direction did he take, directionless as he was? There is no plot to Wordsworth's first residence in London, but there was plenty of movement: 'Month after month I *ranged* at large through the metropolis . . . free as a colt at pasture on the hills' (IX.18–20; my italics). A 'ranger' in London slang was a man of the town on the prowl, as in the contemporaneous *Ranger's Magazine*, an illustrated guide to the prostitutes of Covent Garden, listing names, addresses, prices, and specialities.[20] Is that 'colt' ranging at pasture another one of Wordsworth's naturalizing metaphors?

For the most part, he walked, a four-month urban tour to complement his recent three-month mountain tour of the Picturesque-Sublime. He lived 'chearfully abroad / With fancy on the stir from day to day, / And all my young affections out of doors.' Especially noteworthy, in light of his later reputation, is Wordsworth's fascination with dramatic spectacle. He went to shows of all kinds, especially at the lower end of the price scale. One still goes to London to see as many shows as possible, and Wordsworth took in the whole city as a show, from jugglers and prostitutes and beggars in the streets, through legitimate and illegitimate theatre, to popular Anglican and Dissenting preachers and the stirring debates in Parliament. Later, in *The Prelude*, he remembered all this as a 'domination of the eye' from which he had to recover, but at the time, on the spot, he experienced it as a passion. The seventh book of *The Prelude* is one of the most exciting representations of the energy of urban life in English literature; it compares favourably to the achievement of London's later presiding literary genius, Charles Dickens.[21]

Thinking of modern London, it may not seem excessive to roam about the city for four months. But London in 1791 was far smaller than it is now, and since Wordsworth spent most of his time outdoors his coverage was very thorough indeed. The city, including Westminster and Southwark, had barely a million inhabitants – though this made it, to be sure, the largest city in Europe. The entire metropolis was only about four miles across in any direction, no challenge for a walker like Wordsworth. He could easily on any day go from his lodgings in the City to one edge of the city, then back across to the opposite edge, and still return to his rooms in good time for dinner at nine o'clock.

His movements in the first four months of 1791 can be charted along two axes. One, running from east to west, was the great thoroughfare formed by Cheapside, Ludgate Hill, Fleet Street and the Strand, to Charing Cross, thence curving down to Whitehall. No less an authority than M. de Saussure, the conqueror of Mont Blanc, considered this the finest street in all Europe. Wordsworth arranged his description of London roughly along this line, conducting us on a walking day tour that we can still follow. His other, less travelled route went from south to north, from the City out to 'half-rural Sadler's Wells' and the open fields beyond.

Stepping westward on his favourite walk from Cheapside, he came immediately into St Paul's Churchyard, the centre for bookshops and printers. He entered the lively shop of his future publisher, Joseph Johnson, at no. 72, where he might see on any given day the rising stars of the exploding radical publishing universe, William Godwin, Mary Wollstonecraft, even Tom Paine himself – and perhaps glimpse Johnson's strange engraver, William Blake. All of them were arming for the polemical wars provoked by Burke's *Reflections on the Revolution in France*, which Wordsworth himself would enter two years later. One street north, in Paternoster Row, was the shop of his future longtime publisher, Longman-Owen-Rees. At the time, however, he had more regard for 'for the humble Bookstalls in the streets.'[22] These specialized in pathetic ballads, sensational accounts of robberies and murders, and ghost and monster stories, frequently illustrated with engravings 'of the altogether most horrible contents.'[23] This was the kind of literature that Wordsworth would later take it as his life's mission to counteract, but he loved it as a child, and its appeal was not lost on him yet: 'Wild produce, hedgerow fruit, on all sides hung / To lure the sauntering traveller from his track.'[24]

Pushing through the massive congestion on Ludgate Hill, Wordsworth crossed Old Bailey. He heard 'the brawls of lawyers in their courts,' and saw the need for more heroic work like John Howard's (who had died the year before) to improve prison conditions. At the bottom of the hill, to enter Fleet Street, he crossed New Bridge Road, which led to 'the river proudly bridged': Blackfriars Bridge, barely twenty years old and considered the most beautiful bridge in the country. He could still glimpse the little Fleet River, or ditch, soon to be entirely covered by pavements. London's first covered sewer ran into this, but it was still ten years in the future, so he picked his way carefully.[25]

Entering Fleet Street, he found more bookshops and printers, the beginnings of the modern newspaper industry. The *Morning Advertiser* was in the first block, at no. 127. The liberal *Morning Post* (founded 1772) was regaining ground against its new rival, *The Times* (1785), and would soon, under the editorship of Daniel Stuart, return to a fully competitive position, partly by employing brilliant young university men like Coleridge, Southey, and Wordsworth. However, the fledgling newspaper offices were less evident than the inns, which from the Fleet to Charing Cross set up shows in their yards to pull customers out of the passing tide of humanity.

He frequently paused at Chancery Lane, a busy corner then as now, for his observations here are particularly exact. Isaac Newton's head was one of the 'physiognomies of real men' (VII.180–82) over the door of Rackstraw's Museum of dead monstrosities near the corner at no. 197; it soon became the *Albion*, where Charles Lamb joked that it was 'our occupation . . . write treason'[26] – another example of a Romantic writer facetiously distancing himself from his Jacobin youth. Across the street was Mrs Salmon's waxworks, featuring effigies of England's kings and queens. This was 'the waxwork' Wordsworth saw in 1791, conflated by the time he came to write *The Prelude* with Mme Tussaud's collection, brought over to London in 1802, and offering, as competition for Mrs

Salmon, effigies of the dead bodies of France's royal victims of the Terror.[27] Dead and disgraced royalty were coming to be more marketable than live ones, as the modern era dawned.

From Chancery Lane, Wordsworth takes us forward with a darting skill that cannot be matched by paraphrase. He gives 'the look and aspect of the place,'

> The broad highway appearance, as it strikes
> On strangers of all ages, the quick dance
> Of colours, lights and forms, the Babel din,
> The endless stream of men and moving things,
> From hour to hour the illimitable walk
> Still among streets, with clouds and sky above,
> The wealth, the bustle and the eagerness,
> The glittering chariots with their pampered steeds,
> Stalls, barrows, porters, midway in the street
> The scavenger that begs with hat in hand,
> The labouring hackney-coaches, the rash speed
> Of coaches travelling far, whirled on with horn
> Loud blowing, and the sturdy drayman's team
> Ascending from some alley of the Thames
> And striking right across the crowded Strand
> Till the fore-horse veer round with punctual skill . . .
>
> (VII.155–70)

The breathless sequence ends with the kind of arresting detail that we might call Dickensian, but it is indubitably Wordsworthian. It brings us exactly to the neighbourhood of the Savoy, where the Fleet took on a 'broad highway appearance' as it passed out of the City at Temple Bar and flowed around St Clements Church to become the Strand.

Moving 'into the throng' of the Strand, Wordsworth came into the heart of his urban delights. First, directly opposite Somerset House and the Savoy, he saw Exeter 'Change, the location of the menagerie he describes in VII.246–47, and of Phillipe de Loutherbourg's 'Eidophusikon' ('moving-image machine'): 'the painter—fashioning a work / To Nature's circumambient scenery.' It also housed Robert Barker's 'Panorama.'[28] When Wordsworth cites 'The Firth of Forth, and Edinburgh, throned / On crags,' he is exactly contemporary and accurate, for Barker's panorama featuring these views was the only one in London in 1791. Such detailed coincidences increase our confidence that much of the rest of *Prelude* VII is equally contemporaneous. Barker's Edinburgh perspective was soon replaced by one of London itself, painted from the top of the huge Albion Sugar Mills at the south end of Blackfriars Bridge (see print) – an unique view, as it turned out, since the mills burned down in March of 1791.[29]

A few steps up from Exeter 'Change brought him to the Drury Lane Theatre, where Sarah Siddons and her brother John Kemble were the stars, under the brilliant, erratic direction of Richard Brinsley Sheridan, leading playwright of the preceding generation and a politician very much of this one. Mrs Dorothea ('Dora' or 'Dolly') Jordan, 'the Muse of Comedy' to Siddons's Tragic Muse, left the theatre and her lover of five years, Richard Ford (son of Sheridan's partner), in 1791 to set up housekeeping with George III's son William, the Duke of Clarence.[30] Both she and Ford would touch significantly on Wordsworth's life before the decade was out. It was here, 'within the walls of Drury's splendid house,'[31] that Wordsworth saw one of his most startling urban sights, a prostitute's child seated on the bar during the interval of a play.

> Upon a board,
> Whence an attendant of the theatre
> Served out refreshments, had this child been placed,
> And there he sate environed with a ring
> Of chance spectators, chiefly dissolute men
> And shameless women—treated and caressed—
> Ate, drank, and with the fruit and glasses played,
> While oaths, indecent speech, and ribaldry
> Were rife about him as are songs of birds
> In springtime after showers.
>
> (383–92)

As with his sight of Poor Susan, it is the starkness of contrast that stimulates the visionary moment that follows, where the child is compared to the children of Israel in Nebuchadnezzar's fiery furnace. But the image itself is from 1791, when Wordsworth himself was among the 'chance spectators' at the bar. Many actresses were prostitutes, and some prostitutes were actresses; the area around Drury Lane and Covent Garden was rife with them. The coffee houses in this area were considered little better than brothels, but they were so well-established that they were not considered 'disorderly' houses in contemporary usage.[32] Pre-eminent among them were The Rose, featured in Hogarth's *The Rake's Progress*, and The Shakespeare's Head, mentioned in Wordsworth's London progress poem (VII.182).

Coming back down into the Strand from this detour, Wordsworth found himself opposite the Beaufort Buildings, soon the residence of the radical orator John Thelwall, fast rising to public prominence, who sometimes held meetings in his rooms here to frustrate infiltration by Pitt's informers. Wordsworth knew of Thelwall in 1791; Thelwall gradually learned about Coleridge from his political speeches and essays during the 1790s; by the end of the decade he would seek out Coleridge and Wordsworth in their West Country retreat as almost his last friends in the country.

Continuing west, Wordsworth came to the Royal Adelphi Terraces, abutting the Adelphi Wharves, and dominated from the Strand by a huge sign of 'the attractive head / Of some quack-doctor, famous in his day' (182–83).[33] This was James Graham (1745–1794), an enterprising Scotsman whose 'Temple of Health and Hymen' was notorious for its 'Celestial Bed,' a supposed cure for sterility and impotence, aimed at the idle rich and noted for its fantastic advertising (see cartoon). Here, for the staggering price of £50, a couple could lie on a nine-by-twelve foot mattress, 'filled with the strongest, most springy hair, produced at vast expense from the tails of English stallions which are elastic to the highest degree.'[34] Circulating magnets added their potency to the 'elastic' powers of stallions' hair. The contraption was calculated to produce 'both pleasure and results, for the bed could be tilted after coition, presumably to aid conception.'[35] The scientific aura of the place was meretricious; if a patron didn't have a partner, he could select one from the teenage Goddesses of Youth and Health assisting the good doctor, one of whom was the beautiful Emma who later became Lady Hamilton. The price for this early sex clinic was of course far too high for any but the very rich; it was a marketing ploy that we would now call a 'loss-leader,' since for the (comparatively) trifling sum of two guineas one could gain admission to see the amazing device and hear a lecture on sex and health. This reduced rate did not return Graham a sufficient profit, but the advertising he gained by the business helped him succeed in his next venture, cosmetic mud baths.

Wordsworth singles out this one of London's sights for emphatic mention, a fact all the more noteworthy because it quite likely *was not there* in 1791. Graham had sold out in 1783, but his immense sign was still there, and Wordsworth seems to have been very interested in Graham's notorious sex machine, for he returned to it in his Juvenal satire of 1795. By then he was scoffing at Graham's mud bath business, but he concludes with a particularly detailed sarcasm recollecting Graham's earlier sensation:

> For them [the rich] though all the portals open stand
> Of Health's own temple at her Graham's command
> And the great high-priest baffling Death and Sin
> Earth [i.e., bury] each immortal idiot to the chin,
> Ask of these wretched beings worse than dead
> If on the couch celestial gold can shed
> The coarser blessings of a Peasant's bed.[36]

The concluding rhetorical question seems to want a negative response, but its reference is ambiguous, as to whether it means producing children or sexual pleasure, or both. That the question was important to Wordsworth is indicated by his Miltonic allusion to Graham as Satan, in his encounter with the most perversely incestuous couple in English literature, his daughter Sin, whom he conceived and then raped, and her offspring Death, who continually rapes and gets children upon his own mother. No allusion to Milton is innocent in Wordsworth's poetry, but those with sexual overtones usually indicate heavily loaded psychological material. Such historical and literary details are recondite, but they match perfectly with other more obvious points of reference in Wordsworth's particular, but by no means abnormal, fascination with the spectacles of sexuality in London.

Immediately after the Adelphi Terrace, Wordsworth crossed Buckingham Street and in all likelihood stopped at the bookshop of William Mathews's father, at no. 18 Strand. Mathews himself was at this time struggling unhappily to harness himself in the profession of schoolmaster in Leicester, but Wordsworth would have been very rude not to have introduced himself, for Mathews was one of his best friends, and he knew that Mathews's father was a kind man, despite the Methodist zealots who infested his shop, making young Mathews's life a misery.[37]

At Charing Cross, Wordsworth turned down Whitehall to Westminster, passing 'from entertainments that are such / Professedly, to others titled higher . . . Where senators, tongue-favoured men, perform, / Admired and envied' (VII.517–24). Wordsworth was not 'tongue-favoured' for speech-making, though he often held forth at length in private conversation. But he envied those who were, particularly the three great speakers who dominated Parliament at this time: William Pitt the Younger, Edmund Burke and Charles James Fox. Their oratory has rarely been matched in parliamentary annals, and in the spring of 1791 they clashed on issue after issue provoked by the French Revolution, Pitt and Fox performed a virtual duet throughout the session, rising about forty times each to speak; Burke spoke twenty times, but his speeches were very long: he earned the nickname Dinner Bell because members often fled for the exits whenever he rose.

From early February to early June, almost exactly the period of Wordsworth's London residence, Parliament was in one of the most dramatic sessions in its history, reaching a climax on 6 May when Burke and Fox had their final falling-out. Their rupture signalled the fact that men of good will could no longer agree to disagree on the significance of the French Revolution, but would have to take stands that broke old patterns of proper behaviour and, indeed, old conceptions of human nature itself. British enthusiasm for the French Revolution had just reached its crest, but it soon began to recede rapidly. The fashion for republican-style cropped hair began in 1791, and Wordsworth adopted it instead of the 'rimey' powder he had used at Cambridge. Burke's *Reflections*, which had appeared the preceding November, was the breakwater which eventually stemmed the tide of revolutionary zeal, but it was being badly battered in early 1791; Burke lamented that it 'stood an object of odium.'[38]

The first attraction was Pitt, whose brilliant orations had already attained the new standard for modern mass politics: they sounded impressive even though it was hard to say exactly what he meant. Wordsworth attested that he had 'often seen Mr Pitt upon . . . the floor of the House of Commons,'[39] and he makes a pun on the prime minister when he describes 'the beating of the heart / When one among the *prime* of these rose up' (VII.524–25). But Wordsworth's apparent praise is only a set-up for a satiric undercutting, as Pitt's manner soon outstrips his matter: 'Words follow words, sense seems to follow sense— / What memory and logic!—till the strain / Transcendent, superhuman as it is, / Grows tedious even in a young man's ear' (VII.540–43).

Fox and Burke made the more lasting impression. Wordsworth said that one 'always went from Burke with your mind filled; from Fox with your feelings excited; and from Pitt with wonder at his having the power to make the worse appear the better reason.'[40] Wordsworth added his praise to the 'Genius of Burke!' to Book VII in 1832, but in the first drafts of the addition he gives almost equal homage to Fox. His details suggest that he saw them as they sat and talked, for they were close enough to overhear each other's whispers: Westminster Hall was a much smaller room than the present parliamentary chambers. Wordsworth pictures Fox as one of the 'younger brethren' who sat 'Listening beside thee—no longer near / Yet still in heart thy friend. Illustrious Fox / Thy grateful Pupil. In the power of words / Thundering & Lightening when *his* turn shall come / A British Pericles.'[41] But by 1832, the year of the passage of the Reform Bill that he bitterly opposed, Wordsworth could only draft, not finally include, this praise of the liberal, reformist Fox in his increasingly retrospective account of the growth of his mind; all praise by then went to the conservative 'genius' of Burke.

It is quite likely that Wordsworth was in attendance for the confrontations between Fox and Burke, for he was there 'night by night,'[42] and sessions often ran into the early morning hours. We could expect him to have been present on 18–19 April, when Wilberforce made his motion against the slave trade. Pitt, Fox, and Burke all supported him, but to no avail; the motion lost, 163 to 88. After temporarily uniting on this lost liberal cause, Fox and Burke immediately resumed their sparring. Public attention to their conflict was intense; their speeches were fully reported in the newspapers, and it was clear at the adjournment on 29 April that the two men must confront each other when debate resumed after a week's recess. On 6 May, Burke began laboriously by casting himself as an old man, very much put upon. When Fox rose to answer, his first words deprecated his own 'feeble powers . . . compared to those of his right honourable friend, whom he must call his master, for he had taught him everything he knew in politics.'[43] Wordsworth's manuscript lines about Fox as Burke's 'grateful Pupil' seem to catch this moment exactly, like a contemporary newspaper cartoon, 'The Scholar lamenting the departure of his Master,' which featured Fox as snivelling urchin schoolboy and Burke as a stern old pedagogue.

Wordsworth's lines in *The Prelude* praising Burke are not simply evidence of his elderly conservatism. They actually give a fuller view of his earlier self, and of the tremendous impact of these mighty antagonists on 'a youth . . . in ancient story versed, whose breast had heaved / Under the weight of classic eloquence,' and who could not but 'sit, see, and hear,' thankful and inspired.[44] Both Fox and Burke loaded their speeches with classical and literary allusions, and Wordsworth's later predeliction for alluding to *Paradise Lost* and *Macbeth* when writing about the French Revolution was certainly stimulated by Burke's rhetoric.[45] On the fateful sixth of May, Burke satirically cast the revolutionaries and their English sympathizers as the witches in *Macbeth*, full of 'Hubble bubble / Toil and trouble,' when they stirred the pot of social ferment – leaving the hint, for those who wished to take it, that Fox was the Macbeth of the moment.

Leaving these heated scenes of national passion, Wordsworth walked through fashionable Westminster, passing 'processions, equipages, lords and dukes' until he came to 'the King's palace' (VII.110–11). This was the new town mansion built by the Duke of Buckingham in 1762, recently bought by George III as a residence for his large family. Ever the devoted husband, he wanted to call it 'The Queen's Palace,' but the name never caught on, and through many expansions that have dwarfed the original structure it is still associated with the name of Buckingham.

More frequently, he headed in the other direction from Parliament, visiting the nearby pleasure park of Ranelagh, across the market gardens of Chelsea, or, crossing over Westminster Bridge, Vauxhall Gardens:

> Vauxhall and Ranelagh, I then had heard
> Of your green groves and wilderness of lamps,
> Your gorgeous ladies, fairy cataracts,
> And pageant fireworks.
>
> (VII.123–26)

He visited Ranelagh first, for, besides being the more fashionable of the two,[46] it was an all-weather facility, and he arrived in February. It featured a huge open fireplace in its central rotunda, where hundreds of diners could be accommodated at a single sitting, looked down on by wealthier patrons seated in galleries on the curved walls opposite. Later in the spring Vauxhall re-opened across the river in Lambeth, a rural fantasia that appealed more to Wordsworth. It declined steadily in gentility through the 1790s, attracting increasing numbers of London 'cits,' and a good many of its 'gorgeous ladies' were prostitutes, who were encountered at these pleasure gardens as reliably as at Covent Garden, though here they cultivated a more elegant appearance: 'Where each spruce nymph from city compters free / Sips the froth'd syllabub or fragrant tea.'[47]

From here, at the end of a long day, Wordsworth turned back home, retracing his steps back through Westminster and along the Strand and Fleet to his lodging in the City. He took this long east–west walk, with countless variations and detours, many times during his four months in London.

His other favourite walking route was more northerly, past Smithfield and Gray's Inn to Sadler's Wells at New River Head, and into the fields between Clerkenwell Green and the hamlet of Pentonville. Sadler's Wells was only a mile-and-a-half away from Wordsworth's lodgings near the Exchange, and not far removed in time from when it had been a watering hole for horse-saddlers. In this rural amusement arcade, among the 'lowest' and 'humblest' the city had to offer, Wordsworth 'more than once . . . took my seat' to see 'singers, rope-dancers, giants and dwarfs, / Clowns, conjurors, posture-masters, harlequins, / Amid the uproar of the rabblement, / Perform their feats' (291–97). When he later scorned those who talked about 'a *taste* for Poetry . . . as if it were a thing as indifferent as a taste for Rope-dancing,' he knew whereof he spoke, on both amusements. The literalness of his description is, as usual, noteworthy. A young German lady visiting Sadler's Wells five years earlier, gives details of a very similar programme: 'In three hours we witnessed nine kinds of stage craft. First, a comedy, then a ballet, followed by rope-walker, after this a pantomime, next some balancing tricks, an operette, and the most miraculous feats by a strong man, another comedy, and finally a second operette.'[48]

Past Gray's Inn, the streets were 'wider,' allowing 'straggling breezes of suburban air' (VII.207). 'As on the broadening causeway we advance' (215) – City Road or Gray's Inn Road – Wordsworth saw a beggar whose very name, neighbourhood, and mode of operation have been identified:

> Behold a face turned up towards us, strong
> In lineaments, and red with over-toil:
> 'Tis one perhaps already met elsewhere,
> A travelling cripple, by the trunk cut short,
> And stumping with his arms.
>
> (VII.216–20)

This was Samuel Horsey, a.k.a. 'The King of the Beggars,' later recalled in Lamb's essay on 'The Decay of Beggars in the Metropolis' for his 'sailor-like complexion.'[49] Horsey's main beat was very much in Wordsworth's neighbourhood, running from Bow Church in Cheapside north along

Wood Street, and then back down Aldgate to St Paul's. Hence he was more than likely 'one perhaps already met elsewhere,' with no 'perhaps' about it. There was general agreement that, though 'half a Hercules,' he was twice a man, for he openly kept two wives, satisfying them both with his vigour. We often skip over such pictures of urban energy in Wordsworth's London, in our haste to fasten on his more pathetic solitaries, such as the Blind Beggar. But the facts of Horsey's frank, successful bigamy surely resonated at some level of Wordsworth's mind when he wrote Book VII's lines the about Mary of Buttermere's bigamous seducer, not to mention his own ambivalent romantic attachments.

On his other route out to Sadler's Wells, Wordsworth passed by Lamb's 'old blind Tobits that used to line the wall of Lincoln's Inn Garden . . . casting up their ruined orbs to catch a ray of pity, and (if possible) of light.' One of these could very well have been Wordsworth's Blind Beggar:

> . . . who, with upright face,
> Stood propped against a wall, upon his chest
> Wearing a written paper, to explain
> The story of the man, and who he was.
> My mind did at this spectacle turn round
> As with the might of waters, and it seemed
> To me that in this label was a type
> Or emblem of the utmost that we know
> Both of ourselves and of the universe . . .
> (612–20)

His conclusion, though rhetorically impressive, is a bit histrionic for the twenty-one-year-old urban tourist who saw the beggar, though not for the transcendentalist thirty-four-year-old poet who made him into a symbol. Wordsworth's amazement that so many people could live so close to each other without knowing each other is certainly a reaction of 1791; the generalizations he built upon it are a later growth.

After a day in the suburbs, he returned 'homeward through the thickening hubbub' (VII.227), to his quarters in the City. More foreigners lived in this mercantile section than anywhere else, with its India House, South Sea House, and Post Office, and Wordsworth drew upon the fact to conclude his perambulatory catalogue with a stylized representation of the four points of the world's compass in his own London neighbourhood:

> . . . all specimens of man
> Through all the colours which the sun bestows,
> And every character of form and face:
> The Swede, the Russian; from the genial south,
> The Frenchman and the Spaniard; from remote

> America, the hunter Indian; Moors,
> Malays, Lascars, the Tartar and Chinese,
> And Negro ladies in white muslin gowns.
>
> (236–43)

The strong contrast in the last detail had, as contrasts always did for him, a strangely conclusive effect. Wordsworth was always struck by the sight of black people in England, as in another of his London snapshots, 'the silver-collared negro with his timbrel' (VII.677). That Wordsworth participated in the cultural racism of his time is not surprising; the biographical point here is that this strong, black-and-white sense of difference graphically illustrates the contrasts of London which set his mind in motion at almost every turn. The last and most dramatic of these came at Bartholomew Fair.

He was very familiar with the fair's location, in Smithfield, especially during his residence in 1791, for the Smithfield markets began at the head of Wood Street, just west of the Barbican.[50] St Bartholomew's Day is 3 September; the fair dates were technically 3–7 September, but it ran for a good two weeks, by far the largest of London's many fairs. He presents the fair's wild hodge-podge of novelties as ostensibly destructive of 'the whole creative powers of man' (655), but the verbal energy of his description belies his thesis, matching that of Rowlandson's print (see illustration), and wonderfully summing up the visual attractions that drew him on throughout his 'Residence in London'.

> . . . the open space, through every nook
> Of the wide area, twinkles, is alive
> With heads; the midway region and above
> Is thronged with staring pictures and huge scrolls,
> Dumb proclamations of the prodigies;
> And chattering monkeys dangling from their poles,
> And children whirling in their roundabouts;
>   . . . buffoons against buffoons
> Grimacing, writhing, screaming; him who grinds
> The hurdy-gurdy, at the fiddle weaves,
> Rattles the salt-box, thumps the kettle-drum,
> And him who at the trumpet puffs his cheeks,
> The silver-collared negro with his timbrel,
> Equestrians, tumblers, women, girls, and boys,
> Blue-breeched, pink-vested, and with towering plumes.
> All moveables of wonder from all parts
> Are here, albinos, painted Indians, dwarfs,
> The horse of knowledge, and the learned pig,
> The stone-eater, the man that swallows fire,
> Giants, ventriloquists, the invisible girl,

The bust that speaks and moves its goggling eyes,
The waxwork, clockwork, all the marvellous craft
Of modern Merlins, wild beasts, puppet-shows,
All out-o'-the-way, far-fetched, perverted things,
All freaks of Nature, all Promethean thoughts
Of man—his dulness, madness, and their feats,
All jumbled up together to make up
This parliament of monsters. Tents and booths
Meanwhile—as if the whole were one vast mill—
Are vomiting, receiving, on all sides,
Men, women, three-years' children, babes in arms.

(VII.663–95)

It requires a very special perspective to call a city crowd enjoying itself a 'parliament of monsters' – which is not to say that Bartholomew Fair was innocent. But the detail that makes this an impression from 1791, that fits best with other urban details in Wordsworth's synoptic account in Book VII, is the final sequence, running backwards from men to women to children to babies, like the nauseating produce of a human regurgitation machine. Such perverted connections stimulated his earliest experiences of the City where, amid all its shows, his attention was always most forcefully arrested by the sight of 'woman as she is to open shame / Abandoned, and the pride of public vice.' At such moments, 'a barrier seemed at once / Thrown in, that from humanity divorced / The human form, splitting the race of man / In twain, yet leaving the same outward shape' (VII.419–27). The 'barrier' was not simply that between men and women, but between human beings lost to shame (mostly women, in Wordsworth's judgment) and those who managed to retain their self-respect. In Wordsworth's London of 1791 this demarcation ran along gender lines more often than not.

CHAPTER TWELVE

The Mighty Mind

Wales, 1791

> Upon the lonely mountain when the scene
> Had passed away . . . it appeared to me
> The perfect image of a mighty mind
> (XIII.67–69)

Towards the end of May, Parliament about to rise and his funds running low, Wordsworth decided to accept Robert Jones's standing invitation to visit him in Wales. By leaving London, he missed some of the wildest demonstrations of popular enthusiasm for reform, but they would reach out to touch him, oddly, in deepest Wales.

He took the Liverpool coach as far north as Chester, then hopped a local wagon to Ruthin and walked the remaining five miles to the Jones's family rectory, in the Vale of Clwyd between Ruthin and Denbigh.[1] It was called Plas-yn-Llan, meaning mansion in the churchyard (or village), and it was – and still is – a very accommodating residence. A Jones family plot, protected by tall iron railings, still holds pride of place next to the churchyard's main entrance, announcing to all who enter, 'This vault belongs to the family of JONES who resided many years at *Plas-yn-Llan* in this Parish.'

Once again young Wordsworth found himself ensconced in a spacious country house. As the rectory for St Cynhafal's church in Llangynhafal, it was almost as big as the church itself, a rambling Tudor house with a courtyard as big as a country inn's, and a separate kitchen as large as a modern townhouse. Plas-yn-Llan still stands out, glowing like a colour feature in *Country Life*, far the most impressive house in the neighbourhood. It is beautifully situated, just a few hundred yards below the top of the Clwydian Range, looking out over the highly satisfactory prospect of the five-mile-wide Vale of Clwyd, long and broad and green. One feels here very much master of all one surveys, a feeling that William conveyed

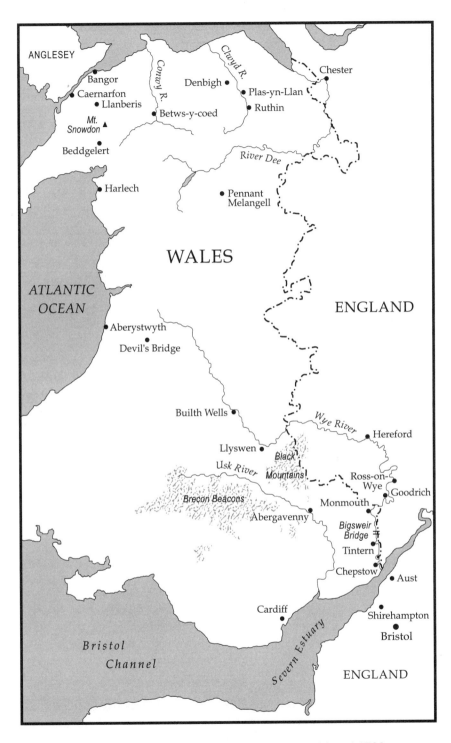

Wordsworth's Wales: North 1791; South 1793 and 1798

to Dorothy as the Vale of Meditation, 'the most delicious of all Vales, the Vale of Clwyd!'[2]

The young men soon decided to repeat their wonderful adventure of the previous summer, this time through the popular picturesque 'sights of Wales. They took three weeks preparing for their ramble, but there was no need for the detailed research of the previous year, for Jones was now on home ground, ready to function as Wordsworth's guide, and personally acquainted with the current experts on all matters pertaining to Welsh topography and history.

They began their tour by striking briefly eastward, back over the Clwydian range to Holywell, where they visited Thomas Pennant, a noted travel writer, amateur geologist, and leader in the burgeoning Welsh national revival. He was the author of *A Tour in Wales* (1778–1784), dedicated to John Jones, Robert's grandfather, from which the two young men derived their itinerary: its special feature was an elaborate description of a sunrise ascent of Snowdon. Pennant's *Tour* set their course: a roughly counter-clockwise oval, west along the north Wales coast to the Menai Strait, then southerly past Caernarfon, Snowdon, Harlech Castle, and Cadair Idris, down as far as Aberystwyth, then eastward past Devil's Bridge and back northeasterly via the River Dee and Betws-y-coed to the Jones family manse.[3] It was a good three hundred miles, but with six weeks to devote to it, Wordsworth and Jones explored North Wales in much greater detail than any part of their European tour the previous summer.

Wordsworth never wrote a separate poem describing this tour, but in his dedication of *Descriptive Sketches* to Jones (1793) he listed the places he remembered best:

> With still greater propriety I might have inscribed to you a description of some of the features of your native mountains, through which we have wandered together, in the same manner, with so much pleasure. But the sea-sunsets, which give such splendour to the vale of Clwyd, Snowdon, the chair of Idris, the quiet village of Bethgelert, Menai and her Druids, the Alpine steeps of Conway [sic], and the still more interesting windings of the wizard stream of Dee, remain yet untouched.[4]

There are two places in this catalogue from which one *cannot* see the sun set over the sea: the village of Beddgelert and the river Dee. And these were the only two places on the tour which Wordsworth found things 'still more interesting' than he had expected.

When they came to Snowdon, Wordsworth, following Pennant, wanted to see the sunrise. The most famous mountain climb in his entire oeuvre, the ascent of Snowdon which concludes *The Prelude*, derives from this trip. As in crossing the Simplon Pass, his expectation of landscape sublimity, formed by cultural models – Gray's 'The Bard' (1757) is set there – was again disappointed, and his mind surprised into poetry by the difference.

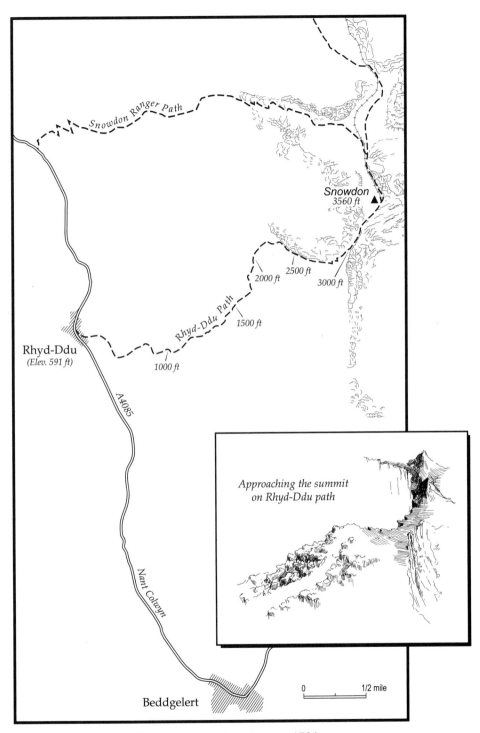

Snowdon Ranger Path

Snowdon
3560 ft

Rhyd-Ddu Path

2500 ft

2000 ft

3000 ft

1500 ft

1000 ft

Rhyd-Ddu
(Elev. 591 ft)

A4085

Nant Colwyn

*Approaching the summit
on Rhyd-Ddu path*

0   1/2 mile

Beddgelert

Climbing Snowdon, August 1791

Matched against the mountain itself, Wordsworth's description of ascending Snowdon is a masterpiece of his ability to wed literal details to visionary interpretation, the two polar opposites of his creative genius. Large quantities of critical ink have flowed into explaining his explanation of his vision (XIII.66–119), written in his transcendental idiom of 1804, but little or no indication has been given of how exact his description of the climb itself is (XIII.1–65). They were following Pennant very closely, for his 'Journey to Snowdon,' complete with a separate title page, takes up the first half of the second volume of his *Tour of Wales*. Wordsworth's and Jones's route began near the hamlet of Rhyd-Ddu west of Snowdon, about seven miles north of Beddgelert. They took the Rhyd-Ddu path because only by this route would they be able to see the sun rise in front of them as they reached the top. Easier routes from the east and north had the drawback that the sun creeps up behind one by degrees, whereas they were aiming for the maximum dramatic impact of seeing the sun rise up in front of them.[5] They would not have started climbing from Beddgelert, for such a route, if there were one, would have taken them up and down many intervening foothills, and both were from mountainous districts and could read the lay of the land better than that. Wordsworth says they left at 'couching-time,' a country phrase for sheeps' bedtime, about midnight, and this is about right: if they wanted 'to see the sun rise from the top of Snowdon,' they would, in July, have had to be on the top between 4 and 5 a.m. Even modestly accomplished walkers can get to the top in three hours or less along this path, weather permitting, which means they would have had to set off from the bottom about 1 a.m. The seven miles from Beddgelert to Rhyd-Ddu on a dark and foggy night would probably require another two hours, so we can imagine them setting off from their lodgings at about 11 p.m. If anything, they were too eager, for they arrived too early.

Reaching 'the cottage at the mountain's foot,' they 'rouzed up the shepherd who by ancient right / Of office is the stranger's usual guide'; Pennant recommended him by name, Hugh Shone.[6] Hugh gave them some 'short refreshment,' probably a stiff drink, because they'd already been walking for two hours. They needed a guide to find the best path, not yet marked out by thousands of tourists, because 'It was a summer's night, a close warm night, / Wan, dull, and glaring, with a dripping mist / Low-hung and thick that covered all the sky' (XII.10–12). They also needed the shepherd because only their 'faith in our tried pilot' assured them that such an unlikely night would result in a morning on which one could actually see the sun rise. As Pennant said, 'It is very rare that the traveller gets a proper day to ascend the hill; for . . . by the evident attraction of the clouds for this lofty mountain, it becomes suddenly and unexpectedly enveloped in mist.'[7] Wordsworth's shepherd, however, knew his weather signs well, for they eventually emerged out of the mist into the clear well before sunrise.*

Wordsworth's description fits a Rhyd-Ddu ascent precisely. Though it is true that he 'hardly needed to go near a mountain, let alone have a specific occasion in mind,' to compose his first version of the event, the *Prelude* account is extremely circumstantial.[8] Like the Rhyd-Ddu route itself, Wordsworth's description is broken roughly into thirds. First, there is a gradually ascending base plateau ('thus did we breast the ascent') across sheep-grazing land marked by holding pens, in which 'the shepherd's cur' might well 'unearth a hedgehog . . . to his own great joy' (XIII.23), and the hikers might comfortably engage in 'ordinary travellers' chat' (17). Second, there is a much steeper middle section, through huge boulders and so covered with rocks of all sizes it is difficult to find anything resembling a path. Here one no longer 'breasts' the ascent, but, more accurately, 'with forehead bent / Earthward, as if in opposition set / Against an enemy, I panted up . . . thus might we wear perhaps an hour away' (29–33).[9] This section does take about an hour, and one is too busy keeping one's balance and breath, especially if it's dark and foggy, to engage in much conversation. Third, there is a wide plateau of about two miles to the summit as one surmounts this rocky steep, from which, 'At distance not the third part of a mile,' is the edge of a very steep precipice of horseshoe cliffs, falling away from the western summit of Snowdon, hundreds of feet straight down, 'a blue chasm, a fracture in the vapour, / A deep and gloomy breathing-place, through which / Mounted the roar of waters, torrents, streams / Innumerable, roaring with one voice' (56–59). Here, where the mountain falls sharply downward, the mists resume, but with a gap in mid-air, because they do not lap as smoothly on the cliff face as they do on more gradual slopes. This is the 'dark deep thoroughfare' where Wordsworth said 'Nature lodged the soul, the imagination of the whole.' The sound of falling waters is audible, especially when there has been rain, but its source is mysterious and invisible because the streams come out of crevices in the cliffs: they are apparently 'homeless' (63). Nor can one hear these waters from any place but the top of the mountain.

---

* Accurate predictions are not easy in the mountains of North Wales, where any day, even in midsummer, can produce thick mist and rain that obliterates everything. I arrived there one splendidly sunny afternoon and the park ranger recommended I ascend immediately to take advantage of the weather. He was right. At three the next morning it was misty and overcast, and looked unlikely to produce any visible sunrise. Being lazier than Wordsworth, I finally arrived 'at the mountain's foot' about 5 a.m., and saw what little sunrise there was to see from the bottom, not the top, of Snowdon. By the time I reached the top about 7:30, it was swathed in mist so thick that I had to hurry back down immediately before I lost all visibility – having climbed the mountain twice in the space of eight hours with no romantic vision for my pains.

Sometimes readers think Wordsworth heard the sound of 'the sea, the real sea,' but that is too 'far, far beyond' to be heard from the top of Snowdon. It was here that Wordsworth had his visionary sight, for only here could 'a light upon the turf / [fall] like a flash,' since there is little or no turf to speak of until one reaches this plateau.

But the light Wordsworth saw was the moon, not the sun. It was all the more startling because they didn't become aware of its light in advance, as they would have with the sun, which would have brightened the mist around them by degrees. The moon, being much less bright than the sun, just hung there, 'naked in the heavens at height / Immense above my head,' invisible until Wordsworth suddenly emerged from the sea of mist as if emerging from under water, 'and on the shore / I found myself of a huge sea of mist' (XIII.41–43). They were still well in advance of the dawn for the contrast to be so sharp: their shepherd-guide had underestimated the climbing prowess of his two young tourists. In fact, Wordsworth never does say if he saw the sun rise, so much did this unexpected, contrary vision move him. Well might he here invoke Milton's account of the creation of the world – 'A hundred hills their dusky backs upheaved / All over this still ocean'[10] – for it is exactly here that one begins to see again all of the neighbouring summits, after a hard climb with one's forehead bent 'earthward.'

The 'meditation' that 'rose in [him] that night' was not written down until thirteen years later, but though its idiom is Wordsworth's transcendental language of 1804, the process of imaginative transformation that it explains must have begun very soon. As in the Simplon Pass, Wordsworth's mind was affected by the sight of something quite different than what he had expected. The language of his first version of this experience, transferred to Switzerland for *Descriptive Sketches*, borrows heavily from his favourite youthful model, Beattie's *Minstrel* (1771).

> . . . oft the craggy cliff he loved to climb,
> *When all in mist the world below was lost,*
> *What dreadful pleasure! there to stand sublime,*
> *Like shipwreck'd mariner on desert coast,*
> And view th'enormous waste of vapour, tost
> In billows, lengthening to th'horizon round,
> Now scoop'd in gulfs, with mountains now emboss'd!
> *And hear the voice of mirth and song rebound,*
> *Flocks, herds, and waterfalls, along the hoar profound!*
> (*The Minstrel*, I.xxiii)

Wordsworth recollected his experience in very similar terms:

> Far stretch'd beneath the many-tinted hills,
> *A mighty waste of mist the valley fills,*
> *A solemn sea!* whose vales and mountains round

Stand motionless, to awful silence bound.
A gulf of gloomy blue, that opens wide
And bottomless, divides the midway tide.
Like leaning masts of stranded ships appear
The pines that near the coast their summits rear.
Of cabins, woods, and lawns a pleasant shore
Bounds calm and clear *the chaos still and hoar:*
Loud thro' that midway gulf ascending, sound
Unnumber'd streams *with hollow roar profound.*
Mounts thro' the nearer mists the chaunt of birds,
And talking voices, and the low of herds,
The bark of dogs, the drowsy tinkling bell,
And wild-wood mountain lutes of saddest swell.
(*Descriptive Sketches,* 492–507)

Wordsworth's description in *The Prelude* draws from both sources, particularly the image of a mariner shipwrecked on a coast. But both Beattie and his own earlier version are mainly frameworks that he invests with his own experience: they have no shepherd's cur, no forehead bent against an enemy, no chasm so precisely 'the third part of a mile' away from the exact spot where he was standing: no unique details at all. Beattie's Minstrel and the narrator of *Descriptive Sketches* are generic figures; but Wordsworth is himself, nowhere more so than in his vast generalization to something far beyond Beattie's range: 'the perfect image of a mighty mind.'[11] He needed no source for mountain mists; he had seen them all his life. What he had to account for was the surprise of *different* sights and sounds. This, as in London and Switzerland, is what released his mind from its planned itineraries and helped him to create himself as the poet of the unexpected. His 'perfect image of a mighty mind' refers not only to the constituent parts of the vision he perceived – mist/moon/ mountain/sea – but also to the image *he* created there, of

> . . . the glorious faculty
> Which higher minds bear with them as their own.
> This is the very spirit in which they deal
> With all the objects of the universe:
> They from their native selves can send abroad
> Like transformation, for themselves create
> A like existence . . .
> . . . They build up greatest things
> From least suggestions . . .
> (84–99, *passim.*)

Few greater passages of poetry have been built up from lesser suggestions – cur, hedgehog, and guide – than Wordsworth's redaction of his midnight ascent of Snowdon's Rhyd-Ddu path in July 1791. But the creativity of his 'native self' depended equally on his cultural reading, in this case from James Beattie and Thomas Pennant.

But here his narrative stops short. His eye was blanked out by his mind, and the physical itinerary became completely unimportant. We hear no more of Wales in Wordsworth's poetry until he recorded a similar reassessment of imaginative power above Tintern Abbey on the Wye in South Wales seven years later. But the 1791 tour went on after Snowdon without incident.

This lasted until they came to the summer country house of Thomas Pennant's neighbour, Thomas Thomas, at Pennant Melangell, in the midst of the barren Berwyn range. Here, in another border country, not far from 'the wizard stream of Dee,' Wordsworth had another liminal experience. Again, as on Snowdon, it had something to do with his misperception of the countryside, but this time the confusion arose in political, not aesthetic terms.

Since Wordsworth's recollection (written in 1829) is the only account we have of the incident, we can let him tell it, as he says it was 'so characteristic of the Cambro Britons that I will venture upon a recital of it.'

> I was introduced to Mr Thomas by my old friend and fellow Pedestrian among the Alps, Robert Jones, fellow of St John's Cambridge. One day we sat down une partie quarrée at the Squire's Table, himself at the head; the Parson of the Parish, a bulky broad-faced man between 50 and 60 at the foot and Jones and I opposite each other. I must observe that 'the Man of God' had not unprofessionally been employed most part of the morning in bottling of the Squire's 'Cwrrw' anglisé strong Ale, this had redden'd his visage (we will suppose by the fumes) but I sat at table not apprehending mischief.

Having set up his protagonist for a coming fall, Wordsworth continues,

> The conversation proceeded with the cheerfulness good appetite, and good cheer, naturally inspire – the Topic – the powers of the Welsh Language. 'They are marvellous,' said the rev[d] Taffy. 'Your English is not to be compared especially in conciseness, we can often express in one word what you can scarcely do in a long sentence.' 'That,' said I, 'is indeed wonderful be so kind as to favour me with an instance?' 'That I will,' he answered. 'You know perhaps the word Tad?' 'Yes.' 'What does it mean?' 'Father' I replied. 'Well,' stammer'd the Priest in triumph, 'Tad and Father there you have it' – on hearing this odd illustration of his confused notions I could not help smiling on my friend opposite; whereupon, the incensed Welshman rose from his chair and brandished over me a huge sharp pointed carving knife. I held up my arm in a defensive attitude; judge of the consternation of the Squire, the dismay of

my friend, and my own astonishment not unmixed with fear whilst he stood threat[e]ning me in this manner and heaping on my poor English head every reproachful epithet which his scanty knowledge of our language could supply to lungs almost stifled with rage. 'You vile Saxon!' I recollect was one of his terms, 'To come here and insult me an ancient Briton on my own territory!' At last his wrath subsided 'et me servavit Apollo.'[12]

Wordsworth's account would not please Welsh readers even today, with its pattern of archly condescending linguistic puns in English, Welsh, French, and Latin. He is the outlander smiling at the natives, and he had touched a nerve of political nationalism that in 1791 was coming close to the surface of everyday life. Jacobitism was still a vital memory in Wales and Ireland as well as Scotland, especially for people (like the parson) fifty or sixty years of age. Welshmen were well represented in the various liberal groups pressing for reform in England: the Reverend Richard Price, whose sermon touched off Burke's *Reflections*, was a Welshman.

Welsh does strike the native English speaker as a 'long' rather than a 'short' language, especially its proper names, though a place-name like Plas-yn-Llan, for example, is nominally more concise than 'the mansion in the church-village.' The priest chose to take insult in territorial terms, but Wordsworth might have reflected that beneath the surface of good manners among social equals, he was the only foreigner present, a guest, and a much younger one at that. The 'characteristic' of the Welsh was, in his view, that they take offence when they think their language is being laughed at by outsiders, but this is hardly a 'Cambro Briton' peculiarity. It may even be that the parson was having Wordsworth on in a complex set of cultural association jokes involving 'long knives,' exaggerated boast-curses, and strategically coded uses of Welsh (*Sais yw ef syn* = 'He is a Saxon, beware').[13] The shock of the situation was not its foreignness (the parson's 'scanty knowledge of our language' is belied by Wordsworth's own report), but rather finding *himself* regarded as foreign. It was as surprising in its way as coming to the top of Snowdon and finding not the sun but the moon standing naked in the heavens. And, as on Snowdon, he explains his surprise in terms not unlike those of 'the glorious faculty' of his own 'higher mind' he used there: 'et me servavit Apollo' (and Apollo preserved me).

The parson, who was probably the vicar, Ezekiel Hamer, may have been touchy about apparent condescension from Wordsworth, since the absentee rector who held the living as a sinecure was, like Wordsworth's Uncle Cookson, a chaplain to George III, and resided at Winchester as a prebendary at the cathedral. The fact that the major income of his parish flowed out to an English priest in comfortable circumstances like the young visitor's uncle may have made the priest particularly ill disposed to suffer smirks from a young, unemployed Bachelor of Arts. Welsh parsons were traditionally the poorest of the poor among clergy, receiving about £35 per annum for the care of up to four parishes.[14] One hopes Wordsworth did not call him Reverend Taffy to his face, even as a joke. But if ethnic slurs were on anyone's mind (e.g., 'Taffy was a Welshman, Taffy was a thief'), the parson had good reason to think of non-resident English priests – those in possession and those in prospect – as the real culprits.[15]

The incident reminded Wordsworth of the precarious position of curates who cared for a parish while the substantial 'living' went to an absentee who might hold several of them. Hence when the tour was over, back at Plas-yn-Llan, he read with mixed emotions a letter that awaited him. It was from John Robinson, informing him that Robinson was prepared to make him curate of a parish in Harwich (Robinson's parliamentary district for nearly twenty years), with a good possibility that the living itself would soon be his. The post was already in the family, its present occupant being Aunt Cookson's brother, William Cowper (not the poet of that name), who had fallen into debt and fled to Holland to avoid imprisonment.[16]

Wordsworth soon bade farewell to Jones and his sisters and travelled back to London in early September. His purpose, however, was not to take up the living that at the last possible moment seemed to rescue him from aimlessness. He went instead to thank John Robinson – and explain that, as he was not yet twenty-three, he could not technically take up orders yet! As if Robinson and Cookson, who had collaborated on the deal, did not know how old Wordsworth was, and – equally well – how easily this regulation could be bent ('anticipated' was the technical term[17]) for the intervening nineteenth months.

Arriving to pay his compliments and give his excuses, Wordsworth came once more into contact with the powerful tangent in his family universe which, had he been willing to follow it, could easily have been the making of his independence. Some part of the difference that marks Wordsworth off from a Crabbe, a Cowper or a Beattie, a difference that we now call 'Romanticism,' has to do with the refusals that he made in the next two months to offers that would have rescued him from his feckless university career and set him on a proper way after all. The difference between what he was giving up and what he was choosing (essentially, nothing at all) began to focus his mind as he rode back to London.

John Robinson resided at Wyke House in Isleworth, just west of London, not far from Heathrow, on a manor he had purchased in 1778 after switching his allegiance from Sir James Lowther to the King, which also allied him with Lowther's main northern antagonists, the Dukes of Norfolk and Northumberland. The neighbourhood was a sort of suburban fiefdom of Robinson's new friend, the Duke of Northumberland, Hugh Percy, whose seat, Syon House, 'one of the most conspicuous ornaments of the county of Middlesex,' was directly across the Great Western Road from Robinson's. Wyke House was the next biggest villa in the neighbourhood, reflecting Robinson's success in his lifelong ambition of raising his social status. Living with him were his daughter, Mary, and her husband of ten years, Henry Nevill, soon to become Earl of Abergavenny: that is, Wordsworth's second cousin by marriage. Brother John was now an officer of, and would later become master of, the *Earl of Abergavenny*, which had just returned on 19 August from another successful voyage; John had his position through Robinson's influence, and would soon stop by to pay his respects as well.[18]

Robinson's initial perplexity at Wordsworth's begging off the proffered curacy soon changed to anger. Here was the nephew who, four years earlier, had sworn to his brother, Admiral Hugh Robinson, to apply himself at university and be 'Senior wrangler or nothing!' Four years later he had achieved – if that is the word – the second alternative. Robinson had no special obligation to help William: there were fifteen other Wordsworth second-cousins of his generation to be helped, not to mention the thirteen nieces and nephews that Mary Myers was producing for his old but virile brother Hugh. One wonders just how Wordsworth expressed his reservations. To Mathews, referring to 'a gentleman you have most likely heard me speak of' (Robinson), he said only, 'I thought it was best to pay my respects to him in person, to inform him that I was not of age.'[19] It took a certain amount of courage to confront Robinson directly at Wyke House, but it also looked like effrontery to turn down such a favour for such a reason.

Wordsworth may have been bluffing his uncle, refusing a small but certain income against the possibility of a much larger independence. In late February, the courts had dissolved the Earl of Lonsdale's nuisance injunction against the Wordsworth claimants, and by late spring Dorothy's letters were full of hope that she and her brothers might at last be coming into their independence: 'We shall either be well off in regard to money matters or be left without a farthing.'[20] In late August her hopes seemed realized, for the Carlisle Sessions found in favour of the claimants. The court ordered Lonsdale to pay the administrators of the Wordsworth estate an amount to be determined by arbitration in London. But in the event, Dorothy's fears, not her hopes, came true, for Lowther contrived to get some of his own lawyers appointed to the board establishing the amount of restitution. One held John Wordsworth Sr's old post and had been recently been rewarded with the Cockermouth seat in Parliament: probably the man least likely in the kingdom, after Lonsdale himself, to look sympathetically on the claims of the Wordsworth children. This kind of chicanery allowed the process to drag on into the next year and peter out in the deadlock of endless rounds of meetings and negotiations for which rich men retain lawyers. But the idea that he might soon come into something approaching £1000 may have emboldened him to decline Robinson's offer.

The wonder is that Robinson did not wash his hands of this trouble-some nephew once and for all. Wordsworth did not stay long after the reason for his visit had become clear. As soon as Cookson heard the outcome of his interview with Robinson, he peremptorily ordered Wordsworth to Cambridge. When he returned there, he found some vacant rooms at St John's before the bulk of the students arrived. He had first to deal with a deeply depressed letter from William Mathews, who sounded near breakdown. Wordsworth's response was supportive, assuring Mathews of his interest in his welfare. He urged Mathews to look at things more positively, basing his advice on his own recent experience. 'It is an observation to whose truth I have long since consented that small certainties are the bane of great talents.' He and Mathews, like most of their Cambridge friends, were convinced of their talents. The question of how talent could survive and prosper, free of the entanglements of influence, was a cultural topic of great importance throughout the eighteenth century; many of the men who made the French Revolution were middle-class lawyers who despised the system of advancement they faced. To Mathews's desperate proposal that they should throw up all efforts at conventional advancement and adopt the wandering life, Wordsworth says he would prefer it 'to vegetating on a paltry curacy' – his estimate of Robinson's offer – 'were I [not?] so situated, as to be with relations to whom I were accountable for my actions.' He had strange notions of accountability, if he was turning down such offers for alter-natives that looked little better than Mathews's fantasy of the wandering life.

Cookson demanded an accounting of his reasons for turning down Robinson's offer. The refusal was especially galling to Cookson, who not only had first-hand information about William's university failures, but who also had painful memories of the nearly ten years through which he and his fiancée had waited and schemed for an offer like the one which had now dropped into their nephew's lap, only to be thrown away.

But Cookson was more forebearing than Robinson; he had another idea. William should undertake the study of Oriental languages – i.e., Hebrew and Aramaic, plus more Greek and Latin – with a view toward either becoming a more learned clergyman, or a university tutor. Cookson thought this field 'the best field for a person to distinguish himself as a man of Letters.'[21] It appears that Cookson talked seriously to his nephew about what he wanted to do with his life, and understood that it was something in the field of letters. What he *did* have in mind was hard to say, even for him. Yet Cookson reasoned, not unsympathetically, that William was good at languages, had taken considerable French and Italian instruction already, and was teaching himself Spanish, so why not study languages?

Wordsworth's reaction to this decent compromise was extreme: 'What must I do amongst that immense wilderness, who have no resolution, and who have not prepared myself for the enterprise by any sort of discipline amongst the Western languages? who know little of Latin, and scarce anything of Greek. A pretty confession for a young gentleman whose whole life ought to have been devoted to study.' The last sentence sounds as it were adapted straight from the mouth of William Cookson. And the sentence about little Latin and less Greek was an allusion – as he and Mathews knew very well – to Ben Jonson's praise for the supposedly minimal language skills of another young English poet in hard family circumstances: William Shakespeare.*

Cookson's plan would also have had the advantage of keeping William occupied for the next two academic years, at which point it might still be possible to install him in the Harwich curacy with no pettifogging excuses about ineligibility. At first, in early October, Wordsworth apparently agreed to this plan, so far as Dorothy knew: 'He is going, by the advice of Uncle Wm., to study Oriental languages.'[22] But then, to disengage himself from this plan, Wordsworth came up with the idea of improving his French so as to become a tutor for young noblemen on the Grand Tour. For this, the best method would be to go to France: 'in some retired Place in France which will be less expensive and more improving than in England.'[23] He pledged himself to take up Cookson's plan after a year in France, if no other employment was forthcoming.

One must admire Cookson's forebearance, or smile at his naïveté, in accepting William's alternative, which was much less plausible than the ones he and Robinson had offered. By trying to help their irresponsible nephew in the autumn of 1791, Cookson and Robinson contributed a good deal to the creation of the Poet Wordsworth. Pressing his duties upon him, they forced him to dream up other alternatives. Had they left him alone, he might have returned to Cumberland, to do God knows what, very possibly never to be heard of again. By giving him options that he could refuse only with difficulty, Robinson and Cookson forced him to find a way of escape. Even on its surface the French option looked dubious; there was still the small matter of finding the requisite young nobleman to tutor, and going to France in the autumn of 1791, just as the crestfallen Louis XVI was being forced to accept the new constitution, cannot have seemed the wisest course of action. It would have been like going to Moscow in 1917 to improve one's Russian.

John Robinson relented a little at the last minute. Despite William's ungrateful foot-dragging, Robinson suggested that he visit his sister-in-law, the bestselling poet and novelist Charlotte Smith, at Brighton before his departure. Finding himself delayed by unfavourable weather, and

---

* Jonson's line was, 'though thou hadst small Latin, and less Greek' ('To the Memory of My Beloved . . . Mr William Shakespeare' [1623], line 31).

remembering his pleasure in her *Elegiac Sonnets*, William did call, and was very kindly received by her. Smith's kindliness is all the more notable because she was no longer on good terms with Robinson. He was a trustee of her suit to recover her husband's estate, another runaway debtor like Mrs Cookson's brother. But she had become disenchanted with his desultory handling of the case and was contemplating filing suit against him, which she finally did in 1793. In her just-published novel, *Ethelinde, or The Recluse of the Lake* (1790), she had satirized Robinson in the thinly-disguised figure of Mr Royston, an unprincipled place-buying politician. (By 1798, in *The Young Philosopher*, he had become Sir Appulby Gorges, reminding those who knew that his rapacious political career had begun in the Lowther interest at Appleby.) But none of this affected Smith's welcome to young Wordsworth: perhaps she sympathized with him for having such hard relatives.

Wordsworth seems to have visited her several times during the week he was waiting for his ship, and copied down some of her poems.[24] If they discussed her latest novel, he would have been surprised to recognize a virtual allegory of parts of his own life, for *Ethelinde* is set in a renovated (but fictitious) Grasmere Abbey, remodelled into the pleasure retreat of a set of jaded London aristocrats. Smith was already hard at work on her fourth novel, *Desmond*, in which she would openly declare her sympathies for the French Revolution, and she now provided Wordsworth with letters of introduction to several important people she knew in France, principally Helen Maria Williams and Jacques-Pierre Brissot, that would materially influence his experiences there.

He sailed for France on the evening of 26 November, fourteen months after his return from his European walking tour, ending a year of aimless wandering in which he had ten different addresses. He would never enjoy such a randomly free year again during his early life, for much of what he did henceforth was motivated and determined by the sequence of events set in motion by his residence in France.

CHAPTER THIRTEEN

Revolution and Romance

Residence in France, 1791–1792

'Oh, happy time of youthful lovers!'
(IX.556)

Wordsworth crossed from Brighton to Dieppe on the night of 26 November, proceeding to Rouen next day, where he spent two days waiting for the diligence to Paris.[1] Wandering among the churches and towers associated with Joan of Arc, he learned that Helen Maria Williams had been there just before him. Throughout the coming year, their paths kept approaching each other but never quite crossed.[2] Williams had been visiting her friends Thomas and Monique du Fosse, whose happy story of true love triumphing over *ancien* privilege formed the opening episode in her immensely successful *Letters from France* (eight printings in 1790 alone). It told how Thomas, a young aristocrat, wooed a local merchant's daughter, despite furious opposition from his father, the old Count, who imprisoned him by *lettre de cachet*. The young man escaped by scaling a fifty-foot wall, fled clandestinely to England with his beloved (where Helen Williams became her tutor), and returned after the privileges of the nobility were dissolved to dance with his bride around a Liberty Tree planted on his ancestral estate, the very image of the world well lost for love. Three thousand copies of Williams's letter of thanks to the Rouenais for their enthusiastic reception of her work had recently been printed up and distributed; some were still in circulation when Wordsworth arrived. Williams's account of the du Fosses had a wide currency in Rouen as evidence of the Revolution's promises coming true. But Wordsworth could not have dreamed how useful the story would be to him as a way of framing, and disguising, the events of his exciting, frustrating year in France. It would eventually provide the base – or the cover – for his extremely *un*happy story of Vaudracour and Julia, his literary representation of his love affair with Annette Vallon in Orléans and Blois.

Paris

Arriving in Paris on Wednesday night, 30 November, he spent five efficient days criss-crossing the city, visiting the ruins of the Bastille and the Faubourg St Antoine in the east, the Pantheon and the Carmelite convent in the south, the National Assembly (since 1 October, the Legislative Assembly), the Jacobin Club, and the Champ de Mars in the west, and Montmartre in the north. This was pre-Terror Paris, jubilant in liberation despite internecine political struggles and war clouds gathering on France's northern borders. Wordsworth stayed in the exact centre, near the Palais-Royal, in the neighbourhood of the old Bibliothèque National. Possibly he took a room at White's Hotel, facing Notre-Dame des Victoires in Place des Petits-Pères, just off the rue de la Banque, where most polite English visitors congregated. Or if this was too expensive, he may have walked two or three streets east to the Hôtel d'Angleterre, which still stands, abandoned and dilapidated, at no. 56 rue Montmartre. The British who stayed at the d'Angleterre tended to be more actively engaged in French affairs, and included many Scots and Irish, among them the extremely radical Colonel John Oswald, one of those unbelievable characters rendered plausible by the intense pressures of the time. Once a hack journalist in London, Oswald had travelled to India, become a vegetarian and nature-mystic, walked back to Europe overland, and threw himself into the French Revolution with the intention of carrying it back to England. Wordsworth undoubtedly knew about this extremist, who lodged in his imagination as the figure of revolutionary excess that he would try to purge from his psyche in the character of Oswald in *The Borderers*.[3]

Each day Wordsworth sallied out from his room and 'coasted round and round the line / Of tavern, brothel, gaming-house, and shop' in the arcades of the Palais-Royal: 'Great rendezvous of worst and best, the walk / Of all who had a purpose, or had not' (IX.51–54). He of course was in the latter category, and he, like many young men on their first visit to Paris, was both shopping and perhaps sampling its pleasures. The arcades and cafés of the Palais-Royal, owned by the Anglophile Duc d'Orléans, were 'the centre in Paris not just of high politics and high ideals, but also of low pleasure.'[4] Even the apparently innocent 'shop' Wordsworth mentions could have been very seductive, if it were the bookstore of Orléans' secretary, Choderlos de Laclos, author of *Les liaisons dangereuses*, which stocked an extensive erotic inventory. Its gardens had long been the resort of prostitutes; since the outbreak of the revolution their number had increased dramatically, especially of very young girls.[5] To coast 'round and round the line' of such temptations indicates extensive reconnoitring: just looking? Or does his use of Milton's verb ('coasted') for Satan's approach to Paradise suggest a determination to test temptation?

He 'stared and listened with a stranger's ears to hawkers and haranguers, hubbub wild,' another Miltonic allusion for this modern Pandemonium, but he was far from being a complete stranger.[6] On the contrary, among his letters from Charlotte Smith was one addressed to Jacques-Pierre Brissot, who was just at this moment rising to the crest of his brief fame as the next ill-fated leader of the revolution.[7] Going to Paris in 1791 carrying an introduction to Brissot would have been approximately like going to Moscow in 1919 with a letter for, say, Trotsky. 'The stage beginning with the Legislative Assembly in October 1791 and ending with the September Massacres in 1792 belonged to Brissot': just about exactly the time-frame of Wordsworth's residence in France.[8] Brissot, a lawyer-journalist-*publiciste* like so many of the Revolution's leaders, was rapidly advancing his influence as a speaker for the most radical wing of the Jacobin Club, favouring immediate war against the German princes and the *émigrés*.[9] Although Wordsworth did not actually stay at Brissot's house in this neighbourhood as was later rumoured,[10] he was introduced into the Assembly by him, and on 2 December to a lively meeting of the Society of the Friends of the Constitution, or Jacobin Club, so called in Paris because it met in rented rooms at a former Jacobin convent off the rue Saint Honoré (see map).

Brissot took some interest in his young English visitor because he, a Protestant, had lived and worked (and been imprisoned for debt) in England in the early 1780s, and was well known to people in Wordsworth's orbit, such as Charlotte Smith, and especially Wilberforce, for lobbying against the slave trade through his humanitarian organization, Les Amis des Noirs. Wordsworth confidently reported to his brother Richard that 'I shall profit [by this acquaintance] on my return to Paris.'[11]

Wordsworth's association with Brissot is usually interpreted as a sign of his 'Girondism,' signifying a liberal rather than radical view of the Revolution. But this is truer after Wordsworth's return to Paris in October 1792, than of his arrival in December 1791. In late 1791, Brissot, like Jean-Louis Carra and Antoine-Joseph Gorsas (journalists known to Wordsworth), was still a leading member of the Jacobin Club, indeed of its radically militant minority. Brissot was at this moment more radical than Robespierre, who distrusted Brissot's war policy because he suspected (rightly, in many cases) the loyalty of the officer corps. And Jean-Baptiste Louvet, another Jacobin whom Wordsworth would praise as the one man brave enough to stand up against Robespierre, was at this time breathing fire in the same vein: 'with the swiftness of lightning let thousands of our citizen soldiers precipitate themselves upon the domains of feudalism. Let them stop only where servitude ends; let the palace be surrounded by bayonets, let the declaration of rights be deposited in the cottage.'[12]

Brissot welcomed his tall, quiet young visitor not only because of his letter from Charlotte Smith, but also because young English men and women were much in demand during the year of Wordsworth's residence in France. Parisians were '*devenus fous des Anglois*', according to Helen Maria Williams, and people in power like Brissot were extremely receptive to delegations from London and provincial corresponding societies.[13] Drawn by the excitement of the Revolution, the politics of these British fellow travellers ranged from sympathetic 'Friends of Liberty' to activists hoping to export revolution to England. Some were government spies or commercial double-agents, adding zest to the mixture. Besides Helen Williams, young people well known to Wordsworth (then or later) who were in and around Paris between late 1790 and late 1792 included James Losh, brother of his Hawkshead schoolmate; Felix Vaughan, the Fellow of Jesus; Tom Wedgwood, the ceramicist's son; Francis Tweddell, brother of Wordsworth's friendly rival at Cambridge; and James Watt, Jr, son of the great scientist and inventor, who was there as a travelling salesman for a Manchester carpet company.[14]

Only for Watt do we have hard evidence that Wordsworth knew him there and then, but it is quite emphatic: 'I went over to Paris at the time of the revolution in 1792 or 1793, and so was *pretty hot in it*; but I found Mr James Watt there before me, and *quite* as warm in the same cause.' It is in fact doubtful that Watt was there when Wordsworth arrived, and he had departed by the time Wordsworth returned to Paris the next autumn.[15] But the significance of the statement is that Wordsworth said it at all, and in tones of such sympathetic identification. Even if he was not physically present with Watt, he clearly knew what Watt was doing, and just as clearly allied himself with the same actions and opinions.

Wordsworth began to take instruction in the new politics immediately, from one of the hottest items being sold by the 'hawkers' outside the Palais-Royal, *L'Almanach du Père Gérard*, by Jean-Marie Collot d'Herbois. This was a simple catechism explaining the new constitution by means of conversations between virtuous peasants and Michel Gérard (1737–1815), a respected old delegate from Brittany to the first National Assembly of 1789. This little volume was the great-granddaddy of Mao Tse-tung's 'Little Red Book' and thousands of other simplified revolutionary tracts. It appeared on the streets in great quantities late in November, and on 2 December, at the meeting of the Jacobin Club Wordsworth attended, the newly appointed procurer of the commune, Pierre Manuel, promised to carry a copy with him always, the better to stay true to revolutionary principles. Members were invited to come to a special morning meeting on 5 December to witness Collot, Robespierre, and the 'schoolmaster Jacobin,' Léonard Bourdon (future petty-dictator of Orléans and mortal enemy of Annette Vallon's brother), instructing a group of children in this new catechism. An English translation by John Oswald, called *The Almanack of Goodman Gerard*, appeared almost simultaneously.[16]

Another publication involving Oswald appeared at this same time, whose influence can also be traced in Wordsworth's subsequent development. This was the *Chronique du mois*, a monthly journal of sophisticated essays on politics, philosophy, and the arts, for intellectuals who wanted deeper analyses of events than they got from the stream of partisan pamphlets which flooded the streets.[17] The *Chronique* is ranked 'among the most important and enduring journals of the Revolution,' and its existence (November 1791–July 1793) neatly brackets – like the period of Brissot's ascendancy – Wordsworth's time in France.[18] It was the kind of journal Wordsworth had in mind – quite literally, I believe – when he explained his ignorance of politics at the time by saying he had 'read, and eagerly . . . the master pamphlets of the day,'[19] but couldn't grasp the big picture because he had

> never chanced
> To see a regular *chronicle* which might shew—
> If any such indeed existed then—
> Whence the main organs of the public power
> Had sprung, their transmigrations, when and how
> Accomplished (giving thus unto events
> A form and body) . . .
> (IX.100–06; italics added)

This is exactly what the *Chronique du mois* did, and to believe that Wordsworth 'never chanced' to see it is to believe he wasn't much interested in reading, for it was exactly the kind of journal he would be most likely to pick up. His disingenuous disclaimer, 'if any such existed then,' gives him away.

Oswald was on the *Chronique*'s board of editors as British correspondent, listed as the friend of Tom Paine, James Mackintosh, and John Horne Tooke, and charged with 'destroying the popular prejudices which have so long sown discord and rivalry between two nations truly distinguished for their love of justice.'[20] Modelled on the *London Chronicle* (where Oswald had also worked), the *Chronique du mois* was published by the Cercle Social, a sort of liberal-masonic think-tank devoted to worldwide liberation and regeneration, which has been called 'the prototype of a modern revolutionary organization.'[21] The Cercle absorbed Brissot's Amis des Noirs, and the *Chronique* became the primary organ of French abolitionists. The *Chronique*'s mixture of political and literary reviews, coupled with general essays on geography, philosophy, history, science, and reprints of Enlightenment classics (Montesquieu, Rousseau, Hume),[22] provided a strong precedent for the 'monthly miscellany' to be called *The Philanthropist* which would shortly become Wordsworth's main literary project, for personal as well as political reasons.[23]

From fellow-travellers like Helen Williams and John Oswald to journalist-politicians like Brissot, Louvet, and Gorsas, Wordsworth was exposed throughout his year in France not simply to politics, but to politics mediated by actively interventionist writers who sought to shape the reality they described. Over five hundred new journals were started up in France between 1789 and 1792, 'an unprecedented number that reflected a separate revolution in the history of journalism.'[24] Brissot exclaimed on 2 August 1791, in his *Patriote français*, that 'the great tribune of humanity has been found: it is the press.' Publishers and writers – and politicians – were not such different roles as they usually are today; the repeated designation of 'publiciste' in many revolutionary biographies indicates how often they were one and the same person. Brissot, Carra, Gorsas, and all the others reported and defended their own actions as deputies in the pages of their journals: the line between politics, print, and profit described a complete and satisfactory circle.

None of this was lost on Wordsworth when, a year later, he had to return to London to raise money fast by his own publishing exertions. But in the first week of December 1791 he was not yet very 'hot in it.' He was still primarily a tourist, and revolutionary Paris did not long deter him from his plans. He went to the Bastille, 'and from the rubbish gathered up a stone, / And pocketed the relick in the guise / Of an enthusiast.' Of all the things he saw, the only one he 'hunted out' was Charles le Brun's painting of *The Repentant Magdalene* (1657), in the Carmelite convent in the Faubourg St Jacques: 'A beauty exquisitely wrought—fair face / And rueful, with its ever-flowing tears' (IX.79–80). Hung with special lighting, featuring recommended viewing stations for different perspectives, and accompanied by organ music, its baroque sensuality was so voluptuous that the Magdalene looked as much like a woman in the throes of passion as of repentance – or, with her imploring eyes, in the passion of being abandoned.

Orléans

Sticking to his plan, Wordsworth left Paris on 5 December – the day Mozart died in Vienna – and travelled seventy-five miles southwest to Orléans. Leaving Paris for Orléans, he was leaving the future for the past. Orléans was still a royal city, as the entire Loire valley had been the playground retreat of French aristocracy for centuries. Lord Gower, the British ambassador, considered the Loire to be the dividing line between monarchical and anti-monarchical France. These qualities made Orléans a favourite resort throughout the eighteenth century for English visitors eager to cultivate French fashions and manners, and sons of prosperous middle-class families were regularly sent there to learn the language and get some continental polish.[25]

Orléans in late 1791 was falling out of step with the times. Helen Williams, arriving shortly before Wordsworth, quickly sized it up as 'confined, illiberal, and disagreeable,' and departed almost on the day he arrived, heading for Paris where the action was. But Williams was already committed to political change, and Wordsworth was not. The established, conservative nature of Wordsworth's sense of himself at this time, for all his rebelliousness against his family's wishes, is illustrated by the fact that his activities were virtually identical with those of young Joseph Jekyll, son of a prosperous Whig merchant, who visited Orléans and Blois in 1775–76, when he also was twenty-one. Almost everything Jekyll did, Wordsworth did too: came to learn French, spent a week in Paris, stayed in the Rue Royal in Orléans, danced and flirted and gamed there, visited the parks and villas at La Source near Orléans, proceeded to Blois, thought Blois provincial but interesting, found the company of women the most agreeable way of learning the language, noted the frequency of poor girls winding distaffs while they led cows to graze, visited the famous chateaux of the Loire, and was finally called home by his father for spending too much money.[26]

But the conservativeness of what Jekyll called 'that stupid town of Orléans' suited William quite well at the outset. He told Richard he looked forward to meeting 'the best society this place affords.'

> I loitered, and frequented night by night
> Routs, card-tables, the formal haunts of men
> Whom in the city privilege of birth
> Sequestered from the rest . . .
>
> (IX.115–18)

In the way that foreign travel often takes us above our usual social strata, Wordsworth was now moving in better circles than he had in either London or Paris, and more elegant than the company of fellows at Cambridge. It was very much the kind of society frequented by those young gentlemen whom he was ostensibly training himself to accompany on their Grand Tours.

He stayed first at Les Trois Empereurs, the best hotel in the city, where he had knowledgeably made advance reservations.[27] When he learned he had just missed Helen Williams, 'this circumstance was a considerable disappointment to me.' But meeting her might have been a shock, since her ideas of 'best society' were already very different than his. He wrote Richard that he had found 'almost all of the people of any opulence are aristocrates [*sic*] and all the others democrates [*sic*]. I had imagined there were some people of wealth and circumstances favourers of the revolution, but here there is not one to be found.'[28] At first, 'the chief of [Wordsworth's] associates . . . were men well-born . . . the chivalry of France' (IX.130–33), military officers who were royalist sympathizers. These officers tried to convince Wordsworth of the justice of their cause, while making allowance for his youth, his awkward language, and his nationality – 'born in a land the name of which appeared / To license some unruliness of mind,' as he suavely put it.

Eager to demonstrate his frugality to Richard, he soon moved out of Les Trois Empereurs and found lodging above the shop of M. Gellet-Duvivier in the rue Royale, Orléans' main street, for eighty livres a month. The impressive buildings, modelled on those in Paris's rue Royale, provided an address well suited to a young English gentleman abroad. Living there with two or three royalist cavalry officers, and with his native frugality, Wordsworth seemed well set for months to come.

But, during his hunt for cheaper lodgings, he came across a 'very agreeable' family whose rooms were too expensive, but they struck up an acquaintance, and by 19 December he was telling Richard that 'I have passed some of my evenings there.' This was the home of André-Augustin Dufour, a magistrate's clerk living in the rue de Poirier near the rue Royale. One of Dufour's tenants was Paul Vallon, a lawyer's clerk working nearby, who was being visited that holiday season by his youngest sister, Marie-Anne, age twenty-five, called Annette.[29] This was the woman who changed the course of Wordsworth's young life.

Annette Vallon was not a great beauty, though her presumed miniature is certainly attractive. But everyone who met her soon commented, or complained, about her vivacity. 'Vivacious' was not a lively enough word for most, who called her, depending on their political perspective, either an 'active intriguer' of 'unscrupulous astuteness,' a woman combining 'great sensibility with a very vivid and impassioned imagination [and] rare firmness in her designs,' or 'a sort of Scarlet Pimpernel.'[30] Annette was as full of outgoing energy as Wordsworth was of power held in reserve, 'gifted with that natural intrepidity which was to make her a model conspirator.'[31] She took initiatives in hundreds of matters in dozens of different ways, braving the secret police of, successively, the Terror, the Directoire, and Napoleon. No doubt she often went too far. But she was a dynamo of action, a Théroigne de Méricourt or Olympe de Gouges of the Right, and, if not as stunning as those Revolutionary beauties, far more politically astute and successful than they. Olympe ended on the scaffold and Théroigne in a madhouse, but Annette, an underground fighter against the Revolution, was ultimately pensioned as a heroine of the royalist resistance to Napoleon: 'the valiant Chouanne of Blois,' a young woman as devoutly attached to king and country as her region's dominant historical figure, the Maid of Orléans.[32]

The contrast between this first love of Wordsworth's life and his second, mild Mary Hutchinson, could hardly be greater. But Annette's intensity was not very different than Dorothy's, and Annette eventually found in Dorothy a true soul mate. That Annette swept William off his feet with her energy, as a relatively independent woman four years his senior, is doubtful. He was reserved, but he was not shy. Dorothy spoke of his 'violence of Affection,' and the judgment that he was 'a dangerous young man . . . if there were unattached feminine hearts in the vicinity' seems just.[33] Their passion seems to have been gratifyingly mutual.[34]

Whatever else she may have been, Annette was one of the best things that ever happened to Wordsworth. Commentators on this love affair take sides even more than is usual with other people's affairs, but both he and she seem to have acted with exemplary sensitivity and understanding through it all – never perfect, but far above what might be considered the norm in such a tangled affair. One is glad to know that young Wordsworth had enough liveliness to attract a woman of Annette's spirit, just as one admires Annette's loyalty in never marrying, and calling herself Mrs or Widow (Veuve) William, or Williams, for the rest of her life. To put their affair in perspective, we have only to consider how many love affairs there were between foreigners and French men and women in these times of 'perturbing promiscuity,'[35] how many might have resulted in illegitimate births, and how few of the principals stayed in touch with each other as long as William and Annette did. On this scale, William Wordsworth and Annette Vallon have few equals for constancy as lovers in the French Revolution, even though, as is always the case, each was true to the other in her fashion, in his way.

The Vallon family home was in Blois, and they were of only slightly lower social class than Wordsworth. Like William, Annette had uncles who were clerics; both had duly taken the oath of the Civil Constitution, and one of them was at this time vicar to the great bishop Grégoire, who had taken office in Blois in March 1791. Her uncles (actually older first cousins) were sometimes called the 'Welsh uncles,' not because they were Welsh, but because the entire family had Jacobite connections, dating back to the Scots and Irish who had come over to France with James II in 1688. At that time the family was called Léonard, which was still the middle name of Annette's father and her younger uncle, corrupted to Léonnar.

These British family connections were one of those nice coincidences that gave the two young people something to talk about at first, things they already had in common to help explain their uncommon interest in each other. Annette may have been, initially, only an item in Wordsworth's frugal budget. 'I do not intend to take a [language] master,' he reported to Richard, 'I think I can do nearly as well without one.' This must have startled Richard, since the whole point of William's elaborately arranged trip was to learn the language to a *professional* standard. But William was employing another method, well known to young men abroad, learning the language by falling in love – or falling in love while learning. Annette, along with her tremendous physical energy, loved to talk,[36] and Wordsworth was for once disposed to listen.

Few expressions better capture the first enthusiasm that greeted the French Revolution than Wordsworth's 'Bliss was it in that dawn to be alive, / But to be young was very heaven!' But we must appreciate Annette's part in creating Wordsworth's bliss, for there are also not many expressions that better capture the transfiguring effect of young love at first sight than Wordsworth's description of Vaudracour's vision of Julia:

> Oh, happy time of youthful lovers—
> . . . .
> —he beheld
> A vision, and he loved the thing he saw.
> Arabian fiction never filled the world
> With half the wonders that were wrought for him:
> Earth lived in one great presence of the spring,
> Life turned the meanest of her implements
> Before his eyes to price above all gold,
> The house she dwelt in was a sainted shrine,
> Her chamber-window did surpass in glory
> The portals of the east, all paradise
> Could by the simple opening of a door
> Let itself in upon him . . .
>
> (IX.556, 582–93)

Whenever Wordsworth uses 'Oriental' diction like this, invoking Arabia, India or Babylon, his imaginative commitment is at its highest emotional pitch.

Annette's language matched Wordsworth's passionate expressions, though no one has seen fit to translate her accurately in print. At the end of her letter of 20 March 1793, after symbolically embracing Caroline in his stead and expressing her concern at worrying Dorothy, she turns to state directly her feelings for him: 'Aime toujours ta petite fille et ton Annette qui t'embrasse mil fois *sur la bouche, sur les yeux et mon petit que j'aime toujours, que je recomande bien à tes soins.*'[37] This is a series of increasingly intimate embraces, 'on the lips, on the eyes and [on] my little [one] that I still love, and that I warmly commend to your care.' 'Mon petit' is not Caroline; it is lover's code for something masculine, and in his keeping.

By allying himself with Annette, Wordsworth put himself directly athwart one of the two most important political issues threatening to rend France apart at that time: the treatment of non-juring priests. The other was the treatment of *émigrés*. Fierce laws against both groups had been adopted on 29 November, exactly when Wordsworth arrived in Paris. The two issues were closely connected in the popular patriot mind, because conservative priests were seen as fanatical fifth columnists plotting sabotage at home, while providing a network of information and supply for the feared invasion of *émigré* armies from the frontiers.[38] At the same time, in conservative areas like Orléans, renegade actions against constitutional priests also increased. The Vallons were the kind of family that was driven out of their initial sympathy with the Revolution by its harsh policies

toward *réfractaires*. The fact that Annette's two priestly uncles had taken
the civil oath immediately, and were important local council officials in
Blois both during and after the Terror, shows how these issues could
simultaneously divide and protect members of the same family.

Wordsworth said he left Orléans because he tired of royalist
proselytizing, but he covers his motive for leaving town in double-edged
language:

> But 'twas not long ere this
> Proved tedious, and I gradually withdrew
> Into a noisier world, and thus did soon
> Become a patriot—and my heart was all
> Given to the people, and my love was theirs.
>
> (IX.121–25)

This sounds like a political decision, but it was not purely so. The 'noisier
world' was Blois, the 'not long' was less than two months after he arrived
in Orléans, and the person among those people to whom he had given his
'heart' and 'love' was of course Annette – who was hardly 'a patriot' in
current usage.[39]

Blois

Wordsworth followed Annette home to Blois sometime between early
February and mid–April 1792. He was following as an ardent lover, but by
the later date he would already have been a prospective father, since they
conceived a child in mid–March. The affair must have been first
consummated in Orléans for him to make such a precipitous move, for
Blois figured nowhere in his plans.

In his next communication home Wordsworth's sense of time is clearly
that of a man in love: 'Since my arrival day after day and week after week
has stolen insensibly over my head with inconceivable rapidity.'[40] Some
huge difference lay between this and his last letter to Mathews the
previous November, when he had yawned, 'I am doomed to be an idler
throughout my life.' Now, he was full of 'confidence and resolution' about
finding 'some method of obtaining an Independence.' He directed
Mathews to scout about for 'some little corner . . . [in] the field of Letters
. . . which with a little tillage will produce us enough for the necessities,
nay even the comforts, of life.'[41] Obviously, something had happened in
the interim to motivate him: something beyond his control. If Mathews
does not find something in the literary line, Wordsworth says he will take
orders, accepting the intervention of Reverend Cookson despite the
personal humiliation: 'My Uncle the Clergyman will furnish me with a
title. Had it been in my power I certainly would have wished to defer the
moment.' But events were no longer in his power.

In coming to Blois, a mere thirty-five miles west of Orléans,

Wordsworth was entering a more attractive town, but a more vexed political climate. It was smaller (population 12,000), less royalist, and much more divided than Orléans. It was a mustering centre for a battalion of volunteers being raised in the new department of Loire-et-Cher. Its chapter of the Jacobin Club (known everywhere outside Paris by its proper name, Les Amis de la Constitution) was more radical than the one in Orléans, especially under its new leader, the constitutional bishop, Henri Grégoire, who had been elected president in November. Grégoire was one of the admirable idealists of the time, a Jansenist Catholic who sought to reform past ecclesiastical abuses with republican virtues while at the same time softening the excesses of revolution with Christian charity. Under his leadership, the Blois Amis de la Constitution was a much more open debating society than its mother club in Paris, which Grégoire regarded as a 'factious hell.'[42] His time as Bishop of Blois (October 1791–September 1792) coincides almost exactly with the period of Wordsworth's residence there. His chief aide was Annette's uncle Claude, and he would have been particularly receptive to Wordsworth if he came recommended by Brissot, since he was also a member of Brissot's Les Amis des Noirs and the fight against slavery (and anti-Semitism) remained his chief cause long after the Revolution had lost its original claims to virtue.[43]

On 3 February, two Englishmen were given permission to attend meetings of Les Amis de la Constitution, the only Englishmen ever referred to in the records of the Blois Amis.[44] Since Wordsworth had been introduced at the Paris headquarters, it is not unlikely that he would have been furnished with a letter or ticket of entry for use in the provinces. The Blois chapter was particularly associated with the Brissotins at this time[45] – as was Wordsworth – and Brissot's name continued to gain lustre. On 15 March he became in effect the prime minister of France, when Louis asked him to form a new ministry.

But at the same time Blois was becoming a zealous centre of the counter-revolution, rife with agents from the Vendée further west. 'Vendée' was a term used loosely to signify royalist insurrections all over the west of France, including not only the Vendée proper, south of Nantes, but also Normandy and Brittany. Many of these royalist Catholic agents were later tracked by the police to the residence of 'the demoiselles Vallon, one of whom is married to an Englishman named Williaume.'[46]

Yet, for all its divisions, Blois was (and is) a cosier town than Orléans. The Comte de Cheverny, though no republican, found it much preferable to Orléans for its lack of class distinctions, friendly family-like gatherings, and elegantly dressed women and pretty marriageable girls.[47] Annette was one of these, and it was her home town; all her family were there, she was better known, and 'better looked after.'[48] These were mixed blessings for the two lovers, who had had more freedom in the relative anonymity of Orléans. But in the heady days of first love in springtime – 'One great presence of the spring' – they were free to walk about, down the rue du Pont, the busy shopping street where she lived, to the river, and up into the old medieval district by the convent where she had been educated.

But Annette needed more care as the months went by, and was more dependent on family and friends, who were not pleased by her connection to an unemployed and evidently not rich young Englishman, who was at best a Protestant and at worst a republican – and a poet. Wordsworth was in no position to provide practical help, and as a result was left more on his own, far less disposed than before to devote himself to the charade of learning French to become a travelling tutor; that career option was now completely out of the question. He was slowly determining himself to marry and provide for Annette. It was in this mixed state, of deep passion, desperate responsibility, and wandering loneliness, that his acquaintance with Michel Beaupuy ripened quickly into deep friendship – indeed, as *The Prelude* freely acknowledges, the most important male friendship of his life before Coleridge.

Michel-Arnaud Bacharetie de Beaupuy (1755–1796) is known in English, if at all, as a character in one part of Wordsworth's long poem on 'the growth of my own mind.' But he is honoured in France as one of the heroic generals who died protecting the Revolution in its vulnerable infancy. In 1798 he was celebrated posthumously as 'le Nestor et l'Achille de notre armée', and his fame has endured. Napoleon's marshals are the military names we most remember from this period, but in the early 1790s France's fate hung upon the skill and bravery – and loyalty – of other generals, several of them foreign freedom fighters, who gave their lives for the Revolution or were destroyed by it, men like Charles-François Dumouriez, Theobald Dillon, Francisco Miranda, Adam Philippe de Custine, and Louis-Lazare Hoche.

Beaupuy's father, like Wordsworth's, had been a steward of aristocratic estates.[49] On his mother's side, he was descended from Montaigne; the family stressed education and public service for its sons: a complete edition of Diderot's massive *Encyclopédie* dominated the family library. Beaupuy had been one of the first to speak out in Mussidan in favour of the changes which led up to the revolution. He supported the call sent out in October 1790, by the leaders of the Limoges Amis de la Constitution for a deputation to be sent to London to meet with English sympathizers. Hence he was happy to meet an Englishman in Blois, especially one so ripe for the final stages of conversion to the good new cause.

At the time they met in February 1792, Beaupuy was rising fast in rank as mobilization, war, and desertions multiplied opportunities. It is unlikely that Wordsworth would have become well enough acquainted with him by 3 February to have been introduced to the Amis by him, but it is very likely that Wordsworth met him there, since Beaupuy was a regular member, and on the two previous Sundays had repeated, by popular demand, his speech on the dangers of excessive mistrust in politics.[50] His regiment, the Thirty-second Bassigny, was in Blois to raise itself to full strength before leaving for service on the Rhine. By his friendship with Beaupuy, Wordsworth became personally involved in the other great political issue racking France at this time: the proper attitude toward aristocrats, particularly those in the military, and most especially those who might become dangerous *émigrés* if given command of troops near the volatile frontier. Beaupuy's speeches on 22 and 29 January against excessive political mistrust were thus very timely, and he was much in advance of the rest of his class in moving rapidly beyond support of limited constitutional monarchy toward full-blown republicanism.[51]

Wordsworth claimed that Beaupuy was 'with an oriental loathing spurned as of a different cast[e]' by his fellow officers (IX.297–98). But this is an imaginative transference of the attitudes of the officers with whom Wordsworth had mixed in Orléans, the better to set off Beaupuy's republican virtues. It is one of several ways in which Wordsworth makes a coherent story out of his 'residence in France' by treating it as though it all happened in *one* unnamed 'city on the borders of the Loire.' Beaupuy was so admired at the Amis that he cannot have been as lonely and scorned as Wordsworth paints him, especially since the 'brothers' of the Thirty-second Bassigny took the oath of allegiance to the Assembly there on 3 February (the same day the two Englishmen were given attendance privileges), and on 14 March the regiment was invited to assist at meetings.[52] But if his aristocratic fellows did scorn his friendship, Beaupuy was all the more receptive to a young, open-minded Englishman. Wordsworth, listening to Beaupuy speak before the local Jacobins, improved his French in a different register than he used with Annette. His political education now began to accelerate rapidly, for here as throughout France the most basic questions of citizens' rights and responsibilities were thrashed out night after night, often with immediate consequences in action the next day.

After meetings of the Amis, Beaupuy elaborated on the questions of the day for his new friend.

> Oft in solitude
> With him did I discourse about the end
> Of civil government, and its wisest forms,
> Of ancient prejudice and chartered rights,
> Allegiance, faith, and laws by time matured,
> Custom and habit, novelty and change . . .
>
> (IX.328–33)

These topics marked the range of contemporary debate, from Burke ('custom and habit') to Paine ('novelty and change') in English terms. If these lines reflect Beaupuy's interests and not simply Wordsworth's change of heart by 1804, they indicate that Beaupuy took longer views in conversation than he may have been able to in debate, though his speeches indicate he was capable of resisting popular hysteria.

But they were still young men of their class, in process of transition to new political allegiances, and they both took 'more delight,' when they were alone, Wordsworth confesses 'freely,'

> In painting to ourselves the miseries
> Of royal courts, and that voluptuous life
> Unfeeling where the man who is of soul
> The meanest thrives the most, where dignity,
> True personal dignity, abideth not . . .
>
> (352–56)

There is a touching realism in this detail of two young men discussing such a topic at such a time and place, when 'royal courts' themselves were soon to pass out of existence, amid far worse 'miseries.' Beaupuy and Wordsworth were talking about the difficulty of advancing in the kinds of careers their families and training had set before them – based on influence and connections – just as the arena for this particular historical form of institutionalized meanness was disappearing. New career models were being created, in which both Wordsworth and Beaupuy would succeed in ways they could as yet barely conceive.

On weekends they ranged further afield, walking out into the profound silences of the great oak and beech forests of the chateaux south and east of Blois. Wordsworth mentions Chambord and Romarentin by name, in addition to 'the imperial edifice of Blois' itself, and alludes to others, such as Beauregard and, north of the Loire, Vendôme.[53] The chateaux themselves, then as now, give grand testimony to both the power and the price of passion, since the story behind many of them is one of beautiful mistresses demanding of their 'royal knight' some magnificent demonstration of his love – Diane de Poitiers' Chenonceaux being only the most stunning example. Indeed, from Joan of Arc through Diane de Poitiers to – for young Wordsworth – Annette Vallon, the power of women controlling politics through passion is a sensation one can still feel strongly all through the Loire Valley.

In the deep woods of these immense pleasure palaces, Wordsworth and Beaupuy talked of two topics especially: individual heroism and, as a dramatic example of it, rescuing damsels in distress. Wordsworth mentions Ariosto's Angelica and Tasso's Erminia, but his own Annette was the real case in point. No one ever asks if Wordsworth mentioned Annette to Beaupuy, but he must have, given the older man's reputation as a gallant. In the rich confusions of life and literature which Wordsworth concocted out of this period of his life, one can almost wish his Julia had met Beaupuy instead of Vaudracour.

Beaupuy brought Wordsworth's romanticizing up short. One day they came upon 'a hunger-bitten girl' following along after her heifer, to which she was looped by a cord, 'busy knitting in a heartless mood of solitude.' ''Tis against *that* which we are fighting,' said Beaupuy, startling Wordsworth from his romantic daydreams (*1850*, 517–18). Beaupuy touched here on the most elusive promise of this and all future democratic revolutions, that after liberty and fraternity would come equality, or something nearer to it:

> that poverty,
> At least like this, would in a little time
> Be found no more, that we should see the earth
> Unthwarted in her wish to recompense
> The industrious, and the lowly child of toil
>
> (IX.522–26)

This was the issue that successively more radical leaders in Paris could never get ahead of, either by means of a maximum imposed on the price of bread, or by a reign of terror instituted against those who were supposedly hoarding its supply or speculating on its scarcity.

Beaupuy departed from Blois and from Wordsworth's life on 27 July 1792. He died at Emmendingen in 1796, but Wordsworth in *The Prelude* says he died fighting on 'the unhappy borders of the Loire,' in action against the Vendéan counter-revolution of 1793. If Wordsworth ever learned the truth, he never corrected it, and it is more fitting dramatically that *his* Beaupuy should have died there rather than in Germany. In a sense, Beaupuy's 'death' on the Loire may be said to represent the death that Wordsworth courted by returning to France in 1793 – a poetical 'sacrifice' of his heroic friend, representing the heroism he could not achieve.

After Beaupuy left, Wordsworth remained in Blois until early September, tending to Annette as much as he could, and attending Grégoire's meetings even more than he had. He wrote the final drafts of *Descriptive Sketches* in late spring and summer of 1792, and the influence of Grégoire's millennial republicanism is clearly evident in the sections of the poem devoted to Switzerland. Grégoire referred to places Wordsworth had actually been, to make a conventional point about natural republicanism: 'On the brow of the mountains of Appenzell and the Alps one often still finds man in all his dignity, gifted with exquisite reason, manly virtue, and even crowned with broad understanding; but it is also there that at the head or the rear of his flocks he marches carrying a sword, a crook, and some books.'[54] Wordsworth virtually sets the images in this passage to verse, with the added licence of poetic diction:

> here
> The traces of primaeval Man appear.
> The native dignity no forms debase,

The eye sublime, and surly lion-grace.
The slave of none, of beasts alone the lord,
He marches with his flute, his book, his sword.

(IX.528–33)

His motives for going to Switzerland in 1790 had been formed by traditional idealizations of the Swiss cantons as bedrocks of mountain republicanism. But, drafting the final version of the poem in 1792, this ideal republicanism was infused with his daily experience of the debates that were creating a modern republic in the largest country in Europe. Grégoire's religious interpretation of the process fitted well with Wordsworth's secular motives of 1790. But when the monarchy was dissolved, two weeks after Beaupuy's departure, the new state was bathed in blood. The first Republic was declared on 21 September – on a motion by Grégoire[55] – and these idealized pieties became harder to sustain.

Wordsworth could hardly have found two more congenial mentors for his conversion to republicanism than Beaupuy and Grégoire. Each was a convert himself, from the old Estates of the nobility and the church, and each tried to preserve the best of the old while seeking to realize the best in the new. But his change of opinions was both quickened and complicated by Annette's ambivalent attitude toward the course of events. He met her at almost the last moment when she and her family regarded the Revolution with sympathy; by the time he left her, they were dead set against it. Hence the contrary motions of love and politics at work on Wordsworth in 1792 had an extremely strong torque: a bishop and a nobleman, natural enemies of revolution and republic, persuaded him to accept it; a daughter of the Third Estate, the bourgeois professional class which created the Revolution, increasingly urged him against it. Paris was too far to the left for him, Orléans too far to the right; only in Blois did the right combination fall fortuitously into place. He was 'radicalized' in love and politics simultaneously, and it is moot to say which came first, though it is true that one would not have occurred without the other. But who could have predicted the odd ways in which they came to him? It is not unlikely that Annette's social conservatism helped make her attractive to him. But it is equally clear that conservative nobles and clergymen had earned his contempt in both France and England, whereas his respect for *constitutionnels* like Grégoire – and Annette's uncles – stayed with him to the end: 'he had known many of the abbés and other ecclesiastics, and thought highly of them as a class; they were earnest, faithful men.'[56]

Political events soon began to outstrip personal affairs for Wordsworth, as they did for everyone else in France. Between Beaupuy's departure and Wordsworth's next letter to Richard, on 3 September, events moved so fast that 'the soil of common life' became 'too hot to tread upon' (IX.169–70), especially for a young man trying to arrange very complicated personal affairs in a very unstable foreign country. On 25 July the German Duke of Brunswick issued his infamous Manifesto, threatening an 'exemplary vengeance' on the city of Paris and its inhabitants if they did not submit to the rule of their king. Two days later, Beaupuy's regiment and many others were hastily called up to the front.

Then, on 10 August, came the successful assault on the Tuileries by the aroused Paris *sections*. Six hundred of the king's Swiss guards were massacred, prelude to worse to come. The Assembly immediately suspended the monarchy and imprisoned the king, dissolved itself into a National Convention, and on 11 August appointed its own ministers: the audacious Danton at Justice, the earnest Roland for the Interior. The new ministry, with the extraordinary powers of the 11 July decree – '*la patrie en danger!*' – began ordering the arrest of hundreds of prisoners, particularly priests and nuns (many of British descent), who were easy to accuse of complicity in a much-feared invasion of *émigré* and foreign armies. With the news on August 23 of the fall of the border fortress of Longwy to the *émigré* princes, followed a week later by the loss of Verdun, fear grew to panic and suspicion to paranoia, because both losses were widely believed to be the result of internal subversion and betrayal. Refractory priests were attacked by a new decree on 26 August and rounded up. For two weeks the jails filled, and the stage was set for the signal to be given for the horrible massacres of 2–5 September. Half the prison population of Paris, over a thousand persons, most of them non-political, were butchered in their cells by the infamous *septembriseurs*, freelance murderers drunk on blood, and the Revolution was set on its course toward Terror. The head of the Princess Lamballe on one pike and her torn genitalia on another are all the symbolism one needs to trouble thoughts of the 'inevitability' of democracy's progress.

Orléans Again

In the midst of these fever-pitched days, Annette's family spirited her away, possibly without telling Wordsworth. She was now in her sixth month, and her appearance had begun to raise comment, so she was removed to Orléans. The circumstance is recorded in *The Prelude*, and has no parallel in Helen Williams's account of the du Fosses.

> To conceal
> The threatened shame the parents of the maid
> Found means to hurry her away, by night
> And unforewarned, that in a distant town
> She might remain shrouded in privacy
> Until the babe was born.
>
> (IX.612–17)

Vaudracour's desperation at this moment is similar to Wordsworth's, judging by his letter to Richard of 3 September, demanding more money. His last words, added after his French *adieux*, are, 'You will send me the money immediately.'[57] Given his initial capital of £40, his proposed budget of expenses, and the continuing decline in the value of the *livre*, he should not have been in such bad straits. Richard sent the money, enough for several more months, but some word of why William needed it must have reached the two uncles who had to approve these disbursements, for they refused a subsequent request, forcing Wordsworth home within four months, 'compelled by nothing less than absolute want of funds for my support' (IX.190–91).[58] What he really needed, of course, were funds adequate to support a wife and child.

He posted his letter from Blois on 3 September but he left town in a hurry, because he was in Orléans at the time of the September Massacres, which continued to the 5th, with further outrages reported in the provinces until the 9th. Annette may have stayed at the townhouse of her friends the du Fours, near Wordsworth's old quarters in rue Royal, since Mme du Four attended at Caroline's birth in mid-December.[59] But it is also possible, on the evidence of *Descriptive Sketches*, that she stayed outside of town in a cottage near the little river Loiret, just south of the city. Wordsworth places the conclusion of *Descriptive Sketches* on the Loiret, and the last seventy lines of that poem are some of the most contemporaneous lines he ever wrote, where his emotion is least 'recollected in tranquillity.' They are set under the mild light of 'October clouds,' which can only be October of 1792.

If we bring together the conclusions of *Descriptive Sketches* and the story of Vaudracour and Julia, the difference between them reveals a space in which we can compare Wordsworth as he was in 1792 and as he chose to represent himself in 1804. In *Descriptive Sketches* he says nothing directly about a birth. Conversely, in his tale of Vaudracour and Julia he says little about the French Revolution, though we know his attitudes toward it were very much affected by his affair with Annette. 'The voice of freedom' could not rouse Vaudracour from 'personal memory of his own deep wrongs.' By contrast, in *Descriptive Sketches*, the voice of Freedom is very loud ('on ten thousands hearths his shouts rebound'), and seems to promise everything.

All this arises confusingly on a first-time reader of *Descriptive Sketches*, who would think until this moment that he is still in the Alps. But the poem's conclusion swerves several hundred miles west with no explanation. Its closing scenes on the banks of the Loiret are ruminations in the mind of a speaker who can hear 'the rumbling drum's alarm' and see 'the red banner' of martial law being raised.[60] Orléans was close to civil insurrection at the time Annette and Wordsworth returned to it, hardly an ideal place for having a baby, making Annette's removal to a suburban cottage all the more plausible.

Descriptive Sketches hopes for universal freedom in every cottage in every valley, but acknowledges that at this moment of crisis such hopes are hard to entertain: 'no more thy maids their voices suit / To the low-warbled breath of twilight lute' (748–49). His own domestic cottage fantasies, already shared with Dorothy in 'a thousand dreams of happiness,' are here interwoven with a commonplace contrast of revolutionary rhetoric, between court and cottage. Wordsworth has mixed in his idealized recollections of Swiss cottages with the cottage where Annette, his own sad maid, was lodged, so that apparently innocuous phrases like 'the little cottage of domestic Joy' (601) and 'the central point of all his joys' (571) become loaded with significance, upon examination.

Rousseau's cottage-ideology of a universal republic seemed to be embodied in concrete form with the declaration of the new French republic on 21 September, which was reinforced locally by a public festival in Orléans the next day, presided over by Bishop Grégoire.[61] This day, 22 September 1792, the autumn equinox, would become Day One of Year One of the new republican calendar. The speaker in *Descriptive Sketches* is in the countryside beside the Loiret, and though he can hear the rooster (the Gallic cock of republican liberty) 'crow . . . with ear-piercing power 'till then unheard,' in his own mind 'the falling leaf' chases these 'delightful dreams' of freedom away, awaking 'a fainter pang of moral grief' (769). What seemed publicly so promising – if dangerous – was privately distressing. This is Vaudracour's situation as well, bringing these two solitary characters (Vaudracour and the speaker of *Descriptive Sketches*) into a proximate identity:

> Nor could the voice of freedom, which through France
> Soon afterwards resounded, public hope,
> Or personal memory of his own deep wrongs,
> Rouze him, but in those solitary shades
> His days he wasted, an imbecile mind.
>
> (IX.931–35)

By the time he wrote these lines, Wordsworth knew very well the further excesses to which the Revolution descended in order to defend itself. But in the earlier poem he, unlike Vaudracour, is able to imagine a new birth because he personally is very near to one about to occur, and he can, unlike Vaudracour, combine them symbolically, and sympathetically:

> Lo! from th'innocuous flames, a lovely birth!
> With it's [*sic*] own Virtues springs another earth:
> Nature, as in her prime, her virgin reign
> Begins, and Love and Truth compose her train;
>
> (782–85)

As Wordsworth walked alone at night along the Loiret, near the cottage where Annette was lodged, he tried to imagine how the Revolution might eventually overthrow 'every sceptred child of clay' and restore peace and quiet to all villages and village maids with *its* newborn child. This hope for a coincidence between his own personal situation, disguised here, and the terrible events of the Revolution threatening to engulf him and Annette, is indeed the only thing that enabled Wordsworth to bring *Descriptive Sketches* to a close. It is exactly the failure of this coincidence between private and public hopes that led Wordsworth twelve years later in *The Prelude* to represent that *un*worthy heart, Vaudra-cour, as the most tragic figure appearing anywhere in the poem 'on the growth of my own mind': 'His days he wasted, an imbecile mind.'

Paris Again

Wordsworth left Orléans for Paris on 28 October 1792. He did not intend to return soon, for he authorized M. Dufour, Paul Vallon's landlord, to represent him as father when the child was baptized.[62] His paternity legally acknowledged, he turned homeward to seek some means to support his new family. He intended to marry Annette as soon as he was sure he could provide for her responsibly, but this would require considerable funds. He determined to take church orders, the position he had so long avoided but now so desperately needed, or to exercise his second option, an advance in anticipation of the payment of the Lowther debt. This seemed more plausible at the time than it does now, and is alluded to in *The Prelude*, for no one imagined how long Lowther's technical objections would be strung out:

> The lovers came
> To this resolve—with which they parted, pleased
> And confident—that Vaudracour should hie
> Back to his father's house, and there employ
> Means aptest to obtain a sum of gold,
> A final portion, even, if that might be;
>
> (IX.645–50)

There were difficulties in the way of marriage in France as well. Wordsworth's religious opinions were not so strong that he would have cavilled much at a Catholic ceremony for Annette's sake, but a Catholic wife would have scandalized Reverend Cookson and his arch-Evangelical friends like Wilberforce. However, Annette's family would have been equally unhappy with a constitutional marriage to a liberal, free-thinking English Protestant, and a secret marriage before a non-juring priest would have been, strictly speaking, illegal.[63] Here too there were fateful double-binds. Just at this time, on 20 September to be exact, the Convention completed the legislation which made the recording of marriages entirely a civil affair. But this new law, which would have suited Wordsworth well, made marriage more difficult for the Vallons, although Annette's two uncles were constitutional priests who could have performed the ceremony in manner acceptable to their family's feelings and loyalties. This issue, like all others, was very much up in the air at the time. The new republic might be defeated or fall apart at any minute. Indeed, this added ambiguity may have determined Wordsworth to go home to see what he could accomplish at his end.

Annette, in her letter of the coming March, speaks without hesitation about her desire to get married as soon as possible. One detail in particular made it urgent: she was not allowed to keep her baby at home because of her unmarried state. Nor does Annette try to disguise how much this circumstance hurt her. But the baby had a father even if Annette did not have a husband, and so the two lovers made their farewells, and Wordsworth set off. Now indeed was he like a hero in romance, setting out to seek his fortune, and as a land of adventure Paris in October of 1792 could hardly be improved on.

With his gift for being at the right place at the right time, he arrived back in Paris on 29 October and awoke next morning to the cries of street vendors hawking Louvet's *Denunciation of the Crimes of Maximilien Robespierre*, potentially one of the most decisive publications of this incredibly literate revolution. Louvet had daringly taken up Robespierre's challenge to Brissot's attack on him two days before in the Convention: that anyone who suspected him of aiming at supreme power – dictatorship – should say so. Crypto-royalism was the more damning form of the charge: the French title of Louvet's pamphlet is *A Maximilien Robespierre et ses royalistes*. After a terrific pause, Louvet rose from his seat and walked to the rostrum, declaring 'Moi, Robespierre, je t'accuse!' The moment had great theatrical effect, but like many such moments at the time, its apparent spontaneity was carefully orchestrated. Louvet's pamphlet was closely modelled on Brissot's *A tous les républicains de France sur la Société des Jacobins de Paris*, written after his expulsion from the Jacobins on 10 October, and published immediately both as a pamphlet and in the *Chronique du mois*.[64]

Brissot, Louvet, and other erstwhile Jacobins were finally starting to realize that Robespierre and the more radical delegates were isolating them for blame in the massacres and the unsuccessful prosecution of the war. Louvet's speech and pamphlet had instant popularity, for Robespierre was always more feared than admired among his fellow delegates, though the galleries loved him, especially the women. But Louvet and the other Girondins (whom Brissot and the other Paris liberals joined only now) were publicists more than politicians. They – like young Wordsworth – expected that words alone could accomplish their desires, hopefully turning a tidy profit as well. Instead of following Louvet's accusation with a motion of no confidence against Robespierre, these new converts to moderation rewarded Louvet with the editorship of a new tabloid, *Bulletin des amis de la vérité*, the Girondins' belated attempt to begin influencing *sansculottes* opinion: their 'Friend of Truth' was to oppose Marat's 'Friend of the People.' Hence it is a mistake to attribute too much personal heroism to Louvet's 'hardihood' and the weakness of his 'irresolute friends,' as Wordsworth does, though in retrospect they certainly appeared so.

Left surprisingly alone, Robespierre, who had been utterly incoherent in the uproar produced by Louvet's accusations, prepared an effective defence of himself, which Wordsworth would certainly have read. For him, walking out from his lodgings as before to see the new revolutionary sights, this pamphlet war was but one of several concrete signs of the immense change that had come over the city in the year he had spent in the provinces. If Orléans had gone bad, Paris was much worse. Brissot's *A tous les republicains de France* warned that the country was passing beyond participatory democracy into manipulated anarchy, a charge that Wordsworth echoes. A year earlier, to be the friend of a friend of Brissot's was enough to gain one entrance to the Jacobin Club, but now Brissot was no longer a member, and Louvet and Roland were ejected on 26 November. Similarly, the revolutionary sites that Wordsworth visited in late 1791 had been places of honourific mass demonstrations or celebrations: the Assembly, the Champ de Mars, the Pantheon, and the ruins of the Bastille. Now they were sites of murder and imprisonment: the Place du Carrousel, where the King's Swiss guards had been killed and their bodies burned on 10 August, and the Temple, 'the prison where the unhappy monarch lay . . . with his children and his wife' (X.42–43). The change was evident even in the way people looked and moved.[65] People kept close to the walls, avoided eye-contact, were more guarded in conversation, and adopted a studied uniformity of dress and demeanor, in contrast to their earlier zany costumes and harmless outlandish behaviour. Strange people began turning up in public whom nobody seemed to know. They were variously identified as rabble from the *sections*, 'scum of all nations, Genoese, Corsicans, Greeks,' or 'a convocation from hell,' as Buzot characterized the mob organized by Marat to pack the galleries at the Convention.

Wordsworth was scared by the new atmosphere: 'The fear gone by / Pressed on me almost like a fear to come' (X.62–63). Thinking about the massacres, he could not sleep at night, and seemed to hear, like Macbeth, a voice crying 'to the whole city, "Sleep no more!" ' (77) 'It seemed a place of fear . . . Defenceless as a wood where tigers roam.' This was no metaphor, or not Wordsworth's metaphor alone, for 'tigers' was consistently the word most commonly applied to the *septembriseurs* and the tough-looking thugs now swaggering on the boulevards. Within a year, it became the epithet for virtually one man alone, Robespierre.

Why then did Wordsworth stay in Paris, 'at a time so exciting,' for nearly six weeks? Few questions have exercised his biographers more. Their apparent assumption is that, with all his personal problems, he should have hurried home to try to make arrangements for a new life with Annette. But this is an excessively anti-romantic judgment. If he had gone straight home, with such mighty changes working all around him, we would probably fault him for that. He now saw clearly the *causes* of what he had registered only as effects in Orléans and Blois:

> now
> In some sort seeing with my proper eyes
> That liberty, and life, and death, would soon
> To the remotest corners of the land
> Lie in the arbitrement of those who ruled
> The capital city;
>
> (X.106–11)

He was 'in some sort seeing with my proper eyes' because, among other reasons, he was using them to read Brissot, for Brissot's main point was that Robespierre was trying to elevate the Paris Commune above all the other departments, and that Robespierre's insistence on the unity of the republic masked his determination to consolidate his control of it.[66]

Wordsworth's possible reasons for delaying his departure to the Channel ports range from the mundane to the portentous. He might have had trouble securing a passport, no small matter at the time, when a desire to go to the frontier could be interpreted as the first step toward treason. The British military attaché and spy, Captain Munro, used these hassles as his cover story for staying in town – the better to relay reports on the identities and activities of the English community back to Whitehall. Or, Wordsworth might simply have been sticking to his original plan, as he had explained to his brother, 'I shall return that way [via Paris] and examine it much more minutely.' And a new kind of fantasy was now available, that Wordsworth indulged to the full, as he had with Beaupuy: imagining oneself as the heroic saviour of the Revolution:

> Inly I revolved
> How much the destiny of man had still
> Hung upon single persons . . .
> . . . not doubting at that time—
> (Creed which ten shameful years have not annulled)
> But that the virtue of one paramount mind
> Would have abashed those impious crests . . .
>
> (X.136–38, 177–80)

This was not Wordsworthian egotism; it was the thought of almost anyone involved in public affairs in Paris at the time, when fantasies about turning private thoughts into world-shaking actions were rife, and not at all unrealistic. It describes the actions of Louvet, Brissot, and Robespierre, as well as the 'one paramount mind' Wordsworth alludes to at the end, Bonaparte's.

As events moved to an ever-higher pitch of intensity, public life entered that state of gigantic humanity which Wallace Stevens characterized as the condition of imagination in time of war. The spaces between thought, word and deed became smaller and smaller. Talking, writing, and reading became non-stop activities, as daytime debates in the Convention were followed by night-time meetings in the clubs, which usually adjourned about ten. Each night was capped with visits to the theatres, where new plays were rapidly composed, or old ones adapted, to reflect – and influence – the events of each day, and were then keenly reviewed for whiffs of treason. To fill up any remaining time, there were the dives and cafés of the Palais Royal and, for people of Wordsworth's class and associations, the salons. Helen Maria Williams's in rue du Bac was the leading English one, a half-dozen streets away from its French sister, that of Manon Roland in the rue Guenegaud. They interchanged visitors regularly. Here informal commentary and conversation were honed and polished into more rhetoric for the next day's public appearances. The great Girondin orator, Vergniaud, improvised and rehearsed his speeches in both ladies' apartments.[67]

Though we cannot place Wordsworth definitely at either of these salons, he clearly spent time at the theatre. An adaptation of Schiller's *Die Räuber* ('The Robbers'), the base text for Wordsworth's *The Borderers* (1796), was one of the most popular propaganda plays of 1792. As *Robert, chef de brigands*, it played at Beaumarchais' Theatre du Marais five or six times during Wordsworth's stay in Paris in November and December.[68] Schiller's play, like Wordsworth's, was a psychological study of remorse for assassination. But the version at Beaumarchais' theatre, as adapted by Jean-Henri Lamartelière, was more like a justification of it. *Robert* gained even more political relevance once the idea of putting Louis XVI on trial for his life was broached at the Convention by Saint-Just on 13 November. Lamartelière, whose play had been attacked in March by royalists as 'a school for brigandage' when it opened, was now denounced by *sansculottes* for unfavourable depictions of republicans in his sequel, *Le tribunal redoutable*, which alternated with *Robert, chef de brigands* – and which he retitled *Robert républicain* after an instructive visit from the Committee of Surveillance.

Wordsworth, attending the plays, listening to the gossip, and reading the scandal sheets, absorbed powerful lessons about the range and limits of literature's ability to influence public events. His subsequent close attention to the relations between 'the revolutions not of literature alone but likewise of society itself' (preface to *Lyrical Ballads*) was first cast in this crucible. His development throughout the 1790s is marked, first, by an attempt to bring his writing much closer into contact with politics, and then by an effort to distance it from immediate public reference, while still maintaining a symbolic topicality.

Hence it is not surprising that Wordsworth imagined putting himself at the service of the Revolution: 'Yet would I willingly have taken up / A service at this time for a cause so great, / However dangerous.' But his modesty about his situation is somewhat overstated: 'An insignificant stranger and obscure.' He had more than adequate connections for a twenty-two-year-old Englishman. He knew Brissot, he was a friend of Beaupuy, he had probably talked with Grégoire on more than one occasion. And he must by this time have made the acquaintance of Gorsas, if his later statement that 'I knew this man' has any meaning at all.[69] His connections in the English community were equally good, but he was also known to be closely associated with a prominent royalist and clerical family in Orléans and Blois.

Granting that to imagine serving the Revolution was the most natural thing in the world at the time for a young man of active imagination, what kind of 'service' did he have in mind, and for which country? Writer or orator, messenger or spy, agitator or assassin? Wordsworth was not given to indulging passing fancies, and when he said he 'doubtless should have made a common cause / With some who perished' (X.194–95), he doubt-less meant it, for he had 'great self-control, tenacity, courage, enthusiasm, and depth of conviction.'[70] He had the advantage now of being fluent in French, which was more than some important figures like Tom Paine could say. The flood of English sympathizers rose to a crest between September and November, and the Convention redoubled its efforts to disseminate favourable views of the revolution to England.[71] Some of this involved concrete matters like raising money, or soliciting and shipping quantities of shoes, pikes, and even cannon for the patriot armies, to which service men as diverse as Francis Place, the radical London tailor, John Hurford Stone, businesman and lover of Helen Williams, and Robert Burns lent their aid.[72] Others, like John Oswald and many Irishmen, were rumoured to be involved in plots to assassinate George III, in synchronization with the widely expected execution of Louis XVI. Although Wordsworth said, truthfully, that he was 'all unfit for tumult and intrigue,' it is worth noting that the one thought that he said now came to him 'with a *revelation's* liveliness' was, 'that tyrannic power was weak' – because dedicated idealistic assassins like Harmodius and Brutus could kill it (X.158–67; italics added).

However, the reports of Captain Munro to Whitehall concentrate on the *writing* being done by Paine, Oswald, and Priestley (who was not even there), and some eight or ten 'others' around them, of whom he mentions only young Watt (who had left 7 October), Thomas Wilson (of

Manchester), Stone, and Mackintosh, 'who wrote against Burke.' They are said to be 'writing a justification of democracy and an invective against monarchy,' a description that fits very well the 'Letter to the Bishop of Llandaff' that Wordsworth began writing about a month after his return to London. Every scene in Paris at this time is crowded, and the backgrounds of the crowd are necessarily indistinct. We cannot clearly see a tall, awkward-looking young Englishman in any of these groups, but we can say without hesitation that his actions when he got back to England were highly congruent with theirs.

The increasing concentration of English sympathizers culminated in the creation of a 'British Club' in October, officially called 'The Friends of the Rights of Man associated at Paris.' They met at White's Hotel, in Wordsworth's neighbourhood, if he was not actually staying at the hotel himself. Two of its leaders were referred to by the French as 'the two best poets in England': William Hayley, Blake's patron, and Robert Merry, the 'Della Cruscan' poet of the English colony in Florence. Hayley was also a close friend of Charlotte Smith and William Cowper.[73] The British Club's meetings were devoted to discussing how the spirit of revolution and reform might best be exported back to England. Great extremes of opinion jostled there, from those who simply wanted to keep open channels of sympathetic communication between the two countries, to those who wanted to provoke a revolutionary uprising in England.

On 18 November, about a hundred of these British sympathizers gathered at White's to draw up a manifesto of solidarity with the National Convention, celebrating General Dumouriez's triumphant entry into Brussels. 'It doubtless appertained,' the address continued, 'to the French nation to enfranchise Europe, and we rejoice to see it fulfilling its great destinies.' The document is dated 24 November, but due to delays in final preparation, it was not presented to the Convention until 28 November, *after* the Edict of Fraternity had been passed, offering aid to all peoples wishing to overthrow tyrants and 'recover' their natural liberty. Hence a cheerful message of congratulations sent by visiting Britons to the armies of the new republic was turned by the rapid movement of events into an endorsement of exporting revolution and a direct challenge to the British constitution – signed, for all the French knew, by fifty leading British citizens.

Wordsworth's name is not among the fifty signatories, who were chosen by vote from among the more than one hundred English there that night. But Francis Tweddell, brother of his Cambridge friend, signed, and, given Wordsworth's associations, it is not hard to believe that he was somewhere in the company. Helen Maria Williams was there: as unofficial hostess of the event, she sang a composition of her own to the tune of the 'Marseillaise.'[74] She was toasted along with Charlotte Smith and Anna Barbauld as representatives of the women of England who had distinguished themselves by writing in favour of the Revolution. Many of the signatories were of Wordsworth's age and class. Half of them were middle-class, university-educated professionals, and a quarter were young men in their twenties.[75] Some who were chosen to sign chose not to (like John Hurford Stone) for various expedient reasons, and Wordsworth too had good reasons for demurring. He was not afraid for himself, but he now had others to think of. For the sake of Annette and their child, he could not afford to get into trouble, either in France or in England.

Events rapidly went beyond the depth of most of the British sympathizers, and the club, formed in October, fell apart in less than three months. Bishop Grégoire made a formal reply to the 18 November resolution, hoping that he might soon address 'the National Convention of England,' to which non-existent body he conveyed the greeting of its French sister.[76] In doing so, he was merely responding to the resolution's claim that 'the great majority of our countrymen' would share their sentiments 'if public opinion were consulted as it ought to be, in a national convention.' Whether by mistake or design, the Convention appeared to be challenging the British government. This was alarming to more than a few of the British Club, for it implied the calling of a constitutional convention, the dearest hope of the burgeoning correspondence societies in England, and the worst-case scenario, short of open rebellion in the streets, of not only Pitt and his ministers, but of most of the English property-owning class. A preliminary 'national' convention held in Edinburgh in December immediately provoked a chain reaction of arrests, treason trials, and transportation to 'the fatal shore' of Botany Bay for the convicted leaders.[77]

This implicit constitutional challenge to George III was underscored by the debates on the trial of Louis XVI, already underway. The vexed questions of whether he should be tried, by whom, and with what punishment if found guilty consumed the Convention's energies for the next two months, and ruined the Girondins in the process. Only the most radical British sympathizers were prepared to associate themselves with a republicanism that entailed regicide; the English Revolution gave no comforting precedent here, and the French did not give them any cause for optimism.

On 29 November the Convention forced Louis to send a double-edged message of peace and warning to the other European powers, saying that France wished them no ill, but that if they continued to plot against her they would approach not with the olive branch but with the sword.[78] By the kind of coincidence that one comes to expect in these heated times, this was the same day on which the Convention received England's response to Grégoire's message of 19 November: a formal note of protest against its language as tantamount to meddling in England's internal affairs. But Pitt's next action was no coincidence: on 13 December, Tom Paine was formally charged *in absentia* for sedition, putting republicanism on trial in England as a foil to the show trial of monarchy in France.

And on 15 December, in the Orléans cathedral, Father Perrin, the episcopal vicar, certified that he had 'baptized a girl, born the same day in this parish to Williams Wordwodsth [*sic*] an Englishman, and Marie-Anne Vallon, her father and mother; named Anne-Caroline by Paul Vallon and Marie-Victoire-Adelaide Peigne, wife of André-Augustin Dufour. Williams Wordsodsth [*sic*], being absent, was represented as the child's father by the aforesaid citizen André-Augustin Dufour, recorder of the court of the district of Orléans, by virtue of a power of attorney *ad hoc* presented to us and signed "Williams Wordsworsth" [*sic*].'[79] The official certificate managed to get his name wrong three different ways in as many attempts, stumbling on those consonantal combinations of 'th' and 'rdsw' so taxing to the French tongue. 'Vaudracour' would have been much easier, and Annette opted for 'Williams' as her new family name, but there was no doubt as to who the child's father was.*

It was perhaps very nearly on this day that Wordsworth finally decamped from Paris to return to London, for on 22 December Dorothy is reporting that he 'is in London [and] writes to me regularly.' On 21 December Captain Munro informed Lord Grenville that 'young Mr Woodfall' would be the bearer of his latest report to the Foreign Ministry.[80] This was William Woodfall, Jr, son of the propietor and editor of *The Diary; or Woodfall's Register*. But one can also wonder if a 'young Mr Wordsworth' might not have been deputized to carry the text of a placard to be printed in England, and dated as if from the 'Friends of the Rights of Man associated at Paris, December 4.' This was a frankly republican but carefully non-inflammatory statement, in which the signatories (though no signed copies survive) expressed their happiness for three things: 'that our temporary residence in this enlightened and regenerated capital enables us [1] to become the organ of communicating knowledge on the most interesting subjects, [2] of administering to the moral improvement and social happiness of a considerable portion of our fellow-men, and [3] of undeceiving the minds of our countrymen, abused by the wretched calumnies of a wicked Administration . . . [about] the glorious exertions of the French.'[81] The placard's first claim to happiness fits Wordsworth's personal experience and political conversion during 1792, the second describes the new aim of his writings from 1793 to 1800, and the last accurately characterizes the short-term polemic of his 'Letter

---

* Wordsworth's name is misspelled on every French document relating to his parentage of his daughter. On the baptism certificate: Wordwodsth, Wordsodsth, and Wordsworsth; on the marriage certificate, Wortsworth. Only Caroline, signing the latter with the name of the father she loved and admired, got it right, confidently signing, 'A. C. Wordsworth.' (*WFD*, 29–30, 38).

to Llandaff' and the long-term ideals of his proposed *Philanthropist*. On either side of the political fence, innocuous young men like Woodfall or Wordsworth were entrusted with dangerous information or errands: they did not raise much suspicion, and were in any case expendable – 'poor mistaken and bewildered offerings' – if they got caught.

Leaving Paris in mid-December 1792, Wordsworth was leaving at almost the last possible moment. The British Club was falling apart, wrecked on the rocks of regicide. Munro reported on 27 December that, 'from being levellers and enemies of our constitution, many are now become friends of Royalty,' and considered the few remaining English sympathizers to be persons of no consequence, 'really much beneath the notice of anyone.' He observed 'the greatest confusion imaginable in all the coffee houses,' and he firmly expected either a massacre of the Convention or a civil war,[82] both of which came soon enough, in the purge of Girondins and on the killing grounds of the Vendée.

CHAPTER FOURTEEN

Castaway

> . . . more like a man
> Flying from something that he dreads, than one
> Who sought the thing he loved.
>
> ('Tintern Abbey,' 71–73)

If Wordsworth was dilatory in Paris, he made up for it as soon as he returned to London. In little over a month, he prepared and saw through the press not one but two quarto volumes, *An Evening Walk* and *Descriptive Sketches*, over 1200 lines of poetry, which were printed and sold by the most distinguished liberal publisher of the time, Joseph Johnson, at his shop in St Paul's Churchyard.

He accomplished this in an atmosphere that was almost as hysterical as in Paris. He arrived in the midst of a journalistic outcry against the government's disinformation campaign concerning an 'infernal' plot, planned by foreigners. French agents were rumoured to be assassinating pedestrians, poisoning the Thames, and occupying the Tower.[1] This was the infamous 'insurrection that wasn't,' the climax of the 'heresy hunt' of 1792 against the reform societies.[2] The charges (a plot to subvert the capital) and the danger (foreign invasion) were similar to those ricocheting between Robespierre, Louvet, and Brissot, and so were the means employed to substantiate them. The government exploited the newspapers, in an early instance of news-management.[3] Suborned journalists manufactured facts in government-subsidized newspapers, particularly the *Sun* and the *True Briton*.[4] Opposition writers were intimidated by government lawyers interpreting their words according to the new theory of close-reading called 'constructive treason.'[5]

It took about a week for even opposition newspapers to notice that none of these dire events were happening, but the panic permitted George III to call out the county militias, making it possible to call Parliament and put the country on a war footing. The evidence that Grenville presented in the House consisted of little more than copies of the congratulatory addresses bouncing back and forth between Paris and England. But he could produce none from England, though cries of 'No King!' and 'Damn Pitt!' could be heard on the streets and read on the walls all the way from London to Edinburgh.[6] Burke crossed over to join Pitt on the Treasury bench for the first time on 15 December, and soon thereafter gave his amazing 'dagger' speech, dramatically throwing a concealed Sheffield knife on to the floor of the Commons and threatening that thousands more were being manufactured for 'domestic consumption.' Like many of his histrionic gestures, this one was immediately exploded by satire, as Whig members demanded he reveal his hidden spoons and forks as well.

William moved into his brother Richard's new rooms at Staple Inn, not far from his haunts of two years earlier. His London spring of 1793 was in some ways a reprise of 1791, but his previous freedom and irresponsibility were now changed to heavy duties and unpleasant confrontations. As he worked feverishly to get *An Evening Walk* and *Descriptive Sketches* ready for the printer, he dissuaded Richard's roommate, Joshua Wilkinson, from writing a sensational 'Jacobin' novel based on the du Fosse episode from Helen Williams's *Letters from France*. He laid claim to this literary option on the moral grounds that he needed to raise money for Annette and Caroline, and on the artistic grounds that his own recent experiences could easily be adapted to Williams's tale. He was so upset generally that Wilkinson and other friends spent a good deal of time simply playing cards with him, to keep him from dwelling too much on his troubles.[7]

Wordsworth is very reticent in all his later reminiscences about the names of his London associates in the 1790s.[8] In his autobiographical memorandum, the next three years are dismissed in a single sentence: 'I came home before the execution of the King [21 January], and passed the subsequent time among my friends in London and elsewhere, till I settled with my only sister at Racedown in Dorsetshire, in the year 1796.'[9] The reason for such circumspection was the usual one for liberal young gentlemen of his generation: covering up their Jacobin youth. His success in securing Joseph Johnson as his publisher shows that his radical credentials were in good order at this time. He had no known prior acquaintance with Johnson, the friend, encourager, and guide of the most brilliant writers of the day: Tom Paine, Mary Wollstonecraft, and William Godwin. Very possibly he came with a recommendation from his new acquaintances in the British Club of Paris.[10] Having so narrowly missed Helen Maria Williams on his entry into France, he now just missed meeting Mary Wollstonecraft, who entered Paris as he left it. With Johnson's assistance, she immediately established contact with Helen Williams. Wordsworth completed this circuit in the other direction, making straight for Johnson's shop in St Paul's churchyard on his return, and had no trouble getting not one but two large, difficult, and expensive books accepted immediately. One might suppose Johnson would have needed some additional recommendation to add the sentimental *Evening Walk* and the picturesque *Descriptive Sketches* to his list. Perhaps it was the latter's revolutionary peroration that convinced him to see more politics than met the eye on the title page, where the author's pedigree was circumspectly announced as 'William Wordsworth, BA, of St John's College, Cambridge':

> Oh give, great God, to Freedom's waves to ride
> Sublime o'er Conquest, Avarice, and Pride,
> To break, the vales where Death with Famine scow'rs,
> And dark Oppression builds her thick-ribb'd tow'rs;
>
> (792–95)

The books were quite well received, especially *An Evening Walk*. Though the print-runs were small, some major reviews commented approvingly on the accuracy of the poet's landscape descriptions, and the novelty of his views of the Alps, though they criticized the obscurity of his hackneyed poetical diction, especially in *Descriptive Sketches*.[11] At a time when journalistic wisdom ranked the insipid Catherine Manners as the best poet of the day, and Mary 'Perdita' Robinson as the best of modern times, such notice and praise was not inconsiderable, especially when political news was rapidly pushing poetry into the margins.[12]

But in October, Thomas Holcroft, an important radical man of letters (his *Road to Ruin* played to enthusiastic audiences all during this year), tore into Wordsworth with a reformer's zeal: 'More descriptive poetry! Have we not enough! Must eternal changes be rung on uplands and lowlands, and nodding forests, and brooding clouds, and cells, and dells, and dingles?' Some seeds of the preface to *Lyrical Ballads* were planted in Wordsworth's mind by this attack, and so, perhaps, were some for *The Prelude*, in Holcroft's closing advice to this cliché *persona*: 'He is the happiest of mortals, and plods, and is forlorn, and has a wounded heart. How often shall we in vain advise those, who are so delighted with their own thoughts that they cannot forbear from putting them into rhyme, to examine those thoughts until they understand them? No man will ever be a poet, till his mind be sufficiently powerful to sustain this labour.'[13]

But by the end of the year, the poems were well enough regarded to be discussed at avant-garde student literary groups at Cambridge, where young Christopher and Coleridge were members, and in provincial literary societies at Exeter and Derby, along with the works of such other leading contemporary poets as Anna Seward ('the Swan of Lichfield'), Charlotte Smith, William Bowles, and Erasmus Darwin (grandfather of Charles).[14]

Good reviews were extremely important to Wordsworth at this juncture. When he told Mathews a year later that he had 'huddled up' these two poems for publication, his use of the university slang term for exam-cramming accentuated his motive: 'as I had done nothing to distinguish myself at the university, I thought these little things might show I could do something.'[15] Who, in particular, did he intend to 'show'? Preeminently, William Cookson, an intention underscored by his title-page identification with Cambridge University. Though he had pointedly *not* 'huddled' for his university exams, he was now, exactly two years later, trying to show that he could 'do something'. There is an endearing earnestness in Wordsworth's hope that his poems would please his elders. Having spurned or deflected both Cookson's and Robinson's last best offers for his future in the autumn of 1791, he was now working very hard to show himself worthy of the formerly despised Harwich curacy.

But his long-suffering benefactors turned him down flat. His very reason for wanting the curacy became their reason for refusing it: Freud himself could hardly have imagined a clearer instance of the double-binds so characteristic of the 'family romance.' Wordsworth had to make his reasons clear, but with each one he put the curacy further and further out of reach: a mistress, a Frenchwoman, a Catholic, and an illegitimate child. 'Anything more?' one can imagine the weary Cookson inquiring. Annette's royalism might have been one forlorn hope in her favour, to the chaplain and the paymaster, respectively, of George III. But the illegitimate child was literally a scandal, and the Cooksons' shocked reaction to it was heightened by their close friendship with Wilberforce.[16] It is hard to say which of the objections was the decisive one, though a Catholic wife (if acknowledged) was a technical disqualification. Years later, Cookson cited Wordsworth's 'French principles' as the straw that broke the back of his patience.

We do not know exactly when Wordsworth was hit with the news that his strenuous effort to get his two volumes published was all for naught, but we can trace its fallout. In Annette's letters of March, she still pleaded with him not to let Dorothy say anything about their situation to his uncle. But she was out of touch with the pace of events. The news, and the break with Cookson it occasioned, probably came sooner than later, for this shocking refusal propelled Wordsworth into another fast and furious effort of composition. This was his 'Letter to the Bishop of Llandaff,' whose great difference from *Descriptive Sketches* – as regards showing his uncles what he could do – is marked, not to say flaunted, on *its* title page by a much more provocative sign of authorship: 'By a Republican.' He might never have written this, the most outspokenly radical writing of his life, if his uncles had not turned down his *bona fide* effort to gain their favour by publishing *An Evening Walk* and *Descriptive Sketches*: being a curate and attacking an Anglican bishop were mutually exclusive acts. Having shown what he could do in one direction, he proceeded almost immediately to do something in an entirely opposite direction. Just as his uncles' well-intentioned plans to fit him to a place in the established church had forced him to come up with his French language scheme, now their self-righteous retraction of the same plan pushed him over the brink of notional liberalism into declaring himself an enemy of that establishment and just about everything that it stood for. Or rather, almost over the brink, since he did not publish the 'Letter to Llandaff,' a career-saving decision which he probably owed to the cautions of Joseph Johnson. But in written word if not in published deed, he now became an 'active partisan' in the pamphlet wars which had been raging in London since the publication of Burke's *Reflections on the Revolution in France*.[17]

His two poems appeared in Johnson's shop in St Paul's Churchyard on 29 January. The very next day, Richard Watson, the Bishop of Llandaff, fellow of Trinity College (Cambridge), Windermere estate owner, and all-around Lake District success story, republished an old sermon, with a new appendix recanting his former support of the Revolution. Two days later France declared war on Britain, and Pitt's government shortly returned the favour. Given this concatenation of public events, it is no wonder that Wordsworth's private reaction was so strong. The moment was, in fact, Wordsworth's revolution:

> No shock
> Given to my moral nature had I known
> Down to that very moment—neither lapse
> Nor turn of sentiment—that might be named
> A revolution, save at this one time:
> (X.233–37)

The wonder is, rather, that scholars have tended to see Wordsworth's shock primarily in political terms. True, he generalizes it to his whole generation: 'Not in my single self alone . . . / But in the minds of all ingenuous youth, / Change and subversion from this hour' (231–33). But he also admits that the coming of war was perfectly obvious to everybody: 'Nor had I doubted that this day would come.' The reason for his great shock was his deep personal involvement in the stakes:

> Now had I other business, for I felt
> The ravage of this most unnatural strife
> In my own heart; there it lay like a weight,
> At enmity with the tenderest springs
> Of my enjoyments.
> (X.249–53)

This, cut from all later versions, could hardly be clearer. The war was 'an unnatural strife in [his] own heart' because it separated him from Annette and Caroline, 'the tenderest springs' of his enjoyments. The appearance of Watson's Appendix at this moment, matched with his uncles' refusal of the curacy, gave Wordsworth a target on which to vent his frustrations, as the childhood helplessness to which his own father's early death had reduced him now began to have adult consequences.

The arguments in the trial of Louis XVI were fully detailed in the London press, with substantial excerpts from persons known to Wordsworth: Paine, Carra, and Léonard Bourdon. Almost every delegate had dutifully spoken against him, but after his conviction there was a lengthy debate about sentencing in which the unanimity of his accusers broke apart on various extemporizing measures that might avoid the death penalty: exile, house arrest, probation on good behaviour, confiscatory fines, etc. Richard Watson had inserted himself directly into this process — an important point, lest we see him entirely in Wordsworth's perspective as a reactionary renegade. For Watson was *the* most liberal Anglican churchman in his attitude toward the Revolution.[18] The so-called 'levelling prelate,' he complained all his life that he suffered in his preferments for his outspoken support of liberal causes, though it is hard to see how he could have done much better in collecting profitable benefices. He had dined with Talleyrand and several members of the National Assembly at Earl Stanhope's in late 1792, and he subsequently sent to Stanhope, for him to convey to the Assembly, a suggestion that Louis be confined to one of his palaces on a pension of £4000 per year, subject to forfeit on any sign of treasonous behaviour.[19] 'I had no great expectation of success attending the application of an individual, buried in the wilds of Westmorland,' he said, 'yet knowing that the greatest events had often sprung from the slightest causes,' he tried to save the royal family.[20]

When Louis was guillotined, Watson's recoil was the leading edge of a massive tide of reaction. As is frequently the case in politics, those closest to a controversial issue are often the most vehement in distancing themselves from its consequences once they see the cause is lost. The vehicle Watson chose for his recantation was a sermon of 1785 extolling God's almighty wisdom in creating both rich and poor, which he reissued to help 'in calming the perturbation . . . in the minds of the lower classes of the community,' and the 'strong spirit of insubordination and discontent' which he observed among the common people. With the kind of self-satisfied calculation that gives conservatism a bad name, he estimated that the provision for the poor in England was already so liberal as to discourage industriousness.

Wordsworth was infuriated by the smug self-righteousness of Watson's tactic, though he would not have written so vehemently against it without his uncles' refusal to goad him. Watson's Appendix was not however quite so hysterical as Wordsworth's 'Letter' might lead us to believe. It is a liberal defence of the established order, on essentially the same grounds as Burke's *Reflections*. To a degree, it gave fresh life to Burke's polemic, since Burke was by this time being attacked on every possible ground for his melodramatic hysteria. Watson said he had wished the French well at first, hoping they would soon have a constitution to replace their former absolutism. But now they had gone too far, staining the altar of Liberty with the blood 'of the aged, of the innocent, of the defenceless sex, of the ministers of religion.' Watson was writing with the memory of the September massacres still fresh in his mind, and they seemed to have been capped by Louis' execution: Liberty's altar was now 'streaming with the blood of the monarch himself.' This was Watson's most emotional paragraph, and well expressed the widespread revulsion in England against the turn of events in France. But the main thrust of his appendix is to defend the English constitution's guarantee of property rights against the threat of republican theorists: 'the licentious principles of such petulant outcasts of society,' who address themselves to 'the flagitious dregs of a modern nation . . . always ripe for revolutions.' Like Burke, Watson feared that the disaffected might lead the disenfranchised toward fundamental change in the status quo.

Wordsworth, as 'A Republican,' set himself directly against Watson's premises. As a man now literally discontented in his expectations, he made a dramatic shift in authorial stance from that of *Descriptive Sketches*. His 'Letter to Llandaff' is written in the white heat of anger, an anger seen nowhere in his writings up to this time. He lets loose the violence of his passionate nature, which Dorothy had noted with half-proud, half-worried concern: 'a sort of violence,' where objects of his affection are concerned, as Annette certainly was, in the implications of changing English public opinion toward France.[21]

Wordsworth wrote with Watson's volume open on the desk before him, refuting it point by point. This accounts for his letter's laboured structure: one can hardly understand it without Watson's appendix ready to hand. But he also raised objections to many points that are nowhere mentioned by Watson. One would think Wordsworth knew Watson personally, and it is not unlikely that he did, having seen him frequently at Cambridge and at the summer dances at Windermere. The promise and now the disappointment of Watson's *career* particularly drew Wordsworth's scorn, reminding us how often Watson must have been held up before him, by the likes of Cookson and Wilberforce, as the epitome of what a Lake District boy of intelligence but limited means could make of himself. Watson was the son of a headmaster of Heversham grammar school, twelve miles southeast of Hawkshead, one of Hawkshead's main rivals in preparing boys for Cambridge.[22] Hence Wordsworth takes considerable satisfaction, at the beginning of the letter, in imagining Watson falling off the 'immense bridge' of reputation, tumbling through one of its many 'trap-doors, into the tide of contempt to be swept down to the ocean of oblivion.'[23] At the end, to satirize Watson's hypocrisy, he adopts a homelier figure of speech that he could expect Watson to recognize from their common home in 'the wilds of Westmorland': 'In some parts of England it is quaintly said, when a drunken man is seen reeling towards his home, that he has business on both sides of the road.'

So much for Watson's principles and his progress: 'the friends of liberty' are glad to lose such a renegade.[24] 'Besides the names which I' . . . but at this exact point the manuscript ends, any further pages were torn off, just when the writer is about to name names. Probably Wordsworth was going to cite more names like those he has already mentioned, Lafayette and Mirabeau, for their 'insidious mask of patriotism.' But possibly he would have named others who remained true to Liberty, among whom we can certainly include the author himself, a republican who vows not to shrink from stating 'any truths, however severe, which I may think beneficial to the cause which I have undertaken to defend.'

The 'Letter' stated some very 'severe' truths indeed, in the polemical context of 1793, going beyond even what Paine ventured (he was against the death penalty for Louis). But there is another pattern of images in Wordsworth's 'Letter' which is as noteworthy biographically as his outspoken political position: a leitmotif of references to the naturalness of passion in a time of the pregnancy, labour, and birth pangs of a new social order. These are partly conventional metaphors, but Wordsworth could not have employed them without thinking of their personal reference to Annette's recent labour and delivery of their child. These positive metaphors are counterpointed with negative ones of a similar provenance, including the unnatural (i.e., illicit) sexual practices to which the poor are driven by economic hardship. Picking up on Watson's bluff confidence that Englishmen will not 'deluge their land with blood,' Wordsworth turns the question away from French revolutions toward English social problems: 'does your lordship shudder at the prostitution which miserably deluges our streets?' Reflecting his and Beaupuy's hope that the Revolution might ultimately put an end to the poverty which leads to prostitution, his main point is 'that the miseries entailed upon the marriage of those who are not rich will no longer tempt the bulk of mankind to fly to that promiscuous intercourse to which they are impelled by the instincts of nature, and the dreadful satisfaction of escaping the prospect of infants, sad fruits of such intercourse, whom they are unable to support.' He could not write such a sentence without his own experience in mind: he who, not being rich, had just felt the full force of such miseries literally *entailed* on his own wish to marry. His 'dreadful satisfaction' clause is obscure, but it seems to signify, not avoiding conception, but fleeing from the *sight* of infants who are sad because they are poor – because they are unsupported by their fathers. This is what he had just done to Caroline, a cowardly act he had returned to England to find a means of rectifying. In this context, his reference to the times as 'big with the fate of the human race,' and to 'a time of revolution' as 'a convulsion from which is to spring a fairer order of things,' make us see, behind his feminine personification of the lady Liberty, the mother of his own child,

Annette Vallon. Unlike Watson, Wordsworth *can* accept the convulsions of revolution because he can link them to his own – Annette's own – experience, all the more so as he felt guilty for not being there with her.

If published, the 'Letter to Llandaff' would have been one of the most radical of all responses to Burke, Watson, or any other conservative writer on events in France. Though congested, its prose is often eloquently passionate – a characteristic of Wordsworth's prose all his life. Its author, if identified, would have been subject to a prosecution as severe as Paine's, who had been convicted of sedition in December and condemned to death. As an unprotected young man, Wordsworth would have faced punishments at least as severe as those meted out – the pillory, prison, and transportation to Australia – to Thomas Muir, Thomas Fyshe Palmer, and William Skirving, 'the Scottish martyrs', later in the year for their role in organizing the Edinburgh constitutional convention. The Traitorous Correspondence Bill and Seditious Practices Act had just been introduced; though technically aimed at commercial transactions, it also had the intended practical effect of fanning public fears about revolutionary fellow travellers. It was aimed specifically at persons who had recently come from France, who were known to have associated with revolutionists or their English sympathizers, and who now maintained a correspondence with France – all conditions that applied to Wordsworth.

The wise advice of Joseph Johnson is the most plausible reason for Wordsworth's not publishing the 'Letter' in such a repressive climate. Johnson's behaviour was generally careful; he could see that the 'Letter' was simply a ticket to jail. He was recommending exactly the same course of restraint at exactly the same time to another of his authors, Mary Wollstonecraft. Early in the year, she had sent him her 'Letter on the Present Character of the French Nation,' which is, surprisingly, closer to Watson's recantation than to Wordsworth's attack. But Johnson knew that she, like Wordsworth, was affected by both personal and political troubles, and he did not publish her 'Letter.' He could keep Wordsworth from reacting too far toward the left while at the same time preventing Wollstonecraft from reacting too far toward the right.

If Wordsworth had published the 'Letter to Llandaff' he would have set his life on a very different course than the one he took. He would have become a marked man in political discussions throughout the rest of the decade. The name Wordsworth, like those of Burke, Paine, Wollstonecraft, Godwin, Mackintosh, Thelwall, and others would have been indelibly fixed (or sunk) in public memory as one of the participants in the great, failed 'Revolution Debate' of 1790–1795. By not publishing the 'Letter to Llandaff,' Wordsworth saved himself for the future as the history of the 1790s receded into his obscure youthful past. By the end of the decade he had transformed himself into a man of a different era. Much of the language of the 'Letter to Llandaff' is consistent with that of the

Preface to *Lyrical Ballads*, but the subject under discussion has changed dramatically, from politics to poetry, and from the immorality of nobles to the nobility of the poor.

Instead of publishing the 'Letter to Llandaff,' Wordsworth did what he had done at earlier crises in his life: he took a vacation. Sometime during the spring, he became reacquainted with William Calvert, an old Lake District friend, whose father had held the same position for the Duke of Norfolk at Greystoke Castle (near Penrith) that Wordsworth's father did for Lord Lonsdale at Cockermouth. Calvert's father had died two years earlier, and William as eldest son had inherited the substantial estate of a father who had prospered in a rich man's service. He was now a man of very independent means – Dorothy called him 'a man of fortune.' The thought 'there but for the grace of God go I,' can hardly not have crossed Wordsworth's mind when they met.[25]

Most Wordsworth biographers, working backwards from the fact that a bequest of £900 from Calvert's younger brother, Raisley, two years later was the beginning of Wordsworth's independence, take William Calvert's reappearance in Wordsworth's life as part of the providence that genius is heir to. It was not a very unusual coincidence, for there was a northern network of mutual friends and acquaintances in London at the time. (Joshua Wilkinson, for example, was from Cockermouth: his grandfather had built the house Wordsworth was born in.)[26] But there is no record of Wordsworth and Calvert having been particularly close friends at Hawkshead, they probably had not seen each other for at least five years, and Wordsworth did not even know young Raisley Calvert at this time. (Raisley entered Magdalene College, Cambridge, in February.)

Calvert soon proposed to underwrite the expense of a leisurely tour of the west of England during the summer. In June, his brother Raisley passed through town bound on an adventure familiar to Wordsworth: he was off to the Continent, proposing to educate himself by travelling for a few years, having decided Cambridge was too lax and licentious. By degrees, first Calvert and then his younger brother came to play the role of that 'young gentleman' on whom Wordsworth's supposed career plan (travelling tutor) focused at this time. In the late spring Wordsworth's last prospect in this line fell through, when someone else got the position as tutor to Lord Bellmore's son in Ireland, the grandson of the Earl of Buckinghamshire.[27] As often happens, plans projected with high aims were realized in more limited terms: instead of the grandson of the Earl of Buckinghamshire, Wordsworth would 'tutor' the son of the Duke of Norfolk's steward. Wordsworth had a university degree, was more disposed toward a teaching career than anything else, and had substantial credentials as a connoisseur-practitioner of the popular arts of the Picturesque. In Book XI of *The Prelude*, Wordsworth alludes to this as the time when he was most engrossed by the finicky principles of landscape discrimination: he may have been preoccupied with them because he was teaching them to Calvert.

They left London in late June or early July, the third summer in four years that Wordsworth had set off on an ambitious tour: this one was planned to last until October. They began by going to the Isle of Wight, a seaside diversion before tackling their intended object, the west of England. The Isle of Wight was not yet the cosy miniature country it became following the Napoleonic wars, though its touristic potential was emerging. At the time Wordsworth visited it, its ambience was still mainly military, like its history. Its only significant cultural association before Wordsworth's sojourn there was William Davenant's imprisonment in West Cowes Castle in 1649.[28] The centre of the island is dominated by Carisbrooke Castle, where Charles I was imprisoned before his execution. These literary-political associations were known to Wordsworth, since Davenant, successor to Ben Jonson as Poet Laureate, was saved from execution by Milton – and was in turn among those who, like Dryden and Marvell, secured Milton's life following the Restoration. But in 1793 a more familiar recommendation came from John Wordsworth, whose favourite anchorage was Cowes Roads at the northern tip of the island, directly across the Solent from Southampton. John had just sailed in May for China on the *Earl of Abergavenny*, under the captaincy of his cousin John Wordsworth, using the £100 legacy Dorothy had recently received from her grand-mother's estate as part of his investment in the profits of the voyage.[29]

Watching the shoals of pleasure craft scudding along the Solent today, one must multiply and enlarge them many times in the mind's eye to imagine what the region looked like in early summer of 1793. Between Southampton and Portsmouth, and all along the island from Spithead on the east to The Needles on the west, the British navy was busily arming itself for worldwide action against the French in the war declared five months earlier. The naval arm of the British empire, the most powerful military force in the world, was flexing itself as it had not done since the American war, for action against a much more dangerous enemy. Most energy was being expended on behalf of Lord Hood and the Mediter-ranean fleet, which was going to blockade the French republic on its southern flank, with Hood in the flagship, *Victory*. This strategy came near to success, but for the brilliant tactics of a Corsican artillery officer named Buonaparte. Wordsworth recalled spending July 'in view of the fleet which was then preparing for sea off Portsmouth,' and he 'left the place with melancholy forebodings. The American war was still fresh in memory.'[30] But this is a feigned recollection: his mood was caused far less by the ten-years-past American Revolution than by his personally unhappy situation vis-à-vis Annette and the French Revolution.

Under the cover of conducting a rich young gentleman's tour,

Wordsworth could have reconnoitred possibilities for slipping back over to France. Along with its strategic military value, the Isle of Wight was also a headquarters for smugglers, who were currently enjoying a very lucrative business in transporting goods, letters, and passengers across the Channel to Cherbourg and Dieppe. Their usefulness to the government was like that existing between police and criminals at all times: communications could be opened, encouraged, compromised, or confiscated for a wide variety of purposes. The south coast of the island is generally too precipitous for good smuggling operations, but Freshwater Bay at its southwest corner was an excellent spot, complete with rocky caves that might – depending on one's interest – be described either as picturesque or as well hidden.

We have only one written record of Wordsworth's time on the island in 1793, from Book X of *The Prelude* ('Ere yet the fleet of Britain had gone forth,' X.290–305). He is watching a beautiful sunset, accenting for Calvert the best ways to see it. A plausible vista is on the west of the island, near the 'steeps' above Freshwater Bay now known as Tennyson Downs (from another laureate's affection for the place), which give an excellent station for watching the sun set over water.[31] It was the frustration of this 'normal' expectation that started, then blocked, Wordsworth's original version of the passage, giving us a further glimpse into the 'revolution' that was working in his mind that summer.

The lines begin with all the tranquillity of a quiet summer sunset, 'How sweet the walk along the woody steep / When all the summer seas are charmed to sleep.' He continues through ten unexceptional lines, until the setting sun's light hits the warships, and literally breaks the poem apart, as the manuscript shows:

> Now lessened half his glancing disc de[scends]
> The watry sands athwart the forest [   ]
> Flush [   ] radiance not [   ]
> While anchored Vessels scattered fa[r] [   ]
> Darken with shadowy hulks [   ]
> O'er earth o'er air and oce[an] [   ]
> Tranquillity extends her [   ]
> But hark from yon proud fleet in peal profound
> Thunders the sunset cannon; at the sound
> The star of life appears to set in blood
> Old ocean shudders in offended mood
> Deepening with moral gloom his angry flood.
>
> $(8–19)$[32]

The poem's problem, like the 'Letter to Llandaff,' is the speaker's inability to negotiate between social crises and natural beauty. War fleets spoil a beautiful sunset here, as a ruined economy and rigid marriage laws cause promiscuous intercourse and illegitimate children in the 'Letter to Llandaff.' Nature has been violated by Culture: history, politics, and war. Wordsworth is unable to establish any poetic interaction between the natural scene and the shadows of the human institution which lay cross it: the British navy. The 'tranquillity' conventionally associated with a picturesque sunset is cancelled out by the 'sunset cannon.' But, after stuttering through this crisis point, his descriptive powers suddenly revive, yet he ends up with sentiments different from those with which he started. The fragment seems to be a sonnet whose structure has been blown apart by an afterthought, revealing the author's determination to be true to actual experience. Instead of ending at the fourteenth line ('Tranquillity extends her . . .' [peaceful reign?]), five additional lines make a forced editorial comment, which appears to be coming from Nature itself, and for the first time in the poem. Of course, the last three lines are projections of human emotions: Wordsworth's is the shuddering offence, his the deepening anger and gloom, and for deeply personal reasons as well as strongly felt political ones. It would take him almost five years to complete the process of healing the break in the fabric of his imagination which we can first mark, textually, here. Then he will be able to say, 'I have learned / To look on nature, not as in the hour / Of thoughtless youth, but hearing oftentimes / The still, sad music of humanity.'[33]

In early August Wordsworth and Calvert left the island and began their tour of the West Country. Almost immediately, however, their route and plans were changed by an accident. Somewhere near Salisbury, Calvert's horse 'began to caper . . . in a most terrible manner, dragged them and their vehicle into a Ditch and broke it to shivers. Happily neither Mr C. nor William were the worse but they were sufficiently cautious not to venture again in the same way.'[34] Calvert mounted his horse and rode off 'into the North,' while Wordsworth was left with his only 'firm Friends, a stout pair of legs,' and strode off, not to the West Country but to Robert Jones's house in North Wales, more than two hundred miles away.

Whether this accident actually occurred at all, or in quite the way Dorothy reported it, will be considered in the next chapter. For the moment, we can take Dorothy's word for it and accept that Wordsworth and Calvert split up and went their separate ways. Like his mountaintop experiences in the Alps and Wales in 1790 and 1791, Wordsworth's walking 'tour' across Salisbury Plain – if that is the right word for a long trudge by the survivor of a dangerous road accident – produced intense emotional experiences contributing to his poetic self-creation. But the literary results of his experience were – also like those in the Simplon Pass and on Snowdon – barely visible to his contemporaries. In 1793–94, he wrote a poem called 'A Night on Salisbury Plain,' which he revised heavily between 1795 and 1799 into another version, called 'Adventures on

Salisbury Plain.'[35] But that poem did not appear in print until 1842, as a specimen of his juvenilia (though so much reworked as to be anything but that), called *Guilt and Sorrow*.

Our knowledge of what actually happened to Wordsworth on Salisbury Plain in August 1793 is buried between the lines and revisions of these poems.[36] Our warrant for searching through them is provided by a stylized excerpt at the end of Book XII of *The Prelude* (312–53), where we see him 'wandering on from day to day,' 'a youthful traveller,' meeting 'the wanderers of the earth.' The Salisbury Plain poems are the first significant sign, along with his 'Letter to the Bishop of Llandaff,' of something new and different in Wordsworth's life and work: an empathy with the poor people who, from this moment onward, began to suffer immensely from the hardships caused by England's new war against France, which would last for an entire generation.

Wordsworth late in life spoke of 'a couple of days rambling about Salisbury Plain,' including a noontime nap at Stonehenge, overcome with heat and fatigue.[37] The events in the Salisbury Plain poems cover two days, and their opening description clearly reflects firsthand experience. His nap at Stonehenge would have been on his first day out from Salisbury. The narrator looks back regretfully at 'the distant spire' of Salisbury cathedral as he measures each 'painful step' – even 'a pair of stout legs' were sore after an accident that broke a carriage into 'shivers.' He is advancing 'o'er Sarum's plain,' specifically Old Sarum, the ancient castle ruins a couple of miles outside Salisbury: 'an antique castle spreading wide. / Hoary and naked are its walls' (*NSP*, 78–79). He had practical reasons for concern, as he notes 'the troubled west . . . red with stormy fire.' Salisbury Plain is not a place to be caught outside, alone, on a stormy night: all conditions that obtain in the poem. A terrific storm on the plain on 7 August was reported in the London newspapers.[38] An even worse scenario would be to be poor, unprotected, and female, like the Female Vagrant the narrator stumbles on to in 'the dead house of the plain,' a ruined traveller's spital which – the final Gothic twist – is supposed to be haunted, and in which each of the characters at first mistakes the other for a ghost.

Salisbury Plain is not a good place for a leisurely walk. It is one of the most desolate open spaces in England, with little or no shade, hardly a stream, and few human habitations. The villages of the farmers who cultivate it are scattered around the perimeter: 'wastes of corn . . . but where the sower dwelt was nowhere to be found' (*NSP*, 45). In his headnote to the 1842 version, Wordsworth noted that 'though cultivation was then (1793) more widely spread through parts of it, [it] had upon the whole a still more impressive appearance than it now retains.' It has not lost that quality. It is not hard to walk across except where crops are thickly planted, but there are few marked footpaths. Even today, two hundred years later, there are only three roads crossing its twenty-five mile length and breadth, and half of its area has been put permanently off-limits as a firing range and field for war games by the Ministry of Defence. Gilpin's *Observations of Western England* called it 'one vast cemetery,' full of 'mansions of the dead,' referring to its megalithic burial grounds.[39]*

It is not exactly a *plain*, but rather a vast expanse of swales, swelling ridges and slopes, in which the walker is paradoxically more often out of sight of the horizon than he would be in climbing a mountain. Both Wordsworth's traveller and his Female Vagrant comment on this aspect of the plain. 'Long had each slope he mounted seemed to hide / Some cottage,' but there are none, hence place-names like Breakheart Bottom. These and several other details are irrelevant to the narrative, but suggest how close Wordsworth was to the events he narrates.

The Female Vagrant's life story is a wide-ranging account that starts in the Lake District and crosses to America, from whence she has returned, widowed and childless. But her account of her departure and return contain several details which correlate well with the Southampton-Portsmouth area, from which she seems to have recently departed, since both she and the narrator are travelling west. Wordsworth's own situation in early August of 1793 and his subsequent revisions of the poem increase his surrogate narrator's implication in her plight. He was now, for the first time in his life, nearly as 'vagrant' as the woman. This was no long-vacation walking tour, triumphantly conducted. Still less was it the 1791 tour of Wales under Jones's protection, and far less the all-expense-paid jaunt in William Calvert's whiskey. To put it bluntly, Wordsworth suddenly found himself between meal tickets. His only money was what-ever he had left from the five guineas Richard advanced for pocket money when he set off with Calvert. Moreover, his indigent condition was pain-fully symbolic of his life-situation at the moment, with no 'prospects' to speak of, and, like the Female Vagrant, with a spouse and child abandoned in a foreign land torn by civil war, whom he could not get to, and could not help much even if he did.

Like the woman in the poem, he too had lost property and comfortable family circumstances in the Lake District. The first words of her 'artless story' are, 'By Derwent's side my father's cottage stood.' Her family has

---

* A modern version of what Wordsworth calls the 'dead house of the plain' is a purpose-built village near Tilshead for practice in house-to-house fighting, circled around a central 'church,' actually an observation tower. I found myself dodging the sightlines of the watchman in this tower because I didn't relish trying to explain what I was doing there – tracing the footsteps of a poetic refugee from the French Revolution. Later, three tanks clanked up a ridge in front of me, and the leader swivelled its turret toward me for one heart-stopping moment before they filed off in a different direction.

been driven off its land by the machinations of a rich neighbouring land-lord, machinations that Wordsworth was very familiar with, not only from Lowther's treatment of him and his siblings but also from some of John Wordsworth's more unsavoury duties in Lowther's service. The woman's story has been shown to derive from legends of the Philipson family of Calgarth Hall on Windermere,[40] and this detail further connects the story to Wordsworth's experience. For the present tenant of Calgarth Hall, he well knew, was none other than Richard Watson.

In *An Evening Walk* and *Descriptive Sketches*, the unfortunate creatures he describes (such as the vagrant mother of Esthwaite and the Grison gypsy) were genre-figures painted into the landscape, not actual persons with unique histories. But the Salisbury Plain poems zoom in on the conventional beggars and peasants of loco-descriptive poetry, breaking the frame of the convention and opening a way toward a new poetry of social realism. Yet, as is often the case with Wordsworth's notes to his poems, he seems to want to establish several degrees of separation between himself and the actual experience.

A year later, writing to Mathews about the poem, Wordsworth adopts his facetious sophisticated tone, but with a choice of diction that reveals more of the nature of his personal investment in the poem. 'You enquired after the name of one of my poetical bantlings. Children of this species ought to be named after their characters, and here I am at a loss, as my offspring seems to have no character at all. I have however christened it by the appellation of Salisbury Plain, though, A night on Salisbury Plain, were it not so insufferably awkward would better suit the thing itself.'[41] What 'species' of children did he have in mind? To have a 'character' meant also to have a reputable name, something that Wordsworth's eight-month-old 'bantling,' Caroline, barely had, though she was christened with the name of Wordsworth. Thus another difficulty of *naming this poem after its characters* might be that one of its character's names was Wordsworth.

Personal experience and imaginative projections, real children and poetical bantlings were richly mixed up together in Wordsworth's adventures on Salisbury Plain. As the storm abates and the moon comes out, the traveller's interest in the Female Vagrant appears in a new light:

> Gently the Woman gan [*sic*] her wounds unbind.
> Might Beauty charm the canker worm of pain
> The rose on her sweet cheek had ne'er declined:
> Moved she not once the prime of Keswick's plain
> While Hope and Love and Joy composed her smiling train?

> 24
> Like swans, twin swans, that when on the sweet brink
> Of Derwent's stream the south winds hardly blow,

'Mid Derwent's water-lillies swell and sink
In union, rose her sister breasts of snow,
(Fair emblem of two lovers' hearts that know
No separate impulse) or like infants played,
Like infant strangers yet to pain and woe.
Unwearied Hope to tend their motions made
Long Vigils, and Delight her cheek between them laid.

25

And are ye sped ye glittering dews of youth
For this – that Frost may gall the tender flower
In Joy's fair breast with more untimely tooth?
Unhappy man! thy sole delightful hour
Flies first; it is thy miserable dower
Only to taste of joy that thou may'st pine
A loss, which rolling suns may ne'er restore.

(*NSP*, 203–23)

These highly over-determined breasts have a literary source: they are a Renaissance *blason*, appropriate to a poem written in Spenserian stanzas.[42] However, Wordsworth loads them with personally suggestive weight, developing their symbolic capabilities to include memories of past happiness in the Lake District, his love for both Annette and Dorothy (he often compared himself and Dorothy to a pair of Grasmere swans), his infant Caroline ('stranger yet to pain and woe'), the 'glittering dews of youth' that he has enjoyed, only to see his 'sole delightful hour [fly] first,' leaving him (and Annette) with a 'miserable dower' from his uncles, which brings only bitterness, since 'rolling suns' seem unlikely to restore her to him. In addition to all this, they may also describe an attractive destitute woman with whom he sheltered from a storm one night in 1793.

But the poem written out of these experiences was anything but personal. It is a determinedly *im*personal reflection on human suffering. The Female Vagrant's story and the narrator's stumbling upon her are framed in a philosophic perspective that holds them, not simply at arm's length, but at the length of the whole of human social evolution. The first stanzas, paraphrasing Rousseau's *Discourse on Inequality*, ask whether men in developed societies do not suffer more from hardship than primitive men who know nothing else. The only conclusion one can draw from such a hypothesis is Rousseau's uncomfortable paradox, that increased civilization entails increased human inequality and mental suffering.

The poem's conclusion comes not from Rousseau, but from Tom Paine. Between the two of them, the narrator and the woman are but a 'friendless hope-forsaken pair,' confirming the woman's estimate of the 'dreadful price of being' she and her children have paid, following their father through the horrors of the American Revolution: 'dog-like wading at the heels of War . . . a cursed existence with the brood / That lap, their very nourishment, their brother's blood.' Her thoughts stimulate the Wordsworthian narrator to historical reflection on nearby Stonehenge. Though one no longer hears the 'horrid shrieks and dying cries' of human sacrifice, all the 'progress' enlightened reason can show is 'How many [are] by inhuman toil debased, / Abject, obscure, and brute to earth incline[d] / Unrespited, forlorn of every spark divine.' Against this depressing reflection, Wordsworth opposes the hope that some unspecified 'Heroes of Truth' will 'uptear / Th'Oppressor's dungeon from its deepest base' – an obvious allusion to the Bastille – and 'rear / Resistless in [their] might the herculean mace / Of Reason,' an allusion to the young French republic, which Wordsworth like everyone frequently compared to the young Hercules.[43] In contemporary English terms, such a hero was preeminently Tom Paine, the intellectual godfather of Wordsworth's 'Letter to Llandaff,' 'Who fierce on kingly crowns hurled his own lightning blaze' both in *The Rights of Man* and by his participation in the trial of Louis XVI.

Anyone who thinks they can resist such 'Heroes of Truth' is 'insenate' – stupid – like Pitt's administration, which imagines that it is wise policy

> That Exile, Terror, Bonds, and Force may stand:
> That Truth with human blood can feed her torch,
> And Justice balance with her gory hand
> Scales whose dire weights of human heads demand
> A Nero's arm.
>
> (515–19)

These are clear references to the government's actions against its opponents throughout the spring and summer of 1793, culminating in the transportation sentences of Muir, Palmer, Maurice Margarot, and William Skirving. Wordsworth's linking of Stonehenge and the Bastille as symbols of oppression is sincere, but histrionic. The poem's framework is as recklessly confident about the future as his 'Letter to Llandaff,' but Wordsworth's narrative faithfulness to the particulars of his characters' stories works to contradict it.

Once off the Plain, he resorted to public transport or cadged what rides he could. 'From that district,' he recalled, 'I proceeded to Bath, Bristol, and so on to the banks of the Wye, where I took again to travelling on foot. In remembrance of that part of my journey . . . I began the verses – "Five years have passed".'[44] Before he got to Tintern Abbey, however, we can track him near the mouth of the Wye, in two poems he wrote at Chepstow Castle just above Bristol, the first obligatory sight for any picturesque walking tour up the Wye valley.[45] Like the Isle of Wight fragment, and like the Salisbury Plain poems in all their versions, these fragments also show

Wordsworth's landscape vision being complicated, not to say ruined, by reflections on the inhumanity of human history.

The first one is a sonnet, partly torn away in manuscript, but its missing lines can be hypothetically reconstructed by extrapolating from its metre and imagery:

> In vain did Time and Nature toil to throw
> Wild weeds and earth upon these crumbled towers;
> Again they rear the feudal head that lowers
> Stern the wretched huts that crouch below.
> [*Here w*]here the cornfield waved and varied sound
> [*Of rural*] pleasure charmed the Cottage shade,
> [*Along the*] path the careless infant stray'd,
> [*Now the*] [?w]ild deer calls his mates around.
> [*But soon a new breeze*] and a form divine
> [*O'er all the*] [?earth] shall stretch her equal reign
> [*To every humble*] [?home] on every plain,
> [*E'en to a rude*] [Hy]mettus low as thine—
> [*Among the poor she*] dwelt, and loved to shed
> [*Her equal blessings round*] thy honour'd head.[46]

As a three-part Shakespearean sonnet, moving from the unhappy present to an idyllic past, and then pivoting toward an ideal projected future, the poem is over almost before it begins, given its strong opening statement that all is 'in vain.' Chepstow Castle, like Tintern Abbey, was at this time inhabited by vagrants, gypsies, beggars, and outlaws. Their number would swell dramatically during the next five years as the 'Minister's War' spread its ruinous economic consequences.

What Wordsworth imagines as completing the inadequate efforts of Time and Nature to cover over unhappy feudal remnants is not an 'equal reign' of agrarian reform, but a hierarchy of mutual respect in which higher and lower classes still exist, but without the need for any 'lowering' or 'crouching.' In this respect, the fragment is a liberal effort to breathe new spirit into inherited forms, for the sonnet is otherwise an uninspired reprise of those by the extremely conservative Reverend William Bowles which had fired Wordsworth's enthusiasm a few years earlier (for instance, 'Netley Abbey'). Bowles's melancholy emotions are entirely personal, but Wordsworth's poem has a kind of socio-political resolution, with its egalitarian female personification ('a form divine') returning like a messiah of Liberty to distribute equal justice in an 'equal reign' of natural plenty: Hymettus being the mountain near Athens famous in ancient pastorals for wild flowers and honey. One reason this poem about 'wretched huts' remained in manuscript, unlike 'Tintern Abbey' with its similar 'vagrant dwellers,' is that in the intervening five years Wordsworth learned – created – a way of hearing such 'still, sad music of humanity' without

258 · *The Hidden Wordsworth*

feeling that it was a contradiction to the beauty of nature. But in 'Tintern Abbey' he achieves resolution almost entirely in personal terms, with even vaguer social overtones.

A second fragment, thirty-two lines beginning, 'The western clouds a deepening gloom display,' places Wordsworth at Chepstow Castle precisely, with mention of a 'traveller' standing before its high 'central bridge,' and references to torture and executions that recall the castle's role as a prison after the civil war. It recapitulates the problem of the Isle of Wight and 'In vain' sonnets, as well as the Salisbury Plain poems. Again Wordsworth sees a beautiful sunset through or across the ruins of a repressive human institution. He wants to draw a comfortable moral about human progress but can't. The result is that, as in the Isle of Wight sonnet, the poem disintegrates before our very eyes. His eyes 'draw from the streams . . . below [the Wye] / New tints of tender sadness *not their own*' (my italics). What these melancholy tints might be is not specified. He knows that 'moonlight beams' should lie 'still' on flowing waters, but at 'midnight hours' the meditating mind 'starts' at what it thinks.[47] A standard recipe of Picturesque ingredients has failed to provide an antidote, and the poem suddenly reverts to scenes of Gothic horror. At this point the manuscript poem degenerates into a purely escapist conclusion:

> When fragrant Morn forth issues glistering bright
> With heedless music and unaltered smile,
> [No] fond regret the ravage shall excite
> In musing sage or thoughtless [son] of toil.
>
> (29–32)

This comes close to saying, Don't worry, be happy. All we can say is that the 'ravage' the poem describes has shifted from Time's damage to the towers of Chepstow Castle to include the ravages of the meditating mind upon itself, as it explores its 'new tints of tender sadness.'

But we know very well what those tints of sadness were for Wordsworth: almost any thoughts about his life in general, and in particular his thoughts about Annette and his inability to provide for her. In his famous lines in 'Tintern Abbey' about his mood 'when first I came among these hills,' he introduces his twenty-three-year-old self with a strange reverse-hyperbole: he was 'more like a man / Flying from something that he dreads, than one / Who sought the thing he loved' (71–73). He was *not* a man seeking the thing he loved (Annette), he was rather a man flying from something that he dreaded – which may also have been Annette, or the whole collection of circumstances that was keeping him from her (the war, his uncles, and his own growing desperation about what being with her may entail for his life). His effort to be true to his own experience, in poems written mainly to produce pat moral generalizations, ruined his poems of 1793. But these efforts are the point of origin of his immense advance beyond mere landscape poetry into a comprehensive vision which could contain, if only uneasily, both history and the individual consciousness.

The next day's walk brought him to to Goodrich Castle, where he records meeting the little girl of 'We Are Seven,' who insisted that the number of her siblings was undiminished, though 'two are in the church-yard laid.' Wordsworth gave her a slight Welsh identification with her information that 'two of us at Conway [Conwy] dwell,' but the obtuse narrator of the poem, who insists that dead children are dead, buried, and in heaven, is not identical with the young man whose own infant child was much on his mind at the time.

Continuing north along the river, he came to Builth Wells, where he met the 'wild rover' who became Peter Bell. 'He told me strange stories. It has always been a pleasure to me through life to catch at every opportunity that has occurred in my rambles of becoming acquainted with this class of people.' This 'class' were those 'wanderers of the earth' who had for Wordsworth the same 'grandeur which invests / The mariner who sails the roaring sea' (XII.153–54): a pointed comparison, since *Peter Bell* is his land-locked companion to Coleridge's *Rime of the Ancient Mariner*. Such itinerant vagrants interested Wordsworth as long as they were not in groups, like gypsies: 'From many other uncouth vagrants, passed / In fear, [I] have walked with quicker step' (XII.159–60). Sometimes the feeling was mutual, if we may credit some cancelled lines from one of the many manuscripts of *Peter Bell*:

> Now Peter do I call to mind
> That eventide when thou and I
> Over ditch and over stile
> *Were fellow travellers many a mile*
> Near Builth on the banks of Wye.
>
> Oh Peter who could now forget
> That both hung back in murderer's guize?
> 'Twas thou that was afraid of me.
> And I that wast afraid of thee,
> We'd each of us a hundred eyes.[48]

After more than a week on the road on foot, Wordsworth the wanderer looked not much less 'wild' than Peter the rover. One would give a lot to know what Peter's 'strange stories' were, and whether Wordsworth told him some of his own. They may have included of Peter's bigamy (he had six wives), though Wordsworth attributed this behaviour to 'a lawless creature who lived in the county of Durham . . . attended by many women, sometimes not less than half a dozen, as disorderly as himself.'[49] Wordsworth was particularly receptive to stories of bigamy as he laboured up the Wye valley toward Jones's sanctuary, 'more like a man / Flying from something that he dreads, than one / Who sought the thing he loved.'

Peter has trekked all over England and Scotland. One of his early points of reference is close to Wordsworth's recent experience – 'well he knew the spire of Sarum' – and the main action of the poem includes one location that sounds like Salisbury Plain: 'Where, shining like the smoothest sea, / In undisturbed immensity / A level plain extends.'[50] The narrator of *Peter Bell* presents his story as an escapist relief from troubling public events that fit 1793 better than 1798 (its time of composition), though applicable enough to both years: 'what care we / For treasons, tumults, and for wars?' But the closest connection to 1793 is *Peter Bell*'s plot, which is in many respects a reprise of the Salisbury Plain poems. Peter, heartless bigamist that he is, finds an untethered ass staring down into a stream where its master lies drowned. Unnerved, and unable to control the stubborn ass, Peter follows him home, where the owner's daughter at first mistakes him for her lost father ('My father! here's my father!'), but the wife rushes out, 'And saw it was another!' As Peter tells the distraught widow what has happened, her grief works upon him like the Female Vagrant's on the Salisbury Traveller: 'He longs to press her to his heart, / From love that cannot find relief.' But, as in that poem, a denouement that might bring the two sufferers together is precisely the one the author rejects, and it is the ass, not Peter, who subsequently 'Help[ed] by his labour to maintain / The Widow and her family.' Peter, instead, becomes a land-rover prototype of the Ancient Mariner: 'And, after ten months' melancholy, / Became a good and honest man.'

Other traces of Wordsworth's 1793 experiences flicker throughout the poem.[51] However, it is a much smaller detail, or inconsistency, that leads me to think that young Wordsworth's thoughts of Annette and Caroline attached themselves to this wild rover's strange stories. Wordsworth said he walked with Peter 'from Builth, on the river Wye, *downwards* nearly as far as the town of Hay.' But if he met him on the itinerary we are following, he should have being going *upward* from Hay-on-Wye toward Builth Wells. Scholars have tried to account for this apparently small inconsistency, ruling out the easy solution, that Wordsworth simply misspoke himself, on the basis of the poet's usual clarity and accuracy about such matters.[52]

But Wordsworth's movements can be aligned with Peter's if we assume that he did not meet Peter on his way north to Plas-yn-Llan, but his way *back* down south some weeks later, as the news from France and his growing uneasiness of mind about Annette and Caroline finally determined him to slip back across the Channel to France to see what he could do for them. This small detail about which direction Wordsworth was heading when he met the 'wild rover' gives us a fulcrum on which to pivot our hero around and head him back to France on his own, a wilder rover than Peter ever was. The one element in *Peter Bell* that Wordsworth got from no source but his own experience is the hero's remorse for having abandoned his wives and children. Here again, what seems strangest in the saga of Wordsworth's heroes may be closest to his own literal experience.

To explore this possibility we must backtrack a little, and try to put ourselves into Wordsworth's mind from the time of his return from France the preceding December, to imagine what he might have been thinking as he heard about what was happening in France, and how he might have imagined these terrible events affecting his lover and their child.

CHAPTER FIFTEEN

A Return to France?

'A season dangerous and wild'
(X.286)

'that terrible moment, '93'
(Victor Hugo, *Quatre-vingt treize*)

Wordsworth's life in the late summer and early autumn of 1793 presents two very different scenarios, like a 'Choose Your Own Adventure' book for adolescents, where one chapter choice lands you with monsters, while another gets you home free. From late August until about Christmas there exists no firm contemporary evidence as to his whereabouts. One option is to think of him 'quietly sitting down in the Vale of Clwyd,' a long-term house guest of the indulgent Robert Jones, biding his time until he could travel ninety miles east to see Dorothy at Halifax.

The other choice is to imagine Wordsworth embarked on an adventure of astonishing danger: going back to France sometime in September to see, marry, or rescue Annette, passing through intense counter-revolutionary actions in Normandy, entering Paris just as the trial of his former acquaintances among the Girondins began, and witnessing the execution of Gorsas on 7 October. He pushes on toward Blois to try to see Annette, and then in the greatest possible danger escapes north through frozen fields, hiding in caves and forests along the route of the desperate Vendéan army as it skirmished its way toward vainly expected British aid on the Normandy coast. This view has Wordsworth crossing back to England in late October or early November.

The two different accounts return to a single narrative line at Christmas-time, with Wordsworth as guest of his guardian uncle, Richard Wordsworth, at Whitehaven. The first alternative seems eminently more likely, except that there is not a shred of evidence to support it. The second alternative seems more like an excerpt from Victor Hugo's *Quatre-vingt treize* – an English love-episode rejected, one might imagine, even by the great Romantic novelist as too implausible. Yet there are two accounts by trustworthy reporters which place Wordsworth in Paris in 1793, to which we can connect a pattern of associations from Wordsworth's poetry and contemporary records that give this wild surmise more substance than its tame alternative. None of Wordsworth's recent biographers is prepared to reject the evidence for a clandestine return; instead, after carefully turning over the evidence, they make the considered judgement that it is the more likely possibility.[1] What remains to be done, since none of these authorities venture beyond the positive evidence, is, by sifting the evidence more finely, to construct a plausible scenario for it.

The first alternative is easily sketched, a still-life without action. If Wordsworth stayed 'quietly sitting down' in Wales until about Christmas-time, we can imagine him passing his time as Dorothy said, following his cross-country hike from Salisbury Plain, 'as happily as he could desire; exactly according to his Taste, except alas! (ah here I sigh) that he is separated from those he loves.'[2] But along with her desires, Dorothy stressed to her friend Jane Pollard to an inordinate degree the need for secrecy. Above all, she insists that Jane should not betray her knowledge that Dorothy knows that William may soon be there. Thus her letter of 10 July opens with the peremptory caution, *'None of this is to be read aloud, so be upon your guard!'* This secrecy is explainable because of William Cookson's increasing distaste for his nephew. Dorothy did not want to appear as conniving in a plan to meet with a relative who is so much in disgrace with her aunt and uncle.

But the insistence on secrecy has another dimension, which draws our two options for Wordsworth's movements this autumn closer together. William and Dorothy were certainly involved in at least one family plot this autumn: their plot to meet at Halifax 'accidentally,' so that no blame would fall on Dorothy for seeing him. This plot was unsuccessful, since they did not meet there at Christmas. But it may be that all these promised movements and adjurations to strictest secrecy were intended to give William an alibi, placing him firmly in Wales until such time as Dorothy got to Halifax, while he was actually going elsewhere, somewhere that truly could not be communicated to anyone in the family.

Other details from the summer increase the possibility of such a secret plan. We have seen that William's sojourn on the Isle of Wight provided an opportunity for reconnoitring the possibilities for slipping out of some small bay like Freshwater for a safe landing spot on the Normandy coast. Then there is the question of the accident to Calvert's carriage and the oddity that Wordsworth and Calvert separated following it, in two different directions: Calvert to the north and Wordsworth to the west. Did this accident actually occur, or was there some other reason for a parting of the ways? For a whiskey and its occupants to be 'dragged . . . into a Ditch and broke . . . to shivers' was a very serious accident. A whiskey was a very light two-wheeled vehicle, essentially a seat on leather straps attached to springs, that could easily break into 'shivers' if dragged into a ditch. Newspapers carried almost daily accounts of similar accidents, usually accompanied by grave injuries or death, like highway accidents today. So it is a little hard to believe that the two young men got out, unharmed, that one of them mounted that same dangerously capering horse and rode off to the north of England, while the other, with conspicuously noted 'firm . . . stout' legs, headed off toward Wales. Of course this account is possible, but it does raise questions. Why was the tour to the west of England now abandoned? Why did Calvert leave Wordsworth so abruptly? Had their separation been planned? Presumably the whiskey was irreparable, but why didn't Calvert, rich as he was, buy or rent another, or rent a horse for Wordsworth? Their separation is strange, though a serious road accident can damp holiday spirits, even if there are no serious injuries. But it could also be an excuse to cover the fact that the proposed sightseeing tour had other motives. Wales was a plausible destination for either plot, for if anyone could be trusted to keep the details secret, it was Robert Jones, European companion *par excellence*.

It is the essence of good plotting to cover one's movements with other plausible accounts for 'deniability.' With the Wales–Halifax connection firmly established, an England–France connection might be pursued more freely. 'William in France? Good heavens, no! He's with Calvert on the Isle of Wight, he's in the west of England, he's with Jones in Wales, he's just waiting to come over to Halifax . . . anywhere but France!' Wordsworth-in-Wales is one option for the autumn of 1793, but it is not without connections to its dramatic alter-ego, Wordsworth-in-the-Vendée. It is not necessary to link up the Halifax 'plot' with a French one, but it does have the virtue of suggesting that our two scenarios are not mutually exclusive, and that the evidence for one can be used to flesh out the evidence for the other.

The Life Record

It starts with Thomas Carlyle. The year is about 1840. Carlyle had met and talked with Wordsworth on several occasions, at breakfasts and dinner parties. Carlyle admired Wordsworth's 'fine wholesome rusticity,' but found his literary opinions exceptionally narrow: 'Gradually it became apparent to me that of the transcendent unlimited [type of genius] there was, to this critic, probably but one specimen known – Wordsworth himself!' Still, Wordsworth was willing to talk with Carlyle 'in a corner' at these large London social gatherings which neither of them liked very much, and in 'another and better corner dialogue . . . which raised him intellectually some real degrees higher in my estimation than any of his deliverances, written or oral, had ever done,' Carlyle decided to drop literature and to try to get from Wordsworth 'an account of the notable practicalities he had seen in life, especially of the notable men.'[3]

This is what he got:

> He went into all this with a certain alacrity, and was willing to speak whenever able on terms. He had been in France in the earlier or secondary stage of the Revolution; had witnessed the struggle of Girondins and Mountain, in particular the execution of Gorsas, 'the first deputy sent to the scaffold;' and testified strongly to the ominous feeling which that event produced in everybody, and of which he himself still seemed to retain something: 'Where will it end, when you have set an example in this kind?' I knew well about Gorsas, but had found in my reading no trace of the public emotion his death excited, and perceived now that Wordsworth might be taken as a true supplement to my book, on this small point. He did not otherwise add to or alter my ideas on the Revolution, nor did we dwell long there; but hastened over to England, and to the noteworthy, or at least noted, men of that and the subsequent time. 'Noted' and named, I ought, perhaps, to say, rather than 'noteworthy;' for in general I forget what men they were, and now only remember the excellent sagacity, distinctness, and credibility of Wordsworth's little biographical portraitures of them.[4]

They went on to speak about Wilberforce, 'the famous Nigger philan-thropist.' The fact is noteworthy, because it is about Wilberforce that Wordsworth begins speaking as he opens his *Prelude* account of returning from France in late 1792: 'I found the air yet busy with the stir . . . against the traffickers in Negro blood.' That is, his thoughts when speaking to Carlyle about being in France follow the same sequence of subjects as in *The Prelude*.

Antoine Joseph Gorsas was executed on 7 October 1793 in Paris. And Thomas Carlyle, the reigning British expert on the French Revolution, was deeply enough impressed with the 'distinctness' and 'credibility' of Wordsworth's recollections to wish he could add it as 'a true supplement' on this one point. Carlyle was markedly *un*interested in correcting his *The French Revolution* once it was published, hence his extensive analysis of this conversation is especially noteworthy. Newly famous authors are not eager to admit publicly that there are additional facts they wish they could add to their best-known works. Yet Carlyle's credibility is as firm as Wordsworth's, for he readily admits he could no longer remember what other men they talked of, besides Gorsas and Wilberforce, making it that much more likely that his remembrance of what Wordsworth said about these two is clear. Nor does he exaggerate the importance of Wordsworth's information: it is a 'small point,' and 'did not otherwise add to or alter' Carlyle's voluminous store of Revolutionary facts. Finally, he appreciates 'the incomparable historical tone' of Wordsworth's recollections, his 'luminous and veracious power of insight . . . you perceived it to be faithful, accurate, and altogether life-like, though Wordsworthian.'

There are two stages in Carlyle's recollection of Wordsworth's recollection: first, his being in Paris to 'witness . . . in particular the execution of Gorsas,' and then afterwards, when they 'hastened over to England' (this refers to their shift in subject, but could carry overtones of an actual trip). Some aspects of Wordsworth's testimony apply to 1792 almost as well as to 1793, but not the execution of Gorsas. Especially notable are the two internal quotations where Carlyle seems to be recalling Wordsworth's actual words. 'Where will it end?', is very much in the spirit of Wordsworth's nightmare vision that 'all things have second birth' on his return to Paris in October 1792.

The struggle between the Gironde and the Mountain broke into the open in the fall of 1792 and ended a year later with the execution of the leading Girondistes on 31 October. Wordsworth had indeed 'witnessed' it all, if, having been in Paris in October 1792, he returned there a year later. His 'hastening' back over to England could apply to either year. In 1793 his reasons for haste would have been his own safety, whereas in 1792 they had to do with his need to raise money for Annette. 'The ominous feeling' Gorsas's execution produced was not generally public. But it would have been strong among 'everybody' that Wordsworth knew in Paris, to some of whom he would have turned for aid on his dangerous return, and who were wondering, like him, 'Where will it end?' – a feeling that Wordsworth 'still seemed to retain.' But the reference to 'hastening' over to England, whether a textual or a biographical pointer, follows his mention of the execution, and the 'subsequent time' would therefore seem to be after 1793. After sifting alternative explanations, the firmness and accuracy of both Carlyle's and Wordsworth's reports stand up very well.

A second thread of evidence is the marginal notation opposite Gorsas's name in Wordsworth's edition of the collected works of Edmund Burke: 'I knew this man. W.W.' This surely indicates personal acquaintance and some level of conversational familiarity. It would be pointless to take it to mean, 'I knew *of* him,' since many people still retained some knowledge of Gorsas. In fact, Wordsworth virtually picks Gorsas out of a line-up of suspects that Burke has assembled to contrast the dubious characters associated with the Revolution with the higher-quality persons who were in charge of France before the Revolution. It is the only mention of Gorsas in Burke's entire *oeuvre*, occurring in his *Letter to a Noble Lord* (1796), defending himself against attacks on his government pension by the Duke of Bedford. He asks whether Bedford can imagine that the Turennes, the Luxembourgs, the Colberts – all the illustrious governing families of old France –

> that these should be given up to the cruel sport of the Pichegru's, the Jourdans, the Santerres, under the Rollands, and Brissets [*sic*], and Gorsas, and Robespierres, the Reubels, the Carnots, and Talliens, and Dantons, and the

whole tribe of Regicides, robbers, and revolutionary judges, that, from the rotten carcase of their own murdered country, have poured out innumerable swarms of the lowest, and at once the most destructive of the classes of animated nature, which like columns of locusts, have laid waste the fairest part of the world?[5]

In this tally of low-class locusts, assembled by the leading British opponent of the French Revolution, we do not find Wordsworth's notation referring to Brissot, who is immediately adjacent, and where we might better expect to find it. Moreover, Wordsworth was indebted to Burke as early as 1804 for just this imagery, and in precisely this context, in *The Prelude*'s description of France, as a 'land all swarmed with passion, like a plain / Devoured by locusts – Carra, Gorsas . . .' (IX.178–79).

To *sign* one's marginal note suggests a certain amount of wished-for identification, namely, 'among all the many French revolutionaries named here, I, William Wordsworth, *knew this man*.' It is, moreover, the only written comment in the whole of Wordsworth's sixteen-volume set of Burke's works. When he knew him is another question. Knowing or conversing with Gorsas in early October 1793 is not very likely. It is more likely that he knew Gorsas in the autumn of 1792, during his six-week sojourn in Paris, when he was closest to the journalistic milieu of the Revolution.

The third line of evidence placing Wordsworth in Paris in 1793 is equally serendipitous, but goes in the same direction. It is from a biography of the minor publicist Alaric Watts (1797–1864), published by his son in 1884, recounting his father's visits to the London salon of John 'Walking' Stewart, c. 1812–1814. Stewart was an eccentric Scots vegetarian and revolutionary; his eloquent harangues on living according to nature much impressed Wordsworth 'when he had met him at Paris between the years 1790 and 1792, during the early storms of the French Revolution.'[6] This again places young Wordsworth close to the journalistic front of the Revolution, for Stewart was one of the English writers in Paris that the British spy Captain Munro reported to London. Two frequent visitors at Stewart's London open-houses (he returned to London after 1792) were the socialist Robert Owen and 'an old Republican named Bailey, who had been confined in the Temple at Paris with Pichegru [in 1804]. He had met Wordsworth in Paris, and having warned him that his connection to the "Mountain" rendered his situation there at that time perilous, the poet, he said, decamped with great precipitation.'[7]

There are problems with this account, but also plausibilities. Like parts of the earlier lines of evidence, it can be attributed almost as well to 1792 as to 1793. Wordsworth was not associated with the Mountain, although in 1792, when the Mountain and the Gironde were in the process of separating, the distinctions between persons belonging to either group was not clear. Wordsworth, we know, was clearly associated with the Jacobins and with the radical Brissot for most of his 1791–92 sojourn, and Gorsas was one of the Girondins who tried 'to the last minute' to achieve a compromise with the more moderate Montagnards.[8] British sympathizers were rapidly dispersing from Paris in late 1792, but more from demoralization than any sense of peril. But Wordsworth's decamping 'with great precipitation' coincides nicely with Carlyle's ambiguous use of the word *hastening* over to England. His 'connection' with the Mountain may have signified his *wrong* connection with the Mountain, insofar as they harked back to Brissot and Gorsas, since neither in 1792 nor in 1793 would a direct connection with the Mountain have been a danger – quite the contrary. Finally, there is the fact that this recollection is attributed to Bailey, whom Wordsworth clearly knew in Paris, rather than to Stewart, who had left in 1792. That is, knowing an Englishman in Paris in 1792 was not a particularly remarkable thing, but in 1793 it most certainly was.*

The record so far, such as it is, is in good order. There is a fourth strand of textual evidence pulling Wordsworth toward France in 1793. Its existence must be inferred from other texts, but they come from a very authoritative source: Annette Vallon. In her letter of 20 March 1793, confiscated by the French police, this was her train of thought:

> I would feel more comforted if we were married, but at the same time I consider it almost impossible that you risk the voyage if we have war. You could be taken prisoner. But where do my desires lead me? I speak as if this minute I touched my happiness. Write to me what you think on this subject, and do everything you can to hurry the happiness of your daughter and mine, but only if there is not the least risk, but I think that the war will not be too long. I would like to see the two nations reconciled. It's one of my most sincere wishes.[9]

What a pushing and pulling is here, what a provocative 'almost'! You might . . . but no . . . and yet . . . . Is she responding to a possibility Wordsworth has already broached, or introducing it herself? Her last words in the letter return to the same subject: 'Tell me about the war, and what you think of it, because this preoccupies me much.' By 20 March the declaration of war was nearly two months old, so her phrase, 'if we have war,' must mean something like, 'if we have war *here*, in Blois, the destination of your risky voyage.'

Annette's come-hither rhetoric was even stronger in her letter to Dorothy, where she subtly associated her situation vis-à-vis William with

---

* In this connection, it may be significant that the original *Blackwood's Magazine* article, 'A Day with Wordsworth' (January 1927), reports Wordsworth saying 'he went over to Paris at the time of the Revolution in 1792 *and* 1793, and so was "pretty hot in it" ' (italics added), not '1792 or 1793,' as stated in *The Life of James Watt*, p. 494.

Dorothy's, and gracefully co-opted Dorothy into her own desires. She reproaches William for not adequately conveying to her how charming his sister was:

> I would like to reproach him one day when we will be reunited, but when will he come? Oh, how far off I believe he still is! I must still buy him with many sighs. But when we will be reunited, oh my sister, how happy we shall be! . . . you like me are deprived of the happiness of seeing him. How unhappy you are, if his absence is as painful to you as it is to me. Only that you are not as far apart as we are. You receive news about him more often than Annette, you exchange thoughts . . . But I assure you that I could be comforted if I were lucky enough that my dear Williams could make the voyage to France to come to give me the title of his wife. First of all, my daughter would have a father, and her poor mother would enjoy the happines of having him always with her . . . I would no longer make my family blush when I call my daughter, my Caroline . . .

This is indeed buying with sighs, a pleading impossible to ignore. Only by marriage could she gain possession of Caroline. Wordsworth has owned his daughter, why not now legitimize her, even if he cannot – yet – provide for her?[10] If they will not come to her, she suggests wildly, she will go to them, and Dorothy's identification with her will be as complete and as intimate as possible:

> Call your father, my little one, soon I will take you in my arms, I will go to meet this father who costs your mother so many tears. [Vaudracour says, 'Julia, how much thine eyes / Have cost me!'] You will hold him in your little arms, your little lips will give him a tender kiss, he will hold these innocent caresses very dear. Yes, my dear sister, I will go to take him his child. I already showed Caroline the road. I'll go again tomorrrow. We shall call him but he will not hear us . . . I think that she will respond to the goodness and care that you will want to give her, for dear sister, you shall be her second mother . . .
>
> We all four are just one, dear friend; a day will come when, reunited, our union will be unbreakable . . . You wouldn't believe it, but at least *I can assure you truthfully that if it is possible that my friend should come back to give me the glorious title of his wife, despite the cruel necessity which would force him to abandon his wife and child right away, I would suffer a painful absence with more ease.* But I would find in his daughter a recompense which at this moment is forbidden to me.[11]

This clearly supplies both a motive and a plan for Wordsworth's trip.

To be pleaded with and pulled by two different women at the same time, both of whom he loved dearly, both of whom construe his absence as a nearly life-threatening situation for themselves, and from both of whom he is also separated by very strong (though very different) prohibitions, was an incredible burden for the twenty-three-year-old Wordsworth. How long could he hold out against such persuasions? Annette allied herself with Dorothy, and Dorothy allied herself with Annette. The Halifax and French 'plots' come to seem matching halves of the same over-arching goal: to be with William. Annette, as inventive, daring, and energetic here as in her later *chouannerie*, even provides the plan, acceptable to her, that would allow him to do both: come over here, marry me, and then return to Dorothy until such time as we can all four live together.

The Public Record

To return with Wordsworth to France in 1793, we should put ourselves in his mind as well as his shoes. He was suffering a personal crisis which was intimately connected to a national one. But though he could not for the moment bring Annette to England, he could still marry her in France. She referred to them as husband and wife in her letters, and was urging actual marriage on him in the strongest possible terms, for only if she was properly a *wife* would her family allow her to assume publicly the role of a *mother*. By not marrying his mistress, Wordsworth was keeping her from her one source of consolation in distress, her daughter: the double bind Annette presented to him was as bad as his uncles', or worse. Wordsworth was capable of loving very few people strongly, but his moral commitment to those he did love was rock solid. This fact, plus his proven willingness to take foolhardy trips to France in his own interest, create a powerful impetus to send him on his way.

But where, when, and how? Wordsworth watched and calculated his chances, mainly on the basis of newspaper reports, fleshed out by rumours, and interpreted by Annette's occasional and voluminous letters. He was always an avid newspaper reader, but never more so than in 1793. In reviewing the news for 1793, there is little danger of our under-interpreting what Wordsworth might have made of this or that item of information; he would have made the very most of everything. He was not reading about the revolution as a historian, a journalist, or even a poet as he pored over the fine print; he was a young man in love, and with enormous responsibilities and difficulties on his shoulders.

For most of the spring and much of the summer, events seemed to favour the lovers' plight. As Hugo says, ''93 was the war of Europe against France, and of France against Paris,' and it looked as if the war would soon be over, as Annette hoped. Although counter-revolutionary activity ebbed in the winter of 1792–93, following Louis' execution, it began again in March, fuelled in Paris by demands for food and in the provinces by reactions against the *levée* for 300,000 men voted on 24 February.[12] There were riots throughout Normandy and Brittany, and in the Vendée proper, south of the Loire. The central government regained control north of the Loire by early April, but its authority south of the river virtually collapsed, and the Vendéan War began in earnest. By the end of March, the

Vendéans had raised an army of 40,000 men, led by experienced generals of the old nobility, and egged on by fanatical recalcitrant priests. The 'Grande Armée Catholique et Royale,' with the imprisoned Louis XVII as its child commander-in-chief and the Sacred Heart as its emblem (also chosen by Annette for her seal), was established in early April, and immediately sent emissaries to England seeking assistance. '"Long live the English!" is the cry of the rebels.'

Blois, whence Annette had returned after Caroline's birth, was only thirty miles east of Tours, the rebels' prime target along the critical Loire line. Lying just outside the area of conflict, it was an important staging area both for republican thrusts into the Vendée, and for relief efforts secretly channelled to the royalists by families like the Vallons. To Helen Williams, 'it seemed doubtful of which party [royalist or republican] France was destined to be the prey,' for, she thought, the Vendéans controlled the Loire 'almost as far as Paris.'[13] This was an exaggeration, but an expansion as far as Tours – or Blois – was not.

The *sansculottes journées* of 9–10 March failed to purge the Convention of the Girondins, but they did plant the suggestion in the public consciousness that the Gironde, the Bordeaux coastal region immediately south of the Vendée, was sympathetic to the royalist rebels' cause. An anticipation of worse things to come, that would certainly have caught Wordsworth's eye, was the mob's smashing the presses of both Brissot's and Gorsas' newspapers.[14] These March 'days' also established the Revolutionary Tribunal, whose original purpose was to intern foreigners and 'suspects' without passports. 'Foreigner' and 'suspect' were becoming virtually interchangeable terms, so from Wordsworth's perspective at this time, there was every reason to wait and see what would happen before venturing dangerously into France.

However, in early March Annette's brother Paul was implicated in a trumped-up assassination charge made by Léonard Bourdon, the Convention's representative in Orléans.[15] Bourdon was shoved about and slightly wounded on the street in a drunken altercation between celebrating Jacobins and the National Guards at the Town Hall, where Paul was working late. Bourdon revenged himself on his assailants by calling them assassins. (Paul Vallon seems in fact to have been trying to disengage the fighters.) Bourdon formally made the charges in a letter sent to the Convention on 19 March, the day before Annette sent her two (confiscated) letters to William and Dorothy. Knowing that Paul was in trouble added urgency to her tone. By coincidence, Bourdon's letter reached the Convention in the same post that first reported the full seriousness of the new Vendée uprising, and the two were immediately linked as internal and external parts of a monarchist plot, and martial law was re-instituted in Orléans. Forty members of 'notable' families that Bourdon accused were indicted, many were arrested, including

Wordsworth's former landlord of the rue Royal, M. Gellet-Duvivier, while some, like Paul Vallon, went into hiding. The affair of 'the forty notables of Orléans' was used by the English press as a frequent point of reference during the next six months to document the rise of French horrors.

Wordsworth may thus have known as early as March that Paul Vallon, and perhaps his sister and mother, had run afoul of one of the harshest of the Jacobins.[16] Bourdon, the 'Schoolmaster Jacobin' (1754–1807), was one of the leading educational reformers of the new Republic. He makes one blush for teachers, but he was – like many academics – a shrewd survivor: he became president of the Jacobin Club after Robespierre's fall. He was named *greffier au tribunal* (clerk of court) for his role in the 10 August rising, and sent to Orléans the following March. His first antagonists were the local *greffiers*, one of whom was André-Augustin Dufour, the landlord and close friend of Paul, whose wife helped Annette deliver Caroline. Though the Convention gradually began to get a clearer picture of the nature of the assault on Bourdon, he managed to push aside all the documents incriminating him and get nine of his assailants (M. Gellet-Duvivier among them) indicted, arrested, and – on 13 July – executed.

The agreeable prospect that the Revolution might soon be defeated began to change with the second of the three great *journées* of 1793, those of 31 May–2 June, which succeeded where 9–10 March had failed. A mob of 20,000 *sansculottes* invaded the Convention and forced the arrest of twenty-nine deputies – all the main Girondistes, including Louvet, who sat for Loiret. However, every successful revolutionary action had its immediate counter-revolutionary reaction, and *journées* of early June had exactly the opposite result in the provinces. The Vendée revolt now suddenly spread north of the Loire. Five departments in Brittany and three in Normandy leagued together at Caen against the Convention, soon drawing to them a number of the proscribed Girondins: 'the journalists Gorsas and Louvet' among them.[17] This was the beginning of the short-lived 'federalist' revolt. Now 'the Vendée had the Gironde for accomplice' (Hugo).

The Girondins in Normandy immediately began acting like a government in exile. It gained an important convert when General Wimpfen, Commander of the Army of the Coasts of Cherbourg, defected from the Republic and joined their new coalition, with the majority of his troops. Wimpfen was known to have English connections, but that was a plus for the Girondins, as it would have been for any young Englishman contemplating a crossing to the coasts of Cherbourg. By 30 June, battalions from Brittany were reported on their way to Paris under Wimpfen to deliver the city from the Commune and the Jacobins.[18] These battalions got to within fifty miles of the capital before they were routed, also on 13 July, at Pacy-sur-Eure.

But on the day after they decamped, a single person set out from the rebel headquarters at Caen who ultimately did more damage to their cause than any defeat their army suffered. Her name was Charlotte Corday. A young woman of noble family, descended from Corneille and steeped in Plutarch's *Lives*, she had decided to become the Brutus of France. But her assassination of Marat – on 13 July – was the event that began to tip the balance decisively against all counterrevolutionaries, since it demonstrated the reality of the radicals' constant warnings of spies, traitors, and assassins in their midst. By making Marat a martyr, Corday galvanized the majority of the Convention behind the Jacobins' energetic revolutionary measures, and guaranteed almost the opposite of what she intended.

Corday's assassination of Marat in July was insistently linked in British newspapers with the attempt on Bourdon in March. This was easy to do, because of the coincidence that the executions in the Bourdon case were carried out on the very day of Marat's murder: 13 July 1793. There are several reasons that the opening lines of 'Tintern Abbey' repeatedly invite us to subtract five years ('Five years have passed; five summers, with the length / Of five long winters!') from the date we have just read at the end of its title, 'July 13, 1798,' and the connection between these two events in 1793 may be among them. Hereafter, accusations against counter-revolutionaries were routinely made in terms of the Marat and Bourdon assassinations, the one more famous publicly, the other far more important to Wordsworth privately.[19] During the trial of the Bourdon case in late June, parents *and sisters* of the accused were reported pleading for their relatives, a group which in Wordsworth's mind's eye could well have included Annette, since the one item she would certainly *not* have included in her letters was the reassuring news that Paul was safe in hiding and not among those on trial. Among the women crying out, 'Grace! grace!,' there was one known to Wordsworth, M. Gellet-Duvivier's daughter, who pleaded her father's mental instability, to no avail. When the verdict was announced, 'plus nombreuses' of these women fell fainting at the foot of the tribunal, 'et de ce tableau sortaient por intervalle *des cris déchirants et des invocations qui arrochaient l'âme*' [heart-rending cries and pleas which break one's soul].[20] If he imagined Annette in this group, Wordsworth's resolve to rescue her may have been fixed at this point.

About this time, 'les hommes des Londres' became a new bogey for the Terror, following Fabre d'Eglantine's 3 August acccount – exaggerated but true – of English efforts to destabilize the French economy by circulating false *assignats*. England's secret agents – 'la Correspondance,' 'les Amis de Paris,' or 'le Manufacture' were its code names – were just getting organized under the direction of first Evan Nepean and later William Wickham, undersecretaries in the Home Office. They were never very effective,[21] but in the late summer there was active recruiting of young men who could speak French and were willing, for high pay

(£100–£200 per mission), to take the risk of carrying messages to England's agents among the various counterrevolutionary groups and make observations on their troop strength as compared to the republicans.[22] Most of these agents were French royalists from Jersey and Guernsey, but some came from England as well. The British government used them to communicate with the Vendéan army, but Pitt and his ministers held publicly that they could not involve themselves in subverting the French constitution, all the while trying privately to ascertain the chances of such a venture's success. All this activity reached a fever pitch of confidential and secret letters, reports, pleadings, and urgings in late August and early September.[23]

Toulon fell to Admiral Hood on 27–28 August, and in the first week of September the Vendéans won a great victory – their high water mark, as it turned out – at Chantonnay. The republican forces fled all the way back to Saumur, a day's march from Blois. Take-no-prisoners became the Vendéans' response to the republicans' scorched-earth policy; it was now total war on both sides, with unspeakable reprisals: no mercy, no quarter.

Into this new atmosphere of increased viciousness came the news of the *journées* of 4–5 September, which I believe prompted Wordsworth at last to push off for France within the week for his own Normandy landing. These *journées* were the most successful of the entire Revolution, surpassed only by 10 August 1792. They were provoked by the fall of Toulon and the defeat at Chantonnay, and the subsequent need for scapegoats: the as-yet-untried Girondins and Marie-Antoinette were ready to hand. They produced three major results: (1) the creation of the revolutionary army, (2) new steps toward identification and arrest of suspects, and (3) the declaration that 'terror was the order of the day.'[24] All three of these, Wordsworth could see, would directly affect Annette.

The revolutionary army was a corps of roving vigilante troops, each equipped with its own portable red guillotine, sent out across the countryside in search of suspected hoarders and rebels, who were summarily executed. The aim of the Terror was precisely that: to terrorize people into submission, to discourage potential traitors and profiteers. There were more executions in Paris than anywhere else, except for one region: the Vendée and the parts of Brittany and Normandy which joined its revolt.[25]

On 4 September *The Times* gave as its first example of 'those execrable Commissioners [who] have deluged France,' Léonard Bourdon, who 'produces a tumult in Orléans, which, until his arrival, had, during the whole revolution, been tranquil.' Wordsworth knows this is an exaggeration, but reads on: 'He fills the prisons of that unfortunate city with his victims, and when the wives and children of the prisoners come to him to expostulate, he compels them, at the point of a bayonet, to dance and drink, as if displaying a savage triumph at the miseries of their husbands and fathers. A few are provoked to give this Bourdon a drubbing. This is called the assassination of a Deputy, and they have expiated their offense on the scaffold.' To the extent that Wordsworth knew anything about the extent of Paul Vallon's involvement in this affair, such an account would have made his hair stand on end, and finally determined him to act.

Soon there came news – which we know reached Wordsworth – that the ferocity of the revolutionary state against its internal enemies was paying off in success against its external ones. Although Valenciennes (on the Belgian border) had fallen to the beseiging Allies on 28 July, the Duke of York, in a collossal strategic misconception, separated his forces from those of the Prince of Coburg and set off to liberate Dunkirk on the Channel. This shift in tactics soon impinged upon Wordsworth. York took up an unfavourable position near Dunkirk, and on 6 September, at the nearby village of Hondschoote, the English army was routed. This victory gave French morale an enormous lift. It was their first victory in a string of defeats stretching all the way back to March – that is, precisely the period of event watching and decision making we have been reconstructing in Wordsworth's mind. This defeat received Wordsworth's full attention; it is the one he refers to in *Prelude* X, at precisely this point in his narrative's chronology, when he 'exulted in the triumph of my soul / When Englishmen by thousands were o'erthrown, / Left without glory on the field, or driven, / Brave hearts, to shameful flight' (X.261–64).

CHAPTER SIXTEEN

A Return to France

The Evidence of Speculation

> Such ghastly visions had I of despair,
> And tyranny, and implements of death,
> And long orations which in dreams I pleaded
> Before unjust tribunals . . .
>
> (X.374–77)

Sometime between 6 and 17 September, Wordsworth's perception of the connection between increased Terror and the sudden turn in the tide of the war led him to steel his resolve to cross the Channel.[1] The latter date seems more likely because it was the day on which the the Law of Suspects was passed.[2] The first provision of this law was that any citizen of a country with which France was at war should be arrested. Much of its effectiveness lay in its vagueness, as Helen Williams recalled: '*suspected!* that indefinite word, which was tortured into every meaning of injustice and oppression.'[3] In fact, though arrests of Englishmen were called for at various times throughout the year, this law was still not executed rigorously for another month, even longer in the provinces.[4] But Wordsworth would not have been so worried about this, since he must have recognized that the main danger of the law, so far as his own life and prospects were concerned, was not for him but for Annette, for its main application was against counterrevolutionaries, partisans of monarchy, federalism, Girondism, and other enemies of liberty.[5]

A crossing from the Isle of Wight promised the greatest safety. Dover was out of the question; a departure from there would have landed him nearly on the front lines. Brighton boats generally went to Dieppe, north of Rouen, which was firmly in republican control. But from Portsmouth-Southampton one crossed to Le Havre or Cherbourg, or, more to Wordsworth's liking, smaller villages along the coast, east or west of the Cherbourg peninsula. Counterrevolutionaries on the Normandy coast around Caen were actively soliciting Englishmen in the fall of 1793 – and the Foreign Office was actively encouraging volunteers to meet this demand. The royalist Vendéan generals and their strange new bedfellows, the republican Girondistes, had begun to draw up elaborate plans for an English invasion. Their goal, according to Victor Hugo (whom we may now take on board as foreign correspondent for Wordsworth's trip), was 'to get possession of some point on the coast and deliver it up to Pitt.' Hugo recreates the specialized propaganda of that time and place, which linked old national enemies against the new ideological one: 'The English invasion is preparing; Vendéans and English – it is Briton with Breton.'[6]

Once in Normandy, Wordsworth would likely have gone to Caen to make contact with his former acquaintances among the Girondins who were still there: Gorsas and Louvet, to name the most obvious. But we should not forget that for every name that history remembers, there were dozens of others, friends and relatives, hangers-on and spear-carriers, who might have been the young Wordsworth's actual contacts. It may seem unlikely that they would have had much time for him in their current plight, but unknown young Englishmen, interesting enough in Paris in 1792, assumed a disproportionately greater importance to the isolated Girondins in late 1793.

With some help from the Girondins – perhaps carrying their messages – Wordsworth would have advanced fairly rapidly to Paris, more probably on foot than in public transport, where he would have been more likely to be challenged. Here Wordsworth's physique and walking experience stand our scenario in good stead, for it is hard to imagine many young Englishmen better qualified and conditioned to walk across country at a rapid rate, and fluent in French besides. He was bold to foolhardiness and resourceful 'as an Indian scout,' in the circumstances.[7] The challenge to his bravery and presence of mind was immense. He was fairly secure in the Normandy countryside as an Englishman, but the closer he got to Paris, the more he would have had to be ready to change his stripes, because the Vendéans and the republicans had exactly opposite views of who the real 'foreigners' were.[8] From a royalist fifth-columnist, Wordsworth would have had to transmute himself into a fellow-travelling international revolutionary sympathizer, of which there were of course many in the Convention and the armed forces. Since the situation was very much one of shooting first and asking questions later, he would have had to be finely attuned to signs and signals, code words both literal and figurative, and a wide range of discursive attitudes, not excluding body language. The weather conditions were in his favour. The summer of 1792 had been wet, but 1793 was very dry. 'Dry fields make an easy route' (Hugo) – a fact Wordsworth knew well, setting off to hike across French fields for the fourth time in as many years.

In any case, one of our firmest points of reference for this whole

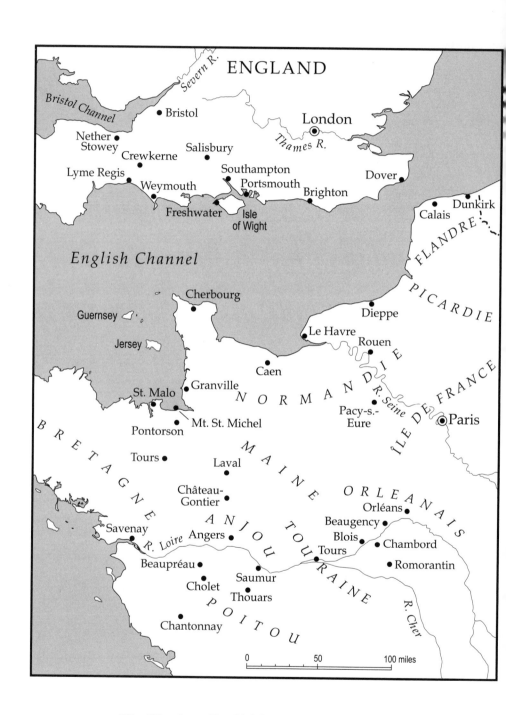

The 'Northern Vendée' (Northwest France), 1793

scenario is 7 October, when Wordsworth said he was in Paris to witness the execution of Gorsas. Wild as it seems, it is not wholly outside the realm of possibility that Gorsas and Wordsworth travelled to Paris together, especially if they already knew each other. They were both desperate men, and Wordsworth was taking a route similar to Gorsas' from Normandy for an identically romantic reason: to visit his mistress. Moreover, they were both making for the same neighbourhood near the Palais Royal, where Gorsas' mistress, Brigitte Mathey, had her bookshop. Gorsas' residence was in the rue Tictonne (or Tiquetonne), three streets east of White's Hotel, very much in Wordworth's old neighbourhood. The English community was still there, largely unmolested despite the Law of Suspects. Helen Maria Williams and her family were not interned until after the middle of October, and Mary Wollstonecraft moved back *into* Paris from the suburb of Neuilly in September, but took the precaution of registering at the American Embassy as the wife of her lover, Gilbert Imlay. This gave her protection as a friendly foreign national in a situation not unlike Wordsworth's: by then she knew she was pregnant with Imlay's child.

Gorsas was arrested on 6 October, at Mme Mathey's bookstore, where he was recognized by a passer-by. He was executed the next day.[9] One group of people who would have been asking themselves, 'Where will it end, when you have set an example in this kind?' as Carlyle reported Wordsworth to have said, is the motley collection of English and Girondiste sympathizers he was associating with around White's Hotel.

Gorsas' execution was a decisive event, which would have forced Wordsworth to get a move on. The concentration of public attention on foreigners, particularly English, was intense for the next three or four days, because the trial of the Girondins was about to begin, and these English residents were seen as persons who might help the Girondins escape, or give them safe hiding.[10] The Convention was readying itself for a decisive purge of its enemies, and it wanted everything under maximum control. On 9 October Robespierre himself for the first time proposed the arrest of all Englishmen remaining in France. The next day, St Just, Robespierre's acolyte and hatchetman on the Committee of Public Safety, gave one of his severest speeches, demanding the government remain 'revolutionary' until a peace was won: i.e., revolutionary laws must be enforced with revolutionary fervour. Robespierre had for weeks been perfecting a speech in which avid gallery audiences were adjured to be ready to 'strike' against 'enemies,' and on 11 October he delivered a hysterical version of it, promising that many such enemies would be 'revealed' on the morrow, with great 'victories' resulting. Many arrests followed, including an Englishman named Rutledge whom Wordsworth had heard speak in the Jacobin Club in November 1791. Marie-Antoinette's trial began on 14 October, and the preliminary examination of

Brissot on the 15th, the ever-present Bourdon serving as one of ten prosecution witnesses. On 18 October, the move against English residents became draconian, and included all Scots, Irish, and even Hanoverians; only children under twelve in French schools and factory workers were excepted.[11] If there were any time that could be called 'favourable' for decamping precipitately from Paris, as old Bailey reported Wordsworth doing, it would have been the week of 7–14 October. Wordsworth confided to Carlyle that he had seen the execution of Gorsas on 7 October; we can be sure that if he had been present in Paris at the time of Marie-Antoinette's trial, he would have said so. Gorsas' death was duly noted in the English press, but details from the queen's trial and execution were printed for months afterwards, and have remained one of the primary sources of anti-revolutionary imagery ever since.

We could of course put Wordsworth en route directly back to England from Paris, on the assumption that things were becoming just too hot. But having come so far, would he not try to go further, to complete his mission? The provinces were always less dangerous than Paris, but as he moved out shortly after 7 October, he went from the frying pan into the fire. Terrible retributions were being exacted, especially against priests, which caused riots and other disturbances in their turn. Coming into this maelstrom, Wordsworth would have had to be ready to reverse his procedure of calculating turncoatism, but this time from rabid republicanism to relative royalism, as he moved cautiously down along the Loire.

Then, on 17–18 October, the fire got even hotter. The Vendéans suffered their strategically decisive defeat at Cholet, twenty-five miles south of the Loire. The revolt could well have ended there, if the republican forces had given pursuit, but the next day the Vendéans began their tragic long march to the sea: 80,000 men, women, and children forded the shallow Loire and headed for the Channel ports, desperately hoping for an English rescue. This move north caught the Convention completely by surprise, for it was thought 'impossible for the Vendée to cross the Loire' (Hugo). Robespierre and the other Jacobin leaders were dumbfounded when they heard that a large rebel army had crossed the Loire, and actually had republican forces on the run again.

This sudden turn of events brings another Wordsworthian figure back into the picture: Michel Beaupuy. He had returned to the Loire valley in late July, commanding part of the Legion du Nord, the fierce garrison forces from Mayence (Mainz), which had been released when the city fell on condition that they would no longer fight against the Allies. They immediately became the Republic's shock troops against the counter-revolution.

If Wordsworth had reached Blois before 17 or 18 October, we could entertain the idea of a secret marriage with Annette, or some other permanent arrangement. A marriage ceremony of some sort might have been performed to legitimize Annette's status, and we could presumably have a record of it, as we do of Caroline's baptism. But priests were scarce, and a civil wedding might have been unsatisfactory to the Vallons, to say nothing of its danger in exposing Wordsworth to the local authorities.

But it may be that, no matter how heroically Wordsworth may have tried to reach Blois, he would have failed because in mid-October some of the fiercest fighting in the entire counterrevolutionary war broke very nearly upon his head. He was now so close to the theatre of operations that he would receive daily reports of what was happening, or exaggerated rumours of what was not happening, or might have happened, or was soon to happen. It seems almost certain that one such rumour came to his ears.

Beaupuy was active in the victory at Cholet, his cavalry cutting down fleeing peasants ruthlessly. Still, he had a high estimate of the Vendéans: 'As soldiers they lacked nothing but the uniform. Troops who have succeeded in defeating such Frenchmen as these can flatter themselves that they can defeat the united armies of the Coalition in the service of Kings.'[12] He was the first republican general to report that the Vendéans had crossed the Loire *en masse*, and to note how small an opposing force might have prevented them from doing so. The republican armies set off in pursuit and decided to attack the royalists again at Laval on the 25th. In a confused action over two days, Westermann, the 'butcher of the Vendée,'[13] with Beaupuy as his second-in-command leading the cavalry, moved back and forth between Laval and Château-Gontier, constantly being ambushed because a member of their general staff was a traitor who passed on all their plans to the enemy. On the 27th, at Entrammes, between the two towns, Beaupuy was ordered to attack well-entrenched rebels, who were at this moment under the leadership of their most charismatic leader, the twenty-one-year-old Henri La Rochejaquelein. Thus the best of the royalists and one of the best of the republicans, the ci-devant nobleman Beaupuy, faced off against each other in a confrontation worthy of Hugo's *Quatre-vingt treize*. But the raw republican recruits were no match for the sharp-shooting Vendéans, and soon fled in panic back to Château-Gonthier, twenty miles north of the Loire, their general Bloss killed, and 'Beaupuy himself mortally wounded' as they attempted to defend the town. News of their deaths spread like wildfire through both camps and the surrounding region, for this was still warfare in which the death of a charismatic leader counted as much as the loss of any number of troops in the field, and Beaupuy was much loved and admired, having been very active in Tours and Blois just the year before, sometimes in company with his tall young English friend. His supposed last words were reported to good effect in the *Moniteur* two months later: 'Je n'ai pu vaincre pour la république, je mourrai pour elle!'[14]

One measure of a theory's persuasiveness is what mathematicians call its elegance, that is, its ability to account efficiently for other pieces of data in the problem under consideration. Just such an important piece in the puzzle of Wordsworth's life in late 1793 falls into place if we account for his erroneous reporting in *The Prelude* of Beaupuy's death 'upon the borders of the unhappy Loire' (IX.432) by the simple fact that he was thereabouts at the time. Beaupuy's biographers report, 'His wound was so grave that they despaired at first of saving him and the news of his death spread among the Vendéans.'[15] This is hardly a report which would have reached Wordsworth in Wales, and though the *Moniteur* of December refers to Beaupuy's severe wounding, this account (supposing Wordsworth saw the French paper) makes it clear that Beaupuy has survived ('blessé à mort . . . n'a cessé, malgré ses blessures').

Furthermore, the victory at Laval was as decisive – temporarily – for the Vendéans as it would have been for Wordsworth. It opened up a path to the sea for both of them. The republicans, having lost over 10,000 men to death, wounds and desertions, fell back to Angers. The Vendéans, fatally led on by promises of British aid, advanced into Normandy without much hindrance. And Wordsworth, trying desperately to stay ahead of the action, would have had small leisure to inquire into the accuracy of the rumours about Beaupuy's death. The distance he had to cover, from the Loire to the Channel, ninety miles, was just about the same as he would have crossed in going from Wales to visit Dorothy at Halifax in his other 'plot.' This was three days' walking for him in ideal conditions, probably more than a week in these wholly unideal conditions. Wordsworth would have had to push on to the coast as rapidly as he could, finding cover as he might, since any persons aiding the escape of 'brigands,' 'insurgents,' or 'foreigners' (all lumped together now) faced an instant death penalty. If we imagine him having missed connections with Annette and hearing of Beaupuy's death more or less at the same time and in the same place, we can begin to grasp the traumatizing effect of this trip, and find strong internal reasons for his repressing it, in addition to many good external reasons for keeping it quiet.

By 13 November the Vendéan army reached the coast and laid siege to Granville, near Mont-Saint-Michel. But the promised English ships did not appear, even though Lord Moira's fleet lay just offshore in the Channel Islands, ready to land if Grenville would give permission. He delayed his decision so long that by the time it came, in December, it was useless. The large contingent of rebels from Poitou, finding themselves with their backs to an apparently unfriendly sea, decided to return home. The dashing La Rochejacquelein was recalled from his push toward Rouen, and on 14 November all the Vendéans began their demoralized flight back south to final defeat. Their Royal and Catholic Army was finally destroyed at Savenay, at the mouth of the Loire estuary, on 23 December. By then, Wordsworth had probably been back in England for a month or more. 'He had accomplished that masterpiece – the most difficult of all in such a war – flight' (Hugo). He spent the Christmas holidays with his kindly uncle Richard Wordsworth and their large family at Whitehaven. The contrast with where he had just been was almost too great to bear thinking of, to say nothing of expression; as Coleridge would later say of the full story of *The Prelude*, it was matter for 'Thoughts all too deep for words!'[16]

The Textual Record
Along with the general incredibility of such an adventure, there is the glaring oddity that we should have so little evidence of it in Wordsworth's own writing. True, we have even less record of any time spent in Wales between August and December, but somehow we don't expect any, given Wordsworth's benign reputation. But if he had such an adventure, wouldn't he have written something about it, as he did about his adventures on Salisbury Plain? Perhaps he did, more than has been recognized.

Nearly two hundred lines of Book X in *The Prelude* (201–380) are devoted to this period. They are oblique, but they do give hints of a French adventure, for their chronology of events and those of Wordsworth's life fit together nicely, once we supply the necessary details. His account of his return to England in late 1792 begins with the lines about Wilberforce's anti-slavery agitation. Wordsworth, we recall, followed his comments on Gorsas to Carlyle with some unflattering observations about Wilberforce, suggesting that the two men inhabited roughly the same time-frame in his memory of his experiences of that time, and for opposite sides of the same reason: 'For me that strife [against slavery] had ne'er / Fastened on my affections.'

Hence, it was relative to liberals' disappointment at the defeat of Wilberforce's anti-slavery legislation that Wordsworth took up his own disillusionment at the much greater shock he experienced: the 'revolution' that occurred in his 'moral nature' when France and England declared war. This passage is usually given a strictly political interpretation: i.e., his idealism was betrayed, first by those in power in England, who would tear 'the best youth in England [from] their dear pride,' and second by France's own Reign of Terror. The phrase, 'a season dangerous and wild,' at this point (286) is thus taken as a reference to the perversion of English patriotic values under Pitt's artificially stimulated war policy.[17] But it may also, given Wordsworth's powerful literalism, refer simply to the weather in France that autumn. A narrowly political interpretation of the lines overlooks the fact that Wordsworth says he actually *did not doubt* that war would eventually break out between the two countries, as indeed few people did. He was shocked because of his personal interest in the event. There was a 'revolution' in his 'moral nature' because, as we noted in Chapter 14, he 'now had . . . other business, for I felt / The ravage of this most unnatural strife / In my own heart' (X.249–51). Indeed he did have 'other business' which the war interrupted: Annette and Caroline. It was an 'unnatural strife' for him especially, since he experienced it as a civil war dividing his own family.[18]

His recollections of the Isle of Wight fall right into place here (290–305). The fleet had 'gone forth' in late July to join Hood in the Mediterranean. When he goes on to say that 'afterwards' he rejoiced in English defeats and French victories, the chronological indicator for a reader in 1805 or 1850, to say nothing of a twentieth-century reader, is very generalized: after *what*? It could be almost any time between February 1793, and the fall of Robespierre in July 1794. But in the immediate context, the battle in which 'Englishmen by thousands were o'erthrown' could only be the Battle of Hondschoote (6 September). By contrast, his feeling 'like an uninvited guest' in a village congregation (266–74) where prayers are offered up for English *victories* refers either to the taking of Valenciennes on 28 July by Anglo-Dutch armies, or to the fall of Toulon to Admiral Hood on 28 August. But the salient point is that he himself was an *in*vited guest, attending services in Jones's parish at Plas-yn-Llan. When he says he felt 'a conflict of sensation without name' (265) it is not only a political dilemma he refers to, but one impossibly conflicted *for him*.

Immediately following his lines of the Isle of Wight, there is a verse paragraph beginning, 'In France' (X.306–345). Normally, this is read as his *report* of what was happening there. But the lines could as well be a *record* of what happened there then, when he went over, from (say) the first week in September to the second or third week in October. Placement may not mean much in a poem as heavily revised as *The Prelude*, but this is exactly where such lines would occur, if Wordsworth were giving a sequential but disguised account of his adventures in France.

Speaking of the 'devilish pleas' of the new French tyrants, he sketches nine different vignettes of types of speakers in the Convention at this time (315–26). This is an extraordinarily detailed set of thumbnail portraits, much more knowledgeable than anything appearing in English newspaper accounts, where the revolutionary leaders were caricatured indiscriminately as devils from hell. In 'the sternness of the just' at the beginning of the catalogue, it is easy to recognize St Just, who was typically very stern, and who had been described standing just so, at the Tribunal which condemned Wordsworth's Orléans landlord to death on 13 July. Similarly, 'the steady purposes of the suspicious' near the end (323) is undoubtedly Robespierre, and 'the blind rage of insolent tempers' (321) would fit Hébert and other *enragés* very well. Wordsworth was given to catalogues of this type, with internal puns, as in the allegory of Folly at the end of his account of his Cambridge residence. Hence his reference to 'the faith of those / Who doubted not that Providence had times / Of anger and vengeance' (316–18) would refer to Bishop Grégoire, who bravely stood his ground during these months when the dechristianization frenzy was at its height, and did not suffer for it, so high was his reputation for integrity. Wordsworth's contrast to Grégoire, those 'who throned the human understanding paramount / And made of that their god' (319–20), would refer to Pierre (Anaxagoras) Chaumette, who finally got his Festival of Reason celebrated at Notre-Dame on 10 November. Finally, 'the hopes of those / Who were content to barter short-lived pangs / For a paradise of ages' (319–21), would be those weak members of the Plain – the 'shoals' of the Convention (Hugo), and the majority at any time – who had sacrificed the Girondins to the prevailing millennarian ideology. Wordsworth's description of the devilish debaters could be applied to other periods in the pre-Terror Convention, but the one that it fits best on all counts is the final trial of the Girondins, beginning with their indictment on 3 October 1793.

When he goes on in the very next line to say, 'Domestic carnage now filled all the year' (330), his chronology is as exact as his generalization is accurate. That 'now,' the execution of the Girondins, was the operative beginning of the Reign of Terror: late October, 1793, 'season dangerous and wild,' when the number of executions began to rise steeply, doubling, tripling and quadrupling by the month.[19] Similarly, such victims as Wordsworth records, or imagines, though usually understood as random vignettes, had close personal parallels for him:

> Domestic carnage now filled all the year
> With feast-days: the old man from the chimney nook, [Gellet-Duvivier?]
> The maiden from the bosom of her love, [Annette from William?]
> The mother from the cradle of her babe, [Annette from Caroline?]
> The warrior from the field [Beaupuy?]—all perished, all—
> Friends, enemies, of all parties, ranks,
> Head after head, and never heads enough
> For those who bade them fall.
>
> (329–36)

Even the imagery of free-falling heads was contemporaneous, as in the newspaper editorials that spurred on Charlotte Corday, or the rhetoric used against the Vendéan rebels: 'Still more heads and every day more heads fall!'[20]

Then comes a temporal indicator – 'meanwhile' (361) – that we can make sense of by a generalized interpretation: i.e., *while* all these executions were going on, 'the invaders fared as they deserved,' referring to the sequence of victories which saved the Republic in late 1793. But this 'meanwhile' also includes one of Wordsworth's most powerful passages describing the Revolution, the 'unjust tribunals' sequence, which closes this entire sequence:

> Most melancholy at that time, O friend,
> Were my day-thoughts, my dreams were miserable;
> Through months, through years, long after the last beat
> Of those atrocities (I speak bare truth,
> As if to thee alone in private talk)
> I scarcely had one night of quiet sleep,
> Such ghastly visions had I of despair,
> And tyranny, and implements of death,
> And long orations which in dreams I pleaded
> Before unjust tribunals, with a voice
> Labouring, a brain confounded, and a sense
> Of treachery and desertion in the place
> The holiest that I knew of—my own soul.
>
> (368–80)

Are these the bad dreams of a man who has vividly imagined the horrors of the Reign of Terror, which had been plentifully detailed in English publications by 1804? Or are these the recollections of a man who has seen the terror whereof he speaks? We must not underestimate the terrific power of Wordsworth's imagination, but we should also never forget his strong tendency to base even his wildest imaginative flights on extremely literal details.

At first, it seems that he is pleading for himself before the 'unjust tribunals,' though in fact very few foreign nationals were actually guillotined. If he saw Gorsas executed, he saw more than one scene like this. But why does he feel betrayed, not before the Revolutionary Tribunal, but in an even sterner court, 'the place the holiest that I knew of – my own soul'? Why should he feel 'a sense of treachery and desertion' there? Has *he* been betrayed and deserted? Or does he feel 'a sense' that he has betrayed and deserted *someone else*? If there has been treachery and desertion in his own soul, does this not mean he feels that he has betrayed and deserted someone else, who could only be Annette? The tribunals were certainly unjust, but the real nightmare in this passage is that the advocate feels untrue to himself.

Closer attention to these lines brings us still closer to Annette and to France in late 1793. His testimony that this is 'bare truth' – written for Coleridge in 1805 – seems unnecessarily strong to attest to the reality of a dream, but not so for a fact. But four or five additional lines were cut before Coleridge saw the early version, from between his 'ghastly visions of despair' and the 'implements of death':

> Such ghastly visions [clung to me of strife
> And persecution—strugglings of false mirth
> And levity in dungeons where the dust
> Was laid with tears, such hauntings of distress

> *And anguish fugitive in woods, in caves*
> *Concealed*, of scaffolds,] implements of death . . .[21]

Where are we here? Accounts of the pathetic mixtures of levity and tears in the prisons of the Terror were a standard feature of newspaper accounts, and by 1804 the genre of *lettres des condamnés* was already initiated, though it did not fully blossom until after the Restoration. But in the second line from the end, we are clearly not in Paris, but in the countryside, most likely the Vendée. Was Wordsworth there? The 'tribunals' were not confined to Paris or the towns, but included travelling detachments of the Revolutionary Army, each with its own portable 'implements of death,' combing the countryside, as suggested in Wordsworth's 'woods [and] caves.' Anyone travelling alone in or near the region of the Vendée uprising had to consider himself a 'fugitive' if he was not known in the neighbourhood, and had to advance by brief furtive sprints from woods to caves, lest he fall foul of vindictive troops from either side. Although 'woods' and 'caves' seem like generic words signifying the countryside, they were of quite specific importance in the Vendée. Hugo speaks of 'the seven Black Forests of Brittany' by name, almost as though they were characters in the action of *Quatre-vingt treize*, for the spiritual and physical comfort they gave the Vendéans: 'this forest of Bocage was the fugitive's auxiliary. He did not flee – he vanished.'[22] Similarly, the caves of the region were often round, narrow wells leading to underground chambers that could hold large numbers of men, as Hugo's Westermann discovered: 'the caves of Egypt held dead men, the caves of Brittany were filled with the living' (II.4.1).

What kind of account would he have given of himself if he had been stopped by republican units? The smartest thing would have been not to say a word about anyone connected with the Vallon family, even though this might well have engendered 'a sense of treachery and desertion' in that other court, 'the holiest that I knew of—my own soul.' Small wonder he imagined himself pleading 'with a voice labouring, a brain confounded.'

When treachery and betrayal come so close to home, it is altogether characteristic of Wordsworth that, having skirted close to revelation, he swerves widely away from present-tense narration into vast generalization, as he does immediately after the 'unjust tribunals' passage: 'When I began at first, in early youth, / To yield myself to Nature . . .' (381–82) We can still parse a continuous general sense here, by saying that Wordsworth shifts from these horrible visions of the Revolutionary Tribunal to his great difficulty at just this moment in trying to move from love of Nature to love of Mankind. But this is not inconsistent with a reading that says the reason such a movement was particularly hard *for him* was because: (a) he was there, and (b) because he had deeply personal reasons, that involved '*a sense* of treachery and desertion' – even if not the actual fact of them – in his own soul, for having gone to rescue Annette, and having failed. We saw such a textual pattern of near-revelation, followed by immediate conceal-ment or self-censorship, on Lake Windermere in 1788 and on Lake Como in 1790, and we see it again here.

In 'Vaudracour and Julia,' published in 1820 without any reference to his own life, and therefore allowing him to be somewhat freer about the story's associations, Wordsworth included seasonal and geographic details that are not in the *Prelude* account. The mental perturbation of the young lovers is represented as their being 'driven by the autumnal whirlwind to and fro,' a line which fits Wordsworth's autumn journey of 1793 very well. It also fits his oblique account of this period in *The Prelude*, where he represented himself as 'a green leaf on the blessed tree / Of my beloved country . . . Now from my pleasant station . . . cut off / And tossed about in *whirlwinds*' (X.254–58). 'Whirlwind' is a naturalistic word weighted with political significance for Wordsworth, as in 'the rage of one State-whirlwind' that threatened the Grande Chartreuse.

His metaphor for the two young lovers' feelings of sympathy with each other even when they were apart foreshadows their coming separation, and also his own experience of it in 1793:

> . . . in their happiest moments, not content,
> If more divided than a sportive pair
> Of sea-fowl, conscious both that they are hovering
> Within the eddy of a common blast,
> Or hidden only by the concave depth
> Of neighbouring billows from each other's sight.
>
> ('V. & J.,' 24–29)

This could well express a feeling of so-near-yet-so-far that afflicted Annette and William as they realized that he was not coming, or was not going to make it to Blois because of the fury of the '*common blast*' – an apt metaphor for *civil war* as well. Images of 'sea-fowl' and 'neighbouring billows' might also have been called up by recollections of a Channel crossing in a small boat in stormy autumn weather.

These seasonal references in 'Vaudracour and Julia' link up with others in the *Prelude* account that suggest firsthand experience. The description of how Vaudracour came to be arrested is best suited to our biographical purposes. His father had a warrant out for him, but he stayed with Julia as long as he dared:

> he lingered still
> To the last moment of his time, and then,
> At dead of night, with snow upon the ground,
> He left the city, and in villages,
> The most sequestered of the neighbourhood,

Lay hidden for the space of several days,
Until, the horseman bringing back report
That he was nowhere to be found, the search
Was ended. Back returned the ill-fated youth . . .

(IX.729–37)

None of this has any parallel in Helen Williams's story, but insofar as the passage refers to Wordsworth's experience in 1793, the return of the 'ill-fated youth. . . back,' would be to England, in very cold weather, consistent with the 'autumnal whirlwinds' and 'common blast' of 'Vaudracour and Julia.' The *Gentleman's Magazine* recorded 'temperature below freezing for several days at the end of October,' just what is needed for 'autumnal whirlwinds' to produce an early 'snow upon the ground.'[23] His lying 'hidden for the space of several days' is consistent with the 'anguish fugitive in woods, in caves concealed' of the lines from the *Prelude* manuscript. Of course, we must make many adjustments for character and action to reconcile these various accounts: the fictional Vaudracour, the real M. du Fosse, many victims of the Terror and of the Vendéan war, and Wordsworth's own fantasies of action are all represented here, as well as what he and Annette may actually have done. But all these variations were written by him, and they all are consistent with the climate, both natural and political, of late October 1793.

The Evidence of Imagination

Even if all these coincidences of imagery derive only from Wordsworth's imagination and not from his experience, they show how powerful that imagination was. For the 'unjust tribunals' themselves are imaginary – literary – *as well as* historical, and in this double aspect we may find a last confirmation, either of the fact of Wordsworth's return to France in 1793, or of the deep emotional impact of his desire to return, and his strong 'sense of treachery and desertion' for not having done so.

As at many of the *The Prelude*'s most powerfully entwined biographical and literary moments, we are again dealing with an allusion from Milton, from *Samson Agonistes*, where the Chorus laments how God deals harshly with those who are 'solemnly elected . . . To some great work, thy glory' (678–80). This was certainly how Wordsworth was beginning to see himself by the time he came to write *The Prelude*: 'thy monument of glory will be raised' (XIII.430). He, like Samson, was a 'chosen Son,' not one of 'the common rout,' not one of those 'Heads without name no more remembered' (674, 677). Yet it is precisely these predestined heroes that God seems to throw down farthest, to the dogs,

Or to th'unjust tribunals, under change of times,
And condemnation of th'ungrateful multitude.

(695–96)

It is not surprising that Wordsworth would call this image to mind, reflecting Milton's experience of civil war in the English revolution, as he wrote about his experience of civil war amid the French revolution.

But what makes the recollection especially potent and revealing at this moment, like so many of the Miltonic depth-charges in Wordsworth's poetry, is what happens next in Milton's text, and our confidence that Wordsworth knew it. After a weak plea to God not to deal so unfairly with Samson, the Chorus suddenly sees Delilah coming. They don't recognize her, but Samson does, blind as he is, and in no uncertain terms: 'My wife, my traitress, let her not come near me.' She is the woman who brought Samson low, and we must wonder if some of Wordsworth's 'sense of treachery and desertion' in his soul applied not simply to his going back to France, but also to his sense of having been foiled in his own career resolves by falling for Annette. Vaudracour was capable of voicing such thoughts to Julia: 'He would exclaim, "Julia, how much thine eyes / Have cost me!"' Delilah, like Annette in her letters, at first weeps profusely for the pain she has brought her foreign husband: 'Like a fair flower sur-charged with dew, she weeps, / And words addressed seem into tears dissolved' (*SA*, 728–29). This would not be an unjust representation of some parts of Annette's letter to Dorothy, where tears are metaphorically distilled into words.

Gradually, the effects of their different countries and religions come into the argument. Delilah blames Samson for entrusting his secret to her in the first place, employing arguments the Philistine officials had used on her. It is fitting that English, Protestant, republican Wordsworth should think of this passage as he remembered the contemporaneous 'unjust tri-bunals' that threatened his attempted reconciliation with French, Catholic, royalist Annette. And by the time he composed this passage in 1804, he knew that Annette had a reputation for political resistance that Delilah, spurning Samson, would also lay claim to: 'among the famousest / Of women . . . who to save / Her country from a fierce destroyer, chose / Above the faith of wedlock bands' (*SA*, 982–86).

No exact correlations are possible here, where text, context, and inter-text lie so closely together, and where Wordsworth's personal experience of love and revolution is so deeply underwritten by Milton's. We cannot simply say, for example, that Wordsworth felt betrayed by Annette as Samson was by Delilah. But more to the point is the realization that we have even less warrant to *deny* that his feelings for Annette were somehow bound up with Milton's representation of Samson's experience. We can-not separate these kinds of evidence neatly into the biographical and the literary: for Wordsworth, the 'literary,' especially if it were Miltonic, *was* biographical. The 'unjust tribunals' were French, they were Miltonic, and they were dream fragments; the sense of betrayal Wordsworth felt there was personal, imaginary, and historical – and real in all of these senses.

*

In the end, the summary of Wordsworth's life in the autumn of 1793 is not a simple choice between a passive or an active hero. If he stayed in Wales, we have not a jot of evidence for it. But if Wordsworth went back to France, it's not simply a new fact that we can now entertain in thinking about him. If he did all these things, or anything remotely like them, such hair-raising adventures would have had permanent consequences of incalculable magnitude for his future development, at least as great as his 1790 walking tour and his affair with Annette itself. An exploit like this would clearly mark one for life. Do we find any telltale scars of it in the body of Wordsworth's work? Or rather, since the effects of such a trip must *already* have manifested themselves, without being recognized, what are the signs of it, which we have heretofore taken as 'natural' birthmarks?

We have seen some from *The Prelude* and 'Vaudracour and Julia,' and we will see others as we follow Wordsworth's life through the 1790s. But there is one body of evidence that clearly refers to 1793: the language of passion in the 'Lines written above Tintern Abbey.' This is the poem, more than any other, which announces the creation of the subject we call William Wordsworth. It is his decisively self-creating text, and is strongly marked by a sense of recovery from traumatic losses. It is set a few miles above the abbey in 1798, and harks back insistently to the time in 1793 when he passed by it en route to Jones's home in Wales. The main point of the poem, very simply put, is to say that his return to this same landscape five years later, in company with Dorothy, reassures him of its value for his present sense of mental recovery. In 1793, he badly needed such reassurance to convince himself that his life had not come to a dead end. It would take him the next five years to complete the cure.

We recognize the poem's language of erotic passion underlying its passionate love for Nature more easily if we reflect that (a) he did not talk about Nature in this way in any of his extant texts from 1793 or earlier, but that (b) he did use such language in writing to Annette, insofar as we can take her letters to him, and his descriptions of Vaudracour and Julia, as indicators of his own love-language.

We have remarked the curiously self-incriminating rhetoric in Wordsworth's presentation of himself as 'more like a man / Flying from something that he dreads, than one / Who sought the thing he loved,' and its aptness to his situation vis-à-vis Annette at the time. He then goes on to present *himself* as a landscape painting, of which he says 'I cannot paint / What then I was' – but then proceeds to do just that, in highly charged erotic language:

> The sounding cataract
> *Haunted me like a passion*: the tall rock,
> The mountain, and the deep and gloomy wood,

> Their colours and their forms, were then to me
> *An appetite: a feeling and a love,*
> That had *no need of a remoter charm,*
> By thought supplied, *or any interest*
> *Unborrowed from the eye.*—That time is past,
> And *all its aching joys* are now no more,
> And *all its dizzy raptures.*
>
> (77–86; italics added)

The metaphoric language of passion in these lines is more explicit than the words referring to the landscape: it is very much the language of infatuation, appropriate to first love affairs. It is also language very similar to that which Wordsworth used in describing the passion of Vaudracour and Julia: 'the raptures of the pair,' 'swarmed with enchantment,' 'some delirious hour.' Vaudracour's regard for Julia is also preeminently an affair of the *eye*, as Wordsworth here says of his first, immature, adolescent attitude toward nature: 'He beheld / A vision, and he loved the thing he saw'; Julia turned everything he saw 'before his eyes to price above all gold' (IX.582–83, 588). Her 'presence' was to him in 1793 exactly as great as Nature's presence in 1798: 'Earth lived in one great presence of the spring' (1793); 'A presence that disturbs me with the joy / Of elevated thoughts' (1798). The later poem is an explanation of why he is still 'a lover' – but of meadows, woods, and mountains, rather than a person. It also gives a reason for his new constancy that is connected to that 'sense of treachery and desertion' we saw him feeling before the 'unjust tribunals' of his soul: 'Nature *never did betray* the heart that loved her.' Does this mean he feels he has been betrayed in love before? Or does it reflect his feeling of having betrayed Annette?

But there is another person present in 'Tintern Abbey': Dorothy Wordsworth. To say that Wordsworth is transferring his former passions to her is, on one level, simply to paraphrase the obvious sense of the poem. But to say that he is also transferring his former passions *for Annette* to her as well, is not inconsistent with an accurate reading of the poem, and furthermore makes sense in the most rudimentary terms of psychological biography. Moorman asks how it was possible for William and Dorothy, 'feeling for one another as they did,' to imagine sharing their cottage with Annette.[24] But the question carries its own answer: feeling for each other as they did, they *needed* some other woman there, lest their passions be tempted in forbidden, taboo directions. Something of the same situation developed with Mary Hutchinson at Racedown in 1797, and eventually in their married life together. Wordsworth's feelings for Annette, as later for Mary, could be accommodated – domiciled – with his feelings for Dorothy. Indeed, they had to be. He sees in Dorothy what he was then, but he also makes her the object of what his passion was then:

> thou, my dearest Friend,
> My dear, dear Friend, and in thy voice I catch
> The language of *my former heart*, and read
> *My former pleasures in the shooting lights*
> *Of thy wild eyes.*
>
> (116–20; italics added)

This reads one way if we suppose he is talking about his attachment to Nature, and another way if we imagine he is talking about his attachment to Annette. But the two readings are not mutually exclusive, for both are positive effects of the influence of nature: 'one great presence of the spring,' or 'a presence that disturbs . . . with the joy of elevated thoughts.'

By the time he comes to 'Tintern Abbey's' peroration, escalating from 'warmer love' to 'deeper zeal' to 'holier love,' it is easy to feel that a process of sublimating human sexual passion into a passion for nature is complete. It is only a small step further to suggest that a transference of passion from Annette to Dorothy has also been effected, and that it has been accomplished by means of a projection outward on to the body of nature, necessary to avoid the prohibitions of the incest taboo. He is proposing a new and different kind of love to Dorothy in July of 1798, but if we take 'Tintern Abbey's' arithmetic as seriously as its passion, we are being strongly urged to identify those agonizing times of 'former pleasures' with July 1793.

Wordsworth's heavily loaded language points to the enormous force of the emotions which made him feel that such a journey was at once his strongest desire and his deepest responsibility. On this view, we should look at the language of all Wordsworth's texts between 1793 and 1798 for evidence of deeply held fantasies about what might have been, as much as for evidence of deeply hidden facts of what was.

CHAPTER SEVENTEEN

Legacy Hunting

Windy Brow, 1794

A youth—he bore
The name of Calvert; it shall live, if words
Of mine can give it life—

(XIII.349–51)

Almost everything Wordsworth did in the next year was dictated by his overriding need for money: for himself, for Annette, for Caroline, and, increasingly, for Dorothy, as she threw her lot and life in with his. Throughout 1794, he moved from one temporary residence or guest house to another, circulating between Halifax, Keswick, Whitehaven, Rampside, and Penrith. He spent two idyllic months with Dorothy at William Calvert's house, Windy Brow, above Keswick in the spring, and three grim months there in the autumn, caring for Raisley Calvert, William's younger brother. It looks like a *Wanderjahr* without a plan, but beneath the surface he was pursuing a strategy for gaining his independence.

William and Dorothy's visits to family and friends in Cumberland in the spring and summer of 1794 seem so 'natural' that nobody questions them. But there was little to call home there any more; in 1794 William had been in the region once in five years, while Dorothy was returning for the first time in fifteen. The only sense in which William and Dorothy's return to Cumberland was inevitable was that they had nowhere else to go. A visit to the Cooksons was unthinkable; William was *persona non grata* there. And Dorothy definitely did not want to return to Cumberland just to visit relatives, especially those in Penrith: 'Perhaps my Uncle Crackanthorpe will invite me into Cumberland . . . but . . . I am not *very* desirous of an Invitation, and shall make my stay as short as possible.'[1] But going with William, to Cumberland or anywhere else, was a different matter altogether. In his effort to establish an income Wordsworth was shifting his theatre of family operations. He was retreating from his influential uncles in the south – who had done all they could to help him only to have their favours rejected – to his poorer ones in the north, the ones legally responsible for him. Like it or not, they were to a certain extent obliged to take him in.

1794 was a good year for retiring into the country and the bosom of one's family, if one was known to have French connections and divisive political opinions. In January, Maurice Margarot and William Skirving were unfairly convicted of sedition by the notoriously corrupt Judge Braxfield in Edinburgh; in February, Thomas Muir and Thomas Fyshe Palmer were led on board the prison ship bound for Botany Bay; in March Joseph Gerrald received the same fourteen-year sentence. These were all middle-class young men, Whigs, university graduates and, variously, lawyers, classical scholars, or high-thinking Unitarians.[2] In May parliament gave Pitt the right to suspend habeas corpus, and King's Messengers began arresting members of the Constitutional and Corresponding Societies in a series of early morning raids. Those rounded up included two known personally to Wordsworth: Thomas Holcroft and John Thelwall. They were arraigned for treason, not for seditious utterance, a charge which all authorities agree would have been sustained. The penalty for conviction was death or, if leniency was granted, fourteen years' transportation. John Horne Tooke, the radical grammarian, showman though he was, was not beyond the mark when he wrote from prison, 'They want our blood – blood – blood!'[3]

Between the Edinburgh convictions in January and November, when the Treason Trial acquittals were announced in London, the national political climate made lying-low a very prudent posture. Wordsworth continued to be very imprudent in expressing his political opinions, but the January–November time-frame neatly encloses the time from his heading north for family visits to his beginning to wish to return to London.

As soon as spring weather was well established in early April, William and Dorothy left their Halifax relatives to visit their closer relations in Cumberland. Their six weeks' stay at Windy Brow may well have been a small declaration of independence to act out the cottage-fantasy which had filled their imaginations for the last five years. Dorothy wrote back to Jane Pollard, 'we set forward by coach towards Whitehaven, and thence to Kendal.'[4] Kendal is only about seventy miles northwest of Halifax, but Whitehaven is nearly that much farther beyond Kendal, so one doesn't go 'towards Whitehaven, and thence to Kendal' unless one backtracks half the distance of one's trip – or unless one gets off the Whitehaven coach at Kendal. But the Windy Brow visit involved a considerable change in plans, since it expanded almost immediately from 'a few days' to 'a few weeks.'

At Kendal, Dorothy fell into step with her brother's wayfaring style, and walked thirty-three miles to Keswick at his side, breaking for an overnight stay in Grasmere. Leaving Kendal in the morning, they advanced to Windermere by noon. They stopped beside the lake for lunch, just before Ambleside at Low Wood, where a 'little unpretending Rill' trickles – still – into the lake. 'Eating a traveller's meal in shady bower,' they shared a basin of milk from the inn on the road, and William gave Dorothy some expert hiking tips, suggesting she slip on her silk stockings to prevent chafing.[5] Dorothy was not used to such long walks, and was justly proud 'of my wonderful prowess in the walking way.' Their lunch at this little rill was still strong in Wordsworth's mind when he came to write a sonnet on it in 1802, from the heightened emotional perspective of his wedding trip. 'The immaculate Spirit of one happy day / Lingers beside that Rill, in vision clear': this refers not to his wedding day, but the day of their lunch in April of 1794. The rill symbolized *them*, 'furrowing its dubious way with shallow will.'

They stopped for the night at Grasmere. This was the first time Dorothy saw it, and she took in the full impact of the valley's vista from its lower entrance at Rydal, extending up to its high terminus over Dunmail Raise. After a night at the old village inn at the centre of Grasmere (not the Dove & Olive Branch that would become their Dove Cottage five years later[6]), they walked the remaining fifteen miles to Keswick next day, and took up their lodging at Windy Brow, a small house perched halfway up the first hills rising toward Skiddaw behind the town. William had a standing invitation from William Calvert to use the house.

Here he met again Calvert's brother, Raisley, who was staying at Ormathwaite, a farm over the hill behind Windy Brow, directly below Skiddaw, one of the several properties he stood to inherit when he came of age in September. Raisley had returned home from his own impetuous jaunt to the Continent in the spring of 1793, and was now trying to recover from the ill effects of strenuous travel on a congenitally consumptive constitution. The two young mens' mildly rebellious attitude toward Cambridge soon ripened into closer friendship. Wordsworth's dire situation was soon made clear to Calvert in the natural opening gambits of youthful conversation: what are you doing? what are your hopes and dreams? what will you do next?

Their friendship was also based on the fact that their fathers had known each other, being employed in identical positions by two of the most powerful landowners in the county, James Lowther, Lord Lonsdale, and Henry Howard, the Duke of Norfolk. Raisley saw more sympathetically than his brother that Wordsworth represented an unhappy instance of what-might-have-been for them. Raisley, like Wordsworth, was a scion apparently not destined to add lustre to the family's connections, and was at present living on an allowance of £100 per year, from a trust fund set up by his late father (d. 1791) and administered by the Duke of Norfolk, who resided occasionally at nearby Greystoke Castle. But he would inherit thousands of pounds when he turned twenty-one in September.

Dorothy's first letters from Windy Brow are like all-points bulletins of newly perceived intentions for her life, revolving around two interrelated topics, the beauty of the country and the possibility of living cheaply in it, both based on the emotional bedrock of 'so full an enjoyment of my brother's company.'[7] She tells Jane, 'you cannot conceive any thing more delightful than the situation of this house . . . it is impossible to describe [the] grandeur' of the view. And the people were as fine as the place, as she described Windy Brow's caretakers:

> I have never been more delighted with the manners of any people than the family under whose roof I am at present. They are the most honest cleanly sensible people I ever saw in any rank of life – and I think I may safely affirm *happier* than any body I know. They are contented with a supply of the bare necessities of life . . . They are fond of reading, and reason not indifferently upon what they read.

She too reasoned not indifferently on what she observed in the life of this family, the Iansons: 'We please ourselves in calculating, from our present expences for how very small a sum we could live.' She and William worked over this equation of natural plus economic simplicity throughout the summer.

They renewed their friendship with the Speddings of Armathwaite, a few miles up the shore of Bassenthwaite behind Windy Brow. Here was another steward's family whose fortunes had been made, not lost, in the interest of the Lowthers.[8] John Spedding was a classmate from Hawkshead, and his unmarried sisters were of Dorothy's age. Mary (twenty-five) and Margaret (twenty) were 'in every respect charming women [who] have read much . . . whose acquaintance [I am] very desirous of cultivating.'[9] The Spedding family, like the Calverts, were immediately attractive because they lived 'in the most beautiful place that was ever beheld,' and because they could afford to. With less native talent than the Wordsworths, they were less crossed by personal worries and family pressures, but these same pressures helped William and Dorothy sharpen their own talents.

Dorothy's unbounded enthusiasm was repeated in a defensive key when her aunt Crackanthorpe from Penrith wrote a most unwelcoming letter, aimed precisely at the desires Dorothy was trying to connect in her new life: 'rambling about the country on foot,' when she could ill afford to do so, either financially or morally. Dorothy answered with her first declaration of independence from her long-suffering dependent status. 'I am much obliged to you,' she wrote, 'for the frankness [in expressing] your sentiments upon my conduct and at the same time extremely sorry that you should think it so severely to be condemned.' Christopher Crackanthorpe's wife had written with the full authority of eighteenth-century domestic tyranny, telling her niece exactly what was wrong with her behaviour and ordering her to change it no uncertain terms. Dorothy defended herself on three grounds, all of which involved William; what was reprehensible in her behaviour became acceptable, even admirable, in his, as a man. (This point should be kept in mind by modern readers disposed to criticize Dorothy Wordsworth for being dependent on her brother: she knew degrees of humiliating dependency compared to which her life with William was an extreme of freedom.) As to the expense, 'I drink no tea . . . my supper and breakfast are of bread and milk and my dinner chiefly of potatoes from choice.' Secondly, as to her being in 'an unprotected situation': 'I affirm that I consider the character and virtues of my brother as a sufficient protection.' Finally, against the charge of 'rambling,' Dorothy defended herself in terms of the new cultural fashion, extending it from young gentleman riding in whiskeys or post-chaises to young women rambling on foot, with the benefit shifted from aesthetics to health: 'I rather thought it would have given my friends pleasure to hear that I had courage to make use of the strength with which nature has endowed me, when it not only procured me infinitely more pleasure than I should have received from sitting in a post-chaise, but [returning to her first line of defence] was also the means of saving me at least thirty shillings.'[10] But she rests her case on her brother, from whom she will not be moved without, Mrs Crackanthorpe is warned, a considerable domestic crisis: she has 'only for a *very few* months' of her entire life enjoyed 'the society of my brother,' and to be forced to give it up now would cause her 'unspeakable pain.'

During these six weeks Wordsworth told William Mathews he was 'quite at leisure,' with more uninterrupted time for concentrated writing than he had had for several years. He began regulating the routines of housekeeping to accommodate those of a professional writer, with Dorothy's full co-operation. His main work was revision of 'A Night on Salisbury Plain' and extensive additions to *An Evening Walk* and *Descriptive Sketches*. He told Mathews the former was now 'ready for the press,' but as with almost every aspect of their life this year, he can only think of it in commercial terms: 'I certainly should not publish it unless I hoped to derive from it some pecuniary recompense.'[11]

Two ultimately contradictory thoughts were growing in his mind. On the one hand, he seemed in his writing to be committing himself to radical social thought and action. On the other, his progressive revisions of 'A Night on Salisbury Plain' show that he was beginning to identify personally with human suffering, but in ways that led to no necessary action, and which disarm all attempts at ideological explanation. Wordsworth's political tendencies led toward agitation for Reform, but his compositional drift was toward empirical psychology or quietism. The extreme rationalism of William Godwin's *Enquiry concerning Political Justice* (1793) promised a way between these extremes, and Wordsworth soon began to fall under Godwin's sway.

An Evening Walk and *Descriptive Sketches* had been failures both in terms of profit and in showing his family 'that he could do something' to make up for his university failures. So he now undertook to revise them along the lines of his own developing interests.[12] To *An Evening Walk*, primarily a landscape poem of private emotions, he added many lines of socio-political commentary; to *Descriptive Sketches*, a generalized view of the Alps with passing social observations and an apocalyptic political conclusion, he added a good deal of physically erotic imagery and intimate personal reactions to it. One might almost think he got his additions mixed up, making *An Evening Walk* more social and *Descriptive Sketches* more private, when the reverse combination would seem more likely, given the underlying subject matter of each poem. But this is so only if we expect Wordsworth's imagination to work in a linear fashion, which it rarely does. Instead, the apparent contradictoriness of his additions can better be seen as his stubborn effort to force his *Evening Walk* landscapes to yield up more by way of moral insight, and, conversely, to make the wide social vision of *Descriptive Sketches* more personally satisfying.

His additions of 1794 thus stand as further advances upon his failed poems of the previous spring and summer, where human history and its institutions (naval fleets, state prisons) fell across the landscapes of England in a way upsetting to their hopeful, naïve viewer. But now his narrator, no longer naïve, expects less by way of congruence between Nature and Society, and can suggest more by way of their revealing contrasts. An unsuccessful trip to France may have driven this point home for him. Or, conversely, when the Nature-Society poles threaten to stand out from each other in painful contrast, he blurs the point of their contact (both its visual point and its moral one) in a way that suggests significant meaning without actually saying what that meaning is. For example, these new lines from *An Evening Walk* at first sound very much like a poetical counterpoint to Dorothy's descriptions of their view over Derwentwater:

> How pleasant, as the sun declines, to view
> The total landscape change in form and hue!
> Here, vanish, as in mist before a flood
> Of bright obscurity, hill, lawn, and wood;
>
> (155–58)[13]

But as the description advances, it gradually moves toward a pure impressionism of light. Skiffs, cottages, 'the industrious oar [of] the char-coal barge' and other human objects and actions only occasionally peep out from the increasing brilliance of a 'thousand thousand twinkling points of light.' The conclusion adds what is implicit in Dorothy's letter, the virtue of *having* such views: 'Blest are those spirits tremblingly awake / To

Nature's impulse like this living lake.' Their spirits are unlike others – such as the Crackanthorpes – 'whose languid powers unite / No interest to each rural sound or sight.' But William and Dorothy are 'different . . . favoured souls.' Their visionary powers comprehend social divisions as well, because it is the vision of

> . . . a soul by Truth refined [who feels]
> Entire affection for all human kind;
> A heart that vibrates evermore, awake
> To feeling for all forms that Life can take,
> That wider still its sympathy extends,
> And sees not any line where being ends;
> Sees sense, through Nature's rudest forms betrayed,
> Tremble obscure in fountain, rock, and shade;
> And while a secret power those forms endears
> Their social accents never vainly hears.
>
> (123–32)

Many things are happening in these excellent passages, not least a rapid advance in the craft of composing fluent imagery. Much of 'Tintern Abbey' and *The Prelude* is here in embryo, lacking only the autobiographical emphasis. But foremost among his advances was Wordsworth's new way of accommodating a sense of social responsibility into his landscape-viewing.

Other additions to *An Evening Walk* give its 'social accents' a more specific identity. The shadowy horsemen suggested by mountain mists are almost purely legendary in the original version, though linked to the border wars by a passing reference to 'the lonely beacon' above Penrith. But in his additions, Wordsworth tried to work up a political situation behind them, asking 'Why, shepherds, tremble thus with new alarms / As if ye heard the din of civil arms?'[14] This was a good if dangerous question in 1794, when the government was doing everything in its power to keep popular mass meetings from spilling out into insurrectionary protests. His imagination keeps playing with the current forms of Britain's warlike past, and he can't avoid the revolutionary tendency of his thoughts, except by swerving abruptly back into beautiful landscape visions:

> Mute Havoc smiling grimly backward slunk.
> Low-muttering o'er the earth that gasped beneath,
> Hung the dim shapes of Solitude and Death,
> And all was theirs save that the plover passed
> With screams and bittern blew his hollow blast.
>
> Now while the solemn evening shadows sail,
> On red slow-waving pinions down the vale . . .
>
> (405–11)

The paragraph break shifts us back into landscape-mode, and we forget that those 'red pinions' might easily, if Wordsworth had stuck with his military metaphors and meditations, have symbolized the red flags of revolution, civil disturbance, and martial law.

The main reason he could not publish a revised *Evening Walk* is the fact that its landscape's 'social accents' were not translated into a consistent meaning, however suggestively they could be conveyed in misty imagery. But he could easily imagine one of the 'favoured beings' who *could* embody this nature-society linkage. For he and Dorothy, 'meek lover[s] of the shade,' have a heroic precursor: 'In dangerous night so Milton worked alone, / Cheared [*sic*] by a secret lustre all his own, / That with the deepening darkness clearer shone.' This is the first explicit mention of Milton in Wordsworth's writing. 'It is understandable that in 1794, an English republican would cite the lonely example of a republican of an earlier age.'[15] But republicanism is not the only issue here, and his image of Milton is not simply a political one. Coming near the end of a set of revisions which change *An Evening Walk* into a significantly different poem, Milton's appearance is highly symbolic. It identifies one name of the 'secret power' that *can* read the 'social accents' of both the landscape and the times. 'The deepening darkness' is both the sun setting across Derwentwater and also England sliding into its own reign of terror, as the mid-1790s increasingly recalled the mid-seventeenth century to thoughtful minds.

For actual republicanism also is at stake here. Richard wrote in late May warning William to be 'cautious in writing or expressing your political opinions. By the suspension of the Habeas Corpus Acts [on 16 May] the Ministers have great powers.' Richard knew very well how political tyranny maintains itself, so he refused to go into detail about his glum view of their chances for success against Lord Lonsdale: 'I have always avoided writing and speaking upon this subject, because His Lordship has so many Spies in every part of the country.'[16] Dorothy replied stoutly, 'I can answer for William's caution about expressing his political opinions. He is very cautious and seems well aware of the dangers of a contrary conduct.'[17] But at exactly this time, William was writing a letter to Mathews about their journal-publishing project that opened with a very 'explicit avowal' of his 'political sentiments': 'I am not amongst the admirers of the British constitution,' which is being perverted by 'the infatuation profligacy and extravagance of men in power.'[18] This certainly could have been brought to trial as 'seditious utterance.'

Towards the end of May William and Dorothy left Windy Brow and set out for Whitehaven, the ostensible first destination of their trip north, to visit with their aunt Elizabeth and uncle Richard Wordsworth. Crossing the Ouse Bridge over the Derwent at the top of the lake, they soon came to

Cockermouth, their birthplace. Dorothy had not seen the grand house by the river since she was six; it was now deserted and marked by neglect: '. . . all was in ruin, the terrace-walk buried and choked up with the old privet hedge which had formerly been beautiful, roses and privots intermingled – the same hedge where the sparrows were used to build their nests.'[19] The ruin of their prospects could hardly have found a better objective symbol as they walked along, moving from playing at adult independence at Windy Brow toward the reality of their dependent status among their Whitehaven cousins.

The sight had a similar resonance for William, though he did not write it down for another year or two. When he did, the impact of seeing his decayed family home is apparent in the cadences of these soon-to-be-famous lines:

> Yet once again do I behold the forms
> Of these huge mountains, and yet once again,
> Standing beneath these elms, I hear thy voice,
> Beloved Derwent, that peculiar voice
> Heard in the stillness of the evening air,
> Half-heard and half-created.[20]

It is as though we are hearing simultaneously the beginning of 'Tintern Abbey' and *The Prelude*, as the memory of time in the former, and that of place in the latter, come together in a literal point of origin for both Wordsworth's life and poetry. He is looking at natural objects and listening to natural sounds while standing near a decayed but unmentioned building, as he also will do above Tintern Abbey. The situation shows how deeply Wordsworth's creative imagination was stimulated by feelings of loss or absence *at the very point from which* it speaks its deepest affirmations. Adapting these lines to the Wye Valley four years later, he changed the name of the river, and the 'huge mountains' (Skiddaw) and local northern elms become the cliffs and sycamores of South Wales. By 1798 this memory would be thoroughly mixed with his recollections of his first trip past Tintern, in 1793, a trip whose motives were in turn very much bound up with his reasons for being with Dorothy at Cockermouth in 1794. Uniting them all was an overwhelming sense of his life returning to its origins, and now beginning to play itself back to him in an adult – and decidedly minor – key. In the perspective of their young adult lives, the neglected mansion of their former hopes gave very little promise for the future.

Passing rapidly on from this solemn moment, they arrived before nightfall in the little village of Branthwaite between Cockermouth and Whitehaven. There they stayed with their uncle Richard, now retired and ailing. Dorothy could see immediately that their uncle would 'never enjoy a *good* state of health.' She spoke truer than she knew, for he died less than a month later. The death of this uncle, the kindliest of the four who were the overseers of their destiny, had immediate repercussions on their lives that summer. As soon as they arrived in Whitehaven, Dorothy wrote a pressing letter to Richard, urging him to do everything he could, and as quickly as he could, to put their financial affairs on a settled basis. 'These things make me very uneasy.' Principally, she was concerned that their Uncle Crackanthorpe be brought 'to an immediate settlement' of the accounts which he co-administered with Richard Wordsworth of Whitehaven, for that very small part of their father's estate which was not contained in the evidently hopeless claim against Lord Lonsdale. As administrators of their nephews' and niece's trust, Richard Wordsworth and Christopher Crackanthorpe had for years been engaged mainly in making advances beyond the present balance of the estate, in anticipation of future repayment.

Dorothy had no hopes for anything on the Lowther front: 'at present it cannot be advancing one step . . . it is said that nothing can be done without applying to the House of Lords.' This was the common view around Whitehaven because, two days before she wrote, Henry Littledale, a local mercer, had finally won a settlement of £4000 against Lowther in the House of Lords, for damages incurred when his house at St Bees sank into a shaft which Lowther's mining company had burrowed beneath it. It had taken three years, but the victory, a very popular one, showed that Lowther could be beaten with perseverance. But after ten years of waiting, Dorothy could only opine regretfully, 'I wish our [cause] had been pursued with equal vigour' – precisely the quality that everybody agreed was lacking in their principal lawyer, Edward Christian.

In their summer visits along the coast, William and Dorothy were passing through the more settled, populous part of Cumberland, which is not identical with the Lake District, though the two terms are often used synonymously by outsiders. None of William and Dorothy's relations lived among the lakes. They were to be found along the coast from Maryport, Workington, and Whitehaven, down to Barrow and Ulverston, either in trading towns like Penrith or in the shipping ports of the coast, where, as ship captains, lawyers, and inn keepers, they earned their livings by working hard. One shouldn't overdo this connecting of people with places, but these were nevertheless the kind of people that Wordsworth's Whitehaven cousins were, not much given to enjoying the 'prospect' of the grey Irish Sea from their town's huge hills.

William and Dorothy stayed with the wife of their cousin John, captain of the ship on which their brother John was serving. These eight living cousins were warm and welcoming for a three-week summer visit. But the question of their cousins' debts was the deep family issue that was on everyone's mind even as they all tried to avoid it in conversation. It could not be wished away, and it was nobody's fault that John Wordsworth had died leaving five young orphans. It came to over £400, the great bulk of it for William's college education – and for his frequent touring expenses.

The question of fault, or deserts, especially crossed the mind of Aunt Elizabeth Wordsworth, as she contemplated paying off the debts of her dying husband's estate, and the looming educational expenses of her youngest child, the promisingly-named Robinson Wordsworth (1775–1856). He had just turned nineteen, and was beginning to seek his place in life. (He found it a year and a half later, when his name paid off, and John Robinson awarded him the lucrative collectorship of customs at Harwich.) Mrs Wordsworth could not avoid comparing her son's prospects to those of his visiting cousin William, the most gifted of her late brother-in-law's children, but the only one who, so far, had shown no sign of getting himself forward in the world in a way to repay the debts that had been contracted on his behalf. The money that had put cousin William through college would now be very convenient for Robinson. It is no bad reflection on Mrs Richard Wordsworth, but quite the contrary as a devoted mother, that she seems to have been the one who began pressing, after a couple more years' lenience, for her own childrens' due.

Even before leaving Windy Brow, William had accepted an offer from Raisley Calvert to share in his allowance in anticipation of the inheritance that would come to him in mid-September. This was a polite formulation of the fact that Raisley was already helping to defray some of the Wordsworths' expenses, as his brother William had the summer before. Wordsworth's letters to Mathews at this time make a small but significant shift reflecting this news, regarding his ability to contribute financially to their proposed journal. On 23 May he said, 'I am so poor I could not advance any thing,' though he did not think 'being in the country would have any tendency to diminish the number or deduct from the value of my communications.'[21] But on 8 June Wordsworth concluded a long letter of detailed suggestions for the magazine by saying he must still decline coming to town, but now for nearly the opposite reasons he had given two weeks earlier: 'I have a friend in the country [Raisley] who has offered me a share of his income. It would be using him very ill to run the risque of destroying my usefulness by precipitating myself into distress and poverty at the time when he is so ready to support me in a situation wherein I feel I can be of some little service to my fellowmen, hereafter, if our exertions are sufficient to support us by residing in London, perhaps I may be enabled to prosecute my share of the exertions with greater vigour.' He then continues, maddeningly, 'Will it not be necessary to free [yourself] from some of those occupations to which your time is at present devoted? . . . As to money I have not a single sixpence of my own to advance . . .'[22]

Wordsworth suffered cruel double-binds at the hands of his uncles, but he seems to have developed the habit of creating them for others: 'I have no money, only a free allowance from a friend. You are gainfully employed, but shouldn't you give up some of your salary in order to give more time to our journal project – the one I dare not invest in?'

*

From Whitehaven, Dorothy went to visit another of her cousins from this family, Elizabeth, who in 1790 had married Francis Barker, and now lived in comfortable circumstances in Rampside, a tiny fishing village directly across Morecambe Bay from Morecambe and Lancaster. The Barkers' house is still standing, large enough to serve as a hotel. William accompanied Dorothy as far as Broughton-in-Furness, where they visited with another cousin, Mary, who in 1789 had married a tavern keeper, John Smith. Francis Barker came to escort Dorothy on to Rampside, while William turned north to ride back to Keswick. Of these shadowy cousins in his youthful biography Wordsworth only recorded later a 'whisper from the heart,' for 'friends and kindred tenderly beloved.'[23]

He spent most of July in Keswick, writing and caring for Calvert, whose health was beginning to deteriorate rapidly. In August William returned to Rampside to spend the month with Dorothy and the Barkers. Rampside is merely a small collection of buildings by the side of the ramp where the ferry from Morecambe puts in. It is also the port, so to speak, for tourist excursions to the closest and smallest of the raggedy little collection islands at the end of the North Lancashire coast, the promontory occupied by the ancient fortress called Peele (or Piel) Castle, originally built to ward off marauding pirates from the Isle of Man.

Short though it was, Wordsworth's summer by the sea at Rampside was marked by two events terrifically amplified in his memory. One was his recollection of this calm time eleven years later, when his brother John drowned off Weymouth and Portland Bill, which hooks out into the sea in much the same way as the Isle of Walney does at Piel Island. The other was his recollection of hearing the news of Robespierre's execution. Both moments exploded in his imagination because of his strong reaction to the sense of difference between a peaceful, naïve 'then' and a violent, tragic 'now.' In this respect, his quiet time at Rampside was a seed-bed for memory, very much as his reaction to seeing his childhood home at Cockermouth anticipated further imaginative growth upon his return to Tintern Abbey.

The 'Elegiac Stanzas, Suggested by a Picture of Peele Castle, in a Storm, Painted by Sir George Beaumont' (1805) stress the dreamy inactivity of that summer – as contrasted with a dramatic picture by Beaumont, his new patron – almost to the point of a paralysis:

> I was thy neighbour once, thou rugged Pile!
> Four summer weeks I dwelt in sight of thee:
> I saw thee every day; and all the while
> Thy Form was sleeping on a glassy sea.
> So pure the sky, so quiet was the air!
> So like, so very like, was day to day!
>
> (1–6)

306 · *The Hidden Wordsworth*

If he could have painted what he saw and felt then, it would have been a picture very different from Beaumont's stormy picture, which he now feels is more realistically suited to life's tragic losses. But in 1794, he would have set the stolid 'Pile' in a 'light that never was, on sea or land . . . Amid a world how different from this!'

Wordsworth's reaction to the news of Robespierre's death also had strong personal dimensions. He had ridden around to the east side of Morecambe Bay on an errand, and he returned by way of Cartmel Priory, where lay the grave of William Taylor, his Hawkshead schoolteacher. Returning to the 'far-secluded privacy' of Rampside, he crossed over the bay at Leven Sands, the shallows at its landward head. A roundabout journey of many miles could be reduced to two miles by crossing here at low tide. There were special guides for it, since the tides of Morecambe Bay are famous for the speed with which they return over their vast shallow expanse; there are many tales of unsuspecting travellers who drowned there.[24] As he rode slowly westward, musing on the schoolmaster who had first encouraged him to poetry and brooding on his present tenuous situation, Wordsworth 'carelessly inquired if any news were stirring,' from the leader a band of travellers being escorted over from Ulverston. The man cried out, 'Robespierre is dead!' Wordsworth's mind turned round with the shock, not only at the news itself, but from its contrast with the delicate frame of mind he was in: memories of careless school days, an encouraging master early dead, dedication to poetry, and his present inability to pursue it.

The shock was as great as that he had experienced in the Simplon Pass. For someone who had seen Robespierre at close range, and whose intimate private life had been complicated by the policies he formulated, the news was an enormous relief: it made thoughts of France and Annette feasible again, a correlation we miss if we see only political emotions in political events. For a few wild moments he fantasized that he was Robespierre's replacement, a saviour coming in 'righteousness and peace' to redeem the world from its enthrallment to these now-fallen devils. Nine months almost to the day after the fall of their Girondin opponents, the Jacobin leaders had suffered their same fate. The news triggered in Wordsworth 'a hymn of triumph' which deserves to stand alongside the paean to Imagination at the similar moment in the Simplon Pass: ' "Come now, ye golden times," / Said I, forth-breathing on those open sands / A hymn of triumph, "as the morning comes / Out of the bosom of the night, come ye" ' (541–44). As in the Simplon Pass, Wordsworth represents himself as quoting from his highest authority: himself. We can hardly overestimate his sense of personal empowerment at this moment: for a few moments he imagined himself to be the central intelligence of the French Revolution: 'Then schemes I framed more calmly, when and how / The madding factions might be tranquillized, [and] / The mighty renovation would proceed' (553–56). This is not simply the reaction of an English liberal to good news from the war front, but the personally implicated reaction of 'an adherent of the French cause,' who looks forward to renewed progress toward the Revolution's original goals[25] – which, coincidentally, may reunite him with his wife and child.

He returned to Keswick toward the end of September, and found Raisley Calvert 'worse than when I left.' Calvert's condition and the date of Wordsworth's return are not unrelated, since Calvert turned twenty-one at mid-month and was now the owner of Ormathwaite farm and other properties and incomes stipulated in his father's will, including an outright cash grant of nearly £900.[26] As his consumption advanced, he thought desperately of travelling to Portugal, a common resort of young Englishmen in these times (William Mathews had lately returned from it, and Robert Southey would shortly go thither). Wordsworth did not oppose this far-fetched plan, despite his dire report of Raisley's condition: 'any person in his state of health must recoil from the idea of going so far alone, particularly into a country of whose language he is ignorant.' As if language were the main problem! Instead, he proposed to William Calvert, very carefully, he (Wordsworth) would accompany Raisley, and that William should give his brother 'as much pecuniary assistance as would enable me to accompany him thither, and stay with him till his health is re-established.'

He then goes further, pressing the idea with a bit of moral arm-twisting: 'This I think, if possible, you ought to do. You see I speak as friend. But then perhaps your present expenses may render it difficult.' This might well have struck William Calvert as presumptuous. But, having intimated that Calvert might not be willing to help his dying brother, Wordsworth then increased the moral pressure: 'Would it not exalt you in your own esteem to retrench a little for so excellent a purpose?'

Having pushed Calvert to the limit, Wordsworth revealed the ground of his importunity. Raisley had been helping out with some of Wordsworth's expenses since June, but this help was now in a fair way to becoming considerably more substantial:

Reflecting that his return is uncertain your brother requests me to inform you that he has drawn out his will, which he means to get executed in London. The purport of his will is to leave you all his property real and chargeable [i.e., all his debts as well] with a legacy of £600 to me, in case that on an enquiry into the state of our affairs in London he should think it advisable to do so. It is at my request that this information is communicated to you [i.e., I am telling you this now because I asked permission of Raisley to do so], and I have no doubt but that you will do both him and myself the justice to hear this mark of his approbation of me without your good opinion of either of us being at all diminished. If you could come over [from Newcastle] yourself it would be much the best. At all events fail not to write by return of post, as the sooner your brother gets off the better. He will depart immediately after hearing from you.

I am dear Calvert,

Your very affectionate friend, W. Wordsworth[27]

This is a very careful, very bold, and very lawyerly letter. It shows the influence of Wordsworth's having had a father, a brother, and some cousins in the legal profession. He is breaking to William Calvert the news that the large amount of ready cash in Raisley Calvert's estate, enough to support a single man for nearly ten years, which William Calvert stood to inherit, was now going to Wordsworth. He is saying, 'Surely you will not take this news badly, or in the wrong way – any more than you would take badly my earnest argument that you support my expenses while I accompany Raisley to Portugal. And you should also pay my travel expenses – even though if your brother dies I will inherit the cash balance of his estate.'

They did in fact set off for Portugal on 9 October – and got as far as Penrith. They returned to Keswick the very next day because Raisley 'found himself worse.' It was the shortest, but by far the most profitable, of Wordsworth's several trips 'abroad' in the 1790s. For William Calvert to have taken Wordsworth's letter in the wrong way would mean that he suspected Wordsworth of legacy-hunting, in one of the most usual situations where such suspicions arise: toward the care-giver of a terminally ill person who is isolated, without family or dependants or any other close friend nearby, in the last months of his life. It is important that we see his actions in their cultural context. Given his and Dorothy's dependent family financial situation when they came north in April, complicated by the claims arising from their uncle Richard's death in June, his positioning himself to inherit something was only common sense, and need not be taken as evidence of morbid plotting.[28]

Far from being underhanded, such behaviour at the imminent death of a friend or relative was perfectly normal for the times, as it still is wherever inheritance is a major way of acquiring wealth. The hope to inherit was a normal kind of 'interest' one had in the dead and dying, perfectly consistent with the constant cultivation of 'interest' among one's influential superiors that was the basis of almost every kind of advancement in eighteenth-century England. Almost all marriages of persons in Wordsworth's class were still arranged on precisely this basis: how much the prospective bride or groom could be expected to bring to the marriage, either directly or in an expected inheritance. Indeed, it might be argued that courting the dying had fewer unfortunate long-term consequences than courtships which produced the many loveless and cruel marriages that women were forced into.

Dorothy's attachment to her brother shared this same economic motivation. Her lack of marriage prospects was directly proportionable to her lack of an estate and her very small 'provision.' These very considerations led William to remind Raisley Calvert of his sister's dependence on him, with the result that Calvert soon increased the amount of his bequest by three hundred pounds to £900: i.e., the full amount of the cash portion of his inheritance, the most liquid, and most useful, part of his estate.[29] In its effect, this additional amount became something like a marriage portion settled on Dorothy.

It would have been ridiculously circumspect, given Wordsworth's circumstances and prevailing social practices, to have behaved in any other way. However, only an excessively sentimental view of the situation could imagine that Wordsworth did nothing to encourage or manipulate Raisley's generosity. The only person who stood to lose anything by Raisley's generosity was his brother William. There are suggestions in Wordsworth's letter to William Calvert that he knew the elder brother did not share his younger brother's enthusiasm for Wordsworth's future: 'He deemed that my pursuits and labours lay / Apart from all that leads to wealth, or even / Perhaps to necessary maintenance, / Without some hazard to the finer sense' (XIII.362–65). Raisley Calvert 'deemed,' that is, what Wordsworth's relatives were also beginning to 'deem' was the case with him in 1794: that he did not seem likely to be able to earn a living. But the Richard Wordsworth family were much less worried about any 'hazard to the finer sense' he might risk by trying to find a job.

Wordsworth's language at the time was a good deal less lofty than his tribute to Raisley Calvert composed ten years later. In two letters fired off to Richard on 10 and 17 October, Wordsworth was in agony of anxiousness lest Raisley die before his intended will could be properly executed and witnessed, and lest his Whitehaven relatives lay claim to this new inheritance for payment of the £400 he owed to his late uncle's estate. He had to satisfy Raisley on the latter count, for Raisley did not want to leave a bequest that could be seized immediately to pay prior debts. In the first of these letters, Wordsworth stumbles all over himself, repeating the interrelated matters of Richard's standing bond to protect him from any claims originating from Whitehaven, the chances of independence the bequest offers him, and his solemn vow that he will repay the debt to his cousins 'if ever I am worth more than this six hundred pounds.'[30] (It was not paid until 1812.) He urged Richard to reply by return post, and then goes further, urging him to leave his London business and travel north to make sure all the legalities were being properly observed. He pushed his case so far he insulted Richard by hinting that Richard might not be willing to be bonded to protect him. This was similar to the provocative moralizing with which he had wheedled William Calvert about paying his travel expenses to Lisbon. We do not have Calvert's replies to such importunings, but we do have Richard Wordsworth's, and it suggests that neither older brother was pleased by such high-handed treatment: 'You will allow me to assure you that I have always had my Sisters yours and my younger Brothers Interest at Hearth [sic] although I have not been fond of making protestations which It could not be my intention to carry into effect. . . . It has been and I hope will always be my [MS torn] to say little upon such heads whate'er my secret intentions may be.'[31] In short: I act, not talk.

After agreeing to enter into the bond that would indemnify William against claims from their Uncle Richard's family, Richard continued more pointedly:

> There is one Circumstance which I will mention to you at this time. I might have retired into the Country and I had almost said enjoyed the sweets of retirement and Domestic life if I had only considered my own Interest. However as I have entered into the Busy scenes of Town life I shall I hope pursue them with comfort and credit. I am happy to inform you that my Business encreases daily and that altho' our affairs have been peculiarly distressing I hope that from the Industry of ourselves at one time we will enjoy more ease and independence than we have yet experienced.

In other words: 'Not all of us can retire so blithely to the country. I am working hard so you may enjoy the "sweets of retirement and Domestic life," and I hope you will soon start doing the same.' He closes with a caution that we may be sure William Calvert, his opposite number in the role of Elder Brother in this family drama, shared: 'I suppose [Raisley] has maturely weighed the matter and taken in to consideration the claims of his Brother to keep any provision he may make for you alone. I cannot get to Cumberland this vacation.'[32]

Wordsworth's reply of 17 October is feverishly fearful that Raisley will die before the will is drawn up. 'It is his wish that the will should be made immediately and yet he is naturally of a dilatory disposition; and one does not wonder that he seizes on any opportunity to defer it, though at the same time his wish is to have it done immediately.' Wordsworth was hardly the one to speak of dilatory dispositions, but the accumulation of excuses and delays drove him nearly frantic: Raisley didn't like his Keswick lawyer (wonderfully named Lightfoot), but the Penrith lawyer wanted a guinea and a half for the trip over, so Raisley thought he'd draw it up himself, but William wasn't sure he knew how to do it correctly. 'At all events no time is to be lost as he is so much reduced as to make it probable he cannot be on earth long.' Finally Raisley convinced William he could draw up a legal document by himself, so William told Richard, in an on-going journal-letter which proceeds almost like a minute-by-minute record of events, 'I retract then what I said about your coming down and think there can be no occasion for it.'[33]

The will was finally signed on 23 October 1794, less than a month after

Wordsworth returned from his seaside vacation to find Calvert 'much worse' than he had left him. It provided 'one or more annuities for his use and benefit' and 'full power to invest any portion for the use and benefit of his Sister Dorothy Wordsworth.' The nervousness was over, but it had been real and justified. £900 was nine years' maintenance, at the allowance rate on which Raisley Calvert had been living: exactly the rate (£100 per year) that Wordsworth told William Mathews he would need before he could consider Mathews's plan of throwing up all their aspirations for wordly success to adopt the wandering life.

Wordsworth's efforts to settle his affairs at this critical juncture in his self-creation were not without costs in friendship and ruffled personal feelings. But, in the course of little over a year, Wordsworth's reacquaintance with William Calvert had moved from being his expenses-paid travelling companion, to the free use of his house at Windy Brow, to sharing his brother's maintenance income, to proposing to be his brother's expenses-paid travelling companion, to becoming Raisley's cash heir in place of William, and finally to beginning to collect the inheritance money within three months of first broaching the news to William.

Raisley Calvert lingered on for three more months, during which William removed him to Penrith for better care. He stayed faithfully at his younger friend's side till the end, and had 'a most melancholy office of it,' as he wrote restively to Mathews. 'I begin to wish to be much in town; cataracts and mountains, are good occasional society, but they will not do for constant companions; besides I have not even much of their conversation, and still less that of books as I am so much with my sick friend, and he cannot bear the fatigue of being read to. Nothing indeed but a sense of duty could detain me here under the present circumstances. This is a country for poetry it is true; but the muse is not to be won but by the sacrifice of time, and time I have not to spare.'[34] He conveys more of a sense of duty than of grieving affection towards Calvert, and he is almost equally reserved about the lakes and mountains of Cumberland.

CHAPTER EIGHTEEN

Philanthropy or Treason?

London, 1795

> . . . demanding proof,
> And seeking it in everything, I lost
> All feeling of conviction, and, in fine,
> Sick, wearied out with contrarieties,
> Yielded up moral questions in despair . . .
>   (X.896–900)

In two long letters to William Mathews in May and June 1794 – just when his family financial predicament was intensifying – Wordsworth had set forth in great detail his plans for a political and moral publication, to be called *The Philanthropist*, which he and Mathews would initiate as soon as they could co-ordinate their time, money, and energy. His proposed editorial policy was firmly republican. Following Godwin's example, he would not begin the project without a full, mutual disclosure of their political views,[1] which he initiated with legalistic formality: 'here at the very threshold I solemnly affirm that in no writings of mine will I ever admit of any sentiment which can have the least tendency to induce my readers to suppose that the doctrines which are now enforced by banishment, imprisonment, &c, &c, are other than pregnant with every species of misery. You know perhaps that I am of that odious class of men called democrats, and of that class I shall for ever continue.'[2]

Penned ten days after the first arrests for the treason trials, such heightened language seems less pompous than brave – or foolhardy, when sent through a post that was being systematically opened by government agents. He was reading the signs of the times very carefully, and his comments on the treason trial acquittals turn shrewdly upon his own situation: 'The late occurrences in every point of view are interesting to humanity. They will abate the insolence and presumption of the aristocracy, by shewing it that neither the violence, nor the art, of power can crush even an unfriended individual, though engaged in the propagation of doctrines confessedly unpalatable to privilege.' He himself was now 'an unfriended individual' in terms of influence and patronage.

Receiving Mathews's 'explicit avowal of . . . political sentiments with great pleasure,' Wordsworth launched into 'a similar declaration of my own opinions.' He proceeds with a deductive logic that leads him to statements that, in the current climate of law, constituted seditious utterance: 'I disapprove of monarchical and aristocratical governments, however modified. Hereditary distinctions and privileged orders of every species I think must necessarily counteract the progress of human improvement.' Coleridge would shortly lecture in Bristol about the risk of such communications: 'If any man, even in a private letter or social conversation, should say a Republic is the best form of government, he is guilty of high treason.'[3]

But Wordsworth feared radical excesses more than government repression: 'the destruction of those institutions which I condemn appears to me to be hastening on too rapidly. I recoil from the bare idea of a revolution.'[4] He was thus opposed to 'all inflammatory addresses to the passions of men,' favouring instead a 'gradual and constant reform' of ministerial extravagance as the best way of avoiding the 'execrable measures' into which the French had been led. This prudence reflects Wordsworth's new familiarity with Godwin's *Political Justice*, which he read very carefully in the winter of 1793–94. Mankind's gradual but inevitable progress toward political justice by the unstoppable force of truth in open discussion was the key element in Godwin's thought. Its necessary corollary was strict avoidance of any kind of writing or public speech that would raise passions to violence which might prove counter-productive to progress.

By mid-February of 1795, Wordsworth was back in London, eagerly checking out journalistic opportunities. Although their plans for the *Philanthropist* had apparently fallen through, he was still persuaded by Mathews's arguments in favour of journalism. In November he had intimated he might even abandon Raisley in favour of his prospects for employment on a London newspaper:

> If he should not recover, indeed whatever turn his complaint takes, I am so emboldened by your encouragement that I am determined to throw myself into that mighty gulph which has swallowed up so many, of talents and attainments infinitely superior to my own. . . . What is the nature of the service performed by you, and how much of your time does it engross? &c &c. You say a newspaper would be glad of me; do you think you could ensure me employment in that way on terms similar to your own? I mean also in an opposition paper, for really I cannot in conscience and in principle, abet in the smallest degree the measures pursued by the present ministry.[5]

Mathews replied by the end of December, and Wordsworth immediately fitted himself to the jobs available. The only thing he ruled out was parliamentary reporting (Mathews's speciality), because he had 'neither strength of memory, quickness of penmanship, nor rapidity of composition . . . [and] my being subject to nervous headaches, which inevitably attack me when exposed to a heated atmosphere or to loud noises . . .'[6] But he was sure he would be able to translate excerpts from the French and Italian gazettes, confidently adding that, 'with two or three weeks reading I think I could engage for the Spanish.' He thought he might also furnish the odd paragraph on current events, 'and now and then an essay on general politics,' but this was just a show of confidence. He really preferred translating – a substantial job, since most newspapers devoted one full page out of four to war reports from the *Moniteur* and other foreign sources.

He had not yet seen Mathews's new paper, the *Telegraph*, which commenced publication on 30 December 1794, but had heard 'that it is democratical, and full of advertisments!' Mathews may well have told him about other young men who were just then signing up for the new paper's staff. In mid-January Coleridge was in London negotiating for a position on it, and by mid-February Southey was its regular Bristol correspondent.[7] Mathews was probably one of the first connections through which knowledge of these future friends came to Wordsworth.

Wordsworth was very insistent that Mathews do something definite for him: 'I cannot be detained long by my present occupation [nursing Calvert], so that you are not likely to give yourself trouble to no purpose.' This was in response to Mathews's annoyed reminder of how much he had done to try to get the *Philanthropist* started, only to have Wordsworth hold back his time and money throughout the summer of 1794. Now he had money, but he was not about to sink his capital into a speculative venture like a new journal. Ironically, the removal of the condition that kept him out of the *Philanthropist* project, lack of money, became his prime motive for launching himself into newspaper work, to protect his nest egg. The Calvert bequest, far from relieving Wordsworth from money pressures, determined him to go to work.

He arrived in the city in early February, staying at first with Mathews at the Middle Temple. On 16 March, there appeared the first issue of the small liberal paper called the *Philanthropist*. It ran for eleven months, through 25 January 1796,[8] and corresponds very well to the *Philanthropist* discussed by Wordsworth and Mathews. Their *Philanthropist* would be opposed to the 'minister's war' with France, and to Pitt's methods of silencing opposition by intimidation, imprisonment and banishment. But, though obviously an opposition paper, it was fundamentally a loyal one. It was to be a reformist, anti-war, non-revolutionary, and pro-British journal, devoted to improving social justice by increasing political justice, and propagating to a mainly middle-class, educated audience, including reformers and Dissenters, 'those doctrines which long and severe meditation [had] taught them are essential for the welfare of mankind.'

Still, their proposed *Philanthropist* would have been considered radical in the hysterical climate of political opinion in England in 1795, more so than the one that actually appeared, at least in its initial numbers. For example, the published *Philanthropist* accepted the existence of the king and the aristocracy as being, along with the clergy, 'admirably adapted to the genius of the English people.' But Wordsworth's and Mathews's journal would have been, like Godwin's, philosophically radical, and need not have troubled the powers that be. 'A vehicle of sound and exalted Morality,' it was devoted to diffusing 'by every method a knowledge of [the] rules of political justice' and to expounding principles of 'social order applicable to all times and places.'

The name of both the proposed and the actual journal was one of the code words of Godwinism, the personified abstraction of his key concept, benevolence. 'Philanthropy' was a fashionable liberal term in the early 1790s, signifying a more-than-nationalistic patriotism, 'a loyalty to the welfare of mankind.'[9] Wordsworth preferred his title to one that Mathews had proposed, which seemed to him 'too common to attract attention.' It is hard to think of a more common word than philanthropy in 1795, but Wordsworth was confident that 'this title . . . would be noticed; it includes everything that can instruct and amuse mankind.'[10]

Almost all the differences between their proposed journal and the actually published *Philanthropist* can be accounted for by the inevitable contraction of aims that often occurs when youthful publishing plans encounter the realities of printing, finance, and editorial decision-making. Wordsworth proposed a monthly miscellany, whereas the published *Philanthropist* was an eight-page penny weekly. But many of the kinds of material Wordsworth proposed for his monthly do appear in the published version. Theirs would 'open with the topic of general politics . . . accompanied with such remarks as may forcibly illustrate the tendency of particular doctrines of government; next should follow essays upon morals and manners, and institutions whether social or political.'[11] Following these 'instructional' essays, Wordsworth proposed a long list of 'essays partly for instruction and partly for amusement': biographical papers, reviews of other philanthropical publications, some poetry (but no 'original communications' [i.e., unsolicited contributions], to avoid 'the trash which infests the magazines'), essays of taste and criticism, works of imagination and fiction, parliamentary debates, and selected state papers.

Each number of the published *Philanthropist* had fewer essays than Wordsworth proposed, but the same kind of essays do appear sequentially in it, and in roughly the same order and proportion as those at the top of Wordsworth's list. Besides essays on general politics, it had several analytical essays illustrating the tendency of particular doctrines of government, and others on social and political institutions generally. Some of these were original essays; others were reprinted from the standard works in the Whig tradition of parliamentary reform (e.g., John Trenchard's *History of Standing Armies in England* and Montesquieu's 'On Liberty'). These essays were neither radical nor scurrilous. The early ones are clearly written, and squarely situated within the Enlightenment tradition of intellectual rhetoric. Their main fault, from a literary point of view, is that they are dull. Although the *Philanthropist* has few 'biographical papers' other than tributes to victims of Pitt's policies, it does contain honourific references to three of the figures Wordsworth proposed for his series of biographical sketches: Algernon Sydney, Milton, and Machiavelli.

More than 'some' verse, the actual *Philanthropist* contained about twenty-five per cent verse, most of which would doubtless have been considered 'trash' by a horrified Wordsworth – thus contributing to his later complex arguments about the relationship between a nation's poetry and its moral character. A good deal of the verse *is* scurrilous, and some of it is funny, but little of it is poetry, strictly speaking, being rather parodic satires upon contemporary personages such as 'your affectionate fellow-swine, Wm. Pitt,' forced into the meter of traditional tunes like 'Oh, Dear, What Can the Matter Be?' However, some of its poetry is close in both spirit and language to poems Wordsworth was writing at the same time, particularly his imitation of Juvenal, and more generally his attempts since 1793 to link descriptions of natural beauty to commentary about human suffering.

These parallels indicate that the congruence between Wordsworth's proposed *Philanthropist* and the one that actually appeared are coincidences 'too large to pass off in a little cough in a footnote [as] scholars have generally done.'[12] And there is more evidence, both external and internal, that corroborates the case for Wordsworth's involvement.

For Mathews and Wordsworth to get the *Philanthropist* into print within six weeks of Wordsworth's arrival in London, there had to be an economic and political climate favourable to such publication, and they would have had to have help. Both of these conditions existed.

There was an unusual window of opportunity in the publishing business as a result of the reformers' apparent victory in the Treason Trials; a liberalized climate of public opinion prevailed through much of 1795. In actual fact, the government's scare tactics in the Treason Trials proved largely successful, and the more knowledgeable reformers began withdrawing from action – wisely, as events showed.* However, all these

---

* Home Office records show that the Duke of Portland, with his under-secretary John King, William Wickham, head of the new Alien Office, and the Bow Street magistrate Richard Ford, began in January to put into operation an elaborate new system of payrolls and pay-offs designed to consolidate Westminster's control

defections from the cause of reform opened the field for more naive and less experienced writers, especially of a more palatable liberal cast: exactly the profile of the *Philanthropist*. Most fortunately for Wordsworth's and Mathews's plans, Daniel Isaac Eaton's *Politics for the People* ceased appearing in March, 1795, and Eaton was the publisher of the *Philanthropist*, which began appearing that same month, and which eventually followed the same format as *Politics for the People*. These various groups were linked by personal ties nearly invisible to the historian's eye. Thus, Eaton's son Henry was John Thelwall's assistant; Thomas Best, one of the two identifiable writers for the *Philanthropist*, worked with Thelwall on the *Imperial and Biographical Magazine*; and William Mathews first met Godwin at Thelwall's chambers in December.[13]

The greatest obstacle in the way of Wordsworth's and Mathews's plans had been money, but an enterprising and fearless publisher like Eaton had the necessary capital investment, and was ready to take on a new organ. At a penny an issue the *Philanthropist* was half the price of *Politics for the People*, but it had the advantage, in a nervous publishing climate, of being by unknown writers who, in its early numbers, held safe opinions about standard liberal issues. The largest single piece of evidence tying Wordsworth's and Mathews's *Philanthropist* to the one published by Eaton is the fact that Wordsworth had proposed to Mathews that they 'communicate to each other a sufficient portion of matter to compose at least two numbers . . . of general not temporary nature.' The first four issues of the *Philanthropist* are exactly that: single-essay issues on the uses of talent (no. 1), the freedom of the press (no. 2), and the Glorious Revolution of 1688 (no. 4). The exception is no. 3, which turns away (with a great show of annoyance) from inculcating 'truths of a very pressing and important nature' to 'the political concerns of the day': the defeat of Fox's recent motion against continuing the war. Wordsworth's letters mention freedom of speech directly in relation to the *Philanthropist*, and the uses of talent was a leitmotif in all his letters to Mathews about what they should do with their lives.

Even with their enthusiasm and ready copy, however, Wordsworth and Mathews could hardly have run such an enterprise on their own. They needed help. Mathews's father was a bookseller but dealt mainly in

---

over the heretofore loose system of unpaid magistrates, honourary local officials, Bow Street 'runners,' and informers of all stripes. Wickham added the innovation of using exposed French spies to find suspicious Englishmen: this strategy would lead the Home Office to Wordsworth and Coleridge in 1797. The complicated budget and payment arrangements needed for all this present a picture of a government extremely worried about internal subversion and possible overthrow. (PRO HO/65/1, *Police Entry Books, Series I: 1795–1921*, Vol. I (1795–1811); Porter, 29–31.)

religious books. Wordsworth could write, though his prose would have needed heavy editing for the *Philanthropist*, and his business skills were negligible.

Our first definite piece of evidence for Wordsworth's whereabouts in London in 1795 points directly to a source for the help he and Mathews needed. It was a gathering of some of the most radical intellectual writers of the day, on 27 February, at the Buckingham Street lodgings of William Frend, the popular former Cambridge don whose 1793 trial for heresy had ended with his dismissal from the university. This tea party, as recorded in Godwin's diary, has all the marks of a meeting for some kind of political publishing venture. Except for Thelwall, who was not present, it is hard to imagine a more radical group of intellectuals than those present that night: 'the centre of political disaffection was to be found somewhere within this circle.'[14]

All the younger men present at Frend's gathering were from Cambridge, slightly older than Wordsworth, but still at university when he arrived. Most were now reading for the law, and all had a lively interest in periodical publications. John Tweddell had published his brilliant classical *Prolusiones Juveniles* in 1793, and was an outspoken admirer of the French experiment. He was the member of their Cambridge set that Wordsworth most often inquired about in his correspondence with Mathews. James Losh was an older brother of Wordsworth's Hawkshead classmate, and probably knew Wordsworth in Paris. At the moment, Losh was busy raising money to pay for the expenses of the Treason Trial's defendants.[15] After returning north in 1797, he briefly published a cautiously liberal farmer's almanac called the *OEconomist*. Jonathan Raine was another northerner, from Northumberland (like Tweddell), and had been one of Frend's lawyers. Thomas Edwards was a fellow of Jesus College, where he had befriended Coleridge; in the next year he would help Coleridge in the production and circulation of his shortlived *Watchman*.

More important for our scenario were the four older men at the gathering: Frend, Godwin, Thomas Holcroft, and George Dyer, all successful polemicists in the pamphlet wars of the day. Godwin (b. 1758) was then at 'the very zenith' of his 'temporary fame,' blazing 'as a sun in the firmament of reputation,' 'in a degree that has seldom been exceeded.'[16] The intellectual success of *Political Justice* had been followed in 1794 by the popular success of his novel, *Things as They Are; or, Caleb Williams*, an attack on England's legal and penal system that managed at the same time to be one of the earliest and most compelling English novels of psychological disintegration. By the end of 1795, Godwin's star would begin to dip, when he published a pamphlet in November daring to suggest that radicals must bear some responsibility for provoking the government into passing the repressive 'gagging acts.' But in February he was still the most famous intellectual in London, and the most admired by all friends of Liberty.

Thomas Holcroft (1745–1809) had become a defendant in the Treason Trials by the headline-grabbing strategy of turning himself in and demanding to be arrested. An early example of what we now call a publicist, he had for twenty years turned his hand profitably to every kind of literary journeyman work: adapting *Les liaisons dangereuses* for the London stage (*Seduction*, 1787), translating Beaumarchais' *The Marriage of Figaro* by memorizing successive performances in Paris, writing the most popular play of the times (*The Road to Ruin*, 1792), and, *inter alia*, tossing off a sharp review of Wordsworth's *An Evening Walk* and *Descriptive Sketches* in 1793. When the introductions were made, Holcroft looked sharply at this young William from Cockermouth, thinking of his own dead son, William, also born there, three years after Wordsworth, during a period when Holcroft lived in Cockermouth as a player in an itinerant theatre company, and well aware of the powerful establishment position held by Wordsworth's father.[17]

Dyer (1755–1841) was a close friend of Wordsworth's revered schoolmaster, William Taylor. He averaged nearly a book a year through the 1790s on all the most timely liberal topics: the price of bread, the treatment of convicts, the theory and practice of benevolence, the Test Acts, and the British doctrine of libel. He was also the author of a biography of another Cambridge liberal, Robert Robinson (d. 1790), which Wordsworth exaggeratedly declared 'the best biography in the English language';[18] extracts from Robinson's *Political Catechism* (1784) are reprinted several times in the *Philanthropist*.

A gathering such as this inevitably turned its conversation to writing for publication, and Wordsworth's ready-formed plans for his *Philanthropist* would have been eagerly seized upon for their flattering congruence with Godwin's rationalist ideology. Godwin was an ardent member of a small debating club called the Philomathean Society ('lovers of learning'); he and Holcroft had to be timed with a small hourglass to keep them within the fifteen-minute time limit for speeches.[19] Given Godwin's passion for 'colloquial discussion,' which turned any social encounter into a kind of seminar (Lamb called him 'the Professor'), the 27 February tea party can plausibly be regarded as a version of a meeting of this group.[20] A publication called the *Philanthropist* can with equal plausibility be considered as one of its likely activities, of the sort that Wordsworth had in mind when he proposed to Mathews that they circulate their essays and look for financial and editorial support 'entirely amongst the dispassionate friends of liberty and discussion . . . whether male or female,' and 'by no means neglect to stir up our friends to favour us with any papers which a wish to add to the stock of general knowledge may induce them to write.'[21]

Among the four senior figures present on 27 February, Dyer and Frend were the most likely aiders and abettors of the younger men, though we should not rule out tough practical lessons in street journalism from

Holcroft. Dyer was a particularly generous encourager of liberal young writers. Coleridge wrote letters to him at this time that sound like verbatim copies of Wordsworth's eager letters to Mathews, particularly one postmarked 10 March, six days before the appearance of the first issue of the *Philanthropist*, in which Coleridge asks, 'Is it possible that I could gain an employment in this new work, the Citizen?'[22] This proposed *Citizen* never appeared, but the *Philanthropist* could have been substituted as safer title for the 'new work,' based on Wordsworth's and Mathews's suggestion. There are more than enough parallels between the style and content of Dyer's voluminous writings and the *Philanthropist* to suggest that he could have been a kindly supervisory master of the work. These men favoured a much simpler, more direct and overtly polemical style of periodical prose than is represented in Wordsworth's contemporaneous writing. Given Holcroft's published opinions, apt though harsh, on Wordsworth's poetry of 1793, any advice from him would have cut very close to the bone if applied to Wordsworth's prose in 1795.

When Wordsworth wrote back to Mathews from Racedown in early 1796 about two of their London associates, he did so in terms of their *style* and his Olympian disapproval of it: 'I have received . . . Godwyn's [*sic*] second edition. I expect to find the work much improved. I cannot say that I have been encouraged in this hope by the perusal of the second preface . . . . Such a piece of barbarous writing I have not often seen. It contains scarce one sentence decently written. I am surprized to find such gross faults in a writer who has had so much practice in composition . . .'[23] Calling Godwin's preface to the second edition of *Political Justice* 'barbarous' is quite gratuitous; Godwin could say outrageous things, but he almost always said them with extreme clarity.[24] Something other than dispassionate literary judgment must have motivated Wordsworth's remark about the man who, a year earlier, he was glad to call his mentor, and whose style and intellectual manner of proceeding he followed scrupulously in setting forth his plans for the *Philanthropist*.

The circumstances of the *Philanthropist*'s production suggest a good deal of instability in editorial control. It was a reckless vehicle, obviously in flux politically, a battleground on which liberals and radicals fought for ascendancy, first one, then the other, winning control for the space of a few issues. This would have terrific ramifications for Wordsworth, who initiated the idea, only to suffer the indignity of seeing it wrested out of his control.

Five distinct phases of editorial policy can be identified during its short existence. The first two phases are the most Godwinian, unexceptionally liberal: this was its period of high-minded moral journalism, from the first issue through the fourth (6 April). After its fourth number, the *Philanthropist* interrupted its regular publication schedule for three weeks, suggesting a sudden lack of available copy. When it resumed again, on 27 April, it began printing smaller pieces sent in by contributors, just the sort of 'reliance on any accidental assistance' which Wordsworth said they should avoid. After another three issues, it fell back on Eaton's practice in *Politics for the People* of filling whole issues with reprints from older works, a sure sign of flagging contributions. The next three months are an unstable period from 27 April (no. 5) through 13 July (no. 16), in which some provocative antiwar and anticlerical satires in nos. 5–7 are counterbalanced, as if correctively, by nine numbers given over almost entirely to reprints from the Society for Constitutional Information's 'Address to the People' and from Trenchard's *History of Standing Armies*.

The third period, from late July to late October, is the *Philanthropist*'s radical phase, containing attacks on government policies, defences of convicted 'traitors' like Gerrald, and, most dangerously, celebrations of French victories. The fourth period, like the second, is a mixed one, and also begins after a temporary hiatus in publication (on 26 October), and runs into early December. These numbers are marked by contributions which refer to, and disagree with, each other, suggesting that contributors' wrangling had supplanted any firm editorial policy. The journal's end-game begins on 14 December (no. 37), with an issue given over to an essay by 'W.' Alas for confirmatory evidence, this is not Wordsworth, but most likely the code initial of a contributor to the Norwich *Cabinet*, one Dr Rigby, 'a thorough-going Democrat of the French type.'[25] But Rigby's essay, 'On the Influence of Some Human Institutions on Human Happiness,' confirms the direction of the *Philanthropist*'s development, for it is implicitly a rejection of the journal's original attraction to Godwinian necessarianism. These late numbers are obviously an attempt to keep the journal outside the scope of Pitt's recently passed 'Gagging Acts.' But the end was clearly in sight. The *Philanthropist* ends at no. 43, with an index which scrupulously records all its contributions, though it is still six weeks away from its first anniversary.

Wordsworth's movements in London correlate suggestively with this account of the *Philanthropist*'s development. He visited Godwin at weekly or bi-weekly intervals during the spring and summer of these 'puzzling lost months,' a highly relevant circumstance when connected to the appearance of so Godwinian a publication as the *Philanthropist*.[26] Godwin's scrupulous diary shows that Wordsworth called on him six times between late February and late April, twice with Mathews alone, and once with Joseph Fawcett accompanying them. The first of these was the day after the 27 February gathering at Frend's rooms. The next five were in March and April. By then, it had become very easy for Wordsworth to call on Godwin: he had moved into rooms at 15 Chalton Street in Somers Town (near the present St Pancras Station), just a few doors away from Godwin, who lived at no. 25.[27] Of these five March–April visits, four are on

Tuesday or Wednesday: that is, a day or two after the *Philanthropist*'s normal publication day, which was Monday. The first Tuesday, 10 March, was the one before the *Philanthropist* commenced appearing, and was probably a meeting of the Philomathean Society, which met fortnightly on Tuesdays.

After late April, there is a long hiatus in Wordsworth's visits to Godwin. Godwin left London after 22 April, not to return until July. After he returned to London, Godwin recorded four attempted meetings with Wordsworth in July (14, 29) and August (15, 18). Only the first of these was successful, but that one visit may be significant, for it was the day after the *Philanthropist*'s last safely liberal appearance: its radical phase began with no. 17 on 20 July. By 18 August, Wordsworth had left London for Bristol. The cooling of relations between Godwin and Wordsworth at this time could be explained by the *Philanthropist*'s leftward lurch and misunderstandings as to who was responsible for it.

In the *Philanthropist*'s early essays there are several resemblances and parallels to Wordsworth's other writings and experiences – though we should keep in mind that little of his prose would have been published without considerable editing.[28] The four essays that filled the first four issues are the most likely to have been contributed by Wordsworth and Mathews. These essays are wholly Godwinian in temper and tendency, commiserating the state of the poor, deploring the frustrations of talent dependent upon patronage, and generally manifesting the Whig interpretation of English history. But it is in the third number, where the *Philanthropist* turns with an almost comically literal tone of regret 'from his original plan and intention' to current events, that we discern language close to Wordsworth's policies for his proposed journal.

'It was the intention of the Philanthropist to have proceeded in a regular discussion of *those subjects*, which involve in their consideration the rights, and happiness, of man, and not to have engaged the attention of the public with the political concerns of the day, till he had *enforced*, and inculcated some truths of a very pressing, and important nature' (3.1). This, stating the reverse of what the writer would really prefer to do, uses the same language for the 'duty' of such a journal that Wordsworth had used with Mathews the previous summer: 'There is a further duty incumbent upon every enlightened friend of mankind; he should let slip no opportunity of explaining and *enforcing those general principles* of the social order which are applicable to all times and to all places.'[29] Wordsworth's statement comes in the middle of his critique of the ministry's lack of 'oeconomy in the administration of the public purse . . . abuses which, if left to themselves, may grow to such a height as to render, even a revolution desirable.' The next issue of the *Philanthropist* returns to exactly that point, telling the King's ministers that if they do not merit the public trust by keeping 'the administration of public affairs just, pure, and uncontaminated,' they had better warn their royal master about his throne's security: 'AS IT WAS WON TO HIM BY ONE REVOLUTION, HE MAY LOSE IT BY ANOTHER' (4.7).

The *Philanthropist*'s first essay, on talent, deserves closest scrutiny, for it is the use and nature of talent, and its differentiation from the greater quality of genius, that forms the leitmotif of Wordsworth's writings throughout the 1790s. Points of contact and congruence between this essay and Wordsworth are abundant. It turns on the rhetorical pivot that the world's neglect of talent is paralleled by society's neglect of suffering humanity. It asks why God gave man talent, and answers: 'to inspire him with a sense of the dignity which he sustained in the creation, to teach him the duties which were due to him from his God, to himself, and to his species, and thus, by awakening within him all those benevolent sympathies . . . which animate to [*sic*] philanthropy . . . to bind him to his fellow-creatures in social charities, and in endearing intercourse' (1.1–2). This perfectly Godwinian thesis is launched off from the antithesis that talent should not be coerced, impeded, or 'its radiance . . . obscured in darkness.' Such motives are not attributed to anyone in particular, but were likely to have been perceived as a general condition by liberal young gentlemen in 1795, especially that one who had enthusiastically thrown himself into London's 'mighty gulph which has swallowed up so many, of talents and attainments infinitely superior to my own.' The implicit subtext of the *Philanthropist's* first essay is: 'If only I could be great, humanity could be too.' It is no disservice to *The Prelude* to say that its subtext is the same.

Wordsworth was a keen connoisseur of talent, his own and others': 'It is an observation to whose truth I have long since consented that small certainties are the bane of great talents.' There are few topics to which he adverts more frequently in the mid-1790s. We hear him saying to Mathews, obviously projecting his own self-image: 'you . . . are furnished with talents and acquirements which if properly made use of will enable you to get your bread . . . you have the happiness of being born in a free country, where every road is open, where talents and industry are . . . liberally rewarded' (19 May 1792). The free exertion of one's talents was a highly political issue throughout the late eighteenth century, as an old order based on patronage was breaking up in favour of – to use Napoleon's exemplary formula for it – 'the career open to talent.'

The *Philanthropist* tries to establish a connection between natural beauty and moral beauty, which Wordsworth pursued in almost all his poetry between 1793 and 1798. But the *Philanthropist* is no more successful than Wordsworth, except to assert the talented individual's *wish* to do good. Like Wordsworth, the *Philanthropist* locates the real tragedy of poverty in its subjective mental effects, 'the tyrannies which have been exercised over the human mind itself.'

> What a gloomy picture . . . is presented to us of the human mind!—We behold the understanding, the genius and the intellect of man prostrated, as it were, before the shrine of the most abominable idols! We behold every faculty of the soul enchained, its best powers either totally annihilated, or perverted to promote the most despicable views of power, rapacity, and ambition! (1.2)

Reading this gloomy history, the writer knows not whether he 'ought the more to commiserate the fortune of a people depressed and enslaved . . . or to execrate the remorseless authors of their afflictions, their sufferings, and their persecutions!' In his lines on the Female Vagrant Wordsworth had already begun exploring the mental perversions caused by poverty. She, 'robb'd of [her] perfect mind,' says her tale 'would thy brain unsettle even to hear.' Her worst suffering is the same as that envisioned in the first *Philanthropist* essay: 'what afflicts my peace with keenest ruth / Is, that I have my inner self abused, / Forgone the home delight of constant truth / And clear and open soul, so prized in fearless youth' (258–61).

A connection between the *Philanthropist*'s attack on the profligate luxury of the upper classes and Wordsworth's later attack on the gaudy splendour of poetic diction is plausible in light of the very special reasons the first essay gives for the failure of the English rich to appreciate the condition of the English poor: 'They read of the afflictions of their fellow-creatures, as they would amuse themselves with a tale or a romance, and they pity the unfriended child of want, perishing for a morsel of bread, as they would pity the desponding and lovelorn hero of the piece, or the unfortunate virgin confined by necromancy in some enchanted castle' (1.6). This is incisive literary criticism in the service of strong social criticism. The larger point, peculiar to what Wordsworth will argue later, is not merely that the rich regard the sufferings of the poor like something in a book, but that they do not understand its significance because they 'read' it like a *bad* book: steeped in vapid tales of Sensibility or escapist Gothic novels, they fail to see the reality around them. It is but a small step in content, though a large one in sophisticated context, from this argument to Wordsworth's lament in the 1800 preface that 'the invaluable works' of Shakespeare and Milton 'are driven into neglect by frantic novels, sickly and stupid German tragedies, and deluges of idle and extravagant stories in verse,' and thence to his suggestive assertion that a 'healthy or depraved . . . public taste' affects 'the revolutions not of literature alone but likewise of society itself' because of the manner in which 'language and the human mind act and react on each other.'

In contrast to those who read about poverty as an item in romance, the *Philanthropist*, like Wordsworth more or less continuously since 1791, has gone out to see for himself: 'The children of fortune and of affluence, have seldom leisure or inclination *to contemplate so melancholy a picture . . . .* But there are some hearts made to sympathize with those that suffer. To some minds it is a *pleasing, though melancholy office*, to leave the sunshine of prosperity, to view awhile amid the gloom of hard necessity and want, the scene of wretchedness in which thousands of their race are engaged' (1.6–7; italics added). This is very close to Wordsworth's statement, that 'the sorrow I feel from *the contemplation of this melancholy picture is not unconsoled by a comfortable hope* that the class of wretches called mendicants will not much longer shock the feelings of humanity' (*Llandaff*, 460–63; italics added).

Finally, coming full circle on its central theme, the link between the terrible mental pains of poverty and the suffering endured by talented minds who would justify their gifts by service to mankind, the *Philanthropist*'s first essay concludes with a poem, 'Address to Poverty.' The quality of the verse is not much below that of the 'Address to the Ocean' and the 'Address to Silence' he wrote in the coming year, and is somewhat above that of the framing narratives in the Salisbury Plain poem of 1793–95, which also concentrate on the mental effect of unwarranted suffering, in ways and words that have close parallels in the *Philanthropist*.

This 'Address' is structured around a long introductory afflatus telling a personified figure of Poverty what ''tis not' in its reign that causes the speaker to mourn: not looks of anguish, famished limbs, nor even 'that voice, whose melancholy tale / Might turn the purple cheek of grandeur pale.' Halfway through, it comes to the point of Poverty's real evil: 'But chief, relentless Power, thy hard controul, / *That to the earth bends low* the aspiring soul, / Thine iron grasp, thy fetters drear, which bind / *Each generous effort of the struggling mind!*' This is close in theme, image, and rhyme to one of Wordsworth's perorations in the 'Salisbury Plain' lines of 1793–94, similarly addressed to a personified abstraction, 'Oppression': 'How many by inhuman toil debased, / Abject, obscure, *and brute to earth incline* / Unrespited, forlorn of *every spark divine?*' (*SP*, 439–41; italics added.) As these excerpts make clear, there is little if anything to distinguish between Wordsworth's poem and the *Philanthropist*'s on the basis of artistic quality.

It may be objected that most of this, prose and poetry alike, does not sound much like Wordsworth's style, however close it may be to his literary and political concerns. Indeed it does not: compared to the turgid 'Letter to Llandaff,' the *Philanthropist's* first essays are much clearer and more to the point, though their strident exclamations sometimes are less effective than Wordsworth's sardonic brooding. However, the difficulty of proving Wordsworth's authorship, or partial authorship, of these and other parts of the *Philanthropist* is part and parcel of the hypothesis which makes his involvement in the enterprise plausible. Proving it requires that we abandon the convenient fiction of single, or even unitary, authorship. Wordsworth was certainly not a consistent sum of political opinions and literary options in 1795 (if he ever was), and neither was the *Philanthropist*.

When it resumed publication on 27 April, the *Philanthropist* introduced verse, the sort of 'trash' that Wordsworth hoped to avoid. Did they abandon this decidedly conservative editorial policy and try to control the journal's productions in this department by using their own compositions? The sonnet from 'Sylvanus Amicus' in no. 7 suggests as much. Its pseudonym, some of its lines, and even its verb tenses point toward the Wordsworth of later reputation:

> Who but must feel his indignation strong,
> On Nature's honest, broad, and gen'ral plan,
> Against that head, that heart, that hand, that tongue,
> Which makes mankind a foe to fellow-man?
>
> (7.8; lines 5–8)

Compare:

> If I these thoughts may not prevent,
> If such be of my creed the plan,
> Have I not reason to lament
> What man has made of man?
>
> ('Lines written in early Spring,' lines 21–24)

The connection between apparent design in nature and its obvious frustration in society was a commonplace in eighteenth-century sentimental morality. Thelwall has been suggested as a more likely author for these lines, another incarnation of the 'Sylvanus Theophrastus' of his own earlier journal, *The Peripatetic*. The resonant last line, a sentiment as old as human history, had also recently appeared in the epigraph to Godwin's bestselling 1794 novel, *Things As They Are*: 'Amidst the woods the leopard knows his kind; / The tyger preys not on the tyger brood: / Man only is the common foe of man.' Any combination of these possibilities links Wordsworth closer to these writers and their politics than many of his admirers would like to have him, and one of them puts him squarely among those trying to publish – and maintain control of – the *Philanthropist*.

Wordsworth departed from Godwin's neighbourhood in Chalton Street at the end of April; the move also marked a change in his friendship with Mathews. He did not move back in with Mathews at the Middle Temple, but returned to the Inns of Court and began moving with other friends. Wordsworth took up lodgings with Basil Montagu at Lincoln's Inn: another Cambridge contemporary. Montagu was also now regularly exchanging visits with Godwin.[30] He was the acknowledged illegitimate son of the fourth Earl of Sandwich, his mother the society singer, Martha Ray, who had been shot to death outside Covent Garden in 1779 by an estranged lover, the Reverend James Hackman,[31] one of the great scandals of the era. Wordsworth rather tactlessly used her name for the distraught mother in 'The Thorn' who has murdered her child, but much of his early association with Montagu did involve questions about the right and wrong way to raise children. Montagu had married against his father's wishes and found himself disinherited on his father's death in 1792, his young wife died from childbirth complications in early 1793, and he was at this time beginning with difficulty work as a lawyer while taking care of his son, Basil Caroline, named after his parents. Wordsworth's interest was piqued by a boy-child named Caroline whose birthdate was 27 December 1792, two weeks after 'Caroline Williams' (the surname adopted by Annette), and his sympathy naturally went out to a young father whose elders had, like Wordsworth's, been willing to ruin his prospects because they disapproved of his marriage. That he should give Montagu's natural mother's name to the unwed infanticide mother of 'The Thorn' strongly suggests a deep psychological empathy with Montagu's situation.

Montagu's own habits were those of a dissolute and irregular young aristocrat, and in his unpublished autobiography he gave credit to Wordsworth's slow steadiness and apparent maturity for saving him from ruin. 'He saw me . . . perplexed and misled by passions wild and strong. In the wreck of my happiness he saw the probable ruin of my infant. He unremittingly . . . endeavoured to eradicate my faults and encourage my good dispositions.'[32] Montagu was also chronically in need of money, and was now in the habit of borrowing money from the wealthy pupils he tutored. In a gesture at once calculated, generous, and ill-considered, Wordsworth agreed to lend £500 from the Calvert bequest, as soon as he received it, to Montagu at ten per cent interest, and later another £200 to Montagu's 'opulent' friend Charles Douglas at the same rate. This was far above the three to five per cent rate prevailing in bank interest and the consol funds; two years later, when the arrangement began to go bad, one of Wordsworth's first concerns was that he might be liable to prosecution for usury for charging such rates.[33] But his desire for larger gain or his sympathy with Montagu's situation led him into error, for Montagu was soon arrears in his payments, and eventually the whole schedule was disrupted for several years, no interest being paid until about 1800. Thus Wordsworth's precious capital was tied up in ways that again prevented his independence and freedom of movement, and forced him back to borrowing advances from his brother Richard.[34]

Through Montagu, Wordsworth became friends with Francis Wrangham, whom he also knew from the university. For three years after graduation, Wrangham and Montagu had taken in students cramming for the university exams, specializing in the sons of West Indian planters. But in 1793 Wrangham lost an expected fellowship at Trinity Hall because of his sympathy with the French Revolution.[35] At the time he was introduced to Wordsworth, he had just taken a curacy in Surrey, another victim, like William Frend, of the establishment's crackdown on its intellectual opponents. Wrangham had been forced into parish ministry because his French sympathies derailed his plans for a university career; this was similar to Wordsworth's unsteady career path: first avoiding the ministry, then seeking it out, only to be refused when he most needed it, because of his French sympathies. So he and Wrangham met as kindred spirits and fellow sufferers.

One of the closest verbal echoes between the *Philanthropist* and Wordsworth's writings may owe something to his new association with Wrangham. It occurred on 31 August, in no. 23, about two weeks after Wordsworth had left town, in the 'Lines, Addressed to the Editor of the *Philanthropist*, on contrasting it with the general History of this Country, and the Writers of the present Day in particular.' This highly self-conscious piece of literary reflection is by 'Clericus,' who may well have been the Reverend Francis Wrangham. It scorns the government's policies of warfare abroad and repression at home:

> But, Ah! such scenes [of bloody history] delight the men alone,
> Who void of love to man, and fond of war,
> Made dupes by Princes to support the throne,
> That rules by rapine and continual jar,
> *For what can War but endless War still breed,*
> Till truth and right from violence be freed.

The sentiments, and the last two lines, match those from a concluding stanza of Wordsworth's 'Salisbury Plain,' the poem he had brought with him to London, ready to publish if he could realize a sufficient profit from it:

> How weak the solace such fond thoughts afford,
> When with untimely stroke the virtuous bleed.
> Say, rulers of the nations, from the sword
> Can ought but murder, pain, and tears proceed?
> *Oh! what can war but endless war still breed!*
> (505–09)

The identical lines have a common source, Milton's sonnet 'On the Lord. Gen. Fairfax at the Siege of Colchester' (l. 10).[36] But this does not rule out a connection, for Wordsworth had read his Salisbury Plain poem to Wrangham while in London, and Wrangham remembered it well.[37] The epigrammatic quality of the line (not unlike the alliterative bounce of 'what man has made of man') may have been the reason it stuck in his mind – presuming that Wrangham was 'Clericus.' Milton's sonnet's last lines ('In vain doth Valour bleed / While Avarice, and Rapine share the land') also anticipate Wordsworth's indictment of Pitt's policies: 'Insensate they who think at Wisdom's porch / That Exile, Terror, Bonds, and Force may stand: / That Truth with human blood can feed her torch' (514–16). And the passage from the *Philanthropist* develops Milton's idea in the same way: 'Till truth and right from violence be freed. / The philanthropic mind forbears to tell / The carnage, death and slaughter that attend / Contending armies.'

Wordsworth and Wrangham launched almost immediately into a joint project, updating Juvenal's eighth satire on corrupt noblemen. Like Wordsworth's plans with Mathews for the *Philanthropist*, the Juvenal project shows again how well disposed he was toward co-operative ventures on politically volatile subjects. They continued to work on the project over the next two years, but it was a brain-child of the year 1795, and closely related to Wordsworth's involvement with the *Philanthropist*. A complete, continuous version of Wordsworth's and Wrangham's imitation of Juvenal has only now appeared, some two hundred years after they began it, strong testimony to Wordsworth's success at erasing unwanted items from the curriculum vitae of his radical youth.[38]

The light this text shines on Wordsworth's biography is narrow but intense. It is a scathing criticism of the morals of the upper classes, not excluding the royal princes and the King and Queen themselves. If published, and its authors identified, its effect on Wordsworth's reputation would have been almost as bad as if he had published his letter to the Bishop of Llandaff. Wordsworth's nervousness lest Wrangham publish it (in 1806, when he had considerably more to lose) shows that he knew it would be regarded as more than a classical exercise.

Their choice of Satire VIII is noteworthy. Satire VII, on poets, teachers, and poverty, or IX, on the griefs of career men, would have been much closer to their own interests and situations at the time. By choosing VIII, which is addressed to a young Roman nobleman setting out to govern a remote province of the empire, Wordsworth and Wrangham suggest that their satire has an addressee, who is sometimes treated as a target, or at least as someone who should know better, but who on other occasions is regarded as a potential patron. This nobleman was Charles Howard, the eleventh Duke of Norfolk (1746–1815), who was William Calvert's patron and a trustee of Raisley Calvert's estate. Norfolk is addressed in company with the other leading northern peer, Hugh Percy, the second Duke of Northumberland (1742–1817), who was John Robinson's patron and neighbour at Syon House outside London, close to Wrangham's rectory at Cobham. In short, they picked as their putative heroes two men closely connected with persons who had actively sought to help Wordsworth in his confused movements toward a vocation since leaving university. An attack on Norfolk was a bit like biting the hand that fed him, if he had thought of Calvert. But Norfolk's politics were dead set against those of the other northern lord in the poem, James Lowther, Earl of Lonsdale. Toward Lowther, as we might expect, the poem shows no mercy, nor any hope of his return to virtue:

> Must honour still to Lonsdale's tail be bound?
> Then execration is an empty sound.[39]

Wordsworth's habit of attacking authority figures who were in a position to help him suggest a young man who was harder on his friends – or symbolic father-figures – than on his natural enemies.

A secondary theme in their argument against unworthy nobles, also present in Juvenal, is the neglect of low-born worth, which Wrangham and Wordsworth took up with alacrity. The truly noble are the truly virtuous: Juvenal's words are 'nobilitas sola est atque unica virtus'; the poem gives '"The virtuous only are of noble kind"'; the Howards' motto is 'Sola virtus invicta.' These lines are probably by Wrangham, but they seem to be addressed to someone *else* from the north of England, other than Howard or Percy. Wordsworth's segment of the translation pursues this implication into a direct comparison between the speaker's virtues and Percy's, without consideration of rank:

> Were such your servant, Percy! (be it tried
> Between ourselves! the noble laid aside)
> Now would you be content with bare release
> From such a desperate breaker of the peace?
> Your friend the country Justice scarce would fail
> To give a hint of whips and the cart's tail.

The reference to the 'breaker of the peace' might be the Duke of York, or it might be an unidentified 'stripling' who has faults to atone for that resemble the young Wordsworth's: the punishments described are those parish authorities could mete out for adultery or for refusing to acknowledge and support illegitimate children. And John Robinson, Percy's friend and neighbour, had been a country justice in Westmorland.

The eighth issue of the *Philanthropist* includes a 'Satire on Modern Clergymen' that is so close in spirit, form and content to Wordsworth's imitations of Juvenal (e.g., the common attack on corrupt bishops like Richard Watson) that only the most knowledgeable specialists are likely to be able to say which of the following excerpts is from the *Philanthropist* and which from Wordsworth:

> Is Common-sense asleep? has she no wand
> From this curst Pharaoh-plague to rid the land?
> Then to our bishops *reverent* let us fall,
> *Worship* Mayors, Tipstaffs, Aldermen and all.
> Let Ignorance o'er monstrous swarms preside
> Till Egypt see her ancient fame outvied.
> The thundering Thurlow, Apis! shall rejoice
> In rites once offered to thy bellowing voice.
> Insatiate Charlotte's tears and Charlotte's smile

Shall ape the scaly regent of the Nile.
Bishops, of milder Spaniel breed, shall boast
The reverence by the fierce Anubis lost.

So sing the Bishops, when they fast and pray;
That is, in language each may understand,
When Fast-Day Sermons darken all the land.
Unnumbered glories shine around the Bench,
Where sleep the Bishops, fearless of the French;
Ten thousand sylphs and gnomes around them stay,
And—wanton, in their wigs and cassocks play;
The guards of those who sweet Religion guard
Against her countless foes, who press so hard
Upon her life; such are the noble band;
Such men, Church-Militant, the times demand.
In Egypt once, 'tis said in holy writ,
A crowd of locusts came; and there, (to wit),
Destroy'd some corn which flourish'd on the soil . . .

In fact, the first excerpt is Wordsworth's, but the secret agents of the Duke of Portland would not have made nice discriminations between them; both are equally suspicious. If Wordsworth's Juvenal imitations had been published, it would have given ample warrant for keeping an eye on him, and the *Philanthropist* satire is by 'Clericus,' who *may* be Wrangham. The satire of 'Clericus' is modelled on Pope's neo-classical *Rape of the Lock*, a piece of literary sophistication very much on the order of Wordsworth's and Wrangham's adaptation of a classical model for their joint project. The metaphor from Exodus of a plague of locusts to describe contemporary ecclesiastical and political abuses is present in neither Pope nor Juvenal, but is common to both 'Clericus' and Wordsworth.

Wordsworth contributed mostly elaborations of contemporary London scenes he had seen that spring and summer. He sketched vignettes of noblemen's regattas on the Thames, extraordinarily expensive events which the public loved to watch and wager on: 'The cry is six to one upon the Duke' [of Manchester]! He also pointed out, like a society gossip columnist, the Prince of Wales 'wedged in with blacklegs at a boxer's show / To shout with transport o'er a knock-down blow.' The nobility are consistently shown to be encouraging public vice, rather than behaving nobly.

But the two or three most specific glimpses of Wordsworth, or of a *persona* in the poem very like him, are outside the main lines of satiric crossfire, and all are new additions to or significant variations of Juvenal's text. In transition from unrelieved invective, an older voice responds to the broad-brush attacks of the first half of the poem by counselling sympathetic moderation. 'An apologist will say to me, "We too did the same as boys." '[40] But whereas Juvenal cites drinking and whoring, Wordsworth's lines turn strangely inward to other kinds of sin, or shame:

> But whence this gall, this lengthened face of woe?
> We were no saints at twenty, —be it so;
> Yet happy they who in life's [later] scene
> Need only blush for what they once have been,
> Who pushed by thoughtless youth to deeds of shame
> 'Mid such bad daring sought a coward's name.

(146–51)

This is an entirely different order of remorse than Juvenal's crude attack on grog shops and male prostitutes. It goes beyond the Latin text to think, obscurely, about those who are *not* so 'happy,' fixing on youthful indiscretions that will *always* be a cause for shame. 'Thoughtless youth' may be the generic condition of being young, used as special pleading to explain what 'pushed' someone in his early twenties to 'deeds of shame' – deeds which he dared to do, but then turned cowardly toward. Or, 'thoughtless youth' may be some specific young men who pushed someone (who is now 'happy' because he only has to blush for 'what [he] once [had] been') to 'deeds of shame' that he refused, preferring to be called a coward rather than accept such 'bad daring.' This could refer to Wordsworth's work on the *Philanthropist*, or, in light of its editorial history, to some escalation of its provocations that he refused to participate in. Or it could refer to something much worse: 'deeds of shame' is a strong phrase, in Wordsworth's mouth. But whatever the precise reference, since Wordsworth is adding his own language to Juvenal's here, the chances are great that he was writing about something he knew personally.

Among contemporary aristocratic vices that Wordsworth catalogued were illegal faro tables, most notoriously those run by the Earl and Countess of Buckingham at their townhouse. But Wordsworth shunts his attack aside toward something else, which is nowhere in Juvenal. He asks why the police and magistrates do not sniff out this kind of corruption instead of expending their efforts on smaller fry:

> . . . is no informer there [among the rich],
> Or is the painted staff's avenging host
> By sixpenny sedition shops engrossed
> Or rather skulking for the common weal
> Round fire-side treason parties en famille[?]

(179–83)*

Cheap seditious publications and intimate conversations that might be

---

* The 'painted staff' was the mace of office carried by the night-watch patrol in each parish of the city.

deemed treasonous are precisely the two kinds of activities with which we can most closely associate Wordsworth at the time. Daniel Eaton's shop at the Cock and Swine was one such 'sixpenny sedition shop,' where the *Philanthropist* was published, and the meeting at Freud's of radical writers could certainly be construed as a 'fire-side treason party.' A further implication of the lines, in light of his earlier reference to 'bad daring' and 'a coward's name,' is the suggestion that he *knew* of an 'informer . . . skulking' round such gatherings. An entry in Portland's private account book records a payment of £200 on 9 May to George Dyer; Dyer's legendary naïveté may have made him an unwitting pawn – or a highly effective operative – in such machinations.[41]

There is one last tantalizing glimpse of these shadowy London scenes in a nearly illegible text brilliantly recovered recently by Carol Landon and Jared Curtis from one of Wordsworth's manuscript jottings on the Juvenal project:

> These equal liberties [?] [? ?] [?]ing
> One s[?] one gin glass and one broken ring
> Mid beggars   specious [?packs]
> And bowstreet runners [?powerless] on their back
> It[42]

Like a smudged fingerprint on a murder weapon, this little piece of *imagism* teases us to reconstruct the scene, the crime, and the victim. All we can see for sure are a political topic, a pub in a poor neighbourhood, and police officers or undercover agents. Is it about the government's infiltration of 'fire-side treason parties'? The convivial scene and the police are common to both passages. Or is it about the easy recruiting, or suborning, of informers? 'One broken ring' could refer to a secret cadre or cell meeting broken up. We have beggars with false wares – or false beggars – and Bow Street runners either on the backs of their victims or perhaps flipped over on their own backs and rendered powerless like noxious insects. It all smacks of sordid betrayals: not the stirring, broad vision of Liberty which Wordsworth sketched out in his letters to Mathews, but one he evidently saw, in dangerous company and dangerous circumstances, in London 1795.

Finally, this 'Pharoah plague' of corruption spreads over the whole land, and the poem falls into fawningly sarcastic cynicism: 'Then to our bishops *reverent* let us fall / *Worship* Mayors, Tipstaffs, Aldermen and all.'* Placed at the end of the poem, they sound like exit lines. Their penultimate thrust is a sneer at tractable 'Bishops, of milder Spaniel breed,' who for Wordsworth would include the Bishop of Llandaff.

---

* A tipstaff was the constable or bailiff in court, or the head officer carrying the nightwatch's painted staff.

The final couplet is exactly contemporaneous. Corruption has gone on so long it has become general, 'things as they are':

> . . . devotion has been paid
> These seven long years to Grenville's onion head

Wordsworth was not sure how long William Wyndham, Baron Grenville, Pitt's cousin and Foreign Secretary, had 'enjoyed the honour of the peerage . . . five six or seven, I do not know.'[43] In fact it was five years since Wyndham had been given the title in 1790. But Wordsworth knew exactly why he closed the poem on this reference. The King's coach was mobbed in Hyde Park on its way to the opening of Parliament on 29 October, to cries of 'No War! No Pitt! No King! Peace! Bread!' Sticks and stones were thrown at the carriage, breaking two of its large glass panels; the King thought he had been shot at. A man in a green coat leapt on the carriage and tried to drag the King out, before troops galloped up.[44] One of the men leading the carriage back to the stable was trampled to death, and the carriage badly damaged. When the King attended Covent Garden next night there was a riot, with much hooting at the Duke of Portland, the well-known head of the Home Office's secret police. This all looked very near to insurrection, and the government no longer hesitated to implement the plans it had been preparing all year. On 6 November, Grenville introduced the Treasonable Practices Bill; his cousin the prime minister proposed the Seditious Meetings Bill four days later. These were the two Acts which, known as the 'Gagging Acts,' were pushed through parliament by large majorities despite huge public protest gatherings estimated at 150,000 persons. They made it possible for written and spoken *language*, as well as overt actions, to be defined as treason. Wordsworth sent these explicit and graphic lines (none of them in Juvenal) to Wrangham ten days later. By this time he had already left London, but his sudden departure in mid-August was taken with a keen awareness of what might be in store for those who exerted themselves too energetically 'on an opposition newspaper.'

Basil Montagu was also the occasion of Wordsworth's meeting John and Azariah Pinney.[45] He steered Wordsworth their way as a source of income that might substitute for the debts he himself was failing to pay them. John, the elder, was studying law at Lincoln's Inn, and Azariah had been Wrangham's pupil at Cobham.[46] They were the sons of John Pinney Sr, one of the Caribbean 'sugar kings', who owned the largest plantation on the island of Nevis. In the spirit of the times which Hazlitt, thinking in part of this very transaction, characterized as 'not a time when *nothing was given for nothing* [but] the mind opened, and a softness [came] over the heart of individuals,' the Pinney brothers offered Wordsworth their country house, Racedown in Dorset, rent free, as soon as they learned of his situation.

Things had begun to go wrong with the *Philanthropist* in mid-July, and Wordsworth was as eager to leave London as he had been ready to 'throw' himself into it six months earlier. As the government's intentions with regard to internal surveillance and provocation became clearer, the leadership of the radical reform movement began to look to the provinces for safety. Wordsworth was ready to re-establish the housekeeping relationship he had had with Dorothy at Windy Brow the year before, and here was another rent-free situation which provided it. Dorothy's skill with children and Montagu's obvious need in this area came naturally together: William and Dorothy would provide room, board, and tutelage for Basil junior at the Pinneys' house – for an additional £50 pounds per year. This, along with the expected repayments from Montagu, made an attractive package. But the political situation in London made it all the more compelling.

Mary Moorman says 'the alacrity with which Wordsworth accepted the offer of Racedown shows that he had not found it possible to live permanently in London,' but does not say why, except to imply the usual mythology that as a nature lover he could not stand the city, and to conjecture that 'nothing apparently had come of the plan of joining the staff of a newspaper.'[47] But the *Philanthropist* hypothesis provides us with reasons that are real reasons. They were, from Wordsworth's point of view, very compelling. He had certainly not arrived in London as a nature lover and city hater, but quite the opposite ('cataracts and mountains, are good occasional society, but they will not do for constant companions'). The experience of London in 1795 marks his first, and fundamental, revisal of this estimate.

But how can all of this have gone undetected so long, if it really is the case? For one thing, we should recall Wordsworth's success in keeping secret all knowledge of his other youthful indiscretion, with Annette Vallon, until long after all the principals were dead. William Mathews's family would later recall that he was 'remembered by a numerous list of his early associates, men of first-rate talent; amongst who may be mentioned Mr Wordsworth, who was his most intimate friend and correspondent.'[48] They probably knew no more of the contents of his correspondence with Wordsworth than Dorothy and Richard did, which was clearly very little. Given what we know of his activities and associates in London, there is plenty of reason to regard Wordsworth's removal to Racedown as something on the order of flight to a safe house.

But such secrets, if they are secrets, are never really hidden. Rather, like Poe's purloined letter, they are already in front of our eyes, could we but recognize them. If we look to *The Prelude* for information about this aspect of Wordsworth's months in London we do not find much that is definite, since we are dealing with events which he was eager to cover over. However, there are places in *The Prelude* which connect to the *Philanthropist* scenario.

The place to look is in Book X: between Wordsworth's account of hearing the news of Robespierre's death as he crossed Leven Sands in early August 1794, and his departure from London in mid-August, 1795 (567–904). His attachment to Godwinism is easy to document, as 'the philosophy / That promised to extract the hopes of man / Out of his feelings' (806–08). His reference to France's changing 'a war of self-defence / For one of conquest' (792–93) refers to General Pichegru's conquest of the Netherlands in late 1794. But, when 'events' could no longer be trusted to provide 'the immediate proof of principles,' he did what many liberals tried to do in 1795:

> . . . rouzed up, I stuck
> More firmly to old tenets, and, to prove
> Their temper, strained them more; *and thus, in heat*
> *Of contest, did opinions every day*
> *Grow into consequence*, till round my mind
> They clung as if they were the life of it.
>
> (X.799–804)

If we refuse these lines' invitation to keep us wholly in Wordsworth's mental theatre, and try to get out into the fervid atmosphere of London in summer 1795, a phrase like 'heat of contest' provides an exit: it gives a glimpse of Wordsworth arguing with someone other than himself, the kind of situation obtaining for his participation in the *Philanthropist*. He is clearly talking about London when he recalls how 'the street-disturbing Newsman's horn' gave hopes to those who wished to hear of French defeats. But, 'with my ardent Comrades,' he laughed at the foolishness of 'men clinging to delusions so insane.'[49] This indicates that his later statement, 'I was an active partisan' (736), means that he was a partisan active among others of the same persuasion.

This leads to his summary of moral crisis at the heart of *The Prelude* (X.878–904), which may well have occurred at about the same time the *Philanthropist* was undergoing its crisis of identity in July and August. He says he 'was betrayed / By present objects, and by reasonings false / From the beginning.' But it was a mutual process, not one that he suffered alone, for as he was 'confounded more and more,' he was *both* 'misguid*ing*' and 'misguid*ed*' (883–888, *passim.*). He was leading others astray even as he was being led astray. The depth of this crisis, by its placement in *The Prelude*, becomes the fulcrum on which the plot and eventual happy ending of the entire poem turn.

> Time may come
> When some dramatic story may afford
> Shapes livelier to convey to thee, my friend,
> What then I learned—or think I learned—of truth,

And the errors into which I was betrayed
By present objects, and by reasonings false . . .
. . . .
Misguiding and misguided. Thus I fared,
Dragging all passions, notions, shapes of faith,
Like culprits to the bar, suspiciously
Calling the mind to establish in plain day
Her titles and her honours, now believing,
Now disbelieving, endlessly perplexed
With impulse, motive, right and wrong, the ground
Of moral obligation—what the rule,
And what the sanction—till, demanding proof,
And seeking it in every thing, I lost
All feeling of conviction, and, in fine,
Sick, wearied out with contrarities,
Yielded up moral questions in despair . . .
. . . .

    Ah, then it was
That thou, most precious friend, about this time
First known to me, didst lend a living help
To regulate my soul. And then it was
That the beloved woman in whose sight
Those days were passed . . .
. . . .
Maintained for me a saving intercourse
With my true self . . . .

(X.878–915)

Formally, *The Prelude* breaks down at this point, and it swerves without explanation to an entirely different set of terms, places, and persons: from excessive rationality to overflowing love, from a debating hall (or magistrate's court) to the countryside, from London to Dorset, and from his own mind to the hearts of Coleridge and Dorothy. The text itself opens up the gap it must leap over, in the paragraph break. But what it describes, referentially, is what actually happened: Wordsworth left town. The crisis of London, 1795, is thus the crisis that initiates the drama of *The Prelude*, the plot it must resolve in order to reach its conclusion.

Rationalistic argument could no longer provide Wordsworth with a personally persuasive motive for action; instead, he fell back on something spontaneously given, not as the solution to his problem, but as his escape from it: Nature. Here, it means gratitude for his sister's unquestioning love. This is not simply a sentimental generalization but specifically pointed advice: she gave him a 'sudden admonition,' warning him away from certain social definitions of his 'true self' to 'preserve me still / A poet, made me seek beneath that name / *My office* upon earth, and nowhere else': not, as he had tried to be in London, a journalist, an essayist, a political activist, or a moral philosopher.

The passage begins with a hint that fuller revelations might be forthcoming: 'Time may come / When some dramatic story may afford / Shapes livelier to convey . . . what then I learned—or think I learned.' Did this time ever come? The reference is usually taken to be to what became Books III and IV of *The Excursion*.[50] In the character of the Solitary, ostensibly based on Joseph Fawcett, Wordsworth gives details of emotions so intimate that they must arise from something very close to direct personal experience:

> . . . he forfeited
> All joy in human nature; was consumed
> And vexed, and chafed, by levity and scorn,
> And fruitless indignation; galled by pride;
> *Made desperate by contempt of men who throve*
> *Before his sight in power or fame, and won,*
> *Without desert, what he desired . . .*
>
> (II.296–302; italics added)

> *Among men*
> *So charactered did I maintain a strife*
> *Hopeless,* and still more hopeless every hour . . .
> —In Britain, ruled a panic dread of change;
> The weak were praised, rewarded, and advanced;
> And, from *an impulse of a just disdain,*
> *Once more did I retire into myself.*
>
> (III.770–74, 787–89, 827–30; italics added)[51]

Academic readers have often failed, when studying Wordsworth's statements of disaffection with city life and politics in the mid-1790s, to note how heavily they are loaded with the language of wounded self-esteem and personal affront, of frustrated ambition, and a feeling of having been beaten, perhaps unfairly, in some kind of intensely competitive effort. But these are just the kind of emotions he would have had as a young writer, launched percipitously into the 'mighty gulph. . . of talents and attainments infinitely superior to my own,' and forced to work along with other highly promising young men in an enterprise of his own devising but soon taken beyond his control.

Several of his London friends also suffered near-breakdowns at this time, further suggesting that these young men had got involved in something in 1795 that they could not control, with traumatic results. Typical was John Tweddell who suffered the effects of a mysterious 'event' which he described as the wreck of hopes 'madly conceived and cruelly frustrated.' This led him to quit London abruptly on 24 September, for Hamburg, just a month after Wordsworth's departure for Racedown. It could have been a romantic disappointment, but it has also been associated with Tweddell's infatuation with Godwin. Tweddell also recovered soon, travelling through Germany to Russia and eventually to Greece, where he died suddenly of a fever in 1799. At the time of his death, Tweddell was looking forward to returning to England, refreshed and restored, and his anticipation of his return sounds very 'Wordsworthian', as we would now say. He longed to leave the world and its crowd, and 'in the midst of the fields, in the heart of some retreat . . . confine myself to the sweet joys of nature, to the innocent pleasures of the study, and to the exercise of the domestic affections.' This is precisely the condition for which Coleridge in 1798 would urge Wordsworth to write *The Recluse* as an antidote: 'I wish you would write a poem [reviving the spirits of those who], in consequence of the complete failure of the French Revolution have thrown up all hopes of amelioration and given themselves over to [solitude] and the cultivation of the domestic affections.' That is, *The Recluse* should address the condition of their entire generation.

Nor, in this rash of nervous disorders that broke out in Wordsworth's London circle at this time, should we forget William Mathews, who soon found himself dropped from Wordsworth's acquaintance. Always a melancholy character, Mathews described himself as having been 'for several years . . . a disappointed man,' when he set out in 1801 to make his fortune in the West Indies.[52] He died of fever within months of his arrival. Mathews's disappointments were connected with the failure of his various vocational choices, which included Wordsworth and the fate of their *Philanthropist* plans.

Wordsworth's letters to Mathews after his departure from London become increasingly cool and peremptory. Their relationship seems to have slid backwards, from close friendship to mere acquaintance. As to politics, there is nary a word; compared to their detailed and enthusiastic discussions before Wordsworth's arrival in London, it is now difficult to believe that these young men ever talked about anything but their friends, the weather, and poetry – and this, with reference to spying authorities, was very much the point.

One particularly clear indication of the terms of their separation fits neatly with Wordsworth's political retrenchment after 1795. Among the various London errands with which he charged Mathews as his factotum after leaving town, he asked for Mathews's copy of the volume in John Bell's *Classical Arrangement of Fugitive Poetry* which contained 'Poems in the Stanza of Spenser,' including Beattie's *The Minstrel*. In an awkward but revealing gesture, he proposed that they exchange books, Mathews accepting Wordsworth's copy of *Cato's Letters* for his volume of Bell. To make the switch seem more worthwhile to Mathews, he proposed the following very concrete mechanism for carrying it out:

> You will write your name in it as presented to me. If you chuse to take the
> trouble of inserting my name in the Cato's Letters, here it is: you
> may cut it out and paste it in.
>> From W. Wordsworth
>>> to
>> W. Mathews[53]

Unlike his letters to Mathews from Penrith in late 1794, where he brushed
aside all stylistic difficulties in his enthusiasm to connect his writing with
the journalism Mathews was doing, Wordsworth was now migrating from
one textual universe to another. He was bidding farewell not only to
Mathews but also to London and the dangerous world of committed
journalism they had shared there, and he could hardly have hit upon a
more symbolic exchange. For 'Cato' is none other than that John
Trenchard whose work figures so prominently in the *Philanthropist*,
especially when the going got rough and some acceptably traditional liberal
material was needed to fill up issues which might otherwise have been
filled by uncontrollably radical volunteer contributions.

Not everything was politics, however. On 21 August, about three days
after Wordsworth left town, his translation of a French poem called
'L'Education de l'Amour' was published in the *Morning Chronicle* as 'The
Birth of Love,' with an introductory note by Wrangham. In it, Cupid is
precociously aroused by the sight of his mother's breasts ('malgré son
jeune age') so that he cannot nurse: 'by the beauty of the vase beguil'd, /
Forgot the beverage—and pin'd away.' Venus asks for help from 'the most
discreet' of the personified abstractions who are her attendant goddesses.
Hope is chosen, but Enjoyment is jealous, and, disguised as Innocence,
fills her laps with sweetmeats, 'and gave, in handfuls gave, the treach'rous
store. / A wild delirium first the Infant thrill'd; / But soon upon her
breast he sunk – to wake no more.'[54] It seems a strange poem to be translating in London in August of 1795, but not so strange in Wordsworth's
case. A French poem about love, disappointed hope, innocence betrayed,
and destructive enjoyment still had many angles of interest for him, all the
sharper as his distance from Annette seemed to increase. And his writings
of the 1790s show that the attraction of women's breasts and wild
deliriums in their sweet laps were not merely abstract or metaphorical
aspects of his writing, but very much part of his lived experience.

CHAPTER NINETEEN

Of Cabbages and Radicals

Racedown Lodge, 1795–1797

Let us suppose a young Man of great intellectual powers, yet without any solid principles of genuine benevolence. His master passions are pride and the love of distinction. He has deeply imbibed the spirit of enterprize in a tumultuous age. He goes into the world and is betrayed into a great crime.

The influence on which all his happiness is built immediately deserts him. His talents are robbed of their weight; his exertions are unavailing, and he quits the world in disgust, with strong misanthropic feelings. In his retirement, he is impelled to examine the reasonableness of established opinions and the force of his mind exhausts itself in constant efforts to separate the elements of virtue and vice.

(Preface to *The Borderers*, 1797)

Wordsworth left London so hastily that Godwin was not aware of it; he called on 18 August but Wordsworth was already gone. The prospect of exciting remunerative work had brought him rushing to town in February, but a much more leisured prospect now beckoned him out of it, made all the more attractive by the dangers and anxieties he was leaving behind.

There had been a vague plan that Dorothy would join him in London, to help earn money by translating. But now, rather than wait for her, Wordsworth departed immediately to Bristol as the guest of the Pinneys' father. The townhouse that Wordsworth arrived at still stands in Great George Street in the elegant Clifton section of town, commodious enough to house the city's museum of furniture from this era of mercantile opulence. It was a symbol of John Pinney's advancing fortunes, built in 1788 following his return from Nevis. He now ran the Bristol West Indies Trading Company in partnership with John Tobin, 'one of the most prominent and intelligent adversaries of the abolition movement,' and father of two sons, John and James, who both became close friends of Wordsworth.[1]

To the senior Pinney, Wordsworth appeared a gentlemen of some means, if he could afford Racedown. Pinney, a complete arriviste himself, was ready to do the genteel thing by entertaining Wordsworth until his sister arrived with young Basil Montagu. The fact that the boy's father was connected to the Earl of Sandwich was not lost on Pinney; though dis- inherited by his father, Montagu was on good terms with his half-brother, the fifth earl.

John Pinney had just recently completed an extensive four-year reno- vation of his country house; he elegantly renamed it Racedown, rather than Pylemarsh Lodge, the homely local designation.[2] Pinney had originally intended to use it as a safe haven from Nevis, if slave uprisings or a French invasion made it expedient to do so.[3] He was actively looking for tenants for the newly renovated house, but not finding any takers had put it at the disposal of his sons, naturally assuming that the tenant they had found for it was paying rent, since he was charging them £50 a year for the use of it.[4]

John Pinney, Sr, did not participate in the generous feeling of giving things for nothing that Hazlitt recalled as 'the spirit of the age.' He made a religion of his accounts, and spoke in self-help copybook maxims like Benjamin Franklin's.[5] Irritable and energetic, he was a mercantile version of Sir James Lowther. He had not been born rich; his father, Michael Pretor, was reported to be 'worse than a footman,' a reference to his way of gaining access to his lady's favours. But he was lucky; in 1764, he had been named heir to the Pinney fortune by two ageing, childless cousins. He went out immediately to Nevis, returning in 1784, with a profit of £35,000. He never intended to stay longer than was necessary to raise a fortune that would allow him to set up independently in England. 'My greatest pride is to be considered as a private country gentleman . . . [I] shall avoid even the name of a West-Indian.'

He wanted to avoid the name of West-Indian because fortunes gained there were, as everyone knew, built on the backs of slaves. When Wordsworth stayed at Pinney's house, Pinney was the owner of over 200 slaves, working three different plantations. For liberal young men like the Pinney brothers, tutored by even more liberal Cambridge graduates like Montagu and Wrangham, at a time of non-stop talk about revolutionary virtue and the rights of man, this background was an unspeakable embarrassment. Matthew ('Monk') Lewis was another young man in the same bind, as was Charles Douglas, Montagu's friend.[6] John Frederick Pinney, 'a rabid Whig,' wanted to get rid of their plantations as soon as possible.[7] The senior Pinney would not have elaborated on the basis of his fortune if asked by young Wordsworth – who was in no position to inquire about the largesse he was about to receive, and knew better than to thank John Pinney for letting him have Racedown for nothing.

Wordsworth's visit lasted five weeks, during which time he carefully observed the active Bristol political scene. With its broad channel estuary, it was more obviously a seaport than London, and opposition to the war with France was more openly expressed, because the costs of the ill-advised war bore heavily on Bristol's import-export economy. Wordsworth was particularly eager to see two young men who had frequently been mentioned by Mathews, Dyer, and Godwin and others in his London set: Samuel Taylor Coleridge and Robert Southey. Wordsworth reported back to Mathews: 'Coleridge was at Bristol part of the time I was there. I saw but little of him. I wished indeed to have seen more – his talent appears to me very great. I met with Southey also, his manners pleased me exceedingly and I have every reason to think very highly of his powers of mind.'[8] Wordsworth speaks of both men as persons he and Mathews already know about: there was no miraculous first vision of his future soul-mate and collaborator. They might have met at Pinney's house, for though the elder Pinney himself would not entertain anyone as 'democratical' as Coleridge, he could have gained entrée as an acquaintance of Pinney's indulged sons.[9]

Coleridge was already 'a noticeable man,' as was Southey, a well-con-nected local boy who had already published a volume of poetry.[10] Coleridge, it is not too much to say, was to Bristol what Thelwall was to London, and that, in late 1795, was very much indeed.[11] He and Southey and their friends (Charles Lloyd, Robert Lovell, and the Fricker sisters, Edith and Sara) were notorious in the region for their plans to found a utopian community, 'Pantisocracy,' on the banks of the Susquehanna River in Pennsylvania, near where Joseph Priestley, the famous scientist and radical, had fled after the destruction of his laboratory by a Birmingham mob. The Pantisocracy plan (government by all) had involved strenuous local efforts to recruit like-minded communalists, but it had just fallen through in late summer, to bitter recriminations between its principals. This occasioned great glee among their Bristol elders, and became a permanent point of satiric reference throughout Coleridge and Southey's careers. Wordsworth was frequently drawn into these satiric pictures by virtue of their later association in the Lake District, which had similar communal overtones of 'plain living and high thinking.' George Dyer, for example, linked them all together in a footnote in *The Poet's Fate* (1797), advising a young poet to 'join Pantisocracy's harmonious train . . . [where] freedom digs, and ploughs, and laughs, and sings.' The note singles out Southey and Coleridge, but adds the names of 'three young men, who have given early proofs, that they can strike the true chords of poesy': Wordsworth, Charles Lloyd, and Charles Lamb.[12]

Dorothy arrived in mid-September, and she and William set out almost immediately for Racedown, fifty miles to the south. They arrived at midnight on 26 September, rousing up Joseph Gill, a 'ruined and unhappy' cousin of John Pinney's who served as Racedown's family caretaker and custodian, broken down from years of dissipation on Nevis.[13] The house they entered was splendid, three storeys high, glistening with new improvements. Dorothy, ever the keen estimator of domestic arrangements, wrote to Jane Pollard Marshall, 'We found everything at Racedown much more complete with respects to household conveniences than I could have expected. You may judge of this when I tell you we have not had to lay out ten shillings for the use of the house.'[14]

Racedown is now twice as big as it was then, from a nineteenth-century addition, but it was a very commodious house in 1795, as Coleridge rightly pegged it after his first visit: 'the mansion of my friend Wordsworth.'[15] It had a beautiful long parlour running from front to back on the left as one entered, with a pretty view of the croquet ground on the south side, and of the formal pleasure garden to the rear (west), decorated with gilded busts on stone columns – the 'images,' as Joseph Gill queerly called them. It boasted a pianoforte, mahogany furniture, two glass-front bookcases on either side of the fireplace, and a library of over four hundred books.[16]

The house is only eight miles from the sea, but it is hard to imagine that anything as wide open as a sea is nearby, in this region of burly hills crowded together in a remote corner of Dorset thrusting out between Devon and Somerset. The sea 'haar,' a fog which descends frequently, only deepens its atmosphere of obscurity. But a short walk up any hill gives a brilliant sight of the ocean on a clear day, when the countryside shines like an emerald. William and Dorothy could see the Channel from their upper floors in winter, through openings between the hills.

Directly across the road, Pilsdon Pen rises steeply nine hundred feet above the Vale of Marshwood, the highest hill in Dorset. A mile east is Lewesdon Hill, upon which William Crowe wrote a hill-by-hill Whiggish survey-poem in 1788 that Azariah Pinney presented to the Wordsworths for the pleasure of placing themselves in their literary landscape.[17] Crowe's vista of English beauty and prosperity celebrates the unbroken views on all sides, 'save only where the head / Of Pillesdon rises, Pillesdon's lofty Pen.' On 15 November William saw from the top of Pilsdon the West India fleet setting out 'in all its glory.' Two days later he and Dorothy learned it had run into a hurricane; many ships had gone down, and for two weeks thereafter the coast was littered with corpses.[18] Ten years later these moments flashed through William and Dorothy's minds when they learned that John's first command, the *Earl of Abergavenny*, had gone down along the same stretch of coast.

Their first days and weeks were taken up with arrangements for delivery of eggs and butter from the little farms around Racedown. Their domestic arrangements required care because their original plans soon fell through, leaving them considerably worse off than they had expected to be, house-rich but cash-poor. Dorothy had calculated that their annual income

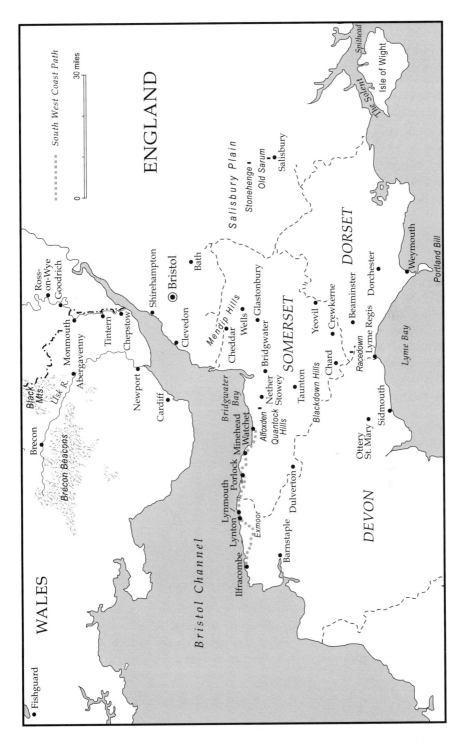

Wordsworth's and Coleridge's West Country, showing their favourite
coastal walk

would be a tidy £180 per year, from the yield of Wordsworth's loans to Montagu and Douglas, plus £50 a year for young Montagu and a similar amount for taking care of the illegitimate daughter their cousin Tom Myers had recently sent back from India.* Dorothy imagined that she and William would be as comfortably situated as their childhood friends the Hutchinsons, whom she had visited near Durham in April. These brothers and sisters, also orphans, had recently inherited £1800 from their uncle, and were now 'quite independent and have not a wish ungratified.' Wistfully, she added, 'You know the pleasure which I have always attached to the idea of a home.'[19]

But these rosy prospects never materialized. Montagu's and Douglas's repayments soon fell in arrears, so they were left with only the £50 per year for Basil, Jr. Even that lasted only two years; by the time they moved to Somerset in mid-1797 they were maintaining little Basil at their own expense.[20] It turned out to be a very good thing they didn't have to pay rent. Far from living a leisured country life as master and mistress of an elegant pre-school nursery for rich colonials, at an income surpassing that of a decent church living, they found themselves instead eking out existence with barely enough cash to cover their basic expenses. The 'plain living and high thinking' that Wordsworth would later idealize was thrust upon them as a rude shock at Racedown.

They were soon forced to turn to gardening for their diet. By the beginning of the new year, Wordsworth was outside helping Joseph Gill, as Dorothy smilingly noted: 'my brother handles the spade with great dexterity.'[21] This was largely because of Gill's inability to get the regular gardener to do anything: talking to him was 'as useless as it would be to sing Psalms to a dead horse.' Gill and the Wordsworths suffered a certain amount of insubordination from the rest of the Racedown staff, because though friends or relations of the Pinney family, they clearly had no money to spare and hence no basis for authority. The expense of coal was one of the first things Dorothy remarked: 'You would be surprized to see what a small cart full we get for three or four and twenty shillings.'[22] Wordsworth knew whereof he spoke when he cast back to Dorset for the setting of 'Goody Blake and Harry Gill' two years later:

> This woman dwelt in Dorsetshire,
> Her hut was on a cold hill-side,
> And in that country coals are dear,
> For they come far by wind and tide.[23]

---

* Tom knew better than William how to avoid mistakes with illegitimate children in the high-stakes marriage game. When he returned from the colonies he married a distant cousin, Lady Mary Nevill, John Robinson's granddaughter and daughter of the Earl of Abergavenny. He was awarded Robinson's Harwich seat when the old politico died in 1802.

Poverty was so widespread and desperate that people had no compunction about stealing from gardens. Once Joseph Gill and Wordsworth had, with difficulty, got their garden in, they managed to prevail on the gardener to build a protective fence around it, only to discover that by-passing wanderers tore out the boards for their fires. Recent laws restricting gleaning rights had made it much more difficult to gather fuel.[24] Thus William partly occupied the position of Harry Gill in the poem, though he foisted Joseph Gill's surname on him. When Wordsworth joked to Wrangham in the spring of 1797 that he had 'lately been living upon air and the essence of carrots cabbages turnips and other esculent vegetables, not excluding parsley the produce of my garden,' he was trying to put a witty face on what had been the reality of their situation.[25]

Gill had done well as a shopkeeper on Nevis, but was a disaster as Pinney's first manager in the 1770s and had to be sent home. Like Wordsworth, he had left a lover behind him in another country, a mulatto woman named Penny Markham whose freedom he bought for £100. He had no more money than the Wordsworths, and once resorted to eating the flesh of a cow that had died in calving, complaining that is was 'cruel hard to be starved to death in a Christian country.'[26]

Wordsworth soon felt the truth of this from the walks he took around the neighbourhood. Prices were rising everywhere because of the war, soon doubling the average cost of living. Between 1790 and 1795, the price of oats rose seventy-five per cent, that of a loaf of bread doubled, and that of a pound of potatoes quadrupled.[27] Dorothy complained, 'everything has been very dear for house-keeping this season; we can get no meat under 6d. and Tea and Sugar, our only luxuries, are rising.'[28] These two luxuries, the main imports of the British East Indian and West Indian imperial trade, respectively – and of John Wordsworth and John Pinney in their immediate acquaintance – were increasing in price also because of the number of merchant ships being commandeered for the war effort.

These economic factors bore hard on the Wordsworths, but they were catastrophic on the rural poor, as Wordsworth soon saw: 'many rich / Sunk down as in a dream among the poor, / And of the poor did many cease to be, / And their place knew them not.'[29] Poverty was bad all over England, but it was worst in the West Country, which was more affected by the war's impact on trade and shipping. Wordsworth's first letter back to Mathews in October conveyed the ambivalence of their situation: 'We are now at Racedown and both happy as people can be who live in perfect solitude. We do not see a soul. Now and then we meet a miserable peasant in the road or an accidental traveller. The country people here are wretchedly poor; ignorant and overwhelmed with every vice that usually attends ignorance in that class, viz—lying and picking and stealing &c &c.'[30] Solitude and happiness, poverty and viciousness: the two extremes lay close together. To 'not see a soul' technically meant they received no visitors, but at Racedown Wordsworth learned to see the 'soul' in wretchedly poor country people like Goody Blake, who had to pick and steal to keep themselves alive. Dorothy too, amid details of their house's furnishings and situation, allotted one sentence to the same contrast: 'The peasants are miserably poor; their cottages are shapeless structures (I may almost say) of wood and clay – indeed they are not at all beyond what might be expected in savage life.'[31]

Wordsworth was in an anomalous position to observe all this. On the one hand, he was to all appearances the lord of the manor, living in a splendour based on the profits of slave labour. Like the Pedlar in his soon-to-be-composed 'Ruined Cottage,' he 'could afford to suffer with those whom he saw suffer.' The point is not that Wordsworth was privileged and the poor were not, or that he was somehow hypocritical in his way-wandering walks on 'lonely roads [which] were schools to me.'[32] On the contrary, his precarious situation gave him a motive to empathize with 'souls that appear to have no depth at all / To vulgar eyes.' He was well aware that he stood blessedly but precariously outside their suffering. The uneasiness of their situation helped to redefine his poetry in a fundamental way over the next two years: How does one write poetry about poverty? How can telling stories about it become part of a solution, rather than part of the problem? Wordsworth had low powers of invention, but at Racedown he began to develop a kind of human inventiveness, the ability to project himself into the minds and bodies of the poor, the old, the senile, and the sick.

During his two years at Racedown, Wordsworth wrote nearly a dozen poems or fragmentary pieces which show these issues working their way haltingly toward his major works of this period, *The Borderers* and 'The Ruined Cottage.' Their subjects, beggars, convicts, deserted mothers and children, are pencil sketches in the genre of Wordsworthian solitude, anticipating the great solitary set-pieces of his mature period: the Discharged Veteran, the Blind Beggar, the Leech Gatherer, and the Solitary Reaper.

The fragments do not lack for verbal power, quite the contrary. What is missing is any explanatory framework in which the suffering they depict might be interpreted. When he made an an effort to supply an explanation, it was manifestly inadequate to the emotional force with which he represented the suffering itself. When he described these experiences in *Prelude* XII, he concluded that such subjects were fit for prophetic poetry: 'the genius of the poet hence / May boldly take his way among mankind / Wherever Nature leads.' But no such confidence is discernible in the manuscripts of 1796–97. These vignettes, taken as a group, cry out for some larger understanding: What are you going to do about *us*? They represent human suffering, very specifically in terms of social conditions in England *c.* 1796, stubbornly persisting independent of any attempt to explain it, or relieve it, or even to sympathize with it.

'The Baker's Cart' is photo-realism from Dorset in the late 1790s. It is set on a road like the one in front of Racedown, where a baker's cart did make rural rounds.[33] Wordsworth overheard a woman mutter seven words, ' "that waggon does not care for us," ' and he swiftly sketched in the entire social malaise around them. The cart does not stop to make its usual delivery at the woman's house as expected by her children, who 'had all come forth . . . at the rumbling of the distant wheels.' The baker's horse, equally innocent, also halts expectantly. But the driver knows the woman has no money, smacks his whip, and moves on, followed by the woman's sullen curse:

> The words were simple, but her look and voice
> Made up their meaning, and bespoke a mind
> Which being long neglected and denied
> The common food of hope was now become
> Sick and extravagant—by strong access
> Of momentary pangs driv'n to that state
> In which all past experience melts away
> And the rebellious heart to its own will
> Fashions the laws of nature.
>
> (17–25)[34]

She is a revolutionary in the making, an anticipation of the amoral villain of *The Borderers*, who fashions 'the laws of nature' to the will of his own heart. Worse than lacking bread, she has been denied 'the common food of hope.' Though Wordsworth implicitly disapproves the woman's words, he offers no judgment on her. The fragment simply says this is what will result if these things happen. Walking about the countryside, Wordsworth had no ready cash with which to relieve the needs of people he met, and could do little more than talk with them. But he heard what they said.

'The Convict' is probably the earliest of these fragments, and its framework reflects the wishful thinking of Wordsworth's London sojourn. It clearly exposes the difficulty Wordsworth had in making some kind of satisfactory statement about such unpromising materials. It is ostensibly about penal reform, but it suggests instead the attractions of giving up hard moral questions in despair. The speaker turns from watching a beautiful sunset on a hill, to ask, ' "And must we then part from a dwelling so fair?" ' This could be Wordsworth on Pilsdon Pen, turning back toward Racedown after watching the sun set over the Channel. The speaker 'repairs' to a place where he has evidently just come from, 'the cell where a convict is laid.' How a dungeon came to be so close to a picturesque viewing station is not explained, though there were rural holding jails, or compters, as in London, and complaints and arrests were being made every day because of all the 'thieving and picking' that hard times had produced. But the jail's proximity to the sunset is mainly a symbolic contrast, in which the 'Nature' alternative is badly defeated. The poem's superficial concern is why aristocratic criminals get better treatment than common ones. But its *object*, the dejected convict with matted hair lying in the back of his cell, raises a quite different question which very nearly ruins the whole composition. A tear runs out of his eye, and 'the silence of sorrow it seems to supply, / And asks of me why I am here.' Good question: why indeed? Wordsworth here puts to himself the question implicit in all these fragments, namely, what is the degree of moral responsibility of a poet who observes the human suffering caused by the action of contemporary British institutions – aided and abetted by the actions of nature (disease, age, bad harvests), and often by the behaviour of the sufferers themselves (jealousy, anger, lust)?

He tries to answer the question, but the weakness of his answer shows why most of the rest of his short pieces of 1796–97 are free-standing icons of pain without commentary:

> 'At thy name though compassion her nature resign,
> Though in virtue's proud mouth thy report be a stain,
> My care, if the arm of the mighty were mine,
> Would plant thee where yet thou might'st blossom again.'
>
> (49–52)

This is merely a wish for an enlightened policy of transportation for criminals, as advocated by John Howard, and most recently pleaded in theoretical terms by William Godwin.[35] The speaker would, if he could, transport ('transplant') the convict to Botany Bay – a good place for blossoming, from the sound of it, but horrifically not so, in reality. 'The Convict' is modern in its emphasis on rehabilitation over punishment, and its sympathy is preferable to the conventional moral self-righteousness it rejects, but its moral is simple: don't despise criminals, try to reform them. This was better than urging more hangings as a solution to the nation's growing crime wave, but it exposes its own weakness when it says, 'if the arm of the mighty were mine,' since it obviously isn't.

Like the *Philanthropist*'s 'Address to Poverty,' 'The Convict' is more concerned about mental than about physical suffering, and this is true of all the Racedown fragments. Though the prisoner lies in 'the comfortless vault of disease,' what Wordsworth really wants to get at are his mental *self*-tortures: 'my fancy has pierced to his heart, and pourtrays / More terrible images there.' This is what Wordsworth will be doing for the next four years at least: trying to see suffering from the inside – including, increasingly, the suffering of the person who observes it.

The 'Argument for Suicide' sums up the moral conundrums of the entire group of 1796–97 fragments. The title is Wordsworth's, but does not make clear exactly whose argument this is:

> Send this man to the mine, this to the battle,
> Famish an aged beggar at your gates,
> And let him die by inches—but for worlds
> Lift not your hand against him—Live, live on,
> As if this earth owned neither steel nor arsenic,
> A rope, a river, or a standing pool.
> Live, if you dread the pains of hell, or think
> Your corpse would quarrel with a stake—alas
> Has misery then no friend?—if you would die
> By license, call the dropsy and the stone
> And let them end you—strange it is;
> And most fantastic are the magic circles
> Drawn round the thing called life—till we have learned
> To prize it less, we ne'er shall learn to prize
> The things worth living for.[36]

We see Wordsworth here in the very act of yielding up moral questions in despair. Is this an argument for or against suicide? And whose argument is it? Someone contemplating suicide? Or someone who is causing death without being charged for murder: the business and military establishments of the opening lines, who kill people legally 'by inches'? Only in the fourth line is the potential suicide addressed directly and warned of eternal damnation, as if the deaths described had been his idea. The 'resolution' of the suicide question proper (9–11) seems to recommend contracting a fatal disease.

But the statement of this sardonic quasi-sonnet is complete, and its method is of a piece with Wordsworth's creation of all these poems: until we cut away the usual explanations for the sanctity of life (here presented as fantastic magical acts), 'we ne'er shall learn to prize / The things worth living for.' End of poem. What these prized things are is not specified, but they are clearly not economic prosperity, military glory, social charity, religious belief, or whatever other excuses society uses to rationalize its behaviour to the suffering poor. The poem is truly if negatively radical, saying that unless people recognize murder and suicide as viable alternatives to the terrible conditions people found themselves living in, we will never come to any truly positive ideas for life.

Efforts like these were not going anywhere for the moment, in terms of poetic closure or development, so once he and Dorothy were well settled in at Racedown, Wordsworth began more concentrated writing in the same way he had at Windy Brow the previous summer, by revising an already completed work: this time, 'A Night on Salisbury Plain' (NSP). But his impulse was directly opposite to that he took with *An Evening Walk* in

1794. There he had taken a decidedly unpolitical poem and filled it with sociopolitical commentary. Now, following several months in London at the nerve centres of agitation for reform, he produced a poem in which explicit political argument is stripped away, by 'alterations and additions so material as that it may be looked on almost as another work.'[37] In revising *An Evening Walk*, he was still focused on the landscape; now, his vision concentrated on the people in it. He gave the revised poem a new title, 'Adventures on Salisbury Plain.' The change in title accurately captures the essence of his changes, for the first version is a relatively static 'night-piece,' a fugue of suffering articulated by the Female Vagrant, whereas the second is a narrative with a beginning, middle and end, and two developed characters whose interactions move the story forward. His main change was to lop off a philosophical and political framework from Rousseau and Paine around the Female Vagrant's story and recast the nameless narrator of the first poem into a new character, a homeward bound sailor, whose story of suffering complements the vagrant woman's and resembles Wordsworth's.

The increased narrative realism makes ASP a better poem than NSP, but not a more reassuring one. The new direction of the poem, toward an unmediated examination of the human condition in England, *c.* 1796, is characteristic of all Wordsworth's Racedown poems. They all display the starkest possible framing of the problem of human suffering, coupled with a determined refusal to offer any kind of interpretation. Giving up moral questions in despair did not mean giving up poetry, only seeking answers more humbly. Rarely have the deprivations and injustice of the English social system been presented in such sombre, unsparing colours.[38] Yet none of these poems were published in their original form at the time; they contributed more to Wordsworth's self-creation than to contemporary debates on the condition of England.

This change in direction is usually interpreted as the sign of Wordsworth's rejection of politics, specifically his revulsion from Godwin's benign necessarianism. This is partly true, but not the whole truth. Retreat from politics became a general condition in 1796, the year in which Coleridge claimed to have 'snapped the squeaking baby trumpet' of his 'sedition' (a clever obfuscation which understates the impact of his radical activities while overstating their criminal status). Far from being a rejection of Godwin, ASP can well be called Wordsworth's 'most Godwinian' work.[39] But it is not Godwin the benevolent necessarian. Rather, it is the Godwin of *Political Justice*, unsparingly criticizing the failure and hypocrisy of social institutions; it resembles the Godwin of *Caleb Williams* even more. The sailor's wanderings and foiled attempts to return home, and the unjust treatment he suffers, are very like Caleb's wanderings to find a fair hearing for his complaints against his cruel, devious master. Both are stark illustrations of Godwin's central critical truth, that circumstances can lead good people into crime.[40]

Revising NSP into ASP, Wordsworth was attempting to strip down his treatment of his chosen materials – the suffering lower classes in the English countryside – to their bare essentials: to see 'men as they are men within themselves.' He rejected all categories of explanation except those provided by his own observation, or else he tried to create new categories of explanation by inductive experiments with his own materials. 'Nature' was the catchall category in which he began to cast for answers to these nearly impossible questions. But the nature he invokes is not the picturesque landscape associated with him from the Lake District, nor is it Nature with any supportive metaphysical principle or god-term behind it. On the contrary, it is more like the grimly competitive nature of Malthus and later of Charles Darwin.[41] Nature here is bleak, barren, sublimely terrifying, and morally unconcerned, simply a given: whatever is just *there*, surrounding mankind, when all support-systems of meaning or help are pulled away, and we seek 'for good in the familiar face of life . . . among the natural abodes of men' (XII.67, 107).

Wordsworth's changes in the plot of NSP turn upon the relationship between the man and the woman, and lay down the lines of what could be an appalling family tragedy. Consciously or unconsciously, Wordsworth now identified with both characters. The woman's story is one of passive suffering and sorrow, commencing with her family's losing their freehold in the Lake District to rapacious estate-builders, reflecting Wordsworth's own early life-experience. The sailor's story is one of unmerited suffering complicated by guilt, reflecting Wordsworth's more recent adult experience in France. Together they stand for *Guilt and Sorrow*, the title under which Wordsworth published the poem many years later (1842).

In both versions, but much more so in the second, Wordsworth raised possibility that the sailor and the female vagrant might support each other in their misery. As it is, the Female Vagrant discovers the sailor's wife dying on a cart near the inn, somehow recognizes her, and rushes back to him to bring them together for an affecting death-bed scene. Wordsworth knew this piling-up of coincidences was too much: 'So much for the vulgar,' he later wryly commented.[42] This would have been a Gothic thriller worthy of 'Monk' Lewis, since Wordsworth proposed to make the Female Vagrant into, variously, the widow, the daughter, or the sister of the very man the sailor has murdered. But such a plot would have left open one denouement which the revised ending dramatically rejects: the sailor and the female vagrant could have stayed together and perhaps lived happily ever after. In NSP, the mutual attraction between the two main characters was represented physically, in the Traveller's kindling interest in the Vagrant's snow-white breasts. In ASP, this strong physical attraction is replaced by a moral one: 'And still the more he grieved, she loved him still the more.' In one kind of moral reasoning, the Traveller, in becoming the Sailor, has moved to a more admirable position: not a man attracted by a woman's body, but a man whose griefs make him attractive to a woman's finer feelings. Similar love-relations exist in all the major poems he wrote over the next three years, from *The Borderers* to 'Tintern Abbey,' where husbands and wives, or lovers, or brothers and sisters, come agonizingly close to being united or reunited. But this solution, close to Wordsworth's personal desires regarding both Annette and Dorothy, is for just that reason held back from being realized.

During the winter months, he and Dorothy read extensively in Racedown's large library. They continued their study of Italian, reading Machiavelli and Boccaccio. There were also Whiggish books of political economy, and a good representation of writing from the English republican tradition: John Frederick Pinney particularly recommended a copy of the works of Algernon Sydney.[43] Though Wordsworth's writings were becoming less overtly political, he had by no means lost interest in politics. Throughout their time at Racedown he requested from his friends in London and Bristol the latest works of political controversy, including the *Monthly Magazine* and the *Analytical Review*. These covered a wide spectrum, from Burke through Coleridge and his Unitarian friend John Estlin, to Thomas Erskine (*The Causes and Consequences of the Present War*). The Pinney library also had a remarkably full collection of seventeenth- and eighteenth-century verse, including both major authors like Milton, Dryden, and Swift, and many now obscure second- or third-rank authors: Sandys, Burnet, Glover, Buckingham, Aubrey, and Blackmore. Wordsworth's poetical education, already prodigious, began to approach the encyclopedic level. A common element linking all these diverse writers was the intricate, various relation between politics and poetics in their art. Wordsworth was reading voraciously not merely to improve his stock of poetry, but because these writers addressed the question that he personally was most troubled by, the social responsibility of the poet.

At the very end of 1795 they received three French books: the memoirs of Madame Roland, written as she awaited execution; those of Wordsworth's one-time hero, Louvet, who had lived to tell about the Terror; and the latest instalment of Helen Maria Williams's *Letters*. These were all people Wordsworth had seen close-up during his residence in France, and perhaps talked to. Their chastened accounts of the crimes committed in the name of liberty reinforced his growing disillusionment with direct political action.

The Pinney boys arrived in a bustle on 2 January for a week, returning again in February for a month which featured a 'grand rout' of winter feast and party. Writing was 'out of the question' when they were there, for the visits of these playboys of the west of England were always festive occasions, devoted to coursing for hares and foxes, in which both William and Dorothy joined enthusiastically.[44] The main use of Racedown to the younger Pinneys was as a hunting lodge; a main benefit of their visits to the young Wordsworths was to replenish the larder with supplies of fresh meat. Azariah noted that 'while we were with him [Wordsworth] he relaxed the vigour of his philosophic nerves so much as to go a Coursing several times, & I assure you did not eat the unfortunate Hares with less relish because he heard them heave their death groans . . . for his usual appetite showed itself at the dining table.'[45]

Azariah Pinney was the 'active and shrewd' son, slated to enter the business, and he shows here a nice ability to take the measure of his man.[46] His keen eye may account for his being not 'so great a favourite' with Dorothy as his brother was. The coolness was mutual: 'Miss Wordsworth has undoubted claim to good humour, but does not possess that je ne sais quoi, so necessary to sweeten the draught of human misfortune.' One wonders what draughts of misfortune this spoiled young man had quaffed, but the sweets he liked are obvious enough. He felt that if a man was a poet he should produce poetry, and asked William to 'write a few lines panegyrical' on the object of John Frederick's affections, helpfully reminding him that her name had three syllables. Panegyric seems to have been called for by the fact that John was under treatment for venereal disease by a London doctor.[47]

John Frederick, as the elder son, enjoyed the privileged status of being 'of no profession,' though he had gone to Oxford, and developed a personality more pleasing to Dorothy: 'a charming countenance and the sweetest temper I have ever observed.' This was not surprising, since he 'had always plenty of money to spend and every indulgence: all these things instead of having spoiled him . . . have wrought the pleasantest and best effects, he is well-informed, has an uncommonly good heart, and is very agreeable in conversation.'[48] The historian of the family takes quite a different view of John Frederick's qualities: 'a showy, peevish nonentity, without any claim to distinction besides an early friendship with Wordsworth and Coleridge, which cannot have gone very deep,' his studies 'a mere show,' and displaying 'all the fretfulness of a weak man.'[49] But the four young people got on well enough, despite these differences in temperament. The Pinneys were flattered to have such advanced intellectual guests, and the Wordsworths were glad to have such generous wealthy admirers.

Nor were John Frederick or Azariah uninterested in literature. They were the main conduit for information and works-in-progress passing between the Racedown solitaries and their new Bristol acquaintances, Coleridge, Southey, and the enterprising Dissenting publisher, picturesque poet, and moral reformer, Joseph Cottle. Azariah took the new version of 'Salisbury Plain' back with him in March to show to Coleridge.

He reported Coleridge's 'lively interest' in 'so valuable a Poem (as he terms it),' and relayed Coleridge's suggestion that Wordsworth publish it in the *Watchman*.[50]

Coleridge made copious comments on 'Adventure on Salisbury Plain' and wrote to Wordsworth urging him to publish it separately as a book. This endorsement of his work was enormously heartening to Wordsworth, and he never forgot the imprimatur of Coleridge's praise: 'That . . . I must then have exercised / Upon the vulgar forms of present things . . . / A higher power . . . / An image, and a character, by books / Not hitherto reflected' (XII.360–362, 365–66). Coleridge probably did say something this extreme; it was part of his character to see immense possibilities in the work of his friends. Writing to John Thelwall in May, Coleridge used Wordsworth's Salisbury Plain poem as an affidavit for his political credentials: 'this man is a republican, and, at least, a *semi*-atheist.' But he added something more important to Wordsworth than his estimate of either Wordsworth's religion or his politics: 'a very dear friend of mine, the best poet of the age.' For Wordsworth this kind of praise coming at this time was crucial. It was the first time he had received such praise from a contemporary whose judgment he respected, and whose own level of achievement he frankly envied: Dorothy and Mathews had been very well in their way, but Wordsworth needed more. His career and sense of himself needed Coleridge far more than Coleridge needed him at this moment, and Wordsworth did all he could in the coming months to keep up his contacts with his new friend.

As soon as the Pinneys left on 6 March, William and Dorothy resumed their busy domestic schedule, which made serious new writing difficult. William was out cutting wood and digging up hedges to help Joseph Gill. Time was taken up with arrangements for fetching coal and walking the seven miles to Crewkerne, to see if Montagu or anyone else had responded to their desperate invitations for company. They planted cabbages, 'and into cabbages we shall be transformed.'[51]

But William managed to crank out a hundred more lines on the Juvenal project and sent them off to Wrangham with some laboured punning. He assured Wrangham of his continued interest in their project: 'I now feel a return of the literary appetite I mean to take a snack of satire by way of Sandwich,' alluding to his intention to throw in a hit at the extramarital adventures of Montagu's father, inventor of the 'sandwich.'

After his fallow spring, Wordsworth was eager for more stimulation. On 1 June, he set off for a six-week visit in London. He supped with Godwin on at least four occasions; his disapproval of the philosopher's style and thought did not affect his personal esteem for him. Wordsworth never dropped Godwin's acquaintance as so many later did, but Wordsworth now began moving in less radical company than he had the previous summer. Godwin's diary makes no mention of William Mathews at any of their meetings, and there is no further record of Mathews in Wordsworth's life after a letter sent to him in March, inviting him to Racedown for a summer visit.[52] Montagu was in attendance at these gatherings, but the other young men were richer, less intellectual, and altogether less impressive than Wordsworth's 1795 circle: the Pinney brothers, the Tobin brothers, and John Stoddart, 'a cold-hearted, well-bred conceited disciple of Godwin's' (according to Lamb). Stoddart eventually became chief justice of Malta, and his sister married Hazlitt. It may have been the experience of listening to Godwin in these less stimulating circumstances that helped push Wordsworth into the sweeping indictment of Godwinism in *The Borderers*, the major work that he began in the autumn. He noticed how Godwin had smoothed his radical edge to accommodate criticisms of *Political Justice* and protect himself in the new atmosphere of repression.

But this London visit also marked the beginning of Wordsworth's lifelong friendship with Charles Lamb, whom he now met, Coleridge having prepared the way by sending Lamb a copy of 'Adventures on Salisbury Plain,' which he read 'not without delight.'

In late November, Mary Hutchinson arrived, escorted by her sailor brother Henry, who was on his way to join his ship at Plymouth.[53] She came directly from nursing her younger sister Margaret's fatal illness, and was in need of a rest. The visit lasted six months, and contributed to William's growing happiness through the winter and into the next spring. He attested to the happiness of this reacquaintance with the childhood friend who would become his wife, in lines set down in the middle of his account of wandering the lonely roads of Dorset. His bleak walks were second in his enjoyment only to

> one dear state of bliss, vouchsafed
> Alas to few in this untoward world,
> The bliss of walking daily in life's prime
> Through field or forest with the maid we love
> While yet our hearts are young, while yet we breathe
> Nothing but happiness, *living in some place,*
> *Deep vale, or anywhere the home of both,*
> From which it would be misery to stir . . .
> (XII.127–34; italics added)

The purposeful vagueness of the locale fits well the conditions of their residence at Racedown. Of course, he could be referring to Dorothy as well, and he probably was.

Yet is Annette not ruled out of this picture, as we see in another fragmentary text he began at this time, a ballad called 'The Three Graves,' which he eventually abandoned as too 'depressing' and turned over to

Coleridge. The ballad's materials are not so depressing as they are psychologically loaded. It is not surprising that Wordsworth abandoned it – nor that he started it – when Mary's presence in the household inevitably stirred up thoughts and desires about his sexual life and his continuing obligations to Annette and their daughter. 'The Three Graves' is only the second ballad that Wordsworth had so far composed in his life, and the first since 1787, when he wrote about Mary Rigge's seduction and betrayal by David Kirkby of Coniston. He produced about two hundred lines, setting out the complications of a potentially incestuous love triangle, or quadrangle. No profound psychoanalytic insight is needed to recognize that the poem projects fantasy materials from his own situation that he could not resolve short of solving the central problems of his life.

The poem concerns the love of Edward for Mary, and the intense jealousy of Mary's widowed mother, which leads her to offer herself to Edward instead. Edward, amazed and disgusted, repulses the mother and, worse, laughs at her, whereupon she casts a curse upon her terrified daughter. The two young lovers leave the house with the mother on her knees in the orchard, gesticulating after them. There Wordsworth's fragment ends. Throughout her trials, Mary is supported by her friend Ellen, who 'though not akin in blood . . . did bear a sister's part' to her. This is exactly the kind of relationship Dorothy and Mary had begun to establish – as had Dorothy and Annette, in correspondence – and after 1802 it would be the pattern of the rest of their life together.[54] These three symbolic parallels are clear enough, but the identity of the 'ruthless mother' is much more problematic.

At first the mother agrees to the marriage, though Mary feared she wouldn't because, as she tells Edward, 'you have little gear' (wealth), like William. But the mother's assent is given on quite different grounds: 'In truth you are a comely man.' The 'course of wooing' goes on 'beneath the mother's eye.' Then, the night before the wedding, she suddenly sends her daughter upstairs with the cry, 'Would ye come here, ye maiden vile, / And rob me of my mate?' The girl flees and the mother offers herself to Edward on the grounds that Mary 'is not fit / To be your paramour.' Edward, of course, is looking for a wife, not a paramour, but a paramour was what, strictly speaking, Annette was to William – just as she was the only 'mother' among the three women in his life at this moment.

As they leave 'this wicked house,' the mother, with weird irony, wishes them well and tells them not to worry about her: 'What can an aged woman do, / And what have ye to dread?' The focus at the end of the fragment is very much on the mother – a mad mother, another version of the emerging dominant character in Wordsworth's poems, whose curse has rebounded upon herself. She is last seen baring her breast to show strangers 'the milk which clinging imps of hell / And sucking daemons drew.' Unless one arbitrarily decides the poem could have nothing to do with Wordsworth's life (exactly contrary to everything we have seen about every text he produced in the 1790s), it is easy to infer that he is imagining the anger or reproaches of Annette if he were to marry Mary Hutchinson, an idea which may now have first been seriously entertained by him, by Mary, and of course by Dorothy.

The whole story is told long after the fact by an old sexton in a churchyard where the three graves of the title are lined up beneath a thorn tree: 'a ruthless mother,' 'a barren wife,' and 'a maid forlorn.' The women are all dead, but where is Edward/William? Is he that blooming thorn near the graves? 'It blossoms sweet,' yet round 'its roots / The dock and nettle meet.' The sexton's tale may be Wordsworth's fantasy of the death of all three of the women troubling his constricted life, and his longing for freedom. Such a possibility seems finally more ordinary than shocking or surprising.

CHAPTER TWENTY

An Independent Intellect

From The Borderers *to 'The Ruined Cottage,' 1796–1797*

> . . . the only law that wisdom
> Can ever recognize: the immediate law
> Flashed from the light of circumstances
> Upon an independent intellect.
> (*The Borderers*, III.v.30–33)

From early October, Wordsworth was 'ardent' in the composition of *The Borderers*, his only surviving drama. He worked on it steadily through a winter of heavy, isolating snows, and brought it to its first complete form by the end of February: two thousand lines of blank verse in less than six months. At the end of 1797 he tried to make it suitable for stage production, but after it was rejected by the manager of Covent Garden he put it aside for over forty years.

Though unsuccessful as a stage vehicle, *The Borderers* was a strong conception, taking risks that face down easy criticisms. Wordsworth was attempting, seven years after the fall of the Bastille, to dramatize a fundamental critique of the spirit of revolution. Several works of English fiction had already taken up the implications of a radical application of reason to human institutions. Robert Bage (*Man As He Is*, 1792) and Wordsworth's old nemesis, Holcroft (*Anna St Yves*, 1792; *Hugh Trevor*, 1794–97), pursued the paradox that 'arguments advanced by one [view of reason] to attack the hypocrisy of institutions were employed by another to sap the foundations of human nature.'[1] Godwin's *Caleb Williams* and Burke's *Reflections* had probed the same paradox.

At its furthest stretch of implication, *The Borderers* asks why noble ideals of human liberation so often become tyrannical in their turn. It confronts the central moral dilemma that has dogged efforts to decide whether the French Revolution was finally worth it after all: How much does it matter that acts of unspeakable brutality are committed in the name

(*Clockwise from top left*) Wordsworth, by William Shuter (1798); Wordsworth, by Robert Hancock (1798); Wordsworth, by Henry Edridge (1806); Wordsworth? (disputed subject, artist unknown; *c.* 1803–1810)

(*Above*) Wordsworth's birthplace, Cockermouth; (*below*) Hawkshead School

Satan in All His Glory,
by James Gillray (8 May 1792)

The satirist 'Peter Pindar' (John Wolcott)
is pleading for mercy in Lowther's suit
against him for libel. Several of the 'glories'
in his halo were familiar to the Wordsworth
family: ruining creditors by non-stop law-
suits, undermining the town of Whitehaven,
bribing witnesses to perjure themselves,
bringing sham trials, and making hell-
hounds of his clerks and attorneys.

John Robinson, by William Ward

Penrith Beacon, from a nineteenth-century lithograph
The structure is approximately thirty feet high. It stands on Beaconhill (937 feet), on the east
edge of Penrith. The hill is part of the Beacon Plantation, property of the Lowther Trust.

Rural Road Scene,
by W. H. Pyne
(published 1824)

Bucks of the First Head, by Thomas Rowlandson (*c.* 1785)

(*Bottom left*) William Wilberforce, age 28 (June 1789), by John Rising
(*Bottom right*) William Frend, Fellow of Jesus College, Cambridge,
by Sylvester Harding (1789)

View of London over Blackfriars Bridge, from Albion Mills Tower (1791)
(The view taken for Barker's Panorama in Exeter Change.)

The Quacks (Dr. Graham and Dr. Katterfello), 1783

'…all the portals open stand
Of Health's own temple at her Graham's command'
(*Imitation of Juvenal*, lines 168–169)

Illustrating Graham's Temple of Health & of Hymen, with its 'Prime Conductor and Gentle Restorer, the Largest in the World'. The thistle marks Graham as that 'Scotch Doctor, famous in his day' (*Prelude*, VII.183, MS. variant [*Thirteen*]).

Bartholomew Fair, by Thomas Rowlandson

'What a hell
For eyes and ears, what anarchy and din
Barbarian and infernal'   (*The Prelude*, VII.659–61)

Near Beddgelert, by Thomas Rowlandson

Imagine, left to right: Jones, Wordsworth, guide and cur

Dorothy Wordsworth, pencil drawing
(The bottom of the sheet has been torn away.)

Helen Maria Williams,
by John Singleton

Presumed miniature portrait of
Annette Vallon, artist unknown

Antoine Joseph Gorsas
(1751–1793)

Jean-Louis Carra
(1742–1793)

'–Carra, Gorsas–add
A hundred other names, forgotten now,
Nor to be heard of more; yet were they powers,
Like earthquakes, shocks repeated day by day
And felt through every nook of town and field.'

(*The Prelude*, IX.179–83)

Henri Grégoire
(1750–1831)

(Detail from Jacques-Louis
David, *Oath of the Tennis
Court, 20 June 1789*)

Grégoire (in black) stands in
the middle of the foreground
group representing the union
of the clergy and the aristocracy. The other priest, representing religious establishments,
was not actually present, but
Grégoire was, representing the
regular parish clergy.

Michel Beaupuy
(1755–1796), artist unknown

'Beapuis – let the name
Stand near the worthiest of antiquity –'

(*The Prelude*, IX.426–27)

Thomas Holcroft and William Godwin at the 1794 Treason Trials, by Sir Thomas Lawrence

John Thelwall addressing crowd behind Copenhagen House, Islington (detail from *Copenhagen House*, by James Gillray, published 16 November 1795)

(in foreground: Charles Lamb (l.) and Robert Southey (r.) as urchins playing a roulette game, 'Equality and No Sedition Bill')

Daniel Isaac Eaton
(published 14 May 1794),
by W. Sharpe

(Motto: Frangas non Flectes:
'Break, Don't Bend')

Joseph Johnson,
by W. Sharpe

Francis Wrangham,
artist unknown

Samuel Taylor Coleridge,
by Peter Vandyke (1795)

Robert Southey,
by James Sharples

Charles Lamb,
by Robert Hancock

William Henry Cavendish Bentinck,
3rd Duke of Portland (1738-1809),
engraving by J. Murphy after
Sir Joshua Reynolds

Richard Ford

'His name is *Wordsworth* a name I think
known to Mr. Ford.'
(James Walsh, Home Office agent, to
John King, under-secretary for secret
service, 15 August 1797)

George Canning, by John Hoppner
(Editor of *The Anti-Jacobin*)

The New Morality, by James Gillray (published 7 August 1798)

'Coleridge & Co.' (detail from *The New Morality*)

Showing, left to right, John Thelwall (reaching out with book of lectures), Joseph Priestley, Gilbert Wakefield, Charles Lamb, Charles Lloyd, Wordsworth? (hand beneath cornucopia), Southey, and Coleridge. In rear, *bonnets rouges* roses, from Erasmus Darwin's *The Loves of the Plants*, and Lord Moira, Francis Rawdon-Hastings (1754–1826), Irish peer and hero of British actions in America, France, and (later) India.

Town End, by T. M. Richardson

Walter Scott,
from portrait by
Henry Raeburn

of admirable political ideals? *The Borderers* does not confront these questions directly, since its villain, Rivers, is no Robespierre, but at best a provincial caricature of him. But it anticipates questions which thoughtful revolutionaries asked themselves, often in crushed despair, over the next two hundred years.

Wordsworth's version of these questions is strongly skewed to produce a negative answer. His villain representing the dark side of revolution is a much stronger character than his naïve hero, Mortimer. Swinburne (who seems like a good authority on such matters) thought the play and its villain 'unparalleled by any serious production of the human intellect for morbid and monstrous extravagance of horrible impossibility.'[2] Mortimer is ready to break the law in order to help suffering poor people, but he cannot quite take the steps urged on him by Rivers, to go beyond all conventional moral considerations and act upon the right as he alone sees it.

Yet Wordsworth was not simply writing a tract for his times. His motives arose from his personal history, dramatizing his emotional involvement in the Revolution, especially his love affair with Annette Vallon, now complicated by his responsibilities for Dorothy.[3] The play enacts his attempt to purge himself of both kinds of personal commitment he had made to revolutionary possibilities since 1792, the emotional and erotic as well as the intellectual and political. Given the scope of its public theme, and the intensity of its private one, it is no wonder that the play fails dramatically. It has well be called 'a failed play of successful repression,' or a play that '*intends* to be a bad play.'[4]

Intellectually, *The Borderers* is a critique of the enlightened moral expediency which Wordsworth learned from Godwin. Rivers's monologues are shot through with the language of *Political Justice*, and the remorse-driven plot and the hero tricked into seeking vengeance are virtually identical to the basic situation of Godwin's popular *Caleb Williams*. Yet the play rarely broaches social or political issues directly, though they are implied by its military ambience: the Crusades and the border wars between England and Scotland. Instead, it enacts the personal dimension of philosophic issues, that arise prior to social action, and in so doing exposes the consequences of egotistically misappropriating the range of 'wild theories [then] afloat,' Godwin's among others.

When placed in the contexts of its larger resonance, the actual plot of *The Borderers* seems more than a bit bizarre. It concerns Rivers's efforts, through five very talky acts, to persuade Mortimer that his beloved Matilda has been groomed all her life by a man who pretends to be her father, the old blind Baron Herbert, to be delivered as a concubine to the depraved Lord Clifford. Herbert, according to Rivers, purchased Matilda as an infant from a beggar woman (actually a woman in Rivers's pay), and has morally bound her to him by telling her moving tales of how he saved her from the flames of Antioch in which her mother and brother died. Rivers goads Mortimer to kill Herbert for these heinous crimes, having beforehand poisoned Herbert's opinion of Mortimer as a lawless free-booter. He does all this because he resents owing gratitude to Mortimer for having once saved his life.

Rivers's deeper motive is a kind of philosophical seduction of Mortimer, to make him repeat a crime that Rivers himself was tricked into en route to Palestine. Convinced by the ship's crew that its captain meant to lead them to destruction, and that he had spoken slightingly of the proud Rivers, he agreed to lead their mutiny. They left the captain stranded on a piece of barren rock to die of starvation at the hand of the elements. Later, when the crew tell Rivers they have tricked him, he flees in remorse. But after three days of self-torment in a Biblical wilderness, he rejects remorse in favour of an ethic of personal expediency, raised to the level of an existentialist philosophy, which he subsequently tries to foist on Mortimer. Mortimer cannot quite bring himself to kill Herbert outright, but, in a duplication of Rivers's crime, abandons him on the barren heath.

The trouble with *The Borderers* is that everybody but Mortimer can see right away that Rivers is evil. It's the kind of play at which an audience wants to cry out, It's the guy in black, stupid! He's the villain! Mortimer's band of borderers virtually foam at the mouth every time they see Rivers, so spontaneously do they mistrust him, and they gleefully dispatch him in a mass stabbing as soon as Mortimer gives them leave in the final scene.

Wordsworth could not easily have solved this problem of plausibility without diluting the philosophical problem that was his real concern. The play, as a psychological thriller, lacks what Alfred Hitchcock called a 'MacGuffin,' some concrete plot device the audience can keep its eye on as the horror grows. A leadership struggle between Rivers and Mortimer would be an obvious solution, or a rivalry for Matilda's love. But any motive that Wordsworth gave Rivers would blur his radical existential focus and weaken his Iago-dimension: the powerful attraction of moral behaviour based solely on a virtuous conviction of the rightness of one's own motives, bolstered by total confidence in the scrupulous accuracy of one's efforts to learn the truth:

> . . . the only law that wisdom
> Can ever recognize: the immediate law
> Flashed from the light of circumstances
> Upon an independent intellect.
>
> (III.v.30–33)[5]

These famous lines, a twisted paraphrase of passages in *Political Justice*, are virtually identical with Wordsworth's description in *The Prelude* of the radical faith in 'the freedom of the individual mind' which ultimately led him to yield up all moral questions in despair.[6]

The Borderers rose from deep psychological roots, but it has many literary sources as well. First among these is Schiller's *Die Räuber*, published in England in 1792 as *The Robbers*. Wordsworth almost certainly saw this play during one of his two stays in Paris in 1791–92, given his predeliction for the theatre and the fact that a French adaptation, titled *Robert, le brigand*, held the stage there regularly for the better part of two years.[7] Schiller's play breathes the quintessence of the so-called new morality, which Coleridge felt with fearful exhilaration when he read it at Cambridge in October of 1795, asking Southey in wonderment, 'Did he [Schiller] write his tragedy amid the yelling of Fiends? . . . I tremble like as Aspen Leaf.'[8]

Schiller's hero, Charles de Moor (or Karl Moor), is a very commanding figure, the leader of a band of roving robbers, not Robin Hoods like Mortimer's band – though Moor's personal impulses have consistency and integrity. Wordsworth made Schiller's hero into a better man but a weaker one, like Vaudracour, who causes evil where he should do good. Legitimizing Mortimer at the level of social value, Wordsworth undercut him at the level of character.[9]

Wordsworth's most fruitful source was Shakespeare. *The Borderers* reads at times as if Hamlet had stumbled into the plot of *Othello*, in a political situation out of *Macbeth*'s Scotland, all set down on the blasted heath from *King Lear*. These Shakesperean echoes and pastiches can be sneered at, but individually they are often very good. In Wordsworth's self-creation, his use of them marks a new access of literary energy. If Wordsworth yielded up moral questions in despair in late 1795, he undertook the literary representation of that despair a year later with a sublime artistic confidence: taking on the best of Shakespeare to write a history play that was simultaneously an intellectual history of the French Revolution and of his own emotional involvement in it.

Finally and most typically, he recast his experience in the light of Milton's *Paradise Lost*. Rivers's temptation of Mortimer – to repeat a fall into sin that he himself has made – is the organizing template that Wordsworth used to organize all his other sources: Rivers is Satan to Mortimer's Eve. But if Rivers acts like Satan, Mortimer talks like him: 'I am weak. – There is my hell.'

With Burke on his right and Godwin on his left, Wordsworth was well equipped to give Rivers speeches that are dramatic paraphrases of the mental actions he attributed to himself at this time in *The Prelude*: when he 'dragged all precepts, judgments, maxims, creeds, / Like culprits to the bar; calling the mind . . . to establish in plain day / Her titles and her honours . . . demanding formal *proof* / And seeking it in everything' until he 'yielded up moral questions in despair.' Rivers has undergone the same process, but emerged in triumph, not despair:

>   Methinks
>   It were a pleasant pastime to construct
>   A scale and table of belief—as thus—
>   Two columns, one for passion, one for proof;
>   Each rises as the other falls: and first,
>   Passion a unit and *against* us—proof—
>   Nay, we must travel in another path,
>   Or we're stuck fast for ever;—passion, then,
>   Shall be a unit *for* us; proof—no, passion!
>   We'll not insult thy majesty by time,
>   Person, and place – the where, the when, the how
>   All particulars that dull brains require
>   To constitute the spiritless shape of Fact,
>   They bow to, calling the idol, Demonstration.
>   A whipping to the Moralists who preach
>   That misery is a sacred thing: . . .
>   . . . We dissect
>   The senseless body, and why not the mind?—
>   These are strange sights—the mind of man, upturned,
>   Is in all natures a strange spectacle;
>   In some a hideous one—hem! shall I stop?
>   (*1842* III.ii.1145–60, 1166–70)

This brilliant speech anticipates *The Prelude*'s mental trial scene, and is as close as Rivers ever comes to self-recognition.

Wordsworth could hardly have stamped the play more strongly with his own imprimatur than he did by setting it in the Borders at the time of the Barons' League against King Henry III, in the late thirteenth century. Mortimer and his gang are 'rievers,' or raiders, operating in the power vacuum created by the Crusades, at the beginning of the Border Wars that continued more or less without interruption until the accession of James VI of Scotland to the throne of England. Its locations are easily identifiable with Penrith and its Border Beacon,[10] the scene of one of his most traumatic early memories of male sexual violence. Almost all the character names in the play have North Country analogues. Besides Mortimer and Rivers (Rivaulx), the Cliffords were the ancient lords of Brougham Castle, whose ruins lie directly between Penrith Beacon and Lowther Castle, in clear sight of both.[11] The name Clifford was commonly associated in Cumberland with aristocratic excess.

The fact that Wordsworth signed two newspaper poems 'Mortimer' around this time clinches the fact, though not the degree, of his identification with the play's issues, as does does the symbolism of his later calling himself 'an outlaw and a borderer of his age.' And, though the play's villain was not renamed Oswald until sometime between 1796 and its publication in 1842, it is now widely accepted that Wordsworth must have had Colonel John Oswald partly in mind when he used the name, from recollections of the bloodthirsty Scottish mercenary he had seen in Paris. Wordsworth may also have been thinking of Kirkoswald in Scotland, named for St Oswald, who is also the patron saint of the Grasmere village church, a medieval soldier-priest. The mixture of two such different characters as namesakes perfectly embodies the ambivalent attractions of Wordsworth's Border villain.

Wordsworth's essay analysing the character of Rivers biographically draws his own experience further into the play. Its connections with the immediately preceding years of his own life are remarkable: 'great intellectual powers . . . pride and the love of distinction . . . talents robbed of their weight . . . quits the world in disgust, with strong misanthropic feelings.' He felt his abandonment of Annette as a 'great crime,' specifically the crime of desertion, which both Rivers and Mortimer commit against their lover's fathers, and which the sailor of 'Adventures on Salisbury Plain' and Robert of 'The Ruined Cottage' commit upon their wives. Wordsworth could well have viewed himself as 'betrayed' into this crime by his uncles' refusal to give him the aid he expected, or by his getting Annette pregnant in the first place by 'trusting' his passion 'to Nature.'[12] In any case, we have an over-supply of motives, just the sort of psychological overdetermination that can lead to intensely cathartic composition.

To stress *The Borderers*'s biographical connections is not strictly to call it an autobiographical work, however. Instead, Wordsworth wrote it from one of the most powerful of all writing perspectives: exploring *tendencies* he recognized in himself, worked out in actions provided mainly by other sources. Both of the play's main characters, Rivers and Mortimer, are aspects of Wordsworth's personality, as their precisely matched fates suggest. Biographically, Matilda would seem to stand mainly for Annette Vallon. But in her dependence on Mortimer, hero of the north, Matilda's character also partakes of Dorothy – and of Mary Hutchinson, currently living with them and literally under Wordsworth's protection. Given these overlapping possibilities in Wordsworth's biography, it is easy to see why *The Borderers* could never have reached a happy romantic ending. Wordsworth deeply wished, wanted, needed to live with both Annette and Dorothy. But he was deeply prohibited from doing so, by distance and political calamity in the case of Annette, and by proximity and cultural taboos in the case of Dorothy.

Baron Herbert, Lord Clifford, and Rivers's captain partake variously of John Wordsworth, James Lowther, John Robinson, William Cookson, and Christopher Crackanthorpe. None of these correlations are exact, but they are all figuratively powerful: the father who abandoned him by dying young, the aristocrat who manipulated the law to deny him his inheritance, the uncles who would not help him when he needed it most. What is astonishing about these connections, however, is that instead of paying them back, Wordsworth shows instead that 'authority is innocent.'[13] Old blind Baron Herbert is just what he seems, Rivers's captain may have been bad tempered but he was no villain, and even Lord Clifford's fiendish reputation is not borne out by the action of the play. Having taken great pains to suggest that established authority is as bad as can be imagined, the play reveals that *it is not so*: violent revolution is not justified. The only authority who is wrong is Mortimer, the hero of the story and the leader of the band, who tries to convince himself that his personal motives serve a higher good.

The play does not examine Wordsworth's personal failings so much as it filters his intense sense of creative individualism through his political and psychological motives. He had identified his growing sense of enormous creativity with the immense power for good represented by the French Revolution. After the Terror, after seeing – and participating in – the extremes to which both French and English ideologues were prepared to go to defend 'the new morality' which produced it, Wordsworth's reaction was not merely one of disillusionment – though it was that too, along with thousands of other European intellectuals. He was forced, in addition, to recognize in his own individualism the same kind of demonic tendencies that goaded the Jacobins, with the result that he was left in an extreme crisis of self-confidence.

Wordsworth was working out these biographical parallels in the context of political allegiances he had formed over the past four or five years, allegiances which he was now in the process of rejecting. At the end of the play, Rivers asks Mortimer how old he is. Mortimer replies, 'Just three and twenty summers': Wordsworth's age in the summer of 1793, when he had composed his regicide pamphlet, and when he went to France to try to rescue Annette – and failed in the basic manly action of saving his lover. (Schiller composed his play at age twenty-three as well.) If ever there was a text in which the personal is the political, Wordsworth's *Borderers* is it. And yet, on the face of it, as on the face of so many Wordsworthian texts, we see none of this. It looks like a failed medieval adventure story, set long ago and far away.

In the play's bleak catharsis there is no redemption for Mortimer. Civil and domestic order are not restored but left in worse shape than when the play opens. Herbert's lands have been restored, but he is dead and his daughter heartbroken; the man who should have been the source of their lives' continuity has been the cause of its destruction. The paradoxes cannot be screwed down any tighter. *The Borderers* is of a piece with Wordsworth's Racedown fragments of unrequited pain: we see everything that's wrong, but nothing that is right. Everyone in the play who is right is weak and helpless, and finally Mortimer is too.

The Borderers develops a situation that Wordsworth returned to constantly in the next few years, where a character perfectly placed to aid or save a suffering and vulnerable innocent person (usually a woman) is simultaneously poised or tempted to destroy that very person. This paradox, highly developed in the poetry of Helen Maria Williams, and implicit in Wordsworth's poetry of 1793–95, now becomes explicit. It relates not only to the play's paradox of arrogant individualism, but also to Wordsworth's questioning of his role as the narrator of many of these poems. To what extent is writing poems about suffering an adequate or justifiable human response to it?

As soon as *The Borderers* was finished, William sent off another section of the Juvenal imitation to Wrangham. He thanked Wrangham for his offer to find some more pupils for him, but finally rejected that vocational option: 'upon a review of my own attainments I think there is so little I am able to teach that this scheme may be suffered to fly quietly away to the paradise of fools.' His tone indicates high good humour, and Dorothy's letters at this time are full of the same report: 'we are as happy as human beings can be; . . . William is . . . as chearful as any body can be; . . . he is the life of the whole house.'[14] Clearly the time of depression and despair was over. At the same time, there came good news of John's safe return from nearly two years as fourth mate on the *Osterly*. He shipped out again in September, for Bengal, as second mate on the *Duke of Montrose*. These voyages were highly profitable to the officer-investors on any ship that did not sink, and John's rapid rise in rank shows he was doing very well indeed. He regularly invested one or two hundred pounds of Dorothy's money along with his own.

In mid-March, Basil Montagu arrived, with more good humour. He and William soon departed for a two-week visit to Bristol, with side trips to fashionable Bath. In Bristol, they paid calls on local society, notably the wealthy Wedgwoods, the pottery industrialists. They were frequently in company with James Losh, now fully recovered from the breakdown that had sent him packing from London in September of 1795.[15] When Wordsworth first saw him in London, Losh was raising money to help pay expenses for the Treason Trials defendants; now he was devoting his energies to the cause of Unitarian Sunday schools in Bath.[16] Both were worthy causes, but their difference in scope indicates the kind of changes in social activism young men of Wordsworth's class and persuasion were making at the time.

Montagu returned to London, but Wordsworth, before returning to Racedown, went down to Nether Stowey to visit Coleridge for a couple of days. This is the first visit of either poet to the residence of the other. He met Sara Coleridge, and observed the Coleridges ensconced in their little cottage at the end of Lime Street; he also got an earful from Coleridge about the difficulties of providing food for three mouths by the labour of one's pen. They talked – alone together for the the first time – of their highest ambitions, the great epic poems they dreamed of producing. The germ of *The Recluse*, Wordsworth's never-to-be-completed philosophical masterwork 'on Man, on Nature, and on Human Life,' was sown in these conversations.

They also discovered they were both writing plays, Coleridge having been urged by Richard Brinsley Sheridan to give him something for Covent Garden. Coleridge soon added his new friend's play to the project, and finishing the two works, *The Borderers* and Coleridge's *Osorio*, became their main work together when Wordsworth moved to Alfoxden.[17]

Through a small passage at the rear of Coleridge's garden, they visited the prosperous local tanner, Thomas Poole. A self-educated radical of the old English type, a self-styled 'Poor Man's Friend' whose charitable actions really merited the title, Poole was also one of the leading businessmen in North Somerset, and Coleridge's benefactor and friend. From Poole, Wordsworth learned that Alfoxden House, a handsome country mansion he had seen on one of his walks with Coleridge, was vacant, and he asked Poole to make some inquiries about the terms of its availability.[18]

Poole, an engaging raconteur, regaled the poets with local stories, providing Wordsworth with incidents that later led to 'The Idiot Boy,' 'The Farmer of Tilsbury Vale,' and 'Poor Susan.'[19] But by far the most compelling story Wordsworth heard from Poole was the account of a murder that had occurred outside Nether Stowey when Poole was a boy. Wordsworth soon turned this into a draft of the so-called 'Somersetshire Tragedy' which he subsequently abandoned, the manuscript of which was destroyed in 1931 by Gordon Wordsworth, as being 'in no way calculated to add to [W's] reputation, and [of] even less poetical merit than "The Convict," the only one of his published poems to which it bears resemblance.'[20]

Fortunately a few scraps of manuscript have been recovered, and accounts of the murder itself are fully recorded. It concerned a charcoal burner named John Walford who was in love with the local miller's daughter, Anne Rice. But his stepmother forbade their marriage. John was 'pursued' and 'solicited' in the woods by a retarded woman named Jenny, by whom he soon had two children. The parish authorities, presented with an illegitimate child, gave Walford the choice of paying for its maintenance or marrying Jenny. Walford chose the latter when the second child came, either to spite his stepmother or to avoid the embarrassment of asking her to help him support it. The marriage was a disaster, soon acted out. One night shortly after the marriage he sent her, or they went together, to the Castle of Comfort Inn (still in business on the A39 near Holford) for some cider. On the way, he murdered her, slitting her throat with a hedge stake, severing the muscles and arteries so thoroughly that the blood soaked his clothes.

Walford pleaded innocence, but was soon convicted by his own construction of the evidence: the shilling he said he had given her for cider was found in his bloody clothes. At his execution a month later a huge crowd gathered; he was reputed to be good-tempered, generous, and popular. As the cart was being positioned under the gibbet he asked if Anne Rice were present. 'Where is Anne?' ran the whisper through the crowd. She was discovered at the edge of the crowd, hiding below the brow of a hill. 'Almost lifeless,' she was dragged up to the gibbet, where she kneeled and Walford talked to her for ten minutes; she said nothing. He tried to kiss her, but an officer prevented him, saying 'You had better not – it can do no good.' He snatched her hand, kissed it, shed tears for the first time, declared he had commited the murder 'without foreintending it,' asked the assembled people and God for forgiveness, and, saying, 'I am now ready,' was hanged.

It is not hard to see why Wordsworth was fascinated with this story. It seemed like a case of life imitating art, so close was its triangular cast of characters to 'The Three Graves.' The ways in which the situation solicited Wordsworth's imagination are legion. Now the 'ruthless mother' would be Walford's stepmother, and an abandoned fiancée named Anne would obviously have stimulated his interest. Here were parental opposition to a desired marriage, and a young man stuck with an illegitimate child which forces him into an undesired marriage. The wife is seduced but then rejected, while the beloved is abandoned until the end, when she is called forth for an excruciatingly public declaration of his love.

What is most extraordinary about all accounts of the case, throughout the nineteenth century and into modern Wordsworth criticism, is the degree of sympathy for 'poor Jack Walford.' Anne Rice is given some melancholy sentimental consideration, but Jenny, the idiot girl, none at all: 'a bad character.' According to Poole, she was 'an ordinary squat person, disgustingly dirty and slovenly . . . but nevertheless she was a woman.' That was enough for John Walford. And no one says anything about his astounding self-dramatizing imposition on Anne Rice at his execution, attended by hundreds of people from all over the region.

No one, that is, but Wordsworth. In the few extant lines that are obviously intended for 'The Somersetshire Tragedy,' his focus is squarely on Jenny:

> Ill fared it now with his poor wife I ween,
> That in her hut she could no more remain:
> Oft in the early morning she was seen
> Ere Robert to his work had cross'd the green.
> She roam'd from house to house the weary day,

> And when the housewife's evening hearth was clean
> She linger'd still, and if you chanc'd to say
> 'Robert his supper needs,' her colour pass'd away.

A disconnected couplet adds, 'Her face bespake a weak and witless soul / Which none could think worth while to teach or to controul.'[21] Exactly: the couplet summarizes the whole history of Somerset commentary on the case, that 'none could think [it] worth while to teach or to controul' the likes of Jenny. Wordsworth alone of all the commentators was not swayed by John Walford's good looks, popularity, 'good temper,' and great strength. In the extant lines of Wordsworth's manuscript, Jenny is not given a name. In her society, she has the lowest status of any of the characters, counts for least, and is Wordsworth's heroine.

One nineteenth-century commentator says the 'sombre' story is better suited to Crabbe 'than to the cheerful poet of Rydal Mount.'[22] But our concern here is with the biographical cost to Wordsworth of achieving that cheerfulness. This is precisely the kind of perspective he was increasingly drawn to: the hardest case, the toughest question, the ugliest person. But he soon decided to give up work on 'The Somersetshire Tragedy' for an equally hard case, Margaret in 'The Ruined Cottage.'

With the negative catharsis of two tragedies behind him, Wordsworth turned immediately to new composition when he returned to Racedown. The new work was first called 'The Ruined Cottage,' then (about 1803) 'The Pedlar,' and finally, as the first book of *The Excursion* (1814), 'The Wanderer'. 'The Ruined Cottage' is the first of Wordsworth's poems that can be called 'major' without qualification. But it was never published by him in its greatest form, nor is it possible to say definitively what its best version is, for its textual status is highly problematic.[23] Yet it is one of the essential Wordsworthian texts, and his struggles with it – for seventeen years before publication, and in every republication of *The Excursion* thereafter, to 1845 – show that, like *The Prelude*, 'The Ruined Cottage' was a poem whose creation was inextricably bound up with his self-creation.

Its story is quickly told. Margaret and Robert live in a Dorset cottage where he does piece-work weaving. They have been fast-forwarded, Stoppard-style, from cameo roles in *The Borderers* as terrified peasants in the barons' wars, to helpless, unemployed small artisans of Dorsetshire, displaced by the 'Minister's War' with France, *c.* March 1797. They have two children and are happy. Then wartime dislocations throw him out of work and bad harvests raise the price of bread. He works around the cottage for a while, making small repairs, but finally the sight of his hungry wife and children becomes too much for him. He secretly enlists for the government's bounty of ten guineas and slips away one morning, leaving the money in a bag on the windowsill. Margaret waits years for his return, neglecting her house, her children, and herself. One child is taken away to an apprenticeship by the parish authorities, the other dies; finally Margaret dies too. End of story. It is another version of the story of an abandoned woman that is Wordsworth's main plot throughout the 1790s. His problem, again, is what to make of such a story. How should it be told? Even harder, how should it be heard?

In its earliest form, the poem does not appear to be something very new in Wordsworth's development. It looks like yet another of the free-standing images of unexplained suffering which he produced steadily throughout 1796–97: indeed, it is the apotheosis of this form. As with many of his poems, he composed its conclusion first. This contains the full force of Margaret's tale without a word of explanation, forty-six for-bidding lines which compress the essence of her experience into a sustained dirge. It begins, 'Five tedious years / She lingered in unquiet widowhood, / A wife, and widow. Needs must it have been / A sore heart-wasting.' And it ends, after remorselessly detailing her pathetic waiting and watching and putting her 'same sad question' about Robert to every passerby,

> Meanwhile her poor hut
> Sunk to decay, for he was gone whose hand,
> At the first nippings of October frost,
> Closed up each chink and with fresh bands of straw
> Chequered the green-grown thatch. And so she sate
> Through the long winter, reckless and alone,
> Till this reft house by frost, and thaw, and rain
> Was sapped; and when she slept the nightly damps
> Did chill her breast, and in the stormy day
> Her tattered clothes were ruffled by the wind
> Even at the side of her own fire.—Yet still
> She loved this wretched spot, nor would for worlds
> Have parted hence; and still that length of road
> And this rude bench one torturing hope endeared,
> Fast rooted at her heart, and here, my friend,
> In sickness she remained, and here she died,
> Last human tenant of these ruined walls.
> (MS B, 512–28)[24]

A child can read this, but what ancient wisdom is necessary to understand it? The simple repetitions and specific indications ('this rude bench,' 'that path,' 'yon gate'), relentlessly underscored by adverbs of time and place (here, here; still, still) build to a climax of almost unbearable power: she stayed here, she kept waiting and hoping, and finally she died doing it.

No one who heard these lines ever forgot them. They were the first thing Wordsworth read to Coleridge when he came for his visit in early

June. Coleridge asked Dorothy to copy them out for him, and many years later he still recalled the impact of 'The Ruined Cottage' on him, and regretted that Wordsworth had not published it in its original form. Lamb, Hazlitt, Southey, and others who heard versions of the poem over the next six months similarly attest its enduring power.

These lines are the summa of the descriptions of human suffering that Wordsworth began with the female beggar of *An Evening Walk* and the Grison gypsy of *Descriptive Sketches*. Symbolic details of the beggar woman – her husband died in war and she also had two children – are made literal in Margaret's tale. In the dirge of 'The Ruined Cottage' almost all the characters of Wordsworth's recent work are reprised: not only the abandoned woman, but the returning soldier and sailor, 'the crippled Mendicant,' and the nameless wanderer who encounters them all – and must tell their tales.

The version that Wordsworth had completed by the time Coleridge arrived was no more than 300 lines long, barely a third the length it would reach six months later, and much shorter than the nearly one thousand lines it contained by the time of its publication in 1814. The poem grew so long, and over so long a time, because Wordsworth had set himself a terrific double challenge: to write a full narrative of how Margaret had come to this end, and to place that narrative in a framework that would comprehend the terrific force of its ending, making it both philosophically plausible and aesthetically palatable. He wanted it to be recognized as a poem making a complete statement, and not to leave begging the ferocious questions such an ending provokes: Why do these things happen? Who is responsible? What are we to do in the face of such dying? These were challenges to the very essence of what he felt his poetic *self* to be. He was determined to get beyond reportage, no matter how powerful, and achieve some kind of satisfactory conclusion. He was never wholly successful in meeting the aesthetic, philosophical, or political challenges posed by 'The Ruined Cottage,' but we should not underestimate the force of these challenges to his ambition and self-confidence.

Political critics on both the left and the right have been driven to distraction by what they see as Wordsworth's unacceptable resolution of the poem. On the right, there are readers like Thomas De Quincey, who nearly stamped himself into the ground like Rumpelstiltskin in his annoyance with both Margaret and Wordsworth for failing to have taken advantage of the several agencies of help and information which existed in communities around her: the local vicar, the magistrate, the war office, the commander of the nearest army post, or almost any responsible citizen. 'To have overlooked a point of policy so broadly apparent as this vitiates and nullifies the very basis of the story.'[25] De Quincey also criticized Margaret severely for 'gadding about' instead of taking care of her house and children. All valid criticisms, but all inadequate to Margaret's tragedy.

On the left, critics in our own time have been very disapproving of Wordsworth's failure to develop the socioeconomic context he established at the beginning of the poem (the war with France) into a thorough-going critique of a political system that wages wars at the expense of its own citizens.[26] For these critics, contrary to De Quincey, there is no meaningful help available: the whole social situation is itself so 'criminal' as to make revolution almost the necessary consequence.

For both sets of critics, the issues are clear: the status quo or the revolution, which will it be? But Wordsworth's problem is, rather, what to *say* about her death, in and as a *poem*.

These are questions Wordsworth would try to answer in January of 1798. But in the first week of June 1797, his immediate problem was finding and keeping an audience. The young narrator of 'The Ruined Cottage' is trapped into a heightened sense of personal guilt by the Pedlar's artful tale-telling, and Wordsworth used something of the same tactics on Coleridge.

Coleridge arrived at teatime. As he came up over the hill, he saw William and Dorothy working in the garden and vaulted the fence gate, running down across the field to greet them. This famous vignette, often used to represent the birth moment of British Romanticism, possibly did not occur where most people think it did: namely, on the road from Crewkerne where a small rise gives a first glimpse of Racedown, its front door less than a hundred diagonal yards away. But William and Dorothy were working in the gardens which, as Racedown's present owner has pointed out to me, have always have been behind the house, to the southwest. If Coleridge had come from Crewkerne he could not have seen them from that road. But if he were coming *via* Chard, which is in a straighter direct line from Nether Stowey, he would have approached the house from the west, the direction of Forde Abbey. From that smaller road he could easily have seen William and Dorothy working in the gardens at the rear, but his famous dash across the fields would have been considerably more demanding: up and down a couple of intervening hillocks, across a bushy stream at the bottom, and up a longish incline to the house, a distance of at least three hundred yards.

Whichever angle Coleridge took, the ordeal that awaited him at teatime was considerably more taxing, reminding us that Romanticism is not simply about running across summer fields to greet friends, but also about hearing poems like 'The Ruined Cottage' at the end of one's run – and, somehow, connecting the two experiences into one. 'The Ruined Cottage' was read to Coleridge immediately; after tea he recited for them the first two and a half acts of *Osorio*. High tea indeed! The hiking endurance of these young people, so often remarked on, was nothing compared to their spiritual stamina. It must have been hard to swallow tea and biscuits after hearing 'The Ruined Cottage' recited by its author, its dirge-like conclusion hammered down from the height of that craggy, melancholy face in stern Miltonic cadences, with images that came right off the roads Coleridge had just been walking.

Coleridge's visit was intended to be a brief one, but it extended for week after week as conversations and re-readings of 'The Ruined Cottage', *The Borderers*, and *Osorio* preoccupied the two young men, implicating them in each other's work and involving them in each other's lives. All three works turned on the question of remorse for a guilt not personally incurred, but caused by sympathetic feelings of implication in unjust situations involving one's friends or loved ones. The friendship of Wordsworth and Coleridge was one of the most productive in the history of literature, and it had many levels. But in the immediate situation of their shared work, it was the aesthetic and philosophic problems of 'The Ruined Cottage' that brought them together.

As June turned into July, and the time came for Coleridge to return home, neither he nor the Wordsworths could bear the thought of separation. Their acquaintance and friendship, kindling slowly over two years, had blazed into love: the kind of passion one would sacrifice almost anything to prolong. Coleridge, ever the entrepreneur, soon thought of ways to maintain it. He returned home to Nether Stowey, but for one reason only: to tell Sara that William and Dorothy Wordsworth were coming for a visit.

CHAPTER TWENTY-ONE

The Spy and the Mariner

Nether Stowey and Alfoxden, 1797

... philosophic thought. . . poetic dreams
In dell romantic . . . and perchance,
Allfoxden's musing tenant, and the maid
Of ardent eye, who, with fraternal love,
Sweetens his solitude . . .

(John Thelwall, 'Lines written at Bridgwater, in Somersetshire, on the 27th
of July, 1797, during a long excursion, in quest of a peaceful retreat')

Coleridge went to Nether Stowey on 28 June, returning next day to collect William and Dorothy for a reciprocated summer visit that he and William had already planned to last much longer. The apparent spontaneity of the Wordsworths' move to Somerset, charming as it seems, was not accidental. Wordsworth had prospected the Stowey neighbourhood during his spring visit, found a vacant house, and set inquiries afoot. Once it became clear at Racedown how well they all got on together, the decision to move was a foregone conclusion.

Coleridge was almost as lonely at Stowey as the Wordsworths were at Racedown. He had come there in January, seeking cheaper living quarters after Charles Lloyd, scion of the banking family, left Bristol, suffering from both physical and mental instability. Lloyd's father had been paying Coleridge £80 a year to maintain his son, but the young man's eccentricities had become impossible to support at any price. Coleridge moved out to the country to continue his independent studies while trying to support his wife and new child by periodical writing. He was assisted by an annuity of £40 that the philanthropic Tom Poole had raised among Coleridge's Bristol admirers to offset the loss of Lloyd's money. He found Coleridge a tiny cottage on Lime Street in Nether Stowey, two rooms down and two up, with a rear garden abutting Poole's orchard of lime and lemon trees. Coleridge made a strong emotional commitment to this cottage, to bolster the image of rural poet he was building up, romanticizing what Sara later termed 'a miserable cottage' and that he himself recalled as 'an old hovel.'[1]

Having lost half his income, Coleridge needed more, and on most Sundays could be found walking crosscountry to preach at Unitarian chapels as far away as Bridgwater and Taunton.[2] One Sunday in April, an old woman on the road asked him if he knew the 'vile Jacobin' who had led astray George Burnett (b. 1776), a young man of the neighbourhood who like Charles Lloyd had fallen for Coleridge's charm, lost his Christian faith, and become addicted to opium.[3] Coleridge (the villain himself) replied that he did not, but commiserated – not ungenuinely – with the woman's complaints about the new 'philosophic' foolishness that had led several young men thereabouts into idealistic schemes like Pantisocracy. Young Burnett, like young Lloyd, had been led astray by 'those two extraordinary young men, Southey and Coleridge,' as Wordsworth had described them to Mathews two years earlier. Five years later, his life still sliding downhill, Burnett would recall that 'the enchantments of Pantisocracy threw a gorgeous light over the objects of life; but it soon disappeared, and has left *me* in ruin.'[4] Coleridge, estranged from Southey, losing Lloyd, and with young men like Burnett and others now among the philosophical walking wounded of the past two years, needed a fresh draft of discipleship.[5] He soon found a new master instead, if not a new deity: 'the Giant Wordsworth, God love him.'[6]

The visit at Racedown had been an intellectual honeymoon; the move to Stowey was more like setting up housekeeping for a lifetime together. The two poets could not get enough of each other's company, and Dorothy was the conduit through which the lively currents of their sensibilities passed. Both of them were in love with her, one way or other. Her personality was similar to Coleridge's: alert, fast thinking, attuned to slights beyond the moral perception of most human beings, her taste (said Coleridge) 'a perfect electrometer – it bends, protrudes, and draws in, at subtlest beauties & most recondite faults.' She and Coleridge were a match even in their initially critical perceptions of each other. She: 'At first I thought him very plain, that is, for about three minutes . . . but if you hear him speak for five minutes you think no more of [his] . . . wide mouth, thick lips, and not very good teeth.'[7] He: 'She is a woman indeed! – in mind, I mean, & heart – for her person is such, that if you expected to see a pretty woman, you would think her ordinary – if you expected to find an ordinary woman, you would think her pretty!'[8] Wordsworth was relaxed and open in Dorothy's presence as with no other person. Though he had known and admired Coleridge for nearly two years, he might never have embraced him so whole-heartedly had it not been for the medium of exchange provided by Dorothy's quicksilver emotions. She translated the Coleridgean fantastic into Wordsworth's more severe natural idiom.

In mid-summer of 1797, the central cast of characters of the first generation of English Romantics began to assemble together on stage for the first time, under the direction of Samuel Taylor Coleridge. He brought William and Dorothy Wordsworth back home with him, and he sent invitations to Charles and Mary Lamb to join them, as well as to John Thelwall and his wife Stella.[9] Charles Lloyd would return briefly in September, his health temporarily restored, but he soon turned vicious in print. Southey, in London, was kept informed of the group's activities by mail. Coleridge's creation of his Romantic generation was the first product of this miraculous year, as *Lyrical Ballads* was its last. In his retrospective on this time in *Biographia Literaria*, twenty years later, Coleridge contrived to make it appear that the production of that highly controversial volume had been the planned outcome of this year. But this was not the case on the ground at Stowey in July 1797, where the idea was – still – the formation of a community of like-minded spirits who would sustain each other in a political climate that was becoming increasingly hostile. Just how hostile, only one of them, Thelwall, really knew.

But for three precious weeks everything seemed like paradise. Dorothy gave Somerset her highest seal of approval, comparing it favourably to her idealized childhood home: 'the brooks clear and pebbly as in Cumberland,' the villages 'so romantic,' and 'the woods are as fine as those at Lowther, and the country much more romantic; it has the character of the less grand parts of the neighbourhood of the Lakes.'[10] All of them began to throw the word 'romantic' about with abandon; normally reserved for exotic scenes and fantastic love stories, it now referred to themselves, their lives and their surroundings. Gradually the word shaded in their usage from its first connotation into the idea of imagination casting a shadow or light across any landscape or person or thought, making it *visible*, as if for the first time, by making it *strange*.

They certainly all seemed strange to the neighbours. Their habit of rambling about the countryside day and night was unusual in a farming region not much used to tourists, and they walked with Coleridge and sometimes with Poole, both known political extremists. In January, Coleridge had distributed a prospectus for six lectures (never delivered) comparing the English and French revolutions, and in May these Stowey liberals had disturbed customers in a tea room with loud exclamations of joy over the news of Napoleon's success in his second Italian campaign against Austria.[11] Wordsworth's severe silences and republican-cropped hair excited 'an impression of awe and mistrust,' and Dorothy's presence was especially noted by conservative country folk who were very sure that a woman's place was in the home, and were not at all sure just whose child Basil Montagu, Jr was.[12] Their strange habits and topics of conversation, their unusual accent, and the fact that they received letters from France made them known as 'the French people.'[13] Silly people thought they might be conjurors, ordinary folk assumed they were smugglers, but the wisest heads assured everyone they must be Jacobins.[14]

They were up and about on the Quantocks from the first day, walking past Walford's Gibbet outside Stowey and up Dowsborough Hill where the ruins of an ancient Roman fortification made them feel masters of all they surveyed. The great thing about the Quantocks, they immediately discovered, was that you can stride along bare open hilltops, your very brain open to the sky because of the hills' percipitous drop to the nearby sea, and then descend quickly into deeply shaded, silent combes that seem to hold secrets as mysterious as the hilltops' revelations.

Within a day or two of their arrival, perhaps on this very first excursion, William took Dorothy on a walk through Holford Combe where they 'discovered' a beautiful house in the woods. This was a nice gesture on Wordsworth's part, almost a lover's ploy, since the route they followed was by no means accidental. Their 'wandering' led them straight from Stowey to Alfoxden House, which he knew from his conversations with Poole was empty and available. The handsome house and its magnificent setting swept Dorothy off her feet, and Poole was immediately instructed to conclude arrangements with its owner.

Alfoxden House, more than two hundred years old, was the largest house on the eastern side of the Quantocks. It was owned by Mrs Anna St Albyn, whose husband, Lancelot, the rector of nearby Stringston, had died in 1791. The St Albyns had no children, and Alfoxden with its well-stocked deer park was much too large for her; it was to be inherited by her grandnephew, who was still a minor. Invasion scares and the unsettled economy had played havoc with country house rentals, especially in the West Country. The Wordsworths were not quite as lucky as they were with Racedown, but Mrs St Albyn was so glad to have the house occupied, by a party recommended by the prosperous (if rather too democratical) Mr Poole, that she agreed to let it out at the very reasonable rent of £23 for a year – payable, in another advantageous perk, at the end of the term, with Poole meanwhile binding himself as security. Wordsworth was becoming a shrewd dealer in matters of rent and inheritance.

Compared to Racedown, which was grand enough, the Wordsworths were getting twice the house at less than half the price. Alfoxden had nine bedrooms and three parlours, 'with furniture enough,' Dorothy exclaimed to Mary Hutchinson, 'for a dozen families like ours.'[15] It is located just where the northernmost Quantocks drop down toward the sea a mile and a half away. From its rear parlour, which soon became Dorothy's favourite, they looked across a sloping fertile landscape, over farms nestling around Kilve and East Quantoxhead to the Bristol Channel. In front, 'it is screened from the sun by a high hill which rises immediately from it. This hill is beautiful, scattered irregularly and abundantly with trees, and topped with fern . . . . The deer dwell here, and sheep, so that we have a living prospect.' It was perfectly situated for their excursions in either direction: up into the hills or down along the sea. It is now a pleasant country hotel, and Dorothy's favourite parlour is the spacious dining room, which can seat forty guests.

A drive curves up to the house from the hamlet of Holford on the main road (A39), past an ancient kennel for hunting dogs, and around a thickly wooded hill which blocks the house from the village commons. Alongside this drive, down a steep bank, runs a little stream where William let Dorothy discover 'a sequestered waterfall in a dell formed by steep hills covered with full-grown timber trees.' This waterfall became the emblem of their year there, and a symbol of the new cultural forms they now began to create. At almost the same time that Dorothy was outlining Alfoxden's grounds for Mary Hutchinson, Coleridge was sketching in its details for Charles Lamb:

> . . . that still roaring dell, of which I told;
> The roaring dell, o'erwooded, narrow, deep,
> And only speckled by the mid-day sun;
> Where its slim trunk the ash from rock to rock
> Flings like an arching bridge; —that branchless ash,
> Unsunn'd and damp, whose few poor yellow leaves
> Ne'er tremble in the gale, yet tremble still,
> Fann'd by the waterfall!
> ('This Lime-Tree Bower My Prison,' 9–16)

The specifically 'romantic' quality they all identified in it was not simply its beauty, but its *strange* beauty: it was dim at noon, its trees' leaves were almost white, not green, even in mid-summer, and they moved not with the wind but were agitated by the air currents from the falling waters.

By 12 July, Poole had concluded the arrangements for Alfoxden, and on 13 July William and Dorothy moved in – yet another significant 13 July for him to remark, to go with those of 1790 and 1793, a series to be culminated a year later in the date of 'Tintern Abbey': 'July 13, 1798.' Charles Lamb had arrived at Stowey on 7 July, partly to celebrate the volume of poetry which he and Coleridge and Lloyd had published in May, but mostly for relief from a family tragedy. His sister Mary in a fit of insanity had stabbed their senile mother to death over a small domestic incident that had unhinged her delicate mind, and she was still under doctors' care. Lamb saved Mary from incarceration in a madhouse by pledging himself to care for her for the rest of her life. Lamb the ebullient, the witty, and the frequently tipsy was not much in evidence during his week's stay, but sat a quiet, recuperative spectator to the enthusiasms of Wordsworth and his sister, watching with 'the silence of a grateful heart.' He now met Dorothy for the first time, though he was already somewhat acquainted with Wordsworth from mutual friends in the Inns of Court.

William and Dorothy took Lamb out on one of their daily jaunts when Coleridge could not join them because Sara had accidentally spilled a pan of the baby's hot milk on his foot. The day's walk was not recorded by its participants, but it lives for posterity in Coleridge's vivid imagining of it in 'This Lime-Tree Bower My Prison,' written as he spent the day in Poole's orchard with his sore foot wrapped up. He imagined the uniquely Quantockian experience of coming up out of the shrouded combes to

> view again
> The many-steepled tract magnificent
> Of hill, fields and meadows, and the sea,
> With some fair bark, perhaps, whose sails light up
> The slip of smooth clear blue betwixt two Isles
> Of purple shadow!
>   ('This Lime-Tree Bower My Prison,' 21–26)[16]

Lamb departed on 14 July, just missing Thelwall, who was expected any day, and who arrived on the 17th, having walked the whole way from London. Lamb very much regretted not seeing 'the Patriot,' and wrote back that he 'was looking out for John Thelwall all the way from Bridgwater, and had I met him, I think it would have moved me almost to tears.'[17] Thelwall had become the literal embodiment of his earlier journal, the *Peripatetic*, being hounded by a government-encouraged campaign of harrassment and intimidation.[18] Three years earlier, he had been public enemy no. 1, as one of the 'aquitted felons' of the 1794 treason trials and the specific target of the second gagging act, directed against large public meetings. By 1797, the Home Office's campaign against him had succeeded. He had folded his *Tribune* in March of 1796, and for the last year had been trying, with dwindling success, to rally the forces and funds of opposition in the provinces. As a public speaker he offered an inviting target. His lectures were broken up by hired ruffians in Norwich, and he had been chased back and forth across the country from Yarmouth to Liverpool, denied protection by local magistrates, heckled into silence by patriotic drunks, and on one occasion 'escorted' out of town by a detachment of the Inniskilling dragoons.[19]

Thelwall had few friends left in the land who were willing to receive him by the time he arrived in Nether Stowey. At the peak of his popularity in London in 1795, Thelwall had been jealous of Coleridge's similar fame in Bristol, but they soon overcame their personal differences, and Coleridge had maintained a frank correspondence since his troubles began in 1796. Like Paine, Godwin, and Holcroft, Thelwall was one of the last of the pure rationalist breed: frank, honest, intelligent men, but rather one-sided personalities. He was well suited to times of crisis when issues had to be presented in their starkest terms. This made him an effective open-air orator: with his personal courage and a strong set of lungs, he could have been England's Danton. But he (also like Danton) was ill suited to times of repression and intrigue that were the coming norm in England. Funding for the newly reorganized secret service reached a new high in 1797, with documentable effect on the poets' year at Alfoxden and their subsequent year in Germany.[20]

Tom Poole's native populism made him receptive to Thelwall as well, though Poole distrusted his enthusiasm for abstract natural rights as much as Coleridge was distressed by his atheism. But Poole's relatives, already upset by his adoption of Coleridge, were shocked when they heard Thelwall had turned up at Stowey. This, following the news that Alfoxden had been 'taken by [another] one of the fraternity,' made young Charlotte Poole wonder, 'To what are we coming?'[21] Another cousin, asked by Poole to sing 'Come, sweet Liberty' from Handel's *Judas Maccabeus* for Wordsworth and Coleridge, demurred, explaining, 'I *could* not sing it. I knew what they meant by *their* liberty.'[22]

Thelwall eagerly entered into the spirit of things at Stowey. He too began to use the fashionable word 'romantic' freely, writing to his wife about 'the Academus of Stowey' and 'the wild, romantic dell in these grounds.'[23] He was obviously enjoying himself, compared to the hazards he had undergone during the preceding year, and he and Coleridge teased each other about things that were no laughing matter to the government. Their best exchange has been improved by much retelling, but it captures this brief moment of ideological stasis, before Thelwall descended into obscurity, and Coleridge and Wordsworth rose up as capitalized Romantics. Beside the strange waterfall which was their holy place, Coleridge mockingly reproached Thelwall, 'Citizen John, this is a fine place to talk treason in!' 'Nay, Citizen Samuel,' Thelwall retorted, 'it is rather a place to make a man forget that there is any necessity for treason.'[24] Wordsworth's recollected version of the same exchange is much tamer; it was certainly *safer*. He thought Coleridge had said that 'it was a place to soften one's remembrances of the strife and turmoil of the world,' and that Thelwall had merely replied, 'Nay . . . to make one forget the world altogether.'[25] No mention of treason here! Before the month was out they were forcibly reminded that though they might forget the 'necessity' to talk treason, there were others who heard them talk and remembered the very different duty of patriotism.

On 23 July, William and Dorothy hosted a housewarming dinner for fourteen people. The guests, besides the Coleridges, Thelwall, and Poole and his secretary Thomas Wade, were Mr and Mrs John Cruikshank, of Castle Hill House in Stowey, like Wordsworth the son of an aristocrat's steward (the Earl of Egmont), who had been admitted at Temple Bar with William Mathews in 1793.[26] In addition, there were the Willmotts from Woodlands, an estate across the main coaching road. He was the son of a

Shelborne silk manufacturer and later became a confidential steward for the Wedgwoods. The remainder were other veterans of Pantisocracy who still flitted around the captivating flame of Coleridge's genius: John Chester, a farmer's son from Dodington who followed him to Germany, and the unhappy George Burnett, 'the wreck of Pantisocracy.'[27] It was a gathering of liberal intelligentsia, like-minded spirits opposed to the present government.

The main course was a leg of Poole's lamb, gaily ordered by Coleridge to be sent over to 'The Foxes' at all-fox-den. The main entertainment was a dramatic reading of *The Borderers* under the trees: a gloomy set of after-dinner speeches, but one that reflected the disaffected mood of the group. During dinner Thelwall, wearing his radical's white hat, 'talked so loud and in such a passion' that he frightened one of the servants, Thomas Jones, so much that he feared to approach the table again. Thomas, who may have been a freelance informer,[28] told his fellow servants about the ranting he had heard. It fitted so well with the gossip that was already accumulating about the strange newcomers that the story travelled rapidly across the country, from kitchen to kitchen, picking up lurid details as it went. In less than two weeks the rumours from Alfoxden had reached the ears of justices of the peace and doctors and lawyers right along the road from Cannington to Bridgwater to Bristol to Bath. Such gossip was part of a national mania for denouncing 'suspicious' individuals, events or publications that had grown steadily since the passage of the gagging acts.[29] The Home Office had all it could do simply to acknowledge the almost daily 'informations' it received from around the country, especially from the southern coastal counties.

On 8 August Dr Daniel Lysons of Bath sent a letter to the Duke of Portland at the Home Office, alerting him to suspicious goings-on at Alfoxden; three days later he followed it up with more details. From his cook, a friend of a woman servant who was a friend of Charles Mogg, who was a friend of Thomas Jones, he had learned that 'the Master of the house has no wife with him, but only a woman who passes for his Sister,' that he and his friends went about the countryside on 'nocturnal and diurnal excursions,' carrying camp stools and 'a Portfolio in which they enter their observations which they have been heard to say were almost finished,' and that they were 'very attentive to the River near them.'[30]

The Home Office reacted instantly. Even before Lysons's second letter arrived, John King, the permanent undersecretary, had dispatched one of his top agents, James Walsh, to investigate. Walsh was already at Hungerford, east of Bath, interrogating Mogg when Lysons's additional information came in. He sent back new particulars (hedging them with the warning that 'Mr Mogg is by no means the most intelligent man in the world'): 'some French people had got possession of the Mansion House' (Alfoxden), that they were taking measures of the house and other places in the country, and that they had asked Christopher Trickie (who had been a huntsman for the St Albyns) whether the waterfall brook was navigable to the sea, 'and upon being informed . . . that it was not, they were afterwards seen examining the Brook quite down to the Sea.' Trickie, who lived by the Alfoxden dog kennel, either misheard the question or served an ill turn to the new tenants of the big house, since anyone who saw that brook would know it could not be navigable anywhere. Wordsworth made Trickie into a pathetic, poor, old, sick, and dying man in 'Simon Lee,' who is excessively grateful for small favours. But the vicar of Over Stowey had a firmer grasp on the real Trickie's character when he called him 'as rascally faced a fellow as ever I met with.'[31]

King replied immediately, on 12 August, instructing Walsh to proceed to Alfoxden to confirm these reports, but to avoid arousing suspicion so that that the tenants might be arrested on the spot, if warranted. Walsh was to get their names and follow their movements. King's instructions clearly reflect the government's increasingly sophisticated handling of internal intelligence matters: all reports were received with initial scepticism and subjected to double-checking.[32]

Three days later Walsh reported from the Globe Inn at Stowey, 'the nearest house I can get any accommodation at.' He had cleared up a good deal of the mystery simply by eavesdropping on his landlord's conversation about 'those Rascalls from Alfoxton.' One of them is 'the famous Thelwall,' who had already left, and the whole 'Nest of them' are protected by Mr Poole, 'a Tanner of this Town.' They were not French, but the landlord assured him 'they are people that will do as much harm, as all the French can do.' Walsh was pretty sure 'this will turn out no French affair, but a mischiefuous [*sic*] gang of disaffected Englishmen.' Just before signing off, he added, 'I have just procured the name of the person who took the House. His name is *Wordsworth* [Walsh's emphasis] a name I think known to Mr Ford.'

By the next day, Walsh had the whole story more or less straight: the Wordsworths' removal from Racedown, Poole's standing in the community and his radical organization, the Poor Man's Club, Coleridge's reputation ('a Man of superior Ability . . . soon to produce a new work'), that Wordsworth's woman servant, Peggy Marsh, called her master 'a Phylosopher,' and that 'a Great Counsellor from London' and a gentleman from Bristol had just arrived (Basil Montagu and Azariah Pinney). This is the last report in the file, and it may have been the end of the affair as far as the Home Office was concerned.

But the significance of this episode was massively forestalled for posterity by Coleridge's hilarious send-up of it in Chapter 10 of *Biographia Literaria* as the 'Spy Nozy' incident. Coleridge cast it as a Shakespearean comic sub-plot, complete with Walsh as red-nosed Bardolph, and Sir Philip Hales, Bart., of Cannington (to whom Undersecretary King directed Walsh to apply for additional assistance) as 'Sir Dogberry.' He says the spy tracked them for three weeks with 'truly Indian perseverance' (three days was more like it), and hid behind their favourite seat at the sea-bank, where he overheard them 'talk of one Spy Nozy.' Walsh supposedly thought this referred to him and his 'remarkable feature,' but was soon convinced 'that it was the name of a man who made a book and lived long ago [Spinoza]'. Coleridge said that Walsh assured his superiors 'that both my friend and myself were as good subjects, for aught he could discover to the contrary, as any in His Majesty's dominions.' This was certainly not Walsh's testimony.

The long-term effect of Coleridge's joke has been to divert attention from the seriousness of the episode and from the idea (still potentially damaging to his career in 1817 when the *Biographia* was published) that he and 'the strange gentleman' could have had anything to do with Jacobinism. It helped to establish the enduring image that they were only harmless poets, not political writers or activists, and that the government was making the kind of mistake that bureaucratic blinders and political hysteria usually produce. This is far from the truth. Whatever we think of Pitt's wartime policy, or of Portland's surveillance of domestic dissent, the government acted correctly and efficiently according to its lights. Pitt's government was very shaky in the spring and summer of 1797 because of the failure of its peace negotiations in late 1796, leading it to intensify its efforts against internal dissent, a policy it could pursue almost with impunity following the Foxite Whigs' 'secession' from Parliament in March for a period of nearly three years. In reaction, a meeting at the Crown & Anchor on 18 May urged all reformers to minimize their differences and maintain solidarity, 'for the reign of Terror and Proscription has begun in England.'[33] The report on 'the Alfoxden gang' thus came in just at the beginning of Pitt's so-called 'reign of terror.' Within a week of its receipt of an unsolicited piece of information from a doctor in Bath, the Home Office had dispatched and funded its top agent, who crossed the country and sent back all the details necessary to dispose of the case. None of the government officers ever suggested that a *mistake* has been made, still less a hilarious one, only that the suspicious persons were not French or French agents, but a gang of disaffected Englishmen, who are well known – and thus accounted for – in their disaffection.

In the summer of 1797, Pitt's main concern was invasion, especially in the West Country, not internal dissent. On 22 February, a small French fleet had appeared off Ilfracombe, just beyond Linton, and engaged in some small depradations as it made its way toward Bristol. Bad weather kept it out of the Bristol Channel, but it landed 1200 troops at Fishguard, in Wales, up around the southwest corner of the Pembrokeshire coast from Bristol. Although the local militia and an army detachment under Lord Liverpool quickly captured this force, which was made up largely of impressed French convicts, subsequent publication of their orders threw the countryside into alarm. They were called the 'Black Legion,' commanded by an American, Colonel William Tate, whose immediate superior was Lazare Hoche, Napoleon's leading admiral, who had commanded the abortive invasion of southwest Ireland at Bantry Bay in December 1796.[34] Tate's orders had been to stage a terrorist raid, disable as much of Bristol's shipping as possible, and then to sail up around the coast to do the same thing at Chester and Liverpool. The strategic aim was to weaken England's ability to respond to a larger Irish insurrection, which came, again unsuccessfully, the next year.[35]

By March newspapers in Bristol and Bath were crying out alarms against enemies and traitors 'insulting' the coasts, and declaring 'there are Englishmen so debased as to be ready to lend a Hand toward enslaving their Country.'[36] These were some of the 'ancestral voices prophesying war' whose echoes are heard in 'Kubla Khan.' There was even a run on the Bank of England.

In April and May there had been huge mutinies in the British fleets at Spithead (Isle of Wight), the Nore (Thames estuary), and Yarmouth, with many officers beaten and put ashore. Traditionally appalling shipboard conditions had been worsened by a nearly tenfold increase in sailors during the decade: the ships were crammed full of impressed 'quota-men' and hundreds of Irishmen ready to revolt against England, as many of their compatriots did the following year. These mutinies did not go unnoticed in the Stowey neighbourhood: Charlotte Poole put them down in her diary as 'occasioned by the black contrivances of the Democrats.'[37]

The reports from Dr Lysons played right into this scenario. But what saved the 'gang' at Alfoxden from further harassment was not their innocence, but their being *recognized*. The government knew all about disaffected Englishmen, thank you very much, Dr Lysons. Walsh had been hounding Thelwall for nearly five years, and they knew each other very well. Walsh had personally arrested Thelwall in London on more than one occasion, and was so well known to Thelwall that he did not dare attend his lectures, for fear of provoking him into an extemporaneous version of his crowd-pleasing performance, 'On Spies and Informers.'[38] The Home Office knew he was in full retreat to a safe hiding place; Walsh had simply uncovered him one more time.

Poole and Coleridge, though two of the most visible antigovernment figures in Somerset, were evidently new to Walsh, who worked mainly in London and Ireland. He ignores any suggestion of political danger attaching to Coleridge, and laid out Poole's threat solely in terms of the number of warm bodies he could command as head of the Poor Man's Club: about 150. This information was relevant to fears of invasion because it was a constant refrain of the warhawks in Paris that a sizeable proportion of the English population would rise up to join a revolutionary invasion force.

The poems of Wordsworth and Coleridge during this period show that these hopes were not entirely unfounded. Coleridge in 'Fears in Solitude,' written the following April in response to another invasion scare, trembles for his country because its rash policy had provoked and deserved one. Wordsworth's vaguely threatening conclusion to 'Goody Blake and Harry Gill' might be said to carry the same message in code: 'Now think, ye farmers all, I pray, / Of Goody Blake and Harry Gill.' Think what? Kind thoughts? Or think about what might happen if the needs of the poor are not attended to?

The only name besides Thelwall's that Walsh underlined in his reports was '*Wordsworth* a name I think known to Mr Ford.' Walsh was not saying that Wordsworth is 'famous' like Thelwall. Nor does he imply that his superior, John King, will recognize the name. Rather, he says he thinks it will be known to Richard Ford, the Bow Street magistrate who was one of the three or four people involved with William Wickham in the liaisons between the Home Office, the Alien Office, and the Foreign Office which were the origin of the modern British secret service. Ford had been Chief Magistrate in all but name since 1794, was consistently rewarded by Portland for his services, and was a particular favourite of the king's; in 1800 he was made superintendent of aliens, and in 1801 knighted and named chief London magistrate.[39] The activities of his group were 'modern' in that they did not simply gather information about undesirable foreigners or disaffected Englishmen, but also operated clandestinely to provoke actions that aided the policies of the government in power: assassinations, disinformation, and fifth-column groups in France and Switzerland, the ultimate goal of which was to defeat and defuse the continuing force of the French revolution by 'underground war.'[40] The new system was called 'preventitive policing.'[41]

How did Walsh know that Ford would probably know Wordsworth's name? Ford's knowledge might have come in one or more of three ways: through the government's interception of letters between Wordsworth and Annette, through its knowledge of Wordsworth's associates and activities in London in 1795, or from the possibility that Richard Wordsworth, as a lawyer, might have known Ford in his capacity as a magistrate.[42] All three possibilities are likely, but especially the first two, for they most closely corroborate the important fact that *Walsh* knew that Ford knew Wordsworth. Letters from Annette had reached Racedown, and the government from 1794 had in place a regular system of interfering with the mails. Walsh knew Thelwall very well, and Wordsworth had come closest to Thelwall (through Godwin) in 1795, when they shared many of the same friends and opinions. It was also in 1795 that Portland's secret accounts book recorded a payment to George Dyer, with whom Wordsworth and Coleridge were frequently in company then. The third possibility, that Ford knew Wordsworth's name because Richard

Wordsworth was also in the legal profession, is the weakest. For if Ford knew Richard in his professional capacity, or socially, these are not the kinds of acquaintance that would have come to James Walsh's attention, except by the merest happenstance.

Both Ford and King, furthermore, knew people who knew Wordsworth and Coleridge, or knew *about* them.[43] Ford and King were intelligent men, not reactionary fanatics; both were interested in the theatre, and good friends of Sheridan. Ford had a large financial interest in Drury Lane, his father had been its manager when Wordsworth was attending it in 1791, the year that Ford's liaison with the actress Dora Jordan had ended (she was frequently called Mrs Ford) when she advanced to better things as mistress of the Duke of Clarence, the future William IV. George Canning, under-secretary in the Foreign Office and soon to be founding editor of the *Anti-Jacobin*, was on extremely friendly terms with John King, whom he considered 'one of the worthiest and best sort of men in the world,' dining with him regularly. King was an intimate personal correspondent of both Grenville and Burke.[44] Canning's good friend George Ellis, another *Anti-Jacobin* contributor, had been tutored by King's brother; Ellis, a very well paid secret service informant, later became a friend of Wordsworth as well as Coleridge. Canning, whose mother was a provincial actress, was also a good friend of Sheridan's; their relationship was so close 'that some believed Canning was [Sheridan's] ward.'[45] Sheridan also knew Coleridge well, and had by this time already asked him to contribute a script for consideration at Drury Lane. So there are plenty of personal and literary relations, as well as public political ones, that could have made the name '*Wordsworth* . . . known to Mr Ford.' We also have to remember how small these offices were; in 1796, the entire Home Office staff, from the Duke of Portland down to the housekeeper, consisted of twenty-five persons,[46] and every piece of business crossed the desks of the two undersecretaries, King and Ford.

Walsh was a hardened professional and his reports from the field were terse and accurate. Whether he construed the stakes to be a foreign invasion or simply keeping his employers happy, he had excellent motives for being as accurate as possible. His knowledge that Ford probably knew Wordsworth is a similarly firm deduction. Walsh clearly expects King to relay the information to Ford, and he also clearly does so by way of confirmatory information, not as a basis for further *action*. Summarized officially, his comments about Thelwall and Wordsworth come to this: We know all about Thelwall in one way, and we know all we need to know about Wordsworth in another way – and that's all we need to know, or do, about this gang at this point. Wordsworth may have appeared to them not merely as a disaffected Englishman, but as one of those liberal, ambitious and poor young Englishmen, often associated with journalism or the theatre, who frequently proved ripe for suborning by the Home Office.

When we see in June 1799 that Portland's secret book records a payment of nearly £100 to 'Mr Wordsworth' these nagging questions about some kind of Wordsworthian connection to the secret service will rise again. The most sinister explanation one could offer of the 'Spy Nozy' incident, if only as a rhetorical counterploy to Coleridge's very successful cover-up, is that Walsh could leave and report the case closed because he had found that another operative was already in place on the ground: our man in Somerset, Mr Wordsworth.

But if Walsh's report closed the government's case, local knowledge that he had been there soon had far-reaching implications for the Alfoxden gang. Mrs St Albyn, already made uneasy by reports of her new tenants' strange habits, now declared that she would not renew their year's lease: very early notice, since they had signed it barely a month before. The lease would expire at Midsummer 1798. The annus mirabilis of English Romanticism had its end in sight almost as soon as it started. But what could be more romantic than to know the exact date when one's paradise will be lost? The constant knowledge that there was a point beyond which its joys could not be prolonged added energy and anxiety to Wordsworth's writing and self-knowledge. Much later, he stoutly denied that the termination of the lease had any effect on his plans, or that he knew the reasons for it, or that he had ever wanted to stay at Alfoxden longer than he did.[47] But this is all mere persiflage to keep covered the evidence of youthful indiscretions. The event was common neighbourhood knowledge, which would hardly have been kept from Wordsworth, the tenant in question, if he was 'caballed against *so long and so loudly.*'[48]

This intense climate of opinion explains Coleridge's letters to Thelwall between 19 and 21 August, responding to Thelwall's wish to become part of the 'literary egotistical triumverate.' Coleridge agreed to make some inquiries, but what he found made him warn Thelwall to go away, at least as far as Bridgwater, until his quiet habits might convince people that his pockets were full of poems, not plans for 'the transportation or ambush-place of a French army.'[49] He informed him of the 'very great odium' which Poole incurred by bringing him (Coleridge) to Stowey. 'My peaceable manners, and known attachment to Christianity, had almost worn it away,' but then Wordsworth arrived, and things went from bad to worse. 'You cannot conceive the tumult, calumnies, and apparatus of threatened persecutions, which the event has occasioned round about us. If *you*, too, should come, I am afraid that even riots, and dangerous riots, might be the consequence . . . *all three* together – what can it be less than plot and damned conspiracy – a school for the propagation of demagogy & atheism?'

This contemporary account by Coleridge of the situation is a lot less humorous than his 'Spy Nozy' version. It also shows that Wordsworth's behaviour or reputation were alarming to people, rightly or wrongly. Coleridge satirically paraphrased locals' commentary on them both: he himself was 'a whirl-brain that talks whatever comes uppermost; but that Wordsworth, he is the dark traitor. You never hear him say a syllable on the subject [politics].'[50] Provincial paranoia, or shrewd country realism?

Thelwall knew all too well what kinds of manifestations his appearance tended to spark off. His 'Lines written at Bridgwater, in Somersetshire, on the 27th of July, 1797, during a long excursion, in quest of a peaceful retreat' show that 'a peaceful retreat' was all he wanted. Like Wordsworth at Tintern Abbey a year later, he wants to escape a world 'that kindness pays with hatred.' (Wordsworth used similar phrases: 'sneers of selfish men . . . greetings where no kindness is.') Like Coleridge's conversation poems and like 'Tintern Abbey,' Thelwall's 'Lines' record the final turn by which the revolutionary hopes and actions of the 1790s turned inward to the form of culture we call Romanticism. In 'solitary haunts' of 'hermit-like seclusion,' with 'some few minds congenial,' he will listen in safety until 'the trump of Truth . . . wakes The Ruffian Crew of Power.' Thelwall hopes to dwell 'in philosophic amity' with Coleridge and their wives, and he *thinks* they might be joined by a third:

> and, perchance,
> Allfoxden's musing tenant, and the maid
> Of ardent eye, who, with fraternal love,
> Sweetens his solitude.

That eye and its love will also appear in 'Tintern Abbey,' when Wordsworth 'catch[es] from thy wild eyes these gleams / Of past existence' [i.e., his 'former pleasures'].

After the flurry of scandal caused by the visits of Thelwall and Walsh things calmed down. As summer waned into September a different set of guests arrived, beginning with Montagu and Azariah Pinney. These two, and James Tobin and Tom Wedgwood, who followed in the second week of September, were, we might say, the second tier of Wordsworth's friends.[51] These young men were neither as brilliant nor as outspoken as Thelwall or Lamb. Tobin was the son of the elder Pinney's partner, a strong defender of the rights of slave traders. As 'dear brother Jem,' he appears in the first line of the original version of Wordsworth's 'We Are Seven.' They were primarily lawyers and businessmen, or the well-off sons of successful entrepreneurs and industrialists.

In their visits and topics of conversation we notice a shift in the interests of Wordsworth and Coleridge: further away from political action, and toward projects that might return a profit while allowing time free for writing. They were not so much escaping from politics as groping toward an idea of *producing human beings* who would be worthy of the new freedoms the French Revolution held out so promisingly. As these hopes dwindled in the sordid machinations of Directory politics and were overshadowed by the rising spectre of Napoleon, the idea of constructing an *education for democracy* began to emerge among this small circle of thinkers, as it had elsewhere in Europe, most notably in Germany in the work of Professor Immanuel Kant at the University of Königsberg, and the circle of writers around Fichte and Schelling at the University of Jena, near Weimar.

Tom Wedgwood, heir to one of the largest industrial fortunes in England, had enthusiastic ideas about liberal social reform and extensive means at his disposal to realize them. His idea was to put Godwin's rationalism into practice by founding a school which would begin training minds at the nursery level, based on Locke's theory of association of ideas, as recently refined in David Hartley's 'vibranticles,' or brain waves.[52] This school would carefully monitor its pupils' sensory experiences, anticipating the 'Skinner box' of behaviourist psychologists in our own time. It shared the drawback of all such purely rationalistic thinking about pedagogical practice: that measurable success would require taking control of infants as early as possible, gathering them together in ever-larger primary schools which would, in their ultimate implication, weaken the nuclear family as the basic unit of society in order to reform humanity from the nursery.

Wedgwood, who had not yet met Coleridge, thought Wordsworth might be a good director for such an experimental school. Wordsworth was associated with ideas of education in the minds of these wealthy young Bristol liberals because of his and Dorothy's care for the son of their friend Montagu, and because they had been considered as possible tutors for the youngest Pinney child. Montagu, who had tutored both of the older Pinney brothers, highly recommended Wordsworth for his success with his son. But Wordsworth's pedagogical credentials for this scheme were almost exactly the opposite of Wedgwood's Godwinian principles. William and Dorothy had succeeded in unspoiling Basil Montagu, Jr by allowing him to run free in the country, with 'no other companions, than the flowers, the grass, the cattle, the sheep,' and by giving him little household duties to perform. Years later, little Basil was notably ungrateful in his recollection of the Wordsworths' 'plain living' programme.[53]

The Wedgwood plan was proto-utilitarian, the sort of education satirized by Dickens nearly half a century later in M'Choakumchild's school in *Hard Times*. But where nineteenth-century utilitarianism sought merely the greatest good of the greatest number, the Wedgwood plan, like Condorcet's in Paris, aimed at the eighteenth century's much higher goal: human perfectibility. Wedgwood's board of directors was virtually a short list of the last pure *philosophes* in England: Godwin, Holcroft, Horne Tooke, and the Bristol physician, Germanist, and minor poet, Thomas Beddoes. Wordsworth's surprisingly sharp satire in Book V of *The Prelude* against the 'dwarf man' and 'monster birth' produced by modern educational theories owes much to this brush with Wedgwood's project, and with the possibility, very real at the time, that he might have to accept it in order to make ends meet. By 1804, he had come to associate such ideas with Coleridge's caricature of their 'Academus of Stowey': 'a school for the propagation of demagogy & atheism.'

But Wedgwood soon decided that Coleridge, not Wordsworth, was the man to invest in for the systematic production of genius. Abandoning the idea of a school, the Wedgwoods in January would settle an annuity of £150 on Coleridge for his own maintenance. The amount was more than twice the proceeds Wordsworth could expect from his legacy from Raisley Calvert, even if his ambitious investment plan for it had worked out, and his comments on Coleridge's good fortune are so restrained as to expose his envy: citing 'the unexampled liberality of the Wedgwoods toward Coleridge,' he soberly 'hope[d] the fruit will be as good as the seed is noble.'[54]

Between rounds of well-heeled guests hatching speculative projects that came to nothing, both Wordsworth and Coleridge were hard at work revising their tragedies for stage production. Their plan was to have Coleridge submit his play, *Osorio*, first, so as not to prejudice Wordsworth's submission: after they'd got Sheridan's reaction to *Osorio*, they would try to strike again with *The Borderers*. Coleridge sent off his manuscript on 16 October, to William Bowles, who relayed it via his friend, the Covent Garden musician William Lindley, to Sheridan.[55] Coleridge then secured Wordsworth an invitation from the Covent Garden manager to read *The Borderers*, and a promise to produce it 'immediately' if he accepted it.

Wordsworth's and Coleridge's plays are similar in their derivation from *The Robbers*, but they are more like each other than they are like Schiller's play. They were much more concerned about guilt and redemption than Schiller, more about the consequences of crime than the crime itself, and especially about *remorse*, as Coleridge made explicit by later giving this title to *Osorio*. Schiller's Karl Moor might be called proto-Byronic, whereas Wordsworth's Mortimer and Coleridge's Osorio are . . . proto-Wordsworthian. Both plays feature two male characters, one of whom is trying to traduce, or kill, the other. Wordsworth focused on an 'amiable' young man who is being tempted into remorse*lessness* by another young man, who has managed to overcome his feelings of remorse. Coleridge, by contrast, shows the belated remorse but final forgiveness of his villain – as if Wordsworth's Mortimer, having learned the causes of Rivers's amorality, were to try to convert him *back* to conventional morality.

Why all this fixation on guilt? the theatre professionals in London might well have asked. If they, like the Home Office, had sent a spy to Alfoxden, they might have learned something about the sources of this peculiarly unspecific guiltiness which seems to have been hanging in the moral atmosphere between Stowey and Alfoxden. Coleridge added a spy passage to his play after the visit of James Walsh: Osorio suborns a Moor to inform on his brother Albert, who is arrested by a despicable representative of officialdom in the play, a prosecutor for the Inquisition. Coleridge's note on Osorio, the evil brother, sounds very much like Wordsworth's essay on Rivers: 'I wished to represent a man, who, from his childhood had mistaken constitutional abstinence from vices, for strength of character – thro' his pride duped into guilt, and then endeavoring to shield himself from the reproaches of his own mind by misanthropy.'[56] In fact, this sounds more like Rivers than like Osorio, whose abstinence from vice is not notable. But it sounds still more like Wordsworth's misanthropic semi-self-portrait in the 'Lines left on a Yew-tree Seat,' which had enjoyed great esteem during the combined Racedown and Stowey visits of June and July. Did Coleridge's essay also represent Wordsworth, and the temptation to self-sufficient individuality that they both felt as they began to exercise their creative powers in each other's company?

Several passages in Coleridge's play echo these possibilities. One versifies his own note on Osorio:

> What if his very virtues
> Had pamper'd his swoln heart, and made him proud?
> And what if pride had duped him into guilt,
> Yet still he stalk'd, a self-created God?
>
> (III.92–95)

'Self-created God' is a phrase similar to the ones Coleridge used indiscriminately in other contexts to praise Wordsworth, and echoes Rivers's flattery of Mortimer: 'self-stationed' to protect the borders of his world. Another passage closely paraphrases the conclusion of Wordsworth's yew-tree lines: 'He was a man different from other men / And he despised them, yet revered himself.' (IV.83–4) (Wordsworth: 'true dignity abides with him . . . who . . . can still suspect, / And still revere himself.') The dangerous attraction the hero represents in both plays is identical: 'Thou blind self-worshipper!'

Wordsworth's and Coleridge's fascination with this kind of amoral, creative, and manipulative character was partly a projection of, and partly a defence against, a temptation they felt strongly themselves. Wordsworth had abandoned Annette and withdrawn from political activism; Coleridge had withdrawn from political writing and from Pantisocracy. This self-centred egotistical character also represented the temptation they felt their entire intellectual generation sliding into; isolated in an utterly polarized political situation, they still felt they should *do* something: cynical detachment was not an option.

*

Finally, in November, with both plays sent off to meet their fate, the three romantic wanderers were left alone to their own devices (Sara had the baby and the washing to look after). They initiated what became a habit during the rest of the year: taking the same walk twice. This had been easy to do, up and around the Quantocks, or back and forth between Stowey and Alfoxden. But it required more time and planning, and cost more money, when they had to stay overnight on longer routes.

Early in the month, they struck out right along the hilltops above the coast, past Minehead and Porlock to Lynmouth and Lynton. The walk was a revelation to William and Dorothy. They felt as if they were on the hills of Cumberland, but with sea views added. The Exmoor downs, though considerably lower than the Cumbrian hills, give a greater feeling of altitude because they rise sharply to over a thousand feet within less than a mile of the level sea, which at just this point broadens out from the Bristol Channel into the Irish Sea.[57]

The breeze off the sea was more than exhilarating in November. They came down, with the hills, at Porlock. Then 'we kept close to the shore about four miles,' where they rose up into the first excitement of this trip. 'Our road lay through the wood, rising almost perpendicularly from the sea.' This brought them to Culbone Church, a very strange little church, reputed to be the smallest in England at thirty-five by twelve feet. This uncanny place, buried between three steep hills, provoked Coleridge to write 'Kubla Khan' – that, and an attack of dysentery (diarrhoea).[58] An attack of dysentery on a walking tour can be a common occurrence, after a none-too-good pub lunch, followed by a four-mile shoreline trek and a sudden uphill push. Coleridge made a quick run up the rest of the steep into the clearings at the top, to find relief at one of the farm houses there.

A good deal of critical ink has been spilled on the question of which 'lonely farmhouse' it was, exactly, where Coleridge composed this orientalist fantasy of English creativity. The claims of Ash Farm and Silcombe Farm seem equally good – both tidy bed-and-breakfasts now – or the vanished Withycombe Farm. But Richard Holmes is surely right to redirect our focus back down to Culbone itself as the real geographic source of 'Kubla Khan.' He remarks the erotic geography of the steep little valley falling down toward the church in the dell, the 'flanks' curving sharply down into the thick foliage, at the bottom of which a stream of water gushed out directly below the tiny church – a Coleridgean fountain to match Alfoxden's waterfall.[59]

> But oh! that deep romantic chasm which slanted
> Down the green hill athwart a cedarn cover!
> A savage place! as holy and enchanted
> As e'er beneath a waning moon was haunted
> By woman wailing for her demon-lover!

> And from this chasm, with ceaseless turmoil seething,
> As if this earth in fast thick pants were breathing,
> A mighty fountain momently was forced:
> Amid whose swift half-intermitted burst
> Huge fragments vaulted like rebounding hail . . .
>
> (12–21)

The 'dome of pleasure' becomes, in this reconstruction of the poem's physical inspiration, the tiny church itself, very odd to see in the middle of those steep woods, making one wonder about the determined act of creation that erected it there, like the creative fiat of a powerful Oriental khan. And the infamous 'person from Porlock' who supposedly interrupted Coleridge in the writing-down of his opium-induced dream (he regularly took laudanum, opium diluted in alcohol, as an 'anodyne' for his ailments) could well have been William and/or Dorothy, who probably returned to Porlock to get some better medication for him. No other person, then or at any other time when he was living at Stowey, would have 'called . . . on business from Porlock,' since no one else would have known he was there. Dorothy had some bemused recollections of their emergency stop there; she took to calling the domestic water cans and chamber pots at Alfoxden 'kubla' cans.[60]

Each of these November walks engendered its own poem project as a way of defraying expenses. By the time they reached the terminus of this first extended walk, the Valley of Stones (or Rocks) west of Lynton, they had decided on their topic: 'The Wanderings of Cain,' modelled after the popular translation (1761) of Solomon Gessner's *Death of Abel*. This work of 'loose poetry' had been widely praised as 'the most finished copy of primeval nature,' a confused judgment that reminds us of the contemporary popularity of Macpherson's 'translation' of Ossian's *Fingal*.[61]

The Valley of Stones added inspiration for this prehistoric theme. It is a desolate enclosed landscape, filled with free-standing rocks that look like ancient monuments. The topic was very like the one they had been pursuing in their dramas, the remorse-racked villain. Picking up where Gessner left off, with Cain setting off into the wilderness with his wife and children, the text of Wordsworth and Coleridge's incomplete prose-poem is obsessively concerned with the effects on Cain's mind of remorse for having killed his brother. Gessner explained how Cain came to commit his murder: Coleridge and Wordsworth wanted to show, instead, how he experienced the consequences of his crime. He has lived out his whole life wracked by remorse, but his remorse is shown to be a delusion. Their Cain is an Osorio who has successfully killed his brother, a Rivers tricked by false spirits.

The idea was for a three-part prose-poem. They would each write one part and whoever finished first would take on the third. Wordsworth's part, the first, was the easiest, since it was mainly to describe Cain being led across the wilderness by a spirit. Coleridge wrote his part, but he recalled with a smile thirty years later the ridiculousness of the plan, so far as Wordsworth was concerned: that 'a mind so eminently original [should] compose another man's thoughts and fancies,' and that 'a taste so austerely pure and simple [should] imitate the Death of Abel':

> I see his grand and noble countenance as at the moment when having despatched my own portion of the task at full finger-speed, I hastened to him with my manuscript – that look of humorous despondency fixed upon his almost blank sheet of paper, and then its silent mock-piteous admission of failure struggling with the sense of the exceeding ridiculousness of the whole scheme – which broke up in a laugh: and the Ancient Mariner was written instead.[62]

This sounds almost as if they went on immediately to compose the 'Rime of the Ancient Mariner,' and this is almost true. They had barely returned from this first walk when, on 12 or 13 November, they set out on a second one, a reprise of the first. Even their departure time, 4:30 p.m., was carefully chosen to get them down to Watchet, five miles from Alfoxden, in time to see the sun set across Blue Anchor Bay. They probably spent the first night at the Bell Inn at Watchet, and here their next joint project was hatched. It was to be, not the wanderings of Cain, but a larger Christian archetype of Cain, the wandering Jew. Many items in the landward geography of this fabulous poem can be located, item by item, along the Somerset coast, from Watchet through Minehead to Lynton: the harbour town from which the Mariner embarks and the hermit in the wood to whom he returns at the end, pleading for forgiveness – surely a denizen of the deep woods around Culbone Church.

Wordsworth's contributions to the 'Ancient Mariner' were considerably greater than he made to 'The Wanderings of Cain,' though it soon became apparent that the poem's metre, mystery, and archaism were beyond, if not his abilities, then his interest. He suggested 'some crime to be committed' which, as in *The Borderers* and 'Adventures on Salisbury Plain,' would bring on to the protagonist 'the spectral persecution, as a consequence of that crime and his own wanderings.'[63] He had been browsing in George Shelvocke's *Voyage Round the World by the Way of the Great South Sea* (1726) just before they left Alfoxden, and noted there the immense wing span of the albatross, sometimes reaching twelve feet. ' "Suppose," said I, "you represent him as having killed one of these birds on entering the South Sea, and that the tutelary spirits of these regions take upon them to avenge the crime." ' We can recognize in these tutelary spirits the guilty but helpless consciences of Wordsworth and Coleridge, and 'these regions' as, not so much Somerset (still less the South Pacific) as the theatre of the mind in which all their poems were now being staged. Having thus accounted for the crime which sets the action going, the main course of the action, and its two most dramatic ocean settings, Wordsworth would seem to merit a rather large share of credit for the 'Ancient Mariner': all Coleridge had to do was write it!

They got back on 20 November, and William and Dorothy departed for London almost immediately, to shepherd *The Borderers* through its first reading in London. Thomas Knight, Covent Garden's principal actor, had expressed 'great approbation' of it, but suggested that Wordsworth come to town to make 'certain alterations.'[64] Wordsworth went with alacrity. Staying again with his old family friend Samuel Nicholson in Cateaton Street, Wordsworth 'curtailed' his play on the spot during the first week of December, trying to follow Knight's suggestions, most probably for the character of Rivers, whom Knight would have acted.

Coleridge got word on 2 December that *Osorio* was rejected because of 'the obscurity of the last three acts.' On the 14th, Knight relayed the same negative verdict on *The Borderers* from Mr Harris, the theatre manager, who pronounced it 'impossible that [the play] could succeed in the representation.'[65] Sheridan's manager and actors must have thought their two aspiring Somerset playwrights were a bit too much in each other's company, for both plays were rejected for the same reason: metaphysical obscurity.

Like many another disappointed playwright, Wordsworth attributed his rejection to the 'depraved' state of the theatre at the time, and he and Dorothy left town in a huff the same day. But before they got the bad news, they went to Covent Garden and Drury Lane as much as they could, since William's temporary status as playwright allowed them 'no difficulty in obtaining orders for Covent Garden, and we have obtained them once for Drury Lane.'[66] They saw Mrs Siddons in *The Merchant of Venice*, Thomas Morton's opera, *The Children in the Wood*, probably Garrick's adaptation of Southerne's *The Fatal Marriage*, a ballet performance of Milton's *Comus*, and Richard Cumberland's new comedy, *False Impressions*.[67]

Wordsworth was combing the theatre for saleable ideas. Six months later, when he was in Bristol supervising *Lyrical Ballads* through the press, he made a point of going to see Matthew ('Monk') Lewis's *The Castle-Spectre*, which had opened in London on the very day *The Borderers* was rejected. Lewis, who had become a millionaire at age nineteen from the success of his salacious Gothic novel, *The Monk* (1795), had struck it rich again: with Dora Jordan featured as the romantic ingenue, *The Castle-Spectre* reportedly earned £18,000 in the three months of its London run. Such figures commanded attention. Wordsworth had Coleridge buy him a copy of the text in January, and went to see the play as soon as he could. He said, 'if I had no other method of employing myself Mr Lewis's success would have thrown me into despair. The Castle Spectre is a Spectre indeed. Clothed with the flesh and blood of £400 received from the treasury of the theatre it may in the eyes of the author . . . appear very lovely.'[68]

This is a mixture of sharp criticism and sour grapes. For though *The Castle-Spectre* is nothing if not transparent, especially when compared to the 'obscurity' of *Osorio* and *The Borderers*, it too is heavily indebted to Schiller's *The Robbers*, as Lewis cheerfully acknowledged. In a lightweight vehicle, Lewis had succeeded with the representation of a theme essentially identical to the one that mesmerized Wordsworth and Coleridge. His play also features two characters, brothers, one who has apparently murdered the other and whose life is eaten away by remorse as a result. Similarly, Lewis's purpose is 'To lay th'exulting villain's bosom bare.'[69] But for the existential aspect of amoral action, he created a separate character, the villain's black African bodyguard, Hassan, who directs vengeance 'at large against [white] mankind' because slave traders murdered his wife and child. This strategy solves (too easily, no doubt) the problem bedevilling Wordsworth's and Coleridge's plays, by casting their motiveless malignity onto a minor, exotic character whose philosophical rantings could be disregarded by members of the audience who wanted to concentrate on the conventional Gothic revenge-romance in the play's main action. Hassan is Rivers in blackface, relegated to a subordinate position in the band of outlaws. (Lewis's play also has four black bodyguards, corresponding respectively to Wordsworth's borderers and Coleridge's Moors.)

Wordsworth was perhaps a little startled to see how close this enterprising young man had come to concerns so near his own heart. *The Castle-Spectre* is set in the 'romantic' north, with action stretching from Northumberland to Conway Castle in North Wales. Like *The Borderers*, its action occurs during the period of the Barons' League, and its hero, the Earl Percy disguised as a shepherd, cautions his fellow aristocrats to reflect 'that their vassals are man as they are, and have hearts whose feelings can be grateful as their own.' For such lines, and his sympathetic representation of the blacks' sarcasm toward 'European gratitude,' Lewis was attacked for 'sentiments [that] were violently democratic' and for supporting 'the Cause of Equality.'

But Wordsworth must have been most surprised when Mrs Jordan said in the Epilogue, 'My shoulder felt a Bow-Street runner's tap,' accusing her of killing Count Osmond, the play's villain. Protesting in vain against the 'design' of 'Townshend' – the name of an actual 'larned Justice' to whose Bow Street court the runner means to deliver her – she says she has fled to the theatre instead: 'Just is my cause, and English is my jury!'[70] This comic confusion is as much a satire on the government's bumbling as Coleridge's later 'Spy Nozy' episode, showing how active such 'runners' were, and how unpopular the trials for treason and sedition at which they gave their suborned evidence. It makes one wonder if rumours of the

Somerset incident had circulated back to London by this time. The possibility is not far fetched: though Coleridge had a hard time getting word from Sheridan about *Osorio*'s fate, he later heard a scene from it declaimed at a party by a Miss DeCamp, who said she'd got it from Linley the musician, who had also passed it on to Charles Grey, Samuel Whitbread, and Sir Francis Burdett, leading Whig and radical politicians.[71]

If Coleridge's manuscript could be passed around, so could Wordsworth's. When Wordsworth heard the last words of Lewis's play, he indeed thought he was hearing something very familiar. They are delivered by the brother who turns out not to have been killed, but who has spent sixteen years in a solitary dungeon instead, yet who can now forgive the brother who wronged him: 'Oh! in his stately chambers, far greater must have been his pangs than mine in this gloomy dungeon.' This contrast between the moral sufferings of aristocratic villains and the physical pains of prisoners thrown unjustly into dungeons was exactly the one Wordsworth had drawn in 'The Convict,' which appeared over the signature 'Mortimer' in the *Morning Post* on 14 December, the very day *The Castle-Spectre* opened at the Theatre Royal in Drury Lane. Had Wordsworth seen it that night, instead of six months later, he could be forgiven for thinking that Lewis had cribbed his conclusion from a hurried perusal of the morning papers. As it was, the Prologue addressed the play to unhappy youths who 'Mourn slighted talents, or desert opprest, / False friendship, hopeless love, or faith betray'd.' These were states of mind largely identical with those Wordsworth had voiced in his yew-tree lines the previous summer and would repeat in his Tintern Abbey lines in the coming one, and were very much part of a common climate of hopelessness that was penetrating all young liberals' opinions at the time.

CHAPTER TWENTY-TWO

The Mariner and the Recluse

Nether Stowey and Alfoxden, 1798

> Not Chaos, not
> The darkest pit of lowest Erebus,
> Nor aught of blinder vacancy, scooped out
> By help of dreams—can breed such fear and awe
> As fall upon us often when we look
> Into our Minds, into the Mind of Man—
> My haunt, and the main region of my song.
> ('Prospectus' to *The Recluse*)

William and Dorothy spent the Christmas and New Year holidays visiting their wealthy friends in Bristol, the Pinneys and Wedgwoods. By 3 January they were back at Alfoxden, alone, with no prospects of any kind in front of them. 'The play is rejected,' Dorothy glumly informed their friends. But this emptiness was a perfect limbo for writing. In terms of viable writing projects Wordsworth was back where he was when he left Racedown: with an unsatisfactory version of 'The Ruined Cottage' and without Coleridge. Coleridge was in Shrewsbury, investigating a call to a Unitarian church there, presently served by a Reverend Hazlitt. He dazzled the minister's son, named William, and decided to accept the call, which would pay him a badly-needed £120 a year. He was rescued from this hard career decision by the annuity from the Wedgwoods, '£150 for life, legally secured to me, *no condition whatever being annexed*.'[1]

For most of January, William and Dorothy lived their frugal life alone, William writing in the morning while Dorothy tended to household duties with Peggy Marsh. In the afternoons and evenings they walked together over the hills. And they both wrote. Over the holidays, Dorothy had got a small journal in which she began to make a record of what interested her each day. Her 'Alfoxden Journal' is filled with minute descriptions of landscape and weather effects. In five months, the only things she noted beyond their daily routines and nature's various appearances were the receipt of Godwin's *Memoirs* of Mary Wollstonecraft and walking over to the local squire's house at Crowcombe to protest their house tax. Of the French invasion of Switzerland in late January, from which William dated his loss of hope in the French cause, she says not a word, though she does mention meeting 'a razor-grinder with a soldier's knapsack upon his back, and a boy to drag his wheel,' which must have reminded them of the *Anti-Jacobin*'s ferocious satire on Southey's knife-grinder poem.[2]

She was beginning to write down observations it had been her habit for years to notice, stimulated by her brother's descriptive sketches and the widespread fashion of cultivating the Picturesque. Her skill, and her differences from William as a writer, are evident from her first entry, 20 January 1798:

> The green paths down the hillsides are channels for streams. The young wheat is streaked by silver lines of water running between the ridges, the sheep are gathered on the slopes. After the wet dark days, the country seems more populous. It peoples itself in the sunbeams. The garden, mimic of spring, is gay with flowers. The purple-starred hepatica spreads itself in the sun, and the clustering snow-drops put forth their white heads, at first upright, ribbed with green, and like a rosebud; when completely opened, hanging head downwards, but slowly lengthening their slender stems. The slanting woods of an unvarying brown, showing the light through the thin net-work of their upper boughs. Upon the highest ridge of that round hill covered with planted oaks, the shafts of the trees show in the light like the columns of a ruin.[3]

The details in this excellent description can be visualized much more easily than those in her brother's poetry; many readers respond to Wordsworth's nature poetry as though the Wordsworth they are reading is Dorothy, not William. Her description moves down the hills with the water, into their own garden, nourished by those run-offs, and then returns us back to the top of the hills. Like Gilbert White of Selborne before her or Thoreau after, Dorothy's nature-writing moves effortlessly from exact observation to metaphoric intepretation, developing the adjective 'populous' into the striking neologism, 'peoples itself,' and then tapering off into a light personification of the flowers. William immediately recognized these possibilities, and turned them into verse:

> these populous slopes
> With all their groves and with their murmurous woods,
> Give a curious feeling to the mind
> Of peopled solitude.[4]

He has not necessarily improved on Dorothy by putting her words into blank verse. If good writing means showing, not telling, Dorothy's passage is the better of the two. Wordsworth's paradoxical 'peopled solitude' is fine, but so is Dorothy's eerie last phrase, 'like the columns of a ruin,' sharply contrasting all the fecund natural details with a sudden stark reminder of humankind.

Dorothy almost never says 'I think' or 'I felt,' or gives any personal opinion.[5] Many of her entries lack verbs, but are surprisingly active nonetheless: the activity she records is often simply that of *being*. It was her style to project no personality in her writing: in person she was just the opposite. In this she was wholly different from her brother, whose poetic landscapes are informed by, if not actually transformed into, his own mental landscape. This difference is especially clear from his adaptation of her entry for 25 January: 'Went to Poole's after tea. The sky spread over with one continuous cloud, whitened by the light of the moon, which, though her dim shape was seen, did not throw forth so strong a light as to chequer the earth with shadows. At once the clouds seemed to cleave asunder, and left her in the centre of a black-blue vault. She sailed along, followed by multitudes of stars, small, and bright, and sharp. Their brightness seemed concentrated, (half-moon).'

William turned this into 'A Night-Piece':

> The sky is overspread
> With a close veil of one continuous cloud
> All whitened by the moon, that just appears,
> A dim-seen orb, yet chequers not the ground
> With any shadow—plant, or tower, or tree.
> At last a pleasant instantaneous light
> Startles the musing man whose eyes are bent
> To earth. He looks around, the clouds are split
> Asunder, and above his head he views
> The clear moon & the glory of the heavens.
> There in the black-blue vault she sails along
> Followed by multitudes of stars, that small,
> And bright, & sharp along the gloomy vault
> Drive as she drives. How fast they wheel away!
> Yet vanish not! The wind is in the trees;
> But they are silent. Still they roll along
> Immeasurably distant, and the vault
> Built round by those white clouds, enormous clouds,
> Still deepens its interminable depth.
> At length the vision closes, & the mind
> Not undisturbed by the deep joy it feels,
> Which slowly settles into peaceful calm,
> Is left to muse upon the solemn scene.[6]

Just about everything in William's poem is also in Dorothy's journal. Of course, he was walking with her and had his own perceptions of the scene as well as her journal entry to work from. He adds a metaphysical contrast between the sound of the wind in the trees and the apparent silence of the spheres, but his largest addition is 'the musing man' who is excited by the vision. Insofar as 'A Night-Piece' makes a poetic statement at all, its meaning is contained in the slight difference between the observer's musing before and after 'the vision.' Before, he was musing inattentively. Afterwards, he is 'not undisturbed by the deep joy' his mind feels, which gradually settles into a 'peaceful calm' that allows him to return to his musings, but upon a 'scene' which has now become 'solemn.' The delicacy of his sensibility is marked by the way visual changes in the landscape rouse him, with his negative admission he is 'not undisturbed' by joy. This is already a mind whose poetry arises from 'emotion recollected in tranquillity.'

But, close as William and Dorothy were in their writing this winter, the next two or three months were the period of the closest literary collaboration between Wordsworth and Coleridge, as they helped each other complete 'The Ruined Cottage' and 'The Rime of the Ancient Mariner.' Their joint work on these poems is much closer than either their collaboration on *Lyrical Ballads* (mostly composed by Wordsworth between March and May) or their work on their dramas. Between 11 Febuary, when Coleridge came over to Alfoxden after his return from Shrewsbury, and 23 March, when he showed up with a completed version of the 'Rime,' the two poets were in almost daily contact.[7] Their hopes for stage success dashed, they turned to the narrative trunks of two poems, one naturalistic, the other gothic.[8]

'The Ruined Cottage' at this time consisted of approximately two hundred lines which gave the outline of the tale of Margaret: she is now dead, and her story is told by someone like a pedlar ('A wanderer among the cottages') to someone else, who doesn't know her. Wordsworth now expanded this spare narrative to over five hundred lines, then to more than nine hundred.[9] The intertwined stories of Margaret and the Mariner beautifully represent Wordsworth's and Coleridge's imaginative bond at this time, but the close connection between these two poems has been obscured by the fact that the 'Ancient Mariner' appeared in *Lyrical Ballads*, while 'The Ruined Cottage' did not see light until 1814, as the first book of *The Excursion*. If they had been published together, as seemed possible for a brief moment in the spring, they would have given a twist to the beginnings of English Romanticism much different from that provided by *Lyrical Ballads*.

The similarities between 'The Ruined Cottage' and the 'Ancient Mariner' become clear immediately if the two poems are set side by side.

In both, we have a narrative of intense suffering, told by an old and uneducated man to a young man, evidently better educated and of higher class, the effect of which is to fundamentally shatter the young man's immediate preoccupations and which seems likely to change his life forever after. The Wedding Guest, stunned, turns *from* the bridegroom's door and rises the morrow morn, 'A sadder and a wiser man.' Similarly, the young narrator of 'The Ruined Cottage' 'turn[s] aside in weakness' from the Pedlar, almost unmanned by grief after hearing the tale of Margaret's decline and death, and must be rescued from despair by the Pedlar's calm words of wisdom. In two early attempts at a conclusion, Wordsworth had his young narrator reflect on the story's meaning – 'and to myself / I seem'd a better and a wiser man' – or thank the Pedlar for it: 'And for the tale which you have told I think / I am a better and a wiser man.' These phrases draw the ending of the 'Ancient Mariner' directly into the picture, but we cannot be entirely sure which poet took them from which.[10] The Pedlar's wisdom about nature's 'calm oblivious tendencies' parallels, in function if not in doctrine, the Mariner's moral to his tale: 'He prayeth best, who loveth best / All things both great and small.' Both morals are appropriate to their unlettered speakers, but seem very inadequate to the devastating effect of the tales they've told.

Beyond these narrative parallels, there are others: (1) a derelict structure (cottage or ship) set in the midst of (2) a wide, bare natural expanse (common or ocean) which becomes (3) a scene of moral instruction in which (4) ugly or grotesque natural objects (weeds or water snakes) function symbolically as signs of the narrators' agony, but also become the focus of their redemption: the Mariner blesses the water snakes 'unawares' and finds that he can pray at last; the Pedlar, passing the dead Margaret's cottage with troubled thoughts, suddenly sees, in the weeds and spear grass 'silver'd o'er' with mist, an 'image of tranquillity' so strong that he can 'walk along [his] road in happiness.'

In expanding their poems, the two poets articulated the sufferings of their protagonists – spread them out, diversified their time and details, and developed the character of their narrators, as well as their effect on their young auditors. Margaret's sufferings are now drawn out over the course of five years, as stages in an excruciatingly painful decline, which are marked by the Pedlar's seasonal rounds. These additions increase our sense of Margaret's pain both by prolonging it, and by projecting it – the poem's master touch – onto the ruination of her cottage. The Pedlar comes back, winter, summer, spring and autumn, notes signs of decay in Margaret's house and garden, then meets her and has his suspicions confirmed by similar signs of decay in her. It is a cruelly effective strategy for representing a process that would otherwise be almost too painful to read: the slow death of a human being. It depends for its effect on the obtuseness of the Pedlar who, like the Mariner in the action of his rime, is not wise *yet*. It is also a potentially sadomasochistic strategy, as Wordsworth recognized, for he has the Pedlar address exactly this point when he resumes Margaret's story at the urging of his young auditor.

> I begg'd of the old man that for my sake
> He would resume his story. He replied,
> 'It were a *wantonness*, and would demand
> *Severe reproof, if we were men whose hearts*
> *Could hold vain dalliance* with the misery
> Even of the dead, *contented thence to draw*
> *A momentary pleasure* never marked
> By reason, *barren* of all future good.'
>> (MS B.278–85; italics added)

The shocking idea that recounting the sufferings of a dying woman could be a kind of necrophilia is unconsciously censored by most readers of these lines, who interpret them in the perspective of the establishment Wordsworth. But Wordsworth's diction suggests it, line by line, especially his reference to the erotic literary fashion of Cavalier dalliance. The lines respond, self-censoriously, to the Pedlar's first announcement that Margaret, whom he 'loved . . . as my own child,' is dead. Both she and her cottage are represented as flirtatious demon-lovers of the disaster which befell them:

> She is dead,
> The worm is on her cheek, and this poor hut,
> *Stripped of its outward garb* of household flowers,
> Of rose and jasmine, *offers to the wind*
> *A cold bare wall whose earthy top is tricked*
> With weeds and the rank spear-grass. She is dead,
> And nettles rot and adders sun themselves
> Where we have sat together *while she nursed*
> *Her infant at her bosom.*
>> (MS B.157–65; italics added)

Immediately, the Pedlar asks forgiveness – 'I feel I play the truant with my tale' – and he rights the moral balance by introducing Margaret's husband, Robert, 'an industrious man, sober and steady.' But it is clear that his relations with Margaret were deeply passionate (though not sexual), and that he uses this kind of quasi-erotic language to manipulate his young listener's interest in her.

Wordsworth's way of writing about himself is now noticeably different than it had been earlier in the 1790s, because he gives a new spiritual significance to his outdoor childhood adventures, a method of numinous heightening he owed largely to the transcendental philosophy of Spirit he was imbibing almost daily in conversations with Coleridge. This was the language of 'the One Life within us and abroad' that Coleridge had first tried out in 1795 in 'The Aeolian Harp.' This pantheistic philosophy is so often taken as the essence of English Romanticism, especially of the Wordsworthian type, that it is often prematurely installed as the meaning of these fragmentary texts which were being worked out experimentally in situ. What Wordsworth absorbed from Coleridge was a revelation of a spiritual life in all natural things, with which human consciousness could sympathize. More familiar in its lighter form ('One impulse from a vernal wood / May teach you more of man . . . Than all the sages can'), it appears everywhere in the Pedlar's new biography:

> He was a chosen son:
> To him was given an ear which deeply felt
> The voice of Nature in the obscure wind,
> The sounding mountain and the running stream.
> To every natural form, rock, fruit, and flower,
> Even the loose stones that cover the highway,
> He gave a moral life; he saw them feel
> Or linked them to some feeling.
>
> (MS B, 76–83)

This was not the rationalized nature of Deism, but a philosophic transcendentalism with classical analogues from Neoplatonism, given renewed life by Spinoza, that was at this moment gaining a powerful influx of philosophic energy in Germany through the various writings of Kant, Fichte, Schelling, the Schlegel brothers, and Hegel. Their *Naturphilosophie* was an intellectual beachhead against the emotionally deadening consequences of relentless Enlightenment rationalism. The simplistic application of reason to human affairs seemed, by 1798, to have gone disastrously awry in the French Revolution. Both Wordsworth and Coleridge had lent their minds, hopes and energies wholeheartedly to this process, but now both were in full retreat from the chilling religious and political implications they saw in it, and searching desperately for a humane way out.

Wordsworth's strained mental condition made him fascinated by the ways in which minds could be overthrown or broken down. He could never have written *The Prelude* without his preliminary Racedown researches into mental instability. But now he avoids textual and mental breakdown by leaping toward vast natural reassurances. In 'Incipient Madness' an unnamed narrator returned compulsively to a ruined cottage, fascinated by 'a broken pane which glitter'd in the moon / And seemed akin to life.'[11] No indication is given why he does this, but the language anticipates the oddly sexual diction in 'The Ruined Cottage': his 'sickly heart' fastened on this speck 'like a sucking babe,' and 'many a long month / Confirm'd *this strange incontinence*.' The speaker's compulsion appears to be a twisted kind of lover's constancy: 'I alone / Remained . . . / My heart claimed fellowship . . . with the beams / Of dawn and of the setting sun that seemed / To live and linger on the mouldering walls.' (45–49) This is close to the 'cold bare wall whose earthy top is tricked / With weeds and the rank spear-grass' in 'The Ruined Cottage.' But the sunset image which finally enabled Wordsworth to bring this troubling poem to an end is much more benign, indicating how thoroughly he had steeped his Pedlar in Coleridge's pantheism:

> Together casting then a farewell look
> Upon those silent walls, we left the shade
> And ere the stars were visible attained
> A rustic inn, our evening resting-place.
>   (MS D.535–38)

These lines conclude the so-called 'reconciling addendum' which Wordsworth composed in March of 1798, but Wordsworth did not present any this-worldly solutions for the sufferings of Margaret, because they are inadequate to those sufferings as he has presented them. Margaret does not need food or money; her problem is a broken heart, and she will not give it up, though she knows full well she should: ' "I am changed, / And to myself . . . have done much wrong, / . . . I have slept / Weeping, and weeping I have waked; my tears / Have flowed as if my body were not such / As others are, and I could never die." '[12] In her immortal grief Margaret claims kinship with the two female characters Coleridge was creating at the same time: 'the Night-mare LIFE-IN-DEATH' and the demon-lover of 'Kubla Khan': her ruined cottage is a Wordsworthian counterpart to the frightening landscape Coleridge imagined at Culbone Church: 'A savage place! as holy and enchanted / As e'er beneath a waning moon was haunted / By woman wailing for her demon-lover!'

Significant as the twin births of 'The Ancient Mariner' and 'The Ruined Cottage' were, an even larger creative event was occurring simultaneously. Wordsworth was being created as the poet of *The Recluse; or, Views of Nature, Man, and Society*. This was the title of the grand epic poem he announced to Tobin and Losh in early March, a project which stayed with him through the rest of his creative life, as the *magnum opus* to which that life was devoted. Its title may have been suggested by Thelwall, who refers to himself as 'the new Recluse' in his autobiographical preface to his *Poems* of 1801.[13] But images of recluses and hermits were becoming fashionable, as many writers opted for classical expressions of pastoral retreat to escape the oppressive climate against free expression that was settling down over England.

By a strict accounting Wordsworth completed barely half of *The Recluse. The Prelude* was its 'portico,' and *The Excursion* was its second, narrative section, though other parts of it can be identified in his manuscripts or in poems recycled to other contexts.[14] But the project's qualitative importance to him – first as an inspiring ideal, later as a crippling obligation – far outweighs the number of lines he wrote for it. To be the Bard of *The Recluse* was the most comprehensive of Wordsworth's self-creations. The Poet of the Preface to *Lyrical Ballads* and 'the chosen Son' of *The Prelude* are versions of the same identity, only slightly less grand and heroic. In his description of each of these incarnations, he uses hyperbolic language to express the existential divinity of this Poet figure and his proposed accomplishments.

In the verse 'Prospectus' to *The Recluse*, composed two years later, his ambitions go far beyond the 'considerable utility' he claimed for his poem in early 1798: 'I must tread on shadowy ground, must sink / Deep—and, aloft ascending, breathe in worlds / To which the heaven of heavens is but a veil . . . / . . . Jehovah—with his thunder, and the choir / Of shouting Angels, and the empyreal thrones— / I pass them unalarmed' (28–35). In such biblical, Miltonic language Wordsworth projects his best image of himself: a poet-prophet-philosopher, whose words will speak to all people everywhere about everything: Nature, Society, and individual consciousness. The dimensions of this figure are godlike, and if Milton's more traditional epic theme – to justify the ways of God to men – seems left out of these expressions, it is because the divine role has been taken up by the poet himself. These dimensions are so large that they could hardly be filled out by any single human being, and Wordsworth explicitly invoked his need for 'a greater Muse' than Milton's to aid him. When we recoil from Wordsworth's egotism elsewhere in his work, we should keep in mind that the projected form of his ego-image was actually much larger than anything he published in his lifetime.

Coleridge was also present at the birth of this Poet figure, partly as midwife, partly as parent; even more than the *Lyrical Ballads*, *The Recluse* was 'half the child of my own brain.' He did not have even Wordsworth's comparative hesitations when he wrote to Cottle to announce the blessed event:

> —The Giant Wordsworth – God love him! – even when I speak in the terms of admiration due to his intellect, I fear lest those terms should keep out of sight the amiableness of his manners – he has written near 1200 lines of a blank verse, superior, I hesitate not to aver, to any thing in our language which in any way resembles it.[15]

For the next seven years, Coleridge's references to *The Recluse* never fall below the level of these superlatives of greatness, firstness, and largeness. For example, from 1804: 'I prophesy immortality to his *Recluse*, as the first & finest philosophical Poem, if only it be (as it undoubtedly will be) a Faithful Transcript of his own most august & innocent Life, or his own habitual Feelings & Modes of seeing and hearing.'[16]

Wordsworth took much of his vision of total human creativity from Coleridge's *The Brook*, an epic of similar magnitude which he had been dreaming about for years. In his search for its organizing metaphor, Coleridge seized upon their symbolic brook behind Alfoxden House, with results that led the government to suspect him of plotting against the nation's security:

> I sought for a subject, that should give equal room and freedom for description, incident, and impassioned *reflections on men, nature, and society* . . . . Such a subject I conceived to have found in a stream, traced from its source in the hills . . . to the first break or fall, where its drops become audible, and it begins to form a channel; thence to the peat and turf barn . . .; to the sheep-fold; to the first cultivated plot of ground; to the lonely cottage and its bleak garden won from the heath; to the hamlet, the villages, the market-town, the manufactories, and the sea-port.[17]

After the unforeseen results of his search, as reported by Christopher Trickie to the authorities, Coleridge said he planned to dedicate *The Brook* 'to our then committee of public safety as containing the charts and maps, with which I was to have supplied the French Government in aid of the plans of invasion.'[18] But, joking aside, *The Recluse* like *The Brook* was clearly aimed at the fallout from the French Revolution. Coleridge conceived it as 'a poem, addressed to those, who, in consequence of the complete failure of the French Revolution, have thrown up all hopes of the amelioration of mankind, and are sinking into an almost epicurean selfishness, disguising the same under the soft titles of domestic attachment and contempt for visionary *philosophes*.'[19]

In March of 1798, *The Recluse* consisted of the newly-expanded 'Ruined Cottage,' plus two or three other poems, which together add up to the thirteen hundred lines Wordsworth spoke of to Tobin and Losh. The first of these others was 'The Old Cumberland Beggar,' another narrative of unrelieved suffering, drafted the previous year, but now expanded with contemporary political commentary against parish workhouses. The second was Wordsworth's description of his encounter with a figure very similar to Margaret and the Cumberland beggar: the Discharged Veteran he had run into near Far Sawrey in about 1788. These three narratives of suffering were originally free-standing poems of nearly unrelieved bleakness, like Wordsworth's other unpublished Racedown fragments. But now he began trying to incorporate into them lines of explanation and understanding, to achieve a larger perspective of reconciliation. This effort is what makes them parts of the now-christened *Recluse*: 'views of nature, man, and society,' giving 'authentic comment' to the sounds of 'humanity in fields and groves / Pip[ing] solitary anguish' ('Prospectus,' 76–77). A fourth poem, rounding out the 1300 lines, was probably 'A Night-Piece,' which emerged from Dorothy's notebook. It fits the others like a prologue or coda, sketching a visionary perspective on the landscapes through which the other three narratives move. On its open road – the inevitable Wordsworthian *mise-en-scène* – we see 'the glory of the heavens' instead of an old beggar, a sick veteran, or a weaver's abandoned wife. Wordsworth's formidable task was to link their suffering, somehow, to that sense of natural glory.

The first *Recluse* poems portray human suffering, of a very contemporary British kind, to suggest how, *in this context*, it might be understood, or properly cared for. They try to make sense out of suffering, but are far from 'the still, sad music of humanity' of 'Tintern Abbey.' They do not preach a doctrine of acceptance; their goal is more limited: simply to keep the observer (all Wordsworth-surrogates) from being overcome by grief and despair at what he sees. This sense-making comfort comes in the Pedlar's 'reconciling addendum,' in the Discharged Veteran's 'ghastly' trust that God will always provide a Good Samaritan on any road. In 'The Old Cumberland Beggar,' Wordsworth's more provocative political message is that it is better to let such old beggars die 'in the eye of Nature' on their usual rounds in neighbourhoods that know them, than make them captives in the 'HOUSE, misnamed of INDUSTRY.' Whether this life and death in nature is better than the workhouse is hard to say, both as social policy and as poetic statement. 'Tintern Abbey' will say that 'Nature never did betray the heart that loved her,' and recommend that Dorothy should 'therefore . . . let the misty mountain-winds be free / To blow against thee.' But the effects of such weather are a lot worse for beggars:

> let his blood
> Struggle with frosty air and winter snows;
> And let the chartered wind that sweeps the heath
> Beat his grey locks against his withered face.
>
> (173–76)

This policy-statement poem has seemed to many readers a betrayal of the poor to the harsh doctrinal implications of Wordsworth's new religion.

Rhetorically, the three *Recluse* narratives of 1798 do not come to bad conclusions. Rather, their conclusions are unsatisfying in the sense of philosophic conviction or political persuasion. They raise as many questions as they answer. But few philosophic systems or political programmes could answer their question satisfactorily, for it is the problem of undeserved or incommensurate human suffering, which is to say, the problem of evil. This is the problem that Romanticism is always accused of avoiding or slighting, and sometimes did ignore. But Wordsworth's high Romantic argument always forced him to confront this question, for it challenged his great faith in the powers of the creative human imagination. It was the problem that surfaced daily in Wordsworth's and Coleridge's conversations at this time: human suffering and the question of their own guilt or remorse for it, and their possible complicity in it. Wordsworth's determination to face these questions comprehensively led inexorably to repeated imaginative crises which kept the *Recluse* forever unfinished. This paradoxical relation between inspiration and dejection explains better than almost any other set of Romantic texts the uncanny connection between the power of the Romantic imagination and its tendency to produce magnificent fragments at least as often as it produces satisfying aesthetic wholes. The typical Romantic Ode to Dejection is not cynical *weltschmerz*, but the underside of all its Odes to Joy, from Schiller's to Wordsworth's to Thoreau's.

Given the logic of this double bind, clear in two hundred years of hindsight but barely emerging into the light of day in the first week of March 1798, it is not surprising to learn that Wordsworth's announcements to Tobin and Losh are the last we hear of *The Recluse* at this time. Though he said all his 'eloquence' would be devoted to it for the next year and a half, in fact nothing more of it was written for almost exactly that period of time: until he and Dorothy were again ensconced together in a new home, at Grasmere, at the beginning of 1800.

CHAPTER TWENTY-THREE

Triumphs of Failure

Wordsworth's Lyrical Ballads *of 1798*

Readers accustomed to the gaudiness and inane phraseology of many modern writers . . . will perhaps frequently have to struggle with feelings of strangeness and aukwardness: they will look round for poetry, and will be induced to enquire by what species of courtesy these attempts can be permitted to assume that title.

'Advertisement' to *Lyrical Ballads* (1798)

The Recluse project was shelved almost as soon as it was announced. Coleridge, who had fathered the idea, was the cause of its delay. Desperate for cash, he proposed one project after another to Joseph Cottle: a third edition of his *Poems*, or a new edition with a second volume to include 'The Rime of the Ancient Mariner.'[1] But in early March the first payment of the Wedgwood annuity arrived, and Coleridge's great aim in life began to crystallize: an *opus maximum* to answer the materialism of eighteenth-century rationalism.[2] In contemporary philosophic terms, this meant refuting Godwin's *Political Justice* with a view of life that recognized a spiritual dimension, and embraced the value of emotions.[3] To achieve this, he proposed acting on the dream he had been entertaining for over two years: to go to Germany to learn, in their original language, the new transcendental philosophies pouring forth from the fountainhead of Kant and the Jena circle. But this journey, which did succeed in making Coleridge a more profound philosopher, was an all-but-mortal wound to *The Recluse*, which he had conceived as the epic poem of the new philosophy.

The plan was broached at the beginning of March and discussed in earnest during a ten-day visit (9–18 March) of the Coleridges to Alfoxden: the first time Sara and little Hartley had stayed for more than a day. The general idea was to export their small communal group to more congenial surroundings abroad. James Losh and his new wife Cecilia Baldwin (a distant Cumberland cousin of William and Dorothy) were invited, and John Chester, the local farmer's son, volunteered to come along as Coleridge's factotum. Sara was at first included in the plans until the obvious impediment of two small babies was faced seriously. They planned to spend about two years abroad; one for learning the language, a second for gaining mastery of the new philosophy. Coleridge readily accepted William's wish to go along with him, and assumed he would keep on writing *The Recluse*, so high was his estimate of his friend's productive power.

As Coleridge went, so went the Wordsworths. Coleridge was vitally necessary to Wordsworth as a constant source of new ideas and unstinting praise. Wordsworth had an inhibiting effect on Coleridge's poetical production, but Coleridge's conversation was terrifically stimulating to Wordsworth. Everyone recognized that William had been writing with immense power since the beginning of the year. Coleridge told Hazlitt that Wordsworth's 'soul seems to inhabit the universe like a palace, and to discover truth by intuition, rather than by deduction.'[4] Dorothy reported to Mary Hutchinson that 'his faculties seem to expand every day, he composes with much more facility than he did, as to the *mechanism* of poetry, and his ideas flow faster than he can express them.'[5] And by the first week in April, Wordsworth himself confidently reported to Cottle, 'I have gone on very rapidly adding to my stock of poetry.'[6]

Such language, addressed to Cottle, was purposely commercial. For once the decision for Germany had been taken, the question of how to pay for it arose immediately – for the Wordsworths. They were still in bad straits financially. The payments of the Calvert bequest had been delayed, and the payments on Wordsworth's loans to Montagu and Douglas had been even slower. He had touched Poole, Cottle and Tobin for loans at different times during the year, and in June as they were leaving Alfoxden, Dorothy had to ask Richard for money to finish paying its very nominal rent.[7] Coleridge had his annuity, but he was not offering to bankroll the whole enterprise. To raise funds, the poets proposed to sell some of their stock-in-trade, poetry, exactly as they had proposed paying for the expenses of their November walking tour by jointly writing 'The Ancient Mariner.'

They approached Cottle with two proposals. One was to publish *The Borderers* and *Osorio* together, now that hopes for their stage career were at an end.[8] Another was to publish 'Adventures on Salisbury Plain' and 'The Ruined Cottage' together, with a few other poems in a similar vein. Both of these volumes were more or less ready to go to press, and Cottle was ready to give twenty guineas or more for each, a nice sum to set them on their way, since the estimated cost of passage to Hamburg was twenty-five guineas.[9]

Why they did not go forward with either or both of these eminently doable plans is a mystery. Both these volumes were complete, and internally consistent, while a book called 'Lyrical Ballads' was neither, and did not yet exist in anybody's mind as such. The reason they did not go forward with these either of these plans, which would have drastically altered their image in literary history (not necessarily for the worse), seems to have been Wordsworth's astonishing rate of production, stimulated by the German trip. The immediate need was for saleable poems. *The Recluse* might save the world, but it was barely begun, years from being finished, and of doubtful market value in any case. And the frustrated stage career of their two dramas did not augur well for their success as published texts. The combined 'Salisbury Plain' and 'Ruined Cottage' idea was kept alive, but Wordsworth was rightly worried about its lack of 'variety.' The only conditions they insisted on for a new volume were anonymity (mostly Coleridge's idea) and joint publication (mostly Wordsworth's). Wordsworth didn't want to publish his new poems without Coleridge's supporting company and Coleridge's estimate of the market value of their names was succinct: 'Wordsworth's name is nothing – to a large number of persons mine stinks.'[10]

So, under strong personal pressure of his need to raise money in order to follow Coleridge, Wordsworth did a very unusual thing, whose oddity is rarely remarked on, because of the subsequent fame of the volume which resulted. He began writing short poems: ballads and lyrics that could be produced quickly to fill up a volume, of the kind familiar to readers of magazine verse at the time: pathetic narratives of the deserving, picturesque poor and sentimental lyrics expressing melancholy feelings in beautiful natural settings. Between the first week of March and mid-May, Wordsworth composed about a dozen of the nineteen poems by him which finally appeared in *Lyrical Ballads*: a total of nearly fifteen hundred lines of poetry in some sixty days.[11] The regular rhyme and metre of the ballad, and its ease of variation, was the 'mechanism' of poetry which Dorothy noted had become so productive for him. During much of this period, neither he nor Coleridge had definitely in mind the shape or title of the volume that became *Lyrical Ballads*. This open-endedness doubtless helped Wordsworth's rate of production: he just wrote, without worrying very much about the form in which all these poems would be contained.

Wordsworth had, as of March 1798, written only one-and-a-half ballads in his entire life: the tale of lovelorn Mary Rigge of Colthouse, in 1787, and his fragmentary start on 'The Three Graves,' which he turned over to Coleridge. His interest for several years had not been in short poems at all, let alone ballads. He was determined to write long poems, narrative poems in blank verse with strong meditative overtones and heavy moral implications, taking his inspiration not from the ballad revivals of Bishop Percy and Robert Burns but from the epic examples of Milton and

Spenser. Furthermore, he was just now deeply interested in the idea of integrating those long poems into an even larger, quasi-epic framework, *The Recluse*.

His switch to ballads and lyrics at this time is as startling as if the young Beethoven were to have turned from composing his first and second symphonies to writing songs or bagatelles based on five-finger keyboard exercises. This is not to denigrate songs and ballads in favour of symphonies and epics, but to underscore the great difference between what Wordsworth had been doing up to the time the German trip was broached, and what he now undertook to do. The poems he wrote were like much magazine verse of the time, though far better in quality – and far bleaker in their descriptions of human suffering. Ballads deal mainly in the curses of slain heroes and the tears of lovelorn maidens, not the curses of freezing old women on landlords for narrowly enforcing their property rights, or the tears of shepherds who have to sell their sheep in order to qualify for parish relief. But it was not Wordsworth's subjects so much as his handling of them that ultimately differentiated *Lyrical Ballads* from a flood of similar works in this age of 'poetical inflation.'[12] Regarded as an exercise in literary primitivism, the volume was rather behind than ahead of the times.[13] Eighteenth-century universalism had produced a spate of real and fictitious 'primitive' or uneducated poets, such as Stephen Duck, the Thresher Poet, and 'Lactilla,' Ann Yearsley, a Bristol milkwoman.[14] But *Lyrical Ballads* are far more literary than primitive: Wordsworth did not use the same rhyme scheme twice in ten ballads. His psychological and sociological attitude toward his ballad subjects is even more unusual. He is not sentimental; he lets most of his characters speak directly to the reader, without introduction or condescension, and though his delineation of their suffering seems sympathetic, he rarely draws the charitable moral which his description of them seems to be leading up to.

Discussion of Wordsworth's 'lyrical ballads' has been conducted so much in light of the late eighteenth-century ballad revival, of Wordsworth's increasingly defensive prefaces to successive editions of the volume, and of Coleridge's account of their 'experiment' in *Biographia Literaria* (twenty years later), that these familiar categories can well be ignored in favour of what Lamb called the 'living circumstances' of their composition: *The Recluse* and its sudden interruption for the trip to Germany. It should be much better known than it is that the accounts offered by Wordsworth and Coleridge as to how, when, and why the *Lyrical Ballads* of 1798 came to be written differ widely from what the poets were actually doing at the time, or said they were. Many textbooks and innumerable classrooms continue to project the image of Wordsworth and Coleridge coming together in 1797, igniting a spark of mutual creativity that led inexorably to the publication of *Lyrical Ballads* a year later. But recent scholarship has found almost no evidence of a 'plan' they were developing for the volume at this time, and especially not of the division of their labour between supernatural and natural poems that Coleridge suggested in *Biographia Literaria*.[15]

This is not to say that Coleridge and Wordsworth were not talking about many of the issues that appear in the preface and in *Biographia Literaria*. Above all, they were talking about 'common language' poetry, and about ordinary people as fit subjects for such poetry. They were also discussing the ways such subjects and speakers could reveal important truths about the nature of man, even when presented without explanatory frameworks of either traditional (religious) or contemporary (political and philosophical) interpretation, other than 'Nature' itself: i.e., the given world of natural forms around them. But there is little sign of any talk about ballads, or of Wordsworth composing them, or looking for models to practice on, until the announcement of the trip to Germany.

His production of these poems, besides being amazingly rapid, was also astonishingly contemporary: it seemed that all he had to do was read about, or look at, something to turn it into a poem. 'The first mild day of March' was probably exactly that, sometime between the 6th and the 11th, and the 'morning task' Dorothy is asked to set aside ('bring no book') may be her copying work on 'The Ruined Cottage.'[16] His need was not for inspiration but simply for information, from almost any material. Cottle was requested on 7 March to send Erasmus Darwin's *Zoönomia* 'immediately,' and within a week it was sent back, having answered its purpose: the account of superstitious autosuggestion which Wordsworth turned into 'Goody Blake and Harry Gill,' occasionally setting Darwin's own words to metre.[17] The same was true of the 'Complaint of the Forsaken Indian Woman,' quickly adapted from Samuel Hearne's *Journey from Prince of Wales's Fort in Hudson's Bay to the Northern Ocean*, which Wordsworth received on 14 April.

When books were not ready to hand, neighbours were pressed into service. Christopher Trickie was transformed into 'Simon Lee,' as Wordsworth literally enacted his advice to his reader:

> O reader! had you in your mind
> Such stores as silent thought can bring,
> O gentle reader! you would find
> A tale in every thing.
>
> (73–76)

A once-prosperous farmer in Holford became the speaker of 'The Last of the Flock.' He had to sell off all his sheep, one by one, reducing himself to demonstrable poverty before he could qualify for parish charity under the ruinous Speenhamland system. Wordsworth had rarely seen

> . . . a man full grown
> Weep in the public roads alone.
> But such a one, on English ground,
> And in the broad high-way, I met . . .
>
> (3–6)

These poems were not simply vignettes of poverty, but of the emotions it provoked – emotions which Godwin in *Political Justice* had dismissed as uselessly sentimental: gratitude, and affection for one's own property.[18] The incidents they recounted were literally 'incidental' to their emotions, accounting for Wordsworth's ability to make such rapid use of such diverse material. As he said later in the preface, 'the feeling therein developed gives importance to the action and situation and not the action and situation to the feeling.' But what the feeling *is*, is difficult to say, and is often left purposely vague: 'Now think, ye farmers all, I pray, / Of Goody Blake and Harry Gill.' The poems were called both Jacobin and anti-Jacobin,[19] and it is difficult to generalize the attitude toward poverty they express.

People of Wordsworth's class widely viewed poverty as part of the nature of things, to be aided by charity, but not systematically eradicable. The poor might become less poor, but they were not expected to rise out of their condition, which was defined as a permanent social rank: the 'lower orders.' An attitude of sentimental concern for all forms of human weakness had been increasing throughout the eighteenth century, but this is not Wordsworth's attitude in *Lyrical Ballads*. Religiously liberal but socially conservative persons like Hannah More (sponsor of Ann Yearsley), whose *Village Politics* qualify her as a Wordsworth or a Southey of the right, thought conditions in Somerset were unbearable and identified the cause clearly: 'all the land in a parish is swallowed up by a few great landlords.'[20]

The net effect of Wordsworth's channelling his *Recluse* power into the ballads and lyrics of spring 1798 was like directing the Alfoxden waterfall into an ordinary drinking glass. His efforts to control the resulting distortion, and minimize the discrepancy between his homely subjects and the vast range of their implied meanings, is the actual working 'plan' of the 1798 *Lyrical Ballads*: to incorporate a metaphysical faith in spontaneous grace – symbolized by images of natural beauty – with an ethic of concern for all human beings.

He had been failing in this effort, for the very good reason that such a connection is very difficult to establish logically, outside some system of *belief* – Christianity, for example. Wordsworth's failure to advance *The Recluse* in March was not a failure of poetic power. On the contrary, it was a triumph of poetic power unleashed but uncontained, a failure to fit his imagination into recognizable poetic form. Coleridge never forgot the impact 'The Ruined Cottage' had on him, but like the other *Recluse* poems, its power tends to knock readers out of the framework of poetry, or art, altogether, making 'enjoyment' seem a superfluous consideration, and raising questions about the need for social action which are always potentially revolutionary, and not only in the repressive political atmosphere of England in 1798. Wordsworth had arrived at a philosophic impasse, and that is exactly where one does arrive when trying to establish a self-evident, positive connection between natural processes and human, cultural ones.

We might expect the first four *Recluse* poems to have a significant relation to the other poems Wordsworth was composing at this time, and this is exactly what we do find: his lyrical ballads of 1798 are the triumphs of a failure. That is, some very successful poems – successful in achieving poetic closure through generic identity – emerged from his failure to get on with *The Recluse*. But they still carry, vicariously, the power of *The Recluse*'s inspiration, even as they disguise some of its troubling philosophical and political implications in more conventional forms. Wordsworth transferred the vexing power of *The Recluse*'s philosophical burdens and its generic ambiguity into the smaller poetic forms of *Lyrical Ballads* by a single, simple strategy. He divided his work on *The Recluse* into two different types of poems: ballads which pose difficult questions, and lyrics which imply profound answers. These are the two different kinds of poems, announced in the volume's hybrid title, which articulate its imaginative structure. Only at the very last moment, in the 'Lines above Tintern Abbey,' did he try to bring the two concerns back together in the same poem, and then only with the utmost caution.

There are five lyrics of meditative natural description, all identified with the same initial title word, 'Lines,' designating their conventionally informal, sketchy quality. Secondly, there are ten ballads or tales about suffering poor people, especially mothers and fathers and children, making up most of the poems usually understood to be the 'lyrical ballads' of the title: that is, semi-mysterious narratives involving ordinary people, but written in much more intricate rhyme schemes than those typical of the authentic folk ballad. In this respect, it was not the simplicity of the 1798 ballads that set them off from reams of similar contemporary poems, but rather their literary sophistication. (There are, in addition, four 'dialogue' poems, printed together in two pairs, which act out the double thematic aspect of the volume's main division into lyrics and ballads.)

As in the four poems he wrote for *The Recluse* in January–March, the narrative element bulks much larger in Wordsworth's contributions to *Lyrical Ballads* than the lyric element. But the interpretive burden carried by his ballads of March–May is much *less* than that of the *Recluse* poems. By comparison with the narrator-auditor situation in the *Recluse* poems, his lyrical ballads are far simpler. Wordsworth achieved this simplicity by radically reducing the function of the by-standing auditor who 'hears' the tale of woe and 'tells' it to the reader. In the *Recluse* poems, this narrator is a sensitive young man, essentially Wordsworth himself, who feels his mental stability severely threatened by the sad stories he hears. But in his ballads of 1798, there is little danger of such 'contamination' from the suffering object to the narrating subject of the poems, since the narrator is very little present. In most of them, a poor, old, decrepit or deranged person tells his or her life story to a by-passing interlocutor, whose presence is necessary only to get the story going ('I followed him, and said, "My friend, / What ails you? wherefore weep you so?"'), and whose reactions to it are represented very minimally, if at all, in the poem.

'Old Man Travelling' is the hardest poem to place on this spectrum, and Wordsworth's treatment of it shows he was well aware of the specific difficulty he faced. The narrator says quite a lot at the beginning of this 'sketch,' heavily interpreting the 'patience' and 'perfect peace' of the slow-moving old beggar. But the original last six lines, spoken by the old man, about his son dying in the Falmouth naval hospital, appear to question so radically the benign interpretation of his life offered by the narrator that the poem seems to break into two contradictory parts. Wordsworth recognized this flaw and subsequently excised the last six lines altogether, in keeping with his overall narrative strategy in his lyrical ballads (relative to the *Recluse* poems) but in reverse: instead of reducing the role of the narrator to a minimum, he here reduced the speaking voice of the suffering object to nil.

The 'lines' or lyrics in this division of Wordsworth's labours on *Lyrical Ballads* are half as many in number, and proportionately much shorter than the ballads. Just as Wordsworth keeps interpretive commentary to a minimum in his ballads of 1798, so in most of these 'lines' he keeps to a minimum any *narrative* explanation of the speaker's situation, so that they tend to become full, credal statements about 'seeing into the life of things' through natural forms.

The usefulness of this view of the plan of *Lyrical Ballads* can be seen in comparing Wordsworth's worst poem in the volume, 'The Convict,' with his best one, the lines written above Tintern Abbey. 'The Convict' is a companion piece to Coleridge's 'The Dungeon.' Significantly, they are the only two poems in the 1798 volume that approach direct social commentary, both written under the influence of Southey's 'Botany Bay Eclogues' (1794). A large part of 'The Convict's' failure can be explained by reference to Wordsworth's difficulties with *The Recluse*, for it is the only one of his ten ballads or narratives of suffering in which the narrator both directly addresses the suffering person *and* offers to comment directly on the causes or meaning of his suffering. Its situation is similar to what would have obtained if the young man in 'The Ruined Cottage' had come upon Margaret in the last days of her decline, without the company of the Pedlar or the benefit of his philosophical long views, and had tried to say some reassuring words to her.

In contrast to 'Tintern Abbey,' 'The Convict' turns very abruptly from its opening scene of natural beauty to a highly articulated scene of human distress, thus causing an abrupt shift in tone, which, in 'Tintern Abbey,' is managed much more gradually, until Wordsworth can smoothly achieve the harmonic moral tonic of 'the still, sad music of humanity.' The narrator of 'The Convict' defends his presence at the convict's cell – actually a defence of the entire poem – by insisting that he is not 'idle.' Not, that is, a moral prig, as Southey very often appeared in his similar poems of this time, blandly congratulating himself on the difference between his situation and the convict's.

But we are left in a position of impotence at the end of 'The Convict,' wishfully indulging fantasies of power to no purpose, because there is no persuasive authoritative alternative, no wise old Pedlar, for example, to instruct us in 'that secret spirit of humanity' which still endures despite nature's 'calm oblivious tendencies.' The speaker of 'The Convict' is much less successful, has in fact nothing more to say, must almost literally shut up at the point at which his poem ends, rather than concluding it more effectively, because he has attempted to draw *direct* and *immediate* connections between: (1) his appreciation of natural beauty, (2) his sensitivity to human suffering, and (3) his own function as commentator connecting the two, when he undertakes to respond to that portentous tear that 'asks of me why I am here.'

These were precisely the triangulated relationships, 'on Man, on Nature, and on Human Life,' that Wordsworth had been trying to integrate in his *Recluse* poems of early 1798, and had been failing to, because of his narrating subject's 'contamination' by the emotional force of the poor people whose suffering he tries to present and interpret authoritatively. After early March, he pursued these *comparatively* easier experiments successfully by separating the two themes – natural beauty and human morality – he had been trying unsuccessfully to integrate. Instead of fully integrating these themes in a single large poem, Wordsworth could hope, by the artfully juxtaposed arrangement of his poems, that the reader would supply the necessary 'thought,' 'thinking,' or 'reason' variously alluded to throughout the volume – in a word, its philosophy. The *Lyrical Ballads* are not *all* triumphant, of course, but even in the worst of them we can see the seams of Wordsworth's magnificent effort of expediency, which allowed him to snatch triumphs out of his failure.

By mid-April, Wordsworth had added so much to his 'stock' of new poetry that he invited Joseph Cottle to come from Bristol to hear them. But he did not come, and by the time Wordsworth renewed the invitation on 9 May he had added so many more poems to his inventory that he hinted to Cottle of 'another plan which I do not wish to mention till I see you; let this be *very, very,* soon.'[21] He was still promising the Salisbury Plain poem to Cottle, but clearly the new plan, which would become *Lyrical Ballads*, was beginning to gain ascendancy in his mind.

By mid–May, most of Wordsworth's other 1798 lyrics and ballads were finished. He needed a rest. At the same time, another work of creation came to term: Sara Coleridge was delivered of her second son on 14 May, named for the philosopher Berkeley. Two days later, Coleridge set off with Wordsworth and Dorothy on yet another walking tour, to visit the rock formations at Cheddar Gorge, twenty-five miles away in the direction of Bristol. This was an easterly pairing to their favourite westerly walk to the Valley of Stones. Unfortunately for those who expect Romantic poetry to arise naturally out of the landscape, no poetic record was made of this jaunt; Wordsworth had publishing, not landscapes, on his mind. Instead of returning to Stowey with Coleridge and Dorothy, he continued on to Bristol.

His ostensible mission was to bring Charles Lloyd back with him so Lloyd and Coleridge could talk out the hurt feelings caused by Coleridge's publishing three sonnets (by 'Nehemiah Higginbottom') in the *Monthly Magazine* that parodied the stylistic mannerisms of Lloyd, Lamb, and Coleridge himself. Lloyd was not disposed by age or temperament to take the joke well. The incident showed some of the risks of having Coleridge as a collaborator, and illustrates the extent to which friends and enemies alike in the literary world communicated with, or insulted, each other through barely-coded insider jokes: Coleridge's sonnets could as well have appeared in the *Anti-Jacobin*. One of them was the sonnet, 'On a Ruined House in a Romantic Country,' which glanced at Wordsworth's 'Ruined Cottage.'* Lloyd was trying desperately to get rid of the 'Jacobin' label which his association with Coleridge had stuck on him. In the spring he had retaliated with a semi-*roman à clef* called *Edmund Oliver*, which caricatured the sexual, alcoholic, and political aspects of Coleridge's

---

* In 1799, Southey extended this textual debt by publishing his own 'The Ruined Cottage,' a transparent rip-off of Wordsworth's manuscript poem, with Southey taking the role of the Pedlar and 'Charles' (Lloyd or Lamb) playing the young man. The slackening of dramatic tension and devaluation of moral signficance is so great, compared to Wordsworth's poem, that he must have wept more in frustration than in anger when he came to Southey's tepid conclusion: 'I pass this ruin'd dwelling oftentimes, / And think of other days. It wakes in me / A transient sadness; but the feelings, Charles, / Which ever with these recollections rise, / I trust in God they will not pass away.'

dissipated undergraduate career, based on information only Southey could have supplied.

Wordsworth learned that Lloyd was no longer in Bristol before he parted from Dorothy and Coleridge, but this did not deter him, for he had errands of his own in mind: to get Cottle down to Alfoxden to hear the new poems and talk business. Once in town, Wordsworth caught hold of Cottle and bore him home in triumph (in Cottle's chaise) on 22 May for a week's stay.

When Wordsworth and Cottle arrived at Stowey, they found that young William Hazlitt had arrived the day before. Hazlitt, taking up Coleridge's invitation of the previous January, had walked the entire 160 miles from Shrewsbury. For the next three weeks, we have something like life-studies for events at Stowey and Alfoxden, from Hazlitt's retrospective essay, 'My First Acquaintance with Poets' (1823). Hazlitt's recollections, though coloured by time (and his by then long-standing disputes with his former idols), still retain the first impressions of an intelligent young man who was seeing for the first time in his life the great world of ideas which he believed poets inhabited.

Wordsworth burst into the Coleridges' cottage, hungry as a bear, and 'instantly began to make havoc of the half of Cheshire cheese on the table,' sourly commenting that 'his marriage with experience' had given him a better appreciation 'of the good things of this life' than the abstemious Southey. Hazlitt remembered clearly how Wordsworth looked:

'I think I see him now . . . gaunt and Don Quixote-like . . . quaintly dressed (according to the *costume* of that unconstrained period) in a brown fustian jacket and striped pantaloons. There was something of a roll, a lounge in his gait, not unlike his own Peter Bell. There was a severe, worn pressure of thought about his temples, a fire in his eyes (as if he saw something in objects more than the outward appearance), an intense high narrow forehead, a Roman nose, cheeks furrowed by strong purpose and feeling, and a convulsive inclination to laughter about the mouth, a good deal at variance with the solemn, stately expression of the rest of the face.

But Hazlitt was as evenhanded as Wordsworth was single-minded, and when Wordsworth looked out the window to comment, ' "How beautifully the sun sets on that yellow bank!" ' the young man thought, ' "With what eyes these poets see nature!" ' Through Wordsworth and Coleridge, Hazlitt was enjoying the domestication of the Picturesque, seeing nature as an aesthetic object, not as an upper-class pastime but as part of the fabric of everyday life, between hungry mouthfuls of Cheshire cheese after a fast drive in an open chaise.

In Wordsworth's absence, Coleridge had been reading Wordsworth's new poems to Hazlitt at Alfoxden, with Dorothy as their 'frugal' hostess, and the next morning they came back over to Alfoxden to hear

Wordsworth read *Peter Bell*. They sat on the branches of an old ash that resembled a banyan tree, two of its branches growing in and out of the ground, 'which gave to each the appearance of a serpent moving along by gathering itself up in folds.'[22] Hazlitt was enchanted by each poet's voice, and keenly remarked their individual differences: 'Coleridge's manner is more full, animated, and varied; Wordsworth's more equable, sustained, and internal. The one might be termed more *dramatic*, the other more *lyrical*.' Coleridge read as he composed, 'walking over uneven ground, or breaking through the straggling branches of a copse-wood; whereas Wordsworth always wrote (if he could) walking up and down a straight-gravel walk.' The movements of their minds seemed to match their bodies and their voices.

That night, walking back to Nether Stowey, Wordsworth and Hazlitt got into 'a metaphysical argument . . . in which neither of us succeeded in making ourselves perfectly clear and intelligible.' As with almost everything Wordsworth did now, this argument was soon turned into poetry: the matching pair of 'Expostulation and Reply' and 'The Tables Turned.' In both, Wordsworth's natural metaphysics wins out over Hazlitt's earnest Dissenter's insistence on book-learning. Against Hazlitt's Godwinian insistence on the disinterestedness of the human mind, Wordsworth preferred its 'wise passiveness,' open to Nature's action: 'One impulse from a vernal wood / May teach you more of man; / Of moral evil and of good, / Than all the sages can.' Such sentiments, often taken straight as Wordsworthian gospel, were in the context of their composition deliberately reductive provocations, calculated ripostes to the brash confidence of a brilliant but callow young man.

At the end of the week, Cottle went back to Bristol, carrying all these poems with him, except 'Tintern Abbey,' which was neither planned nor dreamed of at this time. The title, *Lyrical Ballads*, seems to have been proposed at or about this time, for Hazlitt recalls Coleridge using it on a walk to Linton, along with his claim that it was to be an 'experiment . . . to see how far the public taste would endure poetry written in a more natural and simple style than had hitherto been attempted.'[23]

Coleridge's contributions to the volume were finally quite small, numerically. The balance they had aimed at was upset by Wordsworth's phenomenal rate of production, and some of Coleridge's comments to Cottle give the appearance of struggling to keep his place in the volume.[24] This was just the reverse of their several previous attempts at collaboration, where Wordsworth had always been the one to drop out. But with 'The Ancient Mariner' as its first, longest, and most striking poem Coleridge more than deserved his title to joint-authorship. Also, given their placement of the poems (three of Coleridge's total of four poems coming first), a reader who went sequentially through the book would have 'heard' Coleridge's 'full, animated, and varied' voice for nearly a third of its length before he came to Wordsworth's 'more equable, sustained, and internal' one.

Wordsworth, having committed himself at last, and with the quit-notice for Alfoxden soon to arrive, threw himself into the preparations for the volume. He followed Cottle to Bristol in late May, and kept returning compulsively, staying two weeks at the beginning of June. He worried Cottle with small changes and matters of detail, delivered with the pompous authority that James Losh noted in Wordsworth's manner at the time: 'pleasant and clear, but too earnest and emphatic in his manner of speaking in conversation.'[25] Coleridge followed their conversations by mail, explaining to Cottle (who was worried about the volume's lack of unity) that they 'are to a certain degree *one work*, in *kind tho' not in degree*, as an Ode is one work – & . . . our different poems are as stanzas, good relatively than absolutely: – Mark you, I say *in kind* tho' not in degree.'[26] This was desperate reasoning, provoked by the fact that 'The Ancient Mariner' is the volumes's most *dis*unifying poem, a tendency exacerbated by placing it at the beginning. Coleridge was, characteristically, using the Aristotelian, scholastic distinction between kind and degree as a rhetorical smokescreen to impress the naive, nervous Cottle. Taken literally, his argument would mean that none of the poems could stand alone on its own merits. But it does point to the truth that the volume's ensemble, ballads of suffering plus lines of natural beauty, produces its unsettling but enduring master-impression.

Postscript

Sometime evidently during his work on 'The Thorn' Wordsworth produced a strange poem which he never published, but which is 'perhaps a reminiscence of his last unhappy days with Annette.'[27]

> Away, away, it is the air
> That stirs among the withered leaves;
> Away, away, it is not there,
> Go, hunt among the harvest sheaves.
> There is a bed in shape as plain
> As from a hare or lion's lair
> It is the bed where we have lain
> In anguish and despair.
>
> Away, and take the eagle's eyes,
> The tiger's smell,
> Ears that can hear the agonies
> And murmurings of hell;
> And when you there have stood
> By that same bed of pain,
> The groans are gone, the tears remain.

> Then tell me if the thing be clear,
> The difference betwixt a tear
> Of water and of blood.[28]

The standard scholarly view is that this is a gothic fragment reminiscent of Wordsworth's earlier work.[29] But it is neither a fragment nor particularly 'gothic,' except as gothic is taken to signify a melodramatic expression of painful emotions. It is a riddle or conundrum poem, like Wordsworth's 'Argument for Suicide,' or Thel's hysterical questions in Blake's *The Book of Thel*: 'Why a tender curb upon the youthful burning boy! / What a little curtain of flesh on the bed of our desire?' The riddle is, 'Can you find the bed I'm talking about? And if you can, can you appreciate the kind of pain it represents?' It has relevance to the tale of infanticide in 'The Thorn,' and scholarly tracings to Burger's 'The Lass of Fair Wone' are useful,[30] but 'Away, away' asks a question both more complex, and closer to Wordsworth's personal experience.

It says you will not find the bed where you are looking for it, but 'among the harvest sheaves': it is a bed of autumn. Its 'withered leaves' and 'harvest sheaves' echo the 'rustling aspins' and 'the falling leaf' at the end of *Descriptive Sketches*, written in October 1793 as Wordsworth lurked outside Orléans, where Annette had been spirited to a bed, hidden from him, for her lying-in. To find this bed requires supernatural capabilities, though its shape carries a plain meaning: namely, you can see clearly that two people have been lying there. But profound resources of understanding are evidently required to grasp the meaning of this plain evidence. The immediate pains are gone, but not the grief: 'the tears remain.' Its final question is, who can adjudicate between two different kinds of pain, and tears, those 'of water and [those] of blood' – indicating perhaps those directly experienced and those indirectly observed. The poem's implied answer is that the answer will *not* be clear.

The poem is as good as similar puzzle-poems in *Lyrical Ballads* of much lighter touch: 'We Are Seven' and 'Anecdote for Fathers.' But the voice of 'Away, away' is masterful and lordly: find it if you can, it dares us, 'Then tell me if the thing be clear' – in the confident expectation that it will not be.

Two kinds of beds came together in Wordsworth's mind here, those where he lay with Annette, and those where he frequently lay with Dorothy. Both women, for different reasons, must be disappointed of his love, but it is impossible for him to say which loss is worse, the tear of water (Annette's?) or of blood (Dorothy's?). On 26 February Dorothy recorded, 'we lay sidelong upon the turf, and gazed on the landscape till it melted into more than natural loveliness.'[31] At about the same time, Wordsworth jotted down that

> In many a walk
> At evening or by moolight, or reclined
> At midday upon beds of forest moss,
> Have we to Nature and her impulses
> Of our whole being made free gift.[32]

Lying down on the ground together was a common practice with them. They would imagine they were dead, listen to their own breathing, pay minute attention to the sounds around them: clearly sensual behaviour, but hard to tell 'if the thing be clear, the difference' between it and sublimated sexual behaviour. In 'The Three Graves,' Edward also lies down in a bower, not with Mary his beloved but with Ellen, her sisterly friend. 'With shut-up senses, Edward lay,' but said, 'See, dearest Ellen! see! / 'Tis in the leaves, a little sun, / No bigger than your ee,' and they pass the time arguing about what colour the rays are. The eye/spy motif is also present here.

Other fragments related to 'Away, away' ask bluntly why Nature does not immediately reflect human suffering, the kind of sentiment that *The Recluse* tries to take seriously, but which comes out in *Lyrical Ballads* only in lighter, teasing questions: if Nature seems to take so much pleasure in its own beauty, 'Have I not reason to lament / What man has made of man?' One of these fragments, only published in 1992, is evidently related to both 'Away, away' and 'The Three Graves':

> Are there no groans no breeze or wind?
> Does misery leave no track behind?
> Why is the earth without a shape and why
> Thus silent is the sky?
> Is every glimmering of the sky,
> Is every [?lamphole] in the world an eye?
> Has every star a tongue?[33]

Here too we have the riddle form, and the idea of nature's 'eyes' spying on mankind, with the question of why nature does not shape itself to the forms of human misery: because *then* its facts and meaning would be clear to everyone.

CHAPTER TWENTY-FOUR

Wye Wandering

O sylvan Wye! Thou wanderer through the woods,
How often has my spirit turned to thee!
('Lines written above Tintern Abbey')

Wordsworth returned to Alfoxden in mid-June to collect Dorothy and their few furnishings. They said goodbye to their wonderful residence on 25 June, paused a week at Stowey with Sara (Coleridge was off rambling with Hazlitt), and departed for Bristol on 2 July.

They spent a few days with Cottle in his lodgings above his new shop in crowded, noisy Wine Street.[1] Dorothy registered the shock of the change immediately: 'You can scarcely conceive how the jarring contrast between the sounds which are now forever ringing in my ear and the sweet sounds of Alfoxden makes me long for the country again. After three years residence in retirement a city in feeling, sound, and prospect is hateful.'[2] She soon got her wish to return to the country.

They sought out James Losh in Shirehampton, a quiet suburb on the Avon (it now consists mainly of industrial fuel storage tanks), but he had gone to Bath for special treatments following a relapse.[3] They went immediately in pursuit, and spent 8 July with him and Cecilia at their rooms in Bath. At dinner that night was Losh's Unitarian friend Reverend Richard Warner, a pacifist opponent of the war, whose *A Walk through Wales, in August 1797* had appeared in February, a day-by-day hiking guide book featuring a frontispiece of Tintern Abbey and little woodcut maps at the head of each chapter to show the day's recommended route. The company admired the new book, which immediately prompted Wordsworth to follow in Warner's footsteps while simultaneously retracing his own from 1793. Warner was glad to meet a fellow landscape enthusiast, and invited the Wordsworths to dine with him next day at his house.

After dinner on the 9th, the Loshes returned to Shirehampton with the Wordsworths. Next morning William and Dorothy set out on a walking tour of the Wye valley, following Warner's route in reverse. This trip resulted in the most famous poem in *Lyrical Ballads* after 'The Ancient Mariner.' But although the 'Lines Composed a Few Miles above Tintern Abbey' masterfully conclude the 1798 volume, there had been no suggestion, as of early July, that another poem was needed for the volume, still less that Wordsworth should take a trip in order to write one. As things stood, *Lyrical Ballads* would have ended with 'The Convict.'

They crossed over to Chepstow by the ferry and walked along the road, which sometimes follows, sometimes avoids, the looping curves of the Wye.[4] This walk can only be taken with difficulty now, as the highway (A466) has no shoulders, and the hiking paths (Wye Valley Walk and Offa's Dyke Path) have been relocated to the tops of the hills and cliffs on both sides of the river. They reached the village of Tintern and its ruined Cistercian abbey early that day (it's only five miles from Chepstow), and had ample time to tour the abbey and its grounds.*

On the morning of the 11th, they set off upriver again, heading for Monmouth and Goodrich and their noted ruined castles. The visual contrast of picturesque ruins with dramatic cliffs and deep woods was the primary focus of all the standard guidebooks for this popular tour, especially Gilpin's *Observations on the River Wye . . . Made in the Summer of 1770* (1782; 3rd ed., 1792), which Wordsworth had with him, as well as newer ones like Warner's, though both of these took more realistic account of current local economic and social conditions than Wordsworth's poem does.

Wordsworth later said he began composing his poem 'upon leaving Tintern, after crossing the Wye.' This suggests that he started his oral composition – his singsong humming to himself in five-beat lines – on the morning of the 11th, since the only bridges crossing the Wye were upriver to the north, at Brockweir and at Bisgweir. His reference to the river's 'sweet inland murmur' and his footnote to this line ('The river is not affected by the tides a few miles above Tintern') support this location, because the river stops being affected by the enormous action of the ocean tides between these two bridges, one to three miles above Tintern. His

---

* The abbey is now splendidly preserved for modern tourism, with the usual gains and losses. A few years ago one of the specials on the menu of the quite good restaurant next to the parking lot was a stuffed salmon called 'The William Wordsworth.' Walkers wishing to approximate Wordsworth's younger, leaner experience should climb up to the ruins of St Mary's Chapel on the hill overlooking the abbey. Though technically off-limits, its mouldering walls, broken floors, and lush, overgrown graveyard give a more powerful feeling of vanished sacrality than the comprehensive archaeological information supplied by the National Trust for the abbey itself. Threatening graffiti ('Beware! This is Holy Ground!') and surprised trysting lovers bring one closer to Wordsworth's experience, as hidden or revealed in his poem, than one might suspect.

opening description seems to record a backward look downriver towards the abbey, moving from the 'mountain-springs' and 'cliffs' where he stood, across the more cultivated 'plots of cottage ground' and 'orchard tufts,' to end with highly selective images of the village, the beggars in the abbey, and the nearby iron and charcoal industries: 'wreathes of smoke sent up in silence' and 'vagrant dwellers in the houseless woods.'

They spent the night of the 11th at Goodrich, and on the 12th they walked all the way back down past Tintern to Chepstow. At the end of the day they took one of the many tour boats that plied the river back up to spend another night at Tintern. Thus Wordsworth was at or around the abbey on every day of this tour, which he said was 'a ramble of four or five days,' but probably four, since they could easily have returned to Bristol on the 13th, and he said he 'composed the last 20 lines or so as he walked down the hill from Clifton to Bristol.'[5] Returning to Cottle's house that evening, he delivered the completed poem, of which he said 'not any part of it was written down till I reached Bristol,' to the printers the next day: 14 July.

This is the bare bones of their itinerary. But in the last fifteen years, 'Tintern Abbey' has become the focus of an extraordinary controversy, that turns very much on where Wordsworth walked, and what he saw on this trip. Where one stands now on 'Tintern Abbey' makes a big difference in Romantic scholarship – whether one stands with Wordsworth, 'a few miles above' the abbey, or with Gilpin, Warner, and many contemporary critics down in the ruins of the abbey itself. Older critics, steeped in Wordsworthian 'nature worship,' praise the poem for its universality, and are actually puzzled to find residual traces of his concern for humanity in it.[6] But contemporary critics, having learned how our 'nature poet' has been homogenized by an adulating tradition, have seized on those same traces as the last evidences of a radicalism Wordsworth was now trying, like Coleridge, Lloyd, Thelwall and many others, to hide.

The debate turns mainly on the 'uncertain notice' that Wordsworth gives to the smoke rising from the trees, since we know that the smoke was rising from the thriving iron industry of small forges in the wooded hills above the abbey, and from the kilns which burnt these trees to produce the charcoal needed for the forges. The river was thick with the traffic of this industry, as well as with boats serving the busy tourist industry. Both were by-products of the war: the iron forges, to produce cannon and other material; the tourists, because picturesque British locales were more in demand with so much of the Continent closed to touring. Furthermore, Wordsworth's tentative suggestion that the smoke 'might seem' to come from 'vagrant dwellers in the houseless woods' touches with extreme delicacy on a fact known to everybody who visited the abbey: that it was the shelter and resort for many beggars and vagabonds, who made their living by cadging from the well-to-do tourists who came to visit it, under the pretext of offering them 'tours.'

Warner's *Walk* gave details about both the beautiful aspects of the scene and the ugly ones that Wordsworth softens. The noise of the forges kept him awake on a hot summer's night, and he could accommodate 'the dingy beings who melt the ore . . . in their horrible employment' to his cultural purpose only by alluding to Virgil: 'we saw Virgil's description realized . . . Etna, the forges of the Cyclops, and their fearful employment.'[7] But he was capable of viewing other human activities in a complementary relationship to nature in a way that anticipated Wordsworth: 'The little cottages scattered at the feet [of the cliffs], neat residences of industrious labour, form a pleasing accompaniement; exhibiting simplicity combined with majesty.' Wordsworth framed this image too: 'These plots of cottage-ground, these orchard tufts . . . these pastoral farms / Green to the very door.'

But though Warner's vistas were fresh in memory from their recent conversation, Wordsworth seems to have relied more on Gilpin's standard guidebook. His reference to 'these steep and lofty cliffs' and the way in which *thought* 'connect[s] / The landscape with the quiet of the sky' was directly indebted to Gilpin's attempt to bring the region's *smoke* into a more pleasing aesthetic perspective: 'Many of the furnaces, on the banks of the river, consume charcoal, which is manufactured on the spot; and the smoke, which is frequently seen issuing from the sides of the hills; and spreading its veil over a part of them, beautifully breaks their lines, and unites them with the sky.'[8]

It is interesting to consider some uses Wordsworth did *not* make of Gilpin, in the light of his demonstrable familiarity with this guidebook. Wordsworth's 'vagrant dwellers,' less pitiable than Warner's 'dingy beings', are far less so than the ones Gilpin encountered in the abbey and described with a shocked candour that quite breaks through his conventional picturesque perspective. Over half the pages Gilpin devotes to Tintern are given over to these distracting beggars. His tone in general is fastidious, not to say mincing, as he recommends one viewing-station or criticizes another. He facetiously proposed, for example, taking a hammer to certain corners of the abbey to make its appearance more ruinous. But when he meets the beggars, his aestheticizing manner breaks down in the shocked honesty of his naked human response: 'The poverty and wretchedness of the inhabitants were remarkable.' They lived in huts among the ruins, and 'the whole hamlet' congregated at the gate, offering 'tours.' Gilpin and his party followed one of these, a 'poor woman [who] could scarce crawl; shuffling along her palsied limbs, and meagre, contracted body.' She led them to what she said was 'the monks' library,' but 'it was her own mansion':

> all indeed she meant to tell us was the story of her own wretchedness; and all she had to shew us, was her own miserable habitation. We did not expect to be

interested; but found we were. I never saw so loathsome a dwelling . . . a cavity between two ruined walls; which streamed with unwholesome dews . . . . We were rather surprised, that the wretched creature was still alive; than that she had only lost the use of her limbs.'[9]

Such a powerfully ambiguous passage, standing out from its bland surroundings in Gilpin, and reinforced by his own experience, had an enormous impact on Wordsworth. Reading this passage, and seeing firsthand what it described, seemed like an image from his own recently-completed ballads, which everywhere recapitulate what Gilpin heard: 'all indeed she meant to tell us was the story of her own wretchedness.' Compare the Female Vagrant: 'She ceased, and weeping turned away, / As if because her tale was at an end.'

In 'Tintern Abbey's' summation of his self-creation, Wordsworth tried, by oblique references to these 'vagrant dwellers' in the Wye's secluded landscape, to bring together the two themes he had separated in most of his compositions since early March, the ballads of suffering and the lyrics of natural celebration. This is clear in the justification he gives for the significance of his return to Nature, and to this landscape in particular:

> For I have learned
> To look on nature, not as in the hour
> Of *thoughtless* youth, but hearing oftentimes
> The still, sad music of humanity,
> Nor harsh nor grating, though of ample power
> To chasten and subdue.
>
> (89–94; italics added)

He has added *thought* to his aesthetic pleasure, of a specifically moral, humanistic kind, such as he recommended at the end of 'Goody Blake': 'Now *think*, ye farmers *all*, I pray, / Of Goody Blake and Harry Gill.'

But so great is his fear of upsetting his new creative balance, that it can be argued with equal cogency that he strove mightily to *prevent* such thoughts from intruding too forcefully into the poem. 'Vagrant *dwellers*' (a cautious oxymoron) are not quite as bad off as vagrants, to say nothing of beggars, especially when they are immediately replaced by 'some hermit,' an entirely picturesque appurtenance, self-sufficient in his isolation: 'where by his fire / The hermit sits alone.' This anachronistic hermit was also suggested by Gilpin: 'a man of warm imagination, in monkish times, might have been allured by such a scene to become an inhabitant of it.'[10]

This is not to say that Wordsworth should have added some ruins, human or architectural, to his landscape a few miles above Tintern Abbey. His loco-descriptive meditative poem is not required to demonstrate the relation between landscape viewing and social responsibility. But the poem itself is full of language which simultaneously invites and resists such probing questions, opening up precisely those areas of concern that it seeks to contain in more manageable aesthetic terms. By posing this ostensibly personal poem of nature worship in such terms, Wordsworth forces us to consider what he is *not* doing as well as what he is doing – and to appreciate how hard-earned his sweeping affirmations in the poem are.

In the only other poem in *Lyrical Ballads* that tries to bring nature and suffering mankind close together, 'The Convict,' Wordsworth maintains his faith by wishful thinking about social reform. Not that 'Tintern Abbey' is more liberal than 'The Convict.' On the contrary, it makes very small claims for what nature's 'forms of beauty' produce by way of moral social action: 'such [feelings], *perhaps*, / As *may* have had no *trivial* influence / On that best portion of a good man's life; / His *little, nameless, unremembered* acts / Of kindness and of love.' Only an extremely quietistic view of morality would call such unknown actions 'the best portion' of anybody's life. But this was as much as Wordsworth was now capable of saying, by way of healing the split in *The Recluse*'s intentions represented by the triumphant 'failures' of his lyrical ballads.

The triumph of 'Tintern Abbey' is, rather, its awareness of its own proximity to failure. Though usually read as a deeply affirmative statement of existential faith, it achieves its affirmations in ways that are shot through with the signs of their own deconstruction. These are more than indications of Wordsworth's emotional sincerity and rhetorical skill, acknowledging honest doubts; it is a risk that at every moment threatens to end the poem. Each of its verse paragraphs after the first one begins with or turns upon language that undercuts the statement it is making: 'If this be but a vain belief,' 'Not for this faint I, nor mourn nor murmur,' 'Nor perchance, / If I were not thus taught,' 'Nor, perchance— / If I should be where I no more can hear / Thy voice,' 'Nor wilt thou then forget.' It is precisely the *dubiety* of thought and belief, of education and of faith, that underscores 'Tintern Abbey's' natural religion.

In each paragraph, these negatives are linked to images of human suffering, usually in cities and always in groups. In the first paragraph, great care is taken that any mention of human activity should not 'disturb the wild green landscape.' In the second, 'the din of towns and cities' and 'hours of weariness' are generalized into 'the heavy and the weary weight / Of all this *unintelligible* world.' In three, it is 'the fretful stir / Unprofitable, and the fever of the world.' In four, it is 'the still, sad music of humanity' itself. And in the fifth paragraph, it is 'evil tongues, / Rash judgements . . . the sneers of selfish men, / . . . greetings where no kindness is, [and] all the dreary intercourse of daily life.'

But what one notices about these statements of social suffering, upon reflection, is that they do not in fact add up to any very great sum of evil, of the kind we usually silently supply when we read the sonorous phrase, 'still, sad music of humanity.' They sound, rather, much like

Wordsworth's experiences in London in 1795, which he was now being sharply reminded of: the lonely feelings of rejection suffered by a sensitive person in conditions of intensely competitive work in urban markets, where gossip, hasty or ill-formed judgment, jealousy, and smooth hypocrisy all contribute to the feverish pace at which one's business fails to move along as profitably as one wishes.

Yet 'Tintern Abbey''s composition, on the one hand so immediate, contemporaneous, and personal, was at the same time so heavily indebted to a variety of poetical sources that it can be considered a *summa* of Wordsworth's literary experience to this point, as well as of his personal history.[11] Besides obvious debts to contemporary poets like Edward Young, it also has distinct echoes of Shakespeare, Milton, and the Bible. The influence of Coleridge's 'conversational poems' is also marked: 'Nature never did betray the heart that loved her' echoes 'Nature ne'er deserts the wise and pure' from 'This Lime-Tree Bower.' Not merely the fact but the *specificity* of Wordsworth's echoes is important. He hears Shakespeare's, Milton's, and the Bible's heroes in their time of crisis, as they contemplate what Wordsworth himself was contemplating: the need, and the cost, *of public action in the world.* Hamlet: 'How . . . unprofitable / Seem to me all the uses of this world' (cf. 'the fretful stir / Unprofitable, and the fever of the world'). Samson: 'So much I feel my genial spirits droop' (cf. 'Nor . . . should I the more / Suffer my genial spirits to decay'). Milton: 'though fall'n on evil dayes, / On evil dayes though fall'n, and evil tongues' (cf. 'neither evil tongues . . . nor all / The dreary intercourse of daily life'). The Psalmist: 'He maketh me to lie down beside the still waters . . . Yea, though I walk through the valley of the shadow of death, I will fear no evil: for thou art with me' (cf. 'For thou art with me, here, upon the banks / Of this fair river').[12]

This broad range of allusive language raises another register of language in the poem to view, which is usually excluded from critical consideration even more than its language of social pain: namely, the passionately erotic language that conveys his feelings for Annette, 'more like a man / Flying from something that he dreads, than one / Who sought the thing he loved.' Through each of its five paragraphs, words of passion are invoked, but only (like its social terms) to be chastened simultaneously by gestures taming that passion. Some of it is physiological: 'sensations sweet, / Felt in the blood, and felt along the heart.' Some of it is moral: 'Feelings too of unremembered pleasure . . . of kindness and of love.' Some of it is human passion projected on to natural objects: 'How often, in spirit, have I turned to thee / O sylvan Wye! Thou wanderer through the woods, / How often has my spirit turned to thee!' And some of it is displaced from himself into eroticized landscape painting: 'The sounding cataract / Haunted me like a *passion*,' the woods and mountains 'were then to me / *An appetite: a feeling and a love.*' But 'that time is past, / And all its *aching joys* are now no more, / And all its *dizzy raptures*.'

Here follows his hard lesson of learning 'to look on nature, not as in the hour of thoughtless youth,' with its resulting transformation: 'Therefore am I still / A *lover* of the meadows and the woods' (103–05). He is still a lover, but now of Nature, not another person. And yet there is another person present in the poem, his sister Dorothy. The final portrait of Dorothy is in fact a portrait of William's passion, as reflected in her eyes:

> in thy voice I catch
> The language of my former heart, and read
> My former pleasures in the shooting lights
> Of thy wild eyes! Oh! yet a little while
> May I behold in thee what I was once,
> My dear, dear Sister!
>
> (117–22)

This language of passion is the more noteworthy because its reference to himself five years earlier is not true in terms of his supposed attachment to nature then. Instead, his language at that time was full of thoughts of Annette, deflected from his and her letters into his erotic description of the Female Vagrant of 'A Night on Salisbury Plain,' and in his extensive sexual heightening of *Descriptive Sketches* in his revisions of 1794. He was not such a lover of nature in 1793, and he is not so much a lover of humanity in 1798.[13] The sequence of his development had been more nearly the opposite: from love of man to love of nature, or rather, from *despair* of loving man to finding relief in nature. What he imagines happening to Dorothy is what he now recognizes has happened to him: 'When these *wild ecstasies* shall be matured / Into a sober pleasure.'

He was about to leave England again, for the first time in five or six years. All his memories of 1793 at this place came flooding back. Repressing his feelings for Annette, he in effect weds himself to Nature via Dorothy (or vice versa) with the invocation of 'a holier love' in nature a few miles above the altar of the ruined abbey in the valley. Thoughts of divorce and marriage sprang to mind from very deep sources in his past. A partial source for his strange definition of the 'best portion of a good man's life' as 'his little, nameless, unremembered acts / Of kindness and of love' is one of Milton's divorce tracts: 'whereby good men in the best portion of their lives . . . are compelled to civil indignities.'[14] But in Milton's text, 'the best portion of their lives' refers specifically to men's sexual happiness in marriage, and 'civil indignities' refers to restrictions against divorce, whereas Wordsworth's 'best portion of a good man's life' includes acts of love so small as to be nameless and unremembered – which would include Caroline Wordsworth, so far as public acknowledgment is concerned.

'Tintern Abbey''s intense mingling of public and private passions was especially volatile because, at the very moment *Lyrical Ballads* was being set up in type, the whole Alfoxden gang was exploded by the *Anti-Jacobin*. In a long, scorched-earth satire called 'The New Morality,' published in its last number, 9 July, it pilloried them as 'ye, five other wandering bards that move, / In sweet accord of harmony and love, / C——dge and S – th – y, L —— d and L – mbe, & Co. / Tune all your mystic harps to praise LEPAUX!' (Larevellière-Lepaux was the current president of the French Directorate, and a patron of the state religion of 'Theophilanthropie.'[15]) 'Coleridge & Co.' were being mopped up as small fry under the influence of the *Anti-Jacobin*'s larger targets, Godwin, Paine, Holcroft, Thelwall, and David Williams (a Welsh radical), in a virtual Who's Who, or last call, of English radicalism in the 1790s. The references to 'wandering' and 'harmony and love' show that the Tory satirists (Canning, Frere, Ellis, and Pitt) knew something about their targets' movements, including the Pantisocracy fiasco, and had studied the contents of their recent volumes carefully. Wordsworth is almost certainly the 'Co.,' since it signifies only one person (to bring the total to '*five* wandering bards') and since he had been identified by name with the other four in George Dyer's well-meaning praise of 'Pantisocracy's harmonious train' in *The Poet's Fate* the year before.[16] The entire 1797–98 run of the *Anti-Jacobin* had contained shrewd assessments of the nature of the 'Jacobin' poetry produced pre-eminently by Southey, and also by Coleridge and Erasmus Darwin among others. Coleridge's poem, 'To a Young Ass,' was the direct target of these lines from 'The New Morality':

> Mark her fair Votaries, prodigal of grief,
> With cureless pangs, and woes that mock relief,
> Droop in soft sorrow o'er a faded flow'r;
> O'er a dead Jack-Ass pour the pearly show'r: –
> But hear, unmov'd, of *Loire's* ensanguin'd flood,
> Choak'd up with slain; —of *Lyons* drench'd in blood;
> Of Crimes that blot the Age, the World with shame,
> Foul crimes, but sicklied o'er with Freedom's name
>
> (140–47)

If 'The New Morality' appeared on 9 July, it arrived in Bristol just before William and Dorothy set off on their tour of the Wye valley. However, the last numbers of the *Anti-Jacobin* are misdated, so though 9 July is usually understood to be the date of its last appearance, there is a possibility that the last number, containing this apocalyptic condemnation, appeared just *after* Wordsworth returned from his tour, on 16 July.[17] The effect of this attack from the very centre of England's political power may well be registered in 'Tintern Abbey''s nervous concluding language about 'the sneers of selfish men.'

Then, before the month was out, but after Wordsworth had turned

'Tintern Abbey' over to Cottle, the *Anti-Jacobin*'s more pedestrian successor, the *Anti-Jacobin Review and Magazine; or, Monthly Political and Literary Censor*, led off the poetry section of its inaugural number with Gillray's famous print illustrating 'The New Morality' (see illustration). Here, Lepaux is represented as 'the holy Hunch-back,' holding the new religion's bible, titled *Religion de la Nature*. A caption, 'Explanation of the Satyrical Print,' reproduced just those lines of Canning and Frere's brilliant satire pertaining to the procession of English liberals and radicals who wanted to enshrine Jacobinism as England's state religion. In this reprint, the names of the 'five wandering bards' are the first proper names to appear, even before 'Paine, W–ll—ms, G–dw–n, H–lc–ft,' 'Th–lw—l, and ye that lecture as ye go.' Someone had also paid close attention to the bards' names, for the spelling of Lamb's name has been corrected from 'L–be,' as it appeared in the last issue of the *Anti-Jacobin*.

In the cartoon, Wordsworth's friends appear smaller than Fox and the major political figures, but closer to the throne of revolutionary atheism. Coleridge and Southey have asses' heads, courtesy of Coleridge's 'To a Young Ass.' Lamb and Lloyd are 'Toad and Frog,' to associate them, by a silly alliterative transfer, with the cartoon's other witches' brew monstrosities and unnatural growths: vipers, monkeys, and crocodiles. They hold their *Blank Verses* in their mouths, dedicated to Southey and published in February by the Arch brothers, who would soon become the London publishers of *Lyrical Ballads*. The two raggedy boys in Liberty caps in front of them may be their human forms, or other youngsters led astray (like George Burnett and Richard Reynell), in which case, by a process of elimination, the large right hand just visible supporting the 'Cornucopia of Ignorance' from below would be that of the fifth partner in their wandering 'Co.': Wordsworth's. The arm and hand appear to belong to a large, strong man, which fits Wordsworth's description. This assumes a good deal of literalism on Gillray's part, but that was precisely his genius: to take physical, personal details and exaggerate them grotesquely, often to the displeasure of Canning, Frere and Pitt.

Such a vehement attack made it abundantly clear that a volume bearing the name of Coleridge would do no good to any other name linked with his, for it would immediately be made to 'stink' too. This was no time to offer the reviewers a double target, especially one that could be associated with the hapless Southey and his flaccid poems sympathizing with the suffering poor, as Wordsworth's ballads assuredly would be by readers who did not bother about fine points of difference. No one was making fine discriminations in this highly polarized climate of opinion. The religion of nature at the end of 'Tintern Abbey' would not have been much differentiated from Lepaux's *Religion de la Nature*. For one thing, it was not all that different.

The 'Advertisement' to *Lyrical Ballads* may have been been written by

Wordsworth at this time, alone in Bristol, under fire, and separated from Coleridge. It lacks Coleridge's subtle persuasive powers. It insults its readers by assuring them that, whatever they may think of these poems, they are most assuredly wrong, either because their taste has been improperly educated or because they have not devoted enough attention to the study of poetry. It speaks with the voice that James Losh complained of, 'too earnest and emphatic.' But if Wordsworth imagined himself to be answering the editors of the *Anti-Jacobin* his assertiveness sounds more brave than pompous. A culture war in political poetics had been waging for the better part of a year, and Wordsworth's 'Advertisement' may best be read as a salvo back in the direction of the 'Introduction to the Poetry of the *Anti-Jacobin*,' from its very first issue. There, the *Anti-Jacobin* had spoken with lordly authority about the true nature of poetry, and lamented the present cultural situation, in which it seemed 'that good Morals, and what We should call good Politics, are inconsistent with the spirit of true Poetry.' This being the case, it elected 'to go to the only market where [poetry] is to be had good and ready made, that of the *Jacobins*' – a frank admission – but to present it 'with such precautions, as may conduce at once to the safety of our Readers' principles, and to the improvement of our own Poetry.'[18] Hence Wordsworth's reference to Sir Joshua Reynolds, '[who] observed [that 'an accurate taste in poetry'] . . . can only be produced by severe thought, and a long continued intercourse with the best models of composition,' was a deliberate invocation of the kind of authority that 'readers of superior judgement' would be disposed to accept. But Wordsworth also made his volume's provocation obvious by imagining the scene that would be created when these poems appeared, like lower-class bumpkins barging into a genteel eighteenth-century drawing room: these sneering 'readers of superior judgement . . . accustomed to the gaudiness and inane phraseology of many modern writers . . . will look round for poetry, and will . . . enquire by what species of courtesy these attempts can be permitted to assume that *title*.' Who are *they*? Who invited *them*?

Wordsworth was, in effect, responding to the *Anti-Jacobin*'s invitation in 'The New Morality' to some 'bashful Genius, in some rural cell' to rise up in response to 'thy Country's just alarms': 'Wield in her cause thy long neglected arms: / Of lofty Satire pour th'indignant strain' (76–77). The main thrust of 'The New Morality' is a call for a strong national poet to rise up and take on the task of moral regeneration which the editors had been preparing for by therapeutic satire. It is not wholly out of the question that they actually had Wordsworth in mind, and hence protectively did not mention his name. They certainly knew who he was, and their description of this ideal poet has many similarities to his career to date:

. . . for who can tell
What bashful Genius, in some rural cell, [Racedown? Alfoxden?]
As year to year, and day succeeds to day, [1796–98?]
In joyless leisure wastes his life away?
In him the flame of early Fancy shone; [*An Evening Walk?*]
His genuine worth his old Companions own; [Frere the old
    Cantab?]
In childhood and in youth their Chief confess'd, [Wordsworth's
    reputation at Hawkshead and Cambridge?]
His Master's pride [William Taylor?], his pattern to the rest.
Now, far aloof retiring from the strife
Of busy talents, and of active life, [London, 1795?]
As, *from the loop-holes of retreat*, he views [remaining contacts with
    London friends?]
Our Stage, Verse, Pamphlets, Politics, and News,
[packets of books and newspapers sent to Racedown and Alfoxden?]
He loaths the world, – or with reflection sad
Concludes it irrecoverably mad; [the *Recluse* plans?]
Of Taste, of Learning, Morals, all bereft,
No hope, no prospect to redeem it left.
               (55–70; italics added, from Cowper, *The Task*)

'Tintern Abbey' may be in part Wordsworth's response to this invitation, adapting it to his only somewhat different purposes. Calls for a great new English poet had been echoing throughout the 1790s, and Wordsworth's self-creation was, as we saw in the links between *The Recluse* and the *Lyrical Ballad* prefaces, intimately connected with an idea of his poetry *and* his life forming a model for national regeneration.

Maybe the *Anti-Jacobin* editors had somebody else in mind, or nobody in particular. But if they knew Francis Wrangham, they may have known that he and Wordsworth had collaborated on a Juvenalian satire very much on the order of the one they call for, calling for renewed moral leadership from the upper classes. Such knowledge on their part is not at all unlikely. Canning, Frere and Ellis, when they were not engaged in the semi-clandestine production of the *Anti-Jacobin*, were regularly in contact with the wholly clandestine operations of the government's secret service run by Wickham, King, and Ford, the latter two of whom had received a full set of reports less than a year earlier on the disaffected Alfoxden gang, naming Coleridge and *'Wordsworth'* in particular. John King's brother had tutored Canning's friend George Ellis, a major *Anti-Jacobin* contributor and well-paid government informer, and Frere had overlapped with Wordsworth for three years at Cambridge, and with Coleridge for one. Despite their differences in political persuasion, the young men who produced the *Anti-Jacobin* and those who produced the *Philanthropist* and

Lyrical Ballads were not very different in class and education, or in their desires for a moral reform of the country, or in their literary brilliance and ambition. Wrangham, Montagu, and Wordsworth had family political backgrounds very much like those of Canning and Frere – rather more conservative than theirs, in fact. Wordsworth in particular had a strong line of connections from his family relations with the Lowthers and the Howards, through his uncles Cookson and Robinson, to Wilberforce and thence right up to Pitt. Pitt himself was an occasional contributor to the *Anti-Jacobin*'s inspired high-jinks, though he kept an eye on it, lest it be too closely connected with his government.

'The New Morality,' a poem widely ignored and underrated in literary history, is one of the last representatives of a grand tradition of English verse satire stretching back at least as far as Dryden. The largest target of this tradition had always been excessive zeal or 'enthusiasm' in religious and political matters, following the terrible events of the English Civil War. Now these excesses were seen to be rising horribly renewed in a French Revolution which some misguided young Englishmen seemed to want to bring back home. In this perspective, the *Anti-Jacobin*'s final appeal to some 'bashful Genius, in some rural cell' could have been to the young Wordsworth, putting in public, patriotic terms the appeal to his better, establishment self that William Cookson and John Robinson had put to him in personal, familial terms throughout the 1790s. If so, it was a last invitation to come in from the cold.

William and Dorothy spent another month at Shirehampton before starting their trip to Germany. At the beginning of August, Coleridge arrived back from a trip to London. William and Dorothy enthusiastically reported their wonderful walk up the Wye, and read him the poem that, he only now learned, formed the great climax of *Lyrical Ballads*. Enchanted, he immediately proposed that they repeat the trip for his benefit: 'a dart into Wales.' This followed the pattern of the past year, where one good walk was always the best excuse for another. As enthusiastic as ever, they set off the next morning at six o'clock, 3 or 4 August.

They took at least a week for this jaunt, making a circular route of it, up the Wye and back down via the Usk valley, ten miles to the southwest – or perhaps the other way around.[19] But on this trip their focus was specifically, not obliquely, political. The turning point of their route was at Llyswen, where the Wye and the Usk come closest together, and where John Thelwall had finally found a place where he thought he was safe from persecution. Thus the annus mirabilis of English Romanticism was framed by Coleridge and Wordsworth's visits with 'the famous Thelwall': prospective and hopeful at Alfoxden in 1797, retrospective and disappointed at Llyswen in 1798. Wordsworth had already set his 'Anecdote for Fathers' at 'sweet Liswyn farm.' The little boy in the poem, clearly young Basil

Montagu, expresses his preference for his former home at 'Kilve by the green sea' (directly below Alfoxden) because, when pressed repeatedly by his obtuse father for a reason, 'At Kilve there was no weather-cock.'

Wordsworth's use of the name of Thelwall's hideaway seems a bit cavalier, since he knew of Thelwall's continuing troubles. Or it may suggest that he empathized with these difficulties more than we have realized. The little boy's desperate nonreason, that there was no weathercock at Kilve, might have an adult subtext: i.e., here at Llyswen, we are too much reminded of which way the winds blow. Wordsworth had not, until this moment, ever been 'here at Liswyn farm,' and he may have revised his earlier composition accordingly. Clearly the adult speaker in the poem regrets intensely his time at or near Kilve, though he will not say why, beyond an almost compulsive repetition of the *Lyrical Ballads*' ubiquitous verb for hidden significances, 'think':

> My *thoughts* on former pleasures ran;
> I *thought* of Kilve's delightful shore,
> My pleasant home, when spring began,
> A long, long year before.
>
> A day it was when I could bear
> *To think, and think, and think again;*
> With so much happiness to spare,
> I could not feel a pain.
>
> (9–16; italics added)

These lines are rarely attended to, given readers' normal concentration on the poem's humorous situation. But it certainly had been 'a long, long year' for all of them.

They had a lot to talk about, recalling the excitement Thelwall's appearance at Alfoxden had provoked almost exactly a year earlier. But there were no more jokes about 'this being a fine place to talk treason in.' The visit of the Home Office agent, eight months of excoriating attacks by the *Anti-Jacobin*, the recent arrest of Joseph Johnson, the subpoena served to Daniel Stuart, Coleridge's editor at the *Morning Post*, and the mounting war fever made them all too aware of the 'the necessity [*not*] to talk treason,' or anything remotely resembling it.* Thelwall called his new

---

* These were only public signs of higher levels of government surveillance; behind the scenes, more dramatic changes were afoot. In January, William Wickham had returned from directing the 'underground war' against France to join Portland and John King at the Home Office. King and Richard Ford now began working together even more closely. Charles Fox paid the new arrangements a bitter compliment, calling them more effective than the secret police of the *ancien* and revolutionary French regimes combined. Wickham would have

home 'an enchanted dormitory,' but his experiences there had been nightmarish. The local parson had stirred up opinion against him as soon as he arrived – on one occasion he was attacked with a pick-axe. He finally issued a general warning to his neighbours that he would shoot any intruder on his grounds.[20] He now considered himself 'the new Recluse,' exiled from the busy scenes of his former triumphs.

Returning to Bristol, they collected their few belongings and left town around mid-August, travelling across country with Coleridge and Basil by foot, wagon, coach, and post-chaise to London.[21] They stayed there till mid-September, hoping to observe *Lyrical Ballads*' reception firsthand, since after 'Tintern Abbey' was handed over to Cottle Dorothy expected the book to appear in six weeks.[22] But instead they found themselves involved in last-minute efforts to make sure it would appear at all.

After all the protracted negotiations with Cottle to publish a book that would help defray their travel expenses, the deal suddenly appeared to be unravelling. Although a stock of books was printed up in Bristol by late August, Cottle seemed to be getting cold feet, for either financial or political reasons or both – reasons not easily separable in the publishing business in England in 1798. He learned that Southey intended to write a negative review of the volume. Though such a motive for selling the impression or its copyright 'seems almost too bad to believe,' it is hardly out of the realm of practical morality in the publishing business then or now.[23] Cottle contacted a large London publisher (Longman) about sharing in the publication in order to spread the risk.[24] Wordsworth initially helped in this effort, but when Longman showed no interest, Wordsworth approached Joseph Johnson on his own, without telling him that Cottle had already purchased the copyright for *Lyrical Ballads*.

Johnson, still the most prestigious liberal publisher in the country, apparently agreed, consistent with his loyalty to his authors, and despite the fact that he was soon to go to jail for six months for publishing Gilbert Wakefield's *Reply to Some Parts of . . . [Bishop Watson's] Address to the People of Great Britain*. This sentence, which Fox considered the final destruction of liberty of the press in England,[25] sent Wakefield into Dorchester jail for two years, from whence he emerged a dying man. (Wakefield's conviction is referred to in 'The New Morality,' both poem and cartoon.) Wordsworth and Coleridge interpreted the sentence very much as the *Monthly Magazine* would two years later on the occasion of Wakefield's death: a sign of the government's determination to pick 'a

---

thought this underestimated them: in his report to Portland in 1801 of what the revamped 'Alien Office' had accomplished, Wickham called it 'the most powerful means of observation and information . . . that ever was placed in the Hands of a Free Government.' See Ann Hone, *For the Cause of Truth: Radicalism in London, 1796–1821* (Oxford: Clarendon Press, 1982), 74–79.

victim of name and character sufficient to inspire a wide alarm.'[26] They were already enough 'inspired' by signs of alarm to have taken steps insuring that they would not be the government's next victims of name and character.

Wordsworth asked Cottle to send his already printed books to Johnson and apply to Richard Wordsworth for whatever money he felt he had coming for his work so far. Cottle however refused, either out of anger or embarrassment that Wordsworth should have so little confidence in his marketing skills. (Wordsworth was right: Cottle went bankrupt eighteen months later.) Instead, Cottle worked out a different proxy arrangement with the reputable Arch brothers in Gracechurch Street, and the famous volume finally hobbled into public view on 4 October, two weeks after its anonymous authors had left the country.

Controversy began as soon as the volume appeared, with the damning review that Southey had primed and ready from his inside knowledge of the authors and their poems – including his knowledge that they would be out of the country when it appeared. Southey excoriated 'the author' for wasting his talents on an ill-conceived language experiment. He blasted almost all the ballads, infamously dismissing 'The Ancient Mariner' as 'a Dutch attempt at German sublimity.'[27] His criticisms are all the more remarkable since Wordsworth's ballads of everyday life in the underclass were the poems most like the 'Botany Bay Eclogues' Southey himself had published in 1797, that drew him into the *Anti-Jacobin*'s main line of fire. But of course that was the very reason for Southey's venom: to get himself out of the 'Jacobin' camp by any means necessary.

Though Wordsworth and Coleridge did not learn about this review for several months, it only confirmed what they already knew, that in England in 1798 it was becoming impossible to tell friends from enemies. This was another reason they were going to Germany. In Wordsworth's case, it may be that he tried to solve the problem by deciding to be friends with his enemies.

CHAPTER TWENTY-FIVE

'Mr. Wordsworth'?

Hamburg, 1798

'To paid Mr. Wordsworth's Draft, £92/12/-'
(Duke of Portland's secret paybook, 13 June 1799)

With John Chester serving as their baggage handler and trip manager, Coleridge and the Wordsworths arrived at Yarmouth on 15 September. They stayed the night, giving Coleridge time to look up the disappointed Pantisocrat, George Burnett, now tutoring Southey's younger brother; they had a long recriminatory conversation. Burnett was politically disillusioned, a common feeling at the time, but he also felt personally betrayed in his former enthusiasm for Coleridge.[1] Wordsworth too was about to learn the costs of following this brilliant lodestar. But in Germany, Coleridge was the one who followed his course, Wordsworth the apparently directionless one, with decisive results for both.

There was also in Yarmouth at this time a Home Office agent named Walsh, son of the James Walsh who had visited Somerset the year before and fingered the 'gang of disaffected Englishmen.'[2] He was there as part of a new arrangement between the Home Office and the Alien Office, to make note of departing and arriving foreigners or other suspicious persons.[3] Given the continuing high level of Home Office surveillance of Thelwall, and Coleridge's notoriety wherever he went, this next stage of the Somerset gang's disaffection was duly noted.[4]

The party of four departed Yarmouth on 16 September and spent two days crossing the North Sea, sailing almost due east from Yarmouth to Cuxhaven at the mouth of the Elbe. They had good winds on a swelling sea. The Wordsworths retired immediately down into their cabin and were, according to Coleridge, 'shockingly' sick the whole time.

Coleridge had a great time crossing, his enjoyment not at all 'decreased by the Sight of the Basons [*sic*] from the Cabin containing green and yellow specimens of the inner Man brought up by the Cabin-boy every three minutes.'[5] His account of it reads like the standard nationalistic traveller's joke, featuring a Dane, a Swede, a Prussian, a Hanoverian, and a Frenchman, the humour based mainly on their poor command of English – by an Englishman who spoke no other modern tongue. The Dane, returning home from his St Croix plantation, latched on to Coleridge: ' "Vat imagination! vat language! vat fast science! vat eyes! – vat a milk vite forehead! – O my Heafen! You are a God!" ' Rich as he was, the Dane 'declaimed like a Member of the Corresponding Society about the Rights of Man; & how . . . he thought the poorest Man alive his Equal.' Coleridge accepted to be identified as 'Un Philosophe,' though he claimed it was a title for which he had 'the greatest disgust.' The Dane proceeded to attack Christianity like 'that rude blunderer, Mr Thomas Paine,' until Coleridge professed his belief in God, whereupon he sank '50 fathoms immediately' in the Dane's graces.

The Hanoverian and the Prussian (who looked suspicious and told obscene stories) were translated by another passenger, the '*English* Youth,' 'a genteel Youth who spoke perfect German perfectly.' By the end of the trip both the young Englishman and the dubious Prussian had got themselves adopted into the Dane's 'Train of Dependents.'

Coleridge hardly slept at all during the trip. On the second night, 'I partook of the Hanoverian's and Dane's wines, & Pine apples – told them some hundred Jokes, and passed as many of my own. Danced altogether a sort of wild dance on the Deck – Wordsworth and Sister as bad as ever.'[6] When everybody else passed out, he turned his roving eye toward nature: 'About 4 o'clock I saw a wild duck swimming on the waves – a single solitary wild duck – You cannot conceive how interesting a thing it looked in that round objectless desart of waters.'

The Frenchman was sick during the crossing, down in the cabins with the Wordsworths, and by the time they got into the calmer waters of the Elbe, 'Wordsworth had introduced himself to a kind of confidential acquaintance with the French Emigrant who appeared a man of sense and who was in his manners a most complete gentleman. He seemed about fifty. It was agreed that if possible we should live together.' This they did, until they left Hamburg for Goslar. The Frenchman, whose name was De Leutre, 'talked with rapture of Paris under the monarchy – & seemed not a little enamored of London, where he had lived in style.' De Leutre was being deported by order of the Duke of Portland because (he said) of the influence of some *émigrés* who were angry at him for refusing to lend them money.[7] 'He seemed very deeply *cut* at heart – a man without hopes or wishes,' though he 'attached no blame either to the Alien act, or to the minister who had exerted it against him,' which suggests a direct personal contact with Portland in the matter. He took it all so calmly that Coleridge asserted 'such a man, I think, I could dare warrant guiltless of *espionage* in any service, most of all in that of the present French directory.'[8] But this may have been exactly the point: not that De Leutre was a French agent, prerhaps a counterrevolutionary one, but that his genteel equanimity, and his interest in Wordsworth, arose from his being an English one, or both.

At Cuxhaven, they negotiated with the ship's captain to take them up the river to Hamburg by packet boat. As soon as they landed in Hamburg, Wordsworth and De Leutre set off in search of lodgings, leaving Chester to guard Dorothy and the luggage, while Coleridge hastened to deliver his letters of recommendation to the Wedgwoods' agents, the Von Axens. To their surprise, most hotels and inns were full, but they found rooms at last in Der Wilde Mann, which Coleridge thought must be named after its landlord. Dorothy was shocked to be shown to her room by 'a *man*,' but they kept their complaints to themselves, for they found the Germans ready to fight if criticized. When Wordsworth complained of the price of bread, the baker knocked the loaf out of his hands and refused to refund his money.[9] Oddly, Wordsworth did not at first stay at the inn with Dorothy but, leaving her in the care of Chester and De Leutre, went to 'The Duke of York' hotel, run by an ex-seaman. He went there to see John Baldwin, the brother of James Losh's wife Cecilia.[10] Why he should have had to stay in the same hotel with Baldwin is not clear, unless he, like Coleridge, was arranging other local contacts.

Hamburg was a neutral city and Germany the only country outside Scandinavia open to travellers, because of the threatening presence of French armies almost everywhere else in Europe.[11] The city was teeming with agents and spies from all European governments. It was the hub of French efforts to keep the German principalities out of the war – and of English determination to draw them into it. Intense political in-fighting had begun in October of 1797, when Napoleon forced Austria out of the war by a combination of military defeats and territorial concessions, ending the so-called First War of the Allied Coalition, ratified in the Treaty of Campo-Formio. This left England alone in the field against republican France. The treaty's terms for settling the peace of Europe were still being worked out in a diplomatic convention at Rastadt, near Baden-Baden in southwest Germany. This treaty, along with the *coup d'état* of 18 Fructidor (4 September 1797), had ended British hopes of influencing French politics by 'electoral' means – that is, by bribing the directors and spending huge sums of money to influence key provincial elections.

These were the set-backs that had determined young George Canning to bring British public opinion solidly behind the war effort. On top of his job as Grenville's undersecretary in the Foreign Office, Canning's zeal led him to start the *Anti-Jacobin* to combat ideological liberalism in the press. The political reverses of autumn 1797 also meant that continuing British clandestine efforts on the Continent came to depend increasingly on the advice and actions of desperate royalists. These efforts were directed by

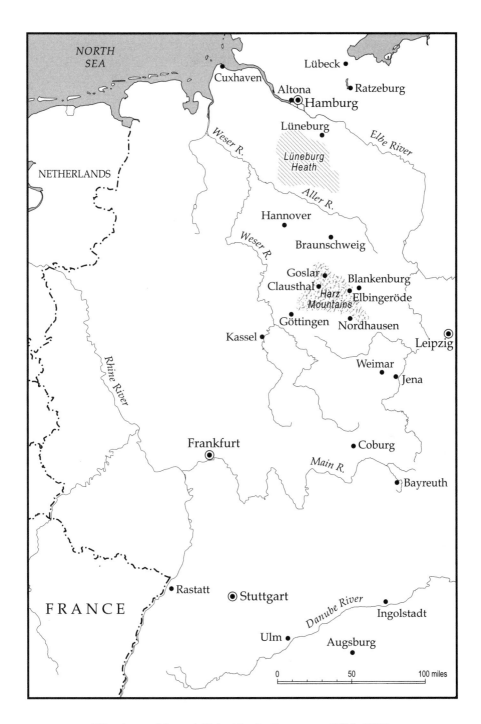

Wordsworth's and Coleridge's Germany, 1798–1799

James Talbot (a.k.a. James Tindal), whose so-called Swabian agency operated in southern Germany, co-operating with the royalist Comité de Bayreute, with the ultimate aim – as Grenville learned with alarm in January 1799 – of assassinating all five members of the new Directory.[12] In September of 1798 Talbot was authorized to spend up to £400,000 to raise and equip an army of Swiss *affidés* (recruits sworn to secrecy) that would be the tool to prise Austria out of the Campo-Formio treaty. Talbot's authorization came in a letter dated 11 September, carried from London by his secretary and confidential courier, his younger brother Robert. The younger Talbot must have taken a ship for Germany close to the time of Wordsworth's departure, making us think of that unidentified '*English Youth*' on the boat who spoke German so fluently.

To monitor these intensified activities in Hamburg, Grenville had set up a British chargé d'affaires in May of 1798, Sir James Craufurd (or Crawfurd), to report on all suspicious persons arriving from Britain.[13] In practice, 'suspicious persons' meant mainly Irishmen, especially after the defeat of the French expeditionary force under Humbert in August, and the demise of a short-lived 'Republic of Ireland.' Irishmen were flooding into Hamburg in September, including leaders like Napper Tandy; this was why the inns and hotels were so crowded. Craufurd was a zealous worker, who considered Hamburg a '*foyer de révolution.*'

There is no mention in Craufurd's dispatches of Wordsworth or Coleridge; their names probably appeared in supplementary lists, now lost, of 'English citizens,' whom Craufurd normally did not comment on. But on 25 September, in the week that Wordsworth and Coleridge were getting settled in Hamburg, Craufurd wrote to Grenville that he had taken an extraordinary risk in order to obtain the names of three agents of the Directory residing in London, of 'some standing in the commercial world.' He had arranged to be hidden in the apartments of the French chargé d'affaires where a council of confidential agents met by night to read over dispatches. Such a risk was unusual for the cautious Craufurd; if he'd been detected it would have caused a serious international incident. But he thought the prize was worth the price: he learned that the three agents were M. Grefulke, a Mr Bibbes, and one De Leutre, 'who we have since heard has been sent away under the Alien Bill.'[14] Hence, Coleridge's character-witness notwithstanding, he and Wordsworth were travelling with a suspected agent of the Directory, with whom Wordsworth soon struck up a 'kind of confidential aquaintance.'

On 28 September, at the end of Wordsworth's and Coleridge's first week in Hamburg, Craufurd wrote to assure William Wickham, Grenville's chief of foreign espionage, that 'you may rely on the most scrupulous caution respecting *the two individuals* mentioned to me in your letter' (Craufurd's emphasis).[15] A month later, after the poets had left town, Craufurd again referred to 'the person whose *name is not to be mentioned*' (his emphasis).[16] Could these two individuals have been Wordsworth and Coleridge? The shift from two to one unmentionable name is noteworthy: they evidently came to Craufurd's attention as a pair, but only one was actually involved in secret business. This circumstance fits well with everything we know about the two poets' behaviour, both at Alfoxden and aboard the ship from Yarmouth: Coleridge talked a lot but was harmless, Wordsworth was silent but 'dark,' and had entered into a 'confidential' relation with at least one suspect person, M. de Leutre. There are other details in Craufurd's subsequent correspondence that could point to Wordsworth: for example, the person in question is clearly operating somewhere in the country away from Hamburg, and has had a prior association with Richard Ford: 'our friend here, who is not to be named . . . has hitherto received [his monthly allowance] through Mr Ford, if I remember well.'[17]

On balance, it is safer to attribute Craufurd's reference to known British agents in Germany, such as James Talbot or James Powell, an infiltrator among the United Irishmen. But to say that the case is difficult to document is to understate the obvious: the whole point then was to make these activities difficult to document (even to other parts of the British government), to say nothing of two hundred years later. As Craufurd himself protested, 'you must be very sensible of the imperfectibility of attaining even a slight knowledge of one tenth of the people who go from hence to England in all kinds of vessels.'[18] Even when reports were made, key documents were routinely destroyed. In particularly sensitive cases, such as this one evidently was, names were not mentioned, and of course many names were false ones. Wickham himself, on whose meticulous record-keeping and collecting so much of our knowledge of this secret service depends, nevertheless destroyed some of his entry books and registers, with the tantalizing notation that they contained 'curious information respecting the ill-intentioned of our own countrymen.'[19] Since he did not destroy many which (like Craufurd's) do mention the names of known spies, we may hazard the guess that he destroyed others to protect the future reputations of persons who were either (a) not professional spies but occasional employees, or (b) not permanent enemies of the state but temporary enthusiasts of the French revolution. The latter category would include both Wordsworth and Coleridge; a faint but persistent trail of names, innuendos, and coincidences throughout the 1790s suggests that the former may include Wordsworth.

The point of these observations apparently becomes clearer the following June, when William Wickham made the following entry in the Duke of Portland's secret payment book for intelligence services rendered: 'To paid Mr. Wordsworth's Draft, £92/12/–.'[20] By itself, this information is not conclusive evidence of Wordsworth's acting on behalf of the new 'Secret Department.' But when we see the context in which the entry is made, its significance would seem to tilt rather sharply toward young Wordsworth:

4/6	Crawfurd	L60
11/6	Ford	L200
13/6	To paid Mr. Wordsworth's Draft,	L92/12/–
15/6	Crawfurd	L170
,, ,,	,,	L185

That is to say, that in Portland's office, where financial accountability had done as much as espionage skills to put the secret service on a modern footing, Wordsworth's name appears in a series of entries of payments made to the chief British agent in Hamburg, and to the Home Office official who James Walsh reported from Somerset in August of 1797 as likely to recognize '*Wordsworth* a name I think known to Mr. Ford.' In a well-run office like Portland's, disbursements to related accounts were made so far as possible at the same time, on vouchers or receipts related to similar items of business. Nor is this proximity of Wordsworth's name to Craufurd's a random accident: a pencilled note on the page opposite this column reads: 'Expended to 4 June 1799, [for?] payment of 3 Bills drawn by Wordsworth and Crawfurd.' The payments to Craufurd and Ford are round lump sums, either regular allotments or bonuses, but the payment made to Mr Wordsworth looks more like the settling of a specific claim or expense.

Why should payments to Craufurd, who was a Foreign Office agent, appear in the books of Portland, the Home Secretary? Ford, we know, was the main liaison between the two offices constituting the 'Secret Department.' The most likely answer again points toward Germany. Wickham, the leader of Britain's underground war against France, had been forced to withdraw from Switzerland in the wake of 18 Fructidor. He retired first to Frankfurt, where he stayed with Captain Charles Craufurd, one of Sir James's brothers.[21] By early 1798 he was back in London, where he was made under-secretary of the Home Office, the same position Canning held in the Foreign Office. Thus the Englishman who knew more than anyone else about the government's intrigues on the Continent became the chief executive officer of the agency charged with domestic surveillance, while his opposite number, Canning, who led a semi-official literary war against the government's domestic opponents (primarily journalists and poets), took over responsibility for correspondence with the remnants of Wickham's operation in Germany and Switzerland. Given the critical nature of England's political and military situation in 1798, when international and domestic affairs were inextricably tangled by combined fears of invasion and insurrection, these two men were in almost daily contact. Whether in all their conversations they ever put together the name '*Wordsworth* . . . known to Mr Ford' with those of 'C—dge and S—they, L—d and L—b, & Co.' known to Canning, we cannot be sure. But we do know they had a constant need for agents whose ability to report and carry messages confidentially could be guaranteed by patriotic loyalty, good pay or threat of exposure. Already a new significance emerges for Wordsworth's 'kind of confidential acquaintance' with M. de Leutre, deported by Portland.*[22]

M. de Leutre himself was well known to members of the French community in Hamburg.[23] He seems most likely to have been Joseph-Antoine Deleutre, from Avignon, who as papal delegate to the National Assembly in 1791–92 protested the atrocities of terrorists in his region. He (or his son) is described as a merchant, 'fort riche et, en politique, ardent légitimiste': hardly a profile calculated to make him persona non grata to the Duke of Portland.[24] He said he was 'an intimate Friend of the Abbé de Lille, the famous Poet' (1738–1813), whom Wordsworth admired very much. De Leutre took William and Dorothy to see a French painter's work on 25 September, where Dorothy noted that 'a very nice chearful looking fille de chambre seemed very glad to see Monsr. de Loutre.'[25] Dorothy was alert to nuances of relations between the sexes, but it is hard to tell if she is being sophisticated or naïve here, noting the effects of De Leutre's charm or his prior acquaintance in Hamburg – the latter possibility badly undercutting the truth of his explanation to Coleridge of his reasons for being there.

John Hurford Stone, Helen Williams's consort, was also in Hamburg when Wordsworth arrived. He had attended the November 1792 banquet at White's Hotel in Paris, and was known to Wordsworth. He was first noticed by Craufurd on 28 September, just before the Wordsworths left town.

Intrigue was so thick in Hamburg that you could cut it, or else too deep to cut through easily to any solid truth; but it certainly could not be avoided. Wordsworth and Coleridge were well known to powerful persons in both the Foreign and Home Offices, and their appearance in Hamburg

---

* For any hypothesis, there must be disconfirming possibilities. The 'Mr. Wordsworth' might be Wordsworth's cousin, Robinson Wordsworth, who had been installed in the Customs Office at Harwich, thanks to the influence of John Robinson. I have found only one reference to Robinson Wordsworth during this time frame: a pro forma instruction from William Wickham on 24 April 1799, that Robinson should release the Captain Cowen he had lately arrested (PRO HO 5/4/43). However, since the first edition of *The Hidden Wordsworth* was published, Michael Durey, citing unspecified documents in the Public Record Office, reports finding a voucher for 'Robn. Wordsworth' dated 16 March 1799, for exactly £92 12s, for expenses incurred in arresting two persons suspected of treason (*Times Literary Supplement*, 10 March 2000, 15).

would not have gone unremarked. Furthermore, they were highly noticeable. As Coleridge noted, 'to be an Englishman in Germany is to be an angel.' Everything, from sticking plasters to carriages, suburban landscaping, coffee houses and hotels were called 'English,' both from long-standing affection for England's Hanoverian kings and dukes, and for England's resistance to Napoleon.[26] Wordsworth and Coleridge were greeted especially warmly arriving when they did, just as the news of Nelson's victory in the Battle of the Nile reached Hamburg, along with that of Cornwallis's victory over Humbert and the Irish rebels at Ballynamuck on 15 September.

With M. De Leutre, Wordsworth and Coleridge attended a performance of Moller's *Count Waldron* (1776), translated for the French theatre. This was probably the play most responsible for Wordsworth's denunciation of 'sickly and stupid German Tragedies' in his 1800 preface to *Lyrical Ballads* as one of the contemporary abuses of language and culture that he aimed to reform. Wordsworth walked out before it was over, but Coleridge's synopsis suggests that *Count Waldron* was very stupid indeed: 'Bless me! why it is worse than our modern English plays!'[27]

They discussed the play, and the sad state of literature it reflected, with Friedrich Klopstock (1724–1803), the grand old man of German poetry. They had met him by chance, because his brother Victor was the business partner of the Wedgwoods' agent; Victor was almost as old as his aged brother, but Wordsworth and Coleridge delighted to call him 'YOUNG Klopstock,' playing on the currency of the adjective all over Europe at this time from the continuing popularity of Goethe's *The Sorrows of Young Werther* (1774).[28]

Although generally disappointed with the old man's opinions and ignorance of English culture, they respected him as 'the father of German poetry.' The subjective perspective and expressive language in Klopstock's *Odes*, written half a century earlier, marks the break with the Spinozistic rationalism of early eighteenth century German literature.[29] Thus Klopstock anticipated the revolution in German literature that Goethe, Schiller and others were at that very moment bringing to fruition, roughly as the odes of the Wartons, Collins, and Gray are said to anticipate the Romantic revolution in English poetry. But Klopstock was an innovator who had lived to see his new directions pursued further than he wished. Although 'he spoke favourably of Goethe,' he found Schiller's *The Robbers* 'so extravagant that he could not read it.' The two young Englishmen agreed with him, but could not have done so very frankly without embarrassment, since their own recent dramatic projects had been firmly based on Schiller's play.

Klopstock had also welcomed innovation in the political sphere, only to recoil from it in a way very familiar to the two younger poets. When he first greeted his visitors, on 26 September, he was in raptures over

Nelson's victory on the Nile. After having been an early supporter of the French Revolution, he was now 'a most vehement anti-Gallican,' Coleridge sympathetically noted.[30] He had originally, like Coleridge, written poems in praise of it, and been, like Joseph Priestley, honoured by the French Assembly and invited to take a seat in it. Coleridge generalized from Klopstock's case to all 'the literary Men' in Germany: 'many *were* [supporters]; but like me have *published* abjurations of the French.' 'When French Liberty metamorphosed herself into a Fury,' Klopstock wrote another ode 'expressing his Recantation.' Coleridge's comment recapitulates the argument and imagery of his own 'France: An Ode,' published in the *Morning Post* as 'The Recantation: An Ode' just before he left England.

The work of literature that Wordsworth and Klopstock talked about in greatest detail was Christoph Wieland's *Oberon* (1780), which had just been translated into English by the poetaster William Sotheby. Wordsworth observed that 'it was unworthy of a man of genius to make the interest of a long poem [12 cantos in 2 volumes] turn entirely upon animal gratification.' He fairly lectured poor old Klopstock on Wieland's sensuality, brushing aside his objection that different poets could choose different subjects, or that such kinds of poems were popular. 'I answered that it was the province of a great poet to raise people up to his own level, not to descend to theirs.' Klopstock, collapsing, agreed, 'and confessed that on no account would he have written a work like the Oberon.'

Oberon does advance through a series of 'Oriental' adventures by means of visual set-pieces describing the naked charms of women, but Wordsworth's stern disapproval may not have been wholly literary. It could also be an embarrassed over-correction of his own former behaviour, since the actions of Wieland's hero, Huon, toward a foreign beauty, the Arab maiden Rezia, parallels his own toward Annette. The lovers' giving in to their natural desires is very close to the reason – that is, the rationalization – that Wordsworth would give to Vaudracour and Julia in *The Prelude*, indirectly explaining his own motives. Indeed, when Vaudracour celebrates Julia's beauties by hyperbole – 'Arabian fiction never filled the world / With half the wonders that were wrought for him' – we can imagine that *Oberon* is precisely the 'Arabian' fiction he has in mind. This love scene occurs in the seventh book. Wordsworth answered Klopstock's inquiry, 'if I was not delighted with the poem,' by saying 'that I thought the story began to flag about the 7th or eighth book.'[31] Quite right: the poem is set up to titillate us with the chances and near-misses of its beautiful protagonists, and once they've experienced what Wordsworth censoriously called their 'animal gratification,' its main point is over.

Wordsworth and Coleridge also briefly discussed with Klopstock the poetry and fame of Gottfried Bürger (1747–1794), whose ballads had enjoyed a huge vogue in England at mid-decade. Wordsworth bought a

German copy of Bürger's works to take with him to Goslar, but his low rate of progress in learning the language makes it doubtful he read very much. Most of Bürger's undeniable influence on Wordsworth had already manifested itself in the 1798 *Lyrical Ballads*, especially 'The Thorn,' from translations of German ballads. But the original title of 'Poor Susan' ('The Reverie of Poor Susan') is a direct translation from Bürger's title, and 'Hart-Leap Well' (1800) is based on an tale from Bürger's poems. Given his moralistic strictures on Wieland, one wonders how much Wordsworth knew of Bürger's pathetic sexual pursuits; Coleridge certainly did, in no uncertain terms: Bürger's third wife 'is now a Demirep & Actress at Hamburgh – A *Bitch*!'[32]

More relevant to Wordsworth's creative life situation was Schiller's extraordinarily damning review of Bürger's poems published in 1791, 'which effectively silenced Bürger as a creative poet.'[33] Schiller's review reads (from Wordsworth's perspective) like a draft toward the 1800 preface. It began by lamenting the decline of lyric poetry 'in the current philosophizing age,' and set forth the 'awesome responsibility' of poetry under these conditions: 'that it should assimilate all the manners, the characters, the entire wisdom of its time,' creating, 'out of the century itself, a model for the century. Such a task . . . called for mature and cultured hands.' Bürger, far from being a *Volksdichter* (folk poet), as he claimed in his preface of 1789, only proved 'that the true *Volksdichter* could no longer exist.' What was wanted was refined simplicity: initiating readers ' "into the mysteries of the beautiful, the noble and the true, it should draw the *Volk* up to it, but Bürger descends to the level of the *Volk*, where he mingles, rather than edifies and elevates his art." '[34]

Between talks with elderly dignitaries and walks out to the suburbs, the party was busy seeking out proper transportation for their planned removal to somewhere cheaper in the country. 'Young' Klopstock suggested Ratzeburg as a likely place: a fashionable aristocratic resort town on a lake near Lübeck, some thirty miles northeast. Coleridge was chosen to reconnoitre with Chester. He departed 22 September and returned, ecstatic, on the 27th. The place was perfect for him, but quite the contrary for the Wordsworths. It was clean and delightful, full of educated though not highly intellectual wealthy people – and very expensive, even for the kind of boarding arrangement they sought, that Coleridge had found in the home of a Lutheran pastor.

As they talked it over the night that Coleridge returned, the difference in their motives for coming to Germany became clearer, as well as the wide difference in their means of realizing them. They had not really thought through what they were going to do when they arrived, and they were quite unprepared for the expense. Wordsworth's main motive in coming to Germany with Coleridge was just that: to go wherever Coleridge went.

Dorothy's goal was to be with William, preferably in Coleridge's company, but with William at all costs.

Coleridge had more serious reasons for being there. Not only was he fulfilling his desire to study German literature and philosophy at the source, he also carried the hopes – and the money – of several influential people who had invested in his ability to turn himself into an expert on German culture: the Wedgwood family primarily, but also Daniel Stuart of the *Morning Post*, and Tom Poole.[35] It was clear that Coleridge would never learn the language to the extent required if he stayed with the Wordsworths. He needed to learn to speak with intelligent persons on abstruse subjects, whereas the Wordsworths were content to learn literary German in the same way they worked on their Italian over the years, reading and translating to each other in front of the fire at night.[36] Both aimed at university study of some sort, but that required learning the language first, and clearly they could not do that on the Wordsworths' budget in Hamburg; still less so, in Ratzeburg. It was another perfect double bind for Wordsworth: he wanted to be with Coleridge but he couldn't be, because it would spoil Coleridge's own wishes.

With these differences in motive painfully underlined by their difference in incomes, they decided to split up. Coleridge and Chester departed for Ratzeburg on 30 September, ten days after their arrival at Hamburg. William and Dorothy began making plans to go to the south, somewhere near Göttingen. The University of Göttingen was very popular with Englishmen, having been founded sixty years before by the Hanoverian George II.[37] Their decision to head for Goslar, 130 miles south of Hamburg, is not so mysterious as it sometimes seems, though the decision to go to such a remote spot ultimately had important consequences for Wordsworth. Old Klopstock was a native of the Harz region, and probably recommended it as the sort of wooded, mountainous country they liked.[38] It was only about fifty miles from Göttingen, and its location fits very well the prospectus Wordsworth had offered Losh in the spring: 'Our plan is to settle if possible in a village near a university, in a pleasant, and, if we can a mountainous, country.'[39]

They settled up their accounts at Der Wilde Mann and also with M. De Leutre, whom they had visited every day after Coleridge's departure. He had stayed at the inn with them until he learned of Coleridge's plans, then he put into effect his own plan to rent an 'English' house in the suburbs along the river. Wordsworth drew £32 7s. 3d. from the Von Axens, and inquired the way into Lower Saxony from Klopstock. William seems to have had a premonition that things might not work out for the best. Among the last letters they posted before leaving Hamburg, he asked Tom Poole to keep an eye on Alfoxden for him, in case 'any series of accidents should bring it again into the market we should be glad to have it, if we could manage it.'[40]

Lamb and Southey and Lloyd shared a few sneers when they heard that 'the two noble Englishmen have parted no sooner than they set foot on German earth.'[41] The whole scheme had seemed hare-brained, especially to envious eyes, and it was not unpleasant to old friends in various states of disaffection and alienation to learn that all was not going well.

The *separation* of Wordsworth and Coleridge in Germany was as crucial to their development as poets as their 'amalgamation' at Alfoxden and Stowey had been. It is common to regard the German adventure as a failure for Wordsworth and a success for Coleridge. But this is only true insofar as what they did matches what they had projected to do. Wordsworth, who had planned to stay one or two years, returned home in less than eight months; Coleridge, who had planned to stay only three months, stayed for nine. In fact the separation made the trip successful for both of them, but in ways that Wordsworth especially could not have foreseen. For yet another time in his young life, the disappointment of a projected goal created a shock of surprise that led to a huge re-evaluation of what he was about and resulted in important new creative work. Like his 'failures' on Simplon or Snowdon, his frustration in Germany provoked creative work that he did not realize he had in him. Thus the German trip became for him, like the 1798 *Lyrical Ballads* which were supposed to pay for it (but dismally failed to), another triumph snatched from failure.

For this process to have the result it did, Wordsworth's being without Coleridge was as essential as being with Dorothy. We can learn a great deal about Coleridge's German experiences from his letters and notebooks, but much less about his inner life. He gives more details about Goslar after passing through it for a few hours the next spring than Dorothy or William recorded – or preserved – of their five months there. But, in terms of this same creative economy, Coleridge wrote very little poetry in Germany other than metrical or translation experiments, and occasional or memorial verses written for specific persons or places. 'My poor Muse is quite gone,' he admitted. For all the entrepreneurial and intellectual success of Coleridge's stay, his poetical output is much overbalanced by Wordsworth's statement, 'I have been obliged to write in self-defence.'

CHAPTER TWENTY-SIX

Writing in Self-Defence

Goslar, 1798–1799

As I have had no books I have been obliged to write in self-defence. I should have written five times as much as I have done but that I am prevented by an uneasiness at my stomach and side, with a dull pain about my heart. I have used the word pain, but uneasiness and heat are words which more accurately express my feeling. At all events it renders writing unpleasant. Reading is now become a kind of luxury to me. When I do not read I am absolutely consumed by thinking and feeling and bodily exertions of voice or of limbs, the consequence of those feelings.

(Wordsworth to Coleridge, Goslar, December 1798)

William and Dorothy climbed up into the diligence at five o'clock in the afternoon of 3 October, and arrived in Goslar three days later. It was a wretched trip. Dorothy was as sick from the pitching of the coach as she had been crossing the North Sea. On the first stage, they travelled all night, plunging along corrugated roads to arrive in Lüneburg in time for breakfast. Hamburg had been bad, but this was worse: 'all seemed lifeless and dead.' Continuing on across the great Lüneburger Heath, Dorothy noted desperately, 'the country becomes occasionally rather more interesting for its strangeness.'[1] They sought out 'English' inns at every stop, hoping for a higher standard of comfort, for they were now in the realm of England's king, but 'in the Hannoverian dominions . . . the inns were more strange and more miserable.' At Brunswick, the last stop before Goslar, the fare at 'The English Arms' was thankfully somewhat better: 'potatoes after the English fashion . . . beds excellent with blankets etc. as in England.'[2]

They arrived exhausted and thoroughly disoriented, as if they had come to the ends of the earth. Dorothy's last entry in her German journal is, 'It was on Saturday the 6th of October when we arrived in Goslar at between 5 and 6 in the evening.'[3] Except for five letters and fragments of four others, we have no more direct indications of what they did during the rest of their stay in Germany until the last week of April. But we do have a very large amount of poetry written by Wordsworth at Goslar, which shows quite clearly what he did there: he thought and wrote about himself, in self-defence, especially his formative boyhood experiences. Wordsworth, poet of Englishness par excellence, was conceived in France and born in Germany. The beauties and excitements of France (and Switzerland) stimulated his sensual imagination in its young adulthood, but the loneliness and depression of Germany brought him to 'manhood now mature,' as he would redundantly say of himself, safe home at Grasmere, a year later.

The Wordsworths found rooms in the centre of town, in the substantial house of Frau Deppermann, widow of a former town senator and linen-draper, at no. 107 Breitestrasse.[4] William was duly listed in the town's roll of lodgers as 'William Waetsford, ein Englander.'[5] Wordsworth called Goslar 'an old decaying city'; Coleridge called it 'this ugly silent old desert of a city.' From what they say of it, it sounds like the setting for a Kafka story or an especially bleak Bergman film.

Their house was very cold; that winter was the coldest recorded in the century. They had to put on overcoats to go from one room to another, and they wrapped themselves up in furs when they went out walking, which they indefatigably did, 'at least an hour every day, often much more.'[6] William, wrapped up in a dark fur gown and wearing a sort of helmet lined with black dog's fur, looked, Dorothy thought, 'like any grand Signior.'[7] He had to protect himself because his own room was above an uninsulated passageway; the phlegmatic natives calmly assured him he could expect to freeze to death some night. The one contemporary portrait he gives of himself is a projection of his own feelings onto a fly he observed crawling on their heating stove: 'a disconsolate creature . . . a child of the field or the grove . . . Alas! how he fumbles about the domains . . . He cannot find out in what track he must crawl . . . there he stands like a traveller bemaz'd.'[8]

This unhappy Wordsworthian fly contrasts with the lightsome Coleridgean one described in a letter to Sara, for both were creatures of the poets' housing arrangements: 'no Fly unimprisoned from a boy's hand, could more buoyantly enjoy its element, than I this clear & peaceful [Lutheran pastor's] house, situated in this wholesome Air!'[9] The Wordsworths had hoped to find what Coleridge had found, a family or *pensione* arrangement such as William had had in Orléans, where they could begin learning German by participating in the life of the household. But what they got instead was a boarding house where they met the other residents only at meals. Besides their taciturn landlady, a young apprentice of the house who came and sat with them in the evenings, and a friendly deaf man they met in town, 'we have no other society except that of a French Emigrant Priest.'[10] What was *he* doing in godforsaken Goslar?

With their slow progress in German, it was quite a while before they could talk to anybody but this priest. Given the hints already dropped about the possibility of some sort of clandestine activity by Wordsworth, this nameless priest should not go unremarked, though we cannot identify him. *Émigré* priests were some of the leading operatives and couriers for the British Swabian agency, particularly 'the abbé Jean François André, alias de La Marre . . . *voyageur* par excellence, flitting about Europe and turning up in London, Paris, Mittau or Augsburg as required.'[11] The priest Wordsworth knew was not André, but every agent and courier had his contacts and his safe houses. The mention of Mittau, in what is now Latvia, is pertinent, since that is where Louis XVIII went, as guest of the half-mad Paul I of Russia, following the two worst years of his long exile – which were spent in Blankenburg, a 'nasty little town' of Brunswick, about twenty-five miles southeast of Goslar.[12] He had left in February of 1798, but his residence there was well known. Louis XVIII – 'Monsieur,' Duc de Provence, the late Louis XVI's brother – was the focus of all plots for and against a Restoration: an event that between 1795 and the end of 1799 seemed to be always just around the corner.[13] Some of his retainers lingered on, and it was safer for them to stay in a neighbouring town like Goslar, for Louis and his entourage were quite unpopular: he never rode out, for fear of assassins. It may be impossible to account for the presence of 'a French Emigrant Priest' in Goslar in the winter of 1798–99, but Louis XVIII's recent proximity and Wordsworth's arrival is one way of doing so. Had his 'confidential' friend M. de Leutre suggested Goslar as a good place to learn the language, and for other reasons as well?

As for making acquaintances among the gentility of the town – the method Coleridge employed to great advantage among the petty nobility at Ratzeburg – that turned out to be impossible for two reasons, or rather, two versions of the same reason: Dorothy. As a man and a woman constituting a kind of household they were expected to receive visits as well as pay them, which they could not afford to do. And many people, beginning with Frau Deppermann, did not believe that Dorothy was really William's sister: 'sister' being here 'considered as only a name for Mistress,' as Coleridge told Sara. 'It is next to impossible for any but married women . . . to be introduced to any company in Germany.'[14] To Wordsworth's complaints about their situation Coleridge gave two reasons, but no solutions: 'your not loving to smoke; and your sister.'[15] Dorothy's free and easy behaviour, her walks and wild eyes, did little to dispel these suspicions.

The question arises, To what extent these perceptions were entirely mistaken? Love between brothers and sisters was already a romantic fashion in Germany, not merely a personal fact, as it was for the Lambs and the Wordsworths. Schiller's works ran compulsively on the theme, and Goethe said his deep feelings for Frau Charlotte von Stein arose in part because she reminded him of his sister Caroline.[16] Indeed, as a cultural fashion, the Germans thought that in this one, as in so many others, they were following the lead of the English. Goethe had voiced this common German conception of Englishmen abroad in his journal of his Italian tour (1786): 'Heute gesellten sich, reitend, ein Herr und eine Dame zu uns, ein Engländer mit einer sogenannten Schwester [with his so-called sister].'[17] In an era when arranged marriages were still the norm, especially among the rising middle classes trying to consolidate their capital gains, the idea of a *romantic* marriage was a threat to established order. Passions doomed to find no satisfactory outlet in marriage often turned to those other beloved men or women, with whom marriage was out of the question, but with whom intimate personal knowledge and sympathy were facts of experience from immemorial infancy.

William and Dorothy had no household routine to attend to, a trying circumstance for her, who had been in charge of her brother's domestic life for three full years.[18] They were thus thrown more on each other's company, further frustrating their chances of learning German. They talked to each other about what their life had been like and what it had come to: 'Was it for *this*?' All their measures of Germany had been computed in terms of England, and now they began to measures themselves in those terms. Hadn't they been happy once? Their only shared passion was for each other, and for Coleridge, whose letters they awaited with something like lust. 'Let me speak,' Dorothy says at one point, 'of the joy we felt at seeing your handwriting again; I burst open the seals and could almost have kissed them in the presence of the post-master.'[19] To the degree that they could – or could not – love each other directly, they did so through their shared passion for Coleridge. Coleridge reciprocated their passion in an experiment in English hexameters, stimulated by Goethe's recently published *Hermann und Dorothea*: 'William, my teacher, my friend! dear William and dear Dorothea!' The poem is filled with the passion of absence: 'many a wearisome mile are ye distant.' Its last lines said all he could, or need, say:

> William, my head and my heart! dear William and dear Dorothea!
> You have all in each other; but I am lonely, and want you![20]

But Coleridge was busy with many other people, and not nearly as pre-occupied in thinking about the Wordsworths as they were about him. Wordsworth said plaintively, 'I need not say how much the sentiment [your hexameters] affected me.'[21]

While I do not believe there was a physically incestuous relation between William and Dorothy Wordsworth, it is equally hard to believe that the possibility did not often cross their minds, whether as a temptation or a threat. The 'Lucy' poems give access to more psychological details here, but we must get to them *via* Wordsworth's other 'self-defence' poems, for it is in his sense of himself that he most clearly expresses his feelings for Dorothy and his determination to control them – against her advances.

In the absence of any English books to read, Wordsworth began to 'write in self-defence,' but the cure was almost as bad as the ailment: 'an uneasiness at my stomach and side, with a dull pain about the heart. I have used the word pain, but uneasiness and heat are words which more accurately express my feeling.' We can call these pains psychosomatic, but they were nonetheless real. As the soma of his psyche, they sound like birth or labour pains. That was certainly their result. He was compensating for apparently minor losses (lack of books and company) with mighty gains: a series of apparently disparate poems that, taken together, show the Wordsworthian self-creation machine shifting into high gear. The idea of gain snatched from loss, triumph from failure, applies to Wordsworth's entire German sojourn, but most of all to the 'mass' of poems (as Dorothy described them) he wrote in five winter months at Goslar: an output nearly as great in quantity as his five months at Alfoxden at the beginning of the year. The Goslar poems are much more serious than most of the lyrical ballads of early 1798, and their seriousness results from a massive turn inward, toward what we would call 'psychological' perspectives, and away from sociopolitical ones.

The idea that writing poetry could be more significant moral action than philosophy connected in his mind to his conversations with Coleridge about Bürger. Wordsworth gave Bürger credit for being 'always the poet . . . never the mobbist, one of those dim drivellers with which our island has teemed for so many years.'[22] As he tried to separate his project from that of Godwin and the philosophical radicals, his comment on Bürger further delimits it, distinguishing him from the wrong *kind* of poets, who produced the sentimental 'drivel' with which well-intentioned liberal writers ('mobbists') like Southey flooded the magazines. Wordsworth also criticized Bürger because 'I see everywhere the character of Bürger himself . . . I wish him sometimes at least to make me forget himself in his creations.' This shows how deeply Wordsworth himself was caught up in the contradictions between subjectivity and objectivity which necessarily afflict – and energize – all attempts to speak authoritatively from one's own experience for other people. We rarely forget Wordsworth in any of his creations; in the *Prelude* lines he now began composing, he found himself as a man by remembering himself as a child.

As he confronted the necessity of writing without Coleridge, Wordsworth wrote three different kinds of poems, whose similarities in tone, theme and purpose are far more revealing than their superficial differences in subject matter. They are (1) his first drafts of 'the poem on the growth of my own mind,' or 'the poem to Coleridge' (*The Prelude*); (2) the Matthew poems, on a village schoolmaster-figure, essentially William Taylor, but incorporating features of other older men who befriended the boy Wordsworth; (3) the Lucy poems, on the death of a young woman or girl who is the speaker's love or inspiration: Dorothy, in psychological terms, though not literally.

All these poems are concerned with the origins of Wordsworth's imaginative growth – and, almost as much, a fear of losing contact with those sources. They are celebrations, but we miss their point if we lose sight of the fact that, for the most part, they launch themselves into expression out of a fear of losing the very quality or person celebrated. They are celebrations under threat, *determinedly* joyful overcomings of strong feelings of depression and dejection: essentially Wordsworth's mood in Goslar. In all of them Wordsworth emerges as the poet of natural fullness and human relationship not 'naturally,' but because he feels so strongly that such possibilities may not be natural at all. It is precisely here that the orthodox interpretation of Wordsworth as the sage of 'wise passiveness' in nature goes astray, not as an account of the evident meaning of most of the subsequent poems in his *oeuvre*, but as an account of the process of self-creation that led him to make those affirmations.[23] They frequently hold up his Lake District childhood as a 'blessed retreat,' but he enters into it under something like a curse, the self-accusing 'Was it for this?'

In mid-December, he and Dorothy finally wrote a long letter to Coleridge. For this, their first report of work in progress, Dorothy excerpted three passages from the 'mass' of early childhood vignettes Wordsworth had written. At bottom, these short passages were a therapy constructed out of desperation, Wordsworth pulling himself up by the bootstraps of memory. His life seemed to have come to its worst dead-end so far, and he started taking stock of himself to see where or how it had all gone wrong. The three passages sent to Coleridge became the skating scene and the rowboat scene from *Prelude* I, plus a version of what became 'Nutting.'

All three passages have the same pattern of gain recovered from loss, matching the entire structure of Wordsworth's biographical experience in Germany. In each of them, it is not the part of the poem describing nature that makes them uniquely Wordsworthian, but the parts he *cannot* describe, because it is not simply 'nature.' Each time, he starts off 'going with nature,' but then that movement breaks, and something far greater than natural forms invades his consciousness. This 'something' is what Coleridge meant when he said, of the conclusion of the Boy of Winander passage, 'Had I met these lines running wild in the deserts of Arabia, I should instantly have screamed out, "Wordsworth!"' Only Wordsworth could have written them because they suggest that behind these ordinary Lake District scenes there was a landscape of imagination as threateningly alien as if it were another planet.

The same pattern, infinite gain from finite loss, is repeated throughout the notebook from which Dorothy copied these excerpts, which forms the foundation of the first book of *The Prelude*.²⁴ William began it with a page of short, desultory 'inspiration' passages where he tried to invoke Nature directly as his Muse: 'a mild creative breeze / a vital breeze that passes gently on.' But each effort to frame Nature as 'a mild creative breeze' is quickly frustrated, and produces instead 'a redundant energy / Creating not but as it may / disturbing things created'; or 'vexing its own creation,' as he put it in the final version.²⁵ Then he broke off this normal poetic start-up procedure and asked himself instead the famous self-accusing question, 'Was it for this?' that launched him into his life-work. The fragmentary invocations have no pronouns at all, but one turns over the journal leaf and suddenly they flood out across the page: 'I . . . I . . . I . . . my . . . my . . . my.'

This paradoxical sense of creative power as destructive is at the heart of Wordsworth's first description of his early experience of his own imagination. It was hard to get started, and when it did, it destroyed its own productions. This was the power he had hoped to harness by linking it to Coleridge's philosophical range and depth. On his own again, without Coleridge's philosophical ballast, he was frustrated again. He *felt* everything that had gone to make him a creative force, but he could not produce a poem because he had no story line to hang it on, no theme, no philosophy, not even a collection of anecdotes in which to invest it, as he had done with Erasmus Darwin's case histories and local Somerset lore in the spring. He was trying to attach conceptions of intellect and spirit to natural forms, but he had no vehicle for doing so. Or rather, he discovered he had nothing but himself, and frustrated, he asked himself in exasperation, 'was it for this / That one, the fairest of all rivers, loved / To blend his murmurs with my nurse's song . . .?' An initial question as to the possible uselessness of his whole life up to this point is set down on paper, and repeated three times in the immediately following lines. It is then answered by a similarly repeated insistence that it *was not* in vain: 'Ah, not in vain . . . Ah, not in vain . . . I may not think / A vulgar hope was yours.'²⁶ The huge force and length of his affirmative answer (eventually, the 8000 lines of *The Prelude*) is proportionate to the depth of the negative doubt that provoked it. Wordsworth clung to the earth, to Nature, because he feared indeed that there *was* nothing but himself and the rest of the universe: such intense self-consciousness demands the earth itself as its ground – '*even as if* the earth had rolled / With visible motion her diurnal round.'

But the question, 'Was it for this?' is also an old literary convention, a variation on the *ubi sunt* motif, with many antecedents from Virgil to Pope, most recently from Godwin's *Caleb Williams*, where Caleb asks himself whether his heroic efforts to achieve simple justice (i.e., to justify his whole life) have been worth it.* It is also an inevitable human question, arising about the direction of one's life, or, more often, about that of one's offspring (Was it for this that I worked so hard to raise you?). But whatever its rhetorical provenance, 'in the loneliness and self-questioning of Goslar, the question was as urgent as death itself.'[27] Many readers of literature think that writers always know where they are going; readers of Wordsworth, hooked on his 'naturalness,' have developed this habit into an addiction.

His insistent repetition that it was 'Ah, not in vain' recalls the self-interrupting structure of the poem he had most recently completed, 'Lines Composed above Tintern Abbey,' with their similar-sounding topic sentences: 'If this be but a vain belief.' The beginnings of *The Prelude* pick up right where 'Tintern Abbey' left off, with the same rhetorical form, of temporary doubts silenced by ultimate affirmations. The main difference is that his retrospective time frame has been extended from 'five years, and the length of five long winters' to as far back as he can remember: 'from the dawn almost of life.'[28]

This is perfectly clear when we hear the echo of Wordsworth's July lines on the Wye ('If this be but a vain belief, yet, oh! how oft – . . . in spirit, have I turned to thee, / O sylvan Wye!') in his December lines on the Derwent:

> was it for this
> That one, the fairest of all rivers, loved
> To blend his murmurs with my nurse's song
> And from his alder shades and rocky falls
> And from his fords and shallows sent a voice
> To intertwine my dreams, for this didst thou
> O Derwent—travelling over the green plains
> Near my sweet birth-place didst thou beauteous
> Give ceaseless music to the night & day
> Which with its steady cadence tempering
> Our human waywardness composed my thought
> To more than infant softness giving me
> Amid the fretful tenements of man
> A knowledge, a dim earnest of the calm
> That Nature breathes among her woodland haunts . . .[29]

Their conclusions are also similar: 'Nor perchance, / If I were not thus taught, should I the more / Suffer my genial spirits to decay: / For thou

---

* 'Was it for this that I had broken through so many locks, and bolts, and the adamantine walls of my prison; that I had passed so many anxious days, and sleepless, spectre-haunted nights; that I had racked my invention . . .; that my existence had been enthralled . . .?' (*Caleb Williams*, Vol. III, Chap. XII).

art with me ' ('TA,' 111–14); 'Yet, should it be / That this is but an impotent desire . . . / . . . need I dread from thee / Harsh judgements' (*1799*, i.450–60). Only the addressee has been changed, from Dorothy in July to Coleridge in December. Another echo shows why: 'Nor while, though doubting yet not lost, I tread the mazes of this argument . . . may I well / Forget what might demand a loftier song' (*1799*, i.118–23). For Dorothy, it was enough that she remember him: 'Nor wilt thou then forget . . . with what healing thoughts / Of tender joy wilt thou remember me, / And these my exhortations!' Coleridge wanted him to be the Recluse, for the world; Dorothy wanted him only to be William, and hers.

But even as he began the 'poem to Coleridge,' Wordsworth was simultaneously drafting a new 'poem to Dorothy' in the form of the Lucy poems. The Matthew poems are intermediary between these other two groups: poems to fatherly teachers, rather than poems to brotherly or sisterly teachers. The Matthew poems show Wordsworth's mind running on the death of another source of childhood inspiration: not his reckless adventures outdoors in the natural world, but the nurture he received from culture, in the form of the schoolteachers who befriended him at Hawkshead.

The Lucy poems bring sharply into focus the fact that almost all the poems Wordsworth wrote in Goslar are about persons who are dead, or whose main action in their poems is to die. (The *Prelude* fragments insist that that little boy is not dead, or did not live 'in vain.') But they are also about a person – the speaker – who is strangely obtuse about or surprised by death, living in a kind of trance: 'a slumber did my spirit seal,' 'in one of those sweet dreams I slept.' They are not simply about the death of a small girl or beloved young woman; they are about the death of a female figure who is/was the poet's inspiration, especially in her immediate connection to nature. If 'the poem to Coleridge' is about 'the growth of my own mind,' these poems to Dorothy are about the loss of her inspiration. Lucy is Wordsworth's Muse, and the group as a whole is a series of invocations to a Muse feared to be dead. Just as the first *Prelude* jottings invoked a 'mild creative breeze' that became instead 'a redundant energy vexing its own creation,' so the Lucy poems are powerfully inspired poems on the theme of *loss* of inspiration. Their operative question is not 'Was it for this?' but 'What if?' As epitaphs, they are not sad, a very inadequate word to describe them, but breathlessly, almost wordlessly aware of what such a loss would mean to the speaker: 'oh, the difference to me!'

These 'poems to Dorothy' have a much greater range than their point of origin in Wordsworth's love for Dorothy, but there can be little doubt that Dorothy is the biographical form of the spiritual Lucy. Every Lucy in Wordsworth's poetry is not to be equated with Dorothy, but there are several poems, like 'The Glow-Worm,' in which we know that 'Lucy' does refer directly to her. When she copied out 'Strange fits of passion' for

Coleridge she added a note, with an interesting slip of the pen: 'The next poem is a favourite of mine – i.e. of me Dorothy – ' That is, it is both mine, and *of* me. The last stanza of the version sent to Coleridge, cancelled before publication, indicates that Wordsworth was indulging an adult fantasy in imagining the death of his beloved:

> I told her this, her laughter light
> Is ringing in my ears;
> And when I think upon that night
> My eyes are dim with tears.

Which night does he have in mind? The night he rode to Lucy's cottage and watched the moon 'drop' behind it as he advanced up the hill, or the night he told her his fantasy? The latter possibility is transferred to the beginning of the poem in the new stanza Wordsworth wrote for publication –

> Strange fits of passion I have known:
> And I will dare to tell,
> But in the Lover's ear alone,
> What once to me befell.

But when he dropped the last stanza, its comfortably 'adult' conclusion is lost sight of, and we are no longer sure of the distance between the emotion felt and the tranquillity expressed.

Coleridge, copying out 'A slumber did my spirit seal' for Poole, as part of his own complicated response to the news that his baby son Berkeley had suddenly died, made a positive identification of Lucy in the poem, but with only an oblique awareness of its significance. 'Some months ago Wordsworth transmitted to me a most sublime Epitaph / whether it had any reality, I cannot say. —Most probably, in some gloomier moment he had fancied the moment in which his Sister might die.'[30] Does 'I cannot say' signify doubt or a prohibition? Years later, speaking to Crabb Robinson about Dorothy, Coleridge envied Wordsworth's having such a sister and lamented his own lost one: 'he also spoke of incest.'[31] Thomas De Quincey noted that Wordsworth 'always preserved a mysterious silence on the subject of that "Lucy" repeatedly alluded to or apostrophised in his poems.'[32]

But trying to prove that Dorothy is literally Lucy or that the Lucy poems refer directly to Dorothy is pointless, or beside the point. Most of them work like conundrums, to make us ask, Who is Lucy, what is she, that this swain so adores her? The powerful feelings which Wordsworth sublimates in these poems are not simply sexual, but sexual and fraternal feelings expressing, as in the *Prelude* and Matthew poems, a fear of failing inspiration. Dorothy was not about to die, though Coleridge's pinpointing the 'the *moment* in which [she] might die' is an astute perception, and in *fancying* her dead, Wordsworth may be exploring a death wish, insofar as the double binds which kept him with her were the same ones that kept him from enjoying the good life with Coleridge.[33] But in either sense, immediate or lifelong, she must be dead *to him*: this is the 'difference' that he expresses in the poems.

The possibility that the Lucy poems express a theme of psychological incest was first proposed forty years ago.[34] The theory has often been rejected, more often ignored, but never systematically refuted, probably because it is so obviously relevant, though finally unprovable. If 'Tintern Abbey' shows Wordsworth in love with Dorothy, the Lucy poems, according to psychoanalytic theory, represent his determined effort to 'refuse conscious recognition' of that fact under pressure of the new intensity in their relationship created by their isolation in Goslar.[35] But to reduce the meaning of these magical poems to a conscious or unconscious repressing of sexual feelings is an expense of spirit in a work of shame. Yet equally wrong-headed is the determination, in supposedly defending our nature moralist, to deny the power of such feelings in their creation.

For the purely psychological agenda of the poems, the reason that Lucy is dead, and curiously sexless for a lover, is obvious: she must be killed off, and presented as never having been a *sexual* temptation in the first place, despite her highly sensual identification with the natural world.[36] If her naturalness is pushed hard enough, she will no longer be human: this is the shock recorded in 'A slumber did my spirit seal': 'No motion has she now, no force . . . Rolled round in earth's diurnal course, / With rocks, and stones, and trees.' A more pragmatic psychological explanation, that Lucy's death expresses Wordsworth's frustation at not being able to be with Coleridge, is far from saying Wordsworth wished Dorothy were dead. Rather, the poems are simultaneously expressions of and defences against the trauma of that event.[37]

An alternate version of 'Nutting' has long been available, recently published in fuller form, which makes the identification of Dorothy with Lucy clearer, and also suggests that the incest prohibition being worked out in the poems was a temptation coming as much from Dorothy's direction as from William's.[38] This version shows that the 'dearest maiden' suddenly addressed at the end of it is clearly Dorothy of 'Tintern Abbey.' In its published form the moral of 'Nutting' about not violating Nature is stated bizarrely, as the narrator describes himself as a little boy, cutely decked out in old clothes for his nut-gathering expedition, who imagines in astonishingly precocious sexual terms the 'one dear nook' he will raid:

> the hazels rose
> Tall and erect, with milk-white clusters hung,
> A virgin scene! – A little while I stood,
> Breathing with such suppression of the heart

> As joy delights in; and with wise restraint
> Voluptuous, fearless of a rival, eyed
> The banquet . . .
>
> (19–25)

He toys with the setting like a man who, frankly, has his pleasure right where he wants her, and delights to prolong the anticipation: 'In that sweet mood when pleasure loves to pay / Tribute to ease . . . of its joy secure.' This highly sexed language makes the speaker's admonition *to her* to 'touch' these woods 'with gentle hand' sound more than a bit hypocritical.

But in the longer form of the poem, the maiden has just broken off a branch of a tree herself: 'Ah what a crash was that,' it begins, and goes right into the admonition: 'with gentle hand / Touch those fair hazels; my beloved Maid.'[39] Thus Wordsworth's published version mystifies a situation whose biographical reference in its original form was much clearer. True, he produces a better poem as a result. But in the original form the speaker proceeds to give the maiden a lesson in the proper way to express passion, as Wordsworth did in 'Tintern Abbey,' but now much more explicitly. He says the woods all 'shrink' from such 'rude intercourse,' and sets forth the kind of passion he would like to see in her face, as compared with the kind he actually does see – and fears:

> While in the cave we sat thou didst o'erflow
> With love even for the unsubstantial clouds
> And silent incorporeal colours spread
> Over the surface of the earth and sky.
> But had I met thee now with that keen look
> Half cruel in its eagerness, thy cheek
> Thus rich with a tempestuous bloom, in truth
> I might have half believed that I had pass'd
> A houseless being in a human shape,
> An enemy of nature, one who comes
> From regions far beyond the Indian hills.
>
> (6–16)

That is, he would have thought she was a gypsy, a category of persons always fascinating and upsetting to Wordsworth. Her coming from 'far beyond the Indian hills' is like Coleridge's claiming he would have recognized the Boy of Winander in the 'deserts of Arabia,' but Wordsworth is incredulous to think that he should cry out 'Dorothy!' on meeting such a passionate creature. So he asks her to calm down and modulate her feelings, to let her passion 'o'erflow' more tranquilly, for him:

> Come rest on this light bed of purple heath
> And let me see thee sink into a dream

> Of gentle thoughts till once again thine eye
> Be like the heart of love and happiness,
> Yet still as water when the winds are gone
> And no man can tell whither.
>
> (17–22)

This hardly needs interpretation: Please be calm and don't alarm me with your passionate looks. Then he makes an awkward transition to the story of 'Nutting,' presented as his own lesson in learning how to control passion, but only after he has resettled her comfortably for such edification:

> And dearest maiden, thou upon whose lap
> I rest my head, oh! do not deem that these
> Are idle sympathies.
>
> (44–46)

The transition is awkward – in fact, it breaks the poem apart – because Wordsworth is trying to negotiate his supposedly 'usual' passage from natural to human morality, which is very much harder, if not actually impossible, to cross than his naïve admirers realize. It is also hard to recognize in his poetry because he has so well covered his tracks with the artistry of disguise. The sympathies he teaches Dorothy are far from 'idle'; their force is highly sexual, as the language of the ensuing boyhood incident makes clear, language that rightly puzzles or shocks readers who come upon it with the orthodox image of Wordsworth in their minds.

In a closely related version of the poem the maiden is addressed as, 'Thou, Lucy, art a maiden "inland bred." '[40] This confirms that the 'maiden' of 'Nutting' is Lucy-Dorothy, and reveals more besides. The internal quotation is from *As You Like It*, where the lines apply to the hero, Orlando, who must be gentled and tamed by Rosalind, the play's charming heroine, because Orlando is an intruder in the romantic Forest of Arden. Wordsworth's switch in genders shows that the boy/speaker and the Lucy/maiden are in effect *interchangeable*, a possibility entirely typical of such loaded psychological fantasy-material. It also points up the fact that the problem being explored in all three versions of 'Nutting' is one that the speaker and the maiden share.[41]

The incest thesis is greatly strengthened by this new textual evidence, which shows that Wordsworth was desperately determined to 'repress a disruption of natural sibling relations.'[42] The blunt fact is that, prurience aside, whether or not Wordsworth had sexual relations with his sister is none of our business. But as the possibility – or his resistance to it – increases our understanding and appreciation of his poetic development, it is very much our business.

Some twenty years later, Wordsworth reflected on these 'early hours' he spent with Dorothy in a pair of odes to 'Lycoris,' the name of the lost love of the shepherd Gallus in Virgil's tenth and last *Eclogue*. Thinking of those times, Wordsworth muses,

> We two have known such happy hours together
> That, were the power granted to *replace* them (fetched
> From out the pensive shadows where they lie)
> In the first warmth of their original sunshine,
> Loth should I be to use it: passing sweet
> Are the domains of tender memory!
> ('To the Same,' 47–52; italics added)

No prospect is so revealing as the retrospect, in Wordsworth, and these 'domains' are precisely those of 'Nutting,' as four lines he inserted from the 1798 MS make clear. In the cave where he and 'Lycoris' lie down to rest and cool themselves, he asks,

> There let me see thee sink into a mood
> Of gentler thought, protracted till thine eye
> Be calm as water when the winds are gone,
> And no one can tell whither. Dearest Friend!

Why, in 1820, should he be wary of 'replacing' those hours unless the happiness they held were somehow felt to be suspect or ambivalent? As usual, Wordsworth's editors take pains to keep him clean on his odd use of the name Lycoris: 'It has no special significance for him.'[43] But this is unlikely for a poet who knew Virgil as well as Wordsworth did. He would have known from his schooldays the significance of the tenth eclogue: it is Virgil's sad farewell to the pastoral mode as he continues his career's ascent toward the epic. This significance of Eclogue X had been famously kept up in English by Milton's 'Lycidas.' In Virgil's poem, this valedictory gesture is contained in a negative lesson: Gallus should give up mourning his lost Lycoris, but he can't. Eighteenth-century classical scholarship may or may not have known that Lycoris was a real person, an actress named Cytheris (a.k.a. Volumnia), mistress of several Roman poets and a friend of Antony, but it certainly knew who Cornelius Gallus was: a military leader, a statesman, and a poet, one of the few historical persons named in the *Eclogues*.[44] And the poem itself indicates whither she has fled with her new lover: 'among the Alpine snows or over the frozen Rhine.' Here is a reason for thinking of, or responding to, her name that took Wordsworth in 1820 straight back to frozen Goslar of 1798–99. Gallus is trapped in the pastoral mode. He cannot stop thinking about Lycoris, nor can he adapt to the pleasant love-'em-and-lose-'em rhythms of literary pastoral; a rough soldier, he condemns himself to a life of exile in the forest, where he will roam about carving his lover's name on trees. Ovid's *Ars Amoris* cites Lycoris as an example of a woman made famous by her poet.[45] She was not made famous by Wordsworth, but this late appearance by her in his poems is – by this series of displacements – exposed as a screen or mask for the woman he *did* make famous, his 'Lucy', who by another skein of displacements must be seen as essentially identical to that other woman he made famous, but in far different contexts, his sister Dorothy.

That Dorothy was a more passionate person than her brother is everywhere a matter of record. Her eyes are called 'wild' as regularly as his expression is called 'calm.' 'The shooting lights of thy wild eyes' in 'Tintern Abbey' are clearly reflected in 'the keen look / Half cruel in its eagerness' of the 'Nutting' manuscripts. Her dominating presence in these manuscripts confirms, by sheer force of contrast, Wordsworth's determination to elide her emotional affect in the Lucy poems.[46] Given Wordsworth's transposal of gender roles from his Renaissance and classical inter-texts, it seems clear that not only the 'Nutting' versions but all of the Lucy poems are, in varying degrees, evidence of his effort to deny Dorothy a love she wanted. She had turned twenty-seven in 'the cold of [a] Christmas day . . . not equalled even in this climate during the last century,' alone with him. She knew by now she would never marry, and that she was in a real sense wedded to her brother for life.[47] It is hard to argue that Dorothy missed out on a writing career for her devotion, but it is certainly the case that she sacrificed herself *as a woman* to William's (vocational) desires.

The Lucy poems register some of the cost of this sacrifice, which we should not condescend to by anachronistically presuming to know what was 'normal' for young women at the end of the eighteenth century. Dorothy knew William had had mature sexual experience, that he had a 'wife' and daughter with whom she herself was also intimate, and whose frustrating separation from William she also felt deeply. She was a 'maiden' too, without sexual experience but with much erotic curiosity, and she trusted him wholly and completely. He had to teach her otherwise, but schooling her away from 'such rude intercourse' was the same lesson he had to learn himself. This necessity is represented in one of several passages that contain versions of the same lessons as the 'poem to Coleridge.' When he attested that even as

> A child I held unconscious intercourse
> With the eternal beauty drinking in
> A pure organic pleasure from the lines
> *Of curling mist or from the smooth expanse*
> *Of waters coloured by the cloudless moon,*[48]

we can recognize in this landscape a sublimated lover's body, of the sort we saw Wordsworth drawing as early as his boyish metaphor of 'the tufted grove' of Grasmere's cottage 'peeping through . . . the veil . . . flutter[ing] . . . loosely chaste o'er all below' his lover's neck. Its last two lines chime exactly with the way William said in 'Nutting' he preferred to experience Dorothy's love:

> While in the cave we sat thou didst o'erflow
> With love even for the unsubstantial clouds
> *And silent incorporeal colours spread*
> *Over the surface of the earth and sky.*[49]

The whole effort is to render their passion 'unconscious,' 'pure,' and 'incorporeal.' Wordsworth had to gain control of his passion for Dorothy in order to relay the same lesson to her. He said in 'Tintern Abbey' she would be the future bearer of his 'holy' love for nature, 'when these [her] wild ecstasies shall be matured / Into a sober pleasure.' In the longer version of 'Nutting' he becomes the instructor of that maturing process; the *Prelude* fragments show it occurring in his childhood, and the other Lucy poems show the pain of his renouncing her. Their 'gloomier' moment was not, as Coleridge *could not* say, his fancying the moment when she might die, but his recognizing the moment when she must die *for him*.

Some devout readers of Wordsworth's poetry will insist forever that 'Nutting' and its related texts are only about trees and reverence for nature. They *are* about this, but their highly charged erotic language shows that Wordsworth's reverence for natural bodies went well beyond trees, and any interpretation that insists on a literal reading of these loaded images and metaphors will find itself forced to explain a far stranger passion – for hazel nuts – than the altogether common and eternal one of a lonely brother and sister for each other, so mysteriously and powerfully confronted – and magnificently tamed – by the Lucy poems and their related inter-texts.

The Goslar lyrics are more 'refined' and apparently more 'universal' than the Alfoxden ballads and lyrics, but not simply because Wordsworth has removed most of the social context or immediate emotion of the poems written that spring.[50] They are more refined (that is, tranquil) and more universal precisely because they are more personal and deeply, intimately emotional, though Wordsworth carefully excised or sublimated almost all the signs of that intimacy out of them. If the Lucy and Matthew poems make the loss of a loved one 'a constant of human experience,'[51] it is because Wordsworth knew that loss so intimately, and also knew that there were other ways than death of losing loved ones.

CHAPTER TWENTY-SEVEN

Destination Unknown

Southern Germany, February–April, 1799

I travelled among unknown men,
In lands beyond the sea;
Nor, England! did I know till then
What love I bore to thee.

(c. 1801)

Life was claustrophobic in Goslar that polar winter, and both William and Dorothy longed to be out and away. They had proposed leaving Goslar very shortly after they arrived, and were still talking of doing so in December. They stayed on, probably because William was writing so well, and soon found themselves frozen in. But by early February, when it was still quite cold, they directed a series of letters to friends and family members concerned about them, announcing their intention to leave Goslar and travel south, probably to Weimar, possibly as far as Switzerland. William drew on his Wedgwood account for the remainder of the total amount he expected to spend in Germany, £40, in case 'we should prolong our stay beyond our expectations.' The £40 was more than the total (£32) he had spent in four-and-a-half months, for a tour they said would last no longer than two months, and when they got back to Hamburg at the end of April he drew out another £25. Well over half their total expenditure in Germany was laid out during the two months they spent somewhere in the south of Germany, primarily for transportation and perhaps for lodging, since their frugal eating habits always saved them money. Where did they go and what did they do?

On 23 February they left Goslar. They walked through the forests along the base of the Harz mountains for four days, passing through Claustal and Osteröde and other small towns, arriving at Nordhausen on 27 February, a total distance of about fifty miles (see map). In Osteröde, they were required to show their passports to some suspicious soldiers and were held up until their letters arrived in the trunk that was following them by wagon. 'After he had seen our letters,' the Burgomaster let them continue.[1] Were these the letters of introduction they had for Weimar, or just routine travel documents? In any case, they guaranteed safe conduct the rest of the way to Nordhausen.

Nordhausen was the terminus for diligences to all the major towns of Saxony, especially Weimar and Jena, another fifty miles further south. But at Nordhausen the Wordsworths' trail runs cold, and we see or hear no more of them for two months, when they pass hurriedly through Göttingen on 20 April, staying only one night, appearing 'melancholy and hypp'd' [depressed] to a perplexed Coleridge, before hurrying on to Hamburg and home.

There is a confused report that would place them in Göttingen in mid-March for a couple of days, but though this might account for their whereabouts from 27 February to *c.* 14 March (that is, they might have travelled from Nordhausen down to Weimar and back up to Göttingen), it still leaves more than a month unaccounted for.[2]

So we come to the third and last set of 'lost' months in young Wordsworth's life, to add to the autumn of 1793 and the six months in London in 1795. By the most cautious judgment, their travels that spring, without any other alternative explanation, 'must have been far different from what was originally projected if their only visit [to Göttingen] was that of late April.'[3] The next interesting question is, *How* 'far different'?

There are three possibilities for accounting for this time. The first is that they did what they said they would: toured around more southerly locales until time, the weather, expenses, boredom or discomfort drove them home – where, as their early February letters indicate, they had decided to go anyway.

The second possibility is that they went to Weimar to see the splendid court and intellectual life that was unfolding there. Goethe was there, at the height of his powers, resuming work on *Faust*, staging parts of Schiller's *Wallenstein*, and reintegrating himself into the official and cultural life of a place and a time that ranks among the most brilliant in the world history of arts and letters. Schelling, Fichte, and the elder Schlegel were visiting frequently from Jena; Steffens and Novalis were not far away.[4] Goethe's friendship with Schiller (often compared to Wordsworth's with Coleridge) was ripening through correspondence, though Schiller did not actually come to live in Weimar until December. Dorothy said they had letters of introduction for Weimar, and if they did (from Klopstock? from the Thomas Beddoes, the Bristol Germanist?) it is a wonder they did not go.

The third possibility is that they were embarked on some kind of errand for the Foreign Office, possibly having to do with closing the 'Swabian Agency' run by James Talbot and his brother Robert. Talbot was informed by a letter from Grenville in early March that he was to 'hand over the whole of his Mission to an Officer who would be sent out,' primarily the more than £75,000 that had been forwarded to him (of £400,000 authorized) for paying his subagents, bribing French royalists, and helping to arm and outfit Swiss volunteer troops and some regular Austrian army units.[5] The policy decision to close the agency had been taken in mid-January, when Grenville discovered that the wild Lord Camelford, his own brother-in-law and Pitt's cousin, had been detained at Dover with evidence on his person of a plot to assassinate some or all of the five French Directors.[6] This was the plot, Grenville now realized with horror, that Talbot had been aiding and abetting all along, with funds that, if not recouped, would lead to a public accounting by the Treasury, forcing Grenville to repay from his personal fortune, probably costing him his position in the government as well, possibly forcing a new election, and discrediting England abroad.[7]

Not a word, not an image, not a memory survives that is traceable to these two months. This fact alone, it seems safe to say, rules out the Weimar possibility. That Wordsworth should have been in Weimar and never say a word about it is even more incredible than that he should have been all set to go there, letters of introduction in hand – and then not gone! This is one of the great near-misses of literary history, that the young Wordsworth did not meet the mature Goethe at the height of his powers, when he was only fifty miles away from him and apparently fully intending to go there.

The first possibility, touring the south, is of course the most likely in default of other evidence: they did what they planned to do, and then never said a word about it to anyone. Dorothy's letters provide meticulous information about their four days' walk from Goslar to Nordhausen, but what happened to the next two months?

The fact of complete silence fits the third possibility very well, for that is exactly what we would expect for a mission into southern Germany to relay orders, or pick up papers or money as part of the process of closing Talbot's Swabian mission. Not that Wordsworth himself was the 'Officer . . . sent out.' For a mission of such delicacy, this was probably Grenville's own brother, Tom, who arrived in Germany in March as an envoy to the German courts.[8] But the decisive tactical decisions were taken in London between 22 March and 25 May, covering the period of Wordsworth's disappearance, especially the first week of this period, when Grenville was totally in charge of all foreign policy decisions, Pitt having fallen into a funk of discouragement over the war effort.[9]

There are references to a 'lost' journal that William and Dorothy kept together which might shed light on this period.[10] This may not be a separate booklet, but could refer to fourteen pages torn out of the 'Hamburg journal' or to some fifty pages torn out of the 'Christabel

Notebook,' since these notebooks were not discrete units, but were used for many different purposes.[11] It is remarkable, though certainly not impossible, that they should lose a whole journal. But ripping out pages that contained compromising information would make sense.

Coleridge seems to refer to this 'lost' journal in 1800 when he explained to the publisher Thomas Longman why he hadn't yet delivered his promised account of Germany. But his explanation raises as many questions about this putative journal as it answers. Coleridge said Wordsworth 'offered me the use of his Journal tho' not of his name,' for an 'account of Germany farther south than I had been' (that is, below Göttingen). Coleridge proposed to substitute chapters adapted from this journal for his own 'obnoxious' account 'of the Illuminati [which] would raise a violent clamour against me and my publisher.'[12] The Illuminati were a secret brotherhood of freethinking intellectuals, akin to the Freemasons, who were active in southern Germany.[13] Though officially disbanded in 1785, they continued to figure prominently in some of the wildest conspiracy theories of the French Revolution, which was already well on its way to becoming the great grandmother of all modern political conspiracy theories. The influence of the Illuminati persisted especially in the universities, most particularly at Göttingen, where the English influence gave plausibility to charges of 'religious infidelity,' the usual code-phrase for presumed revolutionary conspiracies.[14] The *voyageurs* of the royalist underground, James Talbot informed his superiors, communicated by 'universally known passwords and signs, "given as in Freemasonry," which enabled political travellers to receive help wherever they went.'[15] Hence the implied contents of Wordsworth's journal are not very reassuring for a neutral interpretation of it: it was less 'obnoxious' than an account of the Illuminati, but still something that Wordsworth did not want his name associated with. Why not, if he and Dorothy were just touring? Was there something about simply being present in southern Germany that he knew would compromise him with some people, or blow his – or their – cover?

Their earliest plans had included a trip southward. Dorothy had been hoping to visit Switzerland when she wrote to Aunt Rawson the previous summer explaining the German trip: 'if the state of Europe will permit . . . we shall travel as far as the tether of a slender income will permit.'[16] Christopher Wordsworth's *Memoir* hints that his aunt and uncle went pretty far south, 'to a more genial climate.'[17] By Feburary of 1799 their travel hopes had contracted to a trip of 'a couple of months,' or a wish to 'saunter about for a fortnight or three weeks.'[18] For one thing, they had less money than they had hoped for, and all of it was borrowed. For another, 'the state of Europe' did *not* permit unrestricted rambling, especially in southern Germany, since in October Austrian and Swiss troops had reoccupied some towns in Switzerland and engaged the French in skirmishes both above and below the border between Switzerland and the German principalities.[19] This was the beginning of General Suvorov's famous campaign, in which his English liaison officer was Robert Craufurd, Sir James's brother, following in the footsteps of their other brother, Charles, who had been invalided home the previous year, via Frankfurt, where he was visited by Wickham in retreat from the debacle of 18 Fructidor, the end of England's efforts to infiltrate and control the Directory.[20] So English communications between Hamburg and the south were well kept up, on both the highest professional and most intimate personal levels. James Craufurd was in regular contact with his brother Robert and with James Talbot, and with several other secret agents in the south, whose number could have included Wordsworth, or he may merely have been one of Craufurd's channels of communication.

In the spate of letters William and Dorothy sent off in early February, they informed almost everybody they knew about their plans and possibilities. This was just good sense, when heading in the direction of warfare in a foreign country, though their relatives, if they had had anything like modern access to news, would have been stunned at the folly of a tour in that direction. They had had reason to wonder similarly about William's trips to the Continent in 1790 and 1791 – to say nothing of 1793, when they may have been similarly manipulated precisely so as *not* to have anything to remark. William and Dorothy also left themselves little escape clauses. They would tour around, 'unless we should meet with so pleasant a residence in Saxony as should induce us to stay here longer than seems at present likely. If we do not, we shall go to Hamburgh at the end of two months'; their mail would be forwarded, 'if we should prolong our stay beyond our expectations.'[21] This is just about what they did do, but they did not see anything past Nordhausen worth recording, or, if recorded, not worth saving.

Have we seen this kind of behaviour somewhere before in the biographies of young William and Dorothy Wordsworth? Indeed we have. Their open-plan excursion into Saxony sounds like their double, and perhaps duplicitous, accounts of William's projected tour to the West of England in the summer and autumn of 1793 and their proposed reunion at Halifax at the end of it, to provide a plausible cover-story for William's clandestine trip back to France (Chapter 15). The large number of letters they sent off at one time (eight in all though only three survive[22]) could suggest a deliberate misinformation campaign with the same aim: tell everybody concerned where we're going, so each person's report would confirm others' inquiries, and then go somewhere else, that can't be traced or checked – and keep quiet about it forever after.

What would Wordsworth have been doing, if he was on a mission, even if only as a sub-contracted courier, for the Foreign Office? For this, we have not a clue, but only educated guesses: some kind of pick-up or delivery, of a message to the Swabian agency's main area of operations, which was one to two hundred miles south of Nordhausen? Although called the Swabian agency by the British, the French royalists called themselves the Comité de Bayreute, and its agents were centred there and at Coburg, closer to Nordhausen and Weimar. Though Louis XVIII had gone into Russia, his agents were still in place, 'all of whom had subordinate agents in the provinces,' of whom the Wordsworth's 'French Emigrant Priest' in Goslar could have been one.[23]

Although the 'Mr. Wordsworth' entry in Portland's paybook must now be discounted, other evidences of the British secret service's knowledge of Wordsworth, accented by this gap in his life record, which in turn coincides with the winding up of the Swabian agency, lend these conjectures some warrant. Some kind of hypothesis seems required. As with the 1793 trip to France, the mildest possibility seems the most plausible (he stayed in Wales then, he toured southern Germany now). But there is no evidence to support it. In both cases, the available evidence tends towards the wildest possibility.

Whatever Wordsworth thought about spies and provocateurs in Germany, he – 'that *dark* one' – wasn't saying anything. His acquaintance with M. de Leutre was so 'confidential' that neither he nor Dorothy ever said anything about it. Coleridge was well aware of spies' presence everywhere in Germany. Later that spring, after the Wordsworths had gone home, he rang an early change on his 'Spy Nozy' motif:

>—On Mr. Ross, usually cognominated *Nosy*,
>I fancy whenever I spy nosy
> Ross
>More great than Lion is Rhynose-
> ros.[24]

This notebook entry follows one on the tomb of Lucas Cranach, in Goslar, so there is a good possibility that it was written in or near Goslar. James Ross is clearly someone Coleridge knew, a suspected spy in the community of British students at Göttingen, some of whom (like Coleridge) the Foreign Office might have wanted to keep an eye on. Would some such fear have made the Wordsworths go through town in such a hurry in April, the only time they had seen their beloved friend since October? Or was it the even worse fear, of being recognized and *acknowledged* by the likes of Ross?*

The Foreign Office had no trouble keeping track of Wordsworth; four of the five extant letters he and Dorothy sent to England, including three

---

* 'Lion' was the nickname of a senior British diplomat, Lord Malmesbury, Ross's superior, just then passing through Göttingen on mission to Russia, based on his pride in his mane of powdered hair.[25]

of the eight sent off detailing their travel plans in early February, were franked through the Foreign Office – as of course was almost all British subjects' correspondence. And the person in that very small office who was directly in charge of controlling Talbot and communicating with Craufurd was George Canning, the undersecretary, late editor of and main contributor to the *Anti-Jacobin*, whose last long blast at British sympathizers with 'The New Morality' of republican ideology and Theophilanthropic/ Masonic mumbo-jumbo had been directed against 'C—ridge and S—they, L—d and L—mbe, & Co.'

Wordsworth was well aware of the insecurity of the post, for he 'dare[d] not trust . . . to a letter' his final communication from Nordhausen, about 'a new invention for washing' they had seen, which they hoped to patent when they returned, assuring Coleridge that 'you shall be a partner, Chester likewise.'[26] What modern convenience was lost to posterity when the Wordsworth washing machine failed to go into production? Wordsworth only went so far as to explain that 'only one washing bason [would be] necessary for the largest family in the kingdom.' Needing money as badly as they did, and 'wishing not to be in debt when I return,' they didn't want their get-rich-quick scheme to fall into other hands, because they knew that the mails were opened. That is one explanation for their guardedness. Or is this a coded reference to something else? Something that could *guarantee* his not being 'in debt when I return'? Certainly the debts of one 'Mr. Wordsworth' were notably relieved by Portland's payment in June.

How Wordsworth got himself into this position (if he did) is a matter that requires further conjecture. In a sense, he had passed from the surveillance, or control, of the Home Office to that of the Foreign Office, via the *Anti-Jacobin*. He could have been a man marked for compromising as early as 1791, and his associates and activities in France in 1792–93 and London in 1795 would not have removed him from suspicion; quite the contrary. If we presume that he knew far more than he let on about James Walsh's report in 1797, we can readily imagine that he was horrified to find himself suspected by the government, and that he volunteered his services as a way of dispelling suspicion, or at least agreed to serve when asked.[27] His name was already 'well known' to Richard Ford by then: how so? If he was a government courier now, had he also been one in the late summer of 1793, when presented with another opportunity to mix business with pleasure, or to cover private business with public business? Southey and Lloyd took no less self-serving steps, and far more public ones, to try to remove their 'Jacobin' labels.

Perhaps William Cavendish, the Duke of Portland, saw in the various kinds of reports about young Wordsworth he received from his operatives James Walsh, Richard Ford, John King, and George Canning an opportunity to reclaim – to *turn*, in the technical espionage term – the wandering son of the hapless lawyer who had prepared Sir James Lowther's brief against Portland in their dispute over Inglewood Forest thirty years earlier (Chapter 1). Portland was already using Wordsworth's cousin Robinson in similar capacities, and Robinson's need for such employment was not unrelated to William's failure or refusal or inability to pay back those parts of the Lowther debt on which he had drawn heavy advances for the education, social life, and foreign tours of that work-in-progress, the *bildungsroman* of his young life. Hence Portland's draft in favour of 'Mr. Wordsworth' returns us to the scenes of Wordsworth's childhood in a way that uncannily parallels – even as it materially supports – those first drafts of *The Prelude* in which Wordsworth, 'writing in self-defence,' sought to recover and preserve himself as a poet. Whether the offer ever came from the Home Office, and in friendly terms or as blackmail, Wordsworth's changing opinions on revolution and social reform would have made co-operation palatable, especially if sufficiently lucrative.

For he was also developing a vast sense of the entitlements of genius. In Goslar he composed several hundred lines of blank verse 'argument' about the necessary independence of the creative mind.[28] They dwell upon the negative effects on genius of the 'law severe of penury' and the need to earn a living; they form an economic subtext to the ideology of genius presented in the grander passages of nature worship interleaved with his boyhood 'spots of time.' They urge the need for mental freedom if men are to perform good actions, since economic hardship will prevent, and prudential moralisms will not sufficiently produce, the spontaneity that is the hallmark of true morality. But at bottom they are efforts to construct a philosophical justification of the need for the Poet to be financially independent in order to be morally and creatively independent. He was very concerned not to be in debt when he returned to England, and he knew he had been accumulating nothing *but* debt during his months in Germany.

Furthermore, he and Coleridge had now seen themselves, as Englishmen, in a far different light than the revolutionary 'angels' he and Robert Jones had seemed to be to the 'saucy' Frenchmen when they sailed down the Rhône in 1790. They saw that England was regarded as Europe's last best hope against a revolutionary republicanism that had turned to imperial expansion. As Coleridge said, 'being abroad makes every man a Patriot and a Loyalist – almost a Pittite!'[29] His young friends in Göttingen were impressed by Coleridge's keen appreciation of the political difficulties Pitt faced in getting England through the crises of 1798-99, despite Coleridge's evident opposition to the war and his continuing loyalty to Fox.[30] Wordsworth returned to England in 1799 far less 'disaffected' than Walsh had reported him in 1797, or than Canning had satirized 'Coleridge & Co.' for being in 1798. He was still three years away from the great 'Sonnets on

National Independence and Liberty,' but on the way to them he wrote a late 'Lucy' poem which looked back to the 'melancholy dream' of Goslar with a firm statement of its outcome:

> I travelled among unknown men,
>> In lands beyond the sea;
> Nor, England! did I know till then
>> What love I bore to thee.

This is a kind of *re*-conversion poem, underscored by the same deep signature of all his inspiration in Goslar, the death of Lucy: 'And thine [England] too is the last green field / That Lucy's eyes surveyed.'

This was already their mood when they stopped overnight with Coleridge on 20–21 April, 'melancholy and hypp'd.' Coleridge noted 'they burn with such impatience to return to their native Country, they who are all in all to each other.'[31] He walked five miles out of town with them along the coach road toward Hannover and Hamburg. Coleridge felt that 'dear Wordsworth appears to me to have hurtfully segregated & isolated his Being / Doubtless, his delights are more deep and sublime; but he has likewise more hours, that prey on his flesh & blood.'[32]

They left Hamburg as soon as they got there, sometime between 26 and 28 April, just as Europe began to fall apart behind them. On 28 April George Harward, Craufurd's sub-agent at Cuxhaven, began to think that all this surveillance had gone far enough. He hoped that an Austrian victory over the French would 'perhaps allow us to despise the efforts of insignificant individuals' to travel to and from England.[33] William and Dorothy Wordsworth might have appeared as just such 'insignificant individuals,' but Harward's liberal hopes were misplaced, for on that very day the French deputies to the Rastadt peace conference were assassinated by some Austrian hussars. This assassination solidified French distrust of all monarchies, confirmed their worst fears about 'perfidious Albion,' and assured the re-entry of Austria into the war on the side of the allies. Though not in the way James Talbot intended when he fruitlessly spent thousands of Grenville's pounds in *his* assassination plot, the Austrian hussars had achieved part of the public goal the British Foreign Office had been working toward since 1793: widening the war with France. (Its private, secret goal was to end the war by subverting the Directory internally.) But like most political assassins, the hussars got far more and much worse than they bargained for. Wordsworth left Germany and returned home just as the die was cast that would lead, by November, to the end of the Directory and the transfer of power to a new form of government, headed by a 'consul': the 18th Brumaire of Napoleon Bonaparte.

At this same time in April, Sir James Craufurd in Hamburg closed the net he had been carefully positioning all year, arresting the Irish republicans and their French agents.[34] Craufurd's arrests were timed to co-ordinate with arrests of United Irishmen conspirators in London taverns in March and April under the direct supervision of Pitt, Portland, and Wickham, the precise timing of which had been their main preoccupation since late February: coincidentally, the time at which Wordsworth left Goslar and disappeared.[35]

The creation of the Poet in Germany involved not only his declaration of independence from Coleridge's mind ('Was it for this?'), and his declaration of independence from Dorothy's heart ('with gentle hand touch . . . beloved Maid'), but also a declaration of *de*pendence on the nation-state that he now admitted, after a terrible year of isolation and self-exile, he 'had learned to know the value of.' If he was to avoid the penalty of the 'law severe of penury' which 'blocks out the forms of nature,' he may have decided that his 'liberty of mind' made it worthwhile to strike a deal, either with himself or with the 'Secret Department,' that might have been hard to refuse anyway.[36] His justification for this higher liberty is expressed in language that shows that his conception of it went beyond the law. Or rather, that it put him outside the bounds of law, so that, like Rivers in *The Borderers* – but as a member of the establishment rather than an outlaw – he acts by 'the light of circumstance,' putting himself (in his own estimation) beyond conventional judgments for betraying – or in this case co-operating with – the powers that be:

> we know
> That *when we stand upon our native soil,*
> Unelbowed by such objects [like financial obligations] as oppress
> Our active powers *those powers themselves become*
> *Subversive* of our noxious qualities:
> And by the substitution of delight
> And by new influxes of strength *suppress*
> *All evil*; then the being spreads abroad
> His branches to the wind; and all who see
> Bless him, rejoicing in his neighbourhood.
> *There is one only liberty; 'tis his*
> *Who by beneficence is circumscribed;*
> 'Tis his to whom the power of doing good
> Is *law and statute, penalty, and bond,*
> *His prison, and his warder,* his who finds
> His freedom in the joy of virtuous thoughts.[37]

This is a very unusual way to define the 'freedom of the universe' derived from the 'active principle alive in all things.' The whole passage uses political language – but of a police state – as a metaphor for the individual's internal regulation of his own higher morality. Those to whom such freedom is granted are first made 'subversives' against their own evil ('noxious') tendencies, and are then locked up in the prison-house of their own virtue, rather than in 'the close prison-house of human laws.' The 'freedom of the universe' operates, internally, almost like a secret police against our own worst impulses, far more effective than 'chains . . . shackles, and . . . bonds' (26–27)—not unlike the operation of the 'Secret Department,' whose chief organizational merit (as Wickham explained to Portland) was linking the Home Office with the Foreign Office in such a way that 'no other office could ever know anything of what was passing there, unless instructed from the Fountain Head.'[38] A similar mode of operation characterizes Wordsworth's conception of the moral force of his imagination, flowing from its fountainhead, in language that seems purely metaphorical but that, upon closer examination, appears – as we have seen so often in texts deriving from the contexts of his young life – to be literally descriptive as well.

PART III

WHAT IS A POET?

1799–1807

CHAPTER TWENTY-EIGHT

'We have learnt to know its value'

Sockburn-on-Tees, May–December 1799

It is a grazing estate, and most delightfully pleasant, washed nearly round by the Tees, (a noble river,) and stocked with sheep and lambs which look very pretty, and to me give it a very interesting appearance.

(Dorothy Wordsworth)[1]

Disembarking at Yarmouth at the end of April after seven upsetting months abroad, William and Dorothy rapidly pushed on north to the Hutchinson family estate at Sockburn-on-Tees, just south of Darlington. The Hutchinsons were just about the last people left in England to take them in. This family of young adults, two men and three women, had been living independently for five years after coming into an inheritance of over £2000.[2] Mary was twenty-nine, the same age as Wordsworth, Sara twenty-four, and Joanna nineteen. George and Thomas were twenty-one and twenty-six, respectively; their eldest brother, Henry, was at sea. Sockburn-on-Tees was a self-sufficient estate on its own isolated peninsula in the Tees, eight miles east of Scotch Corner, the gateway to Scotland.[3] The farm, a low-maintenance grazing estate, produced about £200 year. Although of very similar background to the Wordsworths, the Hutchinsons enjoyed a much more comfortable lifestyle, a difference that had long distressed Dorothy: 'they are quite independent and have not a wish ungratified, very different indeed is their present situation from what it was formerly when we compared grievances and lamented the misfortune of losing our parents at an early age and being thrown upon the mercy of ill-natured relations.'[4]

In her first letter after returning, Dorothy said, 'We are now at Sockburn with Mary Hutchinson.'[5] Mary was the focus of their visit, as she now became the object of William's affections, slowly intensifying over the next three years. His new romantic interest was not a conscious decision, but rather a feeling acted on spontaneously, provoked in part by the frustrating relations that had surfaced between him and Dorothy in Goslar.[6] More than erotic relief (which was surely not explicit), Mary and her siblings represented *domesticity*: feelings of home and family that had been starved in a strange land. The moment was that precious though precarious one of young adults living out the last days of youth. Ideas of marriage and settling down were in the air. Living at Sockburn for the next seven months, William and Dorothy saw the embodiment of their oldest dream: brothers and sisters living together, unmarried, in great harmony – and substantial comfort. The feeling of, 'Nor, England! did I know till then / What love I bore to thee,' began at Sockburn, stimulated by relief at escaping from the claustrophobia of Goslar, compounded with a new appreciation of England's role as the opponent of tyranny, and all brought together in an idyllic English manor house, surrounded by old childhood friends.[7]

Despite sexual and political tensions lurking beneath the surface, the idyll of Sockburn-on-Tees restored Wordsworth's spirits. He responded by composing most of Part Two of the 1799 *Prelude* there, inspired by feelings of joyous community precisely contrary to the feelings of alienation in Goslar that had forced him into the fragments that became Part One.[8]

He wrote bluffly to Cottle that they were 'right glad to find ourselves in England, for we have learnt to know its value,' but the new feelings between him and his country were not exactly reciprocal: 'I am in want of money.'[9] He owed over £100 to the Wedgwoods, and he and Dorothy wanted to contribute something to their maintenance, as their visit stretched into summer and autumn. Before they could decide where to live, they had to get their finances in order.

William began by trying to discover the fate of *Lyrical Ballads*. Little had gone as planned. Cottle still owed him twenty of the thirty guineas promised as an advance, and had not turned over the volume's copyright to Joseph Johnson as Wordsworth had asked. The Arch brothers' sales of the book had been satisfactory, though not sensational, and Cottle was very vague as to its prospects. 'Can you tell me whether the poems are likely to sell?' Wordsworth asked exasperatedly.[10] The earliest review, Southey's quick and dirty ambush, had not helped, and was extremely aggravating since *Lyrical Ballads* had been a money project from the start. It was still the only property Wordsworth had for producing income, and he continued to regard it very much in that light. Even his objection to Southey's review was not to his hypocrisy or his judgment but his motive: 'He knew that money was of importance to me. If he could not have spoken differently of the volume, he ought to have declined the task of reviewing it.' His own motives were unabashedly commercial: 'I care little for the praise of any other professional critic but as it may help me to pudding.'[11]

Other professional critics, though, began to take notice of the book and helped him toward pudding. Most reviews of *Lyrical Ballads* (1798) appeared after the Wordsworths' return in 1799, so enormous the glut of poetry on the marketplace: the years around the turn of the century saw one of the few poetry 'booms' in the history of English literature. Almost every reviewer found something to admire as well as criticize; they tended to divide most sharply on 'The Idiot Boy' and 'The Thorn.' 'Tintern Abbey' was most frequently singled out for praise, and 'The Mad Mother' ('Her eyes are wild') seemed a bizarre favourite with everyone. Dorothy Jordan, the leading actress in Sheridan's melodrama-pantomime, *Pizarro*, a big hit when it opened on 24 May at Drury Lane, proposed to sing a few stanzas of 'The Mad Mother' when the play was staged again.[12] The interest of London's most popular actress brought its still-anonymous author to the leading edge of London cultural gossip.

The first new review Wordsworth saw after his return was by Dr Burney (father of Fanny) in the *Monthy Review* for May 1799, representing conventionally liberal middle-class opinion. Burney complained of the general 'gloom' of the volume, astutely locating its source in its 'implied criticism of the social system.'[13] He saw some dangerous Rousseauism in the attitudes expressed in the 'Yew-Tree Seat' lines, an excess of tenderness for convicted criminals in 'The Dungeon' and 'The Convict,' and 'a general stigma on all military transactions' in 'The Female Vagrant.' These are all accurate observations, and Wordsworth agreed with most of them: he dropped 'The Convict' for ever, and excised the most strident stanzas from 'The Female Vagrant' ('dog-like, wading at the heels of war . . . with the brood / That lap . . . their brother's blood'). Burney encouraged the author to treat 'more elevated subjects and in a more cheerful manner,' and Wordsworth by and large followed this advice. Though there is nothing in the 1800 *Lyrical Ballads* quite as elevated as 'Tintern Abbey,' there is a good deal more cheerfulness. Six months earlier Wordsworth had confidently lectured old Klopstock on an author's moral necessity to rise above market considerations, but when his own 'pudding' was concerned he was ready to follow the opinion of professional reviewers.

More painful when it came to Wordsworth's ears was the word of mouth about *Lyrical Ballads* circulating among their family and friends. Relatives sometimes see anything less than total success as failure, especially when it concerns things they're not familiar with. Margaret Spedding thought the poems were 'really such queer odd sort of things that if everybody was of my mind, profits would not answer for a journey.'[14] Sara had written to Coleridge that they 'were not well esteemed here, but the Nightingale and the River Y.' To Poole, she was blunter: '*Lyrical Ballads* are laughed at and disliked by all with very few excepted.'[15] By the time Coleridge returned to London, Wordsworth was so touchy about the volume's reception that when Coleridge reported having heard Godwin comment favourably on it to no less a personage than Fox, Wordsworth sulkily impugned Godwin's motives, intemperately calling him 'a polite liar [and] a worse philosopher . . . ergo the account is smoke or something near it.'[16]

But gradually, as late reviews came trickling in, and the need for money did not go away, and sales continued until the first edition was exhausted in just over a year, Wordsworth began to consider another edition or another publication. He turned over his pile of manuscripts to see what might be serviceable.[17] He began to 'hew' down *Peter Bell* and think about its compatibility in a volume with either 'The Ruined Cottage' or 'Adventures on Salisbury Plain.' But he responded to reviewers' comments on the 'gloominess' of *Lyrical Ballads* by turning most of his new work in a lighter direction than these depressing narratives, so that none of these long poems saw the light of day for at least another fifteen years. He had about a dozen new poems from Germany, concerning two mysterious characters named Lucy and Matthew, of no relevance to any casual reader though massively relevant to 'the poem to Coleridge' he kept working on, despite its manifest unprofitability. But he was not, in any of his thoughts about publishing in 1799, concerned with expanding *Lyrical Ballads* except by way of increasing his profits from them.

His only income was a twice-yearly dividend of £7 10s. on the 3 per cent consols Richard had purchased while he was in Germany.[18] He soon learned from Richard that his loans to Montagu and Douglas from the Calvert bequest were faring as badly as ever; they were not paying up; out of their sight, he had slipped their minds. The best Montagu could do was to keep up premiums on an insurance policy on his life, Wordsworth's desperate measure against losing almost everything he'd got from Calvert five years before. William made Richard take a hard line with Montagu: 'I shall be under the absolute necessity of pursuing those steps which will be extremely distressing to myself and unpleasant to you unless you immediately remit me the Balance due.'[19] Montagu still did not remit anything, but no action was taken against him. His friend Douglas finally paid his £100, putting Wordsworth in a position to pay back the Wedgwoods at last, to whom he had been sending a string of extenuating letters about his debt, 'owing to irregularities, mistakes respecting the publishing of my poems, and other causes.'[20] But there is no evidence that he repaid this [Wedgwood] debt in 1800. Instead it was John, the only entrepreneur in the family, who instructed Richard to pay the debt, prompted by Dorothy's inquiry if it would be proper to invest the £100 received from Douglas in John's next voyage, which indicates that they still had the sum at their disposal.[21]

Assuming that their financial mess would eventually get better, since it could hardly get worse, William and Dorothy began thinking about where to go. Though they were now standing at the gateway to the north, they had no immediate plans to visit, let alone live in, the Lake District. Sockburn became the jumping-off point for their probes in that direction in the autumn, but in the spring their only motive toward the Lakes remained that of Dorothy's flirting invitation to Coleridge from Goslar: 'wherever we finally settle you must come to us at the end of next summer, and we will explore together every nook of that romantic country.'[22]

The Hutchinsons were in transition too, for by the next spring their own idyll split up under the constant bourgeois pressure to increase the size of estates. George went to a new property at Bishop Middleham near Durham, taking Sara as his housekeeper, and Thomas went to Gallow Hill near Scarborough, taking Mary with him. Joanna traded visits between them.[23] The Hutchinsons' discussions about moving gave the Wordsworths an extra push, but William's development toward poetical independence did not initially involve thoughts of going to live in Cumberland or Westmorland, regions that were still for him and Dorothy, as for most people, places for 'romantic' holidays, not permanent residence.

Coleridge expected Wordsworth to return to Alfoxden, which suggests that the row over their behaviour in 1797 had subsided, and that their opinions which prompted it had also changed. A drama was shaping up that neither of the principal actors quite foresaw. Coleridge expected that Wordsworth would follow *him*, as he had without hesitation for the past two years, 'unless he should find in the north any person or persons who can feel and understand him, and reciprocate and react on him.'[24] 'As I do,' is the unspoken complement of the sentence. Wordsworth did not find any such persons; the Hutchinsons were great old friends but not creative soul mates. Instead, it was 'the north' itself that began to draw him, in no small measure because he continued writing about it constantly in the poem to Coleridge, which now intensified the function that it had started to have in Germany: a means of drawing Coleridge after *him*.

Plans shuttled back and forth during the summer to little purpose, but Coleridge was being drawn toward Wordsworth as if by magical incantation, in his role as the addressee of the expanding proto-*Prelude*, which Wordsworth now brought to an end by incorporating Coleridge into it. At the end of Part One, Coleridge was asked to listen sympathetically to Wordsworth's 'lengthen[ing] out / With fond and feeble tongue a tedious tale' (i.448–49). This alliterative joking was appropriate to their situation in Germany, where Wordsworth admitted he was indulging 'the weakness of a human love for days disowned by memory' instead of writing *The Recluse*. 'Yet should it be . . . / That I by such inquiry am not taught / To understand myself,' he knew he need not 'dread from thee / Harsh judgements' (458–59). During the summer and autumn of 1799, Coleridge did not give 'harsh judgements' on the poem that became *The Prelude*, but he repeatedly wished Wordsworth were writing *The Recluse* instead, neither man having yet divined that Wordsworth's 'preparatory' poem for the more philosophical *Recluse* was itself 'the philosophic song' he was destined to write.

In his first renewed comment on *The Recluse*, however, Coleridge provided Wordsworth with a new rationale for it, which Wordsworth immediately co-opted into *The Prelude*. 'I wish you would write a poem, in blank verse, addressed to those, who, in consequence of the complete failure of the French Revolution, have thrown up all hopes of the amelioration of mankind, and are sinking into an almost epicurean selfishness, disguising the same under the soft titles of domestic attachement and contempt for visionary *philosophes*.' This charge appears, with only minimal alteration for blank verse, as the new conclusion of 'the poem to Coleridge':

> . . . if in these times of fear,
> This melancholy waste of hopes o'erthrown,
> If, 'mid indifference and apathy
> And wicked exultation, when good men
> On every side fall off we know not how
> To selfishness, disguised in gentle names
> Of peace and quiet and domestic love—
> Yet mingled, not unwillingly, with sneers
> On visionary minds . . .
>
> (ii.478–86)

He hasn't fallen off, Wordsworth concludes, because his 'gift is yours / Ye mountains, thine O Nature.' Suddenly, the 'tedious tale' of his life has been given a point and a mission: it could save their entire generation from the dashed hopes of the French Revolution.

Most specifically, the 'good men' falling off on every side refers to James Mackintosh (1765–1832), who had been their acquaintance among the wealthy intelligentsia in Bristol. Mackintosh would soon be instrumental in persuading his brother-in-law Daniel Stuart to make Coleridge his highest-paid contributor.[25] But Coleridge did not let gratitude interfere with despising this man who, as he rightly saw, was leading the tide of apostasy away from liberal reform ideas. Mackintosh's *Vindiciae Gallicae* (1791), the most closely reasoned of all responses to Burke's *Reflections*, has been called 'the ablest ideological defence of the French Revolution ever written.'[26] But between February and June of 1799 he delivered a series of lectures on 'The Laws of Nature and of Nations,' attacking the course of the Revolution and refuting the arguments of his own pamphlet. Mackintosh remained throughout his career a liberal Whig, but these lectures became the public symbol of liberal intellectuals abandoning all hope of encouragement from the example of France. Hazlitt sourly recorded their devastating effect, bitterly rating them the best speeches Mackintosh ever gave in a long public career. 'The volcano of the French

Revolution was seen expiring in its own flames, like a bon-fire made of straw: the principles of Reform were scattered in all directions, like chaff before the keen northern blast. . . . As to our visionary sceptics and Utopian philosophers, they stood no chance with our lecturer.'[27]

Coleridge spent most of his time after returning from Germany making emotional repairs with his family and friends. Mending two fences at one stroke, he reconciled with Southey, and the two brothers-in-law spent the late summer touring the West Country with their wives and children. He joined in toasts to king and country in a new access of patriotism that was, like Wordsworth's, as genuine as it was expedient.[28] A friend of his brother's muttered against his continuing association with 'dark-hearted Jacobins,' and Coleridge readily admitted that some of them were 'shallowists.'[29] He was still under official surveillance, and dashed of another variation on his 'Spy Nosy' theme, this one 'On Naso Rubicund, Esq. a dealer in Secrets' (identified as Sir William Anderson).[30]

But for most of the autumn he dithered. What finally got him up north were increasingly alarming accounts of Wordsworth's health. These were not wholly fictitious, but they were psychosomatic: the pains around his heart that he reported in Germany when, as now, he was working on the poem that invoked his friend as Muse, pleading for his approval of its account of the creation of the Poet.

Wordsworth, it turned out, was not so sick after all, or else his illness was part of the plan to 'decoy' Coleridge to them. Coleridge arrived on 26 October, having commandeered Cottle and his chaise, and William popped out of bed the next day, ready for a month-long walking tour in harsh November weather. Of his first impressions of Sockburn and the Hutchinsons, Coleridge only had time to note, fatefully, 'Few moments in life so interesting as those of an affectionate reception from those who have heard of you yet are strangers to your person.'[31] The Hutchinsons had been hearing about the 'wonderful' Coleridge for nearly four years, but this was their first meeting. 'Interesting' seems a mild word to describe the meeting that would lead to the heartbreak of his life, his passion for Mary's sister, Sara, a name whose mocking repetition of his wife's name he never tired of twisting into symbolic permutations, especially as the 'Asra' of his great 'Dejection: An Ode.'

They set out next morning, Wordsworth and Coleridge and Cottle. But Cottle, mounted on Sara's mare, Lily, turned aside almost immediately at Greta Bridge, barely twenty miles on the way. Very likely Wordsworth could not resist expressing some dissatisfaction with Cottle's handling of *Lyrical Ballads*. But Cottle probably sensed that the two friends wanted to be alone. Even Dorothy was left behind, who had imagined 'follow[ing] at your heels and hear[ing] your dear voices again,' when she teased Coleridge about exploring 'every nook of that romantic country.' She had to wait her turn.

With Cottle gone, the two friends took a coach over the Stainmore wastes of the Pennines. They were headed for Penrith, but at Temple Sowerby, the last stage before Penrith, a very odd coincidence occurred. Wordsworth 'learned from the address of a letter lying on the table with the Cambridge post mark, the Letter from Kit to Mrs C[rackanthorpe] that he was gone to Cambridge. I learned also from the Woman that John was at Newbiggin. I sent a note – he came, looks very well – '[32]

But Dorothy knew very well why he was at Temple Sowerby. It was on the main road a mile from Newbiggin, the closest thing left to an ancestral estate in which the Wordsworth siblings had a legitimate interest. Christopher Crackanthorpe had just died, on 15 October, and John and Christopher were there for the funeral, along with their uncle Cookson.[33] Both William and Dorothy had known at Sockburn of his final illness, as she was Uncle Christopher's favourite niece. William would not have gone to the funeral in any case, for he despised this uncle. But his brief stop at Temple Sowerby provided the essential news that led him there in the first place: 'Your Uncle has left you [Dorothy] £100, nobody else is named in his Will.'[34] He was doing the quite usual thing, checking to see what they'd got from the estate. Dorothy reacted more in pity than in anger: 'He did not so much as name the name of his brother [William Cookson] or one of his nephews.' That is to say, not one of them would inherit, not even the dutiful John or Christopher. The worst had happened: all the estate that Christopher Cookson had inherited passed entirely out of family hands into those of his widow, née Cust, William and Dorothy's aunt Crackanthorpe, 'despised by everyone for her excessive pride.' Once again the Wordsworths had to face the blunt reality that their relatives would not help them and that they must help themselves.

Still, they had linked up with John, a much better companion than Cottle. William had not seen him for over two years, and Coleridge now met him for the first time. Coleridge wrote Dorothy, 'Your Br. John is one of you; a man who hath solitary usings [*sic*] of his own Intellect, deep in feeling, with a subtle Tact, a swift instinct of Truth & Beauty.'[35] John, the 'silent poet,' had the physique of his older brother and the quick sensibilities of his sister, strangely combined in a taciturn sea-faring officer of great responsibility and growing wealth, whose hazardous profession was now made more dangerous by war.

Few people can have experienced a guided tour of the Lake District such as Wordsworth now gave Coleridge. And yet, for all its natural splendour, even in 'savage and hopeless' November weather,[36] it was a case of life imitating art: not a voyage of discovery, but of confirmation. During the next three weeks, Wordsworth brought Coleridge directly into most of the scenes from his childhood that he had been writing about for him over the course of the past year. The tour was a tour de force, to show Coleridge the places on which the imaginative power of *The Prelude* was based, as the necessary foundation of *The Recluse*. Coleridge had at last been decoyed into that 'romantic country,' and he was, on this tour with this guide, a sitting duck. Of course, it knocked him over.

They made two large contiguous loops through the whole district, first down past Windermere to Hawkshead and up to Keswick over Dunmail Raise (with a week's stay at Grasmere in the middle), then west around through Ennerdale and Wast Water and back up again to Keswick via Borrowdale, with side trips into Buttermere and Crummock Water, and possibly to Cockermouth.

Starting from Penrith, they made straight for Hawkshead. They stopped to inspect a small property of Richard's at Sockbridge near Barton, where they had lunch with Reverend Thomas Myers, father of Wordsworth's cousin and Hawkshead and St John's schoolmate. They moved rapidly along the route that Wordsworth had often taken in his boyhood trips back and forth to school. Between Barton and Bampton they saw Lowther Castle to the east, and the next day, as they passed under Walla Crag on Haweswater, Coleridge learned a local superstition, with contemporary commentary: 'On the bold rock Lord Lonsdale's Father's spirit. Walla Crag – Sir James would let them rest in Lowther Hall.'[37] Robert Lowther (1681–1745), a former Governor of Barbados who suppressed Jacobite sympathizers there amid charges of corruption, libel, and bigamy, died of a heart attack during the last Jacobite invasion of Westmorland, despite the brave success of his steward, Wordsworth's grandfather, in saving his gold and plate. His corpse was said to have refused to stay in its grave at Lowther, so a priest put the body under a large rock at Walla Crag.[38] Coleridge's comment (learned from Wordsworth, of course) implies that even Sir James, 'the bad Earl,' would not be so inhospitable. As they went along, Wordsworth's mind ran much on the injustices of his situation because of the Lowthers, as obscurely indicated by another of Coleridge's journal entries: 'Universities – Pox – Impotence – Lord Lonsdale.'[39]

Low-hanging mists prevented them from going directly over the mountains to Ambleside, so they crossed Kentmere Common, and came out of the hills at Troutbeck, into Windermere. Here too picturesque appreciation mixed with social criticism of Wordsworth's old antagonists. Wordsworth was 'much disgusted with the New Erections and objects about Windermere,' and Coleridge noted at the 'Head of the Lake of Wynandermere – Mr. Law's white palace [at Brathay] – a bitch! – Matthew Harrison's House where Llandaff lived [Calgarth] / these and more amid the mountains!'[40] Richard Watson still lived at Calgarth, and when Coleridge came to live in the Lakes he expanded his attacks on this liberal but dangerous antagonist of their generation: 'that beastly Bishop, that blustering Fool, Watson, a native of this vicinity, a pretty constant Resident here, & who has for many years kept a Rain-gage, considers it as a vulgar Error that the climate of this country is particularly wet.'[41]

At Hawkshead, Wordsworth sadly observed 'great change amongst the People since we were last there.'[42] He especially regretted the loss of the 'grey stone of native rock' which was the 'centre' of the schoolboys' games, now 'split and gone to build / A smart assembly-room that perked and flared / With wash and rough-cast, elbowing the ground / Which has been ours' (ii.31–39). Happy as he was to be back, his commentaries suggest a sense of resentful displacement. The saddest change 'amongst the People' was the death of Ann Tyson three years before, which William and John learned of only now.

They hurried on to meet those 'divine sisters, Rydal and Grasmere,' where Coleridge said he 'received I think the deepest delight.'[43] Grasmere is the natural hub at the centre of the Lake District, and they spent nearly a week there, staying at the old inn near the church and taking day trips out. Grasmere was one of the places on the tour where Wordsworth had not spent any time as a child. In his letters to Dorothy, William's growing enthusiasm for it closely correlated with *Coleridge*'s fascination with the place, and his own 'mad' plan was roused by Coleridge's admiration: 'C. much struck with Grasmere and its neighbourhood and I have much to say to you, you will think my plan a mad one, but I have thought of building a house there by the Lake side.'[44] Coleridge's first sight of the vale – 'Embraced round by Hill's arms behind – before us what ridges & on the side of that little spot of Lake What an awful mount!'[45] – was repeated in one of the most ecstatic passages of 'Home at Grasmere': 'Embrace me then, ye Hills, and close me in!'

John left them on the 5th to return to the business of finding investors for his next voyage. They walked with him as far as Grisedale Hause and Tarn below Helvellyn. Something of the difference between Coleridge's and Wordsworth's descriptive language, and of their personalities, is revealed by what they said about this day. Wordsworth merely noted, 'This day was a fine one and we had some great mountain scenery – the rest of the week has been bad weather.'[46] Wordsworth's descriptive powers are weaker than they are often assumed to be; what he saw in landscape were emotions, human figures supported or destroyed by nature, and, above all, himself. But Coleridge, who was collecting images for his notebook, gives both more details and more emotion:

> On the top of Hevellin
>
> First the Lake of Grasmere like a sullen Tarn / then the black ridge of mountain – then as upborne among the other mountains the luminous Cunneston Lake – & far away in the Distance & far to the Lake the gleaming Shadow, Wynandermere with its Island – Pass on – the Tairn – & view of the gloomy Ulswater & mountains behind, one black, one blue, & the last one dun – [47]

They also disagreed occasionally on the character of country people. Wordsworth cared less for the scenery, but he stuck up for the people, while Coleridge noted, 'People in the country – their vindictive feelings –'[48] For Wordsworth, the people and the landscape went together, but for Coleridge as often as not, they clashed. Admiring the sweeping curve of the northern outlet of Grasmere Vale, between Helm Crag and Stone Arthur, his view suddenly dropped to the bottom: 'all between on both sides savage & hopeless – obstinate Sansculottism.'

Back down at Rydal, they again ran afoul of aristocrats' efforts to control the landscape. They entered the grounds of Rydal Hall, seat of Sir Michael Le Fleming, who had erected a small house over Rydal Beck to provide a framed view of Lower Rydal Falls. It was open by permission to acceptable persons, but the two poets' appearance was evidently not acceptable: 'While at Sir Fleming's a servant, red-eyed &c, came to us, to the Road before the Waterfall to reprove us for having passed before the front of the House.' Coleridge responded with the new landscape authority he had learned from Wordsworth: 'our Trespass of Feet [was nothing to] the Trespass on the Eye by his damned White washing!'[49] But Wordsworth said nothing of the sort about the incident: 'The evening before last we walked to the upper Water fall at Rydal and saw it through the gloom, and it was very magnificent.'[50]

After the week at Grasmere they crossed over the 'inverted Arch' of Dunmail Raise to Keswick, and began the third week of their tour with a swing through the western lakes. Probably they visited the Speddings, for they spent a night at Ouse Bridge at the top of Bassenthwaite, but it is not clear if they went to Cockermouth, even though they seemed headed in that direction. Coleridge later noted, 'Cockermouth – and why I never went there.'[51] 'Why' might be, in the context of this tour, because Wordsworth wanted to go back alone, or didn't want to go there at all, for reasons too emotional to contemplate with tranquillity. His and Dorothy's sight of their old home in 1794 had been upsetting, and he had already come across more than enough reminders of how his various inheritances in the region had been denied him, without seeking out more.

At Buttermere on 11 November they first saw Mary Robinson, daughter of the landlord at the Fish Inn, where they spent the night.[52] Mary was just a local beauty then, though a striking one. But she would become a national *cause célèbre* three years later when she was seduced into marriage by a bigamist, John Hatfield, posing as an MP and the brother of the earl of Hopetoun. Like the grey stone of Hawkshead broken up to make a 'smart' assembly-room, this Mary Robinson became for Wordsworth a symbol of the ways in which his native district was being exploited by outsiders, tourists, developers, and venal aristocrats. She, 'the artless daughter of the hills,' was symbolically related to him, Nature's 'chosen Son,' because 'we were nursed – as almost might be said – / On the same mountains,' and connected, he suggests, by the umbilical cord of the River Cocker, he at its mouth and she at its source in Buttermere (VII.342–43).

Next day, over in Ennerdale, they heard the story of James Bowman and his son, both of whom fell to their deaths from crags while tending their sheep, the son apparently while sleepwalking.[53] This became one of the incidents in 'The Brothers,' the first poem Wordsworth began composing when he and Dorothy moved to Grasmere. It is also informed by his recent experience of having been with John for two weeks, since the brother who returns to his home vale is a seaman, while the one who stayed and died was the shepherd. True to Coleridge's perception of the region's names and Wordsworth's imaginative installation of himself in it, the shepherd is given a new name symbolizing his fatal place, James *Ew*bank.

Returning to Keswick, Coleridge found a letter waiting for him from Daniel Stuart, offering him a place as lead writer for the *Morning Post*; he would become its highest-paid contributor, with his mornings free.[54] It was an offer he couldn't refuse, and he determined to return to London immediately. Wordsworth felt his prey slipping from his grasp just when he thought he had netted him. A sense of déjà vu must swept over him as he thought of himself almost five years earlier, rushing off to London from nearly the same spot to join William Mathews in newspaper work, though of a far less certain nature. They ran into William Calvert, reminding Wordsworth of Raisley and all he owed to him from that same hopeful moment, though his gift was now precariously tied up in uncertain debts.

They headed back to Penrith for Coleridge to get the stage. Wordsworth looked heroic to Catherine Clarkson, wife of the great anti-slavery agitator, at whose country estate, Eusmere, at the head of Ullswater, they made their last stop on 17 November. 'He has a fine commanding figure is rather handsome & looks as if he was born to be a great Prince or a great General.'[55] She also noted his partiality to Coleridge: 'He seems very fond of C. laughing at all his Jokes & taking all opportunities of shewing him off & to crown all he has the manners of a Gentleman.' She seems to have expected something worse, probably from family gossip, which she knew well from her husband's close association with Wilberforce and William Cookson.

Coleridge was greatly excited by Ullswater, running up and down the shore recording effects of light and shadow. He drew intricately numbered diagrams to establish the exact visual perspective for William's description of the 'huge cliff' that seemed to stride after him, 'like a living thing,' in his stolen rowboat: probably either Black Crag or Stybarrow Crag.[56] Said Coleridge, 'I turn my Back to the Lake / & what a Cliff!'[57] His descriptions, compared to Wordsworth's, show, for all their energy and detail, not that Wordsworth's are better, but again how different they are.

Wordsworth was more concerned with '*un*known modes of being' that utterly blank out 'familar shapes / Of hourly objects, images of trees, / Or sea or sky, *no* colours of green fields' (ii.124–26).

Wordsworth remained among the lakes, but Coleridge headed for London via Sockburn – a significant detour – where he stayed nearly a week. Back at the Hutchinsons without William, he was the undivided centre of everyone's attention. He fondly quoted to himself a question overheard in conversation on his arrival a month earlier, 'Miss Mary Hutcheson & Cottle immediately after Tea on our arrival, "Pray, what do you think of Mr. Coleridge's [first] appearance?" '[58] The only 'you' to whom this question could have been addressed was Sara Hutchinson, and Coleridge indulged himself in recalling her charmingly embarrassed reply. On his last night, they all played like children in front of the fire, at 'Conundrums & Puns & Stories & Laughter,' and he put his intense recollections into a foreign tongue: 'et Sarae manum a tergo longum in tempus prensabam, and [*sic*] tunc temporis, tunc primum . . . .'[59] The entire Latin passage reads, in translation, 'And pressed Sara's hand a long time behind her back, and then, then for the first time, love pricked me with its light arrow, poisoned alas! and hopeless.' Seven more lines are heavily obliterated in the journal.[60] His recollections continued, helplessly, 'I just about to take Leave of Mary – & having just before taken leave of Sara –. I did not then know Mary's and William's attachment: The lingering Bliss, / The long entrancement of a True-love Kiss.'

If he was half in love with the Lakes, he was now all in love with Sara Hutchinson (and partly with Mary as well, it seems). Some part of his decision the next summer to return to live there was based, fatalistically, on the hope of seeing her more often. As Wordsworth had fallen for that 'divine sister,' Grasmere, under the charm of Coleridge's enthusiasm, so Coleridge had a predeliction for falling in love with the sisters-in-law of his best friends, first with Sara Fricker and now with Sara Hutchinson.[61] It was not mere coincidence that Coleridge should be meeting the love of his life at the same time that Wordsworth was beginning to think about marrying; both of them had prior romantic relationships that were proving, in their different ways, untenable.

His emotions completely aroused, Coleridge began a poem later called 'Love,' which he soon published in the *Morning Post* as 'Introduction to the Ballad of the Dark Ladie.' It records the effect on a beautiful auditor of a minstrel reciting a doleful tale of a lady rescued 'from outrage worse than death' by a knight she had earlier rejected. This story is 'The Ballad' itself, which Coleridge had already composed, but never published. He may have recited it to the company that fateful night, or fantasized about the effect of doing so. One stanza says all that mattered to him:

> She listened with a fitting blush,
> With downcast eyes and modest grace;
> For well she knew, I could not choose
>   But gaze upon her face.[62]

The happy denouement of the ballad is repeated in the happy scene of its telling, when the meaningful look goes in the other direction:

> She wept with pity and delight,
> She blushed with love, and virgin-shame;
> And like the murmur of a dream,
>   I heard her breathe my name.
>
> Her bosom heaved—she stepped aside,
> As conscious of my look she stepped—
> Then suddenly, with timorous eye
>   She fled to me and wept.
>
> She half enclosed me in her arms,
> She pressed me with a meek embrace;
> And bending back her head, looked up,
>   And gazed upon my face.
>   (77-88)

The knight's heroism in the tale is transformed, in the 'Introduction', to the minstrel's creative power in telling it, and each wins his dark lady (Sarah's hair was a beautiful auburn).

William had gone back to Grasmere and spent a week arranging to take a house he had seen. He returned to Sockburn the day after Coleridge left, and found Mary alone. He wrote Coleridge that he 'was sadly disappointed in not finding Dorothy,' but added that 'Mary was a solitary housekeeper and overjoyed to see me.'[63] Occasions were conspiring to make their decisions about where to settle more complicated, for both delight and disaster.

The 'mad' decision to go 'home' to Grasmere did not take long, once Dorothy returned to Sockburn; William returned on 25 November and they left on 17 December. It was a foregone conclusion once William started talking about his tour. Their necessary preparations were minimal, as they had next to nothing in the way of household goods, only their clothes, their books, and a growing collection of William's manuscripts and Dorothy's journals.

They set off on horseback, William riding Lily, and Dorothy mounted behind George Hutchinson.[64] But once past Richmond they continued on foot, a three-day march of some sixty miles in mid-December directly across 'Wensley's long Vale and Sedburgh's naked heights' to Kendal.

'Bleak season was it, turbulent and bleak.'[65] This was another of those arduous, definitive walks on the itinerary of the young Wordsworth, and, in its way, the last of them. It was not his longest, but in the symbolic arc of his career it was a Long March of mythic proportions, through a Wilderness into their Promised Land – the sort of similes he soon began using in 'Home at Grasmere,' where he raised them to even higher levels, Eden and Paradise. Both of them boasted about their rate of progress: twenty-one miles the second day, ten miles in a little over two hours through the highest pass, seven miles in an hour and a half coming down into Sedbergh – not just brisk walking, but almost respectable jogging times.[66]

Wensleydale provides the only road route across this part of the Pennines, but they marked their progress by the three waterfalls they visited, at Aysgarth, Askrigg, and Hardraw Force, which Wordsworth described in a carefully crafted letter to Coleridge, written on Christmas Day from their new home at Grasmere.[67] This letter was not merely an exercise in picturesque description, but, like the November walking tour and the early *Prelude*, part of the Wordsworths' effort to keep Coleridge interested in their surroundings and draw him to them.

Like Coleridge's description of the waterfalls at Alfoxden and Culbone, these contain as much imagination as description. Wordsworth could write effective prose description when he wanted to, but here he manipulates perspective to maximize the effect of seeing one thing through another, particularly the veil or curtain of the falling water itself. His presentation of Aysgarth is delightfully Spenserian, 'such a performance as you might have expected from some giant gardiner employed by one of Queen Elizabeth's Courtiers, if this same giant had consulted with Spenser and they two had finish'd the work together.' By this, he concludes lamely, 'you will understand that with vastness or grandeur it is at once formal and wild.' At Askrigg, the falls seemed more architectural, like 'a tall arch or rather nitch which had shaped itself by insensible moulderings in the walls of an old castle,' and distorted their sense of distance: 'The steeple of Askrigg was . . . not a quarter of a mile distant, but oh! how far we were from it.' But, oh, the difference to them.

Wordsworth's metaphors became even more exotic for their view of 'a *third* waterfall,' Hardraw, where a single column of water drops nearly one hundred feet into a pool. He tried to reproduce 'the enchanted effect produced by this Arabian scene of colour as the wind blew aside the great waterfall behind which we stood and hid and revealed each of the faery cataracts in irregular succession or displayed them with various gradations of distinctness, as the intervening spray was thickened or dispersed.'[68] He knew Coleridge was fascinated by the movement of wind or water across natural objects (like trees) which move, bend and recover without losing their essential form, though streaked by rapid passages of light and colour. The knotty intensity of his descriptions attempts to show how one thing appears *through* another, as Coleridge would generalize it in *Biographia Literaria*'s account of the origin of *Lyrical Ballads*: 'the power of giving the interest of novelty by the modifying colours of imagination. The sudden charm, which accidents of light and shade, which moon-light or sun-set diffused over a known and familiar landscape, appeared to represent the practicability of combining both [truth to nature and novelty]. These are the poetry of nature.'[69] Since they were not painters or watercolourists, they analogized these natural movements to the rhythm and metre of poetry as it went through or across the words in a line, giving life to the images they described.

William had given their walk its symbolic force before they got to these three waterfalls, by a different fall, or leap – of faith and imagination. They said their 'sorrowful' farewell to George Hutchinson near Hart-Leap Well, five miles beyond Richmond. In olden times, according to local legend, a noble stag leapt to its death there, down 'four roods of sheer ascent,' after a thirteen-hour chase by a knight named Sir Walter. The stag breathed his last into a spring at the bottom of the hill, which was his birthplace. Sir Walter raised a pleasure-dome there for his 'wondering Paramour,' and there was much 'merriment within that pleasant bower.' But now 'the pleasure-house is dust: —behind, before, / This is no common waste, no common gloom'; 'Something ails it now; the spot is curst.'[70] Wordsworth said a peasant told them the story of the place, and there is a place called Hart-Leap Well, but like the November walking tour with Coleridge, this was a case of life confirming art rather than inspiring it. For the main incidents of the cursed hunter are present in Bürger's poems which Wordsworth had purchased in Germany. But none of his sources treat the story as a cautionary homecoming tale in the way that Wordsworth does. It is a homecoming sanctified by death, always present at Wordsworth's deepest imaginative moments, and it contains a warning to themselves not to triumph over nature by trying to arrange it to suit themselves: 'Never to blend our pleasure or our pride / With sorrow of the meanest thing that feels.'

Some lines in 'Home at Grasmere' make clear that the millenial 'milder day' of 'Hart-Leap Well' is not far off, and that it will arrive very close to the 'bleak season' of December 1799. The sign of its coming is the journey of William and Dorothy Wordsworth to their new home, cast as Paradise Regained:

> when the trance
> Came to us, as we stood by Hart-leap Well—
> The intimation of the milder day
> Which is to come, the fairer world than this—
> And raised us up, dejected as we were
> Among the records of that doleful place . . .[71]

The 'trance' was a 'Vision of humanity and of God / The Mourner, God the Sufferer,' in which they found a very specific message:

> A promise and an earnest that we twain,
> A pair seceding from the common world,
> Might in that hallowed spot to which our steps
> Were tending, in that individual nook,
> Might even thus early for ourselves secure,
> And in the midst of these unhappy times,
> A portion of the blessedness which love
> And knowledge will, we trust, hereafter give
> To all the Vales of earth and all mankind.
>
> (248–56)

It is important not to back away from the implication of these lines in order to appreciate the final stages of Wordsworth's self-creation as the Poet of the 1800 preface and the 1805 *Prelude*. 'Seceding' (a precisely chosen political word) to their own 'hallowed spot,' they are, like John the Baptist in the Wilderness, precursors to a worldwide regeneration. The 'unhappy times' of revolutionary despair that Coleridge said *The Recluse* should address, and that Wordsworth promptly incorporated into *The Prelude*, were soon to be changed by the example of their private lives. To the extent that their 'secession' was funded by payments or forced by compromises with the government's secret service apparatus, their creation of a mythic 'home' at Grasmere can be regarded as their safe passage out of the world of active, dangerous politics, a retreat to a safe-house in the provinces.

They arrived at Kendal on 19 December, fairly sprinting the last seven or eight miles from Sedburgh. They spent the rest of that day buying necessary furniture and utensils, and on the 20th they proceeded to Grasmere by post-chaise, thus creating a far different impression on their new neighbours than if they had come straggling up the road as the 'Wild Wanderers' they looked like coming off Sedbergh's 'naked heights.'

The house they entered was the first one they came to, descending the old road over from White Moss Common. It had been readied by William's arrangement with an elderly neighbour lady, Molly Fisher, who later told Dorothy, 'I mun never forget t'laal [little] striped gown and t'laal straw Bonnet as ye stood here' (by the fire).[72] The sun set as they entered their 'home within a home [and] . . . love within a love,' bringing a 'composing darkness' to the 'little shed / Disturbed, uneasy in itself, as seemed, / And wondering at its new inhabitants.'[73]

In those first nights, the longest of the year, they saw a good omen in the sky: Jupiter was visible from 20 to 23 December, largest of the planets and king of the gods, William's particular emblem.[74] The next night (24 December) they associated it with another star in another sky, and

Dorothy forever afterwards celebrated Christmas Eve and Christmas Day with recollections of their arrival in Grasmere as much as for the Christian holiday. Nor was the Star of Bethlehem far from William's mind when, soon after, he composed the conclusion to 'Home at Grasmere,' with a prayer to a secularized Holy Spirit ('thou prophetic Spirit, Soul of Man') for what his poetry might become, in the same kind of rhetoric he had adopted to prophesy the coming of the 'milder day' that their advent in Grasmere would bring:

> Thou human Soul of the wide earth that hast
> Thy metropolitan Temple in the hearts
> Of mighty Poets; unto me vouchsafe
> Thy guidance . . . that my verse may live and be
> Even as a Light hung up in heaven to chear
> Mankind in times to come![75]

Home at Grasmere

'Embrace me then, ye Hills, and close me in!'
('Home at Grasmere,' MS. B, 129)

William had rented a cottage at the southern end of Grasmere valley, in a little collection of houses known as Town End, half a mile from the town centre. Once an inn called the Dove & Olive Branch, the house itself was nameless while the Wordsworths lived there (till 1808); its modern name, Dove Cottage, was bestowed later. But Wordsworth rang many variations on Grasmere as the 'Vale of Peace' in the poem he soon began writing, 'Home at Grasmere,' and Coleridge extended the metaphor in his picture of their picnic on the lake's island in July: 'the Image of the Bonfire, & of us that danced around it – ruddy faces in the twilight – the Image of this in a Lake smooth as that sea, to whose waves the Son of God had said, PEACE!'[1]

But Wordsworth in fact found it difficult to achieve peace there, and gradually recognized that he would never find it in any place except in the mind and language of an idealized Poet, 'a man speaking to men.' With this discovery he was, by the end of 1800, poised to enter the final stage of his self-creation.

'My little cabin,' as Wordsworth described it, was small indeed.[2] Compared with the elegant spaces of Racedown, Alfoxden, and Sockburn – and his own grand birthplace in Cockermouth – it seemed like a doll's house, particularly for a man as tall as he. It was even smaller than Coleridge's tiny cottage in Nether Stowey, though divided into more rooms: three-and-a-half down, four up. The entry room – wainscoted in dark oak, with leaded windows and a fireplace – had been the barroom. Dorothy made it her kitchen, next to her bedroom. William's bedroom, upstairs, was next to the large front room which they made their living area. The ceilings were so low that William walked indoors with his head permanently bent.

It is hard to correlate a place with poetry, though we do it to a fault with

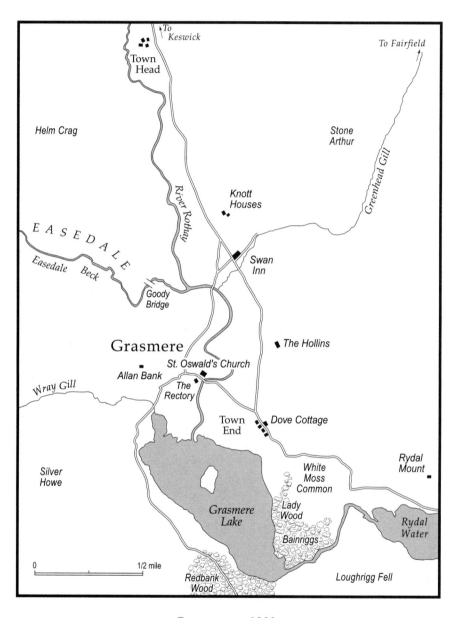

To Keswick

To Fairfield

Town Head

Helm Crag

Stone Arthur

River Rothay

Greenhead Gill

EASEDALE

Easedale Beck

Knott Houses

Swan Inn

Goody Bridge

Grasmere

St. Oswald's Church

The Hollins

Allan Bank

The Rectory

Wray Gill

Town End

Dove Cottage

Rydal Mount

Silver Howe

White Moss Common

Grasmere Lake

Lady Wood

Rydal Water

Bainriggs

0   1/2 mile

Redbank Wood

Loughrigg Fell

Grasmere, *c.* 1800

Wordsworth's outdoor poems. But the 'phenomenological' dimension of Wordsworth's imagination, relative to his bodily living space, is intriguing. At Town End he was in the smallest house he had ever lived in, yet he wrote most of his greatest poetry there. His habit of composing out of doors became a necessity at Grasmere: no house could be less suited for striding about humming words at five beats to the bar. Its Lilliputian dimensions worked like a counterweight to his ambitions, concentrating his mind on giant exertions.

Though small, Dove Cottage was certainly cheap, eight pounds per year, far less than even their nominal rent at Alfoxden.[3] They soon arranged with John Fisher, the local cobbler, across the road in Sykeside cottage, for Mrs Fisher's older sister, Molly, to help with the washing up and other housework, for two shillings, a sixpence more than the going rate.[4]

Expecting little of their neighbours, they were agreeably surprised. 'The manners of the neighbouring cottagers have far exceeded our expectations,' Dorothy wrote to Coleridge soon after their arrival.[5] She had a clear sense of the local hierarchy and of their place in it: 'we are very comfortably situated with respect to neighbours of the lower classes [who were attentive without being servile],' and 'also upon very intimate terms with one family in the middle rank of life, a Clergyman.'[6] This was the family of eighty-five-year-old Reverend Sympson, for forty years vicar of Wythburn, a remote parish on the other side of Dunmail Raise. Sympson had had great prospects in his youth, moving among 'high-born friends.' Both his high expectations and his subsequent disappointments made him more interesting to Wordsworth than the vicar of Grasmere, who disapproved of him and Dorothy for their odd habits, particularly William's not attending church.

Closer to them among the 'middling sort' were the Oliffes at Hollins Farm just north of Town End, named after its profusion of holly trees.[7] Their good friends the Speddings, at the upper reaches of the middle class, were further away, at Mirehouse beyond Keswick. They improved their acquaintances with the Clarksons, at Eusmere at the top of Ullswater, till Catherine Clarkson became Dorothy's most intimate personal friend.[8] But they had nothing to do with the aristocratic Le Fleming family, over the hill at Rydal Hall. Wordsworth had already been warned about trespassing there, but the next year they were given temporary shelter there during a rainstorm, while 'a grand Ball' was in progress.[9]

They soon met their other neighbours, mostly poor people of the village, and explored every nook and cranny in the valley. Like Dove Cottage, the entire Vale of Grasmere appeared 'so narrow,' 'so small,' compared to the high hopes Wordsworth brought with him: 'I looked, I stared, I smiled, I laughed; and all / The weight of sadness was in wonder lost.' The reaction is typical of adult returns to childhood haunts, but there was a huge tension between Wordsworth's 'sadness' and his 'wonder,' a tension that was soon released in his earliest Grasmere poems.

Town End, tucked away into the southeast corner of the valley, has an air of peeping out at the rest of it. Dunmail Raise and Helm Crag were the limit of their horizon to the north, with Easedale and Far Easedale fading away to the northwest – the 'Black Quarter,' Dorothy called it, because the mountain storms came mostly from that direction. But Easedale was their favourite place for walks and poetry composing, being the easiest way to get up quickly into the hills. To the west, Silver How loomed up across the lake, with its perfect little island in the middle. Behind them, hidden from view by the woods along the river Rothay, rose Red Bank and Loughrigg. Immediately beside them, their eastern perspective was closed off by the sharp incline of their 'little orchard plot,' which rose up to How Top, and above that to the whole Fairfield range, making their house the 'rocky corner in the lowest stair / Of that magnificent temple which doth bound / One side of our whole vale with grandeur rare.'[10]

In the 'Poems on the Naming of Places,' Wordsworth started claiming these sites in the name of his own imagination, but he also encountered resistance to their being christened by strangers. It was the same with the neighbours. Their strong first impressions of the Fishers, the Sympsons, the Ashburners, the Greens, and many other families were soon strategically incorporated by William's imagination into poetry, partly as evidence of virtuous country life, but more importantly to show how good country people recovered from life's disappointments.

The Reverend Sympson and his disappointed hopes were one case in point. Another was John and Agnes Fisher, who struggled all their life to pay off the mortgage he had been forced to take out for their marriage – necessitated by a 'mishap' pregnancy. John Fisher summed up the economic situation when he said there would soon 'be only two ranks of people, the very rich and the very poor.'[11] Those who had land were forced to sell or mortgage it for cash, 'and all the land goes into one hand,' a version of the same process in which Wordsworth's father had aided James Lowther. Foreclosures and heavy encumbrances were common in the ruinous economy of the time. Agnes Fisher lost her youth and vivacity and gained only the sense of having wasted her opportunities: 'Bound—by vexation, and regret, and scorn, / Constrained forgiveness, and relenting vows' (*Excursion* VI.712–13). By contrast, it was Wordsworth who succeeded in Grasmere.

The neighbours at least had roofs over their heads, but a constant procession of more unfortunate wayfarers passed by the cottage. Its location made it a natural stopping-place for travellers resting after their climb over from Rydal, or preparing to ascend in that direction. Most who stopped were desperately poor, for the years 1799–1801 saw particularly intense poverty in the northwest of England, with food riots in Lancaster, Wigan, and Birmingham.[12] Hardly a week went by without Dorothy recording her conversation with one of them, some of whom found their way into her brother's poems, most famously the old leech-gatherer whom they encountered just outside their cottage.[13] Their number was legion: 'a widow of Grasmere, a merry African from Longtown' (at the Scottish border); a tall woman whose two small sons denied she was their mother; a slightly mad hatter; the Hawkshead boy who looked surprised when she asked if he had enough to eat; a soldier from Cockermouth of exactly William's age who had lost his leg in battle and returned home, only to find 'he could earn more money in travelling with his ass than at home'; the little girl from Coniston whose 'step-mother had turned her out of doors'; and the woman from nearby Rydal, 'stout and well dressed,' forced to beg because 'these are hard times!'[14]

The friendly reception at Dove Cottage encouraged still more wanderers to stop. Dorothy gave them what penny or scrap she could afford, in exchange for their giving an account of themselves to William. He continued for a while to write poems about these people. He still wanted to know about the mental states their suffering drove them to, or else he imagined them for himself. He was pitilessly interested in what their life-experience had done to their minds, not in their present hunger or debts or rheumatism. His focus on them was the same as on himself: 'the growth of my own mind,' and how their imaginations were 'impaired' or 'restored.'

John returned to them in early January. His behaviour illustrates the enormous emotional pressure surrounding their establishment, after nearly twenty years, of a home in the lakes. He walked out to Town End from the inn near the church, but as he stood in front of the cottage he was overcome by emotion. He returned to the inn and sent word by messenger to prepare William and Dorothy for the shock of this belated homecoming, under the first roof they could call their own since Dorothy was sent away to Halifax in 1778.[15]

In late February, William travelled over to Sockburn to fetch Mary Hutchinson for a visit that lasted six weeks. With devoted friends and family around him, Wordsworth turned again to *The Recluse*, that now became the poetical justification of his career, recasting it in terms of his move to Grasmere. 'Home at Grasmere' is set up to show that he had reached the destination his whole life had been pointing toward. He had everything he wanted, within reason, and no more excuses. It was time to realize his genius as he defined it: the poem's manuscript sub-title is 'Book First, Part First of *The Recluse*.' But it took years to complete just one book of a poem that might have had thirty such books; Wordsworth did not finish it until 1806, after he had completed *The Prelude*. The challenges it presented, and his difficulty in overcoming them, brought him to the final stages of his self-creation as the Poet of the Preface to *Lyrical Ballads*, the hero of *The Prelude*, and the William Wordsworth of subsequent English literary history.

He composed about six hundred lines of the poem in 1800 before its insuperable contradictions forced him to break off composition.[16] These lines constitute a Romantic Ode to Joy in one of the highest keys ever attempted. No small part of Wordsworth's achievement was avoiding the incoherence such odes often fall into, like the youthful effusions of Shelley or Keats. His Ode to Joy launches itself, whether by design or by accident, over the brink of its own ecstasy into the depths of its dialectical contrary, the Ode to Dejection. Unlike the conventional pastoral poet, who writes himself into his chosen landscape as a refuge from worldly suffering and corruption, Wordsworth wrote himself out of it, as he reluctantly acknowledged the social responsibility he was shirking.

The poem opens with a 'spot of time' that may be real or imaginary. He remembers himself as a boy gazing down on the valley and experiencing a visionary moment of notably unboyish thoughts:

> 'What happy fortune were it here to live!
> And if a thought of dying, if a thought
> Of mortal separation could come in
> With paradise before me, here to die.'
>
> (9–12)[17]

'Paradise before me' goes Milton one better, topping *Paradise Lost*'s final vision of 'the earth was all before them.' But Adam and Eve were leaving Paradise, while William and Dorothy are returning to it. Vaunting himself above not only Milton but even Milton's Biblical sources, Wordsworth's thanksgiving hymn vies with *The Song of Songs*, with the striking variation that his erotic language refers not to the expectant community of believers but to the receptive landscape: 'Embrace me then, ye Hills, and close me in!'

He made a vow: 'here should be my home, this Valley be my World.' As he advanced poetically into the landscape that he and Dorothy had just entered physically, there was no expression too extreme for his joy, as he lays claim to the land in the name of his own imagination.

> The unappropriated bliss hath found
> An owner, and that owner I am he.
> The Lord of this enjoyment is on Earth
> And in my breast.
>
> (85–88)

> What Being . . . since the birth of Man
> Had ever more abundant cause to speak
> Thanks . . . ?

The boon is absolute . . .
                . . . among the bowers
Of blissful Eden this was neither given
Nor could be given . . .

(117–25)

This is astonishing language for an essentially non-Christian writer, and one who, as Coleridge said, meant *all* of every word he wrote. Each phrase has to be considered not only as rhetorical hyperbole but as deeply felt personal testament: 'The Lord . . . is on Earth,' 'since the birth of Man.' These are the most extreme expressions of joy in Wordsworth's oeuvre, his least tranquil, most emotional mood; it is an unnerving sight, this human embracing of the divine.

The segments of 'Home at Grasmere' written in 1800 advance by a series of such rhetorical leaps and bounds, each exclamation more sweeping than the last. After the opening boyhood 'spot of time,' the poem follows the sequence of their December walk through Wensleydale and the apparent confirmation of their hopes with the coming of spring and the birds' riotous pleasure in it, reflecting their own inner satisfaction. The poem works toward identification with its very moment(s) of composition, toward saying, Here am I, writing this poem. If all its linguistic peculiarities were compressed into a single sentence, they would collapse all tenses into one: Once upon a time I am living happily ever after. It bursts into – and eventually through – its own moments of inspiration. Every aspect of it strives toward self-identification: it is full of images of reflection and circularity, tautological arguments, and redundant syntax.

It comes as no surprise to any levelheaded reader that this surreal absurdism could not be long sustained, and that the denomination of the first wild days of March 1800 as a unique imaginative entity – new century, new career, new revolutionary agenda – should falter in the face of real time. But it came as an untoward shock to Wordsworth, and we can see the shock waves registered in the poem. At the very height of his '*O altitudo!*' Wordsworth looks down, sees poverty, death, and evil, and plunges to the ground, not to resume the poem for over five years. Just when he seems to be parsing his poem off the page of the landscape, he reads something he doesn't like:

But two are missing – two, a lonely pair
Of milk-white Swans. Ah, why are they not here?
These above all, ah, why are they not here
To share in this day's pleasure?

(322–25)

The repetitions, the reiterated gasp, the insistent questioning – all the poem's self-reflective characteristics implode in upon it. And the reason is presented as nakedly as the ecstasy: he and Dorothy have identified themselves with these two swans to an extraordinary extent: 'to us / They were more dear than may be well believed.' But we can believe it, when we see what their disappearance does to the poem, for William and Dorothy had radically invested themselves in their symbolic identification with the swans:

> ... their state so much resembled ours;
> They also having chosen this abode;
> They strangers, and we strangers; they a pair,
> And we a solitary pair like them.
>
> . . . .
>
> Shall we behold them yet another year
> Surviving, they for us and we for them,
> And neither pair be broken?
>
> (338–41, 348–50)

The poem's extreme symbolism rebounds on to its narrator. Wordsworth pitched his claims for the special qualities of Grasmere so high that this ridiculous literalism threatens to spoil it. He goes immediately on the defensive: the bulk of the remaining lines composed in 1800 show him back-pedalling furiously to restore the damage he has done. But it was no good; he ultimately backs himself into a corner, out of the poem, and breaks off.

The extremes to which he goes to explain the swans' absence are the best guarantee of the utter sincerity of the joy which preceded his discovery of it. His first conjecture, that they may have been shot by Grasmere 'dalesmen,' was a good possibility. Dorothy refers to 'the swan hunt' in her journal, an organized destruction of the decorative species introduced at Windermere twenty years earlier, that were very unpopular with the local residents because they were so noisy and aggressive.[18] But this commonsense explanation leads Wordsworth into an even worse crisis in his poem: lack of moral confidence in Grasmere's natives. He apologizes to both the place and to his poem for even 'harbouring this thought': 'Recall, my song, the ungenerous thought; forgive, / Thrice favoured Region, the conjecture harsh.'[19]

Evidence of human frailty has introduced a complication into the argument which soon became insuperable, forcing him to break off composition. Other human beings have come on the scene, and *The Recluse*'s difficult social theme ('Human Life') disrupts the Man-Nature bonding Wordsworth celebrates. Contrary to sentimental views of Wordsworth's happy return to the Lake District – views which often make much of the phrase, 'home at Grasmere' – the poem of that title challenges and indeed destroys the sentimental view, showing Wordsworth's clear awareness that his greatness as a poet could never be built on Grasmere, the Lake

District, or even all of Nature.* No earthly place was big enough for his godlike conception of imagination: what he learned in these moments of composition in Grasmere in 1800 confirmed what he had already intuited in the Simplon in 1790 and on Snowdon in 1791: the inadequacy of a literal faith in natural transcendence.

Frustrated, he goes on desperately to assert that Grasmere's dalesmen were not swearing, wrathful, selfish, envious people who shoot swans. They may have been poor, hungry and ill-clothed, but 'extreme penury is here unknown . . . they who want are not too great a weight / For those who can relieve' (440–48). This special pleading contradicts plentiful evidence in Dorothy's journal to the contrary. There was no moral counterforce equivalent to nature's mighty forms that could alleviate social poverty and political corruption, or take away from his responsibility to combat them.

When he reached this impasse, Wordsworth could write only a brief coda, which in fact becomes the moral guarantee, in a variety of forms, of all his subsequent failed efforts on *The Recluse*. Falling back into the same rhetorical habit of swerving from unstable argument to assertive personality that he had developed in 'Tintern Abbey', he projected an image of the one spiritual community he could vouch for:

> And if this
> Were not, we have enough within ourselves,
> Enough to fill the present day with joy
> And overspread the future years with hope—
> Our beautiful and quiet home, enriched
> Already with a Stranger whom we love
> Deeply, a Stranger of our Father's house,
> A never-resting Pilgrim of the Sea,
> Who finds at last an hour to his content
> Beneath our roof; and others whom we love
> Will seek us also, Sisters of our hearts,
> And one, like them, a Brother of our hearts,
> Philosopher and Poet, in whose sight
> These mountains will rejoice with open joy.
> Such is our wealth: O Vale of Peace, we are
> And must be, with God's will, a happy band!
> (859–74)

---

* The film shown at Wordsworth's Cockermouth birthplace under the auspices of the National Trust (as of the mid-1990s) exemplifies this simple linking of the 'essence' of his poetry to the Lake District landscape. It is understandable as a device to stimulate tourism: scene after scene is shown in glorious Technicolor, sometimes with a snippet of poetry, but more often with a rich baritone voice-over driving home the lesson that 'this is the place' – precisely the lesson 'Home at Grasmere' is unable to teach.

The upsetting social dimension exposed by the pair of missing swans is finally supplied by an image of an extended family, William and Dorothy, John, the Hutchinson sisters, and Coleridge. This was as far as Wordsworth's social vision could extend with confidence in 1800. The identification of the master poem with the master's life came too quickly. Having cast himself and Dorothy as the Adam and Eve of a new Eden, the strain of saving the world *from this place* soon proved to be too much.

He could not bring his *plot* to a satisfactory denouement, but he did manage to leap to a conclusion: the great 'Prospectus' of *The Recluse*, published with *The Excursion* in 1814. These lines conclude 'Home at Grasmere' by projecting a vision of what *could* fulfill the promises made by the poem. It begins, 'On Man, on Nature, and on Human Life,' the same phrase Wordsworth used to announce *The Recluse* in March of 1798. It establishes a balance between individual integrity and social responsibility in the world-as-given ('Nature'), that constitutes at once the glory and the stumbling block of the democratic Romantic imagination. In this vision, the individual genius is the inspirer, not the leader, of humanity, singing

> Of virtue and of intellectual power,
> Of blessed consolations in distress,
> Of joy in widest commonalty spread,
> Of the individual mind that keeps its own
> Inviolate retirement, and consists
> With being limitless the one great Life—
>   (966–71)

Invocations are supposed to begin, not end, poems. But Wordsworth says that his epic-to-come will surpass Milton's:

> . . . fit audience let me find though few!
>   Fit audience find though few—thus prayed the Bard,
> Holiest of Men. Urania, I shall need
> Thy guidance, or a greater Muse, if such
> Descend to earth or dwell in highest heaven!
> For I must tread on shadowy ground, must sink
> Deep, and, aloft ascending, breathe in worlds
> To which the Heaven of heavens is but a veil.
>   (972–79)

He justifies this out-stripping of Milton (from the invocation to Urania in Book VII of *Paradise Lost*) on the grounds that the heaven and hell of the new epic are higher and deeper than his predecessor's:

> Not Chaos, not
> The darkest pit of lowest Erebus,

Nor aught of blinder vacancy, scooped out
By help of dreams—can breed such fear and awe
As fall upon us often when we look
Into our Minds, into the Mind of Man—
My haunt, and the main region of my song.

(984–90)

Wordsworth's 'egotism' has been much on display in these pages, but it is a measure of his stature to reflect that millions of people believe this now, making their inner consciousness of themselves the psychic bedrock of their reality. In this sense, Wordsworth is not an egoist but a realist.

Having staked out his claim to his 'main region,' Wordsworth proceeded to elaborate its two adjacent territories, Nature and Society. Nature's Beauty is presented as a combination of the Promised Land, the Elysian Fields, and Paradise all rolled into one:

Beauty, whose living home is the green earth,

. . . .

. . . . waits upon my steps,
Pitches her tents before me when I move,
An hourly Neighbour. Paradise and groves
Elysian, fortunate islands, fields like those of old
In the deep ocean—wherefore should they be
A History, or but a dream, when minds
Once wedded to this outward frame of things
In love, find these the growth of common day?

(991–1001)

But Human Life, or Society, is presented far more negatively:

. . . I oft
Must turn elsewhere, and travel near the tribes
And fellowships of men, see ill sights
Of passions ravenous from each other's rage,
Must hear humanity in fields and groves
Pipe solitary anguish, or must hang
Brooding over the fierce confederate storm
Of Sorrow, barricadoed evermore
Within the walls of cities—may these sounds
Have their authentic comment, that even these
Hearing, I be not heartless or forlorn!

(1015–25)

Wordsworth constantly tried, and constantly failed, to integrate a vision of imaginatively redeemed society into *The Recluse*'s epic mission, as he had been doing since 'Tintern Abbey,' which uses some of these same images.

This is what halted his progress on 'Home at Grasmere,' and it continued to do so in each of his efforts to move *The Recluse* forward. His determination not to neglect 'Human Life' spelled the doom of *The Recluse*, but it also gave it its fitful glory, and guarantee that though it could not be finished, it could never be abandoned. It has long been a criticism of Wordsworth's egotism and his 'nature worship' that they lead him, in Matthew Arnold's phrase, to turn his eyes 'from half of human fate.'[20] But the manuscripts of his master-project, largely unpublished until recent times, show that he was determined to turn his vision *toward* 'the tribes and fellowships of men,' determined to give it 'authentic comment.'

He ended the 'Prospectus' with a prayer to a Holy Spirit of poetry for inspiration, that turns finally into a fourth topic, that appears to be an afterthought: himself, William Wordsworth. This shift soon led to his replacing *The Recluse* as his epic subject with a new and better one, the story of his own self-creation, *The Prelude*.

> And if with this
> I blend more lowly matter—with the thing
> Contemplated describe the mind and man
> Contemplating, and who and what he was,
> The transitory Being that beheld
> This vision, when and where and how he lived,
> With all his little realties [*sic*] of life—
> Be not this labour useless.
>
> (1034–41)

However, this was not a 'labour' that in 1800 he could quite conceive of as useful. He had followed Coleridge's orders and got back to work on *The Recluse*, which as Gill wonderfully says was rapidly becoming 'Coleridge's dream and Wordsworth's secret.'[21] He had produced a mythopoeic vision of Grasmere Vale as the Garden of Eden and discovered that, like its original, it could not stand the sight of sin or evil.

While this terrific creative struggle was working in Wordsworth's mind – in essence, the shaping struggle of his entire career – he was living a very ordinary happy life. The spring, summer, and autumn of 1800 were like the extended house-warming party of a newly married couple.

James Losh and his wife Cecilia, their distant cousin, came, the near-recruits of the German tour, first recipient of *The Recluse*'s birth announcement, and editor of *The OEconomist*, a journal devoted to nonviolent social reform. After John Marshall stopped by, the husband of Dorothy's oldest friend, Jane Pollard Marshall, Dorothy re-opened their correspondence. She tactfully tried to smooth over broken connections: 'My dear Jane, I will say nothing of my sorrow and remorse for having neglected you so long; . . . [but] Professions are idle and useless; you are disposed to love and to forgive me and I feel that I must trust to those kindly dispositions for your *entire* pardon.'[22]

In September their new friends the Clarksons came down from Eusmere. Catherine Clarkson rapidly became Dorothy's intimate friend, replacing Jane Pollard Marshall.[23] Also from the November walking tour came the Reverend Thomas Myers, his son Thomas, brother of William's school and college chum, now married to John Robinson's granddaughter, Lady Mary Nevill.

They began to draw some permanent visitors after them. Charles Lloyd came, still hanging on to the vision of creative community they had started in Somerset. He and his new wife moved into a house in Brathay near Ambleside in the autumn.[24] The Wordsworths could hardly object, since, despite the trouble Lloyd inevitably caused, he would soon be related to them by marriage. Christopher, tutoring Lloyd at Cambridge while they were in Germany, had fallen in love with Lloyd's sister Priscilla during a Christmas vacation visit, and they were soon engaged. Coleridge considered Lloyd a 'rascal'; Dorothy defended him, but admitted he was 'a dangerous acquaintance.'[25] Lloyd's main fixation was Coleridge, so he provides a more objective view of the Wordsworths: 'We have not any society except the Wordsworths'. They are very unusual characters. Indeed Miss W. I much like. But her Brother is not a man after my own heart. I always feel myself depressed in his society.'[26] Wordsworth was capable of great animation and vivacity, but only in the presence of a handful of picked people.

John Stoddart, a friend from the Montagu-Pinney set, showed up, returning from a tour of Scotland with his elegant friend, James Moncrieff. Stoddart was a nervy young man, but unlike Lloyd, he could be cultivated to some good. Wordsworth talked with him night and day when he was there, and arranged for him to write a review of the second edition *Lyrical Ballads* whenever it came out, an indication of his increasing professionalism. Stoddart was reading for the law, and would soon advance to the influential position of chief justice of Malta, Britain's primary Mediterranean naval base after Gibraltar.

Finally, there came Robert Jones, boon companion of the 1790 tour, to celebrate his friend's settling down, after a decade of wanderings, in the valley he would never leave.

But far the most important visitor was Coleridge, who arrived on 6 April.[27] He stayed for a month, and by the time he left it was decided he would return to live there – a repetition of the Racedown-to-Alfoxden drama. Dorothy set about making inquiries for suitable accommodation, and soon found Greta Hall in Keswick, a beautifully situated mansion owned by William Jackson, who ran a successful cartage company and was the model for the employer of Wordsworth's 'The Waggoner.'[28] The rent was £42 per year: reasonable, though much more than the Wordsworths were paying. But Jackson was a kindly indulgent soul, and he waived the first six months' rent, gave Coleridge the run of his substantial reference library, and became a sort of grandparent to little Hartley.[29]

Coleridge left for the south on 4 May to collect his family and make arrangements for the move north. On 14 May, William and John left for a visit of nearly a month at Gallow Hill, where Mary Hutchinson was now keeping house for her brother. They were going a–courting, though it was not perfectly clear just who was courting whom. Mary was of age and in possession of her inheritance, she was free to choose any suitor she wished. John was clearly the better prospect of the two, as he pointedly reminded her when he wrote at the end of the year, following his appointment as captain of the *Earl of Abergavenny*, that he expected to be 'a very *rich man*' from the China trade in less than ten years.[30]

In this era of arranged marriages, there are many stories of one brother (or sister) losing out to another in a competition that everyone understood to be fairly open. Jane Austen's *Persuasion* turns on the frustration of right and wrong choices in the marriage game. In real life too, it was by no means rare for the primary suitor's brother to end up as the bridegroom, or for a younger sister to win the bride's place. To the extent that John deferred to, or lost out to, William's courtship of Mary Hutchinson, we can add another item to the cost of the creation of the Poet. But, although William had been regarding Mary with renewed attention since his return from Germany, Mary for all her mildness had an independent mind of her own that chose him over his quiet brother, and she clearly admired the life style at Town End.

The real loser in this mating game was Dorothy. The purpose of the brothers' trip is unmistakeable from the fact of her being left behind, since she would otherwise have been a welcome companion. But the prospect of watching William pay his addresses to Mary would have been too painful to behold.

This is quite clear from her Grasmere journal, which begins precisely at the time of her two brothers' departure. Its opening passages show her feelings projected on to her landscape descriptions.[31] William's absence provoked a new and deeper voice in her journals, giving her landscape descriptions a more profoundly human weight and variety.

May 14th, 1800. Wm. and John set off into Yorkshire after dinner at ½ past 2 o'clock, cold pork in their pockets. I left them at the turning of Lowwood bay under the trees. My heart was so full that I could hardly speak to W. when I gave him a farewell kiss. I sate a long time upon a stone at the margin of the lake, and after a flood of tears my heart was easier. The lake looked to me, I knew not why, dull and melancholy, and the weltering on the shores seemed a heavy sound.[32]

This point at Lowwood is exactly where the 'little unpretending rill' empties into Windermere, the very spot at which she and William, six years earlier, had stopped for lunch on their walk from Kendal to Windy Brow to start living together for the first time in their lives. Steeling her will, Dorothy dedicated her journal to a very specific purpose, a love-offering: 'I resolved to write a journal of the time till W. and J. return, and I set about keeping my resolve, because I will not quarrel with myself, and because I shall give Wm. pleasure by it when he comes home again.'[33]

Two days later she started a letter to Mary, but could not finish it. A walk to Rydal gave her the courage to do so: 'Grasmere was very solemn in the last glimpse of twilight. I had been very melancholy in my walk back. I had many of my saddest thoughts, and I could not keep the tears within me. But when I came to Grasmere I felt that it did me good. I finished my letter to M.H. Ate hasty pudding and went to bed.'[34]

And so the entries continue, shifting from melancholy, to landscape, to restoration, to writing or receiving (or hoping for) letters, all the way through till William's return on 7 June. After three weeks, the letters and the person seemed indistinguishable: 'No letter, no William.' These are the diary entries of a woman whose heart is breaking but who is determined not to lose her mind under the strain.

She did not receive nearly as many letters as she sent, and near the end of the month she got one that called for still more resolve on her part. William wrote, 'When you are writing to France say all that is affectionate to A. and all that is fatherly to C.'[35] This is all that remains of a letter that Gordon Wordsworth destroyed.[36] It reminds us that Annette was always somewhere on their minds, despite the fact that very few letters between them ever made it through, and it opens a crack into their hidden world of intense relations. Dorothy had written to Gallow Hill to tell William about the letter from Annette, but 'all' that was left of the affection between him and Annette was something that it fell to Dorothy to express; he would not write the letter himself from Gallow Hill, nor even wait a week till he returned. He had felt for some time that his emotions were no longer engaged to Annette, possibly when the depths of Dorothy's passions were revealed in Germany, and they both realized the need for him to attach his passions elsewhere. Dorothy was used to writing to Annette, but that she should also be charged to say 'all that is fatherly' to Caroline does seem a cruel imposition.

When Dorothy's hero finally returned, at eleven o'clock at night on 7 June, they stayed up till four in the morning talking about the visit and its implications for their future together.[37] John only came the next day – possibly to give William time to break the news gently to Dorothy that he, not John, was likely to become Mary's husband.

The next three weeks were spent walking, fishing, and making minor household repairs. Coleridge, Sara, and baby Hartley arrived, on

29 June.[38] One fraught set of emotions was added on top of another. Each one of the five adults cramped into the three small sleeping rooms of the cottage had thoughts or dreams troubled by desire, jealousy, hope, and frustration. Any talk about the Hutchinsons made the Wordsworths edgy in ways that only they could know of, while Coleridge was oppressed by the same topic in ways that nobody knew but himself. Relations between Dorothy and Sara Coleridge were never of the best, and to have Sara there, six months pregnant, at such a time and in such close quarters, tried Dorothy sorely. They stayed a month before moving on to Keswick. In the north-south tug-of-war over the location of their creative headquarters, Wordsworth had won.

Wordsworth was pulling Coleridge to him, away from worldly success. While Wordsworth hunkered down in the country, Coleridge had risen to a high level of prominence as what we would now call a columnist. In only five months of writing leading paragraphs and columns for Stuart's *Morning Post*, he had achieved a position in contemporary social debates much more central than he had enjoyed five years earlier, and effectively greater than any he achieved later, except in posthumous reputation.

But urban literary life, for all its excitement, was a scene of intense strife and jealousy, as it always is, and now with the added pressure of dangerous political threats. So Wordsworth's northern blandishments fell on receptive ears. Coleridge like Wordsworth was more concerned about his long-term reputation than his immediate success, and he began to feel 'I have too much trifled with my reputation.'[39] He knew he had 'greatly improv[ed] both in knowledge and in power' as a result of writing under such pressure. But most of Coleridge's poetical contributions to the *Morning Post* were lightweight in comparison to his prose pieces, and he was again occasionally using Wordsworth's rejected poems to help fill out his obligations. He also reprinted seven of Wordsworth's poems from the 1798 *Lyrical Ballads* in the *Morning Post* between April and September, keeping his name before the public in anticipation of the new edition.[40] Still, he had begun to feel that his own days as a poet were numbered.

Both of these impulses, lust for immortality and disgust with the egotistical literary life, one the dark side of the other, connected with Wordsworth's similar concerns in 'Home at Grasmere' and the fledgling *Prelude*. Wordsworth's jealousy of his friend's new success is apparent in passages of 'Home at Grasmere' which try to reorient his provincial hideaway into a position of national centrality, with perhaps some hidden references to his clandestine activities in Germany. Though he and Dorothy were 'a pair seceding from the common world,' he insisted that their choice was actually the more socially responsible one:

> Society is here:
> The true community, the noblest Frame

Of many into one incorporate;

. . . .

    . . . a multitude
Human and brute, possessors undisturbed
Of this recess, their legislative Hall,
Their Temple, and their glorious dwelling-place.
                        (818–20, 825–28)

This is to say that effective social writing could be done just as well in Grasmere as in London: indeed, better. The tug of war between the two poets was not simply one between north and south, but between competing notions of where best to establish a centre of influence in national cultural debates, and with what kind of writing.

When he first came to Grasmere in early April, Coleridge had spent his free time finishing his translation of Schiller's *Wallenstein*. This was the 'money-book' on which he expended a great deal of effort in hopes of financial reward, though he gained very little. But the theme of the play as well as hopes for profit kept him engaged with it. *Wallenstein* was Schiller's effort to get beyond the *sturm und drang* of *The Robbers*, reflecting his reaction against the course of the French Revolution.[41] Like *The Robbers*, *Wallenstein* is a study in power and betrayal, asking how loyalty to the state and political necessity can be maintained when it threatens the integrity of one's principles and personal desires. The same question informs 'Home at Grasmere'.

The emotional temperature in this little gathering of English provincial gentry-professionals at Grasmere in July of 1800 rose to the degrees we usually associate with the more demonstrative Byron and Shelley circles on Lake Geneva in 1816, when creative inspiration, love, sexual attachment, and practical necessity came together in ways that would seem to make productive work impossible, but that became instead the defining creative moments of their existence.

CHAPTER THIRTY

A.k.a. *Lyrical Ballads*

Lyrical Ballads *of 1800*

. . . the human mind is capable of excitement without the application of gross and violent stimulants; and he must have a very faint perception of its beauty and dignity who does not know this, and who does not further know that one being is elevated above another in proportion as he possesses this capability. It has therefore appeared to me that to endeavour to produce or enlarge this capabilty is one of the best services in which, at any period, a Writer can be engaged; but this service, excellent at all times, is especially so at the present day.

('Preface', 1800)

In the supercharged emotional atmosphere of Grasmere, summer 1800, the single most famous edition of poetry in English began to be put together. Wordsworth had been composing at a great rate since arriving in Grasmere; his production in 1800 outstrips even the *annus mirabilis* of 1798. By midsummer he had written roughly the first half of 'Home at Grasmere' and the 'Prospectus' to *The Recluse*, as well as most of the poems that would make up a second volume in the new edition of *Lyrical Ballads*.

The first report of a new volume came from Coleridge to Southey on 10 April. 'Wordsworth publishes [i.e., will publish] a second volume of Lyrical Ballads & Pastorals. He meditates a novel – and so do I – but first I shall write my Tragedy.'*[1] From this report, the first title proposed for the

---

* What novels they were meditating is anybody's guess. Wordsworth had kept in mind since 1792 the idea of adapting Helen Maria Williams's story of the du Fosses to his own experiences; it ultimately became 'Vaudracour and Julia.' The recent letter from Annette, along with his request that Dorothy – not he – answer it, might have prompted him to distance the affair still further into the realm of fiction.

new volume seems to have been *Lyrical Ballads and Pastorals.* This squares with Wordsworth's note to 'The Brothers,' that he had intended to produce 'a series of pastorals, the scene of which is laid among the mountains of Cumberland and Westmorland.' Many of the new poems fit that description, and five have the word 'pastoral' in their sub-titles or notes, suggesting that a still more accurate title for the new volume could have been *Lake District Pastorals.* The title of the new edition was not planned to be *Lyrical Ballads* at all, and it only became so by default, when, despite seven months of Wordsworth's insistence to the contrary, his new publisher, Longman, finally refused his request to call the new publication by the title he really preferred: '*Poems in Two Volumes,* by W. Wordsworth.'[2] This title, not *Lyrical Ballads,* was Wordsworth's repeatedly specified title for the world-famous volumes that finally appeared in January 1801. Wordsworth's preferred title became exactly the title of his next publishing venture, *Poems, in Two Volumes,* by W. Wordsworth, in 1807. Coleridge reported this new title as a fact to Southey, Godwin, and others throughout the summer and autumn, further specifying that the title *Lyrical Ballads* was to be 'dropped' entirely, 'and his "Poems" substituted.'[3]

The title of the 1798 volume was to be dropped (or retained only for the first volume of the new edition) because most of Wordsworth's new poems did not fit the pattern established by his ten 'lyrical ballads' of 1798. They had formed the majority of his nineteen poems in the earlier volume, but only twelve of his much larger number of new poems (forty-one) were ballads at all, and only two of them had that strange quality of social criticism mixed with emotional expressivism that is so marked in 1798 ('Ruth' and 'Poor Susan,' both written earlier). The Matthew poems can be called 'lyrical ballads,' but though the Lucy poems are mysteriously lyrical, they are not ballads, except for 'Strange fits of passion.' His other new ballads were merely sentimental variations on the genre, like 'The Waterfall and the Eglantine' and 'The Oak and the Broom.' Wordsworth wanted nothing to do with his old title, which nevertheless got attached to his new volume. For him, the key word on the title page was not 'Poems.' but 'Wordsworth'.

As late as October, Wordsworth kept up a clear distinction between the old volume and the new one: 'The first Volume of these Poems, under the title of Lyrical Ballads, had already . . . been submitted to general perusal.' But the published preface drops the reference to a former title, with the result that *both* volumes were presumed to be *Lyrical Ballads,* as they have been from that day forward. A great deal of confusion would have been avoided on many counts had Wordsworth got the title he wanted. But a great deal of the controversy generated by his preface would also have been diminished, with incalculable effects for his and Coleridge's long-term reputations. They certainly did not plan it this way, for much of the controversy caused them no end of annoyance, but at the same time its continuance helped immeasurably to make them famous.

If Wordsworth had got the title he wanted, several things would be clearer. First, he did not consider the forty-one poems now published to be lyrical ballads in any meaningful sense, even though a few of them could be linked with the experimental poems of 1798. Secondly, the preface he composed in September did not define a concept that he labelled 'lyrical ballads.' The preface is not in fact concerned with defending hybrid genres, except to attack arbitrary distinctions between poetry and prose. Rather, it argues the need for a thorough renovation of polite definitions of poetry as a whole. Thirdly, because of Longman's insistence on sticking with the original title, all of the forty-one new poems have often, inappropriately, been discussed as lyrical ballads, sometimes with brilliantly ingenious results, but often with glaring inconsistencies – which are hardly surprising, considering that Wordsworth held no brief for them as lyrical ballads.

Having successfully drawn Coleridge to the north after him, Wordsworth now made it clear that he, not Coleridge, was the boss of the new project, enlisting old and new friends in the process. From July to October, he sent a constant stream of finicky, inconsistent directions, pleas, and orders to Cottle and to Humphry Davy, a brilliant young scientist friend of Coleridge's in Bristol whom he had never met, requiring attention to the smallest details of page set-up, white space, type bars, with frequent instances of that most annoying part of the printing process, revisions necessitated not by mistakes but by an author's second thoughts. Wordsworth's second thoughts often ran considerably beyond the number two.[4]

Poole and Wedgwood, who had been worried about Wordsworth's and Coleridge's 'amalgamation' in Germany, were horrified to hear Coleridge's new expressions of abasement before his friend's poetic genius. When Poole protested his 'prostration' before Wordsworth, Coleridge answered that 'since Milton no man has *manifested* himself equal to [Wordsworth].' He told Godwin he considered himself 'unworthy to unloose' the latch of Wordsworth's shoe.[5] To Wrangham, he said that Grasmere and Wordsworth were worthy of each other: 'neither to Man nor Place can higher praise be given.' 'He is a great, a true Poet – I am only a kind of Metaphysician.'[6] Statements like this go beyond admiration to masochism, making it appear that Coleridge had sunk below 'amalgamation' to something bordering on a willed incorporation into the body of Wordsworth's work.

Coleridge's name appears nowhere in the volume, though the five poems by the author's 'Friend' are listed in a note. That Coleridge's name should be so utterly elided seems unnecessary, considering the *éclat* it would have added, following his journalistic successes throughout the year. His name certainly did not 'stink' as it did in 1798, and Wordsworth's keeping it off the volume does not sort well with his telling Coleridge in 1799 not to deny 'the story that the L.B. are entirely yours' because such a story was 'the best thing that can befall them.'[7] The fact is that Wordsworth at the time did not have a clear idea of what he was talking about, as regards the value of a *name* in London's literary marketplace.

The poems which finally appeared in January were notably different than the nineteen poems by Wordsworth from 1798. None of the new poems approached the level of 'Tintern Abbey''s artistic achievement, but it could be argued that the overall level of sheer literary excellence is higher in 1800 than in 1798, when we consider the Lucy and Matthew poems, and 'The Brothers' and 'Michael.' Dorothy hoped that 'the second [volume] is much more likely to please the generality of readers.'[8] Only three of the poems in 1798 had a light or humorous tone, whereas fully a quarter of the 1800 poems are amusing. There were far fewer poems containing the kind of social critique Dr Burney had noticed. There is also much less concern with abnormal states of mind, and with the single clearest cause of this derangement in 1798: people being cast out of their homes or communities.

Instead, Wordsworth's new emphasis is on how communities, or more specifically *pairs or couples* as the smallest units of community, can be preserved. This theme was the motor driving 'Home at Grasmere,' and it continued into 'The Waterfall and the Eglantine,' 'The Oak and the Broom,' 'The Idle Shepherd-Boys,' 'The Two Thieves,' and others. The base situation of the 1798 poems had been a narrator's conversation with a solitary outcast; in 1800, the basic situation is a threatened loss of *partnership*, or a delayed, tragic recognition of its value, heretofore taken naively for granted. Not that the poems of 1800 are all happy ones; far from it. But their unhappiness arises from a suddenly perceived loss of love, in a relationship, a family, or a community, whereas in 1798 the great danger was mental breakdown, caused by apparent rejection from English society itself. The solitaries of 1798 have long since lost their mates or partners, and are struggling to stay in touch with, as the Female Vagrant says, their 'inner self.' The 1800 poems can be called more 'universal,' since they depend less on specific social causes from the late 1790s. But by the same token the losses they express, though real and painful, are much less extreme.

Almost all the poems Wordsworth composed for the second edition of *Lyrical Ballads* are concerned with the proper way to live among simple people in the country, usually explicitly identified as the Lake District. Quite apart from the larger issues Wordsworth addressed in his Preface, most of the poems actually composed in 1800 deal with everyday, practical questions of country living – which is to say, with his and Dorothy's own everyday experience. They are concerned with (1) how their new surroundings should be named or identified (five are gathered together as 'Poems on the Naming of Places'), (2) whether and how one should build there (four fall under the rubric of 'Rural Architecture'), and (3) how one should judge the customs of village folk (five poems like 'The Idle Shepherd-Boys').

Finally, there is a 'control' group of four or five poems dealing with the crisis-question (similar to 'Home at Grasmere') of how *prior love relationships* can be maintained in this new setting – or cannot be. 'The Brothers' is the first of these, and the first Wordsworth began composing after he and Dorothy settled in, while the last of this group, 'Michael,' is last in every way: last composed and also the thematic conclusion of the volume. 'Hart-Leap Well' forms a sort of travelling prologue to this theme, while 'The Waterfall and the Eglantine' and 'The Oak and the Broom' are lighter variations on this love theme.

In 'The Brothers,' a happily anticipated homecoming reunion is spoiled by the death of one of the brothers. This is an unlikely topic for the joyous mood that Wordsworth's return home has assumed in popular cultural mythology, but it is an altogether likely one for the dialectically contrary poet we can recognize in 'Home at Grasmere,' who often expressed the depths of his joy by exploring its opposite. Leonard the mariner has come home after twenty years at sea 'to resume / The life which he lived there.' Wordsworth too had effectively left his family home in 1779, following his mother's death, and returned twenty years later. John Wordsworth, from whom William and Coleridge had parted just a few days before they came to Ennerdale, where they heard the incident on which the poem is based, had gone to sea at age fifteen. Leonard's age is given as twelve at his departure, but Wordsworth changed this to fifteen when he republished the poem in 1815. The two boys were orphans whose grandparents outlived their parents, as also happened to the Wordsworth children. Their grandfather lost the lands which had been in the family for five generations, 'buffeted with bond, interest, and mortgages': a parallel to John Wordsworth Sr's losing his estate to the unpaid debts of Lord Lonsdale – and also to the precise number of generations through which the Wordsworths traced their family's emigration from Yorkshire to Cumberland to rebuild their gentry fortunes.

But all these parallels are given a reverse twist by Wordsworth. Leonard does not reveal his identity to the parish priest who tells him what happened to his brother James, because 'now, / The vale, where he had been happy, seemed / A place in which he could not bear to live.' There are just ten small words in one strong line, revealing Wordsworth's empathy with a self-created situation that holds up a tragic mirror to his own Ode to Joy. Leonard returns to sea, where he is now 'a grey-headed mariner.' This glances at Coleridge's 'old navigator,' but Leonard combines the roles of Ancient Mariner and Wedding Guest, becoming a sadder and a wiser man not from hearing fantastic tales of otherworldly deeds and spirits, but from a homely account of a common accident on the fells.

The five poems on 'The Naming of Places' are less about names than about the moral propriety of bestowing them on places not one's own. Like the broken-pair poems, these Wordsworthian Just-So stories are less explanations of how certain places got their names than cautionary lessons about the risks involved in presuming to *name* anything. As such, they reflect the lessons he learned from the difficulty of composing 'Home at Grasmere.' His textual note on the poems is commonsensical: 'By persons resident in the country and attached to rural objects, many places will be found unnamed or of unknown names, where little incidents will have occurred, or feelings been experienced, which will have given to such places a private and peculiar interest.'

William's identification with nearby Stone Arthur is the most straight-forward in this group. They passed beneath it almost daily on their walks between Town End and Town Head. It is 'the loneliest place we have among the clouds,' so Dorothy gave it 'my name.' But there was also a heavenly portent, whose significance is not revealed in the poem: 'The star of Jove, so beautiful and large / In the mid heavens, is never half so fair / As when he shines above [this eminence].' Jupiter was Wordsworth's planet in the astrology of his imagination, which he linked to the Star of Bethlehem in the 'Prospectus' to *The Recluse* to symbolize his hopes for his poetry. Nobody knew this but Dorothy, which gave her a title of authority to bestow the implied new name, William's Eminence.

'Emma's Dell' is really Emma's Waterfall, hinting that the waterfall in 'The Waterfall and the Eglantine' is also female: Dorothy's wild passion running roughshod over the mild compromises offered by William's eglantine – this replays in coded country allegory the sexual situation of the full version of 'Nutting.' Her waterfall-wildness is stressed repeatedly: 'wild nook,' 'wild place,' and so on. The waterfall hits the traveller with a shock of surprise as he labours up the Easedale path to where Blindtarn intersects with Sour Milk Ghyll. Just when everything seems softened 'down into a vernal tone . . . a deep contentment,' one turns a corner and confronts a waterfall so 'ardent' that all calm is fled. The shock wakes Wordsworth up to the realization that there is something *else*, beyond or different from nature's 'contentment' that is uncontrollably wild, and this quality he associates with Dorothy. Parallel to the language of tamed passion he addressed to Dorothy in 'Tintern Abbey' and in 'Nutting,' this passion will be acknowledged only 'Years after we are in our graves,' by the shepherds to whom he reveals his naming fantasy.

At the other end of the sequence, Mary's Nook is as peaceful as Dorothy's dell is wild. The pool described is in Rydal Upper Park, and '*we* have named [it] for you.' The name is assigned as the joint-title of William and Dorothy, honouring Mary-the-Peaceful. As always in these Grasmere moments of discovery, the title of authenticity is signed by death: the man who 'should plant his cottage here . . . would so love it that in his death hour / Its image would survive among his thoughts.'

'To Joanna' and 'Point Rash-Judgement' correct the other naming-poems' attempts to make one-to-one applications of their names to Grasmere's places. Coleridge makes his only appearance in the latter, but all three walkers – he, Dorothy, and William – are faulted for thinking that the peasant they see fishing should be out helping with the harvest. They have the sturdy middle-class response to the troubles of the working class: 'We all cried out, that he must be indeed / An idle man, who could thus lose a day / Of the mid harvest, when the labourer's hire / Is ample.' But when they came closer, they saw that he is 'too weak to labour in the harvest field.' Unlike similar poems in the 1798 volume, such as 'Simon Lee' and 'Goody Blake,' the thrust of this one is not against the social or human conditions that have worn the poor fisherman down, but against their own status as outsiders and observing moralists, who should know better than to leap to such rash judgments.

Like the morals tacked on to 'The Ruined Cottage' and 'The Ancient Mariner,' this one does not speak at all adequately to the man's condition. The poem's more important meaning comes at its beginning, in the hammer blows it directs at the dreamy scene it establishes, which many readers would unhesitatingly label Wordsworthian:

> . . . in our vacant mood,
> Not seldom did we stop to watch some tuft
> Of dandelion seed or thistle's beard,
> Which, seeming lifeless half, and half impell'd
> By some internal feeling, skimm'd along . . .
>
> (16–20)

But this easy reading of Nature's morality is harshly corrected by human evidence to the contrary, when they see the man 'using his best skill to gain / A pittance from the dead unfeeling lake / That knew not of his wants.'

Wordsworth linked 'Joanna's Rock' to 'Nutting' by saying that these two 'show the greatest genius of any poems in the second volume.'[9] But the stronger point of contact between the two is not their quality but their theme: two young womens' initiation into the mysteries of a religion celebrating an independent life in nature. Nineteen-year-old Joanna Hutchinson at first laughed at William's 'ravishment' when he stood before the 'intermixture of delicious hues' on the side of a tall rock beside the river Rotha between Grasmere and Rydal. But when her laughter echoes hyperbolically through the entire Lake District, from Skiddaw in the north to Kirkstone in the south, 'the fair Joanna' is drawn 'to my side . . . as if she wish'd / To shelter from some object of her fear.' For this involuntary recognition of something akin to the laughter of the gods, Wordsworth carved Joanna's name on the rock, something like enrolling her in an illicit religion, professed by us 'who look upon the hills with tenderness.' His honouring of Joanna's spontaneous fear is set against the disapproval of the old religion, represented by the 'gloomy' Grasmere vicar who chides Wordsworth for apparently 'reviving obsolete Idolatry . . . like a Runic Priest.' Though not a Druid, Wordsworth was becoming in effect the priest of a new dispensation, that finds and worships spirit in different places and in different ways than Christianity.

The four poems on 'rural architecture' present the negative corollary to the positive lessons of the 'Poems on the Naming of Places.' Though he was self-indulgent toward his group's naming of places, he was very hard on any improper building in his paradise. His main complaint was against newcomers whitewashing their houses, making them stand out too starkly from the surrounding landscape. A close second was cutting down stands of native trees to replace them with more 'picturesque' varieties or, worse, plantations of fast-growing, profitable larches for the lumber industry.

The tonic-note of this group is struck by the 'Lines written with a Slate-pencil upon a Stone, the largest of a heap lying near a deserted Quarry, upon one of the Islands at Rydale.' It explains how Sir William Fleming, ancestor of Michael Le Fleming of Rydal Hall, finally did *not* build his 'pleasure-house' on the tiny island just off the shore of Rydal Water. He desisted when he discovered that 'a full-grown man might wade' from the shore to the island, 'and make himself a freeman of this spot.' The place itself prevented him from commiting an outrage upon it, and so his remaining heap of building stones is a monument to his educability. The poem cautions those who, like William and Dorothy, come 'on fire with . . . impatience to become / An Inmate of these mountains . . . disturb'd / By beautiful conceptions.' But the stones of Sir William's *un*built mansion provides a symbolic platform for the right kind of local builders: 'the linnet and the thrush, / And other little builders who dwell here.'

Against this negative example, Wordsworth sets three other examples of architecture that are appropriate to his unique sense of the region. The 'outhouse' or small barn on Grasmere island (a later version of which is still there) makes the obvious connections for modern, post-Romantic readers, though they were more novel in 1800. Though it is 'rude,' and though other buildings 'have maintained / Proportions more harmonious,' still 'the poor / Vitruvius of our village' has here created 'a homely pile' whose form follows its function, of sheltering lambs and heifers. But it also has another more special function, combining the ordinary and the fantastic in a new measure: it provides a place where 'one Poet' can make 'his summer couch' and look out through its door to see 'Creations lovely as the work of sleep, / Fair sights, and visions of romantic joy.'

This 'poor Vitruvius' 'had no help / From the great city,' and Wordsworth in the poem specifically titled 'Rural Architecture' explicitly distances himself from the kinds of work he had seen going forward in cities in the 1790s. He joins some neighbour boys of good family, 'George Fisher, Charles Fleming, and Reginald Shore,' in building a stone man on the top of Great How at the north end of Wythburn (now Thirlmere); they name him 'Ralph Jones, the Magog of Legberthwaite dale.' This stone construction is perfectly attuned to the celebration of both man and nature: when the winds blow it down, 'the very next day / They went and they built up another.' In 1800 Wordsworth included a final stanza that made the application of this simple lesson considerably more pointed:

> —Some little I've seen of blind boisterous works
> In Paris and London, 'mong Christians or Turks,
> Spirits busy to do and undo:
> At remembrance whereof my spirits will flag.
> —Then, light-hearted Boys, to the top of the Crag!
> And I'll build up a Giant with you.
>
> (19–24)

With these lines, we see that Wordsworth joins in the boys' sport as therapy for his traumatic years in Paris and London. The 'spirits busy' there were not building houses but a 'giant' New Man, actively in the French Revolution or abstractly in the perfectibilian extremes of Godwin's *Political Justice*, both of which Wordsworth now regards as 'blind boisterous works.' Running lightheartedly with the neighbour boys to the top of Great How, 'to build up a Giant with' them, Wordsworth also has his own hidden agenda, for an architecture not built with stones but with spirit: *he* is that Giant, but in a new dispensation ('the Giant Wordsworth, God love him').

The deep message of his 'Inscription' for the site of St Herbert's Hermitage on the island in the middle of Derwent-Water is the same: there is now a spirit in these Lake District places that recognizes and can build upon the spirit of the place. According to Bede's *Ecclesiastical History*, St Herbert prayed every night that he might die at the same moment as his former helpmate, St Cuthbert, who had moved to a similar solitary confinement on Windermere. The inscription is thus not really for the building but for the kinds of spirits that inhabit it, and about isolated spots where one stays true to one's beloved. It is thus addressed to a person very like Wordsworth himself and his own present love situation, whether the reference is to Dorothy or Coleridge, or both:

> If thou in the dear love of some one friend
> Hast been so happy, that thou know'st what thoughts
> Will sometimes, in the happiness of love
> Make the heart sink, then wilt thou reverence
> This quiet spot.
>
> (1–5)

This is the state of mind he called 'Strange fits of passion,' and it illustrates his dire need for 'emotion recollected in tranquillity.'

The poems in *Lyrical Ballads* of 1800 about local people and customs are milder versions of the tales of tragic fortitude that Wordsworth added to 'Home at Grasmere' in 1806, to give it moral ballast. Among them, only 'The Childless Father' tries to be serious, and it merely wonders if, 'perhaps,' old Timothy the huntsman thought of his dead daughter when he took the house keys with him as he left to join the fox hunt on 'Hamilton's grounds.' She had died but six months earlier. The spectator-narrator cannot say anything directly about the state of Timothy's moral refinement, for 'in my ears not a word did he speak.' But he is pretty sure on the basis of other evidence: 'he went to the hunt with a tear on his cheek.' Modern readers often treat the title of this poem as if it were the more expectable 'Fatherless Child,' rather than the other way around.

The other local-colour poems treat real or potential moral dilemmas with a much lighter touch. The idle shepherd boys don't attend to their business, daring each other to cross a deep crevice on a narrow out-cropping, and very nearly lose a valuable lamb as a result. They fetch a conveniently nearby 'poet' to rescue it, who 'gently' upbraids them, 'And bade them better mind their trade.' This is brave, when a poetical new-comer instructs the locals in their moral duty, but the man who would 'so converse' with the shepherds was of course Wordsworth. But the trite moral of 'The Idle Shepherd-Boys' is not its point. Instead, its theme is a redaction of *Et in Arcadia ego* with a happy ending, thanks to a saviour who is 'A Poet . . . who loves the brooks / Far better than the sages' books.' There is no reason in the world that he should, except for the fact of his identity: William Wordsworth.

The symbolic consequence of one of the boys' leap across the crevice is to make him appreciate what he has only when he seems about to lose it all, halfway across the arch: 'he hears a piteous moan— . . . his heart within him dies – / His pulse is stopp'd, his breath is lost . . . / And, looking down, he spies / A Lamb, that in the pool is pent / Within that black and frightful rent' (60–66). In this, its moment of truth, 'The Idle Shepherd-Boys' anticipates the two crucial visionary self-recognition scenes of *The Prelude*. They are also on mountains, but their lost sheep is

William Wordsworth, and their 'frightful rent' is 'the mind's abyss' in the Simplon Pass and 'the deep and gloomy breathing-place' on Snowdon.

'Andrew Jones' is about a hateful man who steals pennies from crippled beggars and teaches his children to do the same. Hence Wordsworth's opening line, 'I hate that Andrew Jones,' only seems like comic hyperbole. He really does hate him, and wants to deport him from paradise in the worst possible way, in contemporary terms: '[I] wish'd the press-gang, or the drum / With its tantara sound, would come / And sweep him from the village!' The press-gang and the recruiting officers were villains to Wordsworth's earlier victims, like the sailor and soldier in the Salisbury Plain poems. But here they have become subsidiary demons policing paradise, wishfully called out to rid it of unworthy spirits.

'The Two Thieves' is the comic antidote to Andrew Jones. The 'thieves' were real people, old Daniel MacKeith and his grandson, aged ninety and three, respectively, who went about Hawkshead stealing wood chips, peat, and other small things lying about. But everyone on the village knew Daniel's daughter would 'gladly repair all the damage that's done.' In just letting him be, Wordsworth treats him the same as the Old Cumberland Beggar, and a surprising last line drives this moral home harder than we expect: 'Long yet may'st thou live, for a teacher we see / That lifts up the veil of our nature in thee.' Wordsworth's note to the poem pretends that its moral is the recognition that we may all come to such pitiable senility. But the poem strongly suggests that behind 'the veil of our nature' is a fundamental larceny in our souls, the problem of evil that 'Home at Grasmere' confronted, and that the *Lyrical Ballads* of 1800 tries to defuse.

Finally, little Barbara Lewthwaite, the Wordsworths' next-door neighbour, cannot understand why her 'Pet-Lamb' will not eat or drink: 'Drink, pretty Creature, drink!' she urges. Wordsworth identifies with her to such an extent 'that I almost received her heart into my own,' and the rest of the poem is a kind of poetical transmigration into Barbara's mind and heart, as Wordsworth imagines what she would say if she could write a poem. The apparent subject of the poem is thus the programmatic one for the volume: the poetry implicit in the souls of ordinary folk. But the deeper subject, unstated but strongly implied, is again the troubling one of 'Home at Grasmere,' the question as to whether *either* of its characters, little girl or adult narrator, can penetrate to the sense of loss that makes the *lamb* unhappy:

> —poor Creature can it be
> That 'tis thy Mother's heart which is working so in thee?
> Things that I know not of belike to thee are dear,
> And dreams of things which thou canst neither see nor hear.
>
> (49–52)

The poet tries to interpret the girl trying to interpret the lamb, but it is one thing to receive a little girl's heart into one's own, quite another to inhabit the soul of another species.

The Great Preface

Most of these poems were finished by the beginning of July. During July and August, Wordsworth sent them off in batches to Biggs and Cottle. With this work in train, Wordsworth turned in early September to composing a preface which he thought the new edition needed. But in the immediate circumstances of his life, the famous preface to *Lyrical Ballads* arose from issues having as much to do with *The Recluse* as with the poems in the 1800 edition. Just as the new volume's title was in a real sense inaccurate, or unintended, so the preface is frequently concerned with issues quite different than the poems in the volumes, especially when they are considered 'lyrical ballads.' Like his preferred title (which was still '*Poems*, by W. Wordsworth' at this point, so far as he knew), the preface was more an introduction of himself and his views on poetry than of the individual poems in either volume.

Coleridge promised to help compose the preface; indeed, though its ideas arose out of mutual conversations, 'it was at first intended, that the Preface should be written by me [Coleridge].'[10] This would have been a sensible arrangement: one man writing a preface to a new edition of his friend's work. Coleridge was far better qualified to write such a preface, and he would come to wish very much that he *had* written it, for he spent much time over the next fifteen years explaining which ideas in it were his and which were not, trying to extricate himself from what soon became a permanent English cultural tradition: attacking or defending the claims made in the preface to *Lyrical Ballads*. Defending himself against the excesses of Wordsworth's preface was Coleridge's most important motive for writing his *Biographia Literaria* (1817), which explained his entire literary life in terms of its relations, pro and con, to Wordsworth's theory and practice. For Coleridge clearly recognized what is only now becoming apparent, that much of Wordsworth's preface was itself a literary biography, displacing into another literary genre Wordsworth's other contemporaneous efforts to write himself large, *The Recluse* and *The Prelude*.

Coleridge had had ideas similar to those expressed in the preface about the philosophic tendency of poetical expressions at least since 1796. In his preface to *Sonnets by Various Authors* that year, he spoke of his poems' generating 'a habit of thought' which tends to 'create a sweet and indissoluble union between the intellectual and the material world.' In a brief prefatory note attached to his 'Introduction to the Ballad of the Dark Ladie,' he coyly apologized for publishing 'a simple story, wholly uninspired with politics or personality' in these days when, 'amid the hubbub of Revolutions,' one novelty followed after another 'so rapidly.' This directly anticipates Wordsworth's statement about the debilitating effects of mass media in modern urban life: 'The most effective of these causes [that "blunt the discriminating powers of the mind, and . . . reduce it to a state of almost savage torpor"] are the great national events which are daily taking place.' The two men shared the same conviction, that poetry – their kind of poetry – was more important than these great events, and that it might even provide a way toward solving the dilemmas that they create.

In his notebooks entries in late August, Coleridge spoke of the 'recalling of passion in tranquillity,' and of 'poetry [as] past passion with pleasure,' phrases that clearly anticipate Wordsworth's 'emotion recollected in tranquillity.' In Coleridge's idealist mind-set, any topic was immediately generalized to universal, metaphysical dimensions. While Wordsworth was composing the preface, Coleridge told Davy he was meditating an essay on poetry that 'would in reality be a *disguised* System of Morals and Politics.'[11] This too is an aspect of Wordsworth's preface, for many of the poems in the volumes were still, in the two authors' minds, part of a covert programme of cultural warfare against established moral and political powers as well as literary ones.

So, like *The Recluse*, the preface was a text of philosophical social reform that Coleridge first wanted to write himself, but then urged Wordsworth to write instead.[12] It covers many of the same topics as *The Recluse*, obscurely transposed into issues of rhyme, metre, and diction. The motive of the preface is thus vastly incommensurate with its matter. Not only is 'the intention behind the *Lyrical Ballads* pastorals quite as large as that which had conceived *The Recluse*,' it is in essence the *same* intention.[13] The key terms of *The Recluse* – 'On Man, on Nature, and on Human Life' – are present in the preface's central formulations, as when Wordsworth refers to 'the most valuable object of all writing, whether in prose or in verse, the great and universal passions of men [Man], the most general and interesting of their occupations [Society], and the entire world of nature [Nature].' But the scope of *The Recluse*'s ambition, which was nothing less than the secular redemption of society, was much too big for a preface, especially one that appears to introduce poems that, whatever their merits, are much slighter productions than we would expect for an epic of human secular redemption. Nonetheless, enough of the heroic impulse imbedded in the preface does shine through it to help explain how it achieved its hold on English-speaking audiences everywhere.

Of all the creative confusions and cross-purposes which helped to make the preface to *Lyrical Ballads* such a controversial document in English literature and culture – guaranteeing the centrality of Wordsworth's reputation both as a target of attack and as a rock of defence – none has been more overlooked than this one: that the preface is motivated by the Poet's duty to renew his entire culture, English in the first instance, but implicitly universal. A theory of the creative imagination's role in improving human society is presented mainly in terms of a theory of poetics: metrics, diction, and style. The connections between the two can be worked out, but it takes a lot of time and hard work, far beyond what readers normally expect to give to a preface, and many loose ends are still left hanging.

Once it was clear that Coleridge was not going to help, Wordsworth completed the entire preface, arguably the most influential document of literary theory in English, in the last two weeks of September.[14] He was so full of energy for his self-defining project that he began and nearly finished yet another preface, which would have introduced the second volume. But he decided not to print it because it grew too long from the many quotations that 'must unavoidably be spun into it.'[15] If we take the first preface as a measure of Wordsworth's ideas of length, this second one must have been very long indeed. From his mention of the many quotations in it, it sounds like an early version of the 'Essay, Supplementary to the Preface' that he published with his first collected edition in 1815. That essay is essentially a polemical history of English literature as a spiritual progression leading toward the works of William Wordsworth.

Wordsworth's tone in the 1800 preface is at once very aggressive and very defensive. It is the speech of a man convinced of the purity of his goals and motives, but unsure of the arguments he is using to defend them. Repeatedly, Wordsworth goes further than he needs to in urging his claims, particularly in his long, turgid insistence on the essential identity between the language of poetry and that of prose. He was trying to say everything he most deeply believed all at once, on the first real occasion he had to do so in his life. He strains to unify everything, to assert the kind of moral authority he felt he must have as the bard of *The Recluse*: high seriousness and low subjects, poetry and prose, the great literature of the past and his own poems in the present. He often starts much further down, at the foundations of his subjects, than he needs to, or than most readers would expect him to in a mere preface. But this foundational aspect of the preface is what forces its claims upon our permanent attention: its delving into the nature of the human mind, and the mind's relations to language and the external world.

Wordsworth was implying a full field theory of the way in which language-in-culture affects and even constitutes human nature in social forms. The *presumption* that language and mind do interact in this way to produce culture and society is very largely accepted, two hundred years later, in societies worried about cultural products far more pernicious than 'frantic novels, sickly and stupid German Tragedies, and deluges of idle and extravagant stories in verse.' His interest was partisan, not abstract, because he wished to *change* the present unhappy situation: he clearly believed that 'the present taste' of the country *was* 'depraved.' He set up a standard of value according to which progress could be measured. In a time when talk of 'the rights of man' had begun to sound a bit hollow, if not seditious, Wordsworth proposed a theory not of human equality but a hierarchy based on the value of the healthy human mind in a depraved society. Far from being a 'leveller' as Hazlitt would later describe him, Wordsworth at this point was a democratic elitist. 'One being is *elevated above another* in proportion as he possesses the quality' of *not* requiring 'gross and violent stimulants' for the excitement or healthy exercise of his mind. This sets up a hierarchy of sensibility, or imagination, apart from the civil rights of citizenship. Stimulating this higher type of imagination is 'the best service' that a Writer 'can be engaged in at the present time,' because there are so many more forces working to support and extend these degrading forces than there are counteracting them. They are pervasive and inter-connected: the 'great national events which are daily occurring,' the growth of cities (as poor country people came to find employment in the war economy), the boring, uniform tasks of the emerging industrial system (stimulated by the needs of the war), which produce in turn a craving for 'extraordinary incident,' 'gratified' by 'hourly intelligence' (newspapers), bringing full circle the system of language/mind stimulation and degradation to which Wordsworth alluded at the outset.

The preface thus aims at a whole system of cultural production, setting up a literary Oppositional 'cottage industry' to counter 'great national events.' Wordsworth's confidence is however not based on his poems alone; he is not so unguarded. Rather, it was his faith in 'certain inherent and indestructible qualities of the human *mind*' that gave him confidence to await 'the approach of a *time* when the evil will be systematically opposed by men of greater powers and with far more distinguished success.' No one has ever suggested who these 'men' might be, but from their position at the end of a long sequence of arguments promising a vast vindication in the future, we immediately recognize Wordsworth's rhetorical strategy from 'Tintern Abbey' in 1798, the 1799 *Prelude*, and the 1800 'Prospectus' to *The Recluse*. As at those moments, his point of reference is himself and Coleridge, and he is referring to their major projects, to which *Lyrical Ballads* was, in 1800 as in 1798, dedicated primarily as a prospectus, fund-raiser, and advertising flier.

While Wordsworth was pushing the preface to a conclusion, riding rough-shod through logical impasses, guided by the light of his emerging conception of the Poet, Coleridge, instead of helping Wordsworth's argument, was trying to finish a great work of his own. For about two months, between August and October, the plan was that 'a Poem of Mr Coleridge's was to have concluded the Volumes.' This poem was 'Christabel.'[16] Wordsworth thought that the second preface he drafted was justified by the bulk of a volume that would contain a 'new long poem' by his friend. As late as the first week in October, 'Christabel' was still scheduled with the printers for inclusion.[17]

On 4 October Coleridge read to William and Dorothy at Grasmere all of 'Christabel' that he had completed – largely the poem as we know it today, ending with any further action ominously suspended between the protagonists. Sir Leoline berates his daughter Christabel for her apparently inhospitable looks at Geraldine, the witch who unbeknownst to him has seduced Christabel the night before, after Christabel has rescued Geraldine from what she represents to Christabel as a gang-rape by 'five warriors.' William and Dorothy were 'exceedingly delighted' with it the night they heard it, and they heard it again the next day with 'increasing pleasure.' But Wordsworth soon began to have doubts about it, and three days later it was out of the project. Wordsworth's unilateral decision against 'Christabel' severely damaged Coleridge's self-confidence as a poet. He had crucially recognized Wordsworth as Milton's successor when nobody else in the world would have done so, but Wordsworth's brutal commitment to his poetic programme did not permit him a similar generosity toward Coleridge.

Wordsworth's treatment of 'Christabel' reflected his new attitude toward 'The Ancient Mariner,' because it was in the same suspicious supernatural vein. He felt that 'Christabel,' slightly longer in its final form than 'The Ancient Mariner,' was ill-suited to the contents of the rest of the volumes.[18] He told Longman that 'the style of this Poem was so discordant from my own' that it was better to drop it.[19] In fact, its difference in style, otherwise unexceptionable (it was after all announced as being by another author), amounted to a contradiction in terms, once the high argument of the preface had been set forth at such length.

Coleridge morosely conceded to Davy that Wordsworth 'thought it indelicate to print two Volumes with *his name* [Coleridge's italics] in which so much of another man's work was included – & which was of more consequence – the poem was in direct opposition to the very purpose for which the Lyrical Ballads were published.'[20] What Coleridge wanted, more than credit or profit, was support and encouragement, and this is just what he did not get from Wordsworth. True, he had let Wordsworth down on the preface, he had written none of the poems he promised for the Naming of Places group, and he remained painfully prone to denigrating his own abilities before Wordsworth. Nonetheless, such discouragement at such a time was a nearly mortal wound to his poetic spirit.

By rejecting 'Christabel,' Wordsworth not only lost the justification for his long second preface, he also effectively cut off the last quarter of the second volume as it then stood, presenting himself with the necessity of coming up with a poem or poems of similar length to replace it. This poem was 'Michael.'[21] Publication was delayed for a full three months until Wordsworth could finish it, beginning from 12 October.

'Michael' is the conclusive poem of the 1800 *Lyrical Ballads* in every sense. Aside from unpleasant circumstances of its composition, and the moot question of whether it would have been composed without them, Wordsworth's production of it over the next two months was a remarkable indication of his fully-developed powers as a professional poet. He could, virtually on demand, write a powerful poem to order, appropriate to both the contents of the volume in question and, even more impressive, fully congruent to the theoretical requirements laid down in its preface. 'Michael' is, in this respect, the only poem in the entire collection to have been written to the specification of a previously enunciated theoretical model, since it alone follows rather than precedes the preface in time of composition. It does this particularly with regard to Wordsworth's dictum that, in these poems, unlike most narrative poems, the feeling was to give importance to the action rather than vice versa.

The story's action is quickly told: Michael's son Luke leaves home to earn money to save the family's lands, but falls into dissipation and flees the country. But the *feeling* of the story is almost unspeakable, being entirely contained in the vignette of Michael's repeated returns to the sheepfold the two of them started on the day Luke left: he 'never lifted up a single stone.' Wordsworth confirmed the poem's theoretical importance by claiming that 'Michael' contained his most important 'views.'

It was not easy. Dorothy recorded ten days of discouragement for every one day of good work. There are more than a few similarities – which can hardly be coincidental – between its situation and that of the poem it replaced, 'Christabel,' despite their superficial differences. Both are Lake District family tragedies caused by an excess of fatherly pride: Sir Leoline's, for his reputation, and Michael's, for what amounts to much the same thing, his financial independence and land ownership. In both, a beloved only child is lost to 'dissipation,' though Christabel is overtly seduced by Geraldine whereas Luke gives in to 'evil courses' in the 'dissolute city.' Both poems are set roughly along the western edge of the Helvellyn-Fairfield range of hills. Michael's sheepfold is located in Greenhead Ghyll just below Stone Arthur, and though Sir Leoline's castle is in Langdale, Geraldine's father's house is modelled on Castle Rock of Triermaine, which is at the north end of Thirlmere, just beyond Great How, where Wordsworth had fancied himself helping the local boys build 'the Magog of Legburthwaite vale.' It was also known as 'The Enchanted Castle of St John's.'[22]

At its very beginning, 'Michael' was called simply 'The Sheepfold.' Dorothy records them setting out on 11 October to find it, which they did: 'built nearly in the form of a heart unequally divided.'[23] This means they went looking for a landmark that someone had told them about, perhaps in response to a direct request for some information on which Wordsworth could base a tale, the same method he had used so efficiently in Somerset in writing his first *Lyrical Ballads*. Tales of losing land by foreclosure were so common in the hard times of 1799–1800 that Wordsworth's jottings in 'Ballad Michael' suggest it had become almost the standard story of the region:

> it is the first
> Which in this vale our children hear, perhaps
> A hundred and a hundred years again
> 'Twill be retold among us—[24]

As a place-bonding story 'Michael' has the archetypal quality of telling how someone who left a tightly-knit community suffered bad consequences, and left his family to mourn. This is strongly reinforced by Wordsworth's allusions to tales of the Patriarchs of Genesis and their sons. Since the impulse of young people in provincial places is often to escape, especially when times are hard, such a tale serves as a cautionary threat. Several of the local versions of the story available to Wordsworth were about young men running away from home to seek fame and fortune in the city, sometimes finding it, sometimes not. But all these stories put the onus for blame (or praise) on the young man, whereas in 'Michael' Luke is sent away *by* his father to save the family: he fails, but the responsibility falls back on the father for the course of action he chose for his son.

There were several aspects in this situation that Wordsworth found easy to develop because they applied to his own life in the region. He too had been a promising local boy of suddenly reduced expectations who was sent out into the world to help recoup his family's fallen fortunes. And he, like Luke, had failed in that effort, both in the world's eyes and in the eyes of most of the members of his extended family. To them, and perhaps to himself, it might well have appeared that 'in the dissolute city [he] gave himself / To evil courses,' since this could as easily refer to political activism as to the fleshly pleasures we more usually supply for such a phrase. A 'shame' so great as to drive Luke into exile 'beyond the seas' could only, given the story's circumstances, have something to do with money. But the language that Wordsworth used to describe this 'shame' ('dissolute city,' 'evil courses,' 'ignominy and shame') is so close to that of 'Tintern Abbey' and the yew tree lines that we must feel Luke's experience is very close to Wordsworth's own, in terms of temptations and possibilities if not in literal fact.

Furthermore, Michael's problems arose from the failure of yet another son, 'his brother's son,' to whom Michael had pledged some of his own lands 'in surety.' This is what Richard Wordsworth of Whitehaven had done for the three younger sons of his dead brother, John Wordsworth, Sr.

He had not pledged land in bond to their fiscal responsibility, but he was liable for the bills they contracted, especially those of the eldest of the three, William, who not only contracted many more debts than his brothers John and Christopher, but who had also much less prospect of ever paying him back for his outlays. In addition, Richard Wordsworth's own son, Robinson, had been cruelly inconvenienced at the time of entering adult life (college and marriage), and perhaps compromised into secret government work, by the refusal and inability of that other Prodigal Son, William, to pay off the debts he had accumulated, in process of becoming what he called 'a chosen Son.'

But the poem's blame for this falls hardest on Michael. If we pay attention to the poem, rather than to the sentimental images often conjured up from it, we can see that more goes through the old man's mind than the simple fact that Luke will never return, or even that he may lose half his land and that things will never be the same again. As a Lake District tragedy, and a common one at that, the blame in Wordsworth's poem falls squarely on the hubris of the father – as it does in its supernatural double, 'Christabel,' that it replaced. Michael's decision that Luke should be sent to *earn* the needed bond money sets the tragedy in motion. This decision is what goes through Michael's mind as he contemplates the unfinished sheepfold, not Luke's weakness and errors. Michael is something like the shepherd in 'The Last of the Flock,' but his possessiveness is brought out not by poverty but by pride of ownership. The lands had been 'burdened' (under lien) when they came to Michael and not till he was forty was even half of his inheritance really his. He was a workaholic, and it only occurs to him late in life that he might want an heir to receive all that he has built up: he is sixty-six when Luke is born. He 'lov'd his Helpmate; but to Michael's heart / The Son of his old age was yet more dear,' and he starts taking the boy out to work with him at a very early age. By age five Luke was 'to his office *prematurely* called,' and by age ten he 'could stand against the mountain blasts.'

The pathetic scene of Michael's last conversation with Luke at the sheepfold opens into language that comes close to revealing the selfish tendency of Michael's reasoning. He lays a heavy burden of paternal guilt, or psychological debt, on Luke, telling him how much he has loved him since his birth. He takes the boy on a narrative tour of all the events of his life, and though 'Luke had a manly heart' he soon starts sobbing aloud with gratitude. This finally forces Michael to realize, 'Nay . . . I see / That these are things of which I need not speak.' He then points to the sheepfold as the 'covenant' between them: another bond to be kept, but not by money. 'I knew that thou could'st never have a wish / To leave me, Luke, —thou hast been bound to me / Only by the links of love.' Michael here sounds nearly as much like 'The Mad Mother' as like the father of 'The Last of the Flock' – or like Wordsworth himself at the end of

'Tintern Abbey,' pleading with Dorothy to keep his life in her mind forever.

'Michael' rounds off the defining pattern of broken pairs and broken homes that strikes the dominant note of the new poems Wordsworth wrote in 1800 at Grasmere. In it, the pair poems, the place poems, and the local customs poems of the new volume all come together, in the up-gathering conclusion of the entire volume. The unfinished structure of the sheepfold stands for human disappointment amid nature's beauty. It represents the tragic disappointment of the very hopes that its central symbol was supposed to represent. The unfinished sheepfold is the broken bond of love, as perhaps it seemed to William and Dorothy from the first moment they saw it, looking like 'a heart unequally divided.' In relation to Wordsworth's hopes for Grasmere almost exactly twelve months earlier, this poem, completed on 9 December 1800, represented a strong corrective to what he now recognized as very naïve hopes. Everything is gone: 'the ploughshare has been through the ground / On which it stood.' Like the village tales he later tacked on to 'Home at Grasmere,' 'Michael' shows his awareness that the assumption of an easily enduring link between land, man, and language could not stand the test of reality. In 'Home at Grasmere,' another bonding symbol of the human significance of the natural landscape, the paired swans, was all too easily broken, throwing both poet and his poem into disarray. But 'Michael,' rather than developing an explanation for why this ideal is not tenable, conveys instead the devastating realization that it cannot be so.

Just as the concerns of *The Recluse* are buried beneath the alternatively turgid and splendid arguments of the preface, so are they evident in 'Michael.' Wordsworth defended his reference to 'the earliest of those Tales that spake to me / Of Shepherds' because they spoke to him 'On man, the heart of man, and human life' (33), words virtually identical to those with which he announced the birth of the *Recluse*-project two and a half years earlier. But where 'Home at Grasmere' finally achieved a satisfactory conclusion by Wordsworth's attaching the forward-looking vision of the 'Prospectus' on to its tales of tragedy, Michael gets no such satisfaction: he knows his lands are lost and his dreams destroyed. By telling Michael's story, Wordsworth hoped to achieve what was denied Michael, not in his land holdings but in his own stock in trade, poetry:

> *Therefore*, although it be a history
> Homely and rude, I will relate the same
> For the delight of a few natural hearts,
> And with yet fonder feeling, for the sake
> Of youthful Poets, who among these Hills
> Will be my second Self when I am gone.
>
> (34–39)

This bequeathing of himself to his successors parallels that to Dorothy in 'Tintern Abbey' and to Coleridge in *The Prelude*. Wordsworth will try to perpetuate himself through his poetical 'heirs,' precisely as Michael could not. But like Michael's desire to propagate himself, Wordsworth's legacy is expressed in language that suggest his heirs may get more than they bargained for, or that the gift may entail the assumption of an identity not their own: '*be my second Self* when I am gone.'

This is to read the poem at its deepest autobiographical level, which is concerned preeminently with the creation of the Poet. At the biographical level, Wordsworth's sympathy for the composite character of Michael, great as it is, was not just for the difficulties of poor country life in 1800, nor even for his private cautionary lesson about the danger of naïve identification with the place. It was also a symbol of his own disappointment at his failure to push forward on *The Recluse*. He had piled up 'stones' for it and worked on it 'many a day.' But there were also many days when he too 'never lifted up a single stone.' Michael's sheepfold, begun but never finished, becomes a permanent record of failure. So too did Wordswsorth's *Recluse* manuscripts, as they mounted up through the years.

Rapidly, between 9 December 9 and 25 January, right through the Christmas holidays, Dorothy's birthday, and their anniversary 'homecoming' celebration on 25 December, everything in the volume was brought to a conclusion. *Lyrical Ballads* (1800) actually appeared on 25 January 1801. Also in January, Coleridge's health suddenly collapsed, and for the next three months he confined himself to the upper rooms of Greta Hall.[25] He was suffering a very acute, very early case of the effects of trying to be someone else's 'second Self.'

CHAPTER THIRTY-ONE

Selling the Book, Creating the Poet

Lyrical Ballads, *1801–1802*

. . . what is meant by the word Poet? What is a Poet? To whom does he address himself? And what language is to be expected from him? He is a man speaking to men . . . the rock of defence of human nature . . . carrying everywhere with him relationship and love . . .in spite of things silently gone out of mind and things violently destroyed, the Poet binds together by passion and knowledge the vast empire of human society.

(Preface to *Lyrical Ballads*, 1802)

Well before the actual publication date of the two-volume second edition of *Lyrical Ballads,* Wordsworth had been moving decisively to control its reception, to avoid the lame mistakes and petty disasters that had afflicted the first, single-volume edition. John Stoddart duly delivered his flattering review, which appeared in the moderately liberal *British Critic* in February; the first review in print, it helped to insure that other reviewers, less committed or lazier, would follow suit.[1] The strategy worked – aided, of course, by the poems themselves – and by summer it was clear that the volume would be a success. The *Anti-Jacobin Review*, tepid successor to Canning and Frere's brilliant rag, swallowed the superficial baits of the new volume's sweets, praising its 'genius, taste, elegance, wit, and imagery of the most beautiful kind.'[2] And throughout the year, Daniel Stuart plugged the new volume in the *Morning Post*, reprinting nine of Wordsworth's poems between January and August.[3]

Two weeks before the book appeared, the poets arranged for presentation copies to be sent to eight important public figures.[4] This was a small number by prevailing public-relations standards, but the eight were carefully chosen to represent a wide spectrum of cultural opinion: 'persons of eminence *either in Letters or in the state.*'[5] There were three women and five men, roughly divided between 'letters' and 'state.' The women and man of letters were Dorothy Jordan, the famous actress and mistress of the Duke of Clarence, whose admiration of 'The Mad Mother' was well known; Anna Letitia [Aikin] Barbauld, the popular Dissenting author of children's poetry, supporter of the French Revolution, and author of a poem 'To Mr S.T. Coleridge'; and Matthew 'Monk' Lewis, the popular Gothic novelist and playwright.

The political men were Sir James Bland Burges (1752–1824), possibly because of Wordsworth's admiration for his poem, *Richard Coeur de Lion*, but more probably because of Burges's influential position as a friend of Pitt, Wilberforce, and George III, which included many years of highly paid confidential work in the Foreign Office;[6] William Wilberforce, anti-slavery leader and bosom friend of William Cookson, who had been hearing for years about the vagaries of Cookson's nephew; Charles James Fox, the country's forlorn last hope for reform, still isolated in his self-exile from Parliament; and John Taylor, former editor of the *Morning Post* and later publisher of the *True Briton* and the *Sun* (in which Burges also had an interest). Finally, they sent a copy to the Duchess of Devonshire, Georgiana Cavendish (1757–1806), arguably the most powerful political woman in the land, at least in opposition, from her long friendship and daring efforts on behalf of her dear friend Fox.

Five of these eight letters survive, in copies or replies or other references that allow us to deduce their contents. Their rhetorical flexibility shows how determined the two poets were to succeed, and their willingness to adapt their pitches to a wide variety of readers in order to achieve that goal.

Coleridge, more used to the protocols of literary politics, drafted all the letters except the one to Fox, but all were signed by Wordsworth alone. That half the chosen recipients were key political figures, of both Left and Right, shows how political Wordsworth's sense of his volume's significance still was, despite its avoidance of overt political reference. All of the letters emphasize that *Lyrical Ballads* are 'written on a theory professedly new, and on principles which many persons will be unwilling to admit,' so each of the recipients became, willy-nilly, a specific auditor to some version of the preface's scolding lecture.

The letter to Wilberforce associates *Lyrical Ballads* with Wilberforce's recent *Practical View of the Prevailing Religious System of Instruction* (1797), suggesting that 'in the composition of them I had been a Fellow-labourer with you in the same Vineyard.'[7] This was stretching a slim resemblance, but Coleridge's metaphor connecting the humility of religious workers to the simplicity of the poems' language, which, like a nun, 'walk[s] "in silence and in a veil," ' is completely over the top: hardly a poem in the lot can be associated with that cliché. Nevertheless, it served the purpose of connecting these poetical actions with Wilberforce's religious ones on the basis of their mutually chaste avoidance of 'gaudy ornaments.'

If to Wilberforce the letter writer sounds like a Sunday school teacher, to Burges he sounds like a linguistic scholar. This letter is almost as conservative as Wordsworth's letter to Fox was liberal. The letter takes pains to make sure that the volumes' 'revolutionary' quality, explicitly referred to at the beginning of the preface, will be understood in the old but fast-disappearing sense of the word, as a *return* to good old traditional standards, not abstract innovation for its own sake. It asserts that poems are, or should be, written in the diction of 'the community,' not of the individual. It further asserts blithely that most English writers since the time of Dryden – that is, for more than a century – have ignored this truth (overlooking the strong emphasis in all Neoclassical writing on *decorum*), with the result that 'the simplicity of our national character' has been injured and 'reverence for our ancient institutions and religious offices' weakened.[8] The letter argues, in short, from the corruption of language to the corruption of the state, in a way that anticipates Orwell's 'Politics and the English Language.'

Monk Lewis is addressed as a language *performer*: 'a mind . . . acute . . . in the detection of the ludicrous and the faulty.' Given the hilarity some of the balder *Lyrical Ballads* provoked in many readers, this might look like asking for trouble from the author of *The Castle-Spectre*. But Wordsworth had swallowed his former contempt for Lewis's success and now sought his help to emulate it. His linguistic argument is here twisted around so that printed literature becomes part of the problem to which the accompanying book of printed poems is part of the solution. 'Our written language has been receding from the real language of life' with 'alarming rapidity,' and 'the increasing circulation of books' thus works to 'adulter[ate] our moral feelings,' and hence 'the language of real life itself,' thus 'poisoning our future literature at its best and most sacred source.'[9] Without saying so directly, the letter leaves it to Lewis to draw the tacit conclusion by which the presentation volume can break this viciously circular chain of bad causes: *it* must be written in 'the real language of life.' This ploy worked: John Wordsworth soon relayed to Grasmere a fan letter and complimentary poem he received from Lewis. Both are lost, but from John's comments we can see that Lewis had leapt to the book's social challenge in a way that even Fox would refuse. John called his poem 'quite a caricature of its kind . . . "The Convict" is nothing compared to [it].' 'The Convict' had by now become a family in-joke; it was the most overly political poem of Wordsworth's in the whole collection, and the only one he had cut from the new edition. 'They ought to have made a parson of him instead of a MP,' John concluded, reminding us that Lewis, like Wilberforce and Fox, was a member of the House of Commons.

Wordsworth's letter to Fox is much longer than the other seven. Like the letter to Wilberforce, it tries to connect the programme of *Lyrical Ballads*, 'however feebly,' with its recipient's public work.[10] It sets forth

Wordsworth's position much more clearly than the preface; one wishes he had dared to address the public in this vein. Starting on the defensive – as usual – he acknowledges that these poems might give Fox 'an unfavourable idea of my intellectual powers.' The letter is thus dedicated to removing this presumed negative. It also alludes to another principle we can recognize as the further emergence of the Poet of *The Recluse* in his role as friend of mankind. Wordsworth praised Fox's political flexibility, his ability to deal with men as individuals as well as 'in bodies,' saying it has 'made you dear to Poets; and . . . if . . . there has been a single true Poet living in England, he must have loved you.' As it happened, there *was* one such true Poet, and he here expresses his love for Fox by co-opting Fox's politics to his own poetics.

He then launched into a social critique that went far beyond Fox's stand against the war, though the war was the immediate cause of the 'calamitous effect[s]' which Wordsworth presciently if haphazardly intuited as evils inherent in the new industrial state. He identifies it as the 'rapid decay of the domestic affections among the lower orders of society.' He identifies its causes in the spread of manufacturing, heavy postal taxes, workhouses and soup-shops, and the disproportion between wages and prices. Wordsworth, like almost everyone else in 1801, was only dimly aware of that larger revolution, that we call 'industrial', looming behind the French one. Wordsworth did see clearly, however, that people were being displaced from working at home into centralized workplaces: literally, from cottages to '*manu*factories,' where people became 'hands.'

Wordsworth saw that this movement of people from their home places would have an inevitably dehumanizing effect, which he expressed in terms of their ability to 'read' and express their emotions. People 'read' their homes like a *text*: 'a tablet upon which they [their domestic feelings] are written, which makes them objects of memory in a thousand instances.' It is this domestic attachment which makes them fit subjects for poetry. He quoted an eighty-year-old Grasmere neighbour who had cared for her invalid husband for months, but had now become lame herself: 'it would burst my heart,' she said, if they were 'boarded out among other Poor of the parish . . . having kept house together so long.'[11] Wordsworth interprets her language as arising directly from her domestic emotions: 'These people could not express themselves in this way without an almost sublime conviction of the blessings of an independent domestic life.' A profoundly human language arises, not simply from our sense of place, but from the words wrenched out of us when we fear to *lose* that place.

Summing up, Wordsworth claimed that *Lyrical Ballads* would 'in some small degree enlarge our feelings of reverence for our species . . . by shewing that our best qualities are possessed by men whom we are too apt to consider, not with reference to the points in which they resemble us, but to those in which they manifestly differ from us.' Or, more simply, in a ringing peroration that Fox the great political speaker could appreciate: 'to shew that men who do not wear fine cloaths can feel deeply.' Little more than that need be said to substantiate Wordsworth's claim to have revolutionized the course of English poetry.

Fox's reply, when it finally came in late May, was both gratifying and frustrating. He wrote at some length, but did not take the smallest nibble at the political-linguistic bait Wordsworth offered. Instead, for all his advanced political views (though none as advanced as these), he showed himself to be a member of the old school when it came to poetry. Or rather, of the most acceptable version of the 'new' school, since he declared himself an enthusiastic lover of Cowper.[12] Rather than penetrating to the social implications of 'The Brothers' and 'Michael,' he stopped at their surface, protesting that he was 'no great friend to blank verse for subjects which are to be treated of with simplicity.'[13] Fox frankly said he expressed this reservation only because he admired so many of the other poems, even some of those written in blank verse, surely referring to 'Tintern Abbey.' To his credit as a reader, he chose as his favourites 'Goody Blake,' 'The Mad Mother,' 'The Idiot Boy,' and 'We are Seven,' all from the 1798 volume, and among the most extreme of Wordsworth's socio-linguistic experiments.

The letter to John Taylor was almost the reverse of the one to Fox politically, judging by Wordsworth's answer to Taylor's reply. He asserted that he and Coleridge had the same views on what Taylor 'with great propriety call[ed] jacobinical pathos.'[14] Wordsworth goes to great lengths to give *Coleridge* a clean bill of health for having recognized the error of his ways in using such unfortunate expressions: 'he deeply regretted that he had ever written a single word of that character.' 'Those writers who seem to estimate their power of exciting sorrow for suffering humanity, by the quantity of hatred and revenge which they are able to pour into the hearts of their Readers . . . are bad poets, and misguided men.' He claims, quite otherwise than he had to Fox, that they have shifted from a literature of activism to a literature of emotional universalism: 'Pity, we agreed, is a sacred thing, that cannot, and will not be prophaned.'[15]

That he should make this apologia to John Taylor is as noteworthy as the poets' choosing Taylor to receive a presentation volume in the first place. The *True Briton* was a violently conservative paper, especially compared to the *Morning Post*, Wordsworth's and Coleridge's liberal mainstay and support. That was perhaps reason enough to send a copy to Taylor: to balance their overtures to journalists between Left and Right as they did their political ones. But Taylor had other qualifications that made the poets eager to confess their former political errors to him. Like his father and grandfather before him, Taylor had been the oculist to George III, but he soon became the 'eyes' of the government in another way. He was one of the main journalists providing clandestine information to the government in the mid-1790s.[16] It is unlikely that the young Wordsworth and Coleridge would have known of Taylor's secret activities in the mid-1790s. But it is equally unlikely that they would *not* have known the gossip and innuendo about Taylor's domestic espionage by 1801, given their close association with Stuart, who succeeded him as editor of the *Morning Post*. If one were trying to cover over traces of youthful Jacobinism, what better way than to send a book of reformed poems to a potentially virulent enemy, and then follow it up with a fawning reply agreeing with his strictures against 'jacobinical pathos'?

While these public communiqués were being sent out, private communications were not immediately encouraging. John reported from London that he heard very little mention of the new edition, except that people didn't seem to *get* the poems on first reading.[17] Nevertheless, by the end of the year a young marquis of the Lowther clan, John Lowther Johnstone, saw the queen herself give a copy of *Lyrical Ballads* to a friend; by then, the quantity as well as the quality of the book's readership was assured.[18]

From friends they naturally got praise, but not always enough of it. Charles Lamb's enthusiastic letter of appreciation was similar to Charles Fox's, honestly saying that none of the new poems had affected him as forcibly as 'The Ancient Mariner,' 'Tintern Abbey,' and 'The Mad Mother,' though he singled out the 'Song of Lucy' and 'The Old Cumberland Beggar' among the new ones as especially good. He unfortunately added the quite true observation that the latter was 'too like a lecture.' Fox might say whatever he liked, but from his friends Wordsworth expected nothing but full marks, and Lamb was soon the bemused recipient of letters from both Wordsworth and Coleridge taking issue with his literary judgments.[19] As Lamb wrote to his friend Thomas Manning,

> I had need be cautious henceforward what opinion I give of the 'Lyrical Ballads.' All the North of England are in a turmoil. Cumberland and Westmorland have already declared a state of war. . . . I received almost instantaneously a long letter of four sweating pages from my Reluctant Letter-Writer [Wordsworth] . . . with a deal of stuff about a certain Union of Tenderness and Imagination, which in the sense he used Imagination was not the characteristic of Shakespeare, but which Milton possessed in a degree far exceeding other Poets: which Union, as the highest species of poetry . . . 'He was most proud to aspire to'; then illustrating the said Union by two quotations from his own 2d vol. (which I had been so unfortunate as to miss) . . . . After one has been reading Shakespeare twenty of the best years of one's life, it is hard to have a fellow start up, and prate about some unknown quality, which Shakespeare possessed in a degree inferior to Milton *and somebody else!!*[20]

Lamb had never said that 'he did not *like*' any of the poems, but so much was riding on the volume's reception (for Wordsworth) that any omission was taken as a slight, and Lamb had fatally neglected to say a word about 'Michael.'[21]

The humorous discrepancy between Lamb's reaction and Wordsworth's counterreaction shows how much the ideals of the *Recluse* project suffused the new volumes. But though Lamb was as usual funny, Wordsworth was, as more often than not, right. Yet his 'unknown quality,' linking sublime imaginativeness with humane tenderness, was so new that even Lamb could not adequately recognize it. (John Keats, almost a generation later, would assert that Wordsworth in fact had it to an even greater extent than Milton.) Of course Wordsworth, his head full of expanding notions of the role of the Poet and of himself filling that role, had as usual assumed too much about even his sympathetic readers' intuitions of his meaning. With his mind literally *pre*occupied by the forming shapes of *The Recluse* and *The Prelude*, he could not see how the apparently simple *Lyrical Ballads*, with their hectoring preface, could fail to reveal it. Even less could he see that the apparent discrepancy between the 'low' ballads and the 'high' preface actually worked to obfuscate, not clarify, their relation to his new conception of the Poet. The 'four sweating pages' Lamb received were, like those to Fox, Wordsworth's intensely personal glosses on the preface, and neither the Lamb of letters nor the Fox of politics, though among the most brilliant minds of their era, could quite grasp what they were being offered.

Besides famous, friendly, and unknown correspondents, the little household now began to receive a trickle of visitors, which in the latter years of Wordsworth's life would swell to a procession of holiday-makers. Some gave clear signs of his new cultural importance. Richard ('Conversation') Sharp and Samuel Rogers came in the spring with a letter of introduction from Josiah Wedgwood.[22] Rogers (1763–1855) was the leading poet of mainstream culture during most of Wordsworth's lifetime, somewhat the successor of Samuel Johnson in upholding conventional poetic decorum, though his verse seems soporific now. Wordsworth was careful not to bore him by insisting on his poetical theories. The friendly disposition of culture-brokers like Rogers helped make his poetic revolution look respectable; it led eventually to the patronage of other influential persons, notably Sir George Beaumont, one of the founders of the National Gallery. Conversation Sharp was, as his name implies, an almost equally important acquaintance, for he was the kind of drawing-room wit who was invited to all the best parties, and whose clever repartee could make or break a poet's reputation in high society.

The steady stream of visitors made 1801 a fallow year so far as new compositions went.[23] Wordsworth rested on his laurels and enjoyed the visits, having produced so much under difficult pressures in 1800. But when he and Dorothy went to visit Coleridge in April, they found that his mental health was much worse, especially in his unhappy relations with Sara Coleridge.

They gave some desultory thought to moving closer together again. William Calvert proposed fixing up Windy Brow for them to live in, and adding a little laboratory to attract Humphrey Davy.[24] It was a nice idea, but never very seriously pursued. It was a symptom of their feeling that a small band of like-minded intellectuals was the furthest extent of social vision possible in the repressive climate of England. John Thelwall was still being harassed, in Manchester in July, and it was in July that Coleridge wrote Southey an astonishing letter about taking up sinecure positions as 'Negro-drivers' on the Pinney estate in the Caribbean. 'Now mark my scheme! – St Nevis is the most lovely as well as the most healthy Island in the W. Indies . . . Now between you & me I have reason to believe that not only this House is at my service, but . . . perhaps, Pinny would appoint us sine-cure Negro-drivers at a hundred a year each, or some other snug & reputable office . . . I & my family, & you & Edith, & Wordsworth & his Sister might all go there . . . Wordsworth would certainly go, if I went.'[25] Was he serious? Certainly he was not wholly facetious. It makes one wonder with what degree of moral penetration these astute young men regarded the material base on which their cultural productions rested.

In May, John Wordsworth sailed on his next China voyage, his first as captain of the *Earl of Abergavenny*, having been solemnly sworn in by the East India Company's chairman with a stern official warning against engaging in illegal trade.[26] It was in anticipation of this voyage that John, pressing his own marriage suit, had assured Mary Hutchinson the previous December that he would be 'a very *rich man*.'[27] (His friends were more emphatic: '*a rich dog*.'[28]) He turned down an offer of £5000 to sell his command, believing he'd make a profit of at least £6000 on this trip, a sixty-six per cent return on his investment. But the bottom had dropped out of the woollen market in China, and he lost several thousand pounds instead. He would face other losses of another sort on his return in September of 1802, when he found that William had won Mary's hand in the meantime. But the family financial plan was still that he would make them all rich, and John's £9000 investment in the voyage included over £350 from William and Dorothy.

In June, Longman reported that all but 130 copies of the second volume of the new *Lyrical Ballads* had been sold (the two volumes could be purchased separately) and called for the preparation of a third edition. The second edition had almost sold out in less than six months; this was great success. So after a trip to Scotland in September – his first – to attend the wedding of Basil Montagu,[29] Wordsworth settled down in the autumn and winter of 1801–02 with renewed deliberation to deepen his imaginative control over his most valuable literary property.[30]

'What is a Poet?'

Wordsworth's changes in the texts of the poems and his re-ordering of their position for the new edition of 1802 do not amount to much, but his additions to the preface are of the first importance as indications of his increasingly self-conscious movement toward self-creation as 'the main region' of his song. These are nine long paragraphs on the nature of the Poet which he inserted in the midst of his laboured discussion of 'the strict affinity of metrical language with that of prose.' These additions answer his question, 'What is a Poet?,' by, in effect, pushing the shaky literary theory of 1800 aside in favour of unarguable personal testimony, thus preparing the way for the resumption of *The Prelude* in 1803, not as a distraction from *The Recluse*, but effectively as its replacement.

Theoretically, the 1802 additions to the preface shift Wordsworth's defence of his natural language poetry from a mimetic to an expressive theory of art.[31] In strictly logical terms, he substituted *himself* for the 'class' of human beings on which his linguistic claims were based, instead of the class of rural workers on which his arguments were founded in 1800. In short, 'Wordsworth's new ideas imply that he will, in some sense, write poetry by expressing himself rather than by imitating the utterance of others.'[32] At the same time, he widened his metaphysical criteria for the validity of his argument, from 'permanence' and 'naturalness' to 'general truth,' thus facilitating his 'replacement of the rustic by the poet as the norm of human behaviour,' leading to his new emphasis 'on the poet as his own subject, as representative man.'[33] This new emphasis had even less connection with actual poems of 1798 and 1800 than it did with the preface of 1800, and though its connection to the *Prelude-Recluse* project is much stronger, it remained largely speculative and invisible, given the incomplete state of those poems at this time, not to mention their non-public status throughout Wordsworth's life.

This is not to say, exactly, that Wordsworth had consciously changed his theory of poetry: the claims of the 1800 preface remain intact, taking up roughly the first third and the last third of the preface in its newly expanded form. The logic of his argument in 1800 was shaky enough, though rhetorically splendid, but it is not particularly strengthened by his addition of an expressive theory of poetry. By itself, his expressive theory is stronger logically than his mimetic one: we can argue a good deal about the behaviour and language of rural workers, but not very much about one man's self-report. However, the *appearance* that his mimetic theory was somehow founded on a body of social evidence remains desirable, for, by the same token, we can easily reject or ignore any one person's claims for himself, but it is harder to ignore the claims on our attention of an entire large class of human beings.

Hence it was to Wordsworth's advantage to keep both theories in play, whether or not he recognized their inconsistency, though his additions complicate the logical tangle of the preface immensely. Coleridge sorted out many of these inconsistencies in his chapters on *Lyrical Ballads* in *Biographia Literaria* (1817), but that book has been read even less attentively by most people than the various prefaces of *Lyrical Ballads*. The brief *Advertisement* of the first edition had avoided almost all these problems by presenting the volume as a language 'experiment.' What had been hypothesized in 1798 was theorized in 1800, and now retheorized for 1802. This logical tangle continued to serve in an unintended but highly effective way to keep the issues of Wordsworth's poetry and poetics alive in the public eye, since much of what he said was humanly and democratically so impressive, despite the fact that other things he said were obviously nonsense, and sometimes arrogant nonsense to boot. Wordsworth could hardly have devised a more effective strategy to keep his poems alive than the accumulating and contrasting logical-rhetorical levels of his various prefaces.

These additions, simply as expressions of intention, are the most moving of Wordsworth's statements about himself: 'a Poet . . . is a man speaking to men . . . bringing everywhere with him relationship and love.' They articulate explicitly what he felt he was doing in the 1798 ballads, and yet, considering how literal we usually find Wordsworth to be, when we are in a position to examine the circumstances of his utterances closely, the phrase 'relationship and love,' for all its generality, can also be seen as the simple, concrete fact of the situation in his most powerful narratives. He is out on the road, and he speaks to men and women about their life, about what brought them to the pass in which he now finds them.[34] He could not offer them much – Dorothy was more likely to give a penny than William – but he offered them 'relationship' and, for what it is worth, 'love.' Not to them directly: Wordsworth was not the man to say, 'I love you,' or 'God bless you.' But he loved them enough to make a poem of them, to empathize with their situation enough that their story is immortalized. His poems often continue on from the point where his speakers leave off, as in the case of the Female Vagrant, who '. . . ceased, and weeping turned away, / As if because her tale was at an end / She wept; —because she had no more to say / Of that perpetual weight which on her spirit lay.'

Wordsworth did not continue his man-in-the-street role very long after he settled in Grasmere; for one thing, people began to recognize him, and he was more effective accosting strangers – as Coleridge recognized, calling him *Spectator ab extra*. Not that he was unfeeling. Rather, he was personally so strong in himself that he did not let his own reactions get in the way of attending very closely to what these people had to say. To the despair of his merely political critics, he paid less attention to the causes of their suffering than to its effects, for the effect is what they *feel*: 'what afflicts my peace with keenest ruth / Is, that I have my inner self abused' ('The Female Vagrant').

Wordsworth's argumentative tone continues in the 1802 additions to the preface because he was not very clear himself about the validity of his claims. The lack of fit between his mimetic and expressive theories of the Poet shows up most glaringly when he follows up his apparently friendly claim, that a poet is only a man speaking to men, with a series of qualifications that indicate, if we attend to them seriously, that this is not even remotely so. He says he is using the language we might expect from the Poet as 'a man speaking to men,' but with – 'it is true' – the following list of differences: (1) a more lively sensibility, (2) more enthusiasm, (3) more tenderness, (4) greater knowledge of human nature, (5) a more comprehensive soul ('than [is] supposed to be common'), (6) more pleased with 'his own passions and volitions,' (7) more rejoicing 'in the spirit of life that is in him,' (8) who sees the same spirit 'in the goings-on of the Universe,' (9) or creates them 'where he does not find them,' (10) more affected by absent things as if they were present, (11) with greater ability to conjure up apparently real passions 'than anything which, from the motions of their own minds merely, other men are accustomed to feel in themselves,' (12) a 'greater readiness and power in expressing what he thinks and feels,' and (13) especially such thoughts and feelings as 'by his own choice, or from the structure of his own mind, arise within him without immediate external excitement.' By the end of this sequence of exceptions, we are so far from the nature of rural occupations on which this purified language is supposedly based, and Wordsworth has added so much to his 'man speaking to men,' that he is more like a superman speaking to men.

The 1802 additions are Wordsworth's 'glorious affirmation' of his 'sublime and comprehensive credo' of the role of the Poet.[35] The social role of the poet in the eighteenth century – didactic, moral, or sentimental – was petering out in anti-Jacobin satire and Sunday school religious sentiment, as social problems began to mount up far beyond what poets as gentleman clerics, or London attorneys, or Grub Street hacks, or Oxbridge scholars could offer their educated readers. Wordsworth went deeper, to insist that people were human beings before they were the parish poor, or God's children, or the working class. 'Bringing everywhere with him relationship and love,' the only relationship he could possibly bring with him was that of one human being to another: 'The rock of defence of human nature.' That is why these additions sound so much like Scripture.

Reviewers, trained by profession to look for points of weakness, did not have any trouble finding them in the third edition of *Lyrical Ballads*, with its ever-larger red flag of a preface waving in their faces. This, plus the thoroughly politicized nature of magazine reviewing at the time, guaranteed that the book would be set up as a free-standing target. The *Anti-Jacobin* had singled out 'Coleridge . . . & Co.' in 1798. Now, William Gifford, who in 1802 moved on from the *Anti-Jacobin* to become the first editor of the successful *Quarterly Review*, and knowing full well that Coleridge was the 'Friend' referred to in the *Lyrical Ballads*' preface, and that Wordsworth was his 'Co.', charged his new bulldog, Francis Jeffrey, to keep up the attack. Jeffrey used the same phrase, only now recasting it as 'Wirdsworth [*sic*] & Co.' and linking it directly with 'the laudable exertions of Mr Thomas Paine to bring disaffection and infidelity within the comprehension of the common people.'[36]

It was lucky, in this respect, that the poets had moved to the Lake District, for otherwise they would surely have continued to be belittled as 'Jacobin' poets rather than as 'Lake Poets,' and would have been totally humiliated, like the 'Jacobin' novelists of the era, who have until very recently been effectively erased from the cultural map of the times – names like Godwin, Bage, Thelwall, and Hays. Wordsworth and Coleridge would have been cast as the founders of the 'Jacobin School' of poets, just as Shelley and Byron became the 'Satanic School' and Keats and Leigh Hunt, the 'Cockney School.' Calling them the 'Lake School' or 'Lakers' was in its day a provincial put-down. But its pejorative quality gradually wore off – in no small part because Wordsworth *was* able to create the taste by which he was to be appreciated – so that today the phrase has become not only honorific but even inaccurate and misleading, by identifying the spirit of Wordsworth's poetry too literally with its apparent place of origin.

CHAPTER THIRTY-TWO

Peace, Marriage, Inheritance

> There was a time when meadow, grove, and stream,
> The earth, and every common sight,
> To me did seem
> Apparelled in celestial light,
> The glory and the freshness of a dream.
> Turn wheresoe'er I may,
>   By night or day,
> The things which I have seen I now can see no more.
>   ('Ode: Intimations of Immortality,' Spring, 1802)

In the early autumn of 1801 came news that transformed Wordsworth's life. The two major obstacles that lay between him and his full adult regeneration – ability to provide for a mate and freedom from previous emotional commitments – were removed within months of each other. Shortly after 1 October newspapers reported that preliminary agreement for a truce had been reached at Amiens. The terms were so unfavourable to England that the Peace of Amiens ended in less than a year, but that was time enough for Wordsworth to set his life in order.

Although the peace was not officially signed until 27 March 1802, its terms were sufficiently clear in October, and they included reopening France to travel. William could see Annette again. The importance of Wordsworth's attachment to Annette for every aspect of his life between 1793 and 1801, no matter how invisible it seems at times, is evident from the alacrity with which he moved to resolve it now. Letters now crossed freely between Grasmere and Blois and four months after the peace was signed, William and Dorothy were in Calais, where they spent the entire month of August with Annette and Caroline.

A sense of deep personal relief suffuses Wordsworth's writing in the winter of 1801–02. In December he began three new activities, all crucial steps toward the final creation of the Poet – or rather, crucial missteps. He re-read 'The Ruined Cottage' with a view toward finishing it; he began a rapid course of reading and 'translating' Chaucer; and, on the day after Christmas, he made a stab at extending *The Prelude*.[1] Each of these actions, in the context of his recent additions to the preface, show his growing consciousness that *he* was the Poet he was talking about.

His brief start on *The Prelude* was the least important of these three actions, for it still seemed like a distraction from his main work at hand. In lines that correspond roughly to the first two hundred lines of the present Book III ('Residence at Cambridge'), he started describing his university experience. But only half of them say anything about Cambridge. Instead, he soon fell back into defending the relevance of his subject, repeating a sequence he had been through three times in the last two years: at the conclusion of the 1799 *Prelude*, in the 'Prospectus' lines of *The Recluse* (1800), and, most recently, in his additions to the preface. Once again, he felt he had to reassure Coleridge that he was speaking 'of genius, power, / Creation, and divinity itself . . . *for* my theme has been / What passed within me.' (III.171–74) Once we accept this explanation, the rest of his defence carries the field: 'This is in truth heroic argument.' But what exactly *was* the argument? Here his brief re-start on *The Prelude* faltered: 'I wished to touch [this argument], / With hand however weak—but in the main / It lies far hidden from the reach of words.'

Reading and translating Chaucer was intended as therapy for the mighty poetic issues he was grappling with. Yet Wordsworth did nothing lightly, and when it came to poetry, every issue was an ultimate one. His modernizations of Chaucer's *Canterbury Tales* are quite good; some were published in the 1820s and 1840s. In the economy of Wordsworth's creative development, Chaucer was the only one remaining of the big four in English literature that he had not confronted, challenged, and tried to make his own. He had thoroughly assimilated the languages of Shakespeare and Spenser (i.e., he had mastered them without being over-mastered by them), and Milton's language, mythos, and career were the template of his own. Chaucer seemed an easier challenge because he was still regarded as a coarse comic author writing in a 'primitive' form of English. The result was not very important in terms of poetic product, but in terms of Wordsworth's poetic process of creating the Poet, this winter fireside pastime was very much of a piece with his reviving efforts to make good on the self-advertisements he had just added to the preface to *Lyrical Ballads*.

By far the most difficult and least successful of his three writing efforts this winter was his attempt to bring 'The Ruined Cottage' to a satisfactory conclusion. Beginning in late December and for the next two months, Dorothy's journal records one painful episode after another of William's attempt to make progress on the poem. It gave him headaches, upset stomachs, and bad nights of sleep, all of which she, faithful companion and copyist, fully participated in. Several times they were both reduced to tears, once from reading Book XI of *Paradise Lost* (Adam and Eve's realization that they must leave Paradise) after a particularly unproductive day. Their tears flowed not simply for Milton's grandeur, nor for the discrepancy between Milton's achievement and his own, but for the fact that Milton had succeeded so well in writing the definitive religious version of a story Wordsworth was trying to re-tell in modern, secular terms.

Almost all the signs of Margaret's decline in 'The Ruined Cottage' are presented in terms of her garden: if Wordsworth had called his poem 'The Ruined Garden' its intention as a humanistic tale of fall and redemption would stand starkly revealed. Once again the hopeless tragedy of Margaret's abandonment resonated again with his renewed consciousness of Annette's long 'unquiet widowhood,' as it had in the poem's creation five years earlier. Sometimes his revisions seemed good, but on a second reading they would appear uninteresting: the ratio of bad days to good on this project was about ten to one. On 28 February Dorothy recorded, 'Disaster Pedlar,' and within a week all further work on it came to a halt.[2] Finally, William instructed her to hide all the manuscripts and not to give them to him even if he asked for them, like an addict determined to break his habit.[3] A large measure of Wordsworth's extreme toughness is revealed in this gesture of self-denial.

Turning to 'The Ruined Cottage' at this time was exactly the right thing for him to do at this juncture in his development: having reaffirmed the quasi-divine stature of the Poet in his additions to the preface, it was time to produce the Poem. The problem was that he still could not create a narrator of healing power commensurate with the terrible tale of Margaret's suffering. Not the facts of Margaret's life, but the way they were framed, presented, *and received* was his new concern, if the Poet was indeed to be 'a man speaking to men . . . bringing everywhere with him relationship and love.' The change in his focus is clearly signalled by his change of title to 'The Pedlar': the Pedlar brought those qualities with him, but they did no good to Margaret; hence they must be transferred to whoever *heard* The Tale of Margaret: the young wandering narrator of the whole poem, whose name (or title) would be 'The Poet,' when the much-revised poem was finally published as Book I of *The Excursion*. Like *The Prelude*, 'The Pedlar' is the story of the creation of a poet, by an initiating figure whose authority comes not from education (Nurture) but from Nature.

But Wordsworth could not bring it off, though his manuscripts show clearly enough the kind of figure he intended: by their incorporation of whole sections of the 1799 *Prelude*, they reveal that this figure is not an old Scots peddler, but someone else from the north of England with a wider education and a wider range of travelling experience: the Poet, himself.

*

Instructing Dorothy to hide the manuscripts, Wordsworth soon rebounded from his impasse. Within days of the Pedlar 'disaster,' he began composing a long series of short poems, over thirty in all, that kept him active through the end of July.[4] Two days after 'The Pedlar' was put to rest for his long sleep, Wordsworth began composing 'The Sailor's Mother'; he finished it the next day. This became the new pattern in Dorothy's journal for the next four months: start a poem one day, finish it the next, or very shortly thereafter. The difference from her painful series of 'Pedlar' entries could not be more pronounced. Pushing aside *The Recluse* and starting to plan for his marriage, Wordsworth's poetic confidence was reinforced by strong feelings from every level of his life: personal, financial, and national. A forthcoming settlement of the Lowther estate intensified what was already a time of very good feeling.

This happiness is clearly reflected in the lyrics he composed this spring, which are among his most popular favourites, though not his most characteristic work. They are Wordsworth's easy pieces, poems about butterflies and robins, daisies, and celandines. If not quite as simple as they seem – their author being after all Wordsworth – they are certainly much easier than the poems of either of the two earlier springs (1800 and 1798) when he had also trained his large imagination on small subjects. If the lyrics of 1800 move the human tragedies of 1798 on to the smaller stage of Grasmere, those of 1802 transpose the human problems of 1800 into moralistic symbolisms of plants and animals – a direction already apparent in 'The Waterfall and the Eglantine' and 'The Oak and the Broom,' and now pursued further.

At least this is how they appear when read separately. In the thick texture of Wordsworth's life, their simple optimism is considerably qualified. He began with a few more ballads in his original vein of 1798, like 'The Sailor's Mother' and 'Beggars,' but these are almost the last we see of such characters in his poetry, except for cameo appearances in *The Prelude*. Some of them are only nominally lyrical ballads. 'Alice Fell; or, Poverty' is a sentimental Good Samaritan story, written to order at the request of a Scots friend of the humanitarian Thomas Clarkson, about a little orphan girl who wept inconsolably for the loss of her cloak when it got caught in a coach wheel. The narrator gives money to the innkeeper at the next stop for a new cloak ' "of duffil [sic] grey, / As warm a cloak as any man can sell!" ' In our last sight of little Alice, all her troubles are apparently over: 'Proud creature was she the next day, / The little orphan, Alice Fell!' What the poem tells us about the subject of its sub-title is that the woes of poverty are pretty easily overcome. In 1798 the little girl would not have been so easily placated, but might, like her sister of 'We Are Seven,' have insisted that no cloak could ever replace the one she had lost, the last of her family possessions, literally the last remnant of her family.

Wordsworth soon turned from this small cast of poor people to a large number of natural objects – birds and butterflies, flowers and trees – in which the connection between external nature and human nature is presented in the most uncomplicated manner imaginable. But complications appear when we look more closely, and compare them with Wordsworth's other contemporaneous work. For Wordsworth these simple equations were very hard to maintain, because his mind was evidently filled with feelings of a quite opposite nature. In all of them, he says, more or less, Yes, daisy [robin, linnet, cuckoo, etc.], there you are in your simple beauty, and I will be like you. Or, in his own words: 'We meet thee [daisy], like a pleasant thought, / When such are wanted.' But pleasant thoughts are sometimes very badly wanted, and may be very hard to come by. Some of these poems give lyric expression to the sense of wonder Wordsworth had put in a much higher key in 'Home at Grasmere' and the 'Prospectus' to *The Recluse*.[5] At least they try to: the celandine is called the 'Herald of a mighty band, / Of a joyous train ensuing.' But even this 'Prophet of delight and mirth' is 'Ill-requited upon earth.' The poems as a group might be called conversational transcendentalism, a mode that Wordsworth soon began to elaborate into the full-blown philosophical Idealism of his next stage of development.

Despite the happy surface of these poems, his specifically poetic problem of 1802 was actually far worse than in 1798 and 1800. It did not concern his attitude toward the suffering poor, but the status of his own imagination. In 1798 and 1800 he could turn almost anything into a strong poem, but in 1802 the results were not nearly as impressive. This is evident not so much in individual poems but in the gap between them and another very different kind of poem he was writing. For the happy lyrics of 1802 are countered-balanced – indeed almost negated – by two very different poems, both of which were begun, but neither of which could be finished, at this time: 'Resolution and Independence' (known first as 'The Leech-Gatherer') and the first four stanzas of what became the Intimations Ode. In them we hear indeed the voice of the *Recluse*-bard, a bard very much worried about his staying power.

In 'The Leech-Gatherer' the problem is specifically Wordsworth's lack of confidence in himself as a poet, his deep awareness of the difficulty he faced in maintaining the role of the Poet which he had now fully articulated publicly. The creatures of the other spring lyrics are there in plenty: the stock-dove, the magpie, and the blue jay. But though 'all things that love the sun are out of doors,' and he tries to be with them, he cannot do it:

> But, as it sometimes chanceth, from the might
> Of joy in minds that can no further go,
> As high as we have mounted in delight
> In our dejection do we sink as low;
> To me that morning did it happen so . . .
> (22–26)

These mood swings are soon generalized as a vocational crisis: 'We Poets in our youth begin in gladness; / But thereof come in the end despondency and madness.' 'Madness' is a hard word here, but even harder is the mild-looking conjunction, *thereof*: his gifts are the very source of his present despondency.

William and Dorothy had met the leech-gatherer in Town End in October of 1800. His actual story was considerably worse than in the poem, for he no longer gathered leeches at all, but lived by begging. His wife and ten children were all dead, except 'one, of whom he had not heard for many years, a sailor.' Of this hopeless character Wordsworth makes a stronger one, who still goes about on his 'employment hazardous and wearisome,' but 'with God's good help, by choice or chance . . . in this way he gained an honest maintenance.' However, Wordsworth made him strong not to present a more hopeful picture of poverty in England, but in order that *he* could take sustenance from the old man's perseverance:

> I could have laughed myself to scorn to find
> In that decrepit Man so firm a mind.
> 'God,' said I, 'be my help and stay secure;
> I'll think of the Leech-gatherer on the lonely moor!'

'Resolution and Independence' is a poem about the mental qualities named in its title as necessary ingredients in the character of a major poet, one who would avoid not only the excesses of a Chatterton or a Burns but also the irresponsibility of a Coleridge: 'how can He expect that others should / Build for him, sow for him, and at his call / Love him, who for himself will take no heed at all?' These lines reflect the attitude toward Coleridge's behaviour that was beginning to form, and harden, in the new household at Grasmere. 'The Leech-Gatherer' faces up to the problem of imaginative loss in a stronger way than Coleridge's contemporaneous 'Dejection: An Ode,'[6] but Wordsworth's poem was written in knowledge of his impending marriage and the resolution of his failed past romantic history, whereas Coleridge's was written in the certainty of his marriage's disaster and the heartbreaking knowledge that his desired independence from it would never come.

The same desperate search for assurance is evident in the first four stanzas of the other major poem Wordsworth began that spring, where it is totally undercut by his *lack* of resolution and independence.

> There was a time when meadow, grove, and stream,
> The earth, and every common sight,
>   To me did seem
>   Apparelled in celestial light,
> The glory and the freshness of a dream.

So far, so good. But there is no begetting such 'golden times' again:

> It is not now as it hath been of yore;—
>   Turn wheresoe'er I may,
>   By night or day,
> The things which I have seen I now can see no more.

These are of course the opening lines of the great Ode, 'Intimations of Immortality from Recollections of Early Childhood.' But in 1802 it was Wordsworth's ode to mortality, not immortality, like Coleridge's con-temporaneous companion poem, 'Dejection,' and it arose from the same source: recollections of early childhood which Wordsworth realized he had irrevocably *lost*. Try as he could, through four desperate stanzas, he cannot keep his faith. The last of them begins, apparently like the simple 1802 lyrics, 'Ye blessed Creatures, I have heard the call / Ye to each other make; . . . The fulness of your bliss, I feel—I feel it all.' But it ends, 'Whither is fled the visionary gleam? / Where is it now, the glory and the dream?' He did not know, what we always already know when we sit down to read this poem (that by his order is supposed to stand last in every collection of his verse), that he would finish the poem two years later with seven sombre stanzas, based on the ancient myth of the pre-existence of the soul, that manage to take comfort from the sheer fact of loss. Nor are these four stanzas fragmentary; they make a complete statement that begins very much like the other lyrics of this spring. But they end where none of the rest dared tread, with the sense of imaginative death, brought on by his continuing sense of failure on *The Recluse*, his own challenge to his achieving full poetical maturity.

These contradictory emotions are apparent in poems and letters concerned with the coming happy event of his marriage as well. In January, the day after Mary left following her Christmas visit, William and Dorothy read *Descriptive Sketches*, talked of Lake Como, and thought of Mary.[7] That Wordsworth's youthful erotic experiences on his walking tour should come back to mind – nay, be purposely brought back by reading that part of the poem – shows not only their train of thought but also their frank honesty with each other about their feelings. The coming joys of 1802 were all the more intense for the deep emotions of a quite different nature that had to be kept down.

On 25 April 1802, shortly after his thirty-second birthday, he began 'A Farewell,' which Dorothy referred to in her journal as 'On Going for Mary'; he worked on it for the next two months before getting it right (it was not published until 1815).[8] His difficulties with the poem are significant, for it is apparently a simple piece, merely telling their garden to look after itself while they are gone. As a farewell, it is addressed more to Dorothy than to Annette: the renunciation of the sister had, after ten years, become harder than renouncing the lover. It marks the departure from *their* Grasmere as decisively as 'Home at Grasmere' had marked their arrival two springs before.[9] Their garden 'nook' is addressed as a child – 'Nature's child indeed' – who is being prepared for the new mother coming to take care of her, as if she were the offspring of an earlier marriage. This new mother will not replace her old mother, but will rather be added to the two parents the little garden/child has known so far, who are designated by the poem's consistently first-person plural voice: '*We* go for One to whom ye will be dear.'

The garden would also have to help them with another task, odder yet as an expression of the emotions of a couple returning from their honeymoon: 'Joy will be flown in its mortality; / Something must stay to tell us of the rest.' If Mary was reassured that he was giving up Annette, whom she had long known about, she also being clearly given to understand that he was *not* giving up Dorothy. Twice during the spring Dorothy emphatically put down any suggestion that they might leave Grasmere, no matter how cramped, for Gallow Hill, no matter how spacious.[10] The little poem's ostensible subject, their garden, is heavily over-determined by its real one, the realignment of erotic allegiances. When it at last seemed finished, Dorothy wrote the following carefully indented list on the blotter page of her journal:

> Dorothy Wordsworth
> William Wordsworth
> Mary Wordsworth
> May 29th 6 O clock
> Sitting at small table by window
> Grasmere 1802[11]

The manuscript poem called 'Travelling' was composed at about this same time. Its complicated connections with the full form of 'Nutting' written in Germany three years earlier show how much the memory of their former intimacy rose up to test their resolve for the coming new departures in their life. On the night of 4 May Dorothy repeated its opening words, 'This is the spot,' 'over and over again' to William 'while he was in bed.'[12]

The whole time was fraught with powerful, tender emotions passing between the two households. Dorothy thanked Mary for a 'sweet letter' addressed to a vague but debilitating illness she was suffering: 'I have a kind of stupefaction and headache about me, a feeling of something that has been amiss.'[13] She then informed Mary, 'You must know that we have changed rooms, my regular sleeping bed is [now] William's, I make John's my sick bed.' Sara wrote as well, and William added separate parts of the letter for her and for Mary. Dorothy averts to still-deeper emotions: 'I *could* write far, *far*, more, but William says it does me no good.'[14]

*

In the midst of all this emotional turmoil, on 24 May, another seemingly intractable life problem was solved. Sir James Lowther died of 'a mortification of the bowels,' and his creditors, the Wordsworths among them, began lining up to present their claims on his estate. His successor was a very distant cousin (he had no children), William Lowther, a much more decent man, who soon advertised his wish to honour all just claims on the estate.

In October, brother Richard presented the new viscount (the earldom was discontinued) his family's claim for £10,388 6s. 8d., an enormous amount in terms of the economy that William and Dorothy had been living on for seven years.[15] Richard, with the bookkeeping exactitude of the whole Wordsworth clan, had included in his claim the interest for twenty years of non-payment on an original debt of £4,660 4s. 10d.[16] But William began insisting vociferously that they drop the claim for interest and take a more conciliatory tack. He recommended that they appeal 'to Lord Lowther's Honour and Conscientiousness,' adding, 'It would be proper to state the utter destitution of my Sister on account of the affair.'[17] He did not scruple to suggest that they appeal for help and influence to 'some of my Uncle Wm's [Cookson's] Friends,' such as Wilberforce, or Christopher's new connections in the Church of England hierarchy, such as the Bishop of Norwich, though most of these people cared little for – as they saw it – his self-created problems.[18]

Wordsworth's behaviour resembles his eagerness when Raisley Calvert's estate fell in his way. He would rather be sure of the money than press for more and risk losing it all. He had learned his lesson when it came to dealing with aristocrats' justice: 'What success was a poor man ever known to have against a very rich one in a Law suit?' Richard's claim to the interest was just, but William's preferred approach won out, very likely because he and Dorothy, taken as a unit, needed their shares much more badly than Richard, John, or Christopher needed theirs. A compromise amount of about £8000 was duly paid in early 1803. William's greater need was further pointed up in family terms by John Robinson's will, who also died in 1802. Robinson, long the Wordsworth boys' protector, provided something for Christopher and John, but he left not a penny to William, who had so boldly rejected Robinson's advice ten years earlier about Cambridge and the church.

On 9 July they departed for what could be conceived of as the opposite of a wedding trip, a trip of divorcement.[19] They went via Gallow Hill, and spent ten days at the end of the month with Mary before proceeding to France, discussing what they should say to Annette. They arrived in London 29 July; three days later they were in Calais, where by previous arrangement they met Annette and Caroline at the lodging house of Madame Avril in the rue de la Tête d'Or, where they stayed for the next month.[20]

Of their visit to Calais, we know almost nothing. The sum total of Dorothy's journal for the whole trip is two pages, almost wholly concerned with the beautiful sunsets they saw as they walked on the beach. There is hardly a word describing either Annette and Caroline (though they are named), except for Caroline's reaction ('delighted') to seeing 'the fiery track' of boats' wakes on calm hot nights. But description was hardly necessary; three of the four principals in the affair were together, walking the beach day after day, saying what had to be said. The Wordsworths presented a rather shabby appearance to Annette, coming out of rural retirement in their mended country attire, while she was more vibrant than ever, an active counter-revolutionary with a lengthening police record for harbouring priests and other royalists.[21]

Wordsworth's sense of *déjà vu* was pounding in his head as he compared coming to Calais in August 1802 with his arrival there twelve years earlier, on 13 July 1790. Thousands of English travellers, Charles Fox foremost among them, were flocking through the town en route to Paris, to see the city that had effectively been cut off from London for almost ten years, revolutionized and republicanized in the interim. In a sonnet written on the road to Ardres (ten miles inland) on 7 August, Wordsworth recalled the joy that he and Robert Jones had seen on that 'too-credulous day,' the first Fête de la Fédération, when 'from hour to hour the antiquated Earth / Beat like the heart of Man.' But now, 'sole register that these things were,' he heard two solitary greetings: '"*Good morrow, Citizen!*" a hollow word, / As if a dead man spake it!'

Instead of biographical revelation, his Calais sonnets manifest another form of Wordsworthian displacement, his profound need to recollect his emotions in tranquillity. Now, instead of displacing the political into the personal, he reversed the process and pushed the personal into the political. He could not create a character and a story that would make publishable sense of the life situation he had created for himself ten years earlier. Instead, he ventriloquized Annette as La Belle France, secure in the knowledge that his critical comments about the sad decline of Liberty in France would not be taken personally by Annette if she should ever chance to read them, which was unlikely.

Published together as 'Sonnets on National Independence and Liberty' in 1807, though many appeared in the *Morning Post* during 1802–03, their dates of composition show that Wordsworth's mastery of the sonnet form rose to greatness in the space of just a few months. Dorothy had begun reading Milton's sonnets to him in late May.[22] Two months later, under the intense pressure of one of the most difficult trips of his life, gathering up the ravelled threads of his young manhood, he began writing sonnets at a level that had not been achieved in England since Milton, though Wordsworth had written no more than half a dozen of them to this point in his life. In fact he wrote both more and better than Milton. *The Prelude* does not match *Paradise Lost* as a finished work of art, but Wordsworth's sonnets, especially his political ones, do surpass Milton's, and on virtually the same theme: the disappointment of revolutionary hopes for human redemption. Much of his success, it is true, comes from the fact that he had Milton not only as a precursor, but also as a subject: 'Milton! thou shouldst be living at this hour.' The tension that pervades the sonnets he wrote in Calais is similar to that running between the sweet lyrics and terribles odes of the spring. But now the tension was between his low estimate of England, his even lower estimate of France, and his unhappy acceptance of the need to hang on, if to nothing else, at least to England's past reputation for liberty and manliness: 'Oh grief that Earth's best hopes rest all with Thee!'[23] The friends of his youth rise fresh in his mind, and his hailing of 'Milton!' and 'Toussaint!' (the Haitian leader treacherously jailed by Napoleon) is echoed by similar calls to 'Calvert!' and 'Jones!' 'Great men have been among us' [Sidney, Marvell, Harrington, and Vane] . . . they knew how the genuine glory was put on.' But their knowledge has been lost: 'Lords, lawyers, statesmen, squires of low degree' all post forward to Paris (he saw them going by) in unseemly haste 'to bend the knee . . . before the new-born Majesty' of Napoleon.[24]

We look in vain for a glimpse of Annette or Dorothy in these sonnets, but we can find Wordsworth in them, not as himself, but in his imaginative projection – *not* as Milton, but as the man of the hour himself: 'I grieve for Buonaparte, with a vain / And an unthinking grief! The tenderest mood / Of that Man's mind—what can it be?'[25] He grieved because he imagined that Bonaparte's moods were much like his own, in their wayward violence and destructiveness. But Bonaparte has not learned Wordsworth's lesson: 'The Governor who must be wise and good' must temper 'the sternness of the brain' with 'thoughts motherly . . . and the talk / Man holds with week-day man in the hourly walk / Of the mind's business.' Proposing village small-talk as therapy for Napoleon Bonaparte was like trying to calm intimations of mortality with reassurances from daisies and cuckoos. Throughout these sonnets, the desideratum is a leader of Napoleon's power and Wordsworth's peace: a 'master spirit,' like 'the invincible Knights of old,' and a nation 'risen, *like one man*, to combat . . . for liberty and right.' This personal identification is the source of his new patriotic feelings: 'What wonder if a Poet now and then, / Among the many movements of his mind, / Felt for thee [England] as a lover or a child!'[26] His particular 'wonder' is stimulated biographically by the fact that, at just this time, his feelings for *his* lover and *his* child were being revived and re-engaged, along with his conviction that he was the necessary Poet for these unruly times.

Leaving Annette and Caroline to make their way back to Blois alone, William and Dorothy returned to Dover on September 1, Dorothy looking back to France with 'many a melancholy and tender thought.' But William's joy looked the other way, happily recognizing that of everything he saw: 'all, all are English.' He pushed his personal situation into statements that seem to be solely political and patriotic – 'Thou art free, / My Country!' But they apply equally to him: he too was 'free.'

They spent three weeks in London with Basil Montagu and enjoyed an unexpected family reunion when John landed with the *Earl of Abergavenny* on 11 September. Christopher came up to town to be with them.[27] Reconciliations with other relatives were in order, so Dorothy and William went out to Windsor Castle with Christopher as intermediary to visit Canon Cookson and family, then in residence as the king's chaplain. This was the first time either of them had seen the Cooksons since Dorothy's clandestine escape from Forncett eight years earlier.[28] Formally forgiven, they went back to London to hold a family council to discuss the new arrangements, domestic and financial, that would result from the coming marriage. William and Dorothy were now understood to be one large unit in the group, and a union of the neediest, since unlike Richard and John and Christopher they had no dependable separate income, and *they* now had a wife to support.

But John's latest voyage had not been successful. Besides losing several thousand pounds on his investment, he faced a fine of £300 from 'those vile and abominable Monsters at the India House' for encroaching on the company's monopoly in 'camlets,' a fabric made of silk and wool, in his private trade allowance.[29] Officers' private trading was not smuggling, for the goods were duly registered; this particular practice represented an attempt by the ships' officers to profit from their own company's monopoly. The practice was widely condoned; in 1801 nearly half of all ships' cargoes in camlets were part of the officers' trade allowances.[30] John had merely been caught in one of the East India Company's periodic fits of enforcing its own rules. As he told Dorothy, 'we began to think we had a *right* to smuggle them – We are the first that they have fined and of course we think it very hard and very unjust.'[31] But he had to pay the fine – reduced to £200 through negotiation – before being allowed to sail again. These reverses increased his desperation to realize the profits that would make him a rich man, and permit his brother, the poet, 'to do something for the world' – which meant, in the family plan, completing *The Recluse*. For John, it would mean getting into the even more illegal and dangerous, but vastly more profitable, trade in the commodity that could make a man 'a rich dog' in a single voyage: opium.

There was also some private settling of emotional accounts. John sent a letter to Mary Hutchinson from London on 12 September, the day after he landed.

My dearest Mary,

I have been reading your Letter over & over again My dearest Mary till tears have come into my eyes & I know not how to express myself   thou ar't kind & dear creature   But what ever fate Befal me I shall love thee to the last and bear thy memory with me to the grave.

> Thine aff'ly
> John Wordsworth[32]

He was answering a letter from Mary explaining her reasons for marrying William. But John was plighting his troth, too: like Dorothy, he was vowing never to marry anyone else. Each of them would remain faithful in their own way to the two partners in this marriage, which John and Dorothy now formally accepted as the emotional centre of their lives. William and John had taken their turns, and their chances, wooing Mary over the past two years. William had won out, but John used his brother's words to help deliver a powerfully loaded farewell to his beloved: the last sentence of his letter is a verbatim quotation of Michael's last words to Luke as he him bids goodbye at the sheepfold in Green-head Ghyll, never to see him again. John never saw any of them again: between this time and his death in February 1805 he was in England for a total of nine months, but he never travelled north to visit them.[33]

On 22 September they headed north for the wedding, which took place in Brompton Church near Gallow Hill on 4 October,[34] almost a year to the day after the preliminary Treaty of Amiens had been announced. The arrival, preparations, marriage, and departure of William and Mary and Dorothy for Grasmere all took place within the next ten days. The strange story of the night before the wedding is well known, though Dorothy's symbolic – or symptomatic – behaviour was not so strange in that era of Sensibility as it seems today. She put the wedding ring on her finger when she went to bed. Next morning, she dressed herself all in bridal white and returned the ring to William for the ceremony. But he first slipped it back on her finger and 'blessed [her] fervently.' Dorothy succumbed to a fit of hysteria and threw herself down as if dead until the small party returned from the church at eight o'clock in the morning.[35] She went out to meet them as they returned, but again was overcome and had to be led back to the house.[36]

Like the letters exchanged at the time of 'A Farewell' in May, and the July talks with Mary and the August talks with Annette, the occasion was overloaded with emotions. But they all moved with great deliberation and fortitude to get through it. This was not a wedding to be celebrated with large parties of friends: these would take place gradually over time, at Grasmere. The only known wedding presents were a new gown for Mary – from John Wordsworth – and a set of silver spoons for Dorothy from one of the Ferguson cousins in America.[37] Nor was there any honeymoon:

William, Mary and Dorothy set off for Grasmere immediately after breakfast, along the same route that William and Dorothy had followed in their Long March three years earlier. William and Dorothy kept their thoughts to themselves, of their walk through Wensleydale in 1799, or read them silently in each other's eyes. Never was Mary's natural reticence more of a blessing than on this trip, though it ripened and bore fruit as years went by, as she and William accomplished that most unRomantic and most 'Victorian' of lifeworks, falling more in love after marriage than before. But she also had thoughts of her own to nurse, musing on John's letter.

In less than three months, Wordsworth had definitively reorganized his relations with all three of the women in his life. In the strictly clinical terms of psycho-sexual development, he was at this point young no longer.

The autumn of 1802 was a quiet, tense time of adjustment to complex new living arrangements. Dorothy moved upstairs, giving her old bedroom up to William and Mary, but the 'smallness [of the cottage] and the manner in which it is built [let] noises pass from one part of the house to the other.'[38] Such evidences of the physical part of her brother's marriage that came to her attention troubled Dorothy considerably, and William had to use care in his oral and written expressions – both of which were very frank and intense – of sexual passion for Mary, because he feared Dorothy found them 'obnoxious.'[39] Nonetheless, it was Dorothy, as always, who wrote the necessary delicate letters to Annette about their new life.[40]

What William did was to start translating again, this time from the Italian of Ariosto and Metastasio, advancing as rapidly and fluently as he had through Chaucer's works a year earlier.[41] His translations are excellent, and were published a year later in the *Morning Post*.[42] Much of his energy and fluency in this task came from the subject matter he selected, for all the poems (plus some of Milton's Italian sonnets) are about taking leave of one's beloved, or recalling loves lost long ago and far away. Ariosto's Orlando laments 'his fair Lady lost' – Angelica, Wordsworth's constant fantasy-image of his perfect lover – and Metastasio laments his Laura in words that could only recall Annette to Wordsworth's mind: 'Though far off, still in union, / I will be thy companion; / And thou, who knowst if ever / Thou wilt remember me!'[43]

Peace had been achieved, marriage consummated, and inheritances assured. But each of them at costs – political, financial, and emotional – that remained to be accounted for in the capitalization of the Poet.

CHAPTER THIRTY-THREE

Disciples and Partners

The National Poets of Scotland and the Grasmere Volunteer

> Breathes there a man, with soul so dead,
> Who never to himself hath said,
> This is my own, my native land!
> Whose heart hath ne'er within him burned,
> As home his footsteps he hath turned,
> From wandering on a foreign strand!
> (Scott, *The Lay of the Last Minstrel*, VI.i)

At the beginning of 1803 Wordsworth expanded his role as public poet: eight of his political sonnets appeared in the *Morning Post* between January and September, all signed 'W.L.D.' This was a signature he had last used in late 1795, from the depths of his retreat at Racedown, for a proper little poem, 'On Classick Learning,' in the *Weekly Entertainer*. Then the code-name signified 'Wordsworth Libertati Dedicavit' (Wordsworth dedicated to liberty).[1] Now, eight years later, his dedication to liberty was more patriotic and less reformist. These 'little political essays' are not activist interventions on current events; they view the bustle of political contest from the brooding perspective of a reclusive sage far removed from the world of action.[2]

The previous autumn Coleridge had addressed two letters to Fox in the *Morning Post*, denouncing the cultural bind into which he and his ex-radical friends had been cast by the government's relentless pursuit of men (like Thelwall) who had at first genuinely admired the ideals of the French Revolution. The letters were part of a larger attack on Fox for leading the peace party in its deluded belief that Bonaparte offered any hope for Europe. Wordsworth's sonnets extended this critique. These attacks hurt Fox deeply.[3] Whatever cultural capital Coleridge and Wordsworth had hoped to amass from sending Fox a copy of *Lyrical Ballads* two years earlier, proposing an alliance between his politics and their poetry, was now apparently expended.

Instead, the spring and summer of 1803 were marked by financial transactions more profitable than book sales. On 1 March William and Dorothy
received their share of the first payment on the Lowther debt, over
thirteen hundred pounds, followed by another seven hundred in July.[4] It
came in good time, for Basil Montagu's account with them was still nearly
£500 in the red, over half the total amount of the Calvert bequest on
which William had made his ill-considered loan seven years earlier.[5] Their
new investments were much larger and safer: in July they purchased 2500
consols at 3 per cent for £1315, ploughing two-thirds of their revenue
from the Lowther payment back into low-risk bonds.[6]

Still larger profits lay tantalizingly in view. The total Wordsworth
family investment in John's next voyage (from May 1803 to August 1804)
came to nearly £8000. John had large losses to cover from his last voyage,
but if this one were successful they would soon all be independently
wealthy. But its profit was not at all what they had hoped for: on his
return, he reported he sold his woollen goods 'neither ill nor well . . .
Opium and Quicksilver were the only things in the China market that sold
to any profit,' and he had carried little of either.[7] As a result, he stepped up
his insistence to the major owners of the *Earl of Abergavenny* 'of the
necessity of my having a better than a China direct voyage.'[8] A 'China
direct' voyage meant a non-stop trip out, except for supplies and repairs.
But a scheduled stop on the way, in India, meant that a ship could nearly
double its profits by selling a load of English goods in India and taking on
local goods there for China. The most valuable of these local goods was
opium, which was most easily taken on in Bengal where the East India
Company enjoyed a monopoly on its culture and distribution.[9] On his next
voyage, he got his wish.

Growing fame brought other profit to his brother as well, when he met
Sir George Beaumont, who was renting part of Greta Hall, that summer.
Beaumont, an aristocratic connoisseur and painter, was a regular visitor to
Keswick, having spent his honeymoon there in 1778. He exhibited his
rendition of the view from Greta Hall for his first appearance in the Royal
Academy in 1779.[10] Meeting Wordsworth through the offices of his
fellow-tenant Coleridge (whom Beaumont thought slightly disreputable),
he was so taken with the personal presence of the author of *Lyrical Ballads*
– which he greatly admired – that he arranged for two small pieces of land
at Applethwaite, adjacent to the Calverts' Ormathwaite property, to be
purchased in Wordsworth's name as a token of his esteem.[11] This grand
gesture of implied patronage made Wordsworth wary at first, but
Beaumont charmingly assured him that he expected nothing in return, and
only wanted 'to live & die with the idea that the sweet place with its rocks,
banks, & mountain stream are in the possession of such a mind as yours.'[12]
Thus began a friendship with another upper-class patron that was to be
the most personally affectionate one in Wordsworth's life. As with the new

Lord Lowther, Beaumont's friendship showed Wordsworth how his nature mythology could disguise aspects of his early work that might trouble the established artistic and political classes.

The summer also brought other kinds of discipleship, less grand but more intense. Among the growing number of letters from unknown admirers came one from seventeen-year-old Thomas DeQuincey, who had just returned to his mother's house after running away from school and spending the winter among prostitutes and beggars in London. DeQuincey was in a sense Wordsworth's first literary son, his letter of homage arriving within a month of the birth of the poet's first biological son, John (Johnny), on 18 June.[13] DeQuincey thus became one of the first conscious disciples of a new English brand of Romanticism. He was attracted to the new dispensations announced in *Lyrical Ballads*, just as young men like Charles Lloyd, George Burnett, and Robert Lovell had been the last disciples of Wordsworth's and Coleridge's old school of utopian radicalism.

DeQuincey spent over two weeks drafting his letter, deeply absorbing Wordsworth's own language; it reads like a prose digest of 'Tintern Abbey.' He touched all the right keys: 'the Dignity of your moral character,' 'the transcendency of your genius,' 'your name is with me forever linked to the lovely scenes of nature.' He hinted at the possibility of a visit, with the total abasement – and cheeky self-confidence – of the new convert: 'to no man on earth except yourself . . . would I thus lowly and suppliantly prostrate myself.'[14]

Wordsworth's reply to DeQuincey's youthful excess shows good sense and tact. He appreciated DeQuincey's praise and admiration, but warned him against over-valuing his poetry: 'You are young and ingenuous and I wrote with a hope of pleasing the young and the ingenuous and the unworldly above all others, but sorry indeed should I be to stand in the way of the proper influence of other writers.'[15] He ended by assuring his young admirer 'that it would give me great pleasure to see you at Grasmere if you should ever come this way.'

Over the next four years DeQuincey flirted with the idea of visiting his idol, twice making excursions to the Lakes but losing his nerve both times. Finally in 1807, having cultivated Coleridge and his family during a sojourn in Somerset, he returned to the Lakes as the escort of Sara and the children and imposed himself on the Wordsworths, replacing them as tenant of Dove Cottage after they left in 1808.

In this same July of 1803 Wordsworth also paid the price of another necessary ingredient to a growing reputation: three guineas for a portrait by one of the hundreds of painters who toured about the land, recording the prosperous features and estates of the rising middle class. But this painter was also a disciple of sorts, William Hazlitt, he of the enchanted visit to Nether Stowey in 1798. Hazlitt had come north at Coleridge's invitation, fresh from three months at the Louvre.[16] He painted portraits of both his heroes, but both pictures were universally condemned. Lady Beaumont said he made Wordsworth look more like a philosopher than a poet: this was a criticism. Though this portrait may have been destroyed, the chance that it was not, and that it gives us a picture of Wordsworth exactly at the time he was realizing himself as the Poet of his polemics, makes it an appropriate symbol for a biography of the young poet who in so many other ways hid himself from the gaze of posterity (see illustration). That it looks older than a thirty-three year-old man was part of everyone's reaction at the time, as Coleridge reported: 'Mrs Wilkinson *swears* that your Portrait is 20 years too old for you – & mine equally too old.' Mrs Wilkinson also said they looked 'too lank,' since both had long faces, less appropriate for Coleridge than for Wordsworth.

Hazlitt, 'that roving God Pan,' soon wore out his welcome, but not because of bad painting. Now twenty-five, he was already giving rein to his irascible, independent personality and slovenly disregard for his physical appearance, coupled with an unattractive man's angry lust toward the opposite sex. Wordsworth supported Hazlitt in disputing with Coleridge the existence and nature 'of the Divine Wisdom,' but he was solidly behind Coleridge in disapproving their mercurial disciple's sexual behaviour.

The incident is clouded by contemporary efforts to hush it up and distorted by Wordsworth's and Coleridge's later efforts to put Hazlitt in the worst possible light. What apparently happened is that a girl in Keswick called him 'a black-faced rascal,' whereupon he pushed her down and attempted to rape her. Finding himself thwarted, he 'lifted up her petticoats & *smote* her on the *bottom*.'[17] A gang of the girl's friends soon came looking for the 'out-comer' (outlander), proposing to give him a ducking in the lake. Coleridge and Southey barely got him out of town, leaving his clothes and painting materials behind him. He ran through the countryside, arriving at Grasmere about midnight. The Wordsworths took him in and sent him on his way in the morning, supplied with some clothing and a few pounds to get him home to Shropshire.

At the time, neither Coleridge nor Wordsworth took the defamatory attitude toward the incident that they did in later years. The incident, as reported, sounds very much like Hazlitt's blast against country life in his review of Wordsworth's *The Excursion* in 1814. Taking as his thesis the proposition that 'all country people hate each other,' Hazlitt's diatribe contains several details which echo the scandal of 1803: 'They hate all strangers, and generally have a nick-name for the inhabitants of the next village'; 'Having no circulating libraries to exhaust their love of the marvellous, they amuse themselves with fancying the disasters and disgraces of their particular acquaintance. Having no hump-backed *Richard* to excite their wonder and abhorrence, they make themselves a bug-bear of their own, out of the first obnoxious person they can lay their hands one'; 'They get up a little pastoral drama at home, with fancied events, but real characters.'[18] This was a long way from the pastoral ideology of *Lyrical Ballads*, but in 1803 both Coleridge and Wordsworth were soon writing to Hazlitt in all amicability, especially Wordsworth, who signed himself 'very affectionately yours,' and made no reference to the 'abominable and devilish propensities' he attributed to Hazlitt fifteen years later.

In what would look like the new couple's postponed honeymoon – except for the fact that the bride was not included – William and Dorothy travelled to Scotland from mid-August to mid-September, leaving Mary at home with two-month-old Johnny. They picked up Coleridge along the way, who left Sara in Keswick with their three children. Romanticism did much to bring the ideal of romantic love into general currency, but no one has ever said it was easy being married to a Romantic poet.

The old ménage à trois was on the road again. This was a strange trip for any of them to be taking at this time. Coleridge was always ready to seize any excuse for leaving home, but he was dreaming of a warm climate, which he certainly did not find in Scotland. Dorothy was devoted to her new nephew, yet was leaving him at a time when Mary had barely recovered her strength from a strenuous first delivery. The best explanation seems to be that William and Dorothy were trying to help Coleridge by attempting to revive the spirit of Stowey from six years earlier.

The whole trip had self-consciously romantic overtones. They drove by themselves, in what Dorothy gaily called their 'outlandish Hibernian vehicle,' a small open Irish touring carriage.[19] Their first stop was Carlisle, where Coleridge, 'impelled by Miss Wordsworth,' paid a visit to the cell of John Hatfield, who had just been condemned to death for impersonating an MP in his bigamous seduction of Mary Robinson, 'the Beauty of Buttermere.'[20] Coleridge had scored a big success the previous winter with a series of articles in the *Morning Post* on 'The Romantic Marriage' and 'The Keswick Impostor,' which exaggerated Mary's naïve passion, while intensifying Hatfield's mysteriously malignant motives.[21] It is hard to imagine what Coleridge had to say to Hatfield, whom he did not know. He came to the same conclusion: '*vain*, a hypocrite; it is not by mere Thought, I can understand this man.'[22]

Wordsworth did not accompany Coleridge on his visit to Hatfield's cell. Perhaps it seemed to him a too-literal reprise of his own poem, 'The Convict,' whose 'Jacobincal pathos' he had come to scorn. But it is fitting, though apparently entirely coincidental, that Wordsworth was the one to stop and look at Hatfield's execution site, in Longtown at the Scottish border, on their return trip. The desperation of hardened criminals and ravings of abandoned lovers were subject matter congenial to Coleridge, while Wordsworth's imagination was more stimulated by reflecting on dead ones.

Romantic subjectivity continued unabated once they crossed the border. Their first impressions were of Robert Burns, at Dumfries. William and Dorothy visited Burns's grave with 'melancholy and painful reflections' on the fate of another self-created national poet, whose native-language poetry experiment was even more radical than Wordsworth's, and who had paid the price in ruined reputation for not managing his career according to prevailing standards of what poetry should be like and how poets should live.[23] Burns had died in 1796, but his reputation began declining immediately under politically-motivated attacks on his drunkenness and debts.[24]

Wordsworth admired Burns greatly as a poet and innovator, but the three poems he composed about him from this trip were cautionary lessons about joining the life of the poet and the life of the man too closely together. He could not approve Burns's life style, but neither could he deny his poetry, and most of all he could not avoid identifying with him in an intensely personal, physical way as he meditated on his grave.

> I shiver, Spirit fierce and bold,
> At thought of what I now behold:
> As vapours breathed from dungeons cold
>   Strike pleasures dead,
> So sadness comes from out the mould
>   Where Burns is laid.
>
> And have I then thy bones so near,
> And thou forbidden to appear?
> As if it were thyself that's here
>   I shrink with pain;
> And both my wishes and my fear
>   Alike are vain.
>
> ('At the Grave of Burns,' 1–12)

This weird little Gothic lyric presses on to several more degrees of identification. Wordsworth suggests that he and Burns were neighbours ('Criffel's hoary top' is 'by Skiddaw seen'), 'and loving friends we might have been . . . True friends though diversely inclined.' He claims he grieved more deeply than other 'thousands' when Burns died, because he had hailed Burns's light 'when first it shone,' because it 'showed my youth / How Verse may build a princely throne / On humble truth.' This was sincere, but more true in retrospect than in the actual chronology of Wordsworth's poetical development.

To his credit, Wordsworth had second thoughts – almost always his best ones – and he wrote another poem, 'Thoughts,' commenting on the first. This one pushes aside thoughts of Burns's 'sorrow, wreck, and blight,' and rises to two stanzas that are far the best of the more than two hundred lines in Wordsworth's works devoted to Burns. In them, Wordsworth's identification with Burns becomes complete – or rather, Burns is completely assimilated to the role of Poet Wordsworth had now conceived for himself.

> Through busiest street and loneliest glen
> Are felt the flashes of his pen;
> He rules 'mid winter snows, and when
>   Bees fill their hives;
> Deep in the general heart of men
>   His power survives.
>
> What need of fields in some far clime
> Where Heroes, Sages, Bards sublime,
> And all that fetched the flowing rhyme
>   From genuine springs,
> Shall dwell together till old Time
>   Folds up his wings?
>
>   ('Thoughts,' 43–54)

'Deep in the general heart of men' is where Wordsworth sought to lodge himself. The second stanza is a direct recasting of the 'Prospectus' lines in Burns's honour ('Paradise, and groves Elysian . . . why should they be / A history only of departed things?'). To commemorate this important visit, he and Dorothy bought a one-volume edition of Burns's poetry in Stirling the next day, to put on their shelf next to the Kilmarnock edition that William had bought for Dorothy when he left for Cambridge in 1787.

The weather soon turned terrible, and after two weeks Coleridge left them to go ahead faster on foot, and to escape the inevitable exposure to the elements he suffered in their open touring car. They were making the standard 'Short Tour,' but Coleridge lacked William and Dorothy's willingness to sit and shiver in the rain as they took one detour after another in search of picturesque vistas. Tensions with Coleridge had started almost immediately, and the trip, which had been intended to restore their old camaraderie, showed instead that they were no longer 'one spirit in three persons . . . but one God.' They squabbled over housing and scheduling arrangements and argued about details of Scottish landscape and history that none of them in fact knew very well. Coleridge did not lack stamina: on his own, he walked another 263 miles through the Highlands in eight days![25] But his mental state was awful. He began the terrible 'Pains of Sleep' at this time, with its remorseless, Dantesque exploration of 'the unfathomable hell' within him, as he confronted all his worst demons: 'Thirst of revenge . . . Desire with loathing strangely mixed / On wild or hateful objects fixed. / Fantastic passions! maddening brawl! / And shame and terror over all!'

But their separation was beneficial to Wordsworth, for it meant that his first meeting with Walter Scott came when he was alone with Dorothy, on 17 September, and he did not have to share his host's attention with his dazzling, voluble friend. The meeting, at Melrose, was arranged by John Stoddart through his legal connections with Scott.[26] From it Wordsworth got more valuable lessons on how to set about becoming the Poet of one's nation.

Scott, affable and affluent, was already a laird of the manor in the Borders, in a way that Wordsworth could only conceive in imaginary terms in Cumberland. He was Sheriff of Selkirkshire, a quasi-political legal office that he executed with a combination of fairness and panache that earned him respect throughout the Borders. When financial necessity forced Wordsworth to petition the new Lord Lowther for a similar post ten years later, the office he got – Distributor of Stamps for Cumberland – was, though lucrative, very far from Scott's in popularity, being roughly equivalent to that of a tax collector.

Scott had just published his *Minstrelsy of the Scottish Border*, a three-volume collection of authentic and imitated 'Historical' and 'Romantic' ballads, refined for middle-class tastes, that started his rise to fame. Though close to Wordsworth's common-language project in some ways, its allegiance to the lore of the folk was fundamentally different from Wordsworth's, who always transformed his materials by the force of his own imagination. Where Scott's language normalizes the ancient peasant vernacular, while Burns retained it, Wordsworth can more accurately be said to *ab*normalize it. Scott was just then working on *The Lay of the Last Minstrel*, and recited parts of the first four cantos to William and Dorothy.

It was a pivotal moment in the literary history of the two men and their two countries. If Coleridge had come along it would have been even more interesting, since the *Lay* is very much built upon the fantastic super-naturalism of 'The Rime of the Ancient Mariner' and the Gothic medievalism of 'Christabel.' Stoddart had recently recited part of 'Christabel' for Scott, and Scott immediately appropriated its fast-paced, irregular four-beat metre, as well as many details of setting and mood. Indeed, the *Lay* starts out as a virtual plagiarism of 'Christabel':

> The feast was over in Branksome tower,
> And the Layde had gone to her secret bower;
> Her bower, that was guarded by word and by spell,
> Deadly to hear, and deadly to tell—
> Jesu Maria, shield us well!
> No living wight, save the Ladye alone,
> Had dared to cross the threshold stone.
>
> (I.i.1–7)

There were plenty of other precedents for Scott's poem in the ballad revival and in Gothic fiction, but *The Lay of the Last Minstrel* has good claim to be the original of one of the most popular aspects of British Romanticism: the revival of romance in a fashionably sophisticated mode.

Scott was just then energetically organizing a volunteer cavalry troop of young gentlemen from Edinburgh because of renewed fears of a French invasion following the breakdown of the Peace of Amiens that summer. After dealing with logistics every day (he was the quartermaster), Scott in the evenings recited to the Wordsworths a 'lay' of reunification: the convoluted plot of the *Lay* ends with a marriage that stops the family feud between the Cranstouns and the Buccleuchs, which is celebrated in the context of a still-larger truce between the English, led by Lord Howard, the Earl of Carlisle, and the Scottish border lords. In short, it deals intimately with the mutual neighbours and neighbourhoods, historically magnified, of both young men, thoroughly romanticizing the English-Scottish Border Wars, a three-century-long horror story of 'reiving' (raiding) and feuding of the most unspeakable kind.[27] Scott's *Lay* furthers the cultural work of peaceable assimilation between England and Scotland since the 1707 Act of Union; its lesson is that the two countries have more in common than otherwise.

Politics is to a large extent replaced by poetry in *The Lay of the Last Minstrel*: the bad old days are gone, but poetry lives on, chastened, humble, and humane. The last canto is devoted to a poetry contest at the wedding feast, featuring three poets' versions of failed affairs between lovers on opposite sides of national borders. Both Wordsworth and Scott, young men aged thirty-three and thirty-two, respectively, were already casting themselves as 'last' minstrels, poets of older cultural orders destroyed by present politics. Scott's revolutionary disappointment was 150 years old, but Wordsworth's was still active. Scott took refuge in poeticized history; Wordsworth constructed his refuge, for public consumption, in a poeticized nature, though his private retreat, in *The Prelude*, was more like a personalized history. In 1803, however, both myths were enlisted under the banner of the *Lay*'s most famous words, 'Breathes there a man, with soul so dead, / Who never to himself hath said, / This is my own, my native land!' Possibly the most stirring lines ever written in English in support of nationalism, though by a Scot, they express a sentiment to which both poets were, not without reluctance, bending their imaginations under the twin pressures of foreign invasion and revolutionary disillusionment.

All this was not fully evident at the time, but both men immediately recognized that they shared many interests, and similar social standing, and the friendship which began in 1803 ripened steadily, carefully cultivated by Wordsworth, through the rest of their lives until Scott's death in 1832. As with his visit to Burns's tomb, Wordsworth's visit to Scott stimulated several new poems. The most successful of them, 'Yarrow

Unvisited,' succeeds partly because it is an oblique statement by Wordsworth that he will not be diverted by another man's myth. On their way home, William and Dorothy stopped at the little inn at the crossroads of Clovenford. They had only to walk over a hill to see the picturesque river Yarrow celebrated by Scott, and they had endured far worse discomforts for lesser sights in the earlier part of their tour. Dorothy, recast in dialect as Wordsworth's local 'winsome Marrow' (companion), longs to go, but he bluntly refused: 'Strange words they seemed of slight and scorn.' His reason for this 'strange fit of passion' was to keep Yarrow as an imaginative resource, not to cash it in and be disappointed, as he had been by Mont Blanc, the Simplon Pass, and Snowdon. 'We have a vision of our own; / Ah! why should we undo it?' He was right: the unseen vista was always a more powerful stimulant to his creative imagination than the one seen. 'Yarrow Visited,' written in 1814 when they finally did visit it, tries to say that the 'genuine image' is a fair exchange for the one of 'fond imagination,' but it is a tepid tribute of scene-painting.

The real rival to 'Yarrow Unvisited' is the third poem in this triptych, 'Yarrow Revisited,' composed in 1831, but published only in 1834. And it gains its power from another loss: not of Yarrow but of the 'Great Minstrel of the Border' himself. For it was written on the occasion of their melancholy last visit to Scott, before he departed for Italy in a vain attempt to restore his health. It is a tribute to the power of poetry itself: 'what were mighty Nature's self . . . Unhelped by the poetic voice / That hourly speaks within us?' Wordsworth recalled through the layers of his memory both his 1814 visit and his 1803 nonvisit to Yarrow, collapsing them into a combined image of Scott *and* his last minstrel, standing beneath 'proud Newark's' ruined towers with its 'winding stair that once / Too timidly was mounted / By the "last Minstrel," (not the last!) / Ere he his tale recounted.'

Wordsworth wanted to be the poet of the people, but, in Scotland as in France and Germany, being a stranger in a strange land is what helped him to become the most English of poets. In a larger sense, his otherness was other-worldly: he is in some ways the most *human* of poets because of his deep attraction to states that are not national but extra-terrestrial, the sublime of imagination and the abject of death.

When they returned home, Wordsworth, fired by Scott's example, threw himself into the activities of the Grasmere Volunteers, which had been formed in response to panic fears of a French invasion. The Volunteers were under the general command of Lord Lowther, as lord lieutenant of Cumberland and Westmorland, and they took their training seriously, soon becoming regarded as the best county unit in the north. Wordsworth's participation was not an aberration, nor simply a piece of poetical grandstanding to show solidarity with the local yeomanry à la

Scott. Dorothy drily estimated that if the invading French ever reached Grasmere it would be too late for fighting, but she was correct to say that 'surely there never was a more determined hater of the French [than William] nor one more willing to do his utmost to destroy them if they really do come.'[28] William was one of the tallest and strongest of the recruits, and one of the most fit of those over thirty. His fantasy image of himself as a general and leader of men came close to reality here, a fact he later signalled in his private mythology by using the name 'Oswald' in *The Excursion* for George Dawson, a young Volunteer who died in 1807 of a chill caught swimming in the lake.[29]

Giving the name Oswald to a patriotic militiaman, 'the finest young man in the vale,' was both a literary and literal case of turncoatism, since another Oswald in Wordsworth's life-oeuvre was the anarchic revolutionary of *The Borderers*, based on the radical Colonel John Oswald from Wordsworth's experience in France. We have to look very hard for textual evidence of Wordsworth's migration from radical activist to government agent – whether as intelligence courier or as stamp distributor – but this seems to be one. Wordsworth's creation of Oswald-Dawson is not just a piece of gratuitous praise for a nice young man. It is George Dawson infused with the imaginative spirit of William Wordsworth, world-conqueror and redeemer. Wordsworth picks up on the fact that the Dawson boys 'took more delight in scholarship, and . . . a wider view of social interests than was usual among their associates.'[30] The 'wider view' that he gives Dawson is a close approximation of his own experiences on the Continent, projected on to a scene of the young Oswald teaching the local yokels how to read the map of contemporary Europe: ' "Here flows," / Thus would he say, "the Rhine, that famous stream!" '

> *Thence, along a tract*
> *Of livelier interest to his hopes and fears,*
> His finger moved, distinguishing the spots
> Where wide-spread conflicts then most fiercely raged;
> Nor left unstigmatized those fatal fields
> On which the sons of mighty Germany
> Were taught a base submission.
> (*Excursion*, VII.794–800; italics added)

In context, this refers to Napoleon's victories at Austerlitz (1805) and Jena (1806), but we can be quite sure that young Oswald's 'livelier . . . hopes and fears' were positioned close to the 'tracts' young Wordsworth moved across in Germany in 1799, a likelihood confirmed when his map-description goes on into Switzerland and touches the bases of Wordsworth's 1790 tour and its subsequent recapitulations in *Descriptive Sketches* and *The Prelude*. If there were any doubt that this 'favourite son' (*Excursion*, VII.853) is co-terminous with the 'chosen Son' of *The Prelude*, it is removed by Wordsworth's peroration, which would be ridiculous hyperbole if applied to George Dawson of Grasmere, but is nothing at all beyond the mark in comparison to the kind of rhetoric Wordsworth applies to the Bard of *The Recluse*:

> No braver Youth
> Descended from Judean heights, to march
> With righteous Joshua; nor appeared in arms
> When grove was felled, and altar was cast down,
> And Gideon blew the trumpet, soul-inflamed
> And strong in hatred of idolatry.
>
> (VII.811–16)

Wordsworth's enthusiasm for the Grasmere Volunteers was more patriotic than political, and more poetic than patriotic, but he was determined to save his country, one way or another, even from the consequences of a politics (Pitt's) he abominated.

In November, Thelwall showed up, of all people, starting out on the endless trek that was to continue for the entire remainder of his life. He was trying to eke out a living as another kind of language-professional, an elocutionist, but sooner or later he always suffered the consequences of his early identification with the cause of revolutionary reform, as local authorities or vigilantes discovered his past and ran him out of town. This fate had begun for him – and very nearly so for Wordsworth and Coleridge – during a similar time of invasion-hysteria in Somerset five years earlier. But he was welcomed to dine at the Wordsworth's cottage and stayed on an extra day to talk over old times, and their present career costs.

Thelwall was trying to answer Jeffrey's political smears from a review of April 1803, against his *Poems written chiefly in Retirement* (1802), and wrote in January of 1804 seeking Wordsworth's advice in his pamphlet wars. Thelwall was being tarred with two brushes, one for his actual radicalism, the other for his poems' similarity to the 'Lake School' that Jeffrey had first labelled in his explosive attack in the first number of the *Edinburgh Review*. This review was really aimed at Wordsworth, particularly the revolutionary potential Jeffrey accurately saw in the preface to *Lyrical Ballads*: 'a kind of manifesto that . . . very ingenuously set forth . . . that it was their [i.e., these 'followers of simplicity'] capital object "to adapt to the uses of poetry, the ordinary language of conversation among the middling and lower orders of society." '[31] That object was enough for Jeffrey to call them Jacobins: they were attacking the roots of society by perverting its hierarchies of language usage.

But Thelwall did not get much help from Wordsworth, who pleaded other poetical commitments as his excuse: 'as to the criticisms which you request of me . . . I cannot at present find time to make them. I am now after a long sleep busily engaged in writing a poem of considerable labour' [*The Prelude*].[32] Instead, Wordsworth offered Thelwall some tame improvements in style, and recommended he answer the *Edinburgh* on moral rather than personal grounds, attacking 'their wicked and detestable abstract opinions.' He distanced himself as much as possible from any kind of 'school' of poetry, professing to know nothing about these reviews, while at the same time showing a considerable familiarity with their main outlines. His oblique reference to *The Prelude* at this juncture, and the fact that this is the last extant letter from Wordsworth to Thelwall, suggest that an important corner in the origins of British Romanticism had been turned.

Coleridge too longed to escape from his present existence, but for personal domestic reasons, not public political ones. He was investigating the possibility of being somebody's secretary abroad, but he mostly wanted to get away to a warmer climate. He raised with John Wordsworth the possibility of accompanying him on his next voyage, a crazy idea for which all lovers of English literature owe John a vote of thanks, for dissuading Coleridge from an ill-fated voyage on which two-thirds of the passengers drowned. Coleridge's latest idea, as of December 1803, was to go to Madeira or Sicily, but at the last minute Humphrey Davy's enthusiastic account of Malta, coupled with John Stoddart's new appointment as king's advocate there, sent him to Valletta, England's strategic Mediterranean port. He spent fifteen months there, his immense charm and talents soon raising him to the post of acting public secretary for Sir Alexander Ball, the British governor.[33] Wordsworth did not want Coleridge to leave, not only because he disapproved of what was clearly yet another abandonment of his wife and children, but because he felt Coleridge was abandoning *him*.

CHAPTER THIRTY-FOUR

The End of *The Prelude*

, yet a few short years of useful life,
And all will be complete – thy race be run,
Thy monument of glory will be raised.
(XIII.428–30)

Coleridge's impending departure gave Wordsworth a new excuse to return to *The Prelude*. Coleridge passed through Grasmere just before Christmas on his way to London, and suddenly broke down under the weight of his many ailments: physical, psychological, and psychosomatic. He spent three weeks in bed, screaming from opium nightmares, soothed and nursed by Dorothy and Mary. As he recovered, he tried to get Wordsworth back on track for *The Recluse*, rather than wasting his energies on smaller tasks, or even diverting them to 'the poem to Coleridge.' He wrote to Poole predicting success in this effort, using metaphors from his own coming sea voyage. 'I rejoice . . . that he has at length yielded to my urgent & repeated – almost unremitting – requests & remonstrances – & will go on with the Recluse exclusively. – A Great Work, in which he will sail; on an open Ocean, & a steady wind; unfretted by short tacks, reefing, & hawling & disentangling the ropes . . . this is his natural Element.'[1]

Wordsworth's devoted women were set to copying out the existing parts of the poem, and on 4 January Wordsworth read to him 'the second Part of his divine Self-biography [i.e., Part Two of *1799*].'[2] What neither man fully realized was that the 'divine Self-biography' would shortly become the 'Great Work' itself. Two years earlier, Wordsworth had hesitantly extended the biographical line of the 'poem to Coleridge' beyond his seventeenth year, the point at which the 1799 text ended. There was no strong reason to do this in the structure of the text as it then stood, nor was there now. What *1799* needed to make it a finished poem was more at the beginning – an antecedent to its abrupt opening question, 'Was it for this?' – not more at the end. It certainly did not need over seven thousand additional lines, narrating eleven more years of the author's life, to make his leap into *The Recluse*'s themes of 'Man, Nature, and Human Life' any surer.

In one sense, Wordsworth returned to *The Prelude* by the path of least resistance. In another sense, his return to *The Prelude* was a heroic decision, that effectively turned him away from the older didactic, metaphysical model of *The Recluse* to the new existential, performative model of *The Prelude*. The poem he now resumed was an answer, the only one he knew for sure, to the question he had posed in his expanded preface to *Lyrical Ballads*: 'What is a Poet?' He had listed the essential ingredients and given the basic outline there, but now he had to show that *he* contained those elements and that his own life could fill in the outlines of that ideal Poet-figure. The question 'Was it for this?' would be answered by another, 'What is a Poet?'

The theme of the poem did not change, but he now gave it a much different plot, not just a longer one. Its crisis was now not the loss of his mother or his boyhood fears and ecstasies in the hills of Hawkshead; instead, it was the crisis of his age and his participation in it, including – but not quite revealing – his love affair with Annette Vallon. The conclusion of the two-part *Prelude* had spoken of the political disillusionment of his generation, but failed to give any evidence of the speaker's participation in it. Wordsworth's readiness to write about the subject he knew best – himself – was thus massively complicated by what he recognized it would entail: the need to write about the one contemporary subject on which everybody in his world had an opinion, the French Revolution. And, if he stated the grounds of his own authority – direct participation (both secret and subversive) in many of the Revolution's most exciting events – he would immediately render himself an unreliable narrator, either as a Jacobin sympathizer or as a renegade apostate.

Nevertheless, he persevered and, once committed to his task, the basic composition of *The Prelude* followed rapidly, in another of his amazing biennial bursts of poetic productivity: 1798, 1800, 1802, and now 1804, when most of the new poem was written, especially in the spring.[3] He composed the books that became III-V between January and March of 1804; these were followed in order of composition by VI, IX, and the first half of X between April and July. He added Books VII–VIII and the remainder of X in October–December. There were of course countless additions, deletions, switches, and revisions in this process, to say nothing of the forty-year process of revision that followed, and almost all original composition came to a halt when the tragic news of John's drowning reached Grasmere on 11 February 1805. The completion of the poem, between March and May of 1805, was a hurried affair; it no longer followed the chronology of his life, and used summary material, much of it composed earlier, to create the final books, XI–XIII.[4] But by a rough estimate, he was, between January 1804 and May 1805, often composing at the rate of one hundred lines of powerful blank verse a day.

His decision to resume was certainly liberating. He went straight on through most of 1804, with only a brief summer vacation, completing the entire chronological narrative of the poem as we now have it. At first Wordsworth simply pursued the chronological record of his education through his Cambridge years and summer vacations, apparently intending a five-book *bildungsroman* of the kind familiar to the eighteenth century from such works as Johnson's *Rasselas* or Beattie's *The Minstrel*.[5] But by early March he abandoned this plan and dismantled his manuscript, making the so-called 'five-book' *Prelude* of 1804 a largely conjectural version of the poem.

Neither the two-part version of 1799 nor this hypothetical five-book version are autobiographical poems in the sense that the thirteen- and fourteen-books are. They are preparatory poems or *epyllions*: introductory works to a larger one to follow. For nearly five years, *The Prelude* had assumed this relation to *The Recluse*, but now it took on a life of its own. Despite this large change in direction, Wordsworth pushed on chronologically, though he knew that by describing his 1790 walking tour and his subsequent experiences in France he was forcing his poem beyond any received idea of poetical development possible before 1789. By going into the French Revolution, Wordsworth's poem on the growth of his mind went beyond existing models not only of society but also of human identity and self-definition. Yet he began composing his French Revolution passages at a time when his own reactions to the present form of that cataclysmic event were almost the opposite of what they had been ten years earlier.[6]

There is no telling where Wordsworth's narrative might have stopped had John not drowned. When that occurred, he stopped telling a story. He finished off *The Prelude* when he was thirty-four going on thirty-five, but by February of 1805 he had extended his chronological line only five or six years beyond where *1799* had ended: i.e., from 1787 to *c*.1792–93. The poem's narrative ends with its hero at age twenty-three, with some bits and pieces referring as far forward as age twenty-five. The years 1793–98 are not significantly represented in *The Prelude* at all, the same traumatic 'five long years' from which he had given thanks for his recovery in 'Tintern Abbey.' These are the 'hidden' years of his life, and they are also hidden in his autobiographical poem. They are the years of the probable clandestine return to France, the first hideaway with Dorothy, the London misadventures with the *Philanthropist*, the second hideaway at Racedown, the spy scare in Somerset, and the escape (or mission?) to Germany. In all of these he was very much more involved in political activism and danger than anything in the poem we have, for though Books IX–X are about revolution, they are mainly about French, not English, politics.

John's death changed all this. The grief was too intense, the poem already too long, and the conclusion it was driving toward had already been composed several times. Filling in the years 1793–98 would have embroiled him in hopeless tangles and unexplainable embarrassments which would not aid his narrative but frustrate it as they had his life. Better to summarize how his 'Imagination' had been 'Impaired and Restored' (the running title of the last three books) in Nature (XI), in Society (XII), and in the Mind of Man (XIII): a triad of *Recluse*-terms with which to end *The Prelude*. The end of *The Prelude* thus also marks *finis* to the composition of 'Wordsworth'; the story of young Wordsworth comes to a close at the point where it disappears into Wordsworth's appropriation of it as the basic material of his writing life.

John's death was The End in another sense as well, for it meant that Wordsworth's financial circumstances would never advance much beyond what they already were. Fate, which had smiled so broadly on him in 1802–03, now turned its face the other way. John had expected 'a very good voyage . . . if not a *very great* one.'[7] William and Dorothy were heavily invested in it, taking advances on their share of their Lowther payment to invest even more.[8]

John was confident of a 'very great' return because he had at last prevailed on his ship's main owners to give him one of the routes that stopped in India. He expected it would be the Bombay stop, but when an in-house favourite who had been given the ultimate prize, the Bengal stop, declined it as being too risky, it fell into John's lap. This meant he could off-load his English goods there and take on far more profitable cargo for sale in China: opium.

Though officially forbidden and occasionally regulated, the opium trade had been going on since at least the 1730s, and led eventually to the Opium Wars (or 'Boxer Rebellion') of the 1840s. China had tried to outlaw it again in 1799, but traffic in it more than doubled that year and doubled again in 1800–04, with 60 per cent of it going to China.[9] In the words of John's biographer, it is 'obvious . . . that John and his associates felt no compunction about relying on Bengal's opium as a major asset to private trade on a "better voyage."'[10] It was 'private trade' because the opium was taken on board as part of the officers' private cargo allowance, like the 'camlets' for which John's wrists had been slapped in 1802. But the officers' trade in camlets only interfered with the East India Company's legitimate trade profits; opium was forbidden by company rules and the laws of both governments, though in fact the trade went on very lucratively, condoned by the company and encouraged by the British government. The trade was England's strategy, thinly disguised as private enterprise, to reverse the huge imbalance of payments resulting from the immense increase in tea imports to England.

John needed the opium trade not only to recoup his recent losses, but to realize the great profit that had always fired 'his schemes for making a quick fortune at sea,' which were motivated in turn by his desire to give his brother the independence 'to do something for the world.'[11] His hope and desperation are evident in the size of his total investment in this trip, nearly £20,000, more than double his last voyage, and much of it borrowed. He expected a profit of £10,000 on the first leg alone, even more from his cargo of rice and forbidden opium from Bengal to China, and still more from the teas he would carry on his voyage home.[12]

When his ship left Portsmouth with its fleet and escorts, John was determined 'to arrive in Bengal with the first ship,' and this eagerness tragically contributed to his disaster. For when the fleet turned back to Portland harbour to wait out some heavy weather it encountered, the *Earl of Abergavenny* was the last to put about because it was leading the pack out of the Channel. As a result, it was the last to pick up a pilot to negotiate the tricky turn around Portland Bill into the harbour, and it ran up against the Shambles, a bank of rocks just below water-level off the east tip of the Bill. John's first words to the pilot as they foundered show how much the purpose of the voyage weighed upon his mind: 'O Pilot, you have ruined me!'[13] John's behaviour as captain seems to have been unimpeachable during the seven agonizing hours it took for the ship to sink, though an inquiry afterwards raised several serious questions. Of the 387 persons aboard 155 were taken off the ship or pulled from the water, but John refused to leave his command and went down with the *Earl*. His body washed up on shore months later, not far from where William had seen hundreds of bodies from another wrecked convoy of Indiamen, when at Racedown ten years earlier.

With the loss of the family bottom, the family fortunes were also in shambles. The few hundred pounds William and Dorothy had invested were safely insured, but the huge profits which would have given William Wordsworth full leisure to become the poet of *The Recluse* would now never be realized. It is a material fact worth noting that both of Wordsworth's masterworks came to grief – *The Prelude* prematurely ended, *The Recluse* permanently delayed – in part because of reverses in England's imperial trade operations, particularly in the riskiest, most illegal, and morally reprehensible part of it, the opium 'war' on China. We need not make moral preachments on the fact, but it cannot be set aside as irrelevant to the cost of the creation of the Poet.

John's death not only initiated *The Prelude*'s end-game, it began the transition of the young Wordsworth into the Wordsworth of public memory and literary history. Three strands of life activity bound these poetical events together over the next two years. First, there was the family's wish to leave Dove Cottage, perhaps to leave Grasmere or the north altogether, as a growing family and painful memories there became hard to bear. Second, a subtle competition opened up between Wordsworth's intended major poems, *The Prelude* and *The Recluse*, and his other more saleable poems, in which the latter finally won out, with the fourth edition of *Lyrical Ballads* in 1805 and *Poems, in Two Volumes* in 1807. Thirdly, the public sphere continued to shape his career, as Napoleon's successes on the Continent dashed England's hopes of victory and Wordsworth found himself increasingly a man without any heroes but himself.

The possibility of leaving Town End was raised within a month of the news of John's death and pursued sporadically until late 1807, when the family decided to move to Allan Bank on the north shore of Grasmere. Practical needs motivated these plans and decisions. Thomas Wordsworth was born in June 1806, joining his brother John and sister Dorothy ('Dora'); every bed in the house was now sleeping two persons. But there were strong emotional needs as well, produced by John's death. 'The set is broken!' Coleridge cried out on hearing the tragic news, and some of the old associations of place became very hard to bear, though Wordsworth stoically overcame them, one by one. In the June after John's death he went fishing at Grisedale Tarn with a neighbour but had to leave almost immediately, overcome with grief at the memories of his separations from John at just that spot, in company with Coleridge in 1799 and with Dorothy in 1800. But within days he returned, alone, determined to engage in John's favourite sport, fishing, and his own, composing poems, to recollect his over-powering emotions in an enforced tranquillity. The result, 'Elegiac Verses in Memory of My Brother, John Wordsworth,' is doctrinally routine: Wordsworth's recognition that he must 'with calmness suffer and believe.' But it conveys the horror of the first shocking news:

> Sea—Ship—drowned—Shipwreck—so it came,
> The meek, the brave, the good, was gone;
> He who had been our living John
> Was nothing but a name.

But this fierce attempt to cauterize his emotions by his own poetry could not heal the fact that the days of their youth had ended, and the imminent departure from Dove Cottage was the physical sign that the days of young Wordsworth were numbered.

In the first week of April 1805, after the immediate grief which shook the household had subsided, he composed some lines about John for inclusion in *The Recluse*. These were more than occasional elegiac verses, Dorothy insisted to Lady Beaumont: 'I should not say a *poem* for it is *part* of the Recluse.'[14] That Wordsworth's first return to major composition following John's death was to *The Recluse*, not *The Prelude*, shows how much he regarded the former as the work for which John had been risking his life. Dorothy concurred: 'I trust he will perform something that may mend many hearts, and that his Brother would have approved.' But these lines disappeared into thin air. He 'composed much' by his usual method of outdoor striding and humming, and they 'came from [him] in a torrent,' but they evaporated in his mind; he was 'overpowered by [his] subject.' 'I could not hold the pen myself, and the subject was such that I could not employ Mrs Wordsworth or my Sister as my amanuensis.'[15]

Immediately following this failure he turned to completing *The Prelude*, which he did extremely quickly, assembling Books XI–XIII in the space of a month between late April and late May, mostly by rearranging already composed materials. Here again Wordsworth's mountainous strength is evident. He brought the poem on his life to a close with three books titled 'Imagination, How Impaired and Restored' at the very time his imagination had been *un*restorably impaired by his brother's death.

Completing *The Prelude* was a major step, but with John dead, Wordsworth no longer had the stomach to keep on writing about his own life. His dissatisfaction with *The Prelude*, now widely considered the greatest long poem in English of the nineteenth century, is registered in his letter to Beaumont in June 1805, immediately after he finished writing it. 'It was not a happy day for me I was dejected on many accounts; when I looked back upon the performance it seemed to have a dead weight about it, the reality so far short of the expectation . . . and the doubt whether I should ever live to write the Recluse and the sense which I had of this Poem being so far below what I seem'd capable of executing, depressed me much.'[16] But it gave him a new idea, that 'this work may be considered as a sort of portico to the Recluse, part of the same building, which . . . if I am permitted to bring it to a conclusion, and to write, further, a narrative Poem of the Epic kind, I shall consider the *task* of my life as over.'

Once *The Prelude* was completed, Wordsworth doggedly set himself to meet his implied contract with both John and with Coleridge by pushing *The Recluse* forward. Until Coleridge returned and Wordsworth saw him, he kept his creative eye steadily on *The Recluse*, even as he continued to mark time with smaller pieces. But another sea disaster damaged his hopes in the month before the tragic news about John, when Coleridge reported that Major Ralph Adye (1764–1804), to whom he had entrusted his notes for *The Recluse*, had died of plague en route back to England at Gilbraltar, where all his personal belongings and baggage were burned as a quarantine measure.

This fact may be regarded with a certain amount of scepticism. There really was a Major Adye who did die, and Coleridge probably *had* given him some notes, during Adye's visit to Malta, since producing voluminous notes for other people's poems was one of his most fertile modes of writing. But there are some inconsistencies in Coleridge's account that raise the suspicion he may have used Adye's death as a pretext to explain to everyone who was expecting notes, letters, poems, travel journals, newspaper stories, or anything else from him why they had not got them. Daniel Stuart, the Beaumonts, Sara Coleridge and others all received letters lamenting the fact that the death of 'that good Man Major Adye!' had resulted in the destruction of all Coleridge's writings to them. In one notebook entry, Coleridge's standard formula for the event – 'And Major Adye is dead! There died a good man!' – contains a later insertion, 'as if to retract the preceding sentences' wherein he had intimated his own feelings of failure: 'yet I felt that in telling the Truth I was conveying falsehood.'[17] For good measure, he referred to other sets of letters thrown overboard from the *Arrow*, the *Acheron*, and an unspecified – and thus unspecifiable – 'merchant Vessel.'

But even if we give Coleridge the benefit of the doubt, it remains uncertain whether these notes would have helped much to produce *The Recluse*. After the publication of *The Excursion* ten years later, Coleridge sent Wordsworth a long letter full of regretful suggestions about what *The Recluse* should have been – another favourite Coleridgean perspective. But his observations do not differ fundamentally from what he had been saying about *The Recluse* all along.[18] It was to show how a certain conception of an independent, creative imagination, fostered by 'Nature,' could work to transform and redeem secular society. That is, it was the lesson of *The Prelude* writ large, with 'Wordsworth' rewritten as 'Everyman.'

His inventive powers remained inadequate to the task, but he nevertheless tried: in the summer of 1806 he returned to the portions of 'Home at Grasmere' he had composed in 1800 and completed it, bravely penning, 'Book First, Part First of *The Recluse*,' across the top of the first page of the finished manuscript. He did this by employing materials he had ready to hand: Grasmere neighbourhood stories of human fortitude and moral sensitivity in harsh rural surroundings without benefit of culture and education. For example, there was the local farmer who committed adultery with the family's maid, then let his farm run to ruin from remorse, and finally died broken in spirit. Wordsworth tried to lift these odd moral fables from the literal to the symbolic level. He tried to increase their plausibility by adding a new conclusion which stitched his folksy Grasmere narratives on to the epic, mythic, apocalyptic claims of the 'Prospectus': 'Is there not / An art, a music, and a stream of words / That shall be life, the acknowledged voice of life?'[19] This rhetorical question about a possible transparency between ordinary and artistic language states the intention of *The Recluse* at its best, an intention frequently realized in many of Wordsworth's smaller poems, when freed of the weighty responsibility of *proving* it. But beyond this he could not go.

CHAPTER THIRTY–FIVE

Presenting the Poet

> . . . that Lay
> More than historic, that prophetic Lay
> Wherein (high theme by thee first sung aright)
> Of the foundations and the building up
> Of thy own Spirit thou hast dared to tell
> What may be told . . .
>
> (Coleridge, 'To William Wordsworth: Composed on the Night after His
> Recitation of a Poem on the Growth of an Individual Mind,' January 1807)

All this stop-gap ended abruptly late in October of 1806, when the Wordsworths finally re-established contact with Coleridge. The entire Wordsworth household had been invited to spend several months as guests of the Beaumonts at their estate at Coleorton, between Derby and Leicester. But when the family started south, they learned at their first stop, Kendal, that Coleridge had just returned to the north. Not to Keswick, however. Instead, he had gone to Penrith, hoping to find Sara Hutchinson. Ignoring the bad omen that Coleridge had gone first to see Sara his beloved, not Sara his wife, the Wordsworths immediately sent a message – to Keswick – for him to join them. He came dashing into Kendal almost as soon as the messenger departed, and not from Keswick but from Penrith, for he had set off immediately in pursuit of Sara. They were all shocked by his appearance, and saddened when they learned that he intended to separate from his wife. But they were scandalized when they realized he was trying to act out his fantasy of establishing a connection with Sara Hutchinson. Postponing their trip, they huddled together in strained conversations for two days in the hotel rooms and streets of Kendal, trying to talk him out of his desires while still hoping to re-establish their old relationships.

Reuniting with Coleridge had been the focus of their hopes for the two years since his departure, both for living and for writing (*The Recluse* would emerge when Coleridge returned). But his appearance and his defeated willpower made it clear that all was changed for ever. Coleridge soon did arrange a separation from his wife. But his desperate wish that he might as a result establish a relationship of some sort with Sara Hutchinson involved almost the only woman in the world with whom the Wordsworths could not countenance his having an intimate association. To make matters worse, Coleridge began to form the notion that Wordsworth had supplanted him in Sara's affections and was having an affair with his sister-in-law. This fear did not burst out immediately, but a germ of suspicion was planted at Kendal. On the morning of 28 October Mary and Dorothy and the children climbed into a chaise and departed southward. Sara and William and Coleridge saw them off, and then Coleridge climbed resignedly into the coach heading back toward Keswick. But he knew the rest of the travel plan: that Sara and William would follow the next morning, after staying one more night together in Kendal. The train of morbid thoughts laid down in Coleridge's fervid imagination when he thought about Wordsworth's last night in Keswick exploded at Coleorton two months later.

During the long comfortable winter at Coleorton, they were all guests of the rich and generous Beaumonts, and they had no trouble adapting themselves to this higher style of life (the palatial residence was until recently the headquarters of the National Coal Board). Wordsworth made himself useful by planning an elaborate winter garden on the grounds. He had plenty of leisure time to devote to *The Recluse* if he had wanted to. Instead, he turned from it to more expedient work on his forthcoming *Poems, in Two Volumes*, which appeared in April 1807, arguably the single greatest collection of his works. A cancelled 'Advertisement' in the first of these volumes made clear their relation to *The Recluse*:

> The short poems, of which these Volumes consist, were chiefly composed to refresh my mind during the progress of a work of length and labour, in which I have for some time been engaged; and to furnish me with employment when I had not resolution to apply myself to that work, or hope that I should proceed with it successfully. Having already, in the Volumes entitled Lyrical Ballads, offered to the World a considerable collection of short poems, I did not wish to add these to the number, till after the completion and publication of my larger work; but, as I cannot even guess when this will be, and as several of these Poems have been circulated in manuscript, I thought it better to send them forth at once.[1]

This was certainly honest, but much too exposed, and Wordsworth or his editors did well to cancel it. But it was wholly in keeping with his compulsive notion that any work he produced should be introduced, or defended, by referring to still-larger works and intentions that lay behind it. This habit of posting 'Watch This Space' advertisements for his always-under-construction self provided unfriendly reviewers and pundits with very large targets for fun and satire.

But this was not his only motive for publication. Longman had brought out a fourth edition of *Lyrical Ballads* in the autumn of 1805. Its appearance underscored, for peers and critics who paid attention to this sort of thing, that he had been recycling essentially the same version of his poetry, and of himself, to the reading public for seven years, from 1798 to 1805. What *else* could Wordsworth write? was a question implied in several unsympathetic reviews. Also, the extent to which he was identified solely with *Lyrical Ballads* did his reputation little good in the conservative cultural consensus that was emerging, for *Lyrical Ballads* had by now, through its regular biennial reappearances, become the flagship – and the target – of the 'Lake School' of poetry, that newly dominant reviews like the *Edinburgh* continued to bombard as unreconstructed Jacobinism.

It was not only the shock of Coleridge's appearance that led Wordsworth to redirect his poetic activities in late 1806, but also his perceptions of a changing world that a long visit to London that spring had brought home to him. At the time, Mary was expecting her third child, and William was not much help around the crowded little house, so he was packed off to London in March for a visit of two months. This visit brought him personally closer to the centres of British cultural and political power than he had ever been before, and what he saw and heard forced him to recognize that the world of his youth no longer existed, and convinced him of the need to change with the times.

Pitt had died suddenly in January, heartbroken over the continued failure of his policies against Napoleon, and Grenville was called on to form a new ministry, the hugely promising 'Ministry of All Talents.' Its great promise was not borne out, but for the moment it looked as though the Whig heroes of the 1790s were back in the saddle. Grenville, object of Wordsworth's scorn in his Juvenal imitation of 1795, was prime minister, with the ageing Fox as foreign minister, brought in over the King's objections. Charles Grey entered the Cabinet (he was prime minister when the Reform Bill finally passed in 1832), as did Thomas Erskine, redoubtable champion of the 1794 treason trials.

After visiting with Christopher in Lambeth, Wordsworth moved across the river to Grosvenor Square to be near the Beaumonts and spent much of his time at their spacious town house. He also spent some time with Basil Montagu, who was rising successfully in the law, and on 19 May, near the end of his visit, he attended a 'rout' hosted by Fox's wife. Samuel Rogers introduced Wordsworth to Fox. They had a very satisfactory exchange, which Wordsworth improved over years of retelling it. Fox clearly knew who Wordsworth was, rising from his beloved gaming table with the greeting, 'I am very glad to see you, Mr Wordsworth, though I am not of your faction.'[2] This is all Rogers recorded in his diary, except for the explanation that Fox meant 'he admired a school of poetry different from that to which Wordsworth belonged.' The thrust startled Wordsworth, but he was equal to it, elegantly capping it by replying, 'But in poetry you must admit that I am the Whig and you the Tory.' This is almost the wittiest thing Wordsworth ever said, but it developed over years of reliving the moment and recollecting his emotions about it into tranquillity, for it derives from a manuscript of 1843 prepared by Humphrey Davy's sister-in-law for her children. She said Wordsworth mentioned it, 'the only such mention I ever heard from him,' as 'a *bon-mot* of my own.'[3]

Wordsworth dined with his old radical friends in London, making several calls on Godwin, once in company with Horne Tooke, now seventy. Both were much subdued, older, and radical no more, discredited not only by governmental harassment and amateur vigilantism, but also by geo-politics far beyond their control.

Wordsworth's meetings and reflections on times past were not wholly coincidental. He also dined with John Taylor, part-owner of the *True Briton* and the *Sun*, who had been sent a copy of the 1800 *Lyrical Ballads*. Taylor, true to his informer's habits, gossiped with the painter and diarist Joseph Farington that he found Wordsworth 'strongly disposed to Republicanism.' This meant, according to Taylor, that Wordsworth's 'notions are that it is the duty of every Administration to do as much as possible to give consideration to the people at large, and to have *equality* always in view; which though not perfectly attainable, yet much has been gained towards it & more may be.'[4] Taylor thought 'that all of them [Wordsworth, Coleridge, and Southey] affecting to be simple & natural . . . frequently reduce their expressions to what may almost be called *Clownish*.' We don't know what Wordsworth and Taylor said face to face, but John Taylor was not the man to mask his opinions, and Wordsworth was no more subtle when it came to answering a direct question.

Nonetheless, a sharp inquiry about the legitimacy of his poetry and his politics, to say nothing of having it repeated about town, chimed ominously in his memory with Walter Scott's amused report the previous August (1805) that Lord Somerville, on hearing that Wordsworth had got into Scott's 'good company,' warned Scott he still had doubts about the loyalty of Wordsworth and Coleridge, feeling they were still republican sympathizers; he proudly claimed responsibility for setting the spy on them in 1797 in Somerset.[5] Somerville's comment showed Wordsworth that, even ten years later, memories were still sharp and that clever drawing-room repartee could be based on claiming to have sniffed out Wordsworth's radicalism before it was reformulated as literature. Wordsworth had joined in the laughter at Scott's report, but had not bothered to tell Scott how plausible the government's actions were, given his and Coleridge's and Thelwall's reputations in 1797.

Fox's death in September of 1806 touched a still-deeper chord in

Wordsworth's memory. He composed three poems in response to it, the 'Lines composed at Grasmere . . . after a stormy day, the Author having just read in a Newspaper that the Death of Mr. Fox was hourly expected,' and two fragments, 'The rains at length have ceased' and 'To the Evening Star over Grasmere Water.' His grief for the loss of Fox was so great because, as at the grave of Burns, he felt the general loss personally. 'Many thousands now are sad' was a cliché truism. But when he goes on to say, 'A Power is passing from the earth / To breathless Nature's dark abyss,' the lines thrill because we can hear them echoing Wordsworth's similar lines about himself in the Simplon Pass or on Snowdon. Similarly, 'To the Evening Star over Grasmere Water' remains a twelve-line fragment rather than a finished sonnet because Wordsworth could not bring himself to add the necessary two lines that would complete his identification with Fox, such as he had made in his dedicatory letter of 1801. But we can recognize their connection in the fragment's similarity to 'Hesperus':

> The lake is thine,
> The mountains too are thine, some clouds there are,
> Some little feeble stars, but all is thine,
> Thou, thou art king, and sole proprietor.

Jupiter was his planet, and Hesperus was his star. To say that these lines are egotistical is to miss – or make – the essential point: Wordsworth aspired to an egotism that transcended historical egotism or personal success. At these moments and in these places he began to realize that the epic story of his own imaginative development could never hope for a sympathetic reading in a world dominated by the likes of John Somerville and Francis Jeffrey. With the passing of heroes like Fox, politicians – and readers – who could sympathize even when they disagreed, Wordsworth knew the 'fit audience' he sought was gone, at least for the time being.

Hence he was extremely upset when, within weeks of comfortably settling in after arriving at Coleorton in the autumn, he received a letter from his old friend Francis Wrangham cheerily proposing that they resurrect their Juvenal satire of 1795–97. Possibly Wrangham felt that, with both Pitt and Fox dead, its political bite was now tame enough for safety. Or maybe he thought that its whacks on 'Grenville's onion head' would be great fun now that Grenville was prime minister.

Wordsworth was horrified. Not only were many of the persons named in it still living, and just then returned to power, his own personal and political relations to them had changed markedly. A line like, 'Must honour still to Lonsdale's tail be bound?,' would simply not do, when 'Lonsdale' now signified William, not James, Lowther, a neighbour and benefactor whom Wordsworth was assiduously cultivating, not the tyrant of his youthful life. Individual lines could have been changed, of course, but he wanted to bury the whole ethos of this part of his past, and he was nearly frantic in his determination to quash the project. He was highly successful in doing so, as the full version of this satire has only just appeared.[6]

He fired back at Wrangham a volley of reasons why they should drop the idea, demanding that any verses by him should be immediately destroyed (they weren't). He began with a high-minded literary rationale for declining to participate, 'I have long since come to a fixed resolve to steer clear of personal satire . . . with respect to public delinquents or offenders . . . I should be slow to meddle even with these.'[7] But he ended with a set of practical reasons that arose much more immediately from the present stage of his self-creation as the Poet.

> I would most willingly give them up to you, fame, profit, and everything, if I thought either true fame or profit could arise out of them: I should even with great pleasure leave you to be the judge in the case if it were unknown to everybody that I ever had a concern in a thing of this kind; but I know several persons are acquainted with the fact and it would be buzzed about; and my name would be mentioned in connection with the work, which I would on no account should be.

As in his letters to William Calvert in 1795, Wordsworth's emotions blur his syntax. And with good reason. With *Lyrical Ballads* a sitting target for charges of 'Jacobinical pathos,' with *Poems, in Two Volumes* in the last stages of preparation, and with *The Prelude* finished and waiting Coleridge's arrival for its first performance, such an exposure of his 'youthful errors' was the last thing he needed. It would have confirmed the still-lively suspicions of people like John Taylor and Lord Somerville that Wordsworth was steeped in republicanism. That he no longer was mattered less to him than that he would be *perceived* as such, and he knew that no amount of explanation would satisfy such implacable opponents. His phrase about a 'judge in the case' hints at thoughts about the government's now wholly successful prosecutions for treason and sedition, and his fear that his 'name would be mentioned' by 'several persons . . . acquainted with the fact' could refer equally well to the kind of gossip he had heard about town in the spring or to crown witnesses in a trial. The Juvenal verses were a clear exposure of the young Wordsworth in all his edgy strength; like *The Prelude* and other evidences of this young man's existence (most of them in unpublished manuscripts), they had to be hidden if the creation of the Poet was to succeed.

Hence Wordsworth's thoughts about his career were particularly sharp and sensitive when Coleridge arrived on 21 December, having arranged his separation from Sara Coleridge in an emotional debacle at Keswick in November. In some respects these months together did knit up and restore the old relationships. The Wordsworths had Coleridge to themselves, and could modulate the upsetting effect of Sara Hutchinson's presence on him by daily routines of an ordinary domesticity more in tune with reality. But not before Coleridge tormented himself to the last degree of agony in his amazing fantasy life.

Fate could not have decreed a crueller twist in the final act of creation of the Poet than that Coleridge, in his state, should at this time have had to listen to Wordsworth's first full presentation of *The Prelude*. But he contrived to make matters worse for himself by convincing himself that William was now pursuing an affair with Sara Hutchinson. His fantasy of their sexual encounter seems to have taken up three sheets in his notebook – which, in a gesture of caution highly uncharacteristic in such an unbuttoned account of his private thoughts, he (or a nervous heir) carefully cut out. All that remains is a very precise notation of the time and the place: '**THE EPOCH.** Saturday, 27th December, 1806 – Queen's Head, Stringston [Thringstone], ½ a mile from **Coleorton Church**, 50 minutes after 10.'[8] The words, 'The Epoch,' are written in larger, bolder letters than any other words in Coleridge's huge volume of notebooks. There is no further indication of what might have happened at that time to excite his suspicions, but the emotional debris from it haunted him for the rest of his life, especially over the next two years.

The following September, after quoting a bitter misogynist couplet from Propertius ('What profits it for maids to found temples in honour of Chastity, if every bride is permitted to be whate'er she will?'), he wrote a long, tortured analysis of his desire to make himself worthy of Sara's love, 'even to make her already loving me love me to that unutterableness, that impatience at the not enoughness of dependence, with which I love her!'[9] But even this excruciating meditation on the exquisite reciprocities of love ('to make her Love of me delightful to her own mind'), is crossed by Wordsworth's shadow, at once censorious and lascivious:

> O! what mad nonsense all this would sound to all but myself—and perhaps even She would despise me for it—no! not despise—but be alarmed—and learn from *W* —to pity & withdraw herself from my affections. Whither?—O agony! O the vision of that Saturday Morning—of the Bed/ —O cruel! is he not beloved, adored by two—& two such Beings— /and must I not be beloved *near* him except as a Satellite?—But O mercy mercy! is he not better, greater, more *manly*, & altogether more attractive to any [*sic*] the purest Woman? . . . W. is greater, better, manlier, more dear, by nature, to Woman, than I—I – miserable I!—but does he—O No! no! no! he does not—he does not pretend, he does not wish, to love you as I love you, Sara! . . . No! he is to be beloved – but yet, tho' you may feel that if he loved you, . . . even *partly* as *I* love you, you should inevitably love him . . . yet still he does not *so* love you— . . . I alone love you so devotedly, & therefore, therefore, love me, Sara!—Sara! love me![10]

And in 1808 the 'thunder-cloud' of 'that miserable Saturday morning!' could still break fresh upon him, when he recollected 'the anxious fears, <of which> I scarcely dare be conscious. But *then* was the first Thunder-Peal! But a minute and a half with ME—and all that time evidently *restless & going*—An hour and more with **KK.0XKK.0U** [Wordsworth] *in bed*—O agony!'[11]

That all this is Coleridge's fantasy, not fact, is far the more likely possibility. But the fact cannot automatically be ruled out, given Wordsworth's commanding physical presence and the fact that Sara was much the liveliest and most attractive of the three rather plain women of the household – and the one whose critical opinions about his poetry Wordsworth paid most attention to. But that Coleridge could have fantasized such a scene is not at all out of character for his mercurial imagination. Later in life he was still exorcising the demon of this thought, analysing the 'Strange Self-power in the Imagination, when painful sensations have made it their Interpreter.'[12] His vivid imagination gave a living, breathing sense of reality to something he knew – or should have known – not to be true: 'That dreadful Saturday Morning, at [Coleorton], did I *believe* it? Did I not even *know*, that it *was* not so, *could* not be so? Would not it have been the sin against the Holy Ghost . . . if I had dared to believe it conscientiously, & intellectually! Yes! Yes! I *knew* the horrid phantasm to be a mere phantasm . . . even to this day the undying worm of distempered Sleep or morbid Day-dreams—'[13] One would almost have to *be* Coleridge to imagine how jealousy of Wordsworth could be construed as a sin against the Holy Ghost. But whatever facts he based his fantasy on, their disposition required an unreliable witness and unscrupulous prosector, roles which Coleridge was all too ready to assume, in his mind, especially against himself.

Whether something really had happened that Saturday morning or not, it is in the highest degree amazing that Coleridge could sit still to listen to *The Prelude* delivered in its master's voice later the same week. His ability to hear the poem in a properly receptive frame of mind was beaten down to a nadir of hatred, anger, shame and humiliation. It is a vast tribute to the power of both mens' character that Wordsworth should have finished *The Prelude* and delivered it to its intended auditor at this time, and that Coleridge should rise to the occasion with almost the last significant poem of the remaining twenty-seven years of his life. If the composition of *The Prelude* was brought to an end by John's death, its presentation to Coleridge produced the epitaph for Coleridge's poetical career, written by himself, and titled, 'To William Wordsworth: Composed on the Night after His Recitation of a Poem on the Growth of an Individual Mind.' In drafts written within hours of his first hearing it, Coleridge praised it in terms that magnificently sum up Wordsworth's career achievement:

> that Lay
> More than historic, that prophetic Lay
> Wherein (high theme by thee first sung aright)
> Of the foundations and the building up
> Of thy own Spirit thou hast dared to tell
> What may be told, to the understanding mind
> Revealable . . .

The lines give full emphasis to the importance of the French Revolution in the creation of Wordsworth the Poet, in images recalling the triumphal march of a Roman emperor: 'Where France in all her towns lay vibrating . . . beneath the burst / Of Heaven's immediate thunder . . . thou wert there, *thine own brows garlanded, / Amid the tremor of a realm aglow, / Amid a mighty nation jubilant.*'

The poem is indeed an *homage* to much of Wordsworth's entire oeuvre, from direct allusions to the Intimations Ode ('thoughts all too deep for tears'), to the fact that its overall structure is an amalgam of 'Tintern Abbey' and Coleridge's 'Dejection' Ode. Like the ode's acknowledgment of the imaginative crisis caused by his hopeless love for Sara Hutchinson, 'To William Wordsworth' becomes a farewell to Coleridge's hopes for a poetical career, in humble prostration before Wordsworth's. Even before the reading ended, Coleridge could see his friend 'in the choir of ever-enduring men,' unaffected by Time, 'among the archives of mankind.' As he listened, 'with a heart forlorn,' his spirits revived only to the extent that he knew *he* was lost, 'even as Life returns upon the drowned.' The sense of his life that flooded over him was a terribly unfair indictment of all his failures, both real and imaginary:

> [of] fears self-willed, that shunned the eye of Hope;
> And Hope that scarce would know itself from Fear;
> Sense of past Youth, and Manhood come in vain,
> And Genius given, and Knowledge won in vain;
> . . . [all] but flowers
> Strewed on my corse, and borne upon my bier,
> In the same coffin, for the self-same grave!
>
> (66–69, 73–75)

This is the same kind of death-imagery he used in 'Dejection,' prompted now not simply by a recognition of Wordsworth's greater poetic powers, but also by his excruciatingly painful suspicion of his friend's greater sexual attraction to his beloved Sara Hutchinson. Wordsworth was 'better, greater, more *manly*, & altogether more attractive to any the purest Woman,' both in poetics and erotics. But he did not let such unmanning thoughts destroy his poem: 'That way no more! . . . ill beseems it me . . . To wander back on such unhealthful road, / Plucking the poisons of self-harm!'

Instead, begging Wordsworth's pardon, he returned to a conclusion of praise that summons up Coleorton's prescribed domestic antidote to his violent passion: the scene of all of them listening together, he and Dorothy and Mary and Sara, 'eve following eve, / Dear tranquil time, when the sweet sense of Home / Is sweetest!' A sudden thought reminded him of their trip to Germany. His soul lay passive beneath the power of Wordsworth, 'driven as in surges now beneath the stars, / With momentary stars of my own birth, / Fair constellated foam' – an image he recalled from his night alone on deck during the passage to Hamburg, when 'cloud-like foam dashed off from the vessel's side, each with its own small constellation.'[14] And when Wordsworth had finished, and Coleridge saw 'round us both / That happy vision of beloved faces' – a vision that had been horribly disfigured for him ten short days before – he forgave all, though he never forgot it, in a profound gesture of religious submission: 'And when I rose, I found myself in prayer.'

EPILOGUE

Hiding the Man; or, Emotion Recollected in Tranquillity

Poetry is the spontaneous overflow of powerful feelings: it takes its origin from emotion recollected in tranquillity: the emotion is contemplated until by a species of reaction the tranquillity disappears, and an emotion, kindred to that which was before the subject of contemplation, is gradually produced, and does itself actually exist in the mind.

(Preface to *Lyrical Ballads*, 1800)

After reading *The Prelude* to Coleridge with devastating effect in early 1807, Wordsworth did something unusual, the significance of which was not immediately clear to either man, and which has been almost wholly lost sight of since. But he dealt with it in a manner consistent with many other actions he took in regard to his youth: he hid the poem from public knowledge, keeping it by him during the remaining forty-three years of his life. In this special sense, *The Prelude* is 'The Hidden Wordsworth.'

This decision not to publish 'the poem on the growth of my own mind' inevitably produced the temptation to *keep on* writing it. Not by extending it alongside his ongoing life, but by perfecting its youthful epiphanies through endless revision. At the time, Wordsworth's assumption was that *The Prelude*'s publication would depend on his first finishing *The Recluse*. But this assumption gradually hardened into a retroactive decision against publishing *The Prelude*, as first years, then decades, passed and no *Recluse* appeared, though both poems were announced in the preface of *The Excursion*, published in 1814 and identified as Part II of *The Recluse*.

Instead, the non-appearance of Wordsworth's epic of self-creation matches other acts defining the young Wordsworth. It became yet another hidden aspect of his youthful self, similar to gaps within *The Prelude* itself, such as his affair with Annette Vallon, his political actions on both the left and the right, the aborted business of the *Philanthropist*, the absence of any particulars from the 'five long years,' 1793–98, and the omission of almost all references to the fact that he was writing thousands of lines of poetry while the other life-actions of *The Prelude* were going on.

If he had published *The Prelude* in 1807, even with these omissions – but scandalously more so had he included them – he would have been not only England's first clearly Romantic poet but also her greatest republican poet since Milton. This would have massively complicated Lord Byron's appearance in that role with the publication of *Childe Harold's Pilgrimage* five years later, perhaps the definitive celebrity-creating event in English literature: 'I awoke and found myself famous.' This was the kind of fame Wordsworth had courted all along, but he was not prepared like Byron to accept – nor could he afford to – its consequences, neither the ecstasy of adulation nor the fury of reaction. But *The Prelude* – 'Childe William's Pilgrimage' – was far riskier than almost anything in Byron's lightly-veiled autobiography, not excluding strong hints of sexual attraction involving his sister. Had it appeared in 1807, Wordsworth would have awoken to find himself *in*famous.

The Prelude brought Wordsworth's youth to an end both chrono-logically and compositionally. A question that the present book provokes, '*Was* Wordsworth ever young?' is not, then, facetious but serious, because Wordsworth went to such lengths to bury his youthful self. The young Wordsworth is the hidden Wordsworth, hidden first by omissions and elisions in his autobiographical poem and then buried deeper by keeping that poem out of sight until he was dead. Paradoxically, the public appearance of Wordsworth's youth was delayed until after his death. *The Prelude* was the story he could not tell his nation, only his family and friends. Telling it aloud (so to speak) would have confirmed the suspicions of many readers in 1807 that he was indeed a kind of conspirator, and – as unsympathetic reviewers were already saying of *Lyrical Ballads* – that his poetry reflected his revolutionary ideals and experience.

Anyone who teaches Wordsworth's poetry for very long will occa-sionally toy with the idea of what his image in literary history would be if he had died young – at age thirty-six, for example, Byron's age when he died at Missolonghi, and Wordsworth's age when he read *The Prelude* to Coleridge. In essence, he did die: the story of his youth ends there, so far as public reputation was concerned. I do not propose to kill Wordsworth off, *c.* 1807: more than half his life and much of his best poetry remained ahead of him. But it's not the story I wanted to tell. Neither did he, and how to preserve the story of his youth became the poetic obsession of the rest of his life.

His name for this process was 'recollecting emotion in tranquillity.' We have long thought the phrase applied only to Wordsworth's method of composing, to his ability to draw up images out of 'hiding places ten years deep,' as he said of the twenty-years-delayed *Peter Bell*. Typically, he generalized this process to apply to all poetry, but of course it does not describe the compositional habits of all poets – as we have only to think of his alter-ego, Byron, to realize. But it does apply to Wordsworth's composition of his whole life, both in *The Prelude* and in its posthumous appearance. The very phrase 'hiding places' for wherever he kept his memories of his life is at once a kind of Freudian slip and another of those literal metaphors I referred to in this book's Prologue. 'Hiding places' are not lapses of memory, things forgotten and gone out of mind; they are secret caches of desire, emotion, excitement and shame: Wordsworth's young life is full of them, and they are more numerous, and deeper, than we thought.

The Wordsworth we know and honour is above all the poet of *full presence*: of effort, expectation, and desire, and 'something evermore about to be.' Hence it is not surprising that his absences – his gaps, his lacunae – should be, when we can find them or when we stumble into them accidentally, not shallow but as deep as his heights. He said as much many times, especially when talking about himself as a poet:

> Not Chaos, not
> The darkest pit of lowest Erebus,
> Nor aught of blinder vacancy, scooped out
> By help of dreams—can breed such fear and awe
> As fall upon us often when we look
> Into our Minds, into the Mind of Man—
> My haunt, and the main region of my song.

If the present book has accomplished its mission, it should now be clear that such statements are relevant not only to Wordsworth's philosophical and psychological themes but true to his biography as well.

The hidden and unpublished Wordsworth of *The Prelude* is not an anomaly; on the contrary, he follows a pattern consistent with many of his other works' appearance, or non-appearance. The Salisbury Plain poems and *The Borderers* were not published until 1842, 'The Ruined Cottage' did not appear until 1814 (buried in the turgid *Excursion*), and *Peter Bell* and its companion, *The Waggoner*, radical experiments of 1798, did not appear until 1819. Furthermore, all these and his other published 'juvenilia' are themselves disguised versions of their young author, since they were first carefully doctored by an older man's revisions. The 'Letter to the Bishop of Llandaff' did not appear at all, but it was carefully preserved, and the Imitation of Juvenal, which Wordsworth thought safely destroyed, did not appear in full until two hundred years after its first composition. All of these texts were work of the hidden years, those 'five long years,' 1793–98, and each, in it early form, betrays a more radical author, one far more active in 'the Revolution Debate' of the 1790s than even the language experimenter of the 1798 *Lyrical Ballads*. Wordsworth suffered his fair share of political abuse for *Lyrical Ballads*, and if *The*

Prelude had appeared anytime during the war with Napoleon, or during the postwar years of renewed agitation for reform (and redoubled suppression of it), it would have identified its author far too closely – for *his* success – with the decade of the 1790s. Moreover, if it had included even the breath of a hint that he, a.k.a. 'Mr Wordsworth', also 'had business on the other [Tory] side of the road,' as he sneeringly said of the Bishop of Llandaff, the consequences would have been even worse, as they always are for turncoats and double agents.

Wordsworth might have suffered the fate of Thelwall and Holcroft, or Robert Bage and Mary Hays, or any of the long-forgotten names of England's first 'Lost Generation.' Instead, by cutting, pasting, altering, delaying, or simply denying the appearance of his radical youth, he created and projected a substantially different image of himself as the Poet. First announced in the 1802 additions to the preface, it was first personified in the eponymous character of that name in *The Excursion*, whose only 'action' is to observe and comment on a long argument between a non-political Pedlar and a too-political Solitary (both aspects of Wordsworth himself, as Hazlitt immediately recognized) about the meaning of the French Revolution for England. As the *observer* of the great ideological debate of his era – which *The Excursion* leaves still unresolved – Wordsworth became his audience, or the part of it he had by then identified with: the Poet of *un*reformed England.

Although he published a dozen volumes of poetry after 1807, the number is misleading. Some, as noted, had been written as much as twenty years earlier, while others were very occasional in nature, versified travelogues from his tours, such as *Memorials of a Tour on the Continent, 1820* (1822), though often containing many good poems. Within the poetic economy of the Wordsworth household, moreover, many of these publications were viewed as stopgaps preventing Wordsworth from getting on with *The Recluse*. The temptation to shorter forms that Coleridge had warned against always reasserted itself, especially in sonnet sequences, even though some of these, like *The River Duddon* (1820), are among the best of their kind in English.

The Prelude too continued to prevent *The Recluse*, as it always had, in Wordsworth's cross-grained refusal to accept that he himself was his own best story. And he found another way to expand the image of his life, by, from 1815 on, arranging the poems in editions of his collected works according to the life stages and emotions of an individual human being: 'Poems Written in Youth,' 'Poems Referring to the Period of Childhood,' 'Poems Referring to the Period of Old Age,' and 'Poems of the Fancy' and 'Poems of the Imagination,' interspersed with the tours and memorials and reflections of that same very comprehensive figure. Thus did Wordsworth's works appear to define his life.

Yet, to a surprising extent, Wordsworth's actual life from 1807 to 1850 recapitulates the history of constant textual self-(re)-creation that we see in his sequestering *The Prelude* for posterity. It is an overstatement, but an illuminating one, to say that much of what he did during the last forty-four years of his life was a repetition of what he had already done in his first thirty-six.

This is especially true of his travels. He went to Scotland two more times, in 1814 and 1831, to visit Scott and places in Scott's poetry (like Yarrow) he had missed in 1803. In 1820 he and Dorothy and Mary took the 're-tour' of the Continent that consciously repeated his 1790 walking tour, and in 1828 he travelled on the Rhine with Coleridge, and in 1837 in France and Italy with Henry Crabb Robinson, both trips covering some of the same ground again. And he returned twice to Wales: once in 1824 to visit Robert Jones, his 1790 companion, and once in 1841 – his last extended trip out of the Lake District – to revisit the most important site of all his signature *re*visitations, Tintern Abbey, the Wye Valley, and the Quantock Hills.[1]

But now it was not 'Five years . . . past,' but forty-eight years past. That his past would weigh heavily on his mind in these trips hardly needs arguing, but one detail illuminates how that mind worked upon its past. Coming to Goodrich Castle, Wordsworth sought out the little girl who had assured him in 1793, 'O Master! we are seven.' The enormous retentive power of Wordsworth's early imagination – as well as its egocentrism – is indicated both by his expectation and its frustration: he could not locate the girl because he had forgotten to ask her name. 'It would have given me greater pleasure to have found in the neighbouring hamlet traces of one who had interested me so much; but that was impossible, as, unfortunately, I did not even know her name.'[2] To expect Wordsworth to have asked her name, or to think him egocentric for not doing so, is to wish for a different author, and to assume a very different attitude toward memory and creativity than his. Many of us might have said, What's your name, little girl? But Wordsworth, aged twenty-three, wondered instead, 'a simple child . . . That lightly draws its breath . . . What should it know of death?' She knew more than he did – in his role of the obtuse adult narrator – and what she knew was more important than her name. It was the continuity of life over death that 'interested [him] so much,' and the same interest made his own later life a continuation of his early years.

With his politics as with his travels, Wordsworth repeated himself. The clichéd image of him shows radical youth being replaced by reactionary old age. But his youth was radical because he turned against his conservative world, and then returned to it. Not the label but the process was the essence of his self-creation, in his life, as in poems from *The Borderers* to 'Tintern Abbey.' Continuing his family's generations-long allegiance to the entrenched Lowther interest, Wordsworth in 1812 appealed to Lord

Lonsdale for a public office to help support a family that poetry was clearly not going to be able to. In 1813 he was named Stamp-Distributor for Westmorland, part of the government's tax-collection service, and six years later he was made a Justice of the Peace for Westmorland, exactly as his father had been. This was largely a reward for his strenuous efforts on Lowther's behalf in the decisive post-war election of 1818, canvassing as tirelessly as his father had done and publishing *Two Addresses to the Freeholders of Westmorland*, which helped seal the fate of reform for half a generation more.

Wordsworth worked hard for the conservative Lowther interest in the election of 1818 and vehemently opposed the Reform Bill of 1832 not only because his political ideas had changed. These actions also reflect his career-oriented realization that reform did not fit the image of the Poet that he had decided to present to the public. Though it survived the whirlwind of revolution, his self-image was eventually wrecked on the rocks of reform. In the new era after 1832 Wordsworth was indeed a Lost Leader. As both Tennyson and Browning learned to their sorrow when they published their derivatively Romantic first volumes in 1830 and 1833, most English readers did not want that kind of poetry any more. Self-consciousness, Carlyle declared in his essay, 'Characteristics,' in that same watershed year of 1832, was the disease of the new age, not its cure. His prescription, 'Close thy Byron, open thy Goethe,' meant, Close the book of enthusiastic individualism and open the book of pessimistic social earnestness.

Wordsworth, presciently, had already closed his Romantic book on himself, finished it and hidden it away. His public reputation grew accordingly, as DeQuincey aptly noted: 'Up to 1820 the name of Wordsworth was trampled underfoot; from 1820 to 1830 it was militant; from 1830 to 1835 it has been triumphant.' And the triumph continued: in 1838 Wordsworth was awarded the DCL at the University of Durham, and in 1839 Oxford followed suit. In 1843 he became poet laureate following Southey's death, and in 1846 he was elected an honourary member of the Royal Irish Academy, and would have been named lord rector of Glasgow University but for university political infighting.

Wordsworth was successful in his gamble with posterity for reputation. Inexorably, he became *the* poet of his era. But the costs he paid in compromise were commensurate with his gains. Byron and Shelley were effectively exiled from England and died romantically abroad; defiling their memory became a lively cultural cottage industry in Victorian England, but they have survived with their integrity intact. Blake took an even harder road to artistic integrity, at the terrific cost of almost complete obscurity during his lifetime. Coleridge stayed more in the mainstream of society by making a profession of worrying its margins, religious, political, and educational. Keats alone had a career whose trajectory looks like

Wordsworth's, but he died young, thus preserving his Romantic image intact. Had he lived, he might be remembered as Dr John Keats, a pioneer in, say, the prevention of infectious diseases in industrial slums, who had dabbled in poetry before he too accepted the wisdom of Carlyle's dictum (they were born the same year, 1795), closing his Byron and opening his Wordsworth. The Wordsworth he knew best was the poet of *The Excursion*, which Keats, seeing the gold beneath its dross, hailed as 'one of the three greatest things to rejoice at in this age.' If Wordsworth convinced only this one member of his 'fit audience, though few,' it was enough.

Other poets of the era who compromised with their revolutionary and reactionary times gained their profits immediately: Southey and Rogers and Crabbe among them. Several women writers who enjoyed phenomenal success then are only belatedly being remembered now: Charlotte Smith, Mary Robinson, Anna Barbauld, Felicia Hemans, and others. For the most part, they lost out with posterity. Only Wordsworth hit the right balance between revelation and secrecy. But it cost him – or us – the best image of his soul, for relatively few readers know the Wordsworth of *The Prelude*, let alone its many different versions, to say nothing of the facts it cuts and tailors. Fewer still have ever glimpsed the Bard of *The Recluse*, a shadowy figure as large as any of Blake's Giant Emanations. Instead, they know and love (or hate), the poet of the English Lake District, eminently adaptable to tourism, gardening, calendar art, and mournful private reflections on the impossibilities of modern public life.

There is a view, more English than American, that Wordsworth went wrong when he fell for Coleridge's line that he should write 'the first great philosophic poem' in English. Stephen Gill expresses this succinctly: 'Coleridge was quite wrong. Lyrical utterance was for Wordsworth a natural mode.'[3] Scholars holding this view disapprove of the 'twentieth-century preoccupation' with 'The Ruined Cottage,' *The Prelude*, and 'Home at Grasmere' – that is, with the failed *Recluse*-project in all its dimensions. It will be clear that I share that preoccupation to a considerable extent. And yet it was never, for Wordsworth, simply a matter of deciding to carry on writing one kind of poetry instead of another. If it had been this easy, where are his lyrics of 1795–98? Can the long poems of those years simply be discounted as mistakes? Or, if adherents of the simple, lyrical Wordsworth say that he was, in 1798 or in 1800 or in 1802, finding his 'natural' lyrical voice, how would they account for the marked differences between the *Lyrical Ballads* of 1798 and those of 1800, or the still greater differences between both of them and the simplicities of the lyrics of spring 1802? In which do we hear his 'natural' voice?

In all of them, of course. And what we hear, that makes all of these lyric, dramatic, and narrative poems indubitably 'Wordsworthian,' are the deep echoes of *The Recluse* project, mounting 'like an unfathered vapour' from 'the deep, abyssmal breathing place' of Wordsworth's imagination, to resonate powerfully in simple lyrics about little girls or old beggars, and apparently transparent narratives about shepherd boys and idiot boys.

These resonances are not always, it is true, easy to identify, but they are impossible to account for if one is not aware of their deep sub-structure. Only in 'Tintern Abbey' does this buried presence come close to the surface of the *Lyrical Ballads*. But without *The Recluse* there would be no Margaret, no Lucy, no Matthew, no Michael, no Ruth *as they exist in Wordsworth's poetry*. There never was much of a *Recluse*, though parts of it can be studied with profit. What we have instead, partway between the characters of Wordsworth's narratives (the 'real men' of his preface) and the god-like Bard of *The Recluse*, is the character of the Poet himself, as first announced in the 1802 additions to the preface of *Lyrical Ballads*, and then developed further in his return to the poem 'on the growth of my own mind' between 1803 and 1805.

This is easy to see with the benefit of two hundred years' hindsight, but these relationships only began to emerge in the last hundred years, beginning with A. C. Bradley's lectures at Edinburgh University in the 1890s, published in 1909. It took a good deal of twentieth-century 'pre-occupation' with these inter-relations between parts of Wordsworth's oeuvre to bring them to light, since most serious philosophical inter-pretation of Wordsworth remained stuck with the Idealist metaphysical presumptions he shared with Coleridge, even as both of them were moving beyond them, in practice, to more modern notions of truth based on the contextual consciousness and practices of any truth-claiming subject. But it was not easy for Wordsworth to articulate his self-recognition, not in 1802, nor in the subsequent composition of *The Prelude*, to say nothing of its publication, an event he deferred all the rest of his life because he said that 'it was a thing unprecedented in literary history that a man should talk so much about himself.' It was not quite so unprecedented, even then, but it is a thing with many precedents now, and *The Prelude* itself is one of the most important of them all.

Although the final fair-copy state of *The Prelude* indicates that Wordsworth expected it to be published posthumously, no specific set of written instructions indicating his intentions exists. Even the title was not clearly agreed on, except perhaps by verbal understanding with Mary. *The Prelude*, like *The Excursion* and *The Recluse*, is hardly a striking title for a major poem. All his life, it had been 'the poem to Coleridge' or 'the poem on the growth of my own mind.' There is no '-iad' suffix in English to indicate topicality, like *Iliad* or *Aeneid*, the story or the 'matter' of Achilles and Troy, of Aeneas and Rome. Like them, *The Prelude* is a foundational epic, declaring the independence of the human imagination: The Imagination-iad or Imagiad. To avoid such a barbarism we would have to call it, lamely, Of Imagination. But the real subject of the poem is more specific, and adaptable to the old form of epic titles. It could be called, *The*

Wordsworthiad, or perhaps *The Axiologiad*, referring to its *materia* of semi-revolutionary Wordsworth and demi-revolutionary England. More specifically, given its narrow range, it is not a general treatise on imagination, but the long-withheld story of obscure self-creation: *The Hidden Wordsworth*. That young man's exciting life was the source of the emotions that Wordsworth needed the rest of his life to recollect in tranquillity.

Genealogical Chart Showing Intermarriages between Robinson, Wordsworth, Cookson/Crackanthorpe, and Monkhouse Families

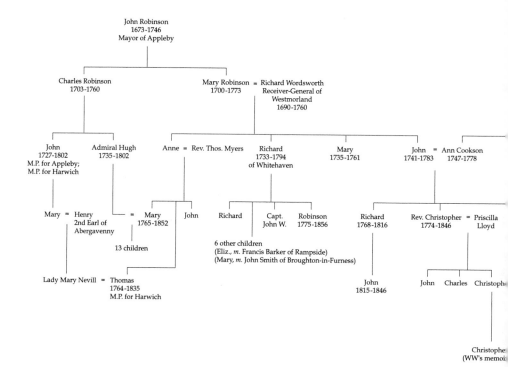

John Robinson
1673-1746
Mayor of Appleby

Charles Robinson
1703-1760

Mary Robinson = Richard Wordsworth
1700-1773   Receiver-General of
               Westmorland
               1690-1760

John   Admiral Hugh   Anne = Rev. Thos. Myers   Richard   Mary   John = Ann Cookson
1727-1802   1735-1802   1733-1794   1735-1761   1741-1783   1747-1778
M.P. for Appleby;   of Whitehaven
M.P. for Harwich

Mary = Henry   = Mary   John   Richard   Capt.   Robinson   Richard   Rev. Christopher = Priscilla
       2nd Earl of   1765-1852   John W. 1775-1856   1768-1816   1774-1846   Lloyd
       Abergavenny

                          13 children   6 other children   John   Charles   Christophe
                                                      (Eliz., m. Francis Barker of Rampside)
                                                      (Mary, m. John Smith of Broughton-in-Furness)

Lady Mary Nevill = Thomas   John
                   1764-1835   1815-1846
                   M.P. for Harwich

                                                                                                                         Christophe
                                                                                                                         (WW's memoi

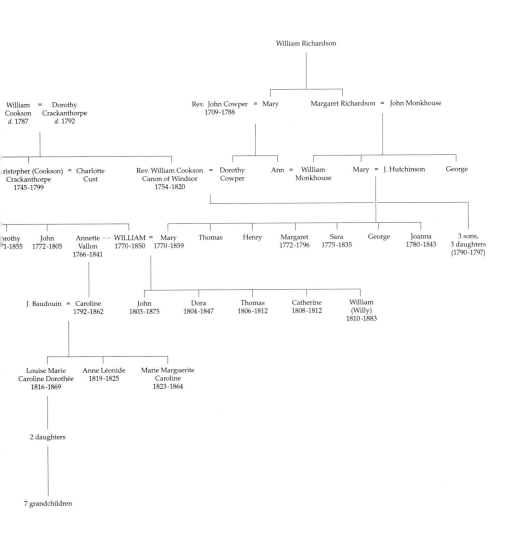

William Richardson

William = Dorothy   Rev. John Cowper = Mary   Margaret Richardson = John Monkhouse
Cookson   Crackanthorpe   1709-1788
d. 1787   *d.* 1792

[C]ristopher (Cookson) = Charlotte   Rev. William Cookson = Dorothy   Ann = William   Mary = J. Hutchinson   George
Crackanthorpe   Cust   Canon of Windsor   Cowper   Monkhouse
1745-1799   1754-1820

[D]orothy   John   Annette - - WILLIAM = Mary   Thomas   Henry   Margaret   Sara   George   Joanna   3 sons,
[17]1-1855   1772-1805   Vallon   1770-1850   1770-1859   1772-1796   1775-1835   1780-1843   3 daughters
           1766-1841   (1790-1797)

J. Baudouin = Caroline   John   Dora   Thomas   Catherine   William
         1792-1862   1803-1875   1804-1847   1806-1812   1808-1812   (Willy)
                                                          1810-1883

Louise Marie   Anne Léonide   Marie Marguerite
Caroline Dorothée   1819-1825   Caroline
1816-1869   1823-1864

2 daughters

7 grandchildren

Abbreviations

BL   *Biographia Literaria*, ed. James Engell and W. Jackson Bate, vol. 7, pt. 2 of *The Collected Works of Samuel Taylor Coleridge*, gen. ed. Kathleen Coburn (Princeton, Princeton University Press, 1983)

BRS   Ben Ross Schneider, *Wordsworth's Cambridge Education* (Cambridge, Cambridge University Press, 1957)

CEY   Mark L. Reed, *Wordsworth: The Chronology of the Early Years, 1770–1799* (Cambridge, Mass.: Harvard University Press, 1967)

CLSTC   *Collected Letters of Samuel Taylor Coleridge*, ed. Earl Leslie Griggs, 2 vols. (Oxford, Clarendon Press, 1956)

CMY   Mark L. Reed, *Wordsworth: The Chronology of the Middle Years, 1800–1815* (Cambridge, Mass.: Harvard University Press, 1975)

CPWSTC   *The Complete Poetical Works of Samuel Taylor Coleridge*, ed. Ernest Hartley Coleridge, 2 vols. (1912; reprint, Oxford: Clarendon Press, 1957)

DC   Dove Cottage

DHRF   Albert Soboul, ed., *Dictionnaire historique de la Révolution Française* (Paris, Presses universitaires de France, 1989)

DNB   *Dictionary of National Biography*

DS   William Wordsworth, *Descriptive Sketches*, ed. Eric Birdsall (Ithaca, Cornell University Press, 1984)

DVE   David V. Erdman, *Commerce des Lumières: John Oswald and the British in Paris, 1790–1793* (Columbia, University of Missouri Press, 1986)

DWJ   *Journals of Dorothy Wordsworth*, ed. Ernest de Selincourt, 2 vols. (New York, Macmillan, 1941)

EL   Emile Legouis, *The Early Life of William Wordsworth, 1770–1798: A Study of 'The Prelude'*, ed. Nicholas Roe (London, Libris, 1988)

EPF   William Wordsworth, *Early Poems and Fragments, 1784–Mid 1797*, ed. Jared Curtis and Carol Landon (Ithaca, Cornell University Press, 1998)

EW   William Wordsworth, *An Evening Walk*, ed. James Averill (Ithaca,

Cornell University Press, 1984)

FO   Foreign Office

GMH1   George McLean Harper, *William Wordsworth: His Life, Works, and Influence*, vol. 1 (London, John Murray, 1916)

Hayden   John O. Hayden, ed., *William Wordsworth: The Poems*, vol. 1 (New Haven, Yale University Press, 1981)

HCR   Henry Crabb Robinson, *Diary, Reminiscences, and Correspondence*, ed. Thomas Sadler, 3 vols. (London, Macmillan, 1869)

HO   Home Office

HRCU   Historical Register of Cambridge University

IF   Isabella Fenwick Notes

LB   William Wordsworth, *Lyrical Ballads and Other Poems, 1797–1800*, ed. James Butler and Karen Green (Ithaca, Cornell University Press, 1992)

LCML   *The Letters of Charles and Mary Lamb*, ed. Edwin W. Marrs, 2 vols. (Ithaca, Cornell University Press, 1975–76)

LEY   *The Letters of William and Dorothy Wordsworth: The Early Years, 1787–1805*, ed. Ernest de Selincourt, 2d ed., rev. Chester L. Shaver (Oxford, Clarendon Press, 1967)

LJW   *The Letters of John Wordsworth*, ed. Carl H. Ketcham (Ithaca, Cornell University Press, 1969)

LLY   *The Letters of William and Dorothy Wordsworth: The Later Years*, 2d ed., ed. by Alan G. Hill, 5 vols. (Oxford, Clarendon Press, 1978–93)

LMY   *The Letters of William and Dorothy Wordsworth: The Middle Years*, 2d ed., rev. Mary Moorman (Oxford, Clarendon Press, 1969–70)

Memoirs   Christopher Wordsworth, *Memoirs of William Wordsworth*, 2 vols. (London, Edward Moxon, 1851)

MM1   Mary Moorman, *William Wordsworth: The Early Years, 1770–1803* (Oxford, Clarendon Press, 1957)

NR   Nicholas Roe, *Wordsworth and Coleridge: The Radical Years* (Oxford, Clarendon Press, 1988)

NSTC   *The Notebooks of Samuel Taylor Coleridge*, notes and text, ed. Kathleen Coburn, 4 vols. (New York: Pantheon Books, 1957)

PP   Pinney Papers

PL   *Paradise Lost*

PRO   Public Records Office

Prose   *The Prose Works of William Wordsworth*, ed. W. J. B. Owen and Jane Worthington Smyser, 3 vols. (Oxford, Clarendon Press, 1974)

P2V   William Wordsworth, *Poems, in Two Volumes and Other Poems, 1800–1807*, ed. Jared Curtis (Ithaca, Cornell University Press, 1983)

PW   William Wordsworth, *The Poetical Works*, ed. Ernest de Selincourt and Helen Darbishire, 5 vols. (1940–49; reprint, Oxford, Clarendon Press, 1967–72)

RH   Richard Holmes, *Coleridge: Early Visions* (New York, Viking, 1993)

SG   Stephen Gill, *William Wordsworth: A Life* (Oxford: Clarendon Press, 1989)

Thirteen   William Wordsworth, *The Thirteen-Book Prelude*, ed. Mark Reed, 2 vols. (Ithaca, Cornell University Press. 1991)

TWT   T. W. Thompson, *Wordsworth's Hawkshead*, ed. Robert Woof (London, Oxford University Press, 1970)

WAG   William Wordsworth, *The Prelude 1799, 1805, 1855*, ed. Jonathan Wordsworth, M. H. Abrams, and Stephen Gill, Norton Critical Edition (New York, W. W. Norton, 1979)

WAV   Emile Legouis, *William Wordsworth and Annette Vallon* (1922), expanded by Pierre Legouis (Hamden, Conn., Archon Books, 1967)

WFD   George McLean Harper, *Wordsworth's French Daughter: The Story of Her Birth, with the Certificates of Her Baptism and Marriage* (1921; reprint, New York, Russell & Russell, 1967)

WL   Wordsworth Library

Notes

Preface

1 For a 'Review of Reviews' of *The Hidden Wordsworth*, see James A. Butler, *The Wordsworth Circle*, 30 (Autumn 1999), 173–75.

2 Francis Parkman, Introduction, *France and England in North America*, 1865 (New York: Library of America, 1983), 16.

3 Kenneth R. Johnston, 'Wordsworth's Mission to Germany: A Hidden Bicentenary?' in *The Wordsworth Circle*, 30 (Winter 1999), 15–22.

4 Michael Durey, 'The Spy Who Never Was,' *Times Literary Supplement* (10 March 2000), 14–15; Kenneth R. Johnston, 'Wordsworth as Spy,' *Times Literary Supplement* (17 March 2000), 17.

5 Conor Cruise O'Brien, *The Long Affair: Thomas Jefferson and the French Revolution, 1785–1800* (London: Pimlico, 1998), 70.

6 'Ode: Intimations of Immortality from Recollections of Early Childhood,' lines 147–48; *The Prelude*, III.62–3 (describing Roubillac's statue of Isaac Newton in Trinty College, Cambridge).

Prologue: Images of Wordsworth

1 Alan Liu, *Wordsworth: The Sense of History* (Stanford University Press, 1989), 36.

2 *Wordsworth at Cambridge: A Record of the Commemoration Held at St John's College, Cambridge, in April 1950* (Cambridge, Cambridge University Press), 70.

3 BRS, 70.

4 CMY, 215; Frances Blanshard *Portraits of Wordsworth* (Ithaca, Cornell University Press, 1959), 142; William Carew Hazlitt, *Memoirs of William Hazlitt*, vol. I (London, R. Bentley, 1867), 103n.

5 'My First Acquaintance with Poets' (1823).

6   J.K. Stephen, 'A Sonnet' ('Two voices are there'), in George Kitchin, *A Survey of Burlesque and Parody in English* (Edinburgh, Oliver & Boyd, 1931), 237.

7   *La Jeunesse de William Wordsworth* (Paris, Masson, 1896); first English ed. tr. J.W. Matthews (London, Dent, 1897). It has recently been reprinted with a valuable introduction by Nicholas Roe (London, Libris, 1988), cited as EL.

8   Stephen Greenblatt, *Renaissance Self-Fashioning: From More to Shakespeare* (Chicago, University of Chicago Press, 1980).

Chapter 1: The Ministries of Fear and Beauty

1   Alexander Carlyle, *Anecdotes and Characters*, ed. James Kinsley (London, Oxford University Press, 1973), 213.

2   Lonsdale letters (16 March 1742), cited in J.V. Beckett, *Coal and Tobacco* (Cambridge, Cambridge University Press, 1981), 15–16.

3   Hugh Owen, *The Lowther Family* (Chichester, Phillimore, 1990), 287 (George III to Lord North, 9 March 1779).

4   Brian Bonsall, *Sir James Lowther and Cumberland and Westmorland Elections, 1754–1775* (Manchester, Manchester University Press, 1960), 67.

5   Ibid., 152.

6   M. Dorothy George, *Hogarth to Cruikshank: Social Change in Graphic Satire* (London, Allen Lane, 1967), 87.

7   Bonsall, *Lowther*, 50.

8   J.V. Beckett, 'The Making of a Pocket Borough: Cockermouth 1722–1756,' *Journal of British Studies* 20 (1980), 140–57 (citing P. Habbakkuk).

9   John Wordsworth, Sr to James Lowther (3 July 1778), Lowther Papers, Kendal PRO.

10   John Cannon, *Parliamentary Reform, 1640–1832* (Cambridge, Cambridge University Press, 1973), 50–51.

11   *LEY*, 65; *LMY*, 2: 410.

12   Appleby lost its representatives to Kendal as soon as the Reform Bill of 1832 was passed (Bonsall, *Lowther*, 152).

13   Eric Robertson, *Wordsworthshire* (London, Chatto and Windus, 1911), 23.

14   Owen, *Lowther Family*, 283.

15   To Captain Hugh Robinson (October 1764). A copy of this letter is on display in the Cockermouth house.

16   WL, MS 1/2; Woof (TWT), 32, n1, 35,n1.

17   *CEY*, 42.

18   Roberston, *Wordsworthshire*, 25.

19   John Beckett, 'Estate Management in Eighteenth-Century England: The Lowther-Spedding Relationship in Cumberland,' in *English Rural Society*,

ed. J. Chartrer and D. Hey (Cambridge, Cambridge University Press, 1990), 69.

20 Ibid., 72.

21 WL MS 8/157.

22 SG, 14.

23 Joanne Dann, 'Some Notes on the Relationship between the Wordsworth and the Lowther Families,' *Wordsworth Circle* 11 (1980), 81.

24 Robertson, *Wordsworthshire*, 12.

25 MM1, 8.

26 MM1, 13.

27 Owen, *Lowther Family*, 298; MM1, 13.

28 Bonsall, *Lowther*, 61.

29 *DNB*; Stephen Ayling, *Fox* (London, John Murray, 1991), 74n.

30 Beckett, 'Estate Management,' 66n29, quoting a letter of 21 May 1751.

31 Bonsall, *Lowther*, 70.

32 Mark Kishlansky, *Parliamentary Selection: Social and Political Choice in Early Modern England* (Cambridge, Cambridge University Press, 1986), 141.

33 Ibid., 146–47.

34 Bonsall, *Lowther*, 104.

35 Wilson Pearson to James Lowther (15 September 1772), Lowther Papers, Kendal PRO.

36 Richard Ferguson, *Cumberland and Westmorland M.P.'s from the Restoration to the Reform Bill of 1867* (London, Bell and Daldy, 1871), 125.

37 24 April 1757; *The Manuscripts of the Earl of Lonsdale* (London, Historical Manuscripts Commission, 1893), 129.

38 Ferguson, 126.

39 Dann, 'Notes,' 81.

40 Bonsall, *Lowther* 89–105.

41 Dann, 'Notes', 81.

42 Bonsall, *Lowther*, 70.

43 *LEY*, 7.

44 *LEY*, 4.

45 Robertson, *Wordsworthshire*, 16.

46 *CEY*, 41 n2.

47 MM1, 15–16.

48 MM1, 4.

49 'Catechizing,' *Ecclesiastical Sonnets*, III.xxii, in *PW*, III.395.

50 'Autobiographical Memoranda,' *Prose*, III.372. All following prose recollections are from this source unless otherwise indicated.

51 *PW*, III.397.

52 GMH1, 21.

53 'Home at Grasmere,' lines 708–14; italics added.

54 *PW*, IV.2, and IF.

55 IF, in 'Composed by the Sea-Shore' (*PW*, IV.397).

56 EL, 233.
57 'To A Butterfly' (1802), lines 6, 9–10, 13–18.
58 'Address from the Spirit of Cockermouth Castle' (*PW*, IV.23).
59 WAG, 9n.
60 The simile, 'like a grave,' is from the earliest version: *1799*, I. 312–13.
61 WAG, 9n.
62 Robertson, *Wordsworthshire*, 12.
63 *CEY*, 45.
64 *TWT*, 33.

Chapter 2: The Vale of Esthwaite

Any account of Wordsworth's Hawkshead must be heavily indebted to the man who wrote the book on it, T.W. Thompson, *Wordsworth's Hawkshead* (London, Oxford University Press, 1970), and to Robert Woof, who organized and edited its veritable thickets of information for publication. In citing my debts to Thompson, I have tried as much as possible to distinguish between his researches and Woof's.

1   Robertson, *Wordsworthshire*, (1911).
2   *CEY*, 47; Woof, TWT, 34nl.
3   GMH1, 35.
4   *CEY*, 55, 64.
5   These time divisions are simplified for clarity. Reed, Thompson (3), and Woof (373) have differing interpretations of the evidence about where the boys spent their summers. Some summer time spent in Hawkshead seems plausible on the basis of the many summertime activities Wordsworth describes there.
6   MM1, 28.
7   TWT, 12.
8   TWT, 71.
9   TWT, 104.
10 TWT, 211–14.
11 TWT, 56.
12 SG, 23.
13 Eileen Jay, *Wordsworth at Colthouse* (Kendal, Westmorland Gazette, 1981), 7, 18.
14 TWT, 71–72; Jay, *Wordsworth*, 20.
15 TWT, 43; paraphrasing his conversations with Mary Hodgson in 1905.
16 MM1, 27.
17 *LLY*, IV.210
18 Woof, TWT, 209n.
19 Woof, citing Liverpool sources, TWT, 209n.
20 Woof, TWT, 209n.

21 *The Prelude*, II.174; TWT, 78–79, 147.
22 *LEY*, 56–57.
23 TWT, 74–76.
24 *Correspondence of Thomas Gray*, ed. Paget Toynbee and Leonard Whibley (Oxford, Oxford University Press, 1935), Vol. III, 1098.
25 MM1, 24.
26 TWT, 246–47.
27 TWT, 248.
28 TWT, 49.
29 Woof, TWT, 131n1, 375.
30 TWT, 53.
31 TWT, 207.
32 IF, *PW*, V.373.
33 TWT, 229, citing 'W.S.' from Kendal.
34 TWT, 230.
35 TWT, 225.
36 TWT, 152.
37 TWT, 165.
38 TWT, 158.
39 TWT, 175.
40 TWT, 263; italics added.
41 TWT, 54.
42 TWT, 53n1.
43 TWT, 53.
44 Woof, TWT, 117n1.
45 Woof, TWT, 129n3.
46 Woof, TWT, xix.
47 TWT, 130.
48 Woof, TWT, 92–93, quoting one of Mingay's newspaper advertisements.
49 Woof, TWT, 131n.
50 J.V. Beckett, 'The Making of a Pocket Borough: Cockermouth, 1727–1756,' *Journal of British Studies* 20 (Fall 1980), 145.
51 Years later, Wordsworth's own son John would marry the granddaughter, also Isabella, of John Christian and Isabella Curwen. (TWT, 21, 127–31; Woof notes, xviii, 374–75).

Chapter 3: 'While we were schoolboys'

1 EL, 31, 55–57.
2 John Burnet, *A History of the Cost of Living* (Harmondsworth, Penguin), 147.
3 Ibid., 158; TWT, 115, 104.
4 MM1, 26.
5 Jay, *Wordsworth*, 28.

6   *Prose*, III.372.

7   *PW*, IV.422; IF note.

8   *LEY*, 56.

9   Cf. Duncan Wu, *Wordsworth's Reading* (Cambridge, Cambridge University Press, 1993); Robert Paul Kelly, 'The Literary Sources of William Wordsworth's Works, 10 July 1793 to 10 June 1797' (University of Hull, unpublished Ph.D. thesis, 1987).

10   E.H. King, 'James Beattie's Literary Essay: 1776, 1783,' *Aberdeen University Review* 45 (1974), 389–401.

11   MM1, 54.

12   Cf. Marlon Ross, *The Contours of Masculine: Romanticism and the Rise of Women's Poetry* (New York, Oxford University Press, 1989); Stuart Curran, *The Cambridge Companion to British Romanticism* (Cambridge, Cambridge University Press 1993); Anne Mellor, *Romanticism and Feminism* (Bloomington, Indiana University Press, 1988) and *Romanticism and Gender* (New York, Routledge, 1993).

13   Bishop Hunt, 'Wordsworth's Marginalia on *Paradise Lost*,' *Bulletin of the New York Public Library* 73 (1969), 85–103; Kelley, 'Literary Sources', 220; Mary Jacobus, *Tradition and Experiment in Wordsworth's 'Lyrical Ballads' (1798)* (Oxford, Oxford University Press, 1976), 244n, 258n.

14   In the Wordsworth Library at Dove Cottage.

15   *PW*, IV, 403.

16   Kelley, 'Literary Sources,' 220.

17   Jacobus gives excellent accounts of Thomson's philosophical influence on Wordsworth's verse, and of such compositional devices as the 'topographical episode' (39–44, 105–09).

18   WAG, 286n6.

19   'How sweet the walk along the woody steep' [Isle of Wight, 1793], Hayden, 116.

20   Edward Walford, 'Life of Bishop Percy,' in his edition of the *Reliques*.

21   *Reliques* (1765), Vol. I, xxi.

22   *LEY*, 100–01.

23   MM1, 73–74.

24   SG, 29n73.

25   George Crabbe, *The Complete Poetical Works*, ed. Norma Dalrymple-Champneys and Arthur Pollard, 3 vols. (Oxford, Clarendon Press, 1988), 668.

26   *LLY*, 348.

27   MM1, 101–02.

28   *The Poetical Works of John Langhorne, D.D.*, ed. J.T. Langhorne [his son] (London, Mawman, 1804), 13. All quotations of Langhorne's work are from this edition.

29   To William Mathews, 7 November 1794 (*LEY*, 135).

30   Hayden, 965.

31 *Poetical Works*, 22. The first sentence is Langhorne's, from 1771, the rest are his son's expansion, published in 1804.

32 Jacobus, 44–51 and *passim.*; also Jonathan Wordsworth, *William Wordsworth: The Borders of Vision* (Oxford, Clarendon Press, 1982), 231–32, 248–49, 295–98, 333–59.

33 *Memoirs*, 11–12.

Chapter 4: 'Verses from the impulse of my own mind'

1 *CEY*, 58–59n.
2 'The Vale of Esthwaite,' lines 469–70.
3 *CEY*, 60.
4 *CEY*, 60.
5 *CEY*, 61.
6 *CEY*, Appendix III, 'Wordsworth's Earliest Poetic Composition,' 298–301.
7 *Memoirs*, I.10.
8 The most thorough, critical account of Wordsworth's earliest poetry is Paul Sheats's *The Making of Wordsworth's Poetry, 1785–1798* (Cambridge, Mass., Harvard University Press, 1973).
9 *CEY*, 298, quoting Justice Coleridge.
10 James Butler, 'The Muse at Hawkshead: Early Criticism of Wordworth's Poetry,' *Wordsworth Circle* 20 (1989), 140.
11 Edmonds translation, 43.
12 Graver comments on Wordsworth's accuracy and stylistic felicities in his comprehensive study, *Wordsworth's Translations from Latin Poetry*, 19–28.
13 Cornish Translation, 53, 55.
14 Hayden, 922; Owen, xvii.
15 *CEY*, 70.
16 TWT, 60.
17 *CEY*, 67.
18 TWT, 66.
19 *The European Magazine* had published favourable reviews of Williams's poetry, as well as other poetic tributes to her (EW, 33).
20 *Memoirs*, I.13.
21 *CEY*, 74–76.
22 *PW*, I.318.
23 *CEY*, 72.
24 'Pale spectres! are ye what ye seem? / . . . / Fix'd are their eyes, on me they bend— / Their glaring look is cold!' ('Irregular Fragments, Found in a Dark Passage of the Tower,' cited by Sheats, 8).

Chapter 5: Stranger, Lounger, Lover

1 SG, 429n17.
2 GMH1, 67.
3 GMH1, 56; *The London Magazine* (1 April 1827), 445.
4 J.M.F. Wright, *Alma Mater; or, Seven Years at the University of Cambridge*, 2 vols. (London, Black, Young and Tavistock, 1827), II.167.
5 If a student did not want to take orders, a Cambridge fellowship could also be used to read for the law at the Inns of Court (BRS, 8).
6 WL, Cookson-Cowper correspondence, 12 April 1788.
7 Percy H. Fitzgerald, *The Royal Dukes and Princesses of the Family of George III: A View of Court Life and Manners for Seventy Years, 1760–1830* (London, Tinsley Brothers, 1882) Vol. II, 248.
8 Bute's wife was Mary Wortley, only daughter of Lady Mary Wortley Montagu, hence James Lowther's wife was the granddaughter of this important woman of letters (James Lee McKelvery, *George III and Lord Bute: The Leicester House Years* [Durham, Duke University Press, 1973], 4); John Brooke, *King George III* (New York, McGraw-Hull, 1972), 87, 102–03.
9 WL, Cookson-Cowper correspondence, 24 April 1782: 'I am told by high authority viz. the King that I look thin.'
10 GMH1, 62.
11 Pollock, *Wilberforce* (London, Constable, 1977), 43.
12 Ibid., 20.
13 Ian Christie, 'John Robinson M.P., 1727–1802,' in *Myth and Reality in Late-Eighteenth-Century Politics* (Los Angeles, University of California Press, 1970), 145–82.
14 *LEY*, 18n4. The letter is dated 6 April 1788, shortly after Robinson received news of Wordsworth's first-class ranking in his first college examination.
15 *LEY*, 694
16 *LEY*, 11n2.
17 MM1, 90; Henry Gunning, *Reminiscences of the University, Town and Country of Cambridge, from the year 1780*, 2d ed., 2 vols. (London, 1855), I.211–20.
18 Arthur B. Gray, *Cambrdige Revisited* (1921; reprint, Cambridge, Par Stephens, 1974), 43.
19 George Pryme, *Autobiographic Recollections* (Cambridge, Deighton, Bell, 1870), 44.
20 E.A. Benians, 'St John's College in Wordsworth's Time,' in *Wordsworth at Cambridge* (Cambridge, Cambridge Ueniversity Press, 1950), 2; Heather E. Peek and Cathrine P. Hall, *The Archives of the University of Cambridge: An Historical Introduction* (Cambridge, Cambridge University Press, 1962), 53.
21 Benians, 'St. John's,' 3; *Prelude*, III.49–50.
22 Wright, *Alma Mater*, I.83–4.
23 MM1, 92.

24 Benians, 'St. John's,' 1.
25 Alec C. Crook, *From the Foundation to Gilbert Scott: A History of the Buildings of St John's College Cambridge*, 1511–1885 (Cambridge, Cambridge University Press, 1980), 16.
26 'After so splendid a start . . . there must be college reasons [for the decline]' (Ibid., 144–46).
27 MM1, 90; Moorman cities only nine names.
28 TWT, 74.
29 *Eagle*, 33–34; SG, 429n9.
30 TWT, 52; Woof (TWT), 357–58; Robert Forsyth Scott, Ed., *Admissions to the College of St John the Evangelist in the University of Cambridge* (Cambridge, Cambridge University Press, 1903), 62.
31 MM1, 154; GMH1, 247.
32 Benians, 'St John's,' 4–5; BRS, 66; Pryme, *Recollections*, 155–58; *DNB*.
33 MM1, 90.
34 Crook, *Foundation*, 70.
35 Benians, 'St. John's', 3; Wright, *Alma Mater*, II.176–77.
36 MM1, 124.
37 BRS, 43–44; Christopher Wordsworth, *Social Life*, 98 ff.
38 Benians, 'St Johns,' 4–5.
39 *LEY*, 19; *Nuts to Crack*, 150.
40 BRS, 3.
41 MM1, 86.
42 Wordsworth's quotation from Thomson's *Castle of Indolence* (WAG, 196n1).
43 *Gradus ad Cantagrigiam*, 85; cited in Christopher Wordsworth, *Social Life*, 378, which also cites *Facetiae Cantabrigienses*, often called 'the complete Lounging Book.'
44 Hunt, 'Wordsworth's Marginalia on *Paradise Lost*,' 167–83.
45 BRS, 46.
46 Christopher Wordsworth, *Social Life*, 142.
47 Gunning, *Reminiscences*, II.147.
48 Wright, *Alma Mater*, I. 98; Christopher Wordsworth, *Social Life*, 397–98, suggests that each of the 'beauties' had her favourite church of resort.
49 Wright, *Alma Mater* I.143.
50 Ibid., I.175.
51 Christopher Wordsworth, *Social Life*, 369–71, 398.
52 Wright, *Alma Mater*, II.119–20.
53 Ibid., I.124.
54 Christopher Wordsworth, *Social Life*, 353, citing Cooper, *Annals*, 409; the date of this letter is 1766.
55 Gunning, *Reminiscences*, II.117.
56 Ibid., I.204.
57 Ibid., I.25–26.
58 Christopher Wordsworth, *Social Life*, 362–63.

59 Wright, *Alma Mater*, II.142–44, I.40n.
60 Gascoigne, 254–55.
61 Pollock, *Wilberforce*, 15.
62 Beth Darlington, ed., *The Love Letters of William and Mary Wordsworth* (Ithaca, Cornell University Press, 1981).
63 MM1, 88.
64 Quoted by Roe, 109, who adds Godwin's observation on Coleridge's condition: 'Loose in sexual morality – spends a night in a house of ill fame, ruminating in a chair: next morning meditates suicide.'
65 Wright, *Alma Mater*, I.223–24, II.108.10.

Chapter 6: Young Love-Liking

1 WL MS. 2.
2 Pollock, *Wilberforce*, 81–83.
3 WAG, 132n8.
4 James Reiger, 'Wordsworth Unalarm'd,' in *Milton and the Line of Vision*, ed. J. Wittreich (Madison, University of Wisconsin Press, 1975), 186.
5 WAG, 141n4 and 5.
6 *Bicentenary Wordsworth Studies in Memory of John Alban Finds*, ed. Jonathan Wordsworth (Ithaca, Cornell University Press, 1970), 434.
7 WAG, 150–51.
8 *LEY*, 10.
9 MM1, 75.
10 *CEY*, 80–84.
11 *CEY*, 90n.

Chapter 7: Weighing the Man in the Balance

1 *Memoirs*, I.14.
2 BRS, 95.
3 *LEY*, 18.
4 *HRCU*, 303, 463–65.
5 *Memoirs*, I.14.
6 *Memoirs*, I.14.
7 Gunning, *Reminiscences*, I.202–04, 206–07.
8 BRS, 105.
9 *Prelude* I.169–238, especially 185–219; cf. Kenneth R. Johnston, *Wordsworth and 'The Recluse'* (New Haven, Yale University Press, 1984), 127–31.
10 Alan Liu, *Wordsworth: The Sense of History* (Stanford, Stanford University Press, 1989), 23–31.
11 BRS, 113–63, and passim.

12 BRS, 106–07.

13 Hayden, 114.

14 MM1, 122–23; *CEY*, 94n.

15 MM1, 122n2.

16 *LEY*, 666–67.

17 BRS, 156–63.

18 BRS, 156–57.

19 Christopher Wordsworth, *Social Life*, 238; Gunning, *Reminiscences*, II.8.

20 C.V. Le Grice, *A General Theorem for a College Declamation* (1796), quoted in BRS, 162–63.

21 *DNB*. It is not improbable that Wordsworth knew Le Grice's satire, since Le Grice, besides being an old schoolfellow of Coleridge and Lamb, was a classmate of Christopher Wordsworth at Trinity from 1792 to 1796, when they were members of the same literary set; Le Grice won the declamation prize – with a serious poem – and Christopher finished second.

22 BRS, 172–73.

23 BRS, 84.

24 BRS, 165.

25 'Thoughts Suggested by a College Examination,' line 72 (first published in *Hours of Idleness*, 1807).

26 Pryme, *Recollections*, 92. This was the standard *c.* 1800.

27 Gunning, *Reminiscences*, I.226–27.

28 BRS, 14; *HRCU*, 464.

29 *HRCU*, 462–67.

30 BRS, 38.

31 Charles H. Cooper, *Annals of Cambridge*, vol. 4 *1688–1849* (Cambridge, Metcalfe and Palmer, 1852), 425.

32 Henry Gunning (quoted in Graham Chainey, *A Literary History of Cambridge* (Cambridge, Pevensey, 1985), 93).

33 Wright, *Alma Mater*, I.122.

34 'A man ambitious of a good place in a Tripos found he could not dispense with a private tutor' (T.G. Bonney, *Memories of a Long Life* [Cambridge, Metcalfe, 1921], 28).

35 Christopher Wordsworth, *Social Life*, 112; *Gradus ad Cantabrigiam*, 62.

36 Benians, *Eagle*, 10.

37 *HRCU*, 465; there were twenty-two senior optimes and sixteen junior optimes; a total of fifty-nine honours degrees.

38 Benians, *Eagle*, 34.

39 Ibid., 9.

40 MM1, 98–99.

41 Chainey, *Litrary History*, 91.

42 MM1, 99–100; also Dorothy Wordsworth, *LEY*, on the tour's pretensions.

43 III.340–41; WAG, 108n9, citing Wordsworth's *Guide to the Lakes* (*Prose*, II.184).

Chapter 8: Something of a Republic

1   BRS, 143.
2   Frida Knight, *University Rebel: The Life of William Frend (1757–1841)* (London, Victor Gollancz, 1991), 80–84.
3   BRS, 7, 118.
4   BRS, 126.
5   Laurence Fowler and Helen Fowler, eds., *Cambridge Commemorated: An Anthology of University Life* (Cambridge, Cambridge University Press, 1984), 132 citing E.H. Barker, *Literary Anecdotes and Contemporary Reminiscences* (1852).
6   Knight, *Rebel*, 85–88.
7   Quoted in BRS, 115.
8   BRS, 59ff. for the facts of Frend's career.
9   BRS, 138–40; Knight, *Rebel*, 86.
10 BRS, 150.
11 Gunning, *Reminiscences*, I.309.
12 BRS, 116–17.
13 Cooper, *Annals*, 362–63.
14 Knight, *Rebel*, 88.
15 *LEY*, 666; 22 March 1789.
16 *CEY*, 91–92, 96; *LEY*, 25n2.
17 *LEY*, 27; 25 January 1790. All quotations in this paragraph are from this letter or that of 30 April 1790 (*LEY*, 24–32).
18 GMH1, 83.
19 WAG, 112n7.
20 Pitt and his running mate, the future Duke of Grafton, polled 351 and 299 votes respectively; their opponents, the old Whigs, got 278 and 181.
21 IF (*PW*, IV.409; italics added).
22 Pryme, *Recollections*, 175.

Chapter 9: Golden Hours

1   *LEY*, 26 July 1791.
2   *LEY*, 37.
3   MM1, 135.
4   Letter 29, describing Mount Grimsel. Coxe's book was well-known in Wordsworth's circle: it had been donated to the Hawkshead School Library by his friends the Raincock brothers and Edward Birkett, along with John Moore's *A View of Society and Manners in France, Switzerland, and Germany*, which contained much discussion of localities associated with Rousseau. (TWT, 361).
5   *LEY*, 37.

6 *CEY*, 97.
7 Helen Maria Williams, *Letters from France*, ed. Janet Todd, vol. 1 (Delmar, N.Y., Scholar's Facsimilies, 1975), 14.
8 GMH1, 100.
9 I follow Harper's hypothesis, entertained by Reed and supported implicitly by Hayden, that they continued south on the Rhône by boat for a day and a half, disembarking at St-Vallier. (GMH1, 90; *CEY*, 102n10; Hayden, *Tour of 1790*, 17–21, 123.)
10 EL, 110.
11 *Correspondence of Thomas Gray*, ed. Paget Toynbee and Leonard Whibley, corr. H.W. Starr (Oxford, Clarendon Press, 1971), I.128.
12 *Prelude* II.122.
13 MM1, 135–36. The 'gleam of arms' Wordsworth saw in 1790 was probably only a contingent of troops on a domiciliary visit, if not simply part of the small detachment of guards that the government had long provided for the protection of the place.
14 WAG, 208n8.
15 *LEY*, 33.
16 'The Tuft of Primroses' (1808), *PW*, V.360–61.
17 EL, 113.
18 Saussure published his *Voyages dans les Alpes* frequently between 1779 and 1796, updating them with new material. His account of his ascent of Mont Blanc was translated into English by Reverend Mr Martyn, Professor of Botany at Cambridge, in 1788 (Coxe, 787–88).
19 Coxe, *Sketches*, 778.
20 Coxe cites modern calculations to debunk ancient accounts of higher mountains, concluding 'that there are no mountains, except those in America . . . which are equal to the altitude of Mont Blanc' (780).
21 Coxe, *Sketches*, 778.

Chapter 10: Golden Days and Giddy Prospects

1 *LEY*, 33 (italics added). For the facts of Wordsworth's Simplon crossing I am indebted to Donald Hayden's account, which summarizes the various findings and interpretations of Moorman, Reed, Wildi, and Bernhardt-Kabisch.
2 VI.565.
3 Max Wildi, 'Wordsworth and the Simplon Pass,' *English Studies* 40 (1959), 228.
4 Again the 1850 version tries to make the place culpable for their error: its 'track . . . held forth / Conspicuous invitation to ascend a lofty mountain' (570–73).
5 The village is Freerberg, in Max Wildi's view (224–32). Ernest Bernhardt-

Kabisch thinks it is an unnamed hamlet, 'Wordsworth and the Simplon Revisited,' *Wordsworth Circle*, X (1979), 381–84.

6   *DWJ*, II.260–61.
7   *LEY*, 34.
8   WAG, 218n6.
9   Johannes von Müller, cited in Pffarer Arnold's *Der Simplon* (1947), cited by Wildi, 230. (The Toggia is another name for the Doveria.)
10 *DWJ*, II.258 (my italics); cited in MM1, 142.
11 The formulation is Geoffrey Hartman's, in his revised preface (1971) to his seminal study of Wordsworth's 'apocalyptic' imagination, *Wordsworth's Poetry*, 1787–1814 (New Haven: Yale University Press, 1964).
12 I am indebted to my late friend Louis Hawes for firsthand information about the Borromean Islands.
13 Wordsworth's itinerary entry; *CEY*, 106; Hayden, *Tour of 1790*, 56–57.
14 *PW*, IV.387–88, 479.
15 *LEY*, 34.
16 Birdsall, in *DS*, 12–14.
17 *DS*, 143–45 (Huntington Quarto transcriptions).
18 *DS*, 149 (Huntington Quarto transcriptions).
19 Hayden, *Tour of 1790*, 64.
20 Ibid., 67.
21 Havens notes that 'most of the memorable experiences recorded in *The Prelude*' *are* unpleasant (429).
22 *DWJ*, II.219–20.
23 *DWJ*, II.243.
24 *DWJ*, II.244.
25 In 1820, the family touring party broke apart for several days because of Dorothy's determination to see exactly where her brother had been on Como in 1790. They first spent two days there, but Dorothy returned with William while Crabb Robinson and the others remained in Milan. *DWJ*, 239.
26 Hayden, *Tour of 1790*, 64.
27 Lane Cooper, *A Concordance to the Poems of William Wordsworth* (New York, E.P. Dutton, 1911), 1002.
28 Wordsworth notes that these two lines are free translations from Petrarch.
29 This is compatible with one of Hayden's options: 'did he backtrack and actually return to the western shore of Lake Como just north of Gravedona?' (Hayden, *Tour of 1790*, 65).
30 *DWJ*, II.223 (Dorothy's italics).
31 *BL*, chapter 4.
32 A proposed revision from 1794 (*DS*, 187).
33 *LEY*, 34.
34 MM1, 146.
35 *DS*, line 564n.
36 Cited in Hayden, *Tour of 1790*, 83.

37   *DWJ*, II.134.

38   *LEY*, 36.

39   GMH1, 92. The fifth 'reverie,' on promenade, is most concerned with this
area.

40   *The Confession of Jean-Jacques Rousseau*, anonymous English translation of
1783 and 1790, ed. A. S. B. Glover (New York, Heritage Press, 1955), 624.

41   Gunther Rothenberg, *Encyclopedia Americana* (1989), vol. 17, 242.

Chapter 11: The Mighty City

1   *LEY*, 37.

2   *CEY*, 115n.

3   *CEY*, 115n29.

4   *LEY*, 46–47; MM1, 150. All references to Dorothy's correspondence in this
section are from *LEY*, 38–47, 50–54 (20 October 1790, and 23 May and 26
June 1791).

5   *DWJ*, II.86.

6   *LEY*, 52.

7   *HRCU* 464–564.

8   MM1, 161.

9   Arthur Beatty, *William Wordsworth: His Doctrine and Art in Their Historical
Relations* (1922, reprint, Madison, University of Wisconsin Press, 1960) 231;
citing *DNB*.

10   *Excursion* II.219–21, *app. crit.* There is no warrant in Fawcett's biography,
however, for Wordsworth's representation of the Solitary's downfall: 'His
sacred function . . . at length renounced; / . . . the course / Of private life
licentiously displayed / Unhallowed actions' (II.263–69).

11   Tantalizingly, a Henry Wordsworth lived in Jewin Street off Aldersgate, one
block away from Wood Street. He signed himself 'Citizen Wordsworth' in a
list of contributors to the defence of the leaders of the London
Corresponding Society who were arrested in May 1794, leading up to the
Treason Trials. (Roe, 'Citizen Wordsworth,' *TWC*, 14 (1983), 21–30.)

12   *PW*, II.217, 507.

13   Peter Manning, 'Placing Poor Susan: Wordsworth and the New
Historicism,' *Studies in Romanticism*, 25 (1986), 351–69; David Simpson,
'What Bothered Charles Lamb about Poor Susan?' *Studies in English
Literature*, 26 (1986), 589–612.

14   *A Treatise on the Police of the Metropolis*, new ed. (London, 1797). Colquhoun
estimated 115,000 persons, or one in nine, were engaged in criminal activity,
which for him included both 'illegal' and 'immoral' behaviour.

15   Mary Cathcart Borer, *An Illustrated Guide to London, 1800* (New York, St
Martin's Press, 1988), 207.

16   'Thy Turtles [? Wilston] and thy Venison, Wright,' *PW*, I.306; Walter

Thornbury, *Old and New London: A Narrative of Its History, Its People, and Its Places* (London, Cassell, Petter and Galpin, 1873–78), 418. Landon and Curtis correct De Selincourt's conjecture of Wilston to Wilchere, owner of the King's Head Tavern; Stephen Wright was a meat provisioner in Charing Cross.

17 In DC MS 47, 29v, an additional line has been inserted between 640–641, and then crossed out, which Reed transcribes as 'From [?door] or [?] or [?] [?breathed]' (*Thirteen*, II.349; I.486).

18 Thornbury, *London*, I.230–31.

19 Pat Rogers, introduction to Boswell's *Life of Johnson*, ed. R.W. Chapman (Oxford, Oxford University Press, 1980), xv–xxviii.

20 André Parreaux, *Daily Life in England in the Reign of George III*, trans. Carola Congrove, (London, Allen and Unwin, 1969), 138–39. The name gained its currency from the character played by Garrick in Benjamin Hoadley's *The Suspicious Husband* (1779), a rake who seduces women but cheerfully lets them go if they love another, thus gaining the sobriquet of 'Honest Ranger.'

21 EL, 170–76.

22 IX.32, MS variant (*Thirteen*, II, 783).

23 George, *Hogarth* (129), citing a turn-of-the-century German visitor's account.

24 IX.33–34.

25 Marjorie and C.H.B. Quennell, *A History of Everyday Things in England*, Vol. 3, *The Rise of Industrialism, 1733–1851*, 5th ed. (London, B.T. Batsford, 1950), III.xxx. There was no central sewer system until 1865.

26 'Newspapers Thirty-Five Years Ago,' in *The Last Essays of Elia*. Lamb noted that 'Already one paragraph, and another, as we learned afterwards from a gentleman at the Treasury, had begun to be marked at that office, with a view to its being submitted at least to the attention of the proper Law Officers.' Such attention helps to account for Lamb's and Southey's appearance in Gillray's cartoon of 1795, 'Copenhagen House,' anticipating their more famous appearance in Gillray's 'The New Morality' of 1798.

27 VI.686; Thornbury, *London*, I.44–45; WAG, 264n7.

28 Richard Altick, *The Shows of London* (Cambridge, Mass., Belknap Press, 1978), 184.

29 Ibid., 128–40, 184.

30 Claire Tomalin, *Mrs Jordan's Profession: The Actress and the Prince* (New York, Alfred A. Knopf, 1995), 72–75, 124–27.

31 MS var. (DC MS 52; *Thirteen*, II, 708).

32 Borer, *Illustrated Guide*, 65, 143; Parreaux, *Daily Life*, 136.

33 The MS makes clear that the quack is Graham, by referring to 'some Scots Doctor' (*Thirteen*, II, 97).

34 Altick, *Shows*, 82.

35 Richard Schwartz, *Daily Life in Johnson's England* (Madison, University of Wisconsin Press, 1985), 88.

36   *PW*, I.306; Juvenal, lines 168–73; *EPF*, 11–12.

37   GMH1, 114.

38   *Parliamentary History*, vol. 29, col. 421

39   *PW*, IV.409.

40   De Selincourt, 565 (citing Haydon's *Autobiography*).

41   *Thirteen*, II.719, 721.

42   *1850* VII.535.

43   All references to the 6 May debate are from *Parliamentary History*, Vol. 29, cols. 365–398.

44   *1850*, VII.540–43.

45   Cf. Mary Jacobus, ' "That Great Stage Where Senators Perform"', *Studies in Romanticism*, 22 (1983), 353–87; Chandler, *passim*.

46   Borer, *Illustrated Guide*, 154 (citing Horace Walpole).

47   Schwartz, *Daily Life*, 80; George, *Hogarth*, 77 (quoting John Hookham Frere, 'Loves of the Triangle', *The Anti-Jacobin*, 7 May 1798).

48   Borer, *Illustrated Guide*, 152, quoting Sophia von La Roche.

49   WAG, 238n5, citing Maxwell edition (Penguin, 1971).

50   Wordsworth returned to London for a few weeks at the end of the summer, after consulting with John Robinson on his future. His other London sojourns in the 1790s do not coincide with the fair's dates, except possibly 1798, when he was busy with last-minute preparations for the trip to Germany.

Chapter 12: The Mighty Mind

1   For most of the geographic details in this section, I am indebted to Donald E. Hayden, *Wordsworth's Travels in Wales and Ireland* (Tulsa, University of Tulsa Press, 1985), 3–16.

2   *LEY*, 109.

3   *CEY*, 317; Hayden, *Travels in Wales*, 4.

4   *PW*, I.43.

5   The present Snowdon Ranger path is another possible route, running roughly parallel to Rhyd-Ddu about three miles further north, but it is longer and easier – neither of which would have recommended it to Wordsworth and Jones.

6   Thomas Pennant, *A Tour of Wales*, 1773 (London, Henry Hughes, 1778–84), 160.

7   Ibid., 165.

8   Jonathan Wordsworth, 'The Climbing of Snowdon,' *Bicentenary Wordsworth Studies*, 453.

9   *1850*: 'a midnight hour.'

10   XIII.45–56; cf. 'the mountains huge appear . . . and their broad backs upheave / Into the clouds' (*PL*, VII. 285–87).

11 WAG, 460n5; also cited as a source is James Clarke's *Survey of the Lakes* (1787), which recounts a walk up Skiddaw at 4 a.m., noting the mist that lies thick in the valley, but which, halfway up the mountain, 'appears so strong that you might walk upon it; I can compare it to nothing so much as to a vast sheet of ice covered with snow' (73), cited in Zera Fink, *The Early Wordsworthian Milieu* (Oxford, Clarendon Press, 1958), 46–47.

12 *LLY*, V, Pt. 2, 78–9 (14 May 1829); Wordsworth places the episode 'five and thirty years ago,' which would put it in 1794, but all authorities agree that Wordsworth's phrase is in an approximation and that 1791 is the actual date.

13 Alan Liu, 'Wordsworth and Subversion, 1793–1804: Trying Cultural Criticism,' *Yale Journal of Criticism*, no. 2 (Spring 1989) 77, 91n16.

14 George, *Hogarth*, 87.

15 I thank my colleague Donald Gray for help on the meaning and connotations of 'Taffy.' It derives from the supposed Welsh pronunciation of David (that is, Dafydd), which is to say, from the English *representation* of the Welsh pronunciation.

16 MM1, 166, n2.

17 MM1, 186n1, citing N. Sykes, *Church and State in the 18th Century*.

18 *LEY*, 60n2.

19 *LEY*, 57–58.

20 *LEY*, 54.

21 *LEY*, 62.

22 *LEY*, 61.

23 Richard Wordsworth to Richard Wordsworth of Whitehaven (7 November 1791), *LEY*, 61n1.

24 *CEY*, 123, citing *LEY*, 66.

Chapter 13: Revolution and Romance

1 *CEY*, 123–25.

2 GMH1, 137; Michael L. Kennedy, *The Jacobin Clubs in the French Revolution: The First Years* (Princeton, Princeton University Press, 1982), 114n4.

3 DVE, 104.

4 James Billington, *Fire in the Minds of Men: Origins of the Revolutionary Faith* (New York, Basic Books, 1980), 29–30; the following details about the Palais-Royal are also from Billington.

5 Raoul Hesdin, *The Journal of a Spy in Paris during the Reign of Terror, January–July 1794* (New York, Harper, 1895), 64–65. A tourist guide to prostitutes in the Palais-Royal neighbourhood was prepared for the Fête de la Fédération in 1790, ostensibly with a view to protecting young men from the provinces. By the time Wordsworth arrived in late 1791, it had gone through five editions (Jean Robiquet, *Daily Life in the French Revolution*, tr.

James Kirkup [New York, Macmillan, 1965], 68).

6 *Paradise Lost*, II.951–52: 'a universal hubbub wild / Of stunning sound and voices' (WAG, 314n1).

7 *CEY*, 125–26. Brissot's first name was Jacques, though in later published attacks on him, his enemies frequently gave his name as Jean Pierre. Eloise Ellery, *Brissot de Warville* (Boston, Houghton Mifflin, 1915), 4.

8 Gary Kates, *The Cercle Social, the Girondins, and the French Revolution* (Princeton, Princeton University Press, 1985), 199.

9 Ellery, *Brissot*, 223–25.

10 Brissot lived in rue Grétry, five or six streets north of the Palais-Royal. James MacGillivray makes a plausible case for locating Wordsworth there, but Wordsworth denied a similar statement in Barron Field's unpublished *Memoirs of Wordsworth*. MacGillivray, 'Wordsworth and Brissot,' *TLS* (29 January 1931), 79; Barron Field's *Memoirs of Wordsworth*, ed. Geoffrey Little (Sydney, Australian Academy of the Humanities, 1975), 26n12.

11 *LEY*, 71.

12 Speech of late November 1791; cited in Donald M. Sutherland, *France, 1789–1815: Revolution and Counterrevolution* (New York, Oxford University Press, 1986), 136.

13 H.M. Williams, *Letters from France*, Vol. I, Letter IX.

14 Eric Robinson, 'An English Jacobin: James Watt, Jr,' *Cambridge Historical Journal*, XI (1953–55), 349–55.

15 *CEY*, 126n15. Watt left Paris hurriedly on 7 October 1792 for Nantes. His route lay through Orléans, and it is just possible he saw Wordsworth there, given the small number of Englishmen remaining.

16 François-Alphonse Aulard, *La société des Jacobins: Recueil de documents pour l'histoire du club des Jacobins de Paris*, 6 vols. (Paris, Libraire Jouaust, 1889–97) III.267; DVE, 122–27.

17 Except where noted otherwise, all details about these Paris journals are from Kates, 177–217, passim.

18 Marcel Reinhard, *Chute de la royauté* (Paris, 1969), 190; cited in DVE, 129n62.

19 'Master pamphlets' refers not only to English tracts like Burke's *Reflections* and Paine's *Rights of Man*, but also to their French counterparts. A bundle of papers identified as 'French Pamphlets and Ephemera' was listed in the sale catalogue of Wordsworth's library after his death (GMH1, 151).

20 DVE, 131 (my translation).

21 Billington, *Fire*, 44; its offices were near the Théâtre Français (the present Odéon Theatre).

22 Kates, *Cercle Social*, 190n27; DVE, 130.

23 *LEY*, 118.

24 Kates, *Cercle Social*, 186.

25 MM1, 174.

26 *The Correspondence of Mr Joseph Jekyll* (London, Algernon Bourke, 1894).

27 *LEY*, 63n1.

28 *LEY*, 70; HMW, *Letters*, II.33–34.

29 Except as noted, all details about Annette Vallon are based on Emile Legouis' pioneering work, *William Wordsworth and Annette Vallon* (1922), expanded by his son Pierre (Archon Books, 1967).

30 The words are those of, respectively, the police prefect of Blois in 1804, a scholar of the French Resistance (Reguis Bouis) in 1944, Guillemin de Savigny, the mayor of Blois in 1818, cited by Pierre Legouis (*WAV*, 90, 156–58), and F.W. Bateson, 92. De Savigny's comments were made as part of a dossier compiled to get Annette a pension after the Restoration for heroic action in the service of the King.

31 *WAV*, 27.

32 *WAV*, 100.

33 *LEY*, 87; Bateson, *Wordsworth*, 85. Dorothy continues: '[it] demonstrates itself every moment of the Day when the Objects of his affection are present with him . . . in a sort of restless watchfulness which I know not how to describe, a Tenderness that never sleeps, and at the same Time such a Delicacy of Manners as I have observed in few Men.'

34 After the facts of Wordsworth's affair became public in the 1920s, some biographers, in a state of Freudian shock, made Annette the key to all Wordsworthian mysteries. Others, determined to defend him from untoward passion, have stressed his youthful naïvete and condescended to Annette as a creature of sentimental excess, 'all sensibility,' 'devoid of intellectual curiosity,' an 'over-generous disposition,' whose 'pathetic strain never relaxes' (*WAV*, 32; *WFD*, 7).

35 *WAV*, 55.

36 *WAV*, 13.

37 *WAV*, 127; italics added.

38 Sutherland, *France*, 132–34.

39 Reed favourably cites MacGillivray's suggestion about the identifications of time and place in this passage (*CEY*, 129n1).

40 *LEY*, 75–76.

41 *LEY*, 62, 76.

42 Ruth Necheles-Jansyn, *The Abbé Grégoire, 1781–1831* (Westport, Conn., Greenwood, 1971), 114.

43 *WAV*, x.

44 Harper, 'Wordsworth at Blois,' 121.

45 GMH1, 168.

46 *WAV*, 48–49, 89, 149. This police report is from 1804, but the Vallons were already being watched when Wordsworth arrived in 1792.

47 *WAV*, 47–48.

48 *WAV*, 19.

49 Facts in this paragraph are from MM1, 192; NR, 55; GMH1, 162; DVE, 140.

50 GMH1, 168.

51 NR, 56.

52 NR, 53; citing *Procés Verbal*.

53 MM1, 196.

54 *Oeuvres de l'abbé Grégoire* (Paris, Editions d'histoire sociale, 1977), III.207.

55 NR, 66.

56 Ellis Yarnall, quoted in *Memoirs*, II.491.

57 *LEY*, 81.

58 *CEY*, 134–35.

59 MM1, 201.

60 NR, 71.

61 NR, 70–71.

62 MM1, 201.

63 *WFD*, 26; following details are from the same source (15–16).

64 All details in this paragraph are from Kates, *Cercle Social*, 235–41.

65 Peter Vansittart, *Voices of the Revolution* (London, Collins, 1968), 167–69, 200; citing Chateaubriand's *Mémoires*.

66 Kates, *Cercle Social*, 241.

67 Favret, 286.

68 On 8, 16, 25, 29 November and 2 and 16 December. Reeve Parker, '"In some sort of seeing with my proper eyes": Wordsworth and the Spectacles of Paris,' *Studies in Romanticism*, 27 (1988), 380–93.

69 In the margin of this copy of Burke's collected works (London, 1803–27), vol. VII (1815), 305; now in the collection of the Wordsworth Library.

70 GMH1, 177. Bateson (96) suggest a minor political post, but this is hard to credit, for either France or England.

71 DVE, 211, 225.

72 Alger, *Englishmen*, 50–51; Goodwin, 510–12.

73 Alger, *Paris*, 346. Cowper berated Hayley for the Revolution's extremes after Louis's execution: 'the French have made me weep for a king of France, which I never thought to do, and they have made me sick of the very name of liberty, which I never thought to be' (29 January 1793; quoted in Brown, *French Revolution*, 89).

74 Alger, *Paris*, 326.

75 These characteristics are based on Alger's description of the signatories (*Englishmen*, 337–42).

76 DVE, 233.

77 Robert Hughes, *The Fatal Shore* (New York, Knopf, 1986).

78 GMH1, 137.

79 *WFD*, 29–30.

80 *Dispatches of Earl Gower*, 262.

81 DVE, 241.

82 *Dispatches of Earl Gower*, 268.

Chapter 14: Castaway

1 DVE, 237.
2 Phillip A. Brown, *The French Revolution in English History* (1918; reprint, London, George Allen and Unwin, 1923), 85.
3 Lucyle T. Werkmeister, *A Newspaper History of England 1792–1793* (Lincoln, University of Nebraska Press, 1967) 92–3.
4 Brown, *French Revolution*, 85–87.
5 'Constructive treason' dates from the fourteenth century, but it came back into its own again in the 1790s. It asked of a text whether its meaning could be 'construed' as 'tending toward' treason – that is, 'compassing or imagining' the death of the king. When enough interpretive pressure was applied, the number of texts that could be found to do so was remarkable.
6 DVE, 238–40, citing Werkmeister's *Newspaper History of England* (134–51).
7 De Quincey, *Tait's Magazine* (April 1839), 238; *Recollections*, ed. V. Sackville-West, 170.
8 MM1, 219.
9 'Autobiographical Memoranda,' in *Prose*, III.374.
10 H.W. Piper, *The Active Universe: Pantheism and the Concept of the Imagination in the English Romantic Poets* (London, Athlone Press, 1962), 66–67.
11 Excerpts are reprinted in the Cornell University Press editions of each (*EW*, 303–06; *DS*, 299–301).
12 Werkmeister, *Newspaper History*, 311; GMH1, 237.
13 *Monthly Review* (October 1793), 216–218; quoted in *DS*, 300–01.
14 GMH1, 186n, citing Christopher Wordsworth's journal for 5 November 1793.
15 *LEY*, 120.
16 MM1, 213.
17 Boulton lists over fifty published responses to Burke between 1791 and 1793 (265–71).
18 EL, 226.
19 GMH1, 215.
20 *Anecdotes of the Life of Richard Watson* (London, Codell and Davis, 1817), 268.
21 *LEY*, 87; GMH1, 217.
22 MM1, 226.
23 *Prose*, I.31. The bridge metaphor is from Addison's 'The Vision of Mirza,' which Wordsworth knew was 'well known to your lordship' since Watson had referred to it in his Appendix. All citations to the 'Letter' are from this edition, 31–49.
24 The portions of *Prelude* X which allude broadly to events of 1793 include several pointed epithets about apostasy or renegadism which apply better to Watson than to almost any other public figure: 'apostasy from ancient faith'

(284); 'scoffers in their pride, / Saying, "Behold the harvest which we reap / From popular government and equality"' (430–32); 'the name of a false prophet' (798); 'Enough, no doubt, the advocates . . . / Of ancient institutions had performed / To bring disgrace upon their very names' (894–51); 'sorrow for the man / Who either had not eyes to wherewith to see, / Or seeing hath forgotten' (857–59).

25 *LEY*, 97 (10 July 1793).

26 *LEY*, 81n2.

27 *LEY*, 193n.

28 Richard J. Hutchings, *Isle of Wight Literary Haunts* (Newport, Isle of Wight County Press, 1989), 18–19.

29 *CEY*, 142.

30 Preface to *Guilt & Sorrow* (1842).

31 MM1, 230n3.

32 *EPF*, 738.

33 'Tintern Abbey,' lines 89–92.

34 *LEY*, 109. (DW to Jane Pollard, 30 August 1793).

35 The definitive scholarly text of both poems is *The Salisbury Plain Poems of William Wordsworth*, ed. Stephen Gill (Ithaca, Cornell University Press, 1975). I refer to this first version as *NSP*, and to the second as *ASP*.

36 Gill cites some of the sources of the poem which do *not* come from Wordsworth's own experience: Rousseau, Chatterton, Spenser, antiquarian writers on Stonehenge, and Lake District memories (438n27).

37 *LLY*, Part III, 616.

38 Gill, 74, citing *The Gentleman's Magazine*, 63 (856–7).

39 Cited in Anne Janowitz, *England's Ruins: Poetic Purpose and the National Landscape* (Oxford, Blackwell, 1990), 96.

40 Fink, *Wordsworthian Milieu*, 88–89, 134–35.

41 *LEY*, 136.

42 Compare the Countess of Pembroke's *Arcadia*, a poem known to Wordsworth: 'The lovely clusters of her brests, / Of *Venus'* babe the wanton nests: / Like pommels round of Marble cleere: / Where azurde veines well mixt appeere. / With dearest tops of porphyrie.'

43 For example: 'The herculean Commonwealth had put forth her arms, / And throttled with an infant godhead's might / The snakes about her cradle' (*Prelude* X. 362–64).

44 *PW* I.330.

45 *CEY*, 146n12.

46 DC MS 11; used by permission of Dove Cottage Trustees. I am grateful to Jared Curtis for help in deciphering some words in the manuscript, and the conjecture of 'Hymettus' in 1.12. A printed version of the fragmentary text appears in his and Carol Landon's edition of the early unpublished poems and fragments in the Cornell Wordsworth series (743). The reconstruction of the missing phrases is entirely my conjecture, the page being torn away at

these points.

47 Hayden's conjectural reading.

48 *PW* II.530 (italics added).

49 IF note, *PW* II.527.

50 Gilpin also compared the plain to the ocean (quoted by Janowitz, *Englands' Ruins*, 104).

51 The dead man's daughter is named Rachel, the name Wordsworth proposed for the Female Vagrant in some revisions of the Salisbury Plain poems. And the widow's thoughts of her orphaned children seems like an adult version of the stout little girl Wordsworth had just met at Goodrich Castle: ' "Seven are they, and all fatherless!" ' (*Peter Bell*, 1120)

52 *CEY*, 316. Donald Hayden purposes an alternative itinerary, back across the Black Mountains from Ross-on-Wye to the Brecon Beacons (*Wordsworth's Travels in Wales and Ireland* 22). But this entails twenty miles of back-tracking down from Builth.

Chapter 15: A Return to France?

1 MM1, 231, 239–42; SG, 77–78; *CEY*, 147–49.

2 *LEY*, 109.

3 *Reminiscences*, ed. J. A. Froude (New York, Harper, 1881), 333. All references are to this edition, 331–37.

4 Ibid., 334.

5 *The Writings and Speeches of Edmund Burke*, Vol. IX, ed. R. B. McDowell (Oxford, Clarendon Press, 1991), 184–85.

6 *Works*, III.106.

7 *Alaric Watts: A Narrative of His Life*, 2 vols. (1884; reprint, New York, AMS Press, 1974), II, 286–87.

8 *DHRF*, 193.

9 *WAV*, 125–26.

10 *WAV*, 26, 31.

11 *WAV*, 128–30, *passim* (italics added).

12 I draw on Sutherland (166–200) for most historical details in what follows, except where otherwise noted.

13 HMW, II.125.

14 Simon Schama, *Citizens: A Chronicle of the French Revolution* (New York, Alfred A. Knopf, 1989), 714.

15 Details are from *WAV*, 40–44, based on records in the Archives National.

16 Louis Jacob, *Les Suspects pendant la Révolution* (Paris, Hachette, 1952), 100, 102.

17 HMW, II.91; DHRF, 511; Schama, 728.

18 Charles A. Dauban, *La Démagogie en 1793 à Paris* (Paris, Henri Plon, 1868), 257.

19 One such accusation ran thus: 'Il avait fait des radiations [erasures] de mots dans les jugements rendus dans les procès des assassins de L. Bourdon et dans celui de Charlotte Corday' (Dauban, *Démagogie*, 300)

20 Dauben, *Démagogie*, 270–271, reporting the words of Harmond de la Meuse.

21 Harvey Mitchell, *The Underground War Against Revolutionary France: The Missions of William Wickam, 1794–1800* (Oxford, Clarendon Press, 1965); Olivier Blanc, *Les Hommes de Londres: Histoire secrète de la Terreur* (Paris, Albin Michel, 1989). Hugo's judgment on Pitt's war policy is very harsh: 'Pitt was in truth a state malefactor. Policy has treasons sure as an assassin's dagger. Pitt stabbed our country and betrayed his own.' (*Quatre-Vingt Treize*, III.1.xvi) Wordsworth's view was substantially the same, in language no less strong: 'base / As vermin working out of reach . . . [to] make an end of liberty.' (X. 275–89, 635–56).

22 Alfred Cobban, *Aspects of the French Revolution* (New York, G. Braziller, 1968), 230–31; Maurice Hutt, *Chouannerie and Counter-Revolution* (Cambridge, Cambridge University Press, 1985), Vol. I, 103–05.

23 HO 98/4.

24 Sutherland, *France*, 200; Richard Bienvenu, ed., *The Ninth of Thermidor: The Fall of Robespierre* (New York, Oxford Universtiy Press, 1968), 21–24.

25 Bienvenu, *Ninth of Thermidor*, 62.

Chapter 16: A Return to France: The Evidence of Speculation

1 Reed establishes the outside parameters for Wordworth's departure from Wales as somewhere between late August and perhaps after 15 September, though not ruling out a date as late as early October (*CEY*, 145).

2 Sutherland, *France*, 226; Dauban, *Démagogie*, 388; Schama, *Citizens*, 766.

3 HMW, II.5.

4 William Kerr, *The Reign of Terror, 1793–94: The Experiment of the Democratic Republic and the Rise of the Bourgeoisie* (Toronto, University of Toronto Press, 1927), 203–04.

5 Sutherland, *France*, 226; Kerr, *Reign of Terror*, 204.

6 III.1.i; II.2.ii. Hugo's republican general has the same view of the situation: 'The ocean no longer belonged to [France]. In this ocean was England . . . a man would fling her a bridge . . . a man would go to Pitt, to Craig, to Cornwallis, to Dundas, to the pirates, and say, "Come!" ' (III.5.ii).

7 George McLean Harper, 'Did Wordsworth Defy the Guillotine?,' in *Spirit of Delight* (New York, Henry Holt, 1928), 53.

8 Schama, *Citizens*, 693.

9 Dauban, *Démagogie*, 454.

10 Details in this paragraph are drawn mainly from Kerr, *Reign of Terror*, 208–20.

11 J.G. Alger, *Paris in 1789–1794* (London, G. Allen, 1902), 144.

12   Quoted in Michael Ross, *Banners of the King: The War of the Vendée, 1793–4* (New York, Hippocrene, 1975), 320. Details of Beaupuy's movements in the post-Cholet campaign are drawn from Ross, except where noted.

13   Le Mercier considered him 'nothing more than a crook from the Palais-Royal,' but he was as brave as he was vicious (Ross, *Banners*, 195).

14   *Moniteur* (27 December 1793), cited by Nichola Roe, 'Wordsworth's Account of Beaupuy's Death,' *Notes and Queries* (1985), 337. Beaupuy's brother Pierre actually was killed in the Vendée (MM1, 197), another source of confusion.

15   George Bussière and Emile Legouis, *Le Général Michel Beaupuy (1755–1796)* (Paris, F. Alcan, 1891), 118; cited by MacGillivray.

16   'To William Wordsworth' (line 11).

17   Strictly speaking, X.278–89 is a passage more obscurantist than oblique, as Wordsworth tries to criticize Pitt's policy without revealing his own, for he himself also had a 'policy' at the time, expressed in the unpublished 'Letter to the Bishop of Llandaff.' WAG, 374n1, explicates these 'four remarkably cryptic points.'

18   These lines were cut from *1850*, following Wordsworth's general policy of revision over forty-five years, of making all historical references less specifically applicable to him.

19   Bienvenu, *The Ninth of Thermidor* calculates twenty-two in August, seventy-two in September, 179 in October, 491 in November. In December and later the numbers began to reach 'industrial levels,' in Schama's chillingly precise phrase.

20   Schama, *Citizens*, 783, quoting Achard; cf. Laparra, president of a Society of Friends of Liberty and Equality in the Vendée: 'Strike, strike great blows against these infamous heads!' (643).

21   *The Prelude*, ed. Ernest De Selincourt (Oxford, Clarendon Press, 1926) 580 (italics added).

22   II.4.i; III.3.xv.

23   James MacGillivray, 'Wordsworth in France,' *TLS* (12 June 1930), 496.

24   MM1, 215.

Chapter 17: Legacy Hunting

1   *LEY*, 94–5.

2   Brown, *French Revolution*, 95–107.

3   BRS, 216.

4   *LEY*, 113.

5   MM1, 243; *PW*, III.4–5.

6   MM1, 244.

7   *LEY*, 113–116. These and the following quotations are from these two letters, both from late April.

8   MM1, 27.
9   *LEY*, 115 (to Jane Pollard).
10   *LEY*, 116–18.
11   *LEY*, 120.
12   Most of these revisions were never published; on the contrary, when Wordsworth reissued the two poems in 1836 he substantially cut them both.
13   *EW*, 136. All citations of Wordsworth's revisions are from this edition.
14   Lines 358–60, 366–67.
15   Lines 686–88; *EW*, 153n.
16   *LEY*, 120n4.
17   *LEY*, 121.
18   *LEY*, 123–24.
19   Letter to Lady Beaumont, August 1805 (MM1 248–49).
20   *PW*, V.340. De Selincourt dates this fragment (which I have quoted in its entirety) from 1795; Moorman estimates 1796 (MM1, 249).
21   *LEY*, 118.
22   *LEY*, 126–27.
23   *CEY*, 151; River Duddon sonnets, XXI.
24   WAG, 386n9.
25   SG, 88.
26   The date of his baptism was 16 September 1773 (*LEY*, 126n1).
27   *LEY*, 129–30.
28   This is far different from the way most of Wordsworth's biographers have presented the matter. They follow Wordsworth's lead in *The Prelude*, taking a view of it based on spiritual insights removed as far as possible from material circumstances. Moorman says that Raisley was 'moved by something in Wordsworth's manner and person . . . [to make] that gallant bet with the future'; Gittings and Manton honour his 'selfless devotion in the face of imminent death.'
29   *LEY*, 130n1. The total cash mentioned in Raisley Calvert Sr's will is £840, but a codicil increased Raisley Jr's cash benefit.
30   *LEY*, 131.
31   *LEY*, 132n1.
32   13 October 1794; *LEY*, 132n1.
33   *LEY*, 134.
34   *LEY*, 134–36; letters of 7 November, 24 December, and 7 January.

Chapter 18: Philanthropy or Treason?

1   'Ought I explicitly to declare the sentiments I entertain?' (*Political Justice*, I.272; cited in NR, 176–77).
2   *LEY*, 119.
3   *Conciones ad Populum* ('The Plot Discovered'), 1795.

4   *LEY*, 124.

5   *LEY*, 135 (7 November 1794).

6   *LEY*, 138 (24 December 1794 and 7 January 1795).

7   *LEY*, 139n2.

8   Mary Moorman says this magazine was of 'extreme radical opinion [and] ran for six months, when Pitt's "Gagging Acts" must have killed it. It was scurrilous in style and contained nothing which could have issued from the pen of Wordsworth' (MM1, 256n). Moorman was the first Wordsworth scholar to examine this journal, but virtually everything she says about it is inaccurate. It ran for eleven months, not six, was not extremely radical in opinion, only intermittently scurrilous in style or content, and contained many things which could have issued from the pen and mind of Wordsworth.

9   Lewis Patton, ed., *The Watchman*, in *The Collected Works of Samuel Taylor Coleridge*, gen. ed. Kathleen Coburn (Princeton, Princeton University Press, 1983), II.xxxix.

10 *LEY*, 125.

11 *LEY*, 125.

12 E.P. Thompson, 'Wordsworth's Crisis,' *London Review of Books* (8 December 1988), 3–6 (reviewing Roe, *Wordsworth and Coleridge: The Radical Years*).

13 Brown, *French Revolution*, 139; Scrivener, *Poetry and Reform*, 96; BRS, 221. Best published a popular book on angling in 1787 (11th ed., 1822) and a long poem, *Matilda*, in 1789. The other identifiable *Philanthropist* writer was William Green, possibly the author of *The Art of Living in London* (1785). A third contributor, George Peopleton, may be a name or a pun. Six other contributors used initials (J. B., B. W., R. F., H. E., A. M. L., and W.); on the last of these, see below. All other contributions are unsigned or use code names: Junius, Common Sense, Liberty Pig, Aristides, Pax, etc.

14 GMH1, 267–68.

15 NR, 192.

16 Hazlitt, *The Spirit of the Age* (1825), 31; Godwin is quoted from MM1, 263.

17 Holcroft, *Memoirs*, 85–88. Holcroft's son shot himself in 1789, as he was being approached by his father on board the *Fame*, on which he was trying to flee the country after stealing some money from Holcroft. The incident created a sensation, and invidious connections were drawn between the boy's death and his father's well-known irascibility.

18 BRS, 150.

19 Binns, *Recollections*, 45; Peter H. Marshall, *William Godwin* (New Haven: Yale University Press, 1984), 87. John Binns was also a member of the Philomatheans.

20 Marshall, *Godwin*, 172.

21 *LEY*, 126, 128.

22 *CLSTC*, i.156; cited in Nicholas Roe, 'Radical George: Dyer in the 1790s,' *Charles Lamb Bulletin*, ns. 49 (January 1985): 22.

23 *LEY*, 170–71.

24 Gill also makes this point, noting that Godwin's preface is 'perfectly well written' (105).

25 Thompson, 'Crisis,' 4.

26 GMH1, 251.

27 *LEY*, 140n2. Wordsworth's address is written on the cover of a letter from Coleridge (but not in Coleridge's hand) to Dyer, dated 10 March 1795.

28 See K.R. Johnston, 'Philanthropy or Treason? Wordsworth as "Active Partisan"' *Studies in Romanticism*, 25 (1986), 371–409. My conclusions are here extended by subsequent work by Roe, Thompson, and Scrivener.

29 NR, 278 (Roe's italics).

30 MM1, 261.

31 MM1, 261.

32 Quoted in MM1, 261.

33 *LEY*, 183–84.

34 Moorman gives the details of these transactions (I.269–70, 297).

35 *LEY*, 156n–157n.

36 Gill, *The Salisbury Plain Poems*, 37n.

37 *LEY*, 159 (20 November 1795): 'I recollect reading the first draft of it to you in London.'

38 *EPF*, 781–821. I am grateful to the editors for allowing me to see a pre-publication typescript of their brilliant reconstruction of this work.

39 *PW*, I.302, ll. 13–14; *EPF*, 808. All citations will be to the latter text.

40 G.G. Ramsay's literal translation, in the Loeb Classical Library edition.

41 'To Cash paid Geo: Dyer Esq. On account of Luttrell Tempest. 200.' Duke of Portland's Secret Service Account Book, 4 verso. Cited courtesy of Wordsworth Library. I have not been able to identify 'Luttrell Tempest.'

42 *EPF*, 821; from the inside cover of DC MS 2. There are seven more brief entries on this cover; the one immediately following this one has an eerie resonance, if we think of Mathews dead in the West Indies in 1801, 'a disappointed man.' It reads, 'And the dead friend is present / in his shade.'

43 *LEY*, 158 (20 November 1795).

44 Binns, *Recollections*, 54–56.

45 Bergan Evans and Hester Pinney, 'Racedown and the Wordsworths,' *Review of English Studies* 8 (1932) 8.

46 SG, 92.

47 MM1, 268.

48 *Memoirs*, 314.

49 Between lines 622 and 24; MS 52, 271v, 272r; *Thirteen*, II.876.

50 WAG, 406n5.

51 These striking parallels to Wordsworth's 1795 London experience are all the more pointed when we consider that this history of disillusionment was *not* very much like Fawcett's, as Wordsworth surely knew. In his old-age note to Isabella Fenwick, Wordsworth said, 'Poor Fawcett, I have been told, became

pretty much such a person as I have described; and early disappeared from the stage, having fallen into habit of intemperance, which I have heard (though I will not answer for the fact) hastened his death.' Hazlitt recalled that the failure of the French Revolution 'preyed upon [Fawcett's] mind and hastened his death' (Holcroft's *Memoirs*, 192n), but also remembered passing 'some of the pleasantest days of my life' with Fawcett in his retirement in Hertfordshire; he was, 'of all the persons I have ever known, . . . the most perfectly free from every taint of jealousy or narrowness.'

52 *Memoirs of Charles Mathews, Comedian*, ed. Anne Mathews (London, Richard Bentley, 1838), 315.
53 *LEY*, 154–55.
54 The poem's author is Vicomte de Ségur; it appeared in *Almanach des Muses, ou Choix Poésies fugitive de 1792, Année 1793* (*CEY*, 24n12; Hayden, I.114–16); the *Morning Chronicle* version is printed in *EPF*, 723.

Chapter 19: Of Cabbages and Radicals

1 Richard Pares, *A West-India Fortune* (Hamden, Conn., Archon Books, 1950), 121.
2 All information on Pinney is from Pares unless otherwise noted.
3 In 1782, Pinney was one of the two planters who arranged the island's peaceful surrender to a French fleet, and who co-operated with the occupiers until they left shortly thereafter. (Evans and Pinney, 'Racedown,' 3.)
4 The records are not clear, but it appears that the younger Pinneys were paying their father for the house (Evans and Pinney, 'Racedown,' 3).
5 Pares, *Fortune*, 63.
6 Ibid., 155.
7 Ibid., 149.
8 *LEY*, 153 (20–24 October 1795).
9 William Knight, *Coleridge and Wordsworth in the West Country: Their Friendship, Work, and Surroundings* (London, Elkin Matthews, 1913), 8.
10 GMH1, 282.
11 Thelwall was keenly aware of Coleridge's success in Bristol (NR, 145–56).
12 *The Poet's Fate*, ed. Donald Reiman (New York, Garland Publishing, 1979), 26–28.
13 Gill lived at Harlescombe Farm, a few hundred yards away from the main house (Evans and Pinney, 'Racedown,' 9, 14).
14 *LEY*, 160 (30 November 1795).
15 *CLSTC*, I.
16 MM1, 205.
17 Crowe's book was not a 'pure' landscape poem, but is imbued with the 'Old' or 'Country' Whig principles that John Pinney, like James Lowther, also represented. The poem projects a vision of free enterprise liberalism that got

644 · Notes to pages 344–55

Crowe into hot water on occasion. The poem he read at a 1793 reception for the Duke of Portland at Oxford was suppressed for its anti-war sentiments. (John Williams, *Wordsworth: Romantic Poetry and Revolution Politics*, Manchester University Press, 1989, 10–18.)

18 *LEY*, 162.
19 *LEY*, 141.
20 MM1, 269.
21 *LEY*, 163.
22 *LEY*, 166 (7 March 1796).
23 Wordsworth cut these lines from the poem after 1815 (*PW*, IV.173, *app. crit.*).
24 Herman J. Wüscher, *Liberty, Equality, and Fraternity in Wordsworth, 1791–1800* (Stockholm, Almquist and Wiskell International, 1980), 97.
25 *LEY*, 168.
26 Information about Gill is from Pares, *Fortune*, 142; Evans and Pinney, 'Racedown,' 14; MM1, 276, 308.
27 Mrs Cecil Thelwall, *The Life of John Thelwall* (London, J. Macrone, 1837), I.319.
28 *LEY*, 184 (7 May 1797).
29 'The Ruined Cottage,' MS B.193–95.
30 *LEY*, 154.
31 *LEY*, 162.
32 XII.163–64.
33 MM1, 314n2.
34 *The Ruined Cottage and The Pedlar*, ed. James Butler (Ithaca, Cornell University Press, 1979), 463.
35 'Will his heart become much either softened or expanded, who breathes the atmosphere of a dungeon? Surely it would be better in this respect to imitate the system of nature, and, if we would teach justice and humanity, transplant those we would teach into a natural and reasonable state of society' (*Political Justice*, II.754–55; quoted in *EPF*, 768).
36 *PW*, I.316.
37 *LEY*, 159.
38 Frederick W. Bateson, *Wordsworth: A Reinterpretation* (London, Longmans, Green, 1954) 119; MM1, 295.
39 SG, 91.
40 MM1, 262.
41 Paul D. Sheats, *The Making of Wordsworth's Poetry, 1785–1798* (Cambridge, Harvard University Press, 1973), 129.
42 *LEY*, 256 (27 February 1799).
43 Leslie Chard, *Dissenting Republican: Wordsworth's Early Life and Thought in their Polictical Context* (The Hague, Mouton, 1972), 219.
44 *LEY*, 169 (21 March 1796).
45 Evans and Pinney, 'Racedown,' 12.

46 Pares, *Fortune*, 166.

47 Woof, *BWS*, 90–91.

48 *LEY*, 165.

49 Pares, *Fortune*, 166.

50 Woof, *BWS*, 90.

51 *LEY*, 169.

52 *LEY*, 169–71.

53 Landon, 'Racedown Period,' 100.

54 'Ellen' was a common literary name, one that Wordsworth regularly used to refer to Dorothy, particularly in poems dealing with the emotional undercurrents of their domestic situation.

Chapter 20: An Independent Intellect

1 EL, 270.

2 *Miscellanies* (London, 1886), 118; quoted by ibid., 269.

3 Richard Matlak, *The Poetry of Relationship* (New York, St Martin's Press, 1997) part one, passim.

4 Ibid., introduction; Liu, 308 (italics added).

5 All quotations from *The Borderers* are from the early version (1797–99) in the edition by Robert Osborn (Ithaca, Cornell University Press, 1982).

6 WAG, 402n8.

7 Reeve Parker, '"In some sort seeing with my proper eyes": Wordsworth and the Spectacles of Paris,' *Studies in Romanticism*, 27 (1988). When Wordsworth was in Paris, on 26 November 1792, an adaptation of *Othello* opened in which Iago's villainy was not revealed until the very end of the play, as in *The Borderers*. In this production, Desdemona is being forced to marry the Duke's son because of her father's opposition to her suitor, the military hero Othello. This twist on the father-daughter-suitor triangle is not found in any other of Wordsworth's likely sources (Parker, 300). This version of the play was published in late September 1793, when Wordsworth may have been in Paris, and performed again on 31 October 1793, the day of the Girondins' mass execution.

8 Quoted by RH, 79.

9 William and Dorothy also read Henry Brooke's *Gustavus Vasa* 'with pleasure' in Racedown's library, a play of 1739 that was still deemed seditious in England for its depiction of an evil minister leading his royal master astray. This story of a young northern prince who freed his country stayed with Wordsworth as the kind of epic story he would have written had he not decided that the growth of his own mind was a better example of such heroism: 'how Gustavus found / Help at his need in Dalecarlia's mine' (I.211–12).

10 Marijane Osborn, 'Wordsworth's *Borderers* and the Landscape of Penrith,'

Transactions of the Cumberland and Westmorland Antiquarian and Archaeological Society, n.s. 76 (1976), 144–58.

11 Marijane Osborne, '*Borderers* and the Landscape of Penrith,' 148–50.

12 Gerald N. Izenberg, *Impossible Individuality: Romanticism, Revolution and the Origins of Modern Selfhood, 1787–1802* (Princeton, Princeton University Press, 1992) 166–67.

13 Ibid., 196.

14 *LEY*, 181.

15 CEY, 194–95.

16 MM1, 309.

17 SG, 120.

18 *LEY*, 190n3.

19 Hayden, I.942.

20 Jonathan Wordsworth, 'A Wordsworth Tragedy,' *TLS* (21 July 1966), 642. Gordon Wordsworth's action was extraordinary, for the man who more than any other is responsible for preserving the collection that forms the basis of the libraries, museums, bookshops, conference centres, and related buildings and activities that now make up the Wordsworth Trust in Grasmere.

21 Quoted by Jonathan Wordsworth, 'A Wordsworth Tragedy,' cited above.

22 W.L. Nichols, *The Quantocks and their Associations* (second edition, 1891), quoted by Jonathan Wordsworth.

23 The definitive account of the early versions of the poem is James Butler's: *'The Ruined Cottage' and 'The Pedlar'* (Ithaca, N.Y., Cornell University Press, 1979).

24 All textual citations are to the Butler edition, MS B, the earliest extant complete version (March 1798).

25 De Quincey, *The Collected Writings*, Vol. VI, 306.

26 Jerome McGann, *The Romantic Ideology* (University of Chicago Press, 1983); Marjorie Levinson, *Wordsworth's Great Period Poems* (Cambridge University Press, 1986); James Chandler, *Wordsworth's Second Nature* (University of Chicago Press, 1984).

Chapter 21: The Spy and the Mariner

1 Margaret E. Sandford, *Thomas Poole and His Friends*, 2 vols. (London, Macmillan, 1888), I.200.

2 GMH1, 307.

3 Tom Mayberry, *Coleridge and Wordsworth in the West Country* (Phoenix Mill, Alan Sutton, 1992), 74; EL, 359.

4 Sandford, *Poole*, II.132–37. Burnett's friends contined to try to help him: the next year, he was a Unitarian minister at Yarmouth, where he tutored Southey's younger brother, and in 1802 he replaced George Dyer as a secretary in Lord Stanhope's house.

5 Richard Reynell was another of these forgotten hangers-on in the circle that became the first generation of English Romantics.

6 *CLSTC*, 325.

7 *LEY*, 189.

8 *CLSTC*, I.330.

9 RH, 152–53.

10 *LEY*, 189.

11 Sandford, *Poole*, I. 211, 219.

12 Ibid. I.238–39.

13 MM1, 338.

14 Mayberry, *West Country*, 96.

15 *LEY*, 190 (14 August 1797).

16 The 'two isles' are lighthouse sand spits, Steep Holm and Flat Holm.

17 *LCML*, 118.

18 Prefatory Memoir, *Poems, written Chiefly in Retirement* (Hereford, 1801). The story of Thelwall's harassment is told by E.P. Thompson, 'Hunting the Jacobin Fox,' *Past and Present*, 142 (1994), 94–140.

19 GMH1, 319.

20 Ann Hone, *For the Cause of Truth: Radicalism in London, 1796–1821* (London, John Murray, 1835) 80.

21 GMH1, 320–21.

22 Sandford, *Poole*, I.244.

23 Quoted by RH, 156.

24 *Specimens of the Table Talk of the Late Samuel Taylor Coleridge* (London, John Murray, 1835), 103.

25 *LLY*, III, 640. (To Mrs John Thelwall, 16 November 1838). Thelwall's own version follows Coleridge's, in his 1801 novel *The Daugher of Adoption* (I.283). My thanks to Geoffrey Carnall for pointing out this parallel.

26 *LEY*, 211n2.

27 Sandford, *Poole*, I.207.

28 NR, 262.

29 EL, 373.

30 PRO HO 42/41; the entire extant correspondence is printed by A.J. Eagleston, 'Wordsworth, Coleridge and the Spy,' *The Nineteenth Century and After* 54 (1908), 73–87.

31 Mayberry, *West Country*, 97.

32 Hone, *Cause of Truth*, 60 ff.

33 Ibid., 29–30, 53.

34 Ian Gilmour, *Riots, Risings and Revolutions: Government and Violence in Eighteenth-Century England* (London, Pimlico, 1993), 416, 441.

35 NR, 257.

36 *Felix Farley's Bristol Journal*, 4 March 1797; cited by ibid., 248.

37 Sandford, *Poole*, I.219.

38 NR, 258–59.

39 Hone, *Cause of Truth*, 69–70; R.R. Nelson, *The Home Office, 1792–1801* (Durham, Duke University Press, 1969), 116; Tomalin, *Mrs Jordan's Profession*, 132.

40 Elizabeth Sparrow, 'The Alien Office,' *Historical Journal* 33 (1990) 366–67; cf. Harvey Mitchell, *The Underground War against Revolutionary France: The Missions of William Wickam 1794–1800* (Oxford, Clarendon Press, 1965).

41 Roger Wells, *Insurrection: The British Experience, 1795–1803* (Gloucester, Alan Sutton, 1983), 37–38.

42 Nicholas Roe, 'Who Was Spy Nozy?' *Wordsworth Circle* 15 (1984), 49.

43 Information in this paragraph is from Hone, *Cause of Truth*, 69–70, Nelson, *Home Office*, 33–36, 115–16, Tomalin *Mrs Jordan's Profession*, 85, 119, and *Canning's London Journal* 33, 36, 282.

44 Dropmore Papers, British Library Add. MSS 69038; Nelson, *Home Office*, 35.

45 Wendy Hinde, *Castlereagh* (London, Collins, 1981), 22.

46 Nelson, *Home Office*, 176.

47 MM1, 339; GMH1, 327–28; *PW*, I.363.

48 *CLSTC*, I.403 (April 1798).

49 *CLSTC* I.343–44.

50 *BL*, chapter 10.

51 *CEY*, 205.

52 MM1 333–37; SG, 130–31.

53 'Autobiographical Memoranda' in Wordsworth Library (MS 17–20).

54 *LEY*, 211, 213.

55 *LEY*, 192n1.

56 *CPWSTC*, 1114; all quotations from *Osorio* are from *CPWSTC*.

57 Mayberry, *West Country*, 101.

58 Most biographers, following Coleridge's dubious lead, assign its composition to October, but I agree with Reed and Margoliouth in assigning its inspiration and much of its composition to the first of their two November tours.

59 RH, 164n.

60 Gittings and Manton, *Dorothy Wordsworth*, 73.

61 John Livingston Lowes, *The Road to Xanadu: A Study in the Ways of the Imagination* (Boston, Houghton Mifflin, 1927), 257–58.

62 *CPWSTC*, I.286–87.

63 Grosart, *Prose*, III.16–17 (IF note).

64 *LEY*, 197.

65 *LEY*, 196.

66 *LEY*, 196.

67 *LEY*, 196n1.

68 *LEY*, 210–11.

69 *The Castle-Spectre* (1798 reprint, Oxford, Woodstock Books, 1990).

70 There were three Townshends connected with the Secret Service during the

1790s, so the name had topical currency: a police officer, an undersecretary, and Thomas Townshend, Lord Sydney, the second home secretary after its reorganization in 1782 (Nelson, *Home Office*, 199).

71 Clement Carlyon, *Early Years and Late Reflections* (London, Whittaker, 1836), I.180.

Chapter 22: The Mariner and the Recluse

1 RH, 178.
2 Entries for 14–15 April and 22 February.
3 *DWJ*, I.1.
4 *PW*, V.341.
5 Robert Gittings and Jo Manton, *Dorothy Wordsworth* (Oxford, Oxford University Press, 1988), 77.
6 Earliest MS text of the poem, established by Beth Darlington *(Bicentenary Wordsworth Studies*, 431).
7 CEY, 218–28.
8 RH, 172.
9 All facts about the poem's composition are from Butler's edition.
10 Paul Magnuson, *Coleridge and Wordsworth: A Lyrical Dialogue* (Princeton, Princeton University Press, 1988), 112–13.
11 Butler, 468–469.
12 MS B.399–410.
13 NR, 235.
14 Cf. K.R. Johnston, *Wordsworth and 'The Recluse'*, *passim*.
15 *CLSTC*, 391.
16 *CLSTC*, 1034.
17 BL I.195–96 (italics added).
18 *NSTC*, I.217 (entry 213).
19 *CLSTC*, 527 (*c*. 10 September 1799).

Chapter 23: Triumphs of Failure

1 *LB*, 6.
2 An edition of the extant portions of the *Opus Maximum*, edited by Thomas McFarland, is scheduled as Volume 15 of Coleridge's *Collected Works*, published by Princeton University Press.
3 SG, 143.
4 Hazlitt, 'My First Acquaintance,' in *The Complete Works*, ed. P. P. Howe, 21 vols. (London, J.M. Dent, 1932), XVII.117.
5 *LEY*, 200.
6 *LEY*, 215.

7   SG, 144.

8   *CEY*, 226.

9   *LEY*, 216.

10 *CLSTC*, I.412 (28 May 1798). Anna Seward, the old 'Swan of Lichfield,' an important figure among the older generation of 'bluestockings,' had never heard of Wordsworth, though she knew and admired the work of Coleridge, Southey, and Lloyd, and considered them a 'school.' (*Letters* [Edinburgh, 1811], cited in Wallace Douglas, *Wordsworth: The Construction of a Personality* [Ohio, Kent State University Press, 1968], 23–26.)

11 *LB*, 10.

12 John E. Jordan, *Why the 'Lyrical Ballads'?: The Background, Writing and Character of Wordsworth's 1978 'Lyrical Ballads'* (Berkeley, University of California Press, 1976), 118, citing Mayo; Jordan lists fifty volumes of poetry that appeared in 1798, several with titles or subjects similar to *Lyrical Ballads* (187–89).

13 Marilyn Butler, *Romantics, Rebels and Reactionaries* (Oxford, Oxford University Press, 1981), 58–64.

14 Jordan, *Background*, 90–93.

15 Mark Reed, 'Wordsworth, Coleridge, and the "Plan" of *Lyrical Ballads*,' *University of Toronto Quarterly*, 34 (1965), 238–53.

16 *LB*, 8.

17 *LEY*, 198, 214; *CEY*, 224, 226.

18 MM1, 382–83; *LB*, 346.

19 RH, 190.

20 MM1, 383n1.

21 *LEY*, 218.

22 IF, quoted in *LB*, 345.

23 Hazlitt, 'First Acquaintance,' 120.

24 RH, 189; SG, 149–50.

25 Losh's *Diary*, cited in *LEY*, 225.

26 *CLSTC*, I.412.

27 MM1, 358n.

28 Hayden, 354; *LB*, 285.

29 De Selincourt calls it 'a curious survival of Wordsworth's earlier and more crudely "romantic" taste' (*PW*, IV.471).

30 Fritz Schulze, 'Wordsworthian and Coleridgean Texts (1784–1822),' in *Strena Anglica*, ed. Gerhard Dietrich and F. Schulze (Halle, 1956), 225–58; cited in *LB*, 455.

31 *DWJ*, 8.

32 *PW*, V.343–44.

33 *LB*, 284.

Chapter 24: Wye Wandering

1 Basil Cottle, *Joseph Cottle of Bristol* (Bristol, Bristol Historical Association, 1983), 9.

2 3 July 1798, *LEY*, 223.

3 *LEY*, 222n1, for details of Wordsworth's visit with Losh and Warner.

4 Detailed accounts of Wordsworth's likely itinerary and timetable by John B. McNulty, Geoffrey Little, and Kenneth R. Johnston are summarized in Donald E. Hayden, *Wordsworth's Travels in Wales and Ireland*, 27–37.

5 *PW*, II.517.

6 EL, 285; John E. Jordan, *Why the "Lyrical Ballds"?* 1–8; Moorman takes this view also, but does wonder, 'did he not claim too much for the all-sufficiency of "Nature"?' (380). This view is continued for posterity in the definitive scholarly edition of *Lyrical Ballads*, which observes that Wordsworth affirms his faith in nature '*in spite of* his "hearing oftentimes / The still, sad music of humanity"' (italics added). I would say Wordsworth's affirmations arise *because* he could still hear that sad music.

7 Richard Warner, *A Walk through Wales, in August 1797* (Bath, Crutwell, 1798), 230 (citing *Aeneid* VIII.431).

8 William Gilpin, *Observations on the River Wye and Several Parts of South Wales, Related Chiefly to Picturesque Beauty, Made in the Summer of 1770* (London, R. Blamire, 1782), 12.

9 Gilpin, *Observations*, 35–37.

10 Gilpin, *Observations*, 32.

11 Mary Jacobus, the leading authority, concludes that, 'more than any other, *Tintern Abbey* is the poem for which Wordsworth's predecessors had smoothed the way' (103–04). She cites particularly Thomson, Akenside, Bowles, and Cowper in the loco-descriptive tradition.

12 *LB*, 357, citing parallels adduced by W. J. B. Owen and Jonathan Wordsworth.

13 SG, 155.

14 De Selincourt, *PW*, II.518.

15 For details about the poem and Gillray's cartoon: Dorothy George, *Catalogue of Political and Personal Satires*, vol. VII (1793–1800), (London: Trustees of the British Museum, 1942), 468–72.

16 SG, 118.

17 In its original newspaper form, nos. 34 and 35 are both dated Monday 2 July; no. 36 (the final number) is dated 9 July. No. 35 carries the following notice under the title: 'The Concluding Number Will Be Published on Saturday next, 7 July.' In the collected editions which began to appear immediately, the date of no. 35 is corrected to 9 July, but no. 36 keeps that same date also. Each of the last three numbers open on a valedictory note: 'Before we take out leave of the Public' (no. 34), 'The Session of Parliament being now closed' (no. 35), and 'We have now completed our Engagement with the

Public' (no. 36). It may also be that two separate issues were published on 9 July to mark the valedictory occasion.

18 *Anti-Jacobin* (20 November 1797), 31–32.

19 Hayden, *Travels in Wales*, 34–37.

20 Thelwall, Prefatory Memoir, *Poems, Chiefly Written in Retirement*, i–xlviii.

21 *CEY*, 245.

22 *LEY*, 226.

23 GMH1, 356–57.

24 Details of these transactions follow Jordan, *Background*, 41–52.

25 Hone, *Cause of Truth*, 48.

26 *Monthly Magazine* (1 October 1801), quoted ibid., 49.

27 *Critical Review*, 2d series XXIV (October 1798), 197–204.

Chapter 25: 'Mr. Wordsworth'?

1 *CLSTC*, I.420.

2 PRO, HO 5/3

3 PRO, HO 5/4.

4 Home Office surveillance of Thelwall in 1798–99 is recorded in PRO, HO 42/43/f.37 and 42/46/fs. 235, 240 (P.J. Corfield and Chris Evans, 'John Thelwall in Wales: New Documentary Evidence,' *Bulletin of the Institute of Historical Research*, 59 (1986), 231–39). A survey of Home Office correspondence preserved from 1798 does not produce any mention of Wordsworth or Coleridge (PRO H.O. 42/43 & 44). But the records are very incomplete: there is only a single item from Yarmouth, registering foreigners who sailed on 28 September, twelve days after the Wordsworths and Coleridge sailed. But in 1798 there would have been hundreds of such reports from every port.

5 *CLSTC*, 421. All references to the crossing are from this letter to Sara, written 3 October from Ratzeburg, and one to Tom Poole of 26 October, unless otherwise noted.

6 *CLSTC*, I.425–26.

7 On 18 August, Wickham acknowledged his receipt on 9 August of a 'letter in favour of M. De Leutre' from the Messrs. Le Chevalier (PRO, HO 5/4/89). This could have been either a defence or a denunciation of his character; 'in favour of' often meant nothing more than 'in regard to' in official correspondence.

8 *BL*, II.179–81.

9 *DWJ*, 27.

10 *LEY*, 229n1.

11 MM1, 409.

12 Information about the general political situation is from Lefebvre, *The French Revolution*, trans. Elizabeth Moss Evanson, 2 vols. (New York,

Columbia University Press, 1962), (II. 192–212); that about the Foreign Office and the Swabian Agency from Sparrow, 'The Swiss and Swabian Agencies, 1795–1801', *Historical Journal* 35 (1992), 873–74

13 PRO, FO 158/3 & 4.

14 PRO, FO 33/15/f.81.

15 Hampshire PRO, Wickham 1/66/f.9 (28 September 1798).

16 Hampshire PRO, Wickham 1/66/f.10 (2 November 1798).

17 Hampshire PRO, Wickham 1/66/f.23 (2 April 1799).

18 Hampshire PRO, Wickham 1/66/f.18 (22 January 1798 – clearly a mistake for 1799).

19 Hone, *Cause of Truth*, 74–5.

20 It has been purchased by the Wordsworth Trust; Reference No. 1994.125.

21 *DNB*, 38–39.

22 Coleridge crossed out a reference to De Loutre in his notebook. In the entry, 'Wordsworth went with the agreeable French Em. to seek a Hotel,' the words 'with the agreeable French' are crossed out; presumably 'Em.' should have been too. Why Coleridge should censor his own notebook is hard to say, unless his fear of surveillance was very great; more likely it was just a correction of fact. (*NSTC*, I.336; *CEY*, 249–50n46.)

23 *CLSTC*, I.459–60.

24 *Dictionnaire de biographie française*, vol. X, Fascicle LVIII, 815. None of the four De Leutres from this period who are listed in biographical dictionaries were titled aristocrats; but none of their English associates could have proved or disproved that.

25 *DWJ*, 24.

26 *CLSTC*, I.429.

27 *BL*, II.183–84.

28 *LEY*, 229n1; *CLSTC*, I.436; *Prose*, I.93.

29 *New Encyclopedia Britannica*, 15th ed. (1993), VI.911.

30 *CLSTC*, I.442.

31 *Prose*, I.93–94.

32 *CLSTC*, I:438.

33 William Little, *Gottfried August Bruger* (New York: Twayne, 1974), 53.

34 Ibid., 53–54; the last quotation is from Schiller.

35 RH, 217.

36 GMH1, 364.

37 Donald E. Hayden, *Wordsworth's Travels in Europe* (Tulsa, University of Tulsa, 1988), 39.

38 L.A. Willoughby, 'Wordsworth in Germany', in *German Studies Presented to Professor H.G. Fiedler* (Oxford, Clarendon Press, 1938), 437.

39 *LEY*, 213.

40 *LEY*, 231.

41 *LCML*, I.141.

Chapter 26: *Writing in Self-Defence*

1   *DWJ*, 33.
2   *DWJ*, 34.
3   *DWJ*, 34.
4   The house is now no. 86 (Hayden, *Travels in Europe*, 39).
5   Willoughby, 'Germany,' 432.
6   *LEY*, 245.
7   *LEY*, 242.
8   'Written in Germany, on One of the Coldest Days of the Century,' lines 11–12, 16, 18, 21 (*LB*, 225–26).
9   *CLSTC*, I.420.
10 *LEY*, 246.
11 Sparrow, 'Swabian Agency,' 873.
12 Mansel, *Louis XVI* (London, Blond and Briggs, 1981), 79.
13 Ibid., 110.
14 *CLSTC*, I.459–60.
15 *CLSTC*, I.440.
16 Peter Boerner, *Johann Wolfgang von Goethe, 1832–1982*, trans. Timothy Nevil and Nancy Boerner (Bonn: Inter Nationes, 1981), 44–45.
17 Cited in Willoughby, 'Germany,' 433n4.
18 SG, 158.
19 *LEY*, 253–54.
20 *CLSTC*, 451–52.
21 *LEY*, 236.
22 *LEY*, 234.
23 Mary Moorman's account may be taken to stand for many: she says Wordsworth in Goslar begins his 'blessed retreat into the past,' joyfully recording his 'early happiness' in childhood (MM1, 419).
24 MS JJ, in the Wordsworth Library.
25 *1799*, 123.
26 *1799*, 124–25.
27 Alastair Conran, 'On the Goslar Lyrics,' in *Wordsworth's Mind and Art*, ed. Alastair Thomson (Edinburgh, Oliver and Boyd, 1969), 158.
28 XI.334–35.
29 MS JJ, 22–36.
30 *CLSTC*, I.479.
31 Willoughby, 'Germany,' 434n, citing Robinson's diaries (ed. Morley, 1922), 38.
32 Frederick W. Bateson, *Wordsworth: A Re-Interpretation* (London, Longmans, Green, 1954), 151.
33 Richard Matlak, 'Wordsworth's Lucy Poems in Psychobiographical Context,' *PMLA*, 93 (1978), 46–65.
34 Bateson, 151–53.

35   Ibid., 151.
36   Ibid., 153.
37   Matlak, 'Wordsworth's Lucy Poems,' 50–60.
38   The history of critical neglect of 'Nutting' is set forth in Gregory Jones, ' "Rude Intercourse": Uncensoring Wordsworth's "Nutting," ' *Studies in Romanticism*, 36 (1996), 213–43.
39   *LB* 302–07, prints the versions from both DC MSS. 15 and 16.
40   DC MS. 16; printed in *LB*, 305–07.
41   Bateson, *Wordsworth*, 153; Jones, 'Rude Intercourse,' 228–43.
42   Douglas Thompson, 'Wordsworth's Lucy of Nutting,' *Studies in Romanticism*, 18 (1979), 287–98.
43   De Selincourt, *PW*, IV.423. Carl Ketcham says Wordsworth used it 'only because it was well established as a pseudonym,' *Shorter Poems, 1807–1820*, ed. Ketcham [Ithaca, Cornell University Press, 1989], 545).
44   Information about the Eclogue X is from the editions by C. Day Lewis (1963) and Robert Coleman (1977).
45   Ketcham ed., *Shorter Poems*, 545.
46   Thomson, 'Lucy,' 288–95.
47   *LEY*, 243.
48   MS JJ, 147–151.
49   DC MS 15, lines 6–9 (italics added).
50   Bateson, *Wordsworth*, 150; SG, 160–61.
51   SG, 161.

Chapter 27: Destination Unknown

1   *LEY*, 252.
2   The report is based on the 1836 memoirs of one of the young men, Clement Carlyon, who was part of Coleridge's hard-drinking set at Göttingen, expanded by a notoriously unreliable literary raconteur, William Howitt, in 1847. Neither Coleridge nor the Wordsworths left any record of such a visit, though Dorothy's statement that they planned 'to saunter about for a fortnight or three weeks at the end of which time you may be prepared to see us in Göttingen,' does fit its time-frame. Clement Carlyon, *Early Years and Late Reflections* (London: Whittaker, 1836), 1:186–97; William Howitt, *Homes and Haunts of the Most Eminent British Poets* (London: R. Bentley, 1847), 2:257–58.
3   *CEY*, 265–65n4.
4   Boerner, *Johann Wolfgang von Geothe, 1832–1892*, trans. Timothy Nevil and Nancy Boerner (Bonn, Inter Nationes, 1981), 64, 98; Willoughby, 'Germany,' 451.
5   Bodleian Talbot MSS., b.27, fos. 54–7 (No. 3) and précis copy PRO, FO 74/23; cited by Sparrow, 'Swabian Agency,' 880n101.

6   Hone, *Cause of Truth*, 129.

7   Sparrow, 'Swabian Agency,' 880.

8   Peter Jupp, *Lord Grenville, 1759–1834* (Oxford, Clarendon Press, 1985), 214.

9   Ibid., 224.

10   MM1, 430.

11   Stephen Parrish, ed., *The Prelude, 1798–1799* (Ithaca, Cornell University Press, 1977), 3 (for MS 19); LB, 717 (for MS 15).

12   *CLSTC*, I.354–55 (15 December 1800).

13   *New Columbia Encyclopedia* (1975), 1315.

14   Carlyon, *Early Years*, III.46.

15   Sparrow, 'Swabian Agency,' 871n51, citing Bodleian Talbot MSS.

16   *LEY*, 221.

17   GMH1, 369.

18   *LEY*, 244, 254.

19   Sparrow, 'Swabian Agency,' 877.

20   Ibid., 868.

21   *LEY*, 244.

22   *CEY*, 262.

23   Mansel, *Louis XVI*, 94.

24   *NSTC*, I.432f50.

25   Elizabeth Sparrow, *Secret Service: British Agents in France 1792–1815* (The Boydell Press, 1999), 99.

26   *LEY*, 257. Since the first edition of *The Hidden Wordsworth* appeared, the likely identity of this washing machine has been established by Prof. and Mrs. David Hiley of the University of Regensburg, in a personal communication to me. It was the invention of Jakob Christian Schaeffer (1718–1790), a Protestant minister with a bent for applied science. Evidently its fame had spread as far north as Nordhausen by 1799, for the Wordsworths to hear of it. But if its reputation was more local, and the Wordsworths actually *in* Regensburg when they saw it, that would place them much closer to the Swabian Agency's headquarters near Ulm.

27   I am grateful to Elizabeth Sparrow for this suggestion.

28   They are printed together in the Cornell edition of *Lyrical Ballads*, 307–16.

29   *CLSTC*, I.510.

30   RH, 233.

31   *CLSTC*, I.484.

32   *CLSTC*, I.490–91.

33   Hone, *Cause of Truth*, 93 (Hampshire PRO, Wickham 1/66).

34   Elizabeth Sparrow, 'Alien Office,' *Historical Journal* 33 (1990), 374.

35   Hone, *Cause of Truth*, 90–1.

36   These quotations are also from the discursive blank verse fragments (i and ii) written at Goslar *LB*, 307–09).

37   From the fragment beginning, 'There is an active principle in all things,' *LB*, 309, lines 29–44; italics added).

38 Hone, *Cause of Truth*, 73 (Wickham to Portland, 3 January 1801; British Library Add. MSS 33107 [Pelham papers], f.1.).

Chapter 28: 'We have learnt to know its value'

1   *LEY*, 142 (mid-April 1795).
2   There were seven children in all: Margaret had died in 1796, age twenty-four.
3   MM1, 436–37.
4   *LEY*, 141–42 (mid-April 1795).
5   *LEY*, 257.
6   Bateson says Mary 'was the real object of their visit' (155).
7   'I travelled among unknown men' (April 1801).
8   Parrish, *1799*, 27.
9   *LEY*, 264.
10 *LEY*, 263.
11 *LEY*, 267–68.
12 *CLSTC*, I.653–54; Tomalin, 179.
13 *LEY*, 267n1.
14 WL; quoted by SG, 163n.
15 *CLSTC*, I.489n1.
16 *LEY*, 276–77.
17 SG, 164–65.
18 *CMY*, 75.
19 *LEY*, 678.
20 *LEY*, 262.
21 *CMY*, 99n62. The final discrepancy, between £100 and the £110 13s. actually owed Wedgwood, 'remains unexplained.'
22 *LEY*, 241.
23 MM1, 438.
24 *CLSTC*, I.491.
25 *LEY*, 276n2.
26 By Melvin Lasky; cited in *Biographical Dictionary of Modern British Radicals*, vol. I, 306.
27 'Sir James Mackintosh,' in *The Spirit of the Age: or, Contemporary Portraits* (1825), in *The Complete Works of William Hazlitt*, ed. P.P. Howe, 21 vols (London, J.M. Dent, 1932), XI.98.
28 RH, 241–42.
29 *CLSTC*, I.528–30.
30 *CLSTC*, I.536; published in *Morning Post*, 7 December 1799 (*PSTC*, II.958).
31 *NSTC*, I.493.
32 *LEY*, 271. William's letter is an extract from a lost manuscript, with some parts missing or not transcribed.

33　*LEY*, 297.

34　*LEY*, 271.

35　*CLSTC*, I.543.

36　MM1, 447–51.

37　*NSTC*, I.510 (text).

38　*NSTC*, I.510 (notes); Owen, *Lowther*, 273–76.

39　*NSTC*, I.520. Lowther was childless due to impotence from syphillis contracted at Cambridge.

40　*NSTC*, I.511 (text).

41　*CLSTC*, II.740.

42　*LEY*, 271.

43　*CLSTC*, I.543.

44　*LEY*, 272.

45　*NSTC*, I.515.

46　*LEY*, 272.

47　*NSTC*, I.515 (text).

48　*NSTC*, I.521 (text).

49　*NSTC*, I.514 (text).

50　*LEY*, 272.

51　Notebook 15, cited in *NSTC*, I 535 (notes).

52　*CEY*, 279.

53　*CEY*, 279.

54　MM1, 452.

55　*CEY*, 280n24, quoting a letter in the possession of Jonathan Wordsworth.

56　WAG, 4n2.

57　*NSTC*, I.549 (text).

58　*NSTC*, I.571 (text).

59　*NSTC*, I.1575 (text); the entry is a recollection from three years later.

60　*NSTC*, I.1575 (notes).

61　RH, 251.

62　*CPWSTC*, I.332.

63　*LEY*, 274.

64　MM1, 453.

65　'Home at Grasmere,' MS B, lines 223, 218.

66　SG, 169.

67　*LEY*, 273–81, and Appendix VI.

68　*LEY*, 280.

69　*BL*, Chapter 14, first paragraph.

70　'Hart–Leap Well,' lines 169–70, 124.

71　MS B, lines 236–41.

72　*LEY*, 661 (25 December 1805); quoted by MM1 468.

73　MS B, lines 261–67.

74　*CEY*, 284.

75　MS B, lines 1027–34.

Chapter 29: Home at Grasmere

1   *LSTC*, I.612.
2   *LEY*, 290.
3   On the authority of James Losh's diary, Reed puts the annual rent at only five pounds per year (*CMY*, 84n44).
4   MM1, 465.
5   *LEY*, 274 (24 and 27 December 1799).
6   *LEY*, 298–99.
7   MM1, 461.
8   *DWJ*, I.60n1.
9   *DWJ*, I.65.
10 'A Farewell,' lines 2–4 (*PW*, II.23).
11 *DWJ*, I.40.
12 Gilmour, *Riots, Risings and Revolutions*, 428–30.
13 David McCracken, *Wordsworth and the Lake District: A Guide to the Poems and their Places* (Oxford, Oxford University Press, 1985), 32.
14 *DWJ*, I.49, 51, 65, 37, and *passim*.
15 MM1, 471.
16 Johnston, *Wordsworth and 'The Recluse'*, 370n10.
17 All line references are to MS B, unless otherwise indicated, in Darlington's edition. This is an earlier version than MS D, which is printed in *PW*, V.313–39.
18 *DWJ*, 67 (17 October 1800).
19 These two lines are from MS D (lines 269–70).
20 'Stanzas in Memory of the Author of "Obermann,' lines 53–54.
21 SG, 190.
22 *LEY*, 293.
23 MM1, 475; *DWJ*, 60n1.
24 MM1, 474.
25 *CMY*, 87; *LEY*, 296.
26 *CMY*, 107n70.
27 *CMY*, 61.
28 RH, 278.
29 RH, 278.
30 *CMY*, 103n64.
31 I am indebted to Anca Vlasopoulos for pointing out this connection between the Grasmere journal and its initiating occasion.
32 *DWJ*, 37.
33 *DWJ*, 38.
34 *DWJ*, 39.
35 *LEY*, 282.
36 *CMY*, 61.
37 *CMY*, 67.

38 *CMY*, 69.
39 *CLSTC*, I.651.
40 Butler and Green, *LB*, 24.
41 RH, 267–68.

Chapter 30: *A.k.a.* Lyrical Ballads

1 *CLSTC*, I.585.
2 Butler and Green, in *LB*, 28; *LEY*, 297, 303–04.
3 *CMY*, 85; *CLSTC*, I.621.
4 *LEY*, 285–311, passim.
5 *CLSTC*, I.582, 620.
6 *CLSTC*, I.658.
7 *LEY*, 281.
8 *LEY*, 298.
9 MM1, 506 (JW to MH, 25 February 1801).
10 *CLSTC*, I.764.
11 *CLSTC*, I.632.
12 MM1, 492.
13 SG, 189.
14 *DWJ*, 61–2.
15 *LB*, 740.
16 *LEY*, 309.
17 *LEY*, 302.
18 MM1, 489–90.
19 *LEY*, 309.
20 *CLSTC*, I.631.
21 Butler and Green, in *LB*, 28.
22 *NSTC*, I.802.
23 *DWJ*, 65.
24 *LB*, 320.
25 RH, 297.

Chapter 31: *Selling the Book, Creating the Poet*

1 *CMY*, 107; MM1, 505n4.
2 *Anti-Jacobin Review*, V (April 1800), 434.
3 Robert Woof, 'Wordsworth's Poetry and Stuart's Newspapers, 1797–1803,' *Studies in Bibliography* (Charlottesville, University of Virginia, 1962), 151.
4 *CMY*, 108.
5 *LEY*, 310; italics added.
6 Burges was the fourth highest-paid of Grenville's secret service operatives

during the 1790s, after Canning, Frere, and George Hammond, receiving a total of £64,541 16*s*. 5*d*. (Dropmore Papers, British Library Add. MSS 69076).

7 *LEY*, 284–85.

8 *LEY*, 683.

9 *LWDW*, Vol. VIII: *A Supplement of New Letters*, ed. A. Hill (Oxford, 1993), 2–3; Reed makes the conjecture that the letter was addressed to Lewis (*CMY*, 108–09).

10 Moorman characteristically downplays the letter's political aspect (MM1, 503), though she is anticipated by Wordsworth himself, who was embarrased when it was published in 1838, by which time he was busily burying all evidence of his youthful Whiggery and Jacobinism (*LLY*, II.957).

11 *LEY*, 314.

12 Ayling, *Fox*, 201.

13 Grosart, *Prose*, II.205–06.

14 *LEY*, 325.

15 *LEY*, 326.

16 John Taylor, *Records of My Own Life* (London, E. Bull, 1832), I.176.

17 MM1, 507.

18 *CMY*, 138.

19 MM1, 506–07.

20 *LCML*, I.245–47.

21 *LEY*, 316.

22 *CMY*, 119.

23 SG, 192.

24 *CLSTC*, II.670; *CMY*, 109.

25 *CLSTC*, II.747–48 (25 July 1801).

26 *CMY*, 120; Ketcham ed., *Shorter Poems*, 29.

27 *LJW*, 76–77.

28 Ketcham ed., *Shorter Poems*, 31.

29 *CMY*, 122–23.

30 *Prose*, I.112; SG, 190.

31 My account of the difference between the 1800 and 1802 prefaces derives largely from W. J. B. Owen's brilliant, dispassionate analysis (*Wordsworth as Critic* [Toronto, 1969], 57–114).

32 Ibid., 65.

33 Ibid., 113, 106.

34 Cf. Frederick Garber, *Wordsworth and the Poetry of Encounter* (Urbana, University of Illinois Press, 1971).

35 SG, 196.

36 *Quarterly Review* IV (1804), 329–30; cited by Marilyn Butler, *Romantics, Rebels and Reactionaries*, 62.

Chapter 32: Peace, Marriage, Inheritance

1   *CMY*, 138.
2   *CMY*, 150–52.
3   *CMY*, 120.
4   *CMY*, 150.
5   SG, 194.
6   SG, 200–01.
7   *CMY*, 141.
8   *PW*, II.468.
9   SG, 205.
10   *CMY*, 155, 176.
11   *CMY*, 174n44.
12   Hayden, I.988.
13   *LEY*, 361–68.
14   *LEY*, 364; Dorothy's italics.
15   *LEY*, 370; MM1 558–60; SG, 207.
16   *LEY*, 371n2.
17   *LEY*, 361.
18   *LEY*, 360.
19   *CMY*, 180.
20   *CMY*, 189.
21   Gittings and Manton, *Dorothy Wordsworth*, 135.
22   SG, 209.
23   'England! The time is come,' line 14.
24   'Great men have been among us,' lines 1, 6; 'Calais, August, 1802,' lines 3–7.
25   '1801,' lines 1–3.
26   'When I have borne in memory what has tamed,' lines 12–14.
27   *CMY*, 191–92.
28   Gittings and Manton, *Dorothy Wordsworth*, 137.
29   *LJW*, 126n3.
30   Ketcham ed., *Shorter Poems*, 215–16.
31   *LJW*, 126.
32   *LJW*, 125–26.
33   Frank Rand, *Wordsworth's Mariner Brother* (Amherst, Mass., Newell Press, 1966), 86.
34   SG, 211.
35   SG, 211.
36   *CMY*, 195–96.
37   Gittings and Manton, *Dorothy Wordsworth*, 139.
38   *LEY*, 140.
39   *LEY*, 157.
40   *CMY*, 198. The letters do not survive, only Dorothy's journal entries about writing 'to France.'

41 *CMY*, 201.

42 Between October and December 1803 (Woof, 'Newspapers,' 184–85).

43 Hayden, 582, 585.

Chapter 33: Disciples and Partners

1 Woof, 'Newspapers,' 159n13; citing Thomas Hutchinson's conjectural translation.

2 Ibid., 155.

3 *CMY*, 202.

4 *CMY*, 211, 218.

5 *CMY*, 210.

6 *CMY*, 218.

7 Ketcham ed., *Shorter Poems*, 37–38; *LJW*, 143.

8 *LJW*, 143; John had 1/16 share in the ship's ownership.

9 Rand, *Mariner Brother*, 46.

10 SG, 218.

11 *CMY*, 217–18; SG, 218.

12 Cited in SG, 219.

13 *CMY*, 213, 218.

14 Quoted in Grevel Lindop, *The Opium-Eater: A Life of Thomas De Quincey* (New York, Taplinger, 1981), 102–04.

15 *LEY*, 400.

16 Ralph M. Wardle, *Hazlitt* (Lincoln, University of Nebraska Press, 1971), 70–80, for details of Hazlitt's visit to the Lakes.

17 *Diary of Benjamin Robert Haydon*, ed. Willard Pope (Harvard University Press, 1960–63), II.470.

18 Hazlitt, *Works*, ed. Howe, XIX.21–24.

19 *DWJ*, I.255.

20 *CMY*, 221.

21 RH, 339.

22 *NSTC*, I.1432.

23 *DWJ*, I.198.

24 James A. Mackay, *RB: A Biography of Robert Burns* (Edinburgh, Mainstream Publishing, 1992), 627–50.

25 Gittings and Manton, *Dorothy Wordsworth*, 145.

26 *CMY*, 234.

27 George Macdonald Fraser, *The Steel Bonnets: The Story of the Anglo-Scottish Border Reivers* (London, Barrie and Jenkins, 1971).

28 *LEY*, 403.

29 *PW*, V.467.

30 *PW*, V.467.

31 *Edinburgh Review*, October 1802; quoted in *LEY*, 432n1.

664 · Notes to pages 579–95

32 *LEY*, 432.
33 Walter J. Bate, *Coleridge* (New York, Macmillan, 1968), 118.

Chapter 34: The End of The Prelude

1   *CLSTC*, II.1013.
2   *NSTC*, I.1801.
3   *CMY*, 247–48. Mark Reed explains the complicated story of the text's composition in *The Thirteen-Book Prelude* (Ithaca, Cornell University Press, 1991).
4   Reed, *Thirteen*, 3–58 (esp. 3–5); WAG, 515–20.
5   Wordsworth and Gill, 'The Five-Book Prelude,' 1–25.
6   GMH1, 298.
7   *LJW*, 41.
8   SG, 213–14.
9   Rand, *Mariner Brother*, 46–7, citing C.N. Parkinson, *Trade in the Eastern Seas* (1937), 78, 350.
10 Ibid., 47.
11 *LJW*, 25.
12 *LJW*, 41.
13 *LJW*, 44.
14 *LEY*, 576.
15 *LEY*, 586.
16 *LEY*, 594.
17 *NSTC*, II.2397 (text and notes).
18 Cf. Johnston, *Wordsworth and 'The Recluse'* (341–48) for discussion of Coleridge's letter and its bearing on the project.
19 'Home at Grasmere,' lines 620–22.

Chapter 35: Presenting the Poet

1   P2V, 527.
2   Rogers, *Table-Talk*, 88.
3   Harper, II.113; *CMY*, 323; SG, 249.
4   Farington, *Diary*, III.249.
5   Kenneth Curry ed., *New Letters of Robert Southey* (New York, Columbia University Press, 1965), I.392, 401.
6   *EPF*.
7   *LMY*, 89 (1 November 1806).
8   *NSTC*, II.2975.
9   *NSTC*, II.3148.
10 *NSTC*, 3148.
11 *NSTC*, II.2975 (notes).

12 *NSTC*, II.2975 (notes); no date given (from Notebook L, ff22ᵛ–23).

13 *NSTC*, II.2975n (quoted from Notebook L ff 22ᵛ–23).

14 When Coleridge printed the poem in *The Friend*, he footnoted these lines with the description from his German notebooks.

Epilogue

1 The only really new trip he took was a visit to Ireland in 1829, with John Marshall, Jane Pollard's husband and MP for Leeds.

2 *PW*, I.362.

3 SG, 202.

Bibliography

Alger, J.G. *Englishmen in the French Revolution*. London: S. Low, 1889.

——*Paris in 1789–1794: Farewell Letters of Victims of the Guillotine*. London: G. Allen, 1902.

Altick, Richard. *The Shows of London*. Cambridge, Mass.: Belknap Press. 1978.

Aulard, François-Alphonse. *La Société des Jacobins: Recueil de documents pour l'histoire du club des Jacobins de Paris*. 6 vols. Paris: Librairie Jouaust, 1889–97.

Ayling, Stephen. *Fox*. London: John Murray, 1991.

Bate, Walter J. *Coleridge*, New York: Macmillan, 1968.

Bateson, Frederick W. *Wordsworth: A Re-interpretation*. London: Longman, Green, 1954.

Beatty, Arthur. *William Wordsworth: His Doctrine and Art in Their Historical Relations*. 1922. Reprint, Madison: Univ. of Wisconsin Press. 1960.

Benians, E.A. 'St. John's College in Wordsworth's Time.' In *Wordsworth at Cambridge*, 2–11, 30–36, Cambridge: Cambridge University Press. 1950.

Benstead, C.R. *Portrait of Cambridge*. London: Robert Hale, 1968.

Bienvenu, Richard, ed. *The Ninth of Thermidor: The Fall of Robespierre*. New York: Oxford University Press. 1968.

Billington, James. *Fire in the Minds of Men: Origins of the Revolutionary Faith*. New York: Basic Books. 1980.

Bimbenet, Jean-Eugène. *Histoire de la ville d'Orléans*. 5 vols. Orléans H. Herluison, 1884–88.

Binns, John. *Recollections of the Life of John Binns*. Philadelphia: Parry & M'Millan. 1854.

Bonsall, Brian. *Sir James Lowther and Cumberland and Westmorland Elections, 1754–1775*. Manchester: Manchester University Press. 1960.

Borer, Mary Cathcart. *An Illustrated Guide to London, 1800*. New York: St. Martin's Press. 1988.

Brown, Phillip A. *The French Revolution in English History*. 1918. Reprint, London: George Allen & Unwin. 1923.

Browning, Oscar, ed. *Despatches of Earl Gower, English Ambassador at Paris from June 1790 to August 1792*. Cambridge: Cambridge University Press. 1885.

Burnett, John. *A History of the Cost of Living*. Harmondsworth: Penguin, 1969.

Bussière, George and Emile Legouis. *Le Général Michel Beaupuy (1755–1796)*. Paris: F. Alcan, 1891.

Butler, James. 'The Muse at Hawkshead: Early Criticism of Wordsworth's Poetry.' *Wordsworth Circle* 20 (Summer 1989): 140.

Butler, Marilyn, *Romantics, Rebels and Reactionaries*. Oxford: Oxford University Press, 1981.

Carlyle, Alexander. *Anecdotes and Characters*. Edited by James Kinsley. London: Oxford University Press, 1973.

Chainey, Graham. *A Literary History of Cambridge*. Cambridge: Pevensey, 1985.

Cobban, Alfred. *Aspects of the French Revolution*. New York: G. Braziller, 1968.

Coleridge, Samuel Taylor. *Biographia Literaria*. Edited by James Engell and W. Jackson Bate. Vol. 7, pt. 2 of *The Collected Works of Samuel Taylor Coleridge*. General editor Kathleen Coburn. Bollingen Series 75. Princeton: Princeton University Press, 1983.

——*The Collected Works of Samuel Taylor Coleridge*. General editor Kathleen Coburn. 16 vols. Bollingen Series 75. Princeton: Princeton University Press, 1983–.

——*The Collected Letters of Samuel Taylor Coleridge*. Edited by Earl Leslie Griggs. 2 vols. Oxford: Clarendeon Press, 1956.

——*The Complete Poetical Works of Samuel Taylor Coleridge*. Edited by Ernest Hartley Coleridge, 2 vols. 1912. Reprint, Oxford: Clarendon Press, 1957.

——*The Notebooks of Samuel Taylor Coleridge*. Notes and text. Edited by Kathleen Coburn. 4 vols. Bollingen Series 50. New York: Pantheon Books, 1957–.

——*Specimens of the Table Talk of the Late Samuel Taylor Coleridge*. Edited by H.N. Coleridge. 2 vols. London: J. Murray, 1834.

Conran, Alastair, 'On the Goslar Lyrics.' In *Wordsworth's Mind and Art*. Edited by Alastair Thomson, 157–80. Edinburgh: Liver & Boyd, 1969.

Cooper, Charles H. *Annals of Cambridge*. Vol. 4, *1688–1849*. Cambridge: Metcalfe and Palmer, 1852.

Cooper, Lane, *A Concordance to the Poems of William Wordsworth*. New York: E.P. Dutton, 1911.

Coxe, William, *Sketches on the Natural, Civil and Political State of Swisserland*. 1776. Reprinted with additions, London: J. Dodsley, 1779.

Crabbe, George. *The Complete Poetical Works of George Crabbe*. 3 vols. Edited by Norma Dalrymple-Champneys and Arthur Pollard. Oxford: Clarendon Press. 1988.

Crook, Alec C. *From the Foundation to Gilbert Scott: A History of the Buildings of St. John's College Cambridge, 1511–1885*. Cambridge: Cambridge University Press, 1980.

Dann, Joanne, 'Some Notes on the Relationship between the Wordsworth and the Lowther Families.' *Wordsworth Circle 11* (1980): 80–82.

Dauban, Charles A. *La Démagogie en 1793 à Paris*. Paris: Henri Plon, 1868.

De Quincey, Thomas. *The Collected Writings*. Edited by David Masson. 11 vols. Edinburgh: Adam and Charles Black, 1890.

Erdman, David V. *Commerce des Lumières: John Oswald and the British in Paris, 1790–1793*. Columbia: University of Missouri Press, 1986.

Evans, Bergen, and Hester Pinney. 'Racedown and the Wordsworths.' *Review of English Studies* 8 (1932): 1–18.

Farington, Joseph. *The Farington Dairy*. Edited by Joseph Greig. 8 vols. London: Hutchinson, 1922–28.

Favret, Mary. *Romantic Correspondence: Woman, Politics and the Fiction of Letters*. Cambridge: Cambridge University Press, 1993.

Ferguson, Richard. *Cumberland and Westmorland M.P.'s from the Restoration to the Reform Bill of 1867*. London: Bell and Daldy. 1871.

Fink, Zera, ed. *The Early Wordsworthian Milieu*. Oxford: Clarendon Press, 1958.

Fitzgerald, Percy H. *The Royal Dukes and Princesses of the Family of George III: A View of Court Life and Manners for Seventy Years, 1760–1830*. London: Tinsley Brothers, 1882.

Fowler, Laurence, and Helen Fowler, eds. *Cambridge Commemorated: An Anthology of University Life*. Cambridge: Cambridge University Press, 1984.

George, M. Dorothy, ed. *Catalog of Political and Personal Satires Preserved in the Department of Prints and Drawings in the British Museum*. Vols. 6–7, *1784–1800*. London: Trustees of the British Museum, 1938–42.

——*Hogarth to Cruikshank: Social Change in Graphic Satire*. London: Allen Lane, 1967.

——*London Life in the 18th Century*. London: Kegan Paul, Trench, Trubner, 1925.

Gill, Stephen. *William Wordsworth: A Life*. Oxford: Clarendon, Press, 1989.

Gilmour, Ian. *Riots, Risings, and Revolutions: Government and Violence in Eighteenth-Century England*. London: Pimlico, 1993.

Gilpin, William. *Observations on the River Wye and Several Parts of South Wales, Related Chiefly to Picturesque Beauty, Made in the Summer of 1770*. London: R. Blamire, 1782.

Gittings, Robert, and Jo Manton. *Dorothy Wordsworth*. Oxford: Oxford University Press, 1988.

Goodwin, Albert. *The Friends of Liberty: The English Democratic Movement in the Age of the French Revolution*. Cambridge: Harvard University Press, 1979.

Graver, Bruce. 'Wordsworth's Translations from Latin Poetry,' Ph.D. diss., University of North Carolina, 1983.

Gray, Arthur B. *Cambridge Revisited*. 1921. Reprint, Cambridge: Par Stephens, 1974.

Harper, George McLean. 'Did Wordsworth Defy the Guillotine?' In *Spirit of Delight*. New York: Henry Holt, 1928.

——*William Wordsworth: His Life, Works, and Influence*. Vol. 1. London: John Murray. 1916.

——*Wordsworth's French Daughter: The Story of Her Birth, with the Certificates of*

Her Baptism and Marriage. 1921. Reprint, New York: Russell & Russell, 1967.

——'Wordsworth at Blois.' In *John Morley and Other Essays*, 111–24. Princeton: Princeton Univ. Press, 1920.

Havens, Raymond. *The Mind of a Poet: A Study of Wordsworth's Thought with Particular Reference to 'The Prelude.'* Baltimore: Johns Hopkins University Press, 1941.

Hayden, Donald E. *Wordsworth's Travels in Europe.* Tulsa: University of Tulsa, 1988.

——*Wordsworth's Travels in Wales and Ireland.* Tulsa: University of Tulsa, 1985.

——*Wordsworth's Walking Tour of 1790.* Tulsa: University of Tulsa, 1983.

Hazlitt, William. *The Complete Works of William Hazlitt.* 21 vols. Edited by P.P. Howe. London: J.M. Dent, 1932.

Hesdin, Raoul. *The Journal of a Spy in Paris during the Reign of Terror, January–July 1794.* New York: Harper, 1895.

Hinde, Wendy. *Castlereagh*, London: Collins, 1981.

——*George Canning.* 1973. Reprint, Oxford: Basil Blackwall, 1989.

Holcroft, Thomas. *Memoirs of the late Thomas Holcroft, Written by Himself, and Continuing to the Time of His Death, from His Diary, Notes, and Other Papers.* London: Longman, Hurst, Rees, Orme & Brown, 1816.

Holmes, Richard. *Coleridge: Early Visions.* New York: Viking, 1993.

Hone, Ann. *For the Cause of Truth: Radicalism in London, 1796–1821.* Oxford: Clarendon Press. 1982.

Hughes, Robert. *The Fatal Shore.* New York: Alfred A. Knopf, 1986.

Hunt, Bishop. 'Wordworth's Marginalia on *Paradise Lost,*' *Bulletin of the New York Public Library* 73 (1969): 167–83.

Izenberg, Gerald N. *Impossible Individuality: Romanticism, Revolution, and the Origins of Modern Selfhood, 1787–1802.* Princeton: Princeton University Press, 1992.

Jacob, Louis. *Les Suspects pendant la Révolution, 1789–94.* Paris, Hachette, 1952.

Jacobus, Mary. *Tradition and Experiment in Wordsworth's 'Lyrical Ballads' (1798).* Oxford: Oxford University Press, 1976).

Johnston, Kenneth R. *Wordsworth and 'The Recluse.'* New Haven: Yale University Press, 1984.

Jordan, John E. *Why the 'Lyrical Ballads'?: The Background, Writing, and Character of Wordsworth's 1798 'Lyrical Ballads.'* Berkeley: University of California Press, 1976.

Jupp, Peter. *Lord Grenville, 1759–1834.* Oxford: Clarendon Press, 1985.

Kates, Gary. *The Cercle Social, the Girondins, and the French Revolutions.* Princeton: Princeton University Press, 1985.

Kelley, Paul, 'The Literary Sources of William Wordsworth's Works. 10 July 1793 to 10 July 1797.' Ph.D. diss., University of Hull, 1987.

Kennedy, Michael L. *The Jacobin Clubs in the French Revolution: The First Years.* Princeton: Princeton University Press, 1982.

——*The Jacobin Clubs in the French Revolution: The Middle Years.* Princeton: Princeton University Press, 1988.

Kerr, Wilfred. *The Reign of Terror, 1793–94: The Experiment of the Democratic Republic and the Rise of the Bourgeoisie.* Toronto: University of Toronto Press, 1927.

Knight, William. *Coleridge and Wordsworth in the West Country: Their Friendship, Work, and Surroundings.* London: Elkin Matthews, 1913.

Lamb, Charles, and Mary Lamb. *The Letters of Charles and Mary Lamb.* Edited by Edwin W. Marrs. 2 vols. Ithaca: Cornell University Press, 1975–76.

Lefèbvre, Georges. *Etudes orléanaises.* 2 vols. Paris: Commission d'histoire économique et sociale de la Révolution, 1962–63.

——*The French Revolution.* 2 vols. Translated by Elizabeth Moss Evanson. New York: Columbia University Press. 1962.

Legouis, Emile. *The Early Life of William Wordsworth, 1770–1798: A Study of 'The Prelude.'* Edited by Nicholas Roe. London: Libris, 1988 [Originally published as *La Jeunesse de William Wordsworth.* Paris: G. Masson, 1896.]

——*William Wordsworth and Annette Vallon.* 1922. Expanded by Pierre Legouis. Hamden, Conn.: Archon Books, 1967.

Lindop, Grevel. *The Opium-Eater: A Life of Thomas De Quincey.* New York: Taplinger, 1981.

Liu, Alan. *Wordsworth: The Sense of History.* Stanford: Stanford University Press, 1989.

Lowers, J.L. *The Road to Xanadu: A Study in the Ways of the Imagination.* Boston: Houghton Mifflin, 1927.

McCracken, David. *Wordsworth and the Lake District: A Guide to the Poems and Their Places.* Oxford: Oxford University Press. 1985.

Mackay, James A. *RB: A Biography of Robert Burns.* Edinburgh: Mainstream Publishing, 1992.

McKendrick, Neil, John Brewer, and J.H. Plumb. *The Birth of a Consumer Society: The Commercialization of Eighteenth-Century England.* Bloomington: Indiana University Press, 1982.

Magnuson, Paul. *Coleridge and Wordsworth: A Lyrical Dialogue.* Princeton: Princeton University Press, 1988.

Manning, Peter. 'Placing Poor Susan: Wordsworth and the New Historicism.' *Studies in Romanticism* 25 (Fall 1986): 351–69.

Mansel, Philip. *Louis XVI.* London: Blond and Briggs, 1981.

Marshall, Peter H. *William Godwin.* New Haven: Yale University Press, 1984.

Mathews, Charles. *Memoirs of Charles Mathews, Comedian.* Edited by Anne Mathews. 4 vols. London: Richard Bentley, 1838.

Matlak, Richard. *The Poetry of Relationship.* New York: St. Martin's Press, 1997.

——'Wordsworth's Lucy Poems in Psychobiographical Context,' *PMLA* 93 (1978): 46–65.

Mayberry, Tom. *Coleridge and Wordsworth in the West Country.* Phoenix Mill: Alan Sutton, 1992.

Moorman, Mary. *William Wordsworth: A Biography*. Vol. 1, *The Early Years, 1770–1803*. Oxford: Clarendon Press, 1957.

Nelson, R. R. *The Home Office, 1792–1801*. Duke Historical Publications. Durham, N.C.: Duke University Press, 1969.

Owen, Hugh. *The Lowther Family*. Chichester: Phillimore, 1990.

Pares, Richard. *A West-India Fortune*. Hamden, Conn.: Archon Books, 1950.

Parreaux, André. *Daily Life in England in the Reign of Geoge III*. Translated by Carola Congreve. London: Allen & Unwin, 1969.

Pennant, Thomas. *A Tour in Wales, 1773*. London: Henry Huges, 1778–84.

Piper, H.W. *The Active Universe: Pantheism and the Concept of the Imagination in the English Romantic Poets*. London: Athlone Press, 1962.

Pollock, John. *Wilberforce*. London: Constable, 1977.

Porter, Bernard. *Plots and Paranoia: A History of Political Espionage in Britain, 1790–1988*. London: Unwin Hyman, 1989.

Postgate, Raymond. *Story of a Year: 1798*. New York: Harcourt, Brace & World, 1969.

Pryme, George. *Autobiographic Recollections*. Cambridge: Deighton, Bell, 1870.

Quennell, Peter. *Romantic England: Writing and Painting 1717–1851*. London: Weidenfeld & Nicolson, 1970.

Rand, Frank. *Wordsworth's Mariner Brother*. Amherst, Mass.: Newell Press, 1966.

Reed, Mark L. *Wordsworth: The Chronology of the Early Years, 1770–1799*. Cambridge, Mass.: Harvard University Press, 1967.

——*Wordsworth: The Chronology of the Middle Years, 1800–1815*. Cambridge: Harvard University Press, 1975.

Robertson, Eric. *Wordsworthshire*. London: Chatto and Windus, 1911.

Robinson, Henry Crabb. *Diary, Reminiscences, and Correspondence*. Edited by Thomas Sadler. 3 vols. London: Macmillan, 1869.

Roe, Nicholas. 'Citizen Wordsworth.' *Wordsworth Circle* 14 (Winter 1983): 21–30.

——'Imagining Robespierre.' In *Coleridge's Imagination: Essays in Memory of Peter Laver*, ed. R. Gravil. L. Newlyn. and N. Roe, 161–78. Cambridge, Mass.: Cambridge University Press, 1985.

——*The Politics of Nature: Wordsworth and Some Contemporaries*. London: Macmillan Academic and Professional, 1992.

——'Radical George: Dyer in the 1790's.' *Charles Lamb Bulletin*. n.s. 49 (Jan. 1985): 17–26.

——*Wordsworth and Coleridge: The Radical Years*. Oxford: Clarendon Press, 1988.

——'Wordsworth, Samuel Nicholson, and the Society for Constitutional Information.' *Wordsworth Circle* 13 (1982): 197–201.

——'Wordsworth's Account of Beaupuy's Death.' *Notes and Queries* 32 (Sept. 1985): 337.

Rogers, Samuel. *Recollections of the Table Talk of Samuel Rogers, to Which Is Added 'Porsoniana.'* London: Edward Moxon. 1856.

Ross, Marlon. *The Contours of Masculine Desire: Romanticism and the Rise of*

Women's Poetry. New York: Oxford University Press, 1989.

St. Clair, William. *The Godwins and the Shelleys: A Biography of a Family*. New York: W.W. Norton, 1989.

Sandford, Margaret E. *Thomas Poole and His Friends*. 2 vols. London: Macmillan, 1888.

Schama, Simon. *Citizens: A Chronicle of the French Revolution*. New York: Alfred A. Knopf, 1989.

Schneider, Ben Ross, *Wordsworth's Cambridge Education*. Cambridge: Cambridge University Press, 1957.

Schwartz, Richard. *Daily Life in Johnson's London*. Madison: University of Wisconsin Press, 1985.

Scrivener, Michael, ed. *Poetry and Reform: Periodical Verse from the English Democratic Press*. Detroit: Wayne State University Press, 1992.

Sheats, Paul D. *The Making of Wordsworth's Poetry, 1785–1798*. Cambridge: Harvard University Press, 1973.

Simpson, David. 'What Bothered Charles Lamb about Poor Susan?' *Studies in English Literature, 1500–1800* 26 (Autumn 1986): 589–612.

Soboul, Albert, ed. *Dictionnaire historique de la Révolution Française*. Paris: Presses universitaires de France, 1989.

Sparrow, Elizabeth. 'The Swiss and Swabian Agencies, 1795–1801.' *Historical Journal* 35 (1992): 861–84.

Sutherland, Donald M. *France, 1789–1815: Revolution and Counterrevolution*. New York: Oxford University Press, 1986.

Taylor, John. *Records of My Own Life; by the Late John Taylor, Esquire*. London: E. Bull, 1832.

Thompson, E.P. 'Disenchantment or Default? A Lay Sermon.' In *Power and Consciousness*, ed. Conor Cruise O'Brien and William Vanech. New York; New York University Press, 1969.

——*The Making of the English Working Class*. New York: Vintage Books, 1966.

Thompson, J.M. *English Witnesses of the French Revolution*. Oxford: Blackwell, 1958.

Thompson. T.W. *Wordsworth's Hawkshead*. Edited by Robert Woof. London: Oxford University Press, 1970.

Thornbury, Walter. *Old and New London: A Narrative of Its History, Its People, and Its Places*. 6 vols. London: Cassell, Petter and Galpin, 1873–78.

Tomalin, Claire. *The Life and Death of Mary Wollstonecraft*. London: Weidenfeld & Nicolson, 1974.

——*Mrs. Jordan's Profession: The Actress and the Prince*. New York; Alfred A. Knopf, 1995.

Tuckerman, Una. 'Wordsworth's Plan for His Imitation of Juvenal.' *Modern Language Notes* 40 (1930): 209–15.

Vansittart, Peter. *Voices of the Revolution*. London: Collins, 1968.

Welford, Richard. *Men of Mark Twixt Tyne and Tweed*. 3 vols. London: W. Scott, 1895.

Wardle, Ralph M. *Hazlitt*. Lincoln: University of Nebraska Press, 1971.

Watts, Alaric. *Alaric Watts: A Narrative of His Life*. 2 vols. London: R. Bentley, 1884. Reprint, New York: AMS Press, 1974.

Wells, Roger. *Insurrection: The British Experience, 1795–1803*. Gloucester: Alan Sutton, 1983.

Wildi, Max. 'Wordsworth and the Simplon Pass.' *English Studies* 40 (1959): 224–32.

Williams, Helen Maria. *Letters from France*. 8 vols. in 2. Edited by Janet Todd. Delmar, N.Y.: Scholar's Facsimiles, 1975.

Willoughby, L.A. 'Wordsworth and Germany.' In *German Studies Presented to Professor H.G. Fiedler*, 432–58. Oxford: Clarendon Press, 1938.

Wollstonecraft, Mary. *The Works of Mary Wollstonecraft*. Edited by Janet Todd and Marilyn Butler. London: Pickering, 1989.

Wordsworth, Christopher. *Social Life at the English Universities in the Eighteenth Century*. Cambridge: Deighton, Bell, 1874.

Wordsworth, Dorothy. *Journals of Dorothy Wordsworth*. Edited by Ernest de Selincourt. 2 vols. New York: Macmillan, 1941.

Wordsworth, John. *The Letters of John Wordsworth*. Edited by Carl H. Ketcham. Ithaca: Cornell University Press, 1969.

Wordsworth, Jonathan. 'The Five-Book Prelude of Early Spring 1804.' *Journal of English and Germanic Philology* 76 (1977): 1–25.

——*Music of Humanity*. London: Thomas Nelson, 1969.

——,ed. *Bicentenary Wordsworth Studies in Memory of John Alban Finch*. Ithaca: Cornell University Press, 1970.

Wordsworth, William, *Descriptive Sketches*. Edited by Eric Birdsall. The Cornell Wordsworth. General editor Stephen Parrish. Ithaca: Cornell University Press, 1984.

——*Early Poems and Fragments 1784–Mid 1797*. Edited by Jared Curtis and Carol Landon. The Cornell Wordsworth. General editor Stephen Parrish. Ithaca: Cornell University Press, 1998.

——*An Evening Walk*. Edited by James Averill. The Cornell Wordsworth. General editor Stephen Parrish. Ithaca: Cornell University Press, 1984.

——*Lyrical Ballads and Other Poems, 1797–1800*. Edited by James Butler and Karen Green. The Cornell Wordsworth. General editor Stephen Parrish. Ithaca: Cornell University Press, 1992.

——*Poems, in Two Volumes and Other Poems, 1800–1807*. Edited by Jared Curtis. Ithaca: Cornell University Press. 1983.

——*The Poetical Works*. Edited by Ernest de Selincourt and Helen Darbishire. 5 vols. 1940–49. Reprint, Oxford: Clarendon Press, 1967–72.

——*The Prelude, 1798–1799*. Edited by Stephen Parrish. The Cornell Wordsworth. General editor Stephen Parrish. Ithaca: Cornell University Press, 1977.

——*The Prelude 1799, 1805, 1855*. Edited by Jonathan Wordsworth, M.H. Abrams, and Stephen Gill. Norton Critical Edition. New York: W.W.

Norton, 1979.

——*The Prose Works of William Wordsworth*. Edited by Alexander Grosart. 3 vols. London: Edward Moxon, 1876.

——*The Prose Works of William Wordsworth*. Edited by W.J.B. Owen and Jane Worthington Smyser. 3 vols. Oxford: Clarendon Press, 1974.

——*The Ruined Cottage and The Pedlar*. Edited by James Butler. The Cornell Wordsworth. General editor Stephen Parrish. Ithaca: Cornell University Press, 1979.

——*The Salisbury Plain Poems*. Edited by Stephen Gill. The Cornell Wordsworth. General editor Stephen Parrish. Ithaca: Cornell University Press, 1975.

——*Shorter Poems, 1807–1820*. Edited by Carl Ketcham. The Cornell Wordsworth. General editor Stephen Parrish. Ithaca: Cornell University Press, 1989.

——*The Thirteen-Book Prelude*. Edited by Mark Reed. 2 vols. The Cornell Wordsworth. General editor Stephen Parrish. Ithaca: Cornell University Press, 1991.

——*William Wordsworth: The Poems*. Vol. 1. Edited by John O. Hayden. New Haven: Yale University Press, 1981.

Wordsworth, William, and Dorothy Wordsworth. *The Letters of William and Dorothy Wordsworth: The Early Years 1787–1805*. Edited by Ernest de Selincourt. 2d ed. Revised by Chester L. Shaver. Oxford: Clarendon Press. 1967.

——*The Letters of William and Dorothy Wordsworth: The Later Years*. Edited by Ernest de Selincourt. 2d ed. Edited by Alan G. Hill, 5 vols. Oxford: Clarendon Press, 1978–93.

——*The Letters of William and Dorothy Wordsworth: The Middle Years*. Edited by Ernest de Selincourt, 2d ed. Revised by Mary Moorman. 2 vols. Oxford: Clarendon Press, 1969–70.

Wordsworth, William, and Samuel Taylor Coleridge. *Lyrical Ballads*. Edited by Michael Mason. London: Longman, 1992.

Wright, J.M.F. *Alma Mater; or, Seven Years at the University of Cambridge*. 2 vols. London: Black, Young and Tavistock, 1827.

Wüscher, Hermann J. *Liberty, Equality, and Fraternity in Wordsworth, 1791–1800*. Stockholm: Almqvist & Wiksell International, 1980.

Index